Lecture Notes in Computer Scien

T0238149

Commenced Publication in 1973
Founding and Former Series Editors:
Gerhard Goos, Juris Hartmanis, and Jan van Leeuwen

Radhia Cousot (Ed.)

Verification, Model Checking, and Abstract Interpretation

6th International Conference, VMCAI 2005
Paris, France, January 17-19, 2005
Proceedings

 Springer

Volume Editor

Radhia Cousot
École Polytechnique, 91128 Palaiseau cedex, France
E-mail: Radhia.Cousot@polytechnique.fr

Library of Congress Control Number: 2004117275

CR Subject Classification (1998): F.3.1-2, D.3.1, D.2.4

ISSN 0302-9743
ISBN 3-540-24297-X Springer Berlin Heidelberg New York

Springer is a part of Springer Science+Business Media

springeronline.com

© Springer-Verlag Berlin Heidelberg 2005
Printed in Germany

Typesetting: Camera-ready by author, data conversion by Olgun Computergrafik
Printed on acid-free paper   SPIN: 11375739   06/3142   5 4 3 2 1 0

Preface

This volume contains the papers accepted for presentation at the 6th International Conference on Verification, Model Checking and Abstract Interpretation (VMCAI 2005), which was held January 17–19, 2005 in Paris, France.

VMCAI provides a forum for researchers from the communities of verification, model checking, and abstract interpretation, facilitating interaction, cross-fertilization, and advancement of hybrid methods that combine the three areas. With the growing need for formal methods to reason about complex, infinite-state, and embedded systems, such hybrid methods are bound to be of great importance.

VMCAI 2005 received 92 submissions. Each paper was carefully reviewed, being judged according to scientific quality, originality, and relevance to the symposium topics. Following online discussions, the program committee met in Paris, France, at the École Normale Supérieure on October 30, 2004, and selected 27 papers.

In addition to the contributed papers, this volume includes contributions by outstanding invited speakers:

- Patrick Cousot (École Normale Supérieure, Paris), *Proving Program Invariance and Termination by Parametric Abstraction, Lagrangian Relaxation and Semidefinite Programming*;
- C.A.R. Hoare (Microsoft Research, Cambridge), *The Verifying Compiler, a Grand Challenge for Computing Research*;
- Amir Pnueli (New York University and Weizmann Institute of Science), *Abstraction for Liveness*.

The VMCAI 2005 program included an invited tutorial by Sriram K. Rajamani (Microsoft Research, Redmond) on *Model Checking, Abstraction and Symbolic Execution for Software*.

VMCAI 2005 was followed by workshops on Automatic Tools for Verification, Abstract Interpretation of Object-Oriented Languages, and Numerical & Symbolic Abstract Domains.

On behalf of the Program Committee, the Program Chair would like to thank the authors of the submitted papers, and the external referees, who provided timely and significant reviews. We owe special thanks to Jacques Beigbeder from the École Normale Supérieure for managing the submission site and the developers of CyberChair for the use of their software.

VMCAI 2005 was held in cooperation with the Association for Computing Machinery (ACM) and the European Association for Programming Languages and Systems (EAPLS).

November 2004   Radhia Cousot

Sponsoring Organizations

The 6th International Conference on Verification, Model Checking and Abstract Interpretation (VMCAI 2005) was held in cooperation with the Association for Computing Machinery (ACM) and the European Association for Programming Languages and Systems (EAPLS).

Program Committee

Agostino Cortesi	Università Ca' Foscari di Venezia, Italy
Radhia Cousot (Chair)	CNRS/École Polytechnique, France
E. Allen Emerson	University of Texas at Austin, USA
Roberto Giacobazzi	Università degli Studi di Verona, Italy
Chris Hankin	Imperial College London, UK
Warren A. Hunt, Jr.	University of Texas at Austin, USA
Ken McMillan	Cadence Berkeley, USA
David Monniaux	CNRS/École Normale Supérieure, France
Amir Pnueli	New York University, USA and Weizmann Institute of Science, Israel
Andreas Podelski	Max-Planck-Institut für Informatik, Germany
Francesco Ranzato	Università di Padova, Italy
Hanne Riis Nielson	Technical University of Denmark, Denmark
Shmuel Sagiv	TelAviv University, Israel
Bernhard Steffen	Universität Dortmund, Germany
Reinhard Wilhelm	Universität des Saarlandes, Germany

Steering Committee

Agostino Cortesi	Università Ca' Foscari di Venezia, Italy
E. Allen Emerson	University of Texas at Austin, USA
Giorgio Levi	Università di Pisa, Italy
Thomas W. Reps	University of Wisconsin-Madison, USA
Andreas Podelski	Max-Planck-Institut für Informatik, Germany
David A. Schmidt	Kansas State University, USA
Lenore Zuck	University of Illinois at Chicago, USA

Organizing Committee

General Chair	Radhia Cousot, CNRS/École Polytechnique
Submission Website	Jacques Beigbeder, École Normale Supérieure
Local Arrangements	Radhia Cousot, CNRS/École Polytechnique
	David Monniaux, CNRS/École Normale Supérieure
	Élodie-Jane Sims, CNRS/École Polytechnique

Referees

Nina Amla
Egon Börger
Christel Baier
Clark Barrett
Jörg Bauer
Bernd Becker
Gerd Behrmann
Sergey Berezin
Bruno Blanchet
Thomas Bolander
Ahmed Bouajjani
Chiara Braghin
Mikael Buchholz
Feng Chen
Horatiu Cirstea
Nicoletta Cocco
Livio Colussi
Scott Cotton
Patrick Cousot
William D. Young
Mila Dalla Preda
Sayaki Das
Jared Davis
Jyotirmoy Deshmukh
Agostino Dovier
Klaus Dräger
Stefan Edelkamp
Cindy Eisner
Alessandro Fantechi
Jérôme Feret
Gilberto Filé
Jean-Christophe Filliâtre
David Fink
Bernd Finkbeiner
Riccardo Focardi
Martin Fraenzle
Han Gao
Angelo Gargantini
Samir Genaim

Walid Ghandour
Ursula Goltz
Sumit Gulwani
Jörg Hoffmann
Hardi Hungar
Michael Huth
Charles Hymans
François Irigoin
Shahid Jabbar
Bertrand Jeannet
Thomas Jensen
Robert Krug
Marta Kwiatkowska
Ruggero Lanotte
Fabrice le Fessant
Stefan Leue
Hanbing Liu
Francesco Logozzo
Markus Müller-Olm
Rupak Majumdar
Oded Maler
Roman Manevich
Shawn Manley
Jacopo Mantovani
Damien Massé
Isabella Mastroeni
Laurent Mauborgne
Tilman Mehler
Flemming Nielson
Gethin Norman
Peter O'Hearn
Peter Padawitz
Carla Piazza
Michele Pinna
Anne Proetzsch
Oliver Rüthing
David Rager
Sandip Ray
Erik Reeber

Jan Reineke
Tamara Rezk
Noam Rinetzky
Eike Ritter
Xavier Rival
Grigore Rosu
Harald Ruess
Andrey Rybalchenko
Rene Rydhof Hansen
Antonino Salibra
Sven Schewe
Francesca Scozzari
Roberto Segala
Helmut Seidl
Ohad Shacham
Vitaly Shmatikov
Élodie-Jane Sims
Fausto Spoto
Jean-Pierre Talpin
Francesco Tapparo
Stephan Thesing
Sarah Thompson
Terkel Tolstrup
Shmuel Tyszberowicz
Antti Valmari
Tullio Vardanega
Arnaud Venet
Vinod Viswanath
Hubert Wagner
Thomas Wahl
Bernd Westphal
Thomas Wies
Kirsten Winter
Enea Zaffanella
Damiano Zanardini
Hormoz Zarnani
Qiang Zhang
Lenore Zuck

Table of Contents

Invited Paper

Numerical Abstraction

Invited Talk

Verification I

Invited Talk

Heap and Shape Analysis

Abstract Model Checking

Model Checking

Applied Abstract Interpretation

Bounded Model Checking

Verification II

Proving Program Invariance and Termination by Parametric Abstraction, Lagrangian Relaxation and Semidefinite Programming

Patrick Cousot

École Normale Supérieure
45 rue d'Ulm, 75230 Paris cedex 05 (France)
Patrick.Cousot@ens.fr
www.di.ens.fr/~cousot

Abstract. In order to verify semialgebraic programs, we automatize the Floyd/Naur/Hoare proof method. The main task is to automatically infer valid invariants and rank functions.

First we express the program semantics in polynomial form. Then the unknown rank function and invariants are abstracted in parametric form. The implication in the Floyd/Naur/Hoare verification conditions is handled by abstraction into numerical constraints by Lagrangian relaxation. The remaining universal quantification is handled by semidefinite programming relaxation. Finally the parameters are computed using semidefinite programming solvers.

This new approach exploits the recent progress in the numerical resolution of linear or bilinear matrix inequalities by semidefinite programming using efficient polynomial primal/dual interior point methods generalizing those well-known in linear programming to convex optimization.

The framework is applied to invariance and termination proof of sequential, nondeterministic, concurrent, and fair parallel imperative polynomial programs and can easily be extended to other safety and liveness properties.

Keywords: Bilinear matrix inequality (BMI), Convex optimization, Invariance, Lagrangian relaxation, Linear matrix inequality (LMI), Liveness, Parametric abstraction, Polynomial optimization, Proof, Rank function, Safety, S-procedure, Semidefinite programming, Termination precondition, Termination. Program verification.

1 Introduction

Program verification is based on reasonings by induction (e.g. on program steps) which involves the discovery of unknown inductive arguments (e.g. rank functions, invariants) satisfying universally quantified verification conditions. For static analysis the discovery of the inductive arguments must be automated, which consists in solving the constraints provided by the verification conditions. Several methods have been considered: recurrence/difference equation resolution; iteration, possibly with convergence acceleration; or direct methods (such

R. Cousot (Ed.): VMCAI 2005, LNCS 3385, pp. 1–24, 2005.

as elimination). All these methods involve some form of simplification of the constraints by abstraction.

In this paper, we explore *parametric abstraction* and direct resolution by *Lagrangian relaxation* into *semidefinite programming*. This is applied to termination (a typical liveness property) of semialgebraic programs. The extension to invariance (a typical safety property) is sketched.

The automatic determination of loop invariant/rank function can be summarized as follows:

1. Establish the relational semantics of the loop body (Sec. 2) (may be strengthened with correctness preconditions (Sec. 2.2), abstract invariants (Sec. 2.3), and/or simplified by relational abstraction (Sec. 2.4));
2. Set up the termination/invariance verification conditions (Sec. 3);
3. Choose a parametric abstraction (Sec. 4). The resolution of the abstract logical verification conditions by first-order quantifier elimination can be considered, but is very often too costly (Sec. 5);
4. Abstract further the abstract logical verification conditions into numerical constraints (Sec. 8) by Lagrangian relaxation (Sec. 6) obtaining Linear Matrix Inequalities for termination (Sec. 6.2) or Bilinear Matrix Inequalities for invariance (Sec. 12);
5. Solve the numerical constraints (Sec. 9) by semidefinite programming (Sec. 7);

After a series of examples (Sec. 10), we consider more complex language features including disjunctions in the loop test and conditionals in the loop body (Sec. 11.1), nested loops (Sec. 11.2), nondeterminism and concurrency (Sec. 11.3), bounded weakly fair parallelism (Sec. 11.4), and semi-algebraic/polynomial programs, for which a further relaxation into a sum of squares is applied (Sec. 11.5). The case of invariance is illustrated in Sec. 12. Potential problems with solvers are discussed in Sec. 13, before concluding (Sec. 14).

2   Relational Semantics of Programs

2.1   Semialgebraic Programs

We consider numerical iterative programs while B do C od where B is a boolean condition and C is an imperative command (assignment, test or loop) on the global program variables. We assume that the operational semantics of the loop is given for an iteration as:

$$[\![B;C]\!](x_0, x) = \bigwedge_{k=1}^{N} \sigma_k(x_0, x) \geq 0 \tag{1}$$

where x_0 is the line vector of values of the n program variables before an iteration, x is the line vector of values of the n program variables after this iteration and the relationship between x_0 and x during a single iteration is expressed as a conjunction of N real valued positivity constraints with $\sigma_k \in \mathbb{R}^n \times \mathbb{R}^n \longrightarrow \mathbb{R}$, $k = 1, \ldots, N$ [1]. Algorithmically interesting particular cases are when the constraints $\sigma_k \geq 0$ can be expressed as linear constraints, quadratic forms and polynomial positivity. Equalities $\sigma_k(x_0, x) = 0$ have to be written as $\sigma_k(x_0, x) \geq 0 \wedge -\sigma_k(x_0, x) \geq 0$.

Example 1 (Factorial). The program below computes the greatest factorial less than or equal to a given N, if any. The operational semantics of the loop body can be defined by the following constraints:

```
n := 0;
f := 1;
while (f <= N) do
    n := n + 1;
    f := n * f
od
```

$$-f_0 + N_0 \geq 0$$
$$n_0 \geq 0$$
$$f_0 - 1 \geq 0$$
$$-n_0 + n - 1 = 0$$
$$-f_0.n + f = 0$$
$$-N_0 + N = 0$$

All constraints are linear but $f - n.f_0 = 0$ which is quadratic (of the form $[x_0\ x]A[x_0\ x]^\top + 2[x_0\ x]q + r \geq 0$, where A is symmetric, q is a column vector, r is a constant, and $^\top$ is transposition), and can be written as follows:

$$[n_0\ f_0\ N_0\ n\ f\ N]\begin{bmatrix} 0 & 0 & 0 & 0 & 0 & 0 \\ 0 & 0 & 0 & -\frac{1}{2} & 0 & 0 \\ 0 & 0 & 0 & 0 & 0 & 0 \\ 0 & -\frac{1}{2} & 0 & 0 & 0 & 0 \\ 0 & 0 & 0 & 0 & 0 & 0 \\ 0 & 0 & 0 & 0 & 0 & 0 \end{bmatrix}\begin{bmatrix} n_0 \\ f_0 \\ N_0 \\ n \\ f \\ N \end{bmatrix} + 2[n_0 f_0 N_0 n f N]\begin{bmatrix} 0 \\ 0 \\ 0 \\ 0 \\ \frac{1}{2} \\ 0 \end{bmatrix} + 0 = 0,$$

or equivalently as $[x_0\ x\ 1]M[x_0\ x\ 1]^\top \geq 0$ where M is symmetric, that is:

$$[n_0\ f_0\ N_0\ n\ f\ N\ 1]\begin{bmatrix} 0 & 0 & 0 & 0 & 0 & 0 & 0 \\ 0 & 0 & 0 & -\frac{1}{2} & 0 & 0 & 0 \\ 0 & 0 & 0 & 0 & 0 & 0 & 0 \\ 0 & -\frac{1}{2} & 0 & 0 & 0 & 0 & 0 \\ 0 & 0 & 0 & 0 & 0 & 0 & \frac{1}{2} \\ 0 & 0 & 0 & 0 & 0 & 0 & 0 \\ 0 & 0 & 0 & 0 & \frac{1}{2} & 0 & 0 \end{bmatrix}\begin{bmatrix} n_0 \\ f_0 \\ N_0 \\ n \\ f \\ N \\ 1 \end{bmatrix} = 0 .$$

□

2.2 Establishing Necessary Correctness Preconditions

Iterated Forward/Backward Static Analysis. Program verification may be unsuccessful when the program execution may fail under some circumstances

---

[1] Any Boolean constraint on numerical variables can be written in that form using an appropriate numerical encoding of the boolean values and embedding of the numerical values into $\mathbb{R}$.

(e.g. non termination, run-time errors). As part of the correctness proof, it is therefore mandatory to establish correctness preconditions excluding such mis-behaviors. Such a necessary termination and absence of runtime errors precondition can be discovered automatically by an iterated forward/backward static analysis [7, 12].

Discovering a Termination Precondition by the Auxiliary Termination Counter Method. Termination requirements can be incorporated into the iterated forward/backward static analysis in the form of an *auxiliary termination counter* k which is strictly decremented in the loop and is asserted to be zero on loop exit. For relational analyzes, this strengthens the necessary termination precondition.

Example 2. The following example is from [3]. The analyzer uses the polyhedral abstract domain [14] implemented using the *New Polka* library [20].

```
while (x <> y) do      {x>=y}                  {x=y+2k,x>=y}
    x := x - 1;        while (x <> y) do       while (x <> y) do
    y := y + 1             {x>=y+2}                {x=y+2k,x>=y+2}
od                         x := x - 1;             k := k - 1;
                           {x>=y+1}                x := x - 1;
                           y := y + 1              y := y + 1
                           {x>=y}                  {x=y+2k,x>=y}
                       od                      od
                       {x=y}                   {x=y,k=0}
                                               assume (k = 0)
```

| Program | Iterated forward/backward | Iterated forward/backward static |
| | static analysis | analysis with termination counter.|

The use of the auxiliary termination counter allows the iterated forward/backward polyhedral analysis to discover the necessary termination condition that the initial difference between the two variables should be even.   □

2.3   Strengthening the Relational Semantics

Proofs can be made easier by strengthening the relational semantics through incorporation of known facts about the program runtime behavior. For example an invariant may be needed, in addition to a termination precondition, to prove termination. Such a loop invariant can be determined automatically by a forward static analysis [8] assuming the initial termination precondition.

Example 3 (Ex. 2 continued). A forward polyhedral analysis [14] yields linear invariants:

```
assume (x=y+2*k) & (x>=y);        assume (x=y+2*k) & (x>=y);
while (x <> y) do                 {x=y+2k,x>=y}
    k := k - 1;                   {loop invariant: x=y+2k}
    x := x - 1;                   while (x <> y) do
    y := y + 1                        {x=y+2k}
od                                    k := k - 1;
                                      x := x - 1;
                                      y := y + 1
                                      {x=y+2k}
                                  od
                                  {k=0,x=y}
```

Program   Forward polyhedral analysis.   □

2.4 Abstracting the Relational Semantics

Program verification may be made easier when the big-step operational semantics of the loop body (1) is simplified e.g. through abstraction. To get such a simplified but sound semantics, one can use any relational abstraction. The technique consists in using auxiliary initial variables to denote the values of the program variables at the beginning of the loop iteration (whence satisfying the loop invariant and the loop condition). The invariant at the end of the loop body is then a sound approximation of the relational semantics (1) of the loop body[2]. The polyhedral abstraction [14] will be particularly useful to derive automatically an approximate linear semantics.

Example 4 (Ex. 3 continued). Handling the operator <> (different) by case analysis, we get[3]:

```
assume (x=y+2*k)&(x>=y);          assume (x=y+2*k)&(x>=y);
{x=y+2k,x>=y}                     {x=y+2k,1>=0,x>=y}
assume (x < y);                   assume (x > y);
empty(6)                          {x=y+2k,1>=0,x>=y+1}
assume (x0=x)&(y0=y)&(k0=k);      assume (x0=x)&(y0=y)&(k0=k);
k := k - 1;                       k := k - 1;
x := x - 1;                       x := x - 1;
y := y + 1                        y := y + 1
empty(6)                          {x+2=y+2k0,y=y0+1,x+1=x0,x=y+2k,x+1>=y}   □
```

3 Verification Condition Setup

3.1 Floyd/Naur/Hoare Invariance Proof Method

Given a loop precondition $P(x) \geq 0$ which holds before loop entry, the invariance proof method [16, 19, 25] consists in proving that the invariant $I(x) \geq 0$ is *initial*

---

[2] The technique was first used in the context of static analysis for context-sensitive interprocedural analysis to compute summaries of recursive procedures [9].

[3] empty(6) denotes the empty polyhedron in 6 variables, that is unreachability $\perp$.

(that is to say holds on loop entry) and *inductive* (i.e. remains true after each loop iteration):

$$\forall x \in \mathbb{R}^n : (P(x) \geq 0) \Rightarrow (I(x) \geq 0), \tag{2}$$

$$\forall x_0, x \in \mathbb{R}^n : (I(x_0) \geq 0 \wedge \bigwedge_{k=1}^{N} \sigma_k(x_0, x) \geq 0) \Rightarrow (I(x) \geq 0) . \tag{3}$$

3.2   Floyd Rank Function Termination Proof Method

Floyd's method [16] for proving loop termination consists in discovering a rank function $r \in \mathbb{R}^n \longrightarrow W$ of the values of the program variables into a well-founded set $\langle W, \preceq \rangle$ which is strictly decreasing at each iteration of the loop. If the nondeterminism is bounded, one can choose $\langle W, \preceq \rangle = \langle \mathbb{N}, \leq \rangle$. In what follows, we will often use real valued rank functions r which are nonnegative on loop body entry and strictly decrease at each iteration by a positive quantity bounded from below[4]. In such a case, and up to an isomorphism, the rank function r can be embedded into $\mathbb{N}$.

In general a loop terminates for some initial values of the variables only, satisfying some loop termination precondition $P(x) \geq 0$ so that the strict decrementation can be requested for states reachable from this initial condition only, as characterized by an invariant $I(x) \geq 0$ in the sense of [16, 19, 25].

Floyd's verification conditions [16] for proving loop termination become:

$\exists r \in \mathbb{R}^n \longrightarrow \mathbb{R}, \exists \delta \in \mathbb{R}$:

$$\forall x_0 \in \mathbb{R}^n : (I(x_0) \geq 0) \Rightarrow (r(x_0) \geq 0), \tag{4}$$

$$\forall x_0, x \in \mathbb{R}^n : (I(x_0) \geq 0 \wedge \bigwedge_{k=1}^{N} \sigma_k(x_0, x) \geq 0) \Rightarrow (r(x_0) - r(x) - \delta \geq 0), \tag{5}$$

$$\delta > 0 . \tag{6}$$

Remark 1. We can also choose $\delta = 1$ but it is sometimes more flexible to let its value be computed by the solver (see later Rem. 4).   □

Remark 2. As proved in [11, Sec. 9, p. 290], the above choice of I and r not depending upon initial states is incomplete so that, more generally, we may have to use $I(\underline{x}, x')$ and $r(\underline{x}, x')$ where $\underline{x} \in \mathbb{R}^n$ denotes the initial value of the variables before loop entry and $x' \in \mathbb{R}^n$ their current value that is x_0 at the beginning of an iteration of the loop body and x at the end of that same iteration.   □

4   Parametric Abstraction

Fixing the form of the unknown invariant $I(x)$ in (2) and (3) or of the rank function r in (4) and (5) in terms of p unknown parameters $a \in \mathbb{R}^p$ to be determined by the analysis is an abstraction [10]. An example is the affine abstraction [21].

---

[4] To avoid the Zeno phenomenon, that is, a strict decrease by 1, $\frac{1}{2}$, $\frac{1}{4}$, $\frac{1}{8}$, ..., which could be infinite.

More generally, a function $f(x)$ can be abstracted in the form $f_a(x)$ where a is a line vector of unknown parameters and x is the line vector of values of the loop variables[5]. For example, the linear case is $f_a(x) = a.x^\top$ and the affine case is $f_a(x) = a.(x\ 1)^\top$. A quadratic choice would be $f_a(x) = x.a.x^\top$ or $f_a(x) = (x\ 1).a.(x\ 1)^\top$ where a is a symmetric matrix of unknown parameters.

After parametric abstraction, it remains to compute the parameters a by solving the verification constraints. For example, the termination verification conditions (4), (5), and (6) become:

$$\exists a \in \mathbb{R}^p : \exists \delta \in \mathbb{R} :$$

$$\forall x_0 \in \mathbb{R}^n : (I(x_0) \geq 0) \Rightarrow (r_a(x_0) \geq 0), \tag{7}$$

$$\forall x_0, x \in \mathbb{R}^n : (I(x_0) \geq 0 \wedge \bigwedge_{k=1}^{N} \sigma_k(x_0, x) \geq 0) \Rightarrow (r_a(x_0) - r_a(x) - \delta \geq 0), \tag{8}$$

$$\delta > 0 . \tag{9}$$

The resolution of these termination constraints in the case of linear programs and rank functions has been explored by [6], using a reduction of the constraints based on the construction of polars, intersection and projection of polyhedral cones (with limitations, such as that the loop test contains no disjunction and the body contains no test).

5   Solving the Abstract Verification Conditions by First-Order Quantifier Elimination

The Tarski-Seidenberg decision procedure for the first-order theory of real closed fields by quantifier elimination can be used to solve (7), (8), and (9) since it transforms a formula $Q_1 x_1 : \ldots Q_n x_n : F(x_1, \ldots, x_n)$ (where the Q_i are first-order quantifiers $\forall, \exists$ and F is a logical combination of polynomial equations and inequalities in the variables $x_1, \ldots, x_n$) into an equivalent quantifier free formula. However Tarski's method cannot be bound by any tower of exponentials. The cylindrical algebraic decomposition method by Collins [5] has a worst-case time-complexity for real quantifier elimination which is "only" doubly exponential in the number of quantifier blocks. It is implemented in MATHEMATICA® but cannot be expected to scale up to large problems. So we rely on another abstraction method described below.

---

[5] The sets of constraints $f_a(x) \geq 0$ for all a may not be a Moore family for the pointwise ordering, in which case a concretization function γ may be used [13]. For simplicity we make no distinction between the representation of the constraint $f_a(x) \geq 0$ and its value $\gamma(f_a(x) \geq 0) = \{x \in \mathbb{R}^n \mid f_a(x) \geq 0\}$. In consequence, the use of a concretization function will remain implicit.

6   Abstraction of the Verification Conditions into Numerical Constraints by Lagrangian Relaxation

6.1   The Lagrangian Relaxation Method

Let $\mathbb{V}$ be a finite dimensional linear vector space, $N > 0$ and $\forall k \in [0, N] : \sigma_k \in \mathbb{V} \longrightarrow \mathbb{R}$ (not necessarily linear). Let $\mathbb{R}^+ = \{x \geq 0 \mid x \in \mathbb{R}\}$. To prove:

$$\forall x \in \mathbb{V} : \left(\bigwedge_{k=1}^{N} \sigma_k(x) \geq 0 \right) \Rightarrow (\sigma_0(x) \geq 0), \qquad (10)$$

the *Lagrangian relaxation* consists in proving that:

$$\exists \lambda \in [1, N] \longrightarrow \mathbb{R}^+ : \forall x \in \mathbb{V} : \sigma_0(x) - \sum_{k=1}^{N} \lambda_k \sigma_k(x) \geq 0, \qquad (11)$$

where the λ_k are called *Lagrange coefficients*. The interest of Lagrangian relaxation is that the implication $\Rightarrow$ and conjunction $\bigwedge$ in (10) are eliminated in (11).

The approach is obviously sound, since the hypothesis $\bigwedge_{k=1}^{N} \sigma_k(x) \geq 0$ in (10) and the positivity of the Lagrange coefficients $\lambda \in [1, N] \longrightarrow \mathbb{R}^+$ implies the positivity of $\sum_{k=1}^{N} \lambda_k \sigma_k(x)$. Hence, by the antecedent of (10) and transitivity, $\sigma_0(x) \geq 0$ holds in the consequent of (10).

Observe that equality constraints can be handled in the same way by requesting the corresponding Lagrange coefficients to be reals (as opposed to nonnegative reals for inequality constraints). Indeed for equality constraints $\sigma_k(x) = 0$, we can use (11) for both $\sigma_k(x) \geq 0$ and $-\sigma_k(x) \geq 0$ with respective coefficients $\lambda_k \geq 0$ and $\lambda'_k \geq 0$ so that the terms $\lambda_k \sigma_k(x) + \lambda'_k(-\sigma_k(x))$ can be grouped into a single term $(\lambda_k - \lambda'_k)\sigma_k(x)$ with no sign restriction on $\lambda_k - \lambda'_k$. Since any real is equal to the difference of some nonnegative reals, we can equivalently use a single term $\lambda''_k \sigma_k(x)$ with $\lambda''_k \in \mathbb{R}$.

Lagrangian relaxation is in general incomplete (that is (10) $\not\Rightarrow$ (11), also called *lossy*). However it is complete (also called *lossless*)) in the linear case (by the affine Farkas' lemma) and the linear case with at most two quadratic constraints (by Yakubovitch's S-procedure [33, Th. 1]).

6.2   Lagrangian Relaxation of Floyd Termination Verification Conditions on Rank Functions

Relaxing Floyd's parametric verification conditions (7), (8), and (9), we get:

$\exists a \in \mathbb{R}^p : \exists \delta \in \mathbb{R} : \exists \mu \in \mathbb{R}^+ : \exists \lambda \in [0, N] \longrightarrow \mathbb{R}^+ :$

$$\forall x_0 \in \mathbb{R}^n : r_a(x_0) - \mu . I(x_0) \geq 0, \qquad (12)$$

$$\forall x_0, x \in \mathbb{R}^n : r_a(x_0) - r_a(x) - \delta - \lambda_0 . I(x_0) - \sum_{k=1}^{N} \lambda_k . \sigma_k(x_0, x) \geq 0, \qquad (13)$$

$$\delta > 0 . \qquad (14)$$

In [29], the constraints $\sigma_k(x, x') \geq 0$ are assumed to be linear in which case the Lagrange coefficients can be eliminated by hand. Then the problem reduces to linear programming (with limitations, such as that the loop test contains no disjunction, the loop body contains no tests and the method cannot identify the cases when the loop does not terminate). We can use semidefinite programming to overcome the linearity limitation.

7 Semidefinite Programming

The *semidefinite programming optimization problem* is to find a solution to the constraints:

$$\begin{cases} \exists x \in \mathbb{R}^m : M(x) \succcurlyeq 0 \\ \text{Minimizing } c^\top x \end{cases}$$

where $c \in \mathbb{R}^m$ is a given real vector, the *linear matrix inequality* (LMI) [2] $M(x) \succcurlyeq 0$ is of the form:

$$M(x) = M_0 + \sum_{k=1}^{m} x_k . M_k$$

with symmetric matrices ($M_k = M_k{}^\top$), and *positive semidefiniteness* is defined as:

$$M(x) \succcurlyeq 0 \stackrel{\Delta}{=} \forall X \in \mathbb{R}^N : XM(x)X^\top \geq 0 .$$

The *semidefinite programming feasibility problem* consists in finding a solution to the constraints $M(x) \succcurlyeq 0$. A feasibility problem can be converted into the optimization program $\min\{-y \in \mathbb{R} \mid \bigwedge_{i=1}^{N} M_i(x) - y \succcurlyeq 0\}$.

8 LMI Constraint Setup for Termination

For programs which invariant and operational semantics (1) can be expressed in the form:

$$I(x_0) \wedge [\![B;C]\!](x_0, x) = \bigwedge_{k=1}^{N} (x_0 \; x \; 1) M_k (x_0 \; x \; 1)^\top \geq 0, \tag{15}$$

the constraints (12), (13), and (14) become LMIs (in the unknown a, μ, δ and the λ_k, $k = 1, \ldots, N$ by parametric abstraction (Sec. 4) of r_a in the form $r_a(x) = (x \; 1) R (x \; 1)^\top$ where R is a real $(n + 1) \times (n + 1)$-symmetric matrix of unknown parameters).

The conjunction of LMIs $M_1(x) \succcurlyeq 0 \wedge \ldots \wedge M_k(x) \succcurlyeq 0$ can be expressed as a single LMI $\text{diag}(M_1(x), \ldots, M_k(x)) \succcurlyeq 0$ where $\text{diag}(M_1(x), \ldots, M_k(x))$ denotes the block-diagonal matrix with $M_1(x), \ldots, M_k(x)$ on its diagonal.

These LMIs can then be solved by semidefinite programming.

Example 5. To show this, we prove the linear termination of the linear example program below, considered as in general semidefinite form (so that the generalization to (15) is immediate). The semantics of the loop body can be determined by a forward symbolic analysis of the loop body assuming the loop invariant (here the loop condition) and by naming the values of the variables at the beginning of the loop body[6]:

```
while (x >= 1) & (y >= 1) do      assume (x0 > 0) & (y0 > 0);
    x := x - y                    {y0>=1,x0>=1}
od                                assume (x = x0) & (y = y0);
                                  {y0=y,x0=x,y0>=1,x0>=1}
                                  x := x - y
                                  {y0=y,x0=x+y,y0>=1,x0>=1}
```

        Program   Semantics of the loop body.

The constraints $\sigma_k(x_0, x)$ are encoded as $(x_0 \ x \ 1)M_k(x_0 \ x \ 1)^\top$. For the above example, we have:

```
Mk(:,:,1) =                       Mk(:,:,3) =
    0    0    0    0   1/2             0    0    0    0    1/2
    0    0    0    0    0              0    0    0    0     0
    0    0    0    0    0              0    0    0    0   -1/2
    0    0    0    0    0              0    0    0    0   -1/2
   1/2   0    0    0   -1            1/2  0- 1/2 -1/2   0

Mk(:,:,2) =                       Mk(:,:,4) =
    0    0    0    0    0              0    0    0    0    0
    0    0    0    0   1/2             0    0    0    0  -1/2
    0    0    0    0    0              0    0    0    0    0
    0    0    0    0    0              0    0    0    0   1/2
    0   1/2   0    0   -1             0  -1/2   0   1/2   0
```

that is in symbolic form:

$$x_0 - 1 \geq 0 \qquad (x_0 \ y_0 \ x \ y \ 1)\text{Mk}(:,:,1)(x_0 \ y_0 \ x \ y \ 1)^\top \geq 0$$
$$y_0 - 1 \geq 0 \qquad (x_0 \ y_0 \ x \ y \ 1)\text{Mk}(:,:,2)(x_0 \ y_0 \ x \ y \ 1)^\top \geq 0$$
$$x_0 - x - y = 0 \qquad (x_0 \ y_0 \ x \ y \ 1)\text{Mk}(:,:,3)(x_0 \ y_0 \ x \ y \ 1)^\top = 0$$
$$-y_0 + y = 0 \qquad (x_0 \ y_0 \ x \ y \ 1)\text{Mk}(:,:,4)(x_0 \ y_0 \ x \ y \ 1)^\top = 0 \ .$$

The termination constraints (12), (13), and (14) now become the following LMIs[7]:

---

[6] As considered in Sec. 2.4, which is different from Rem. 2 where the values of variables were remembered before loop entry.

[7] Notice that if $(x \ 1)A(x \ 1)^\top \geq 0$ for all x, this is the same as $(y \ t)A(y \ t)^\top \geq 0$ for all y and all $t \neq 0$ (multiply the original inequality by t^2 and call $xt = y$). Since the latter inequality holds true for all x and all $t \neq 0$, by continuity it holds true for all x, t, that is, the original inequality is equivalent to positive semidefiniteness of A (thanks Arkadi Nemirovski for this argument).

```
MO-10(1,1)*Mk(:,:,1)-
            10(2,1)*Mk(:,:,2)-10(3,1)*Mk(:,:,3)-10(4,1)*Mk(:,:,4)>=0
MO-M_0-delta-
    1(1,1)*Mk(:,:,1)-1(2,1)*Mk(:,:,2)-1(3,1)*Mk(:,:,3)-1(4,1)*Mk(:,:,4)>=0
```

where >= is semidefinite positiveness $\succeq$ in LMI constraints, the $10(i,j)$ and $1(i,j)$ are the Lagrange coefficients which are requested to be nonnegative for inequality constraints:

$$10(1,1)>=0 \qquad 10(2,1)>=0 \qquad 1(1,1)>=0 \qquad 1(2,1)>=0$$

(where >= is the real comparison for elementwise constraints), the rank function

$r(x) = (x\ 1).R.(x\ 1)^\top$ appears in MO $= \begin{bmatrix} R_{1:n,1:n} & 0^{n \times n} & R_{1:n,n+1} \\ 0^{n \times n} & 0^{n \times n} & 0^{n \times 1} \\ R_{n+1,1:n} & 0^{1 \times n} & R_{n+1,n+1} \end{bmatrix}$ such that

$\forall x : r(x_0) = (x_0\ x\ 1).\text{MO}.(x_0\ x\ 1)^\top$ and in M_0 $= \begin{bmatrix} 0^{n \times n} & 0^{n \times n+1} \\ 0^{n+1 \times n} & R \end{bmatrix}$ such that

$\forall x_0 : r(x) = (x_0\ x\ 1).\text{M\_0}.(x_0\ x\ 1)^\top$ and delta $= \begin{bmatrix} 0^{2n \times 2n} & 0^{2n \times 1} \\ 0^{1 \times 2n} & \delta \end{bmatrix}$ so that $\forall x_0, x :$

$(x_0\ x\ 1).\text{delta}.(x_0\ x\ 1)^\top = \delta$. □

Remark 3. An affine (linear by abuse of language) rank function $r_a(x) = a.(x\ 1)^\top$ where $x \in \mathbb{R}^n$ and $a \in \mathbb{R}^n$ can be enforced by choosing $R = \begin{bmatrix} 0^{n,n} & (\frac{a}{2})^\top_{1:n} \\ (\frac{a}{2})_{1:n} & a_{n:n} \end{bmatrix}$. □

9   Solving the Termination LMI Constraints

Following the extension of the interior point method for linear programming to convex cones [27], numerous solvers have been developed for semidefinite programming such as bnb[8] [23], DSDP4 [1], lmilab [17], PenBMI[9] [22], Sdplr [4], Sdpt3 [32], SeDuMi [31], with common interfaces under MATLAB® such as Yalmip [23].

Example 6 (Ex. 5 continued). Choosing $\delta = 1$ and a linear rank function as in Rem. 3, we can solve the LMI constraints of Ex. 5 using various solvers under Yalmip:

```
r(x,y) = +4.x +2.y -3                                      bnb
r(x,y) = +5.268942e+02.x +4.956309e+02.y -5.270981e+02  CSDP-4.9
r(x,y) = +2.040148e+07.x +2.222757e+07.y +9.096450e+06  DSDP4-4.7
r(x,y) = +2.767658e+11.x +2.265404e+11.y -1.311440e+11  lmilab
r(x,y) = +4.031146e+03.x +3.903684e+03.y +1.401577e+03  lmilab¹⁰
r(x,y) = +1.042725e+00.x +4.890035e-01.y +1.975391e-01  Sdplr-1.01
r(x,y) = +9.888097e+01.x +1.343247e+02.y -1.725408e+02  Sdpt3-3.02
r(x,y) = +1.291131e+00.x +4.498515e-01.y -1.316373e+00  SeDuMi-1.05
```

---

[8] For integer semidefinite programming.
[9] To solve bilinear matrix inequalities.

Since different solvers use different resolution strategies, each one may provide a different solution. Moreover, since there are infinitely many different rank functions (e.g. just multiply by or add a positive constant), the solution may not be the one a human being would naturally think of. Indeed, in the above example, any $r(x, y) = ax + by + c$ with $a \geq 1$, $b \geq 0$ and $a + b + c \geq 0$ will do.   □

Remark 4. It is also possible to let δ be an unknown parameter with the constraint $\delta > 0$ as in (14). In this case, looking for a linear rank function with **bnb**, we get **r(x,y) = +2.x -2** and δ = **8.193079e-01**.   □

Remark 5. It is possible to check a rank function by fixing R as well as δ and then by checking for the feasibility of the constraints (12), (13), and (14), which returns the Lagrange coefficients. For example to check **r(x,y) = +1.x**, we use R = **[[0,0,1/2] ; [0,0,0] ; [1/2,0,0]]** and $\delta = 1$ while performing the feasibility check with **bnb**.   □

10   Examples

The examples illustrate different kind of ranking functions.

10.1   Examples of Linear Termination of a Linear Loop

Example 7. Choosing $\delta = 1$ and a linear rank function for the naïve Euclidean division:

```
assume (y >= 1);
q := 0; r := x;
while (y <= r) do
    r := r - y;
    q := q + 1
od
```

$$y - 1 \geq 0$$
$$q - 1 \geq 0$$
$$r \geq 0$$

$$-q_0 + q - 1 = 0$$
$$-x_0 + x = 0$$
$$-y_0 + y = 0$$
$$-r_0 + y + r = 0$$

The linear semantics of the loop body (with polyhedral invariant) is provided on the right. Solving the corresponding termination constraints with **bnb**, we automatically get the ranking function **r'(x,y,q,r) = -2.y +2.q +6.r**, which is certainly less intuitive than Floyd's proposal $r'(x, y, q, r) = x - q$ [16] but has the advantage not to depend upon the nonlinear loop invariant $x = r + qy$.   □

Example 8 (Ex. 4 continued). For the example Ex. 4 from [3] considered in Sec. 2.2, where the difference <> was handled as a disjunction and one case was shown to be impossible, we get:

```
assume (x=y+2*k) & (x>=y);
while (x <> y) do
    k := k - 1;
    x := x - 1;
    y := y + 1
od
```

$$x - y + 1 \geq 0$$
$$-2k_0 + x - y + 2 = 0$$
$$-y_0 + y - 1 = 0$$
$$-x_0 + x + 1 = 0$$
$$x - y - 2k = 0$$

---

[10] With a *feasibility radius* of ρ = **1.0e4**, constraining the solution x to lie in the ball $x^\top x < \rho^2$ where $\rho > 0$.

With `bnb`, the proposed rank function is `r(x,y,k)` = `+4.k`, proving that the necessary termination precondition automatically determined by the auxiliary termination counter method of Sec. 2.2 is also sufficient.   □

10.2 Example of Quadratic Termination of a Linear Loop

Example 9. Let us consider the program below which oddly simulates `for i = n downto 1 do for j = n downto 1 do skip end end`. The termination precondition has been automatically determined by iterated forward/backward polyhedral analysis. The loop invariant has been automatically determined by a forward polyhedral analysis, assuming the termination precondition. The analysis of the loop body involves a partitioning according to the test `(j > 0)`, as later explained in Sec. 11.1. For each case, the polyhedral approximation of the semantics of the loop body (where initially `(n0 = n)` & `(i0 = i)` & `(j0 = j)`) is given on the right:

```
assume (n >= 0);
i := n; j := n;
while (i <> 0) do
  assume ((j>=0) & (i>=0) &
          (n>=i) & (n>=j));
  if (j > 0) then
    j := j - 1
  else
    j := n; i := i - 1
  fi
od
```

Case $(j_0 > 0)$:

$$n - i \geq 0$$
$$i - 1 \geq 0$$
$$j \geq 0$$
$$n - j - 1 \geq 0$$
$$-j_0 + j + 1 = 0$$
$$-i_0 + i = 0$$
$$-n_0 + n = 0$$

Case $(j_0 \leq 0)$:

$$i \geq 0$$
$$-i + j - 1 \geq 0$$
$$-n_0 + j = 0$$
$$j_0 = 0$$
$$-i_0 + i + 1 = 0$$
$$-n + j = 0$$

Choosing $\delta = 1$ and a quadratic rank function, the resolution of the LMI constraints given in next Sec. 11.1 by `Sdplr-1.01` (with feasibility radius of `1.0e+3`) yield the solution:

```
r(n,i,j) = +7.024176e-04.n^2 +4.394909e-05.n.i -2.809222e-03.n.j...
           +1.533829e-02.n +1.569773e-03.i^2 +7.077127e-05.i.j  ...
           +3.093629e+01.i -7.021870e-04.j^2 +9.940151e-01.j    ...
           +4.237694e+00 .
```

Successive values of $r(n, i, j)$ during program execution are plotted above for $n = 10$ on loop entry. They strictly decrease along the inclined plane.

Nested loops are better handled by induction on the nesting level, as shown in Sec. 11.2.

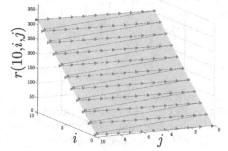

□

10.3 Example of Linear Termination of a Quadratic Loop

Example 10. The following program computes the least factorial strictly greater than a given integer N:

```
n := 0; f := 1;
while (f <= N) do
    n := n + 1; f := n * f
od
```

$$-f_0 + N_0 \geq 0 \qquad -n_0 + n - 1 = 0$$
$$n_0 \geq 0 \qquad -f_0.n + f = 0$$
$$f_0 - 1 \geq 0 \qquad -N_0 + N = 0$$

The non-linear semantics of the loop body (with polyhedral invariant) is provided on the right. It has only one quadratic constraint, a case when the Lagrangian relaxation is complete. The ranking function found by SeDuMi-1.05 (with feasibility radius of 1.0e+3) is r(n,f,N) = -9.993455e-01.n +4.346533e-04.f +2.689218e+02.N +8.744670e+02. □

11   Extension to More Complex Language Features

11.1   Disjunctions in the Loop Test and Conditionals in the Loop Body

Disjunctions in the loop test and/or conditionals within the loop body can be analyzed by partitioning along the values of the boolean expressions [10, Sec. 10.2]. Equivalently, a case analysis of the boolean expressions yields an operational semantics of the loop body of the form:

$$[\![B;C]\!](x, x') = \bigvee_{j=1}^{M} \bigwedge_{k=1}^{N_j} \sigma_{jk}(x, x') \geq 0 . \tag{16}$$

Whichever alternative is chosen, the rank function must strictly decrease while remaining nonnegative. Hence, we just have to consider the conjunction of all terminating constraints for each of the possible alternatives. We have already seen Ex. 9. Here is another one.

Example 11. For the program below:

```
while (x < y) do
    if (i >= 0) then
        x := x+i+1
    else
        y := y+i
    fi
od
```

Case $(x_0 < y_0)$:

$$-x_0 + y_0 - 1 \geq 0$$
$$i_0 \geq 0$$
$$-i_0 - x_0 + x - 1 = 0$$
$$-y_0 + y = 0$$
$$-i_0 + i = 0$$

Case $(x_0 \geq y_0)$:

$$-x_0 + y_0 - 1 \geq 0$$
$$-i_0 - 1 \geq 0$$
$$-i_0 - y_0 + y = 0$$
$$-x_0 + x = 0$$
$$-i_0 + i = 0$$

the cases are listed on the right[11]. The termination constraints are given below (the P(j).Mk(:,:,k) corresponding to the k-th constraint in the j-th case, the corresponding Lagrange coefficients being l0(j).v(k,j) for the nonnegativity and l(j).v(k,j) for decrementation by at least $\delta = 1$. The matrices M0 and M_0 encapsulate the matrix R of the ranking function $r(x) = (x\ 1).R.(x\ 1)^\top$ while $(x\ 1).\mathtt{delta}.(x\ 1) = \delta$ as explained in Sec. 8):

---

[11] Since the alternatives are considered on loop entry, a backward analysis may in general have to be used if some variable involved in a test of the loop body is modified in the body before that test.

```
M0-10(1).v(1,1)*P(1).Mk(:,:,1)-10(1).v(2,1)*P(1).Mk(:,:,2)-...
    10(1).v(3,1)*P(1).Mk(:,:,3)-10(1).v(4,1)*P(1).Mk(:,:,4)-...
    10(1).v(5,1)*P(1).Mk(:,:,5) >= 0
M0-M_0-delta-1(1).v(1,1)*P(1).Mk(:,:,1)-1(1).v(2,1)*P(1).Mk(:,:,2)-...
    1(1).v(3,1)*P(1).Mk(:,:,3)-1(1).v(4,1)*P(1).Mk(:,:,4)-...
    1(1).v(5,1)*P(1).Mk(:,:,5) >= 0
10(1).v(1,1) >= 0
10(1).v(2,1) >= 0
1(1).v(1,1) >= 0
1(1).v(2,1) >= 0
M0-10(2).v(1,1)*P(2).Mk(:,:,1)-10(2).v(2,1)*P(2).Mk(:,:,2)-...
    10(2).v(3,1)*P(2).Mk(:,:,3)-10(2).v(4,1)*P(2).Mk(:,:,4)-...
    10(2).v(5,1)*P(2).Mk(:,:,5) >= 0
M0-M_0-delta-1(2).v(1,1)*P(2).Mk(:,:,1)-1(2).v(2,1)*P(2).Mk(:,:,2)-...
    1(2).v(3,1)*P(2).Mk(:,:,3)-1(2).v(4,1)*P(2).Mk(:,:,4)-...
    1(2).v(5,1)*P(2).Mk(:,:,5) >= 0
10(2).v(1,1) >= 0
10(2).v(2,1) >= 0
1(2).v(1,1) >= 0
1(2).v(2,1) >= 0
```

Solving these LMI and elementwise constraints with bnb, we get r(i,x,y) = -4.x +4.y, that is essentially $y - x$, which corresponds to the intuition. □

11.2 Nested Loops

In the case of nested loops, the loops are handled one at a time, starting from the inner ones.

Example 12 (Manna's original bubble sort). For the bubble sort example below (taken literally from [24, p. 191]), the necessary termination precondition $N \geq 0$ is automatically determined by the iterated forward/backward method of Sec. 2.2. A further automatic forward reachability analysis starting from this termination precondition yields loop invariants:

```
assume (N >= 0);
n := N;
i := n;
loop invariant: {N=n,i>=0,n>=i}
while (i <> 0 ) do
  j := 0;
  loop invariant: {N=n,j>=0,i>=j,i>=1,N>=i}
  while (j <> i) do
    j := j + 1
  od;
  i := i - 1
od
```

The result of this global analysis is used to determine the semantics of the inner loop body as given by its forward analysis:

```
assume ((N=n) & (j>=0) & (i>=j) & (i>=1) & (N>=i));
assume (j <> i);
assume ((N0=N) & (n0=n) & (i0=i) & (j0=j));
j := j + 1
{j=j0+1,i=i0,N=n0,N=N0,N=n,j>=1,N>=i,j<=i}
```

The termination of the inner loop is then proved by solving the correspond-ing termination constraints as shown in Sec. 8. The **bnb** solver yields the rank function $r(N,n,i,j) = +2.n +4.i -4.j -4$.

Next, the semantics of the outer loop body is given by its forward polyhedral analysis:

```
assume ((N=n) & (i>=0) & (n>=i));
assume (i <> 0 );
assume ((N0=N) & (n0=n) & (i0=i) & (j0=j));
j := 0;
while (j <> i) do
      j := j + 1
od;
i := i - 1
{i+1=j,i+1=i0,N=n0,N=N0,N=n,N>=i+1,i>=0}
```

The termination of the outer loop is then proved by solving the corresponding termination constraints as shown in Sec. 8. With **bnb**, we get the rank function $r(N,n,i,j) = +2.n +4.i -3$.   □

In case the program graph is irreducible, the program has to be considered as a whole, with different ranking functions attached to cutpoints (the choice of which may not be unique).

11.3   Nondeterminism and Concurrency

Nondeterministic semantics are similar to (16) in Sec. 11.1. Nondeterminism can be used to handle concurrency by nondeterministic interleaving.

Example 13. The following concurrent program (where atomic actions are square bracketed) does terminate without any fairness hypothesis. If one process is never activated then the other process will terminate and so the remaining one will then be activated.

```
[|                                    while (x+2 < y) do
    while [x+2 < y] do                    if (??) then
        [x := x + 1]                          x := x + 1
    od                                    else if (??) then
||                                            y := y - 1
    while [x+2 < y] do                    else
        [y := y - 1]                          x := x + 1;
    od                                        y := y - 1
|]                                        fi fi
                                      od
```

By nondeterministic interleaving, the program is equivalent to the nondeterministic one on its right. The conditionals in the loop body can be handled as explained in Sec. 11.1. An even simpler solution is to consider an abstract interpretation of the semantics of the loop body through a polyhedral approximation (the resulting constraints are given on the right):

```
assume (x+2 < y);
assume ((x0 = x) & (y0 = y));
if (??) then
   x := x + 1
else if (??) then
   y := y - 1
else
   x := x + 1;
   y := y - 1
fi fi
{y+1>=y0,x<=x0+1,x+y0>=y+x0+1,x0+3<=y0}
```

$$-y_0 + y + 1 \geq 0$$
$$x_0 - x + 1 \geq 0$$
$$-x_0 + y_0 + x - y - 1 \geq 0$$
$$-x_0 + y_0 - 3 \geq 0$$

Establishing the termination constraints as explained in Sec. 8, and solving with bnb, we get the following termination function $r(x,y) = -4.x +4.y -9$.   □

11.4   Bounded Weakly Fair Parallelism

One way of handling fair parallelism is to consider nondeterministic interleaving with a scheduler to ensure bounded weak fairness.

Example 14. The following weakly fair parallel program (where atomic actions are bracketed):

```
[[ while [(x > 0) | (y > 0) do        || while [(x > 0) | (y > 0) do
       x := x - 1]                             y := y - 1]
   od                                      od ]]
```

does not terminate when x and y are initially positive and any one of the processes is never activated. Because of the bounded fairness hypothesis, the parallel program is semantically equivalent to the following nondeterministic program:

```
assume (m >= 1);                       if (s = 1) then
t := ?;                                    if (t = 1) then
assume (0 <= t & t <= 1);                     t := 0
s := ?;                                    else
assume ((1 <= s) & (s <= m));                 t := 1
while ((x > 0) | (y > 0)) do               fi;
   if (t = 1) then                         s := ?;
      x := x - 1                           assume ((1 <= s) & (s <= m))
   else                                 else
      y := y - 1                           s := s - 1
   fi;                                   fi
                                      od
```

The nondeterministic program incorporates an explicit scheduler of the two parallel processes where the turn t indicates which process is running and s indicates the number of atomic steps remaining to run before activating another process. The nondeterminism is bounded by m which ensures the existence of an integer-valued rank function. Notice however that, as found in practice, although the nondeterminism is known to be bounded, it is not known of how much (m can take any positive integer value, including very large ones). The theoretical notion of weak fairness corresponds to the case when m → ∞ that is unbounded nondeterminism, which may require ordinal-valued rank functions. In practice one can use lexicographic orderings on ℕ.

A forward analysis of the program determines the loop invariant {t<=1,s<=m, s>=1,t>=0}. The disjunction in the loop test is handled by partitioning, see Sec. 11.1. There are two cases for the loop test (x > 0), or (y > 0). In each case, the loop body is partitioned according to the value of s which, according to the invariant determined by the forward polyhedral analysis is either (s = 1) or (s > 1). The case (x > 0 ∧ s > 1) is illustrated below (empty(10) stands for ⊥, that is unreachability):

```
assume (t <= 1) & (s <= m) & (s >= 1) & (t >= 0);
assume (x > 0);
assume (s = 1);
assume ((x0 =x) & (y0 = y) & (t0 = t) & (s0 = s) & (m0 = m));
if (t = 1) then x := x - 1 else y := y - 1 fi;
if (s = 1) then
  if (t = 1) then
    t := 0
  else
    t := 1
  fi;
  s := ?;
  assume ((1 <= s) & (s <= m))
  {empty(10)}
else
  s := s - 1
fi
{m=m0,s+1=s0,t=t0,t+y0=y+1,t+x=x0,s+1<=m,t<=1,t>=0,t+x>=1,s>=1}
```

The other three forward analyses are similar and yield the following affine operational semantics for each of the alternatives:

$x > 0 \land s > 1$ {m=m0,s+1=s0,t=t0,t+y0=y+1,t+x=x0,s+1<=m,t<=1,t>=0,t<=y,s>=1}
$x > 0 \land s = 1$ {m=m0,s+1=s0,t=t0,t+y0=y+1,t+x=x0,s+1<=m,t<=1,t>=0,t<=y,s>=1}
$y > 0 \land s > 1$ {m=m0,s+1=s0,t=t0,t+y0=y+1,t+x=x0,s+1<=m,t<=1,t>=0,t<=y,s>=1}
$y > 0 \land s = 1$ {m=m0,s0=1,t+t0=1,t+y=y0,t+x0=x+1,t<=1,s<=m,s>=1,t>=0,t+y>=1}

The LMI termination constraints can then be established, as explained in Sec. 11.1. Solving with SeDuMi-1.05 (with a feasibility radius of 1.0e+4), we get the quadratic rank function:

```
r(x,y,m,s,t) = +8.078228e-06.x^2 +8.889797e-10.x.y +2.061102e-10.x.m
   +2.360326e-11.x.s +2.763786e-09.x.t +9.998548e-01.x +9.770849e-07.y^2
   +7.219411e-07.y.m -1.091400e-07.y.s -2.098975e-06.y.t +6.158628e+02.y
```

```
+4.044804e-06.m^2 -2.266154e-08.m.s +1.794800e-06.m.t +4.524134e-04.m
+7.994478e-06.s^2 -1.899723e-08.s.t -3.197335e-05.s +2.450149e-06.t^2
+3.556544e-04.t +9.696939e+03 .
```
$\square$

11.5   Semi-algebraic/Polynomial Programs

The termination constraints (12), (13), and (14) for semi-algebraic/polynomial programs lead to polynomial inequalities. A necessary condition for $\forall x : p(x) \geq 0$ is that the degree $m = 2d$ of p be even. A sufficient condition for nonnegativity of $p(x)$ is that $p(x) \geq q(x)$ where $q(x)$ is a sum of squares (SOS) of other polynomials $q(x) = \sum_i r_i^2(x)$ for some $r_i(x) \in \mathbb{R}[x]$ of degree d [26]. However the condition is not necessary.

The Gram matrix method [28] consists in fixing a priori the form of the base polynomials $r_i(x)$ in the sum of squares and in assuming that $q(x) = z(x)^\top Q z(x)$ where $z(x)$ is the vector of $N = \binom{n+d}{d}$ monomials of the monomial basis $B_{d,n}$ in any total monomial order (for example $z(x) == [1, x_1, \ldots, x_n, x_1^2, x_1 x_2, \ldots, x_n^d]$) and Q is a symmetric positive definite matrix of reals. Since $Q \succcurlyeq 0$, Q has a Cholesky decomposition L which is an upper triangular matrix L such that $Q = L^\top L$. It follows that $q(x) = z(x)^\top Q z(x) = z(x)^\top L^\top L z(x) = (Lz(x))^\top Lz(x) = [L_{i,:} \cdot z(x)]^\top [L_{i,:} \cdot z(x)] = \sum_i (L_{i,:} \cdot z(x))^2$ (where $\cdot$ is the vector dot product $x \cdot y = \sum_i x_i y_i$), proving that $q(x)$ is a sum of squares.

Finally, $z(x)^\top z(x)$ contains all monomials in x appearing in $p(x)$ and so $\forall x : p(x) - q(x) \geq 0$ can be expressed in the form $\forall x : z(x)^\top M z(x) \geq 0$ where M is a square symmetric matrix depending upon the coefficients of $p(x)$ and the unknowns in Q. By letting X be $z(x)$, the problem can be relaxed into the feasibility of $\forall X : X^\top M X$ which can be expressed as a semidefinite problem. If the problem is feasible, then the solution provides the value of Q whence a proof that $p(x)$ is positive.

The method is implemented by SOSTOOL [30] under MATLAB®.

Example 15 (Logistic map). The deterministic logistic map $f(x) = ax(1 - x)$ with bifurcation parameter a such that $0 \leq a < 1$ has a sink at 0 and every initial condition between 0 and 1 is attracted to this sink. So the following program (where $z > 0$ is implemented as $z \geq \epsilon$ with a small ϵ) terminates.

```
eps = 1.0e-10;
while (0<=a) & (a<=1-eps)
    & (eps<=x) & (x<=1) do
    x := a*x*(1-x)
od
```

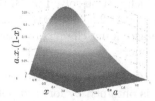

The MATLAB® program below establishes the termination conditions with Lagrangian relaxation (12), (13), and (14):

```
pvar a x0 x1 c0 d0 e0 l1 l2 l3 l4 l5 m1 m2 m3 m4 m5;
eps=1.0e-10;
iv = [a;x0;x1];
uv = [c0;d0;l1;l2;l3;l4;l5;m1;m2; m3;m4;m5];
pb = sosprogram(iv,uv);
pb = sosineq(pb,l1); pb = sosineq(pb,l2);
pb = sosineq(pb,l3); pb = sosineq(pb,l4);
pb = sosineq(pb,c0*x0+d0-l1*a-l2*(1-eps-a)-l3*(x0-eps)-l4*(1-x0)...
                -l5*(x1-a*x0*(1-x0)));
pb = sosineq(pb,m1); pb = sosineq(pb,m2);
pb = sosineq(pb,m3); pb = sosineq(pb,m4);
pb = sosineq(pb,c0*x0-c0*x1-eps^2-m1*a-m2*(1-eps-a)-m3*(x0-eps)...
                -m4*(1-x0)-m5*(x1-a*x0*(1-x0)));
spb = sossolve(pb);
c = sosgetsol(spb,c0); d = sosgetsol(spb,d0);
disp(sprintf('r(x) = %i.x + %i', double(c),double(d)));
```

These polynomial constraints are relaxed by SOSTOOLS v2.00 into a semidefinite program which is then solved by SeDuMi-1.05. The result is:

r(x) = 1.222356e-13.x + 1.406392e+00 .   □

12   Invariance

In the same way, loop invariants can be generated automatically by parametric abstraction (Sec. 4) and resolution of the Lagrangian relaxation (Sec. 6.1) of Floyd's invariance verification conditions (2) and (3). We get:

$$\exists a \in \mathbb{R}^p : \exists \mu \in \mathbb{R}^+ : \exists \lambda \in [0, N] \longrightarrow \mathbb{R}^+ :$$

$$\forall x \in \mathbb{R}^n : I_a(x) - \mu.P(x) \geq 0, \qquad (17)$$

$$\forall x_0, x \in \mathbb{R}^n : I_a(x) - \lambda_0.I_a(x_0) - \sum_{k=1}^{N} \lambda_k.\sigma_k(x_0, x) \geq 0 . \qquad (18)$$

There is an additional difficulty however since the appearance of the parametric abstraction of the invariant on the left of the implication in (3) yields, by Lagrangian relaxation, to the term $\lambda_0.I_a(x_0)$ in (18), which is bilinear in λ_0 and a. For programs which operational semantics has the form $[\![B;C]\!](x_0, x) = \bigwedge_{k=1}^{N}(x_0 \; x \; 1)M_k(x_0 \; x \; 1)^\top \geq 0$, constraint (18) is a bilinear matrix inequality (BMI), which can be solved by BMI solvers, which first appeared only recently, such as PenBMI [22] and bmibnb [23]. Contrary to iterative methods (at least when the ascending chain condition is satisfied), the invariant need not be the strongest one.

Example 16. This is illustrated by the following example from [14] where the invariant is obtained by forward polyhedral analysis:

```
i := 2;                 clear all; yalmip('clear');
j := 0;                 [iv,v] = variables('i','j');
while (??) do           p = parameters('a','b','c', 'm', 'l');
  {j>=0,i>=2j+2}        F = set(a*2+c>=0);
  if (??) then          F = F + set(sos(a*(i+4)+b*j-m*(a*i+b*j+c)));
    i := i + 4          F = F + set(m>=0);
  else                  F = F + set(sos(a*(i+2)+b*(j+1)+c-l*(a*i+b*j+c)));
    i := i + 2;         F = F + set(l>=0);
    j := j + 1          sol = solvesos(F,[],sdpsettings('solver','penbmi'),p);
  fi                    disp(sprintf('%+g*i %+g*j %+g >= 0',double(a),...
od;                                  double(b),double(c)));
```

Solving the given constraints with Yalmip yields the solution:

$$\texttt{+2.14678e-12*i -3.12793e-10*j +0.486712 >= 0,}$$

which is not the strongest possible one. However, satisfiability is easily checked by setting a = 1, b = −2 and c = −2.   □

However one can imagine other methods to discover the parameters (e.g. random interpretation [18]). Then a proof of invariance can be given by semidefinite programming relaxation.

In program verification, the assertions to be proved yields additional constraints which can be useful in the resolution.

Example 17 (Ex. 7 continued). In the Euclidean division of Ex. 7 from [16], we have to prove the postcondition (x=qy+r)&(r<y). For a parametric invariant I=a*x+b*q*y+c*r, the constraints are the following:

```
clear all; yalmip('clear');
[iv,v] = variables('x','y','q','r');
p = parameters('a','b','c','m1','m2','m3','m4','m5','m6','l0','l1',...
               'l2','l3','l4','l5','l6','n1','n2');
I0=a*x0+b*q0*y0+c*r0; I=a*x+b*q*y+c*r;
F = set(sos(I0-m1*(y0-1)-m2*q0-m3*(r0-x0)));
F = F + set(m1>=0);
F = F + set(sos(I-l0*I0-l1*(y0-1)-l2*(r0-y0)-l3*(r-r0+y0)-l4*(q-q0-1)...
               -l5*(x-x0)-l6*(y-y0)));
F = F + set(l0>=0) + set(l1>=0) + set(l2>=0);
P=x-q*y-r;
F = F + set(sos(P-n1*I-n2*(r-y+1)));
F = F + set(n2>=0);
[sol,m,B] = solvesos(F,m1,sdpsettings('solver','penbmi'),p)
disp(sprintf('%+g*x %+g*q*y %+g*r >= 0',double(a),double(b),double(c)));
```

Solving with Yalmip, we get:

$$\texttt{+2.11831e-05*x -2.11831e-05*q*y -2.11831e-05*r >= 0 .}$$

Then, in the other direction (where I0, I, P are respectively replaced by −I0, −I, −P), we get the loop invariant:

$$\texttt{+0.000167275*x -0.000167275*q*y -0.000167275*r >= 0 .}$$

By normalization of the coefficients and antisymmetry, the total correctness proof is finished.   □

13   Potential Problems with Solvers

13.1   Constraint Resolution Failure

The resolution of the termination constraints will definitely fail when the program does not terminate. The same way, the invariance constraints may be infeasible. However, infeasibility of the constraints does not mean "non termination" or "non invariance" but simply failure. First the parametric abstraction of Sec. 4 may be too coarse (so that e.g. a quadratic or even polynomial invariant/rank function may have to be considered instead of a linear one). Second, the solver may have failed (e.g. due to numerical difficulties when handling equalities) but may succeed with some help (e.g. by adding a shift [23]).

13.2   Numerical Computations

LMI/BMI solvers perform numerical computations with rounding errors, shifts, etc. It follows that the parameters of the parametric abstraction are subject to numerical errors and so the logical rigor of the proof may be questionable. Obviously the use of integer solvers or the concordant conclusions of several different solvers will be conclusive, at least from an experimental point of view, anyway more rigorous than mere tests.

Obviously, the hard point is to discover a candidate for the rank function or invariant and it is much less difficult, when it is known, to re-check for satisfaction (e.g. by static analysis or a proof assistant).

14   Conclusion

The resolution of systems of fixpoint (in)equations involving linear, semidefinite, and even polynomial numerical constraints by parametric abstraction and Lagrangian relaxation appears promising thanks to the spectacular progress in semidefinite programming and LMI/BMI solvers this last decade.

The approach seems naturally useful for termination since one is essentially interested in the existence of a rank function, even if it looks "unnatural". This is true of all inevitability/liveness properties for which generalization presents no fundamental problem.

The situation looks different for invariance since unnatural solutions may look less acceptable in the context of static analysis. However, the situation is different for correctness proofs, where the nature of the invariants has no importance provided the proof can be done. A difficulty is nevertheless to establish the form of the parametric abstraction, since the most general form would be costly at higher degrees.

To conclude, beyond numerical programs, parametric abstraction remains to be explored in other non-numerical contexts, such as symbolic computations.

Acknowledgements

We thank É. Féron who introduced us to LMIs [15], D. Henrion for his suggestions in formulating quantified polynomial positiveness as LMIs in Sec. 11.5, J. Löfberg for his help and fixes for YALMIP [23], B. Blanchet, R. Cousot, J. Feret, L. Mauborgne, A. Miné, D. Monniaux, and X. Rival for their comments.

References

1. S. Benson and Y. Ye. DSDP4: A software package implementing the dual-scaling algorithm for semidefinite programming. Technical Report ANL/MCS-TM-255, Argonne National Laboratory, 2002.
2. S. Boyd, L. E. Ghaoui, É. Féron, and V. Balakrishnan. *Linear Matrix Inequalities in System and Control Theory.* SIAM, 1994.
3. J. Brauburger and J. Giesl. Approximating the domains of functional and imperative programs. *Sci. Comput. Programming*, 35(1):113–136, 1999.
4. S. Burer and R. Monteiro. A nonlinear programming algorithm for solving semidefinite programs via low-rank factorization. *Mathematical Programming (series B)*, 95(2):329–357, 2003.
5. G. Collins and H. Hong. Partial cylindrical algebraic decomposition for quantifier elimination. *J. Symb. Comput.*, 12:299–328, 1991.
6. M. Colón and H. Sipma. Synthesis of linear ranking functions. *Proc. 7th Int. Conf. TACAS '2001*, LNCS 2031, pp. 67–81. Springer.
7. P. Cousot. *Méthodes itératives de construction et d'approximation de points fixes d'opérateurs monotones sur un treillis, analyse sémantique de programmes.* Thèse d'État ès sciences mathématiques, Univ. scient. et méd. de Grenoble, 1978.
8. P. Cousot and R. Cousot. Abstract interpretation: a unified lattice model for static analysis of programs by construction or approximation of fixpoints. *4th POPL*, pp. 238–252, 1977. ACM Press.
9. P. Cousot and R. Cousot. Static determination of dynamic properties of recursive procedures. *IFIP Conf. on Formal Description of Programming Concepts, St-Andrews*, pp. 237–277. North-Holland, 1977.
10. P. Cousot and R. Cousot. Systematic design of program analysis frameworks. *6th POPL*, pp. 269–282, 1979. ACM Press.
11. P. Cousot and R. Cousot. 'À la Floyd' induction principles for proving inevitability properties of programs. In *Algebraic Methods in Semantics*, ch. 8, pp. 277–312. Cambridge U. Press, 1985.
12. P. Cousot and R. Cousot. Abstract interpretation and application to logic programs[12]. *J. Logic Programming*, 13(2–3):103–179, 1992.
13. P. Cousot and R. Cousot. Abstract interpretation frameworks. *J. Logic and Comp.*, 2(4):511–547, 1992.
14. P. Cousot and N. Halbwachs. Automatic discovery of linear restraints among variables of a program. *5th POPL*, pp. 84–97, 1978. ACM Press.
15. É. Féron. Abstraction mechanisms across the board: A short introduction. *Workshop on Robustness, Abstractions and Computations*. Philadelphia, 18 Mar. 2004.

---

[12] The editor of J. Logic Programming has mistakenly published the unreadable galley proof. For a correct version of this paper, see http://www.di.ens.fr/~cousot.

16. R. Floyd. Assigning meaning to programs. *Proc. Symposium in Applied Mathematics*, vol. 19, pp. 19–32. AMS, 1967.
17. P. Gahinet, A. Nemirovski, A. Laub, and M. Chilali. LMI Control Toolbox for use with MATLAB®, user's guide. 1995.
18. S. Gulwani and G. Necula. Discovering affine equalities using random interpretation. *30th POPL*, pp. 74–84, 2003. ACM Press.
19. C. Hoare. An axiomatic basis for computer programming. *Comm. ACM*, 12(10):576–580, 1969.
20. B. Jeannet. New Polka. http://www.irisa.fr/prive/bjeannet/newpolka.html.
21. M. Karr. Affine relationships among variables of a program. *Acta Informat.*, 6:133–151, 1976.
22. M. Kočvara and M. Stingl. PENBMI *User's Guide (Version 1.1)*, 2004.
23. J. Löfberg. YALMIP. http://control.ee.ethz.ch/~joloef/yalmip.msql.
24. Z. Manna. *Mathematical theory of computation*. McGraw Hill, 1974.
25. P. Naur. Proofs of algorithms by general snapshots. *BIT*, 6:310–316, 1966.
26. Y. Nesterov. Squared functional systems and optimization problems. In *High Performance Optimization*, pp. 405–440. Kluwer Acad. Pub., 2000.
27. Y. Nesterov and A. Nemirovskii. Polynomial barrier methods in convex programming. *Èkonom. i Mat. Metody*, 24(6):1084–1091, 1988.
28. P. Parrilo. Semidefinite programming relaxations for semialgebraic problems. *Mathematical Programming*, 96(2):293–320, 2003.
29. A. Podelski and A. Rybalchenko. A complete method for the synthesis of linear ranking functions. *Proc. 5th Int. Conf. VMCAI 2004*, pp. 239–251. LNCS 2937, Springer.
30. S. Prajna, A. Papachristodoulou, P. Seiler, and P. Parrilo. SOSTOOLS: *Sum of squares optimization toolbox for* MATLAB, 2004.
31. J. Sturm. Using SeDuMi 1.02, a MATLAB toolbox for optimization over symmetric cones. *Optimization Methods and Software*, 11–12:625–653, 1999.
32. K. Toh, M. Todd, and R. Tütüncü. SDPT3–a MATLAB software package for semidefinite programming. *Optimization Methods and Software*, 11:545–581, 1999.
33. V. Yakubovich. Nonconvex optimization problem: The infinite-horizon linear-quadratic control problem with quadratic constraints. *Systems Control Lett.*, 19:13–22, 1992.

Scalable Analysis of Linear Systems Using Mathematical Programming*

Sriram Sankaranarayanan, Henny B. Sipma, and Zohar Manna

Computer Science Department
Stanford University
Stanford, CA 94305-9045
{srirams,sipma,zm}@theory.stanford.edu

Abstract. We present a method for generating linear invariants for large systems. The method performs forward propagation in an abstract domain consisting of arbitrary polyhedra of a predefined fixed shape. The basic operations on the domain like abstraction, intersection, join and inclusion tests are all posed as linear optimization queries, which can be solved efficiently by existing LP solvers. The number and dimensionality of the LP queries are polynomial in the program dimensionality, size and the number of target invariants. The method generalizes similar analyses in the interval, octagon, and octahedra domains, without resorting to polyhedral manipulations. We demonstrate the performance of our method on some benchmark programs.

1 Introduction

Static analysis is one of the central challenges in computer science, and increasingly, in other disciplines such as computational biology. Static analysis seeks to discover invariant relationships between the variables of a system that hold on every execution of the system. In computer science, knowledge of these relationships is invaluable for verification and optimization of systems; in computational biology this knowledge may lead to better understanding of the system's dynamics.

Linear invariant generation, the discovery of linear relationships between variables, has a long history, starting with Karr [9], and cast in the general framework of abstract interpretation by Cousot and Cousot [6]. The most general form of linear invariant generation is *polyhedral analysis*. The analysis is performed in the abstract domain of all the linear inequalities over all the system variables [7]. Although impressive results have been achieved in this domain, its applicability is severely limited by its worst-case exponential time and space complexity. This has led to the investigation of more restricted domains which seek to trade off

* This research was supported in part by NSF grants CCR-01-21403, CCR-02-20134 and CCR-02-09237, by ARO grant DAAD19-01-1-0723, by ARPA/AF contracts F33615-00-C-1693 and F33615-99-C-3014, by NAVY/ONR contract N00014-03-1-0939, and by the Siebel Graduate Fellowship.

R. Cousot (Ed.): VMCAI 2005, LNCS 3385, pp. 25–41, 2005.

some precision against tractability. The *interval domain* consists of inequalities of the form $a \leq x_i \leq b$. This was first studied by Cousot and Cousot [5]. Miné et al. consider the abstract domain of inequalities of the form $x_i - x_j \leq c$, known as *Difference-Bound Matrices* [12], and more generally, inequalities of the form $\pm x_i \pm x_j \leq c$, known as the *Octagon abstract domain* [13]. The domain has been applied to large programs with impressive results [3]. More recently, Clarisó et al. generalized octagons to *octahedra*, inequalities of the form $a_1 x_1 + \ldots a_n x_n \leq c$, where each a_i is either ± 1 or 0, and applied it to the verification of timing delays in asynchronous circuits [4].

In this paper, we show that an efficient forward propagation-based analysis can be performed in an abstract domain that lies between the interval domain of Cousot&Cousot [5], and the general polyhedra [7]. Our proposed domain can contain any inequality of the form $a_1 x_1 + \ldots a_n x_n + c \geq 0$. It requires the coefficients $a_1, \ldots, a_n$ for all inequalities in the abstract domain to be fixed in advance, and thus is less general than polyhedra. Since $a_1, \ldots, a_n$ can be user specified, our domain neatly subsumes the body of work described above. We show that all such analyses can be conducted in worst-case polynomial time in the program size and the domain size.

The rest of the paper is organized as follows: Section 2 reviews the basic theory of polyhedra, linear programming, system models and abstract interpretation. In Section 3, we describe our abstract domain, followed by the analysis algorithm and strategies on abstract domain construction. Section 4 discusses the complexity of our algorithm, and presents the results of applying it to several benchmark programs.

2   Preliminaries

We recall some standard results on polyhedra, followed by a brief description of system models and abstract interpretation. Throughout the paper, $x_1, \ldots, x_n$ denote real-valued variables, a, b with subscripts denote constant reals and c, d denote unknown coefficients. Similarly A, B denote real matrices, while A_i represents the ith row of the matrix A. We let $a, \ldots, z$ denote vectors. A vector is also a $n \times 1$ column-matrix for $n \geq 0$. The relation $a \leq b$ is used to denote $a_i \leq b_i$ for all $i = 1 \ldots n$.

2.1   Polyhedra

Definition 1 (Linear Assertions) A *linear inequality* is an expression of the form $a_1 x_1 + \cdots + a_n x_n + b \bowtie 0$, and $\bowtie \in \{\geq, =\}$. A *linear assertion* is a finite conjunction of linear inequalities. The assertion

$$\varphi : \begin{bmatrix} a_{11}x_1 + \ldots + a_{1n}x_n + b_1 \geq 0 & \wedge \\ \vdots & \ldots & \vdots & \vdots & \vdots \\ a_{m1}x_1 + \ldots + a_{mn}x_n + b_m \geq 0 \end{bmatrix}$$

can concisely be written in matrix form as $Ax + b \geq 0$, where x and b are n and m-dimensional vectors, respectively. The set of points in $\mathcal{R}^n$ satisfying a linear assertion is called a *polyhedron*. Polyhedra can be represented implicitly by a linear assertion, also known as the *constraint representation*, or explicitly by a set of vertices and rays, also known as the *generator representation* [15]. In this paper we assume that linear assertions do not contain any strict inequalities.

The linear consequences of a linear assertion φ, that is, the linear inequalities that are implied by φ, can be deduced using Farkas Lemma [15]:

Theorem 1 (Farkas Lemma). *Consider the linear assertion*

$$\varphi : \ Ax + b \geq 0$$

over real-valued variables x. If φ is satisfiable, then it implies the linear inequality $c^T x + d \geq 0$ iff there exists $\lambda \geq 0$ such that

$$A^T \lambda = c \ and \ b^T \lambda \leq d.$$

Furthermore, φ is unsatisfiable iff there exists $\lambda \geq 0$ such that

$$A^T \lambda = 0 \ and \ b^T \lambda \leq -1.$$

The main engine behind our analysis is a Linear Programming (LP) solver. We shall describe the theory of linear programming briefly.

Definition 2 (Linear Programming) An instance of the *linear programming (LP) problem* consists of a linear assertion φ and a linear expression $f : b^T x$, called the *objective function*. The goal is to determine the solution of φ for which f is minimal. An LP problem can have one of three results: (1) an optimal solution; (2) φ has solutions, but none is optimal with respect to f (f is unbounded in φ); (3) φ has no solutions.

In principle, an LP problem can be solved by computing the generators of the polyhedron corresponding to φ. If the polyhedron is empty, i.e., it has no generators, then there are no solutions. If the polyhedron has a ray along which the objective function f decreases, then f is unbounded. Also, it has been demonstrated that an optimal solution (if it exists) is realized at a vertex of the polyhedron. The optimal solution can be found by evaluating f at each of the vertices. Enumerating all the generators is very inefficient because the number of generators is worst-case exponential in the number of constraints. The popular SIMPLEX algorithm, although worst-case exponential in theory, is very fast over most problems in practice. Our method scales by taking advantage of this fact. Interior point methods like the *Karmarkar's* algorithm can solve linear programs in polynomial time. In practice, we shall use SIMPLEX for our linear programming needs because of its free availability and its numerical stability.

2.2 Transition Systems and Invariants

As computational model, we use transition systems [11]. For ease of exposition we assume that the transition systems are linear, as defined below. Any transition can be linearized by omitting all nonlinear constructs from the initial condition and transition relations.

Definition 3 (Linear Transition Systems) A linear transition system S : $\langle L, \mathcal{T}, \ell_0, \Theta \rangle$ over a set of variables V consists of

- L: a set of locations;
- $\mathcal{T}$: a set of transitions, where each transition τ : $\langle \ell_i, \ell_j, \rho_\tau \rangle$ consists of a pre-location ℓ_i, a post-location ℓ_j, and a transition relation ρ_τ that is a linear assertion over $V \cup V'$, where V denotes the values of the variables in the current state, and V' their values in the next state;
- $\ell_0 \in L$: the initial location;
- Θ: a linear assertion over V specifying the initial condition.

A *run* of a linear transition system is a sequence of pairs $(l_0, s_0), (l_1, s_1)$, $(l_2, s_2), \ldots$ with $l_i \in L$ and s_i a valuation of V, also called a *state*, such that

- Initiation: $l_0 = \ell_0$, and $s_0 \models \Theta$
- Consecution: for all $i \geq 0$ there exists a transition τ : $\langle p, q, \rho_\tau \rangle$ such that $l_i = p$, $l_{i+1} = q$, and $(s_i, s_{i+1}) \models \rho_\tau$.

A state s is *reachable* at location l if (l, s) appears in some run.

Henceforth, we shall assume that transitions are limited to guarded assignments of the form $\xi \wedge \boldsymbol{x}' = A\boldsymbol{x} + \boldsymbol{b}$, where the *guard* ξ is a linear assertion over V, and A, $\boldsymbol{b}$ are matrices. This form is common in transition systems derived from programs. However, the results easily extend to the general case too.

Example 1. Following is a transition system over $V = \{x, y\}$ with one location and two transitions that update the variables x and y atomically:

$$
\begin{aligned}
L &: \{l_0\} \\
\mathcal{T} &: \{\tau_1, \tau_2\} \quad \text{with} \quad \begin{cases} \tau_1 : \langle l_0, l_0, \left[x' = x + 2y \ \wedge \ y' = 1 - y \right] \rangle \\ \tau_2 : \langle l_0, l_0, \left[x' = x + 1 \ \wedge \ y' = y + 2 \right] \rangle \end{cases} \\
\ell_0 &: l_0 \\
\Theta &: (x = 0 \ \wedge \ y = 0)
\end{aligned}
$$

A given linear assertion ψ is a *linear invariant* of a linear transition system (LTS) at a location ℓ iff it is satisfied by every state reaching ℓ. An *assertion map* maps each location of a LTS to a linear assertion. An assertion map η is an invariant map if $\eta(\ell)$ is an invariant at ℓ, for each $\ell \in L$. In order to prove a given assertion map invariant, we use the theory of inductive assertions [11].

Definition 4 (Inductive Assertion Maps) An assertion map η is inductive iff it satisfies the following conditions:

Initiation: $\Theta \models \eta(\ell_0)$,
Consecution: For each transition $\tau : \langle \ell_i, \ell_j, \rho_\tau \rangle$, $\eta(\ell_i) \land \rho_\tau \models \eta(\ell_j)'$.

It can be proven by mathematical induction that any inductive assertion map is also an invariant map. It is well known that the converse need not be true in general. The standard technique for proving an assertion invariant is to find an inductive assertion that strengthens it. For example, the assertion $x + y \geq 0$ is an inductive assertion for the LTS in Example 1.

2.3 Propagation-Based Analysis

Forward propagation consists of a symbolic simulation of the program to compute an assertion representing the reachable state space. Starting with the initial condition, the assertion is iteratively weakened by adding states that are reachable in one step, as computed by the post operator, $post(\tau, \varphi) : \exists V_0 . (\varphi(V_0) \land \rho_\tau(V_0, V))$ until no more states can be added. This procedure can be described as the computation of a fixed point of the second order function (predicate transformer)

$$\mathfrak{F}(X) = \Theta \lor X \lor \bigvee_{\tau \in \mathcal{T}} post(\tau, X)$$

starting from $\mathfrak{F}(false)$. The least fixed point describes exactly the reachable state space.

This approach has two problems: (1) the sequence $\mathfrak{F}(false), \mathfrak{F}^2(false), \ldots$ may not converge in a finite number of steps, and (2) we may not be able to detect convergence, because the inclusion $\mathfrak{F}^{n+1}(false) \subseteq \mathfrak{F}^n(false)$ may be undecidable. These problems were addressed by the *abstract interpretation framework* formalized by Cousot and Cousot [6], and specialized for linear relations by Cousot and Halbwachs [7].

The abstract interpretation framework performs the forward propagation in a simpler, abstract domain, in which the detection of convergence is decidable. Also the resulting fixed point, when translated back, is guaranteed to be a fixed point (though not necessarily a least fixed point) of the concrete predicate transformer. The problem of finite convergence was addressed by the introduction of a *widening* operator that guarantees termination in a finite number of steps.

The application of abstract interpretation requires the definition of an abstract domain Σ_A, equipped with a partial order $\leq_A$, an abstraction function $\alpha : 2^\Sigma \mapsto \Sigma_A$ that maps sets of states into elements in the abstract domain, and a concretization function $\gamma : \Sigma_A \mapsto 2^\Sigma$. The functions α and γ must form a *Galois connection*, that is they must satisfy $\alpha(S) \leq_A a$ iff $S \subseteq \gamma(a)$ for all $S \subseteq \Sigma$ and $a \in \Sigma_A$.

Forward propagation can now be performed in the abstract domain by computing the fixed point of

$$\mathfrak{F}_A(X) = \Theta_A \sqcup X \sqcup \bigsqcup_{\tau \in \mathcal{T}} post_A(\tau, X) .$$

If the operations $\sqcup$ and $post_A$ satisfy $\gamma(a_1) \lor \gamma(a_2) \subseteq \gamma(a_1 \sqcup a_2)$, and $post(\tau, \gamma(a))$ $\subseteq \gamma(post_A(a))$, and the abstract element Θ_A satisfies $\Theta \subseteq \gamma(\Theta_A)$, then $\gamma(lfp(\mathfrak{F}_A))$ is guaranteed to be a fixed point of $\mathfrak{F}$.

Polyhedra are a very popular abstract domain. Checking for inclusion is decidable, and effective widening operators have been designed. However, manipulating large polyhedra remains computationally expensive and hence, this analysis does not scale very well in practice.

Note. Throughout the rest of the paper, instead of the traditional $\subseteq$ relation, we shall use the models relation ($\models$) between formulas as the order on the concrete domain.

3 Invariant Generation Algorithm

3.1 Abstract Domain

Our abstract domain consists of polyhedra of a fixed shape for a given set of variables $\boldsymbol{x}$ of cardinality n. The shape is fixed by an $m \times n$ template constraint matrix (TCM) T. If T is nonempty, i.e, $m > 0$, the abstract domain Σ_T contains m-dimensional vectors $\boldsymbol{c}$. Each entry c_i may be real-valued, or a special-valued entry drawn from the set $\{\infty, -\infty\}$. A vector $\boldsymbol{c}$ in the abstract domain Σ_T represents the set of states described by the set of constraints $T\boldsymbol{x} + \boldsymbol{c} \geq \boldsymbol{0}$. If the TCM T is empty, that is $m = 0$, the abstract domain Σ_T is forced to contain two elements $\boldsymbol{c}_\top$ and $\boldsymbol{c}_\bot$, representing the entire state space and the empty state space, respectively.

Definition 5 (Concretization function) The concretization function γ_T is defined by

$$\gamma_T(\boldsymbol{c}) \equiv \begin{cases} false & \text{if } \exists c_i = -\infty \text{ or } \boldsymbol{c} = \boldsymbol{c}_\bot, \\ true & \text{if } \boldsymbol{c} = \boldsymbol{c}_\top, \\ \bigwedge_{i \text{ s.t. } c_i \neq \infty} (T_i \boldsymbol{x} + c_i \geq 0) & \text{otherwise.} \end{cases}$$

The value $c_i = \infty$ drops the ith constraint from the concrete assertion, and the value $c_i = -\infty$ makes the concrete assertion *false*. We assume that the standard ordering $\leq$ on the reals has been extended such that $-\infty \leq x \leq \infty$ for all $x \in \mathcal{R}$.

Example 2. Consider the template constraint matrix

$$T = \begin{bmatrix} 1 & 0 \\ -1 & 0 \\ 0 & 1 \\ 0 & -1 \\ -1 & 1 \\ 1 & -1 \end{bmatrix} \quad \begin{matrix} \text{representing the} \\ \text{template assertions} \end{matrix} \quad \begin{bmatrix} x & + c_1 \geq 0 \\ -x & + c_2 \geq 0 \\ & y + c_3 \geq 0 \\ & - y + c_4 \geq 0 \\ -x + y + c_5 \geq 0 \\ x - y + c_6 \geq 0 \end{bmatrix}$$

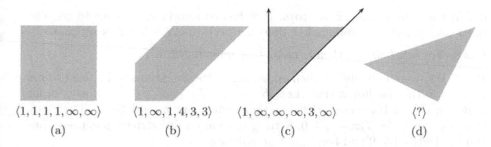

$\langle 1, 1, 1, 1, \infty, \infty \rangle$ $\langle 1, \infty, 1, 4, 3, 3 \rangle$ $\langle 1, \infty, \infty, \infty, 3, \infty \rangle$ $\langle ? \rangle$

(a)   (b)   (c)   (d)

Fig. 1. Polyhedra (a), (b) and (c) are concretizations of the elements in the abstract domain Σ_A of Example 2, whereas (d) is not.

The concretization of the abstract element $c : \langle \infty, 2, 3, \infty, 5, 1 \rangle$ is the assertion

$$\gamma_T(c) : \left[-x + 2 \geq 0 \ \wedge \ y + 3 \geq 0 \ \wedge \ -x + y + 5 \geq 0 \ \wedge \ x - y + 1 \geq 0 \right] .$$

Figure 1 shows three polyhedra that are concretizations of elements in Σ_T, and one that is not.

Definition 6 (Abstract domain pre-order) Let $a, b \in \Sigma_T$,

$$a \preceq b \quad \text{iff} \quad \gamma_T(a) \models \gamma_T(b).$$

Also $a \sim_{\preceq} b$ iff $a \preceq b$ and $b \preceq a$. We set $\bot = \langle -\infty, \ldots, -\infty \rangle$ and $\top = \langle \infty, \ldots, \infty \rangle$, and for T empty, $\bot = c_\bot$ and $\top = c_\top$. Note that $\gamma_T(\bot) = false$ and $\gamma_T(\top) = true$.

The abstraction function α_T maps sets of states into vectors c in Σ_T. Since we restrict ourselves to linear transition systems, we may assume that sets of states can be described by linear assertions $\varphi : Ax + b \geq 0$. Ideally, the value of $\alpha_T(\varphi)$ should be the vector c that represents the smallest polyhedron with shape determined by T, that subsumes φ. Thus, α_T should compute a $\preceq$-minimal c such that

$$Ax + b \geq 0 \models Tx + c \geq 0.$$

To begin with, if φ is unsatisfiable, we set $c = \bot$.

If φ is satisfiable, we use linear programming to determine a suitable c. Consider each half space of the form $T_i x + c_i \geq 0$. We wish to ensure that

$$Ax + b \geq 0 \ \models \ T_i x + c_i \geq 0.$$

Applying Farkas Lemma, we obtain,

$$Ax + b \geq 0 \models T_i x + c_i \geq 0 \quad \text{iff} \quad (\exists \lambda \geq 0) \ A^{\mathrm{T}} \lambda = T_i \ \wedge \ b^{\mathrm{T}} \lambda \leq c_i.$$

To find the smallest c_i that satisfies the requirements above, we solve the LP problem

$$\Psi : \lambda \geq 0 \ \wedge \ A^{\mathrm{T}} \lambda = T_i \ \text{with objective function} \ b^{\mathrm{T}} \lambda .$$

If Ψ has a solution u, c_i is set to u. If Ψ has no solutions, c_i is set to ∞. The third case, where c_i is unbounded, does not occur if $A\boldsymbol{x} + \boldsymbol{b} \geq \boldsymbol{0}$ is satisfiable.

Claim. For satisfiable φ, then c_i cannot be unbounded in Ψ.

Proof. If c_i were unbounded, then appealing to the soundness of Farkas Lemma leads us to the conclusion that $A\boldsymbol{x} + \boldsymbol{b} \geq \boldsymbol{0} \models T_i\boldsymbol{x} + c_i \geq 0$ for all $c_i \leq u$, for some constant u. If φ were satisfiable, then some point $\boldsymbol{x_0}$ satisfies it. Therefore, $(\boldsymbol{x} = \boldsymbol{x_0}) \models \varphi \models T_i\boldsymbol{x} + c_i \geq 0$. Setting c_i to any value strictly less than $T_i\boldsymbol{x_0}$ and u, yields $-1 \geq 0$ and hence, a contradiction.

Example 3. Consider the assertion

$$\varphi : \quad \underbrace{\begin{pmatrix} 1 & 0 \\ 0 & 1 \\ -1 & 1 \\ 1 & -1 \end{pmatrix}}_{A} \begin{pmatrix} x \\ y \end{pmatrix} + \underbrace{\begin{pmatrix} 0 \\ 0 \\ 1 \\ 1 \end{pmatrix}}_{b} \geq \boldsymbol{0} \ .$$

The abstraction $\alpha_T(\varphi)$ mapping φ into the abstract domain of Example 2 is computed by solving six LP problems. For example, c_2 is computed by solving

$$\underbrace{\begin{pmatrix} 1 & 0 & -1 & 1 \\ 0 & 1 & 1 & -1 \end{pmatrix}}_{A^T} \underbrace{\begin{pmatrix} \lambda_1 \\ \lambda_2 \\ \lambda_3 \\ \lambda_4 \end{pmatrix}}_{\lambda} = \underbrace{\begin{pmatrix} -1 \\ 0 \end{pmatrix}}_{T_2} \quad \text{with objective function} \quad \lambda_3 + \lambda_4 \ .$$

The problem has no solutions, yielding the value ∞ for c_2. The value for c_6 is computed by solving the same problem, replacing $T_2 : (-1\ 0)^T$ by $T_6 : (1\ -1)^T$. This problem yields an optimal solution $c_6 = 1$. Solving all the six problems produces $\alpha_T(\varphi) = \langle 0, \infty, 0, \infty, 1, 1 \rangle$.

Definition 7 (Abstraction function) Let φ be the linear assertion $A\boldsymbol{x} + \boldsymbol{b} \geq \boldsymbol{0}$. Given a nonempty TCM T, the function α_T assigns to φ the value $\boldsymbol{c} = \langle c_1, \ldots, c_m \rangle$, such that

$$c_i = \begin{cases} -\infty & \text{if } \varphi \text{ is unsatisfiable,} \\ \min. \boldsymbol{b}^T\boldsymbol{\lambda}, \ s.t. \underbrace{\boldsymbol{\lambda} \geq \boldsymbol{0} \wedge A^T\boldsymbol{\lambda} = T_i}_{\Psi_i} & \text{if } \Psi_i \text{ is feasible,} \\ \infty & \text{if } \Psi_i \text{ is infeasible .} \end{cases}$$

For an empty TCM T, we set $\alpha_T(\varphi) = \boldsymbol{c}_\perp$ if φ is unsatisfiable, and $\alpha_T(\varphi) = \boldsymbol{c}_\top$ otherwise.

Lemma 1 (Abstraction Lemma). *The functions α_T and γ_T form a Galois connection, that is, (1) for all linear assertions φ and abstract elements $\boldsymbol{a} \in \Sigma_A$, $\alpha_T(\varphi) \preceq \boldsymbol{a}$ iff $\varphi \models \gamma_T(\boldsymbol{a})$. (2) Furthermore, for nonempty T, if $\varphi \models \gamma_T(\boldsymbol{a})$ then $\alpha_T(\varphi) \leq \boldsymbol{a}$. That is, $\alpha_T(\varphi)$ is minimal with respect to the standard order $\leq$ on vectors.*

Proof. For empty TCM T, both parts follow easily from Definitions 5, 6, and 7. For the remainder, assume T is nonempty.

(1) ($\Rightarrow$) Assume $\alpha_T(\varphi) \preceq a$. If φ is unsatisfiable, then trivially, $\varphi \models \gamma_T(a)$. Otherwise, let $\alpha_T(\varphi) = c$. By Def. 7 and the soundness of Farkas Lemma, $\varphi \models T_i x + c_i \geq 0$, for each $c_i \neq \infty$. Therefore, $\varphi \models \gamma_T(c)$. By Def. 6 and by assuming $c \preceq a$, we obtain $\varphi \models \gamma_T(c) \models \gamma_T(a)$.

($\Leftarrow$) Assume $\varphi \models \gamma_T(a)$. If φ is unsatisfiable, $\alpha_T(\varphi) = \bot$ and hence trivially $\alpha_T(\varphi) \preceq a$. Otherwise let $\alpha_T(\varphi) = c$. By Def 5, $\varphi \models \bigwedge_{a_i \neq \infty}(T_i x + a_i \geq 0)$, and hence for arbitrary i such that $a_i \neq \infty$, $\varphi \models T_i x + a_i \geq 0$. By Def 7 and the completeness of Farkas Lemma, both c_i and a_i belong to the (nonempty) feasible set of the linear program generated for the implication $\varphi \models T_i x + c_i \geq 0$. Therefore, by optimality of c_i, $c_i \leq a_i$, and hence, $T_i x + c_i \geq 0 \models T_i x + a_i \geq 0$. and hence by Def 6, $c \preceq a$. In fact, we have also established that $c \leq a$.

(2) This follows directly from the second part of (1).

The abstract domain Σ_T is redundant. It contains multiple elements that map to the same concrete element. We eliminate this redundancy by choosing a *canonical element* c_{min} for each equivalence class $[c]$ of the relation $\sim_{\preceq}$.

Example 4. Consider the abstract domain from Example 2. The elements $a_1 = \langle 1,1,1,1,2,2 \rangle$, $a_2 = \langle 1,1,1,1,3,3 \rangle$, and $a_3 : \langle 1,1,1,1,\infty,\infty \rangle$ all map to the rectangle described by $-1 \leq x,y \leq 1 \ \wedge \ -2 \leq x - y \leq 2$, and thus $a_1 \sim_{\preceq} a_2 \sim_{\preceq} a_3$. The reason is that the last two constraints, on $x - y$, are redundant in all these elements. In fact any abstract element $\langle 1,1,1,1,x,y \rangle$, $x \geq 2$, $y \geq 2$ belongs to the same equivalence class.

Definition 8 (Canonical element) Let Σ_T be an abstract domain with ordering $\preceq$. Given an equivalence class $[c]$ of $\sim_{\preceq}$, its canonical element, denoted $can(c)$ is defined as $can(c) = \alpha_T(\gamma_T(c))$.

We need to show that $can(c)$ belongs to the equivalence class of c, and also that the canonical element is unique.

Claim. (1) $can(c) \sim_{\preceq} c$, (2) for any a, such that $a \sim_{\preceq} c$, $can(c) \leq a$, (3) $can(c)$ is unique, i.e., if $a \sim c$, then $can(c) = can(a)$.

Proof. This follows directly from Lemma 1.

Example 5. For the abstract domain of Example 2, $\langle 1,1,1,1,2,2 \rangle$ is the canonical element for the equivalence class represented by

$$[\langle 1,1,1,1,2,2 \rangle] = \{\langle 1,1,1,1,x,y \rangle \mid x,y \geq 2\}$$

Computation of the greatest lower bound of two canonical elements in Σ_T for nonempty T consists of taking the entrywise minimum and canonizing the result.

Definition 9 (Intersection) Let a, b be two canonical elements of Σ_T. For T nonempty, $a \sqcap b = can(\langle \min(a_1, b_1), \ldots, \min(a_m, b_m) \rangle)$, where $\min(x, y)$ is defined as the minimum under the $\leq$ relation. For T empty we define the intersection operation on the elements $\top$ and $\bot$ in the standard fashion.

The following example shows that $\langle \min(a_1, b_1), \ldots, \min(a_m, b_m) \rangle$ is not necessarily a canonical element.

Example 6 (Failure of Canonicity). Consider the abstract domain Σ_T with template constraint matrix $T = (1 \ - 1)^{\mathrm{T}}$, representing the template assertions $x + c_1 \geq 0$ and $-x + c_2 \geq 0$. The entrywise minimum of the elements $\langle 1, 2 \rangle$, and $\langle 5, -2 \rangle$ is $\langle 1, -2 \rangle$. Verify that $\gamma_T(\langle 1, -2 \rangle) = false$, and hence $can(\langle 1, -2 \rangle) = \bot$.

Claim. Let $m = a_1 \sqcap a_2$. Then (1) $m \preceq a_{\{1,2\}}$ and (2) for any $b \preceq a_{\{1,2\}}$, it follows that $b \preceq m$

Proof. If T is empty, $a_1 = \bot$, or $a_2 = \bot$, both parts hold immediately.

(1) If $m = \bot$ then the first part holds immediately. If $m \neq \bot$, then we show that $\gamma_T(m) \models \gamma_T(a_1)$. Since $m = can(\min(a_1, a_2))$, for each row i, $m_i \leq \min(a_{1i}, a_{2i})$. If $a_{1i} \neq \infty$, then $m_i \neq \infty$. Therefore, $\gamma_T(m) \models T_i x + m_i \geq 0 \models T_i x + a_{1i} \geq 0$. Thus, $\gamma_T(m) \models \gamma_T(a_1)$, leading to $m \preceq a_1$. Similarly, $m \preceq a_2$.

(2) Let $b \preceq a_{\{1,2\}}$ and $a_{\{1,2\}} \neq \bot$. For each i, such that $a_{1i} \neq \infty$, $\gamma_T(b) \models T_i x + a_{1i} \geq 0$. Similarly, if $a_{2i} \neq \infty$, then $\gamma_T(b) \models T_i x + a_{2i} \geq 0$. Therefore, for each $m_i \neq \infty$, there are four cases to consider depending on $a_{1i} \neq \infty$, $a_{2i} \neq \infty$. In either case, $\gamma_T(b) \models T_i x + \min(a_{1i}, a_{2i}) \geq 0$. Therefore $b \preceq \min(a_1, a_2) \preceq m$.

Computation of the lowest upper bound of two canonical elements consists of taking the entrywise maximum, and is guaranteed to result in a canonical element.

Definition 10 (Union) Let a, b be two canonical elements of Σ_T. For T nonempty, $a \sqcup b = \langle \max(a_1, b_1), \ldots, \max(a_m, b_m) \rangle$ For T empty the union is the usual result for $\top$ and $\bot$.

Claim. Let $m = a_1 \sqcup a_2$. Then (1) $a_{\{1,2\}} \preceq m$; (2) if for some b, $a_{\{1,2\}} \preceq b$, it follows that $m \preceq b$; and (3) m is canonical

Proof. Proofs for parts (1), (2) are similar to the proof for intersection. For part (3), assume otherwise. Then there exists a vector $b \sim m$, and some position j such that $b_j < m_j$. Assume w.l.o.g., that $a_{1j} \leq a_{2j} = m_j$. Let a_2' be the vector a_2 with a_{2j} replaced by b_j. It follows immediately, that $a_2' \preceq a_2$. $\gamma_T(a_2) \models \gamma_T(m) \models T_j x + b_j \geq 0$, therefore $a_2 \preceq a_2'$, and consequently, $a_2 \sim a_2'$. Thus a_2 fails to be canonical in this case, contradicting our assumptions.

Claim. Let a, b be two canonical elements. Then $a \preceq b$ iff for each i, $a_i \leq b_i$.

Proof. This follows directly from the two claims above, using the fact that $a \preceq b$ iff $a \sqcup b \sim_{\preceq} b$, along with the property that if two canonical forms are equivalent then they are identical.

3.2   Analysis Algorithm

Traditionally forward propagation is performed entirely in the abstract domain until convergence, and the resulting fixed point is concretized. Our analysis algorithm performs the analysis in *multiple abstract domains*: one domain per program location. This allows for tailoring the template constraint matrix to the assertions that are likely to hold at that location. It also complicates the presentation of the *post* operation.

Let $\Psi : \langle L, T, \ell_0, \Theta \rangle$ be an LTS over a set of variables V. Let each location $\ell \in L$ be associated with an abstract domain Σ_ℓ parameterized by the template constraint matrix T_ℓ, with k_ℓ template rows. The objective is to construct an abstract invariant map η that maps each location $\ell \in L$ to a (canonical) element in the abstract domain Σ_ℓ.

We construct this invariant map by forward propagation as follows. The starting point is the map η^0 that assigns to the initial location, ℓ_0, the abstract value of the initial condition, that is $\eta^0(\ell_0) = \alpha_{\ell_0}(\Theta)$, and the element $\perp$ to all other locations.

Example 7. Consider the LTS from Example 1. The associated domain of the single location ℓ_0 has template constraint matrix

$$
\begin{pmatrix} 1 & 0 \\ -1 & 0 \\ 1 & 1 \\ 1 & -1 \end{pmatrix} \quad \begin{array}{c} \text{representing the} \\ \text{template assertions} \end{array} \quad \begin{bmatrix} x & + c_1 \geq 0 \\ -x & + c_2 \geq 0 \\ x + y + c_3 \geq 0 \\ x - y + c_4 \geq 0 \end{bmatrix}
$$

Using this template, the initial condition, $\Theta : x = 0 \land y = 0$ is abstracted to $\eta^0(\ell_0) = \langle 0, 0, 0, 0 \rangle$.

The postcondition operator for a transition leading from location ℓ_i to location ℓ_j computes the element c in Σ_{ℓ_j} that represents the states that can be reached from states represented by the current value of η at ℓ_i. More formally,

Definition 11 (Postcondition operator) Given $\tau : \langle \ell_i, \ell_j, \rho_\tau \rangle$, then

$$
post(\eta(\ell_i), \tau) = \begin{cases} \perp & \eta(\ell_i) = \perp \\ \alpha_j(\gamma_i(\eta(\ell_i) \land \rho_\tau)) & \textit{otherwise} \end{cases}
$$

where α_j is the abstraction function for Σ_{ℓ_j} and γ_i is the concretization function of Σ_{ℓ_i}.

Let T_{ℓ_i} and T_{ℓ_j} be the template constraint matrices for locations ℓ_i and ℓ_j, respectively. Let ρ_τ be $\xi \land x' = Ax + b$. If $post(\eta(\ell_i), \tau) = c$, we require that

$$
\begin{array}{l} (T_{\ell_i} x + \eta(\ell_i) \geq 0) \land \xi \land x' = Ax + b \models T_{\ell_j} x' + c \geq 0, \textit{ equivalently,} \\ (T_{\ell_i} x + \eta(\ell_i) \geq 0) \land \xi \models (T_{\ell_j} A)x + (T_{\ell_j} b + c) \end{array}
$$

In practice, we precompute the TCM $T' = T_{\ell_j} A$ for each transition. We then abstract the assertion $\gamma_j(\eta(\ell_i)) \land \xi$ using this TCM. Care should be taken to subtract $T_{\ell_j} b$ from the result of the abstraction. This yields the post-condition at location ℓ_j w.r.t. transition τ. Note that this technique is also applied to self-looping transitions. Therefore, labeling each location with a different template complicates our presentation but not the complexity of the procedure.

Example 8. Consider the map $\eta^0(\ell_0) = \langle 0,0,0,0 \rangle$ from Example 7 and the transition $\tau_1 = \langle \ell_0, \ell_0, [\, x' = x + 2y \;\wedge\; y' = 1 - y \,] \rangle$. For this transition, $\xi = true$,

$$A = \begin{pmatrix} 1 & 2 \\ 0 & -1 \end{pmatrix} \quad \text{and} \quad b = \begin{pmatrix} 0 \\ 1 \end{pmatrix}$$

We compute $T' = TA$ and $a = Tb$ for performing the abstraction. Abstracting $\gamma_T(\eta(\ell_0)) \equiv (x = y = 0)$, w.r.t T' yields the result $\langle 0,0,0,0 \rangle$. Subtracting a from this yields, $\langle 0,0,-1,1 \rangle$, which is the required post-condition.

Using the postcondition the map at step $i > 0$ is updated in the standard fashion, as follows:

$$\eta^{i+1}(\ell_n) = \eta^i(\ell_n) \sqcup \left(\bigsqcup_{\tau:\langle \ell_m, \ell_n, \rho \rangle} post(\eta^i(\ell_m), \tau) \right)$$

This process does not necessarily terminate. Termination can be ensured by a form of widening that is a natural generalization of widening in the interval and octagon domain. At each location we limit the number of updates to each parameter to a fixed number. If that number is exceeded for a particular parameter, we impoverish the abstract domain at that location by removing the corresponding constraint from the TCM. Clearly this guarantees termination, since for each TCM the number of constraints is finite.

Remark. The reason that we remove the constraint from the TCM, rather than set the parameter to ∞, is that the latter may lead to infinite ascending chains. The problem, as pointed out by Miné [13, 12], is that when a parameter c_i is set to ∞, subsequent canonization may set c_i back to a finite value, effectively bringing back the corresponding constraint.

Example 9. Figure 2 shows the results of applying the algorithm to the LTS in Example 1. The maximum number of updates to any template constraint expression is set to 3. The Figure shows that only three constraints survive, corresponding to the invariants $x \geq 0 \;\wedge\; x + 2y \geq 0 \;\wedge\; x + y \geq 0$.

Instead of directly removing a constraint from the TCM if the number of updates has exceeded the threshold, a more elegant solution is to use a *Local Widening* operator, similar to the widening-upto operator introduced in [8]. Let $T_{\ell,i}x + c_i \geq 0$ be one of the template constraints at location ℓ, such that the number of updates to c_i has exceeded the set threshold. Let τ be an incoming transition at location ℓ. The *local value* of c_i w.r.t τ is obtained by computing the minimum c_i for which $\rho_\tau \models T_{\ell,i}x' + c_i \geq 0$ holds. Assuming that τ can be executed for some state, the corresponding LP problem either shows optimal solution $b_{i,\tau}$, or is infeasible, in which case the local value is set to ∞. As a result, if b_i is the maximum among all the local values of all the transitions τ with target location ℓ, the assertion $T_{\ell,i}x + b_i \geq 0$ is a *local invariant* at ℓ, and c_i can be set to b_i instead of ∞. Thus, the local widening operator computes the

Template	Iteration num.						
	1	2	3	4	5	6	7
$y + c_1$	0	0	2	4	6	x	x
$-y + c_2$	0	3	5	7	x	x	x
$x + c_3$	0	0	0	0	0	0	0
$-x + c_4$	0	1	8	x	x	x	x
$x - y + c_5$	0	2	3	4	x	x	x
$x + y + c_6$	0	0	0	0	0	0	0
$-x - y + c_7$	0	4	8	x	x	x	x
$y - x + c_8$	0	0	9	16	x	x	x
$x + 2y + c_9$	0	0	0	0	0	0	0
$-x - 2y + c_{10}$	0	7	12	17	x	x	x
$x + 3y + c_{11}$	0	0	0	0	1	∞	∞
$-x - 3y + c_{12}$	0	10	17	24	x	x	x

Fig. 2. A run of the invariant generation algorithm.

local value of an expression instead of dropping the expression. In this case the computed value is *frozen*, and further updates to it are disallowed.

Example 10. Consider the template expression $-x + c \geq 0$ and the transition $\tau : x \leq 3 \land x' = x + 2$. The local value of c w.r.t. τ is 5, since $\tau \models -x' + 5 \geq 0$.

3.3   Template Formation

The algorithm presented so far has assumed the presence of a template constraint matrix for every location. In this section we propose some strategies for constructing these templates.

A first source of expressions is the description of the transition system itself: expressions in the initial condition and transition guards are likely to be invariants for some constant values. A second source are expressions present in target properties. A third source are expressions of a certain form such as intervals, $x_i \leq c$, $x_i \geq c$, which are often useful in applications involving array bounds and pointer safety, or octagons, $\pm x_i \pm x_j + c \geq 0$ for each pair of variables [13]. However, these expressions, albeit good candidates, cannot be the only expressions. The reason is that they seldom are inductive by themselves: they need support.

Example 11. Consider the LTS from Example 1 and the assertion $x \geq 0$. Although Example 9 showed that $x \geq 0$ is an invariant, it is not preserved by the transition $\tau_1 : x' = x + 2y, y' = 1 - y$. However, $x + 2y \geq 0 \land x \geq 0$ is inductive. We call $x + 2y \geq 0$ the *support expression* for $x \geq 0$.

Definition 12 (Support vector) Given a coefficient vector $\boldsymbol{a}$ and a transition $\tau : \langle \ell_i, \ell_j, \xi \land \boldsymbol{x}' = A\boldsymbol{x} + \boldsymbol{b} \rangle$, the coefficient vector $(A^{\mathrm{T}}\boldsymbol{a})^{\mathrm{T}}$ is called the support vector for $\boldsymbol{a}$ with respect to τ.

Type	Original		Support	
	TCM	Template expression	TCM	Template expression
bound	1 0	$x \quad\quad + c_1 \geq 0$	1 . 2	$x + 2y + c_2 \geq 0$
bound	-1 0	$-x \quad\quad + c_3 \geq 0$	-1 -2	$-x - 2y + c_4 \geq 0$
bound	0 1	$y + c_5 \geq 0$	0 -1	$- \quad y + c_6 \geq 0$
octagon	1 1	$x + y + c_7 \geq 0$	1 1	$x + \quad y + c_7 \geq 0$
octagon	1 -1	$x - y + c_8 \geq 0$	1 3	$x + 3y + c_9 \geq 0$
octagon	-1 1	$-x + y + c_{10} \geq 0$	-1 -3	$-x - 3y + c_{11} \geq 0$
octagon	-1 -1	$-x - y + c_{12} \geq 0$	-1 -1	$-x - \quad y + c_{12} \geq 0$

Fig. 3. Support vectors for bound and octagon expressions.

Example 12. The support vector for the vector $\langle 1, -1 \rangle$ corresponding with $x - y$ from Example 7, under the update $x' = x + 2y$, $y' = 1 - y$ is $\langle 1, 3 \rangle$ corresponding with $x + 3y$. The table in Figure 3 shows the support vectors and their corresponding template expressions for the interval and octagon expressions in Example 9 with respect to τ_1. Every vector is its own support with respect to transition τ_2. In this case, the table is closed under computing support vectors.

Support vectors are computed for each location. Given template constraint matrices T_{ℓ_i} and T_{ℓ_j} and a transition $\tau : \langle \ell_i, \ell_j, \rho_\tau \rangle$, then a support vector for location ℓ_j with respect to τ is computed from a row of T_{ℓ_j} and ρ_τ and added as a row to T_{ℓ_i}. Note the similarity to computing weakest preconditions.

4 Performance

Complexity. The complexity of our algorithm is polynomial in the size of the program and the size of the template constraint matrix. Consider a transition system with n variables, $|L|$ locations and $|T|$ transitions, and assume that each location is labeled with an $m \times n$ template constraint matrix. Let k be the maximum number of updates allowed to the abstract invariant map. Then the number of post-condition computations is bounded by $(k+1)m|L||T|$. Each post-condition computation requires m LP queries, one for each row in the template constraint matrix, and thus the total number of LP queries is $O(km^2|L||T|)$.

In practice, the number of updates to reach convergence is much less than $(k + 1)m|L||T|$. In addition, the number of LP queries can be reduced further by skipping post-condition computations for transitions whose prelocation assertions did not change.

Practial Performance. We have implemented our algorithm and applied it to several benchmark programs. The results are shown in Figure 4. Our implementation is based on the GNU Linear programming kit, which uses the SIMPLEX algorithm for linear programming [10]. The library uses floating point arithmetic. Soundness is maintained by careful rounding, and checking the obtained invariants using the exact arithmetic implemented in the polyhedral library PPL [1].

Program			Template		Statistics				
name	L	T	#t	#s	t(sec)	t_{lp}(sec)	# LPS	#avg.	#dim.
MCC91 (3)	1	2	11	0	0.05	0.01	227	1.5	15 (20)
TRAINHPR97(3)	4	12	58	3	0.1	0.02	673	0.9	18(25)
BERKELEY(4)	1	3	63	16	0.23	0.11	1,632	1.36	64(96)
DRAGON(5)	1	12	129	157	3.94	2.38	11,426	3.23	202 (298)
HEAPSORT(5)	1	4	33	24	0.34	0.13	1,751	2.45	75(90)
EFM(6)	1	5	506	461	7.65	2.36	10,872	0.69	359(981)
LIFO(7)	1	10	85	79	1.87	0.91	5,401	3.37	141 (174)
CARS-MIDPT(7)	1	2	101	324	3.72	2.21	4,641	6.23	154(329)
BARBER(8)	1	12	128	0	1.97	0.83	9,210	1.96	124(141)
SWIM-POOL(9)	1	6	104	0	0.56	0.27	2,710	2.11	97(118)
TTP(9)	4	20	3,555	127	62.8	40.9	61,263	4.41	574(1032)
REQ-GRANT(11)	1	8	221	18	2.96	1.41	8,635	2.10	241(255)
CONSPROT(12)	2	14	533	40	4.88	2.00	12,487	1.83	266(286)
CSM(13)	1	8	313	73	9.65	5.21	14,890	3.69	380(414)
C-PJAVA(16)	1	14	453	93	35.16	15.19	33,288	5.00	433(567)
CONSPROD(18)	1	14	529	96	38.72	19.43	35,797	5.17	468(663)
INCDEC(32)	1	28	961	267	287.54	110.27	103,841	6.57	877(1294)
MESH2X2(32)	1	32	438	0	43.9	17.5	52,622	4.53	390(506)
BIGJAVA(44)	1	37	864	376	331.98	117.68	122,643	5.25	1018 (1280)
MESH3X2(52)	1	54	1133	0	432.85	192.15	216,600	6.70	930(1241)

Fig. 4. Experimental results for benchmark examples. All timings were measured on an Intel Xeon processor running linux 2.4, with 2GB RAM.

The benchmark programs were taken from the related work, mostly from the FAST project [2]. Many of these programs (eg., BERKELEY, DRAGON, TTP and CSM) are models of bus and network protocols. Other programs, including BIGJAVA, C-PJAVA and HEAPSORT, were obtained by abstracting java programs. Some programs are academic examples from the Petri net literature (eg., SWIM-POOL, EFM, MESHIXJ). These programs, ranging in size from 4 to 52 variables, exhibit complex behaviours and require non-trivial invariants for their correctness proofs. Figure 4 shows for each program the number of variables (next to the name in parentheses), the number of locations ($|L|$) and transitions ($|T|$).

The templates for these programs were obtained in two ways: they were generated from user-defined *patterns* or automatically derived from the initial condition and the transition guards. An example of a user-defined pattern is: "%i + 2 * %j + 3 * %k ". It generates all constraints of the form $x_i + 2x_j + 3x_k + b_{ijk} \geq 0$, for all combinations (x_i, x_j, x_k) of system variables. In many cases the patterns were suggested by the target property. For instance the target property $x \leq K$ for some variable x and constant K, suggests the patterns -%i, -%i -%j and so on. The columns "#t" and "#s" in Figure 4 show the number of template constraints considered initially, and the number of support constraints generated for these initial constraints, respectively. Thus the total number of constraints is the sum of these two values. For each program, the maximum number of updates to each constraint was set to 3.

The statistics part in Figure 4 shows the performance of our algorithm in terms of computation time and number of LP queries solved. The first two columns (t(sec) and t_{lp}) show the total time needed to reach convergence and the time spent by the LP solver, respectively. The last three columns show the number of LP instances solved, the average number of SIMPLEX iterations for each LP call, and the the maximum (and average between parentheses) dimensionality of each LP problem. The memory used ranged from KBs for the smaller examples to 50 MB for BIGJAVA and 67MB for MESH3X2.

Invariants. The invariants obtained for the benchmark programs were of mixed quality. On one hand, the pattern-generated constraints produced invariants that were able to prove the target properties for most examples including the CSM and BIGJAVA. On the other hand, we were unable to prove the desired properties for examples like INCDEC and CONSPROD. In general, like with polyhedra, our technique fails in cases where non-convex and non-linear invariants are required. For all programs the propagation converged within 10 iterations, which is much faster than the theoretical maximum.

5   Conclusions

In this paper, we have demonstrated an efficient algorithm for computing invariants by applying abstract interpretation on a domain that is less powerful than that of polyhedra but more general than related domains like intervals, octagons and the very recent octahedra. In theory, we have thus generalized the previous results and appealed to the complexity of linear programming to show that all of these analyses can be performed in polynomial time. In practice, we have exploited the power of LP solvers to provide time and space-efficient alternatives to polyhedra. We have shown through our benchmark examples that our method is scalable to large examples and has the potential of scaling to even larger examples through a wiser choice of templates. Our support assertion generation greatly improves the ability of our algorithm to infer non-trivial invariants, and exploits the fact that we can support arbitrary coefficients in our assertions.

Future extensions to this work need to consider many issues both theoretical and practical. The analysis can be performed on non-canonical elements. This can greatly simplify the post-condition computation but complicate inclusion checks. Preprocessing LP calls using an equality simplifier could reduce the dimensionality of each call. Possible extensions include the use of semi-definite programming to extend the method to non-linear systems and non-linear templates. The work of Parillo et al. gives us a direct extension of Farkas Lemma for the non-linear case [14].

Acknowledgements

We would like to thank the anonymous referees for their comments and suggestions. We are also grateful to the developers of GLPK [10] and PPL [1] for making their tools public, and hence making this study possible. Many thanks to Aaron Bradley, Michael Colón, César Sánchez and Matteo Slanina for their comments and suggestions.

References

1. BAGNARA, R., RICCI, E., ZAFFANELLA, E., AND HILL, P. M. Possibly not closed convex polyhedra and the Parma Polyhedra Library. In *Static Analysis Symposium* (2002), vol. 2477 of *LNCS*, Springer-Verlag, pp. 213–229.
2. BARDIN, S., FINKEL, A., LEROUX, J., AND PETRUCCI, L. FAST: Fast accelereation of symbolic transition systems. In *Computer-aided Verification* (July 2003), vol. 2725 of *LNCS*, Springer-Verlag.
3. BLANCHET, B., COUSOT, P., COUSOT, R., FERET, J., MAUBORGNE, L., MINÉ, A., MONNIAUX, D., AND RIVAL, X. A static analyzer for large safety-critical software. In *ACM SIGPLAN PLDI'03* (June 2003), vol. 548030, ACM Press, pp. 196–207.
4. CLARISÓ, R., AND CORTADELLA, J. The octahedron abstract domain. In *Static Analysis Symposium* (2004), vol. 3148 of *LNCS*, Springer-Verlag, pp. 312–327.
5. COUSOT, P., AND COUSOT, R. Static determination of dynamic properties of programs. In *Proceedings of the Second International Symposium on Programming* (1976), Dunod, Paris, France, pp. 106–130.
6. COUSOT, P., AND COUSOT, R. Abstract Interpretation: A unified lattice model for static analysis of programs by construction or approximation of fixpoints. In *ACM Principles of Programming Languages* (1977), pp. 238–252.
7. COUSOT, P., AND HALBWACHS, N. Automatic discovery of linear restraints among the variables of a program. In *ACM Principles of Programming Languages* (Jan. 1978), pp. 84–97.
8. HALBWACHS, N., PROY, Y., AND ROUMANOFF, P. Verification of real-time systems using linear relation analysis. *Formal Methods in System Design 11*, 2 (1997), 157–185.
9. KARR, M. Affine relationships among variables of a program. *Acta Inf. 6* (1976), 133–151.
10. MAKHORIN, A. The GNU Linear Programming Kit, 2000. http://www.gnu.org/software/glpk/glpk.html.
11. MANNA, Z., AND PNUELI, A. *Temporal Verification of Reactive Systems: Safety.* Springer-Verlag, New York, 1995.
12. MINÉ, A. A new numerical abstract domain based on difference-bound matrices. In *PADO II* (May 2001), vol. 2053 of *LNCS*, Springer-Verlag, pp. 155–172.
13. MINÉ, A. The octagon abstract domain. In *AST 2001 in WCRE 2001* (October 2001), IEEE, IEEE CS Press, pp. 310–319.
14. PARRILO, P. A. Semidefinite programming relaxation for semialgebraic problems. *Mathematical Programming Ser. B 96*, 2 (2003), 293–320.
15. SCHRIJVER, A. *Theory of Linear and Integer Programming.* Wiley, 1986.

The Arithmetic-Geometric Progression
Abstract Domain*

Jérôme Feret

DI, École Normale Supérieure, Paris, France
jerome.feret@ens.fr

Abstract. We present a new numerical abstract domain. This domain automatically detects and proves bounds on the values of program variables. For that purpose, it relates variable values to a clock counter. More precisely, it bounds these values with the i-th iterate of the function $[X \mapsto \alpha \times X + \beta]$ applied on M, where i denotes the clock counter and the floating-point numbers α, β, and M are discovered by the analysis. Such properties are especially useful to analyze loops in which a variable is iteratively assigned with a barycentric mean of the values that were associated with the same variable at some previous iterations. Because of rounding errors, the computation of this barycenter may diverge when the loop is iterated forever. Our domain provides a bound that depends on the execution time of the program.

Keywords: Abstract Interpretation, static analysis, numerical domains.

1 Introduction

A critical synchronous real-time system (as found in automotive, aeronautic, and aerospace applications) usually consists in iterating a huge loop. Because practical systems do not run forever, a bound on the maximum iteration number of this loop can be provided by the end-user or discovered automatically. The full certification of such a software may require relating variable values to the number of iterations of the main loop. It is especially true when using floating-point numbers. Some computations that are stable when carried out in the real field, may diverge because of the rounding errors. Rounding errors are accumulated at each iteration of the loop. When expressions are linear and when the evaluation of expressions does not overflow, the rounding errors at each loop iteration are usually proportional to the value of the variables. Thus the overall contribution of rounding errors can be obtained by iterating a function of the form $[X \mapsto \alpha \times X + \beta]$. Then by using the maximum number of iterations we can infer bounds on the values that would normally have diverged in the case of an infinite computation.

We propose a new numerical abstract domain that associates with each variable the corresponding coefficients α and β and the starting value M. This

---

* This work was partially supported by the ASTRÉE RNTL project.

R. Cousot (Ed.): VMCAI 2005, LNCS 3385, pp. 42–58, 2005.

$$V \in \mathcal{V}, I \in \mathcal{I}$$
$$E := I \mid V \mid I \times V + E$$
$$P := V = E \mid \textbf{skip} \mid \textbf{tick} \mid \textbf{if } (V \geq 0) \ \{P\} \ \textbf{else} \ \{P\} \mid \textbf{while } (V \geq 0) \ \{P\} \mid P; P$$

Fig. 1. Syntax.

framework was fully implemented in OCAML [7] and plugged into an existing analyzer [1, 2]. We use this analyzer for certifying a family of critical embedded softwares, programs ranging from 70,000 to 379,000 lines of C.

Outline. In Sect. 2, we present the syntax and semantics of our language. In Sect. 3, we describe a generic abstraction for this language. In Sect. 4, we define a numerical abstract predomain that relates arithmetic-geometric constraints with sets of real numbers. In Sect. 5, we enrich an existing analysis so that it can deal with arithmetic-geometric constraints. In Sect. 6, we refine our analysis to deal with more complex examples. In Sect. 7, we report the impact of the arithmetic-geometric progression domain on the analysis results.

2 Language

We analyze a subset of C without dynamic memory allocation nor side-effect. Moreover, the use of pointer operations is restricted to call-by reference. For the sake of simplicity, we introduce an intermediate language to describe programs that are interpreted between the concrete and an abstract level. Data structures have been translated by using a finite set of abstract cells (see [2, Sect. 6.1]). Non-deterministic branching over-approximates all the memory accesses (array accesses, pointer dereferencing) that are not fully statically resolved. Furthermore, floating-point expressions have been conservatively approximated by linear forms with real interval coefficients. These linear forms include both the rounding errors and some expression approximations (see [9]). We also suppose that the occurrence of runtime errors (such as floating-point overflows) can be described by interval constraints on the memory state.

Let $\mathcal{V}$ be a finite set of variables. Let $\texttt{clock} \notin \mathcal{V}$ be an extra variable which is associated with the clock counter. The clock counter is explicitly incremented when a command **tick** is executed. The system stops when the clock counter overflows a maximum value which is defined by the end-user. We denote by $\mathcal{I}$ the set of all real number intervals (including $\mathbb{R}$ itself). We define inductively the syntax of programs in Fig. 1. We denote by $\mathcal{E}$ the set of expressions E. We describe the semantics of these programs in a denotational way. An *environment* ($\rho \in \mathcal{V} \cup \{\texttt{clock}\} \to \mathbb{R}$) denotes a memory state. It maps each variable, including the clock variable, to a real number. We denote by Env the set of all environments. The semantics of an expression E is a function $(\!|E|\!) \in Env \to I$ mapping each environment to an interval. Given a maximum value $\texttt{mc}$ for the clock, the semantics of a program P is a function $[\![P]\!]_{\texttt{mc}} \in Env \to \wp(Env)$ mapping each environment ρ to the set of the environments that can be reached when applying the program P starting from the environment ρ. Returning a set of environments

$$(\!|I|\!)(\rho) = I, \ (\!|V|\!)(\rho) = \{\rho(V)\}$$
$$(\!|I \times V + E|\!)(\rho) = \{b \times \rho(V) + a \mid a \in (\!|E|\!)(\rho), b \in I\}$$
$$[\![V = E]\!]_{mc}(\rho) = \{\rho[V \mapsto x] \mid x \in (\!|E|\!)(\rho)\}$$
$$[\![\mathbf{skip}]\!]_{mc}(\rho) = \{\rho\}$$
$$[\![\mathbf{tick}]\!]_{mc}(\rho) = \begin{cases} \{\rho[\mathtt{clock} \mapsto \rho(\mathtt{clock}) + 1]\} & \text{if } \rho(\mathtt{clock}) < \mathtt{mc} \\ \emptyset & \text{otherwise} \end{cases}$$
$$[\![\mathbf{if} \ (V \geq 0) \ \{P_1\} \ \mathbf{else} \ \{P_2\}]\!]_{mc}(\rho) = \begin{cases} [\![P_1]\!]_{mc}(\rho) & \text{if } \rho(V) \geq 0 \\ [\![P_2]\!]_{mc}(\rho) & \text{otherwise} \end{cases}$$
$$[\![\mathbf{while} \ (V \geq 0) \ \{P\}]\!]_{mc}(\rho) = \{\rho' \in Inv \mid \rho'(V) < 0\}$$
$$\text{where } Inv = \mathrm{lfp}\left(X \mapsto \{\rho\} \cup \left(\bigcup\{[\![P]\!]_{mc}(\rho') \mid \rho' \in X, \rho'(V) \geq 0\}\right)\right)$$
$$[\![P_1; P_2]\!]_{mc}(\rho) = \bigcup\{[\![P_2]\!]_{mc}(\rho') \mid \rho' \in [\![P_1]\!]_{mc}(\rho)\}$$

Fig. 2. Concrete semantics.

allows the description of both non-determinism and program halting (when the clock has reached its maximum value). The functions $(\!|\_|\!)$ and $[\![\_]\!]_{mc}$ are defined by induction on the syntax of programs in Fig. 2. Loop semantics requires the computation of a *loop invariant*, which is the set of all environments that can be reached just before the guard of this loop is tested. This invariant is well-defined as the least fixpoint of a $\cup$-complete endomorphism[1] $f \in \wp(Env) \rightarrow \wp(Env)$. Nevertheless, such a fixpoint is usually not computable, so we give a decidable approximate semantics in the next section.

We describe two toy examples.

Example 1. The first example iterates the computation of a barycentric mean: at each loop iteration, a variable is updated with a barycentric mean among its current value and two previous values.

$$V = \mathbb{R}; \ B_1 = \mathbb{R}; \ B_2 = \mathbb{R}; \ X = 0; \ Y = 0; \ Z = 0;$$
$$\mathbf{while} \ (V \geq 0) \ \{$$
$$\quad V = \mathbb{R}; \ B_1 = \mathbb{R}; \ B_2 = \mathbb{R};$$
$$\quad \mathbf{if} \ (B_1 \geq 0) \ \{Z = Y; Y = X\} \ \mathbf{else} \ \{\mathbf{skip}\};$$
$$\quad \mathbf{if} \ (B_2 \geq 0) \ \{$$
$$\quad\quad X = I; Y = I; Z = I\}$$
$$\quad \mathbf{else} \ \{$$
$$\quad\quad X = I_X \times X + I_Y \times Y + I_Z \times Z + I_\varepsilon\};$$
$$\quad \mathbf{tick}\}$$

where $I \in \mathcal{I}$, $\varepsilon_i > 0$ for any $i \in \{X; Y; Z; 0\}$, $0 < \alpha < 0.5$,
$$I_X = [1 - 2 \times \alpha - \varepsilon_X; 1 - 2 \times \alpha + \varepsilon_X], \ I_Y = [\alpha - \varepsilon_Y; \alpha + \varepsilon_Y],$$
$$I_Z = [\alpha - \varepsilon_Z; \alpha + \varepsilon_Z], \text{ and } I_\varepsilon = [-\varepsilon_0; \varepsilon_0].$$

More precisely, initialization values range in the interval I. The parameter α is a coefficient of the barycentric mean. The parameters ε_X, ε_Y, and ε_Z encode the rounding errors relative respectively to the variables X, Y, and Z in the computation of the barycentric mean. The parameter ε_0 encodes the absolute rounding

---

[1] In fact, we only use the monotonicity of f.

error. The three variables X, Y, and Z allow the recursion (X is associated with the current value, Y is associated with the last selected value and Z is associated with the previous selected value) and the three variables V, B_1, and B_2 allow non-deterministic boolean control. The variable V allows stopping the loop iteration. The variable B_1 allows the selection of a recursive value which consists in shifting the variables X, Y, and Z. The variable B_2 allows the choice between a reinitialization or an iteration step: a reinitialization step consists in assigning the variables X, Y, and Z with some random values in the interval I, whereas an iteration step consists in updating the variable X with the barycentric mean between its current value and the last two selected values. Because of rounding errors, the value associated with the variable X cannot be bounded without considering the clock. Therefore, we can prove that this value is bounded by $[X \mapsto ((1 + \varepsilon_X + \varepsilon_Y + \varepsilon_Z) \times X) + \varepsilon_0]^{(\mathrm{mc})}(M_I)$, where M_I is the least upper bound of the set $\{|x| \mid x \in I\}$. This bound can be discovered using the arithmetic-geometric domain presented in this paper. It is worth noting that the domains that deal with digital stream processing [6] do not help because the value of the variable Y is not necessarily the previous value of the variable X: such domains can only approximate relations of the form $o_n = f(o_{n-1}, ..., o_{n-p}, i_{n-1}, ..., i_{n-q})$ where (i_n) is the input stream and (o_n) is the output stream.

Example 2. The second example iterates a loop where a floating point is first divided by a coefficient $\alpha > 0$ and then multiplied by the coefficient α.

$$V = \mathbb{R};\ B_1 = \mathbb{R};\ B_2 = \mathbb{R};\ X = 0;$$
$$\textbf{while } (V \geq 0)\ \{$$
$$\quad V = \mathbb{R};\ B_1 = \mathbb{R};\ B_2 = \mathbb{R};$$
$$\quad \textbf{if } (B_1 \geq 0)\ \{X = I_1;\}\ \textbf{else } \{\textbf{skip}\};$$
$$\quad X = [\tfrac{1}{\alpha} - \varepsilon_1; \tfrac{1}{\alpha} + \varepsilon_1] \times X + [-\varepsilon_2; \varepsilon_2];$$
$$\quad \textbf{if } (B_2 \geq 0)\ \{X = I_2\}\ \textbf{else } \{\textbf{skip}\};$$
$$\quad X = [\alpha - \varepsilon_3; \alpha + \varepsilon_3] \times X + [-\varepsilon_4; \varepsilon_4];$$
$$\quad \textbf{tick}\}$$

where $\varepsilon_i > 0$, for any $i \in \{1; 2; 3; 4\}$, $\alpha > 0$, and $I_1, I_2 \in \mathcal{I}$.

More precisely, initialization values range in the intervals I_1 and I_2. The parameter α is a coefficient of the example. The parameters ε_1 and ε_3 encode relative rounding errors and the parameters ε_2 and ε_4 encode absolute rounding errors. The variable X contains the value that is divided and multiplied. The three variables V, B_1, and B_2 allow boolean control. The variable V allows stopping the loop iteration. The variable B_1 allows the reinitialization of the variable X before the division, the variable B_2 allows its reinitialization before the multiplication. Because of rounding errors, the value associated with the variable X cannot be bounded without considering the clock. Therefore, we can prove that this value is bounded by $[X \mapsto (1 + a) \times X + b]^{(\mathrm{mc})}(M_I)$ where $a = \alpha \times \varepsilon_1 + \tfrac{1}{\alpha} \times \varepsilon_3 + \varepsilon_1 \times \varepsilon_3$ and $b = \varepsilon_2 \times (\alpha + \varepsilon_3) + \varepsilon_4$, and M_I is the least upper bound of the set $\{|x| \mid x \in I_1 \cup A\}$ with $A = \{\frac{y}{\varepsilon_1 + \frac{1}{\alpha}} \mid y \in I_2\}$. This bound can be discovered using the arithmetic-geometric domain.

3 Underlying Domain

We use the Abstract Interpretation framework [3–5] to derive a generic approximate semantics. An abstract domain $Env^\sharp$ is a set of properties about memory states. Each abstract property is related to the set of the environments which satisfy it via a concretization map γ. An operator $\sqcup$ allows the gathering of information about different control flow paths. The primitives ASSIGN, GUARD, and TICK are sound counterparts to concrete assignments, guards, and clock ticks. To effectively compute an approximation of concrete fixpoints, we introduce an iteration basis $\bot$, a widening operator $\triangledown$, and a narrowing operator $\triangle$. Several abstract domains collaborate and use simple constraints to refine each other. We introduce two domains of simple constraints. The domain of interval $\mathcal{V} \cup \{\text{clock}\} \to \mathcal{I}$ and the domain of absolute value ordering $\wp(\mathcal{V}^2)$. The interval constraints encoded by a map $\rho^\sharp \in \mathcal{V} \cup \{\text{clock}\} \to \mathcal{I}$ are satisfied by the environment set $\gamma_\mathcal{I}(\rho^\sharp) = \{\rho \in Env \mid \rho(X) \in \rho^\sharp(X),\ \forall X \in \mathcal{V} \cup \{\text{clock}\}\}$. The constraints encoded by a subset $\mathcal{R} \subseteq \mathcal{V}^2$ are satisfied by the environment set $\gamma_{\text{ABS}}(\mathcal{R}) = \bigcap_{(X,Y)\in\mathcal{R}}\{\rho \in Env \mid |\rho(X)| \le |\rho(Y)|\}$. The primitives RANGE and ABS capture simple constraints about the values that are associated with variables by weakening the abstract elements of $Env^\sharp$. These constraints are useful in refining the arithmetic-geometric progression domain. Conversely, a primitive REDUCE uses the range constraints that have been computed by the other domains in order to refine the underlying domain.

Definition 1 (Generic abstraction). *An abstraction is defined by a tuple* $(Env^\sharp, \gamma, \sqcup, \text{ASSIGN}, \text{GUARD}, \text{TICK}, \bot, \triangledown, \triangle, \text{RANGE}, \text{ABS}, \text{REDUCE})$ *such that:*

1. $Env^\sharp$ *is a set of properties;*
2. $\gamma \in Env^\sharp \to \wp(Env)$ *is a concretization map;*
3. $\forall a, b \in Env^\sharp, \gamma(a) \cup \gamma(b) \subseteq \gamma(a \sqcup b)$;
4. $\forall a \in Env^\sharp, X \in \mathcal{V}, E \in \mathcal{E}, \rho \in \gamma(a),\ [\![X = E]\!]_{\text{mc}}(\rho) \subseteq \gamma(\text{ASSIGN}(X = E, a))$;
5. $\forall a \in Env^\sharp, X \in \mathcal{V} \cup \{\text{clock}\}, I \in \mathcal{I},$
   $\{\rho \in \gamma(a) \mid \rho(X) \in I\} \subseteq \gamma(\text{GUARD}(X, I, a))$;
6. $\forall a \in Env^\sharp, \{\rho[\text{clock} \mapsto \rho(\text{clock}) + 1] \mid \rho \in \gamma(a)\} \subseteq \gamma(\text{TICK}(a))$;
7. $\forall a \in Env^\sharp, \rho^\sharp \in (\mathcal{V} \cup \{\text{clock}\} \to \mathcal{I}),\ \gamma(a) \cap \gamma_\mathcal{I}(\rho^\sharp) \subseteq \gamma(\text{REDUCE}(\rho^\sharp, a))$;
8. $\triangledown$ *is a widening operator such that:* $\forall a, b \in Env^\sharp,\ \gamma(a) \cup \gamma(b) \subseteq \gamma(a\triangledown b)$; *and* $\forall k \in \mathbb{N},\ \rho_1, ..., \rho_k \in (\mathcal{V} \cup \{\text{clock}\} \to \mathcal{I}),\ (a_i) \in (Env^\sharp)^\mathbb{N}$, *the sequence* $(a_i^\triangledown)$ *defined by* $a_0^\triangledown = r(a_0)$ *and* $a_{n+1}^\triangledown = r(a_n^\triangledown \triangledown a_{n+1})$ *with* $r = [X \mapsto \text{REDUCE}(\rho_k, X)] \circ ... \circ [X \mapsto \text{REDUCE}(\rho_1, X)]$, *is ultimately stationary;*
9. $\triangle$ *is a narrowing operator such that:* $\forall a, b \in Env^\sharp,\ \gamma(a) \cap \gamma(b) \subseteq \gamma(a\triangle b)$; *and* $\forall k \in \mathbb{N},\ \rho_1, ..., \rho_k \in (\mathcal{V} \cup \{\text{clock}\} \to \mathcal{I}),\ (a_i) \in (Env^\sharp)^\mathbb{N}$, *the sequence* $(a_i^\triangle)$ *defined by* $a_0^\triangle = r(a_0)$ *and* $a_{n+1}^\triangle = r(a_n^\triangle \triangle a_{n+1})$, *with* $r = [X \mapsto \text{REDUCE}(\rho_k, X)] \circ ... \circ [X \mapsto \text{REDUCE}(\rho_1, X)]$, *is ultimately stationary;*
10. $\forall a \in Env^\sharp,\ \gamma(a) \subseteq \gamma_\mathcal{I}(\text{RANGE}(a))$ *and* $\gamma(a) \subseteq \gamma_{\text{ABS}}(\text{ABS}(a))$.

Least fixpoint approximation is performed in two steps [4]: we first compute an approximation using the widening operator; then we refine it using the narrowing operator. More formally, let f be a monotonic map in $\wp(Env) \to$

$\wp(Env)$ and $(f^\sharp \in Env^\sharp \to Env^\sharp)$ be an abstract counterpart of f satisfying $\forall a \in Env^\sharp$, $(f \circ \gamma)(a) \subseteq (\gamma \circ f^\sharp)(a)$. It is worth noting that the abstract counterpart $f^\sharp$ is usually not monotonic with respect to the partial order $\sqsubseteq^\sharp$ that is defined by $a \sqsubseteq^\sharp b \iff \gamma(a) \subseteq \gamma(b)$. The abstract upward iteration (C_n^∇) of $f^\sharp$ is defined by $C_0^\nabla = \bot$ and $C_{n+1}^\nabla = C_n^\nabla \nabla f^\sharp(C_n^\nabla)$. The sequence (C_n^∇) is ultimately stationary and we denote its limit by C_ω^∇. Then the abstract downward iteration (D_n^Δ) of $f^\sharp$ is defined by $D_0^\Delta = C_\omega^\nabla$ and $D_{n+1}^\Delta = D_n^\Delta \Delta f^\sharp(D_n^\Delta)$. The sequence (D_n^Δ) is ultimately stationary and we denote its limit by D_ω^Δ. We define[2] $\mathrm{lfp}^\sharp(f^\sharp)$ by the limit D_ω^Δ of the abstract downward iteration of $f^\sharp$. We introduce some lemmas in order to prove that $\mathrm{lfp}(f) \subseteq \gamma(D_\omega^\Delta)$:

Lemma 1. *We have* $f(\gamma(C_\omega^\nabla)) \subseteq \gamma(C_\omega^\nabla)$.

Proof. Since C_ω^∇ is the limit of the upward-iteration, we have $C_\omega^\nabla = C_\omega^\nabla \nabla f^\sharp(C_\omega^\nabla)$. By Def. 1.(8) of the widening, we obtain that $\gamma(f^\sharp(C_\omega^\nabla)) \subseteq \gamma(C_\omega^\nabla)$. By soundness of $f^\sharp$, we also have $f(\gamma(C_\omega^\nabla)) \subseteq \gamma(f^\sharp(C_\omega^\nabla))$. So $f(\gamma(C_\omega^\nabla)) \subseteq \gamma(C_\omega^\nabla)$. $\qquad\square$

Lemma 2. *For all* $a \in \wp(Env)$ *and* $x \in Env^\sharp$, *we have:*

$$a \subseteq \gamma(x) \implies a \cap f(a) \subseteq \gamma(x \Delta f^\sharp(x)).$$

Proof. Let $a \in \wp(Env)$ and $x \in Env^\sharp$ such that $a \subseteq \gamma(x)$. Since f is monotonic, we have $f(a) \subseteq f(\gamma(x))$. Then by soundness of $f^\sharp$, we have $f(\gamma(x)) \subseteq \gamma(f^\sharp(x))$. Thus $f(a) \subseteq \gamma(f^\sharp(x))$. So $a \cap f(a) \subseteq \gamma(x) \cap \gamma(f^\sharp(x))$. By Def. 1.(9), we have $\gamma(x) \cap \gamma(f^\sharp(x)) \subseteq \gamma(x \Delta f^\sharp(x))$. We conclude that $a \cap f(a) \subseteq \gamma(x \Delta f^\sharp(x))$. $\qquad\square$

Lemma 3. *For all* $a \in \wp(Env)$, *we have:*

$$f(a) \subseteq a \implies f(f(a) \cap a) \subseteq f(a) \cap a.$$

Proof. Let $a \in \wp(Env)$ such that $f(a) \subseteq a$. We have $f(a) \cap a = f(a)$. Since f is monotonic, we have $f(f(a)) \subseteq f(a)$. We conclude that $f(f(a) \cap a) \subseteq f(a) \cap a$. $\square$

Lemma 4 (transfinite kleenean iteration). *For all* $a \in \wp(Env)$, *we have:*

$$f(a) \subseteq a \implies \mathrm{lfp}(f) \subseteq a.$$

Theorem 1. *We have* $\mathrm{lfp}(f) \subseteq \gamma(D_\omega^\Delta)$.

Proof. We introduce the sequence (u_n) that is defined by $u_0 = \gamma(C_\omega^\nabla)$ and $u_{n+1} = u_n \cap f(u_n)$ for any $n \in \mathbb{N}$. We can prove by induction that $\forall n \in \mathbb{N}$, we have:

1. $u_n \subseteq \gamma(D_n^\Delta)$;
2. $f(u_n) \subseteq u_n$.

- When $n = 0$: by definition, we have $u_0 = \gamma(C_\omega^\nabla) = \gamma(D_0^\Delta)$ and thanks to Lemma 1, we have $f(u_0) \subseteq u_0$.

---

[2] $\mathrm{lfp}^\sharp(f^\sharp)$ is an approximation of the concrete least fixpoint; it may not be a least fixpoint of the abstract counterpart $f^\sharp$ which is not supposed to be monotonic.

$$\llbracket V = E \rrbracket_{\mathrm{mc}}^{\sharp}(a) = \mathrm{ASSIGN}(V = E, a)$$
$$\llbracket \mathbf{skip} \rrbracket_{\mathrm{mc}}^{\sharp}(a) = a$$
$$\llbracket \mathbf{tick} \rrbracket_{\mathrm{mc}}^{\sharp}(a) = \mathrm{GUARD}(\mathbf{clock}, [0; \mathrm{mc}], \mathrm{TICK}(a))$$
$$\llbracket \mathbf{if}\ (V \geq 0)\ \{P_1\}\ \mathbf{else}\ \{P_2\} \rrbracket_{\mathrm{mc}}^{\sharp}(a) = a_1 \sqcup a_2,$$
$$\text{where } \begin{cases} a_1 = \llbracket P_1 \rrbracket_{\mathrm{mc}}^{\sharp}(\mathrm{GUARD}(V, [0; +\infty[, a)) \\ a_2 = \llbracket P_2 \rrbracket_{\mathrm{mc}}^{\sharp}(\mathrm{GUARD}(V,]-\infty; 0[, a)) \end{cases}$$
$$\llbracket \mathbf{while}\ (V \geq 0)\ \{P\} \rrbracket_{\mathrm{mc}}^{\sharp}(a) = \mathrm{GUARD}(V,]-\infty; 0[, Inv^{\sharp}),$$
$$\text{where } Inv^{\sharp} = \mathrm{lfp}^{\sharp}\left(X \mapsto a \sqcup \llbracket P \rrbracket_{\mathrm{mc}}^{\sharp}(\mathrm{GUARD}(V, [0; +\infty[, X))\right)$$
$$\llbracket P_1; P_2 \rrbracket_{\mathrm{mc}}^{\sharp}(a) = \llbracket P_2 \rrbracket_{\mathrm{mc}}^{\sharp}(\llbracket P_1 \rrbracket_{\mathrm{mc}}^{\sharp}(a))$$

Fig. 3. Abstract semantics.

– We now suppose there exists $n \in \mathbb{N}$ such that $u_n \subseteq D_n^{\Delta}$ and $f(u_n) \subseteq u_n$.
  1. We have $u_{n+1} = u_n \cap f(u_n)$ and $u_n \subseteq \gamma(D_n^{\Delta})$. By Lemma 2, we have $u_{n+1} \subseteq \gamma(D_n^{\Delta} \triangle f^{\sharp}(D_n^{\Delta}))$. By definition of D_{n+1}^{Δ}, we obtain that $u_{n+1} \subseteq \gamma(D_{n+1}^{\Delta})$.
  2. We have $f(u_{n+1}) = f(u_n \cap f(u_n))$ and $f(u_n) \subseteq u_n$. By Lemma 3, we obtain that $f(u_{n+1}) \subseteq u_{n+1}$.

Then let $n \in \mathbb{N}$ be a natural such that $D_{\omega}^{\Delta} = D_n^{\Delta}$. We have $u_n \subseteq \gamma(D_{\omega}^{\Delta})$ and $f(u_n) \subseteq u_n$. By lemma 4, we have $\mathrm{lfp}(f) \subseteq \gamma(D_{\omega}^{\Delta})$.   □

The abstract semantics of a program is given by a function ($\llbracket \_ \rrbracket_{\mathrm{mc}}^{\sharp} \in Env^{\sharp} \to Env^{\sharp}$) in Fig. 3. Its soundness can be proved by induction on the syntax:

Theorem 2. *For any program P, environment ρ, abstract element a, and maximum clock value* mc, *we have:*

$$\rho \in \gamma(a) \implies \llbracket P \rrbracket_{\mathrm{mc}}(\rho) \subseteq \gamma\left(\llbracket P \rrbracket_{\mathrm{mc}}^{\sharp}(a)\right).$$

4   Arithmetic-Geometric Progressions

4.1   Affine Transformations

We introduce, as follows, the family of the affine transformations $(f[a, b])$ that is indexed by two non-negative real parameters a and b:

$$f[a, b] : \begin{cases} \mathbb{R}^+ \to \mathbb{R}^+ \\ X \mapsto a \times X + b \end{cases}$$

Lemma 5. *Let $a_1, a_2, b_1, b_2, X_1, X_2$ be non-negative real numbers in $\mathbb{R}^+$. If $a_1 \leq a_2$, $b_1 \leq b_2$, and $X_1 \leq X_2$, then $f[a_1, b_1](X_1) \leq f[a_2, b_2](X_2)$.*

4.2   Arithmetic-Geometric Progression in the Real Field

We introduce the predomain $\mathcal{D}_\mathbb{R}$ of all the 5-tuples of non-negative real numbers. The predomain $\mathcal{D}_\mathbb{R}$ is ordered by the product order $\sqsubseteq_{\mathcal{D}_\mathbb{R}}$. Intuitively[3], an element (M, a, b, a', b') of this predomain encodes an arithmetic-geometric progression. The real M is a bound on the initial value of the progression. The affine transformation $f[a', b']$ over-approximates the composition of all the affine transformations that can be applied to a value between two consecutive clock ticks. Finally, the affine transformation $f[a, b]$ over-approximates the composition of all the affine transformations that have been applied to a value since the last clock tick.

Thus, given a clock value $\mathsf{vc} \in \mathbb{N}$, we can define the concretization $\gamma_{\mathcal{D}_\mathbb{R}}^{\mathsf{vc}}(d)$ of such a tuple $d = (M, a, b, a', b') \in \mathcal{D}_\mathbb{R}$ by the set of all the elements $X \in \mathbb{R}$ such that $|X| \leq f[a, b]\left((f[a', b'])^{(\mathsf{vc})}(M)\right)$. We now define some primitives to handle the elements of $\mathcal{D}_\mathbb{R}$:

1. The join operator $\sqcup_{\mathcal{D}_\mathbb{R}}$ applies the maximum function component-wise. The soundness of the operator $\sqcup_{\mathcal{D}_\mathbb{R}}$ is established by Thm. 3, as follows:

Theorem 3. *For any* $\mathsf{vc} \in \mathbb{N}$,

$$\gamma_{\mathcal{D}_\mathbb{R}}^{\mathsf{vc}}(d_1) \cup \gamma_{\mathcal{D}_\mathbb{R}}^{\mathsf{vc}}(d_2) \subseteq \gamma_{\mathcal{D}_\mathbb{R}}^{\mathsf{vc}}(d_1 \sqcup_{\mathcal{D}_\mathbb{R}} d_2).$$

Proof. By Lem. 5.   □

2. The primitive $\mathit{affine}_{\mathcal{D}_\mathbb{R}}$ computes a linear combination among some elements of $\mathcal{D}_\mathbb{R}$. Let $n \in \mathbb{N}^*$ be a positive natural[4], let $(d_i) = (M_i, a_i, b_i, a'_i, b'_i) \in \mathcal{D}_\mathbb{R}^n$ be a family of elements in $\mathcal{D}_\mathbb{R}$, let $(\alpha_i) \in (\mathbb{R} \setminus \{0\})^n$ be a family of real coefficients that are all distinct from 0, and let $\beta \in \mathbb{R}$ be a real coefficient. We define the element $\mathit{affine}_{\mathcal{D}_\mathbb{R}}((\alpha_i, d_i), \beta) \in \mathcal{D}_\mathbb{R}$ by $(g(M_i), a_\infty \times \alpha', g(b_i), a'_\infty, g(b'_i))$ where:
   - $a_\infty = \mathit{max}\{|a_i| \mid 1 \leq i \leq n\}$, $a'_\infty = \mathit{max}\{|a'_i| \mid 1 \leq i \leq n\}$,
   - $\alpha' = \sum\limits_{1 \leq i \leq n} |\alpha_i|$ and
   - the function $g : \mathbb{R}^n \to \mathbb{R}$ maps each family (x_i) of n real numbers into the real number defined by $\sum\limits_{1 \leq i \leq n} \frac{|\alpha_i \times x_i|}{\alpha'} + |\beta|$.

   The soundness of the primitive $\mathit{affine}_{\mathcal{D}_\mathbb{R}}$ is established by Thm. 4, as follows:

Theorem 4. *Let* $\mathsf{vc} \in \mathbb{N}$ *be a natural and* $(X_i) \in \mathbb{R}^n$ *be a non-empty family of reals such that for any* i *such that* $1 \leq i \leq n$, *we have* $X_i \in \gamma_{\mathcal{D}_\mathbb{R}}^{\mathsf{vc}}(d_i)$. *Then we have:*

$$\left(\sum\limits_{1 \leq i \leq n} \alpha_i \times X_i + \beta\right) \in \gamma_{\mathcal{D}_\mathbb{R}}^{\mathsf{vc}}\left(\mathit{affine}_{\mathcal{D}_\mathbb{R}}((\alpha_i, d_i), \beta)\right).$$

---

[3] In Sect. 6 we forget this intuition to get a more expressive domain.

[4] The approximation of affine constants has an ad-hoc handling (Cf. Sect. 5.3).

Proof. By Lemma 5, by replacing α_i with $\frac{\alpha' \times \alpha_i}{\alpha'}$, by expanding $f[a,b]^{(vc)}$, and by applying the triangular inequality. $\qquad\square$

3. The primitive $\text{TICK}_{\mathcal{D}_\mathbb{R}} \in \mathcal{D}_\mathbb{R} \to \mathcal{D}_\mathbb{R}$ simulates clock ticks. It maps any element $d = (M, a, b, a', b') \in \mathcal{D}_\mathbb{R}$ into the element $(M, 1, 0, max(a, a'), max(b, b')) \in \mathcal{D}_\mathbb{R}$. Thus, just after the clock tick, the arithmetic-geometric progression that has been applied since the last clock tick is the identity. The progression between two clock ticks is chosen by applying the worst case among the progression between the last two clock ticks, and the progression between any other two consecutive clock ticks. The soundness of this operator is established by Thm. 5 as follows:

Theorem 5 (clock tick). *Let* $vc \in \mathbb{N}$ *be a natural. Then we have:*

$$\gamma_{\mathcal{D}_\mathbb{R}}^{vc}(d) \subseteq \gamma_{\mathcal{D}_\mathbb{R}}^{vc+1}(\text{TICK}_{\mathcal{D}_\mathbb{R}}(d))$$

Proof. By Lemma 5. $\qquad\square$

For the sake of accuracy, we get a more precise definition of the primitive $\text{TICK}_{\mathcal{D}_\mathbb{R}}$ in Sect. 6, by forgetting the intuitive meaning of the elements of $\mathcal{D}_\mathbb{R}$.

4. The primitive $range_{\mathcal{D}_\mathbb{R}} \in (\mathcal{D}_\mathbb{R} \times \{[a; b] \mid a, b \in \mathbb{N}, a \leq b\}) \to \mathcal{I}$ associates an element of $\mathcal{D}_\mathbb{R}$ and an interval for the clock counter with an interval range: we define $range_{\mathcal{D}_\mathbb{R}}((M, a, b, a', b'), [m_{vc}; M_{vc}])$ by $[-l; l]$ where $l = max(u_{m_{clock}}, u_{M_{clock}})$ and for any $vc \in \mathbb{N}$,

$$u_{vc} = \begin{cases} a \times (M + vc \times b') + b & \text{if } a' = 1, \\ a \times \left(a'^{vc} \times \left(M - \frac{b'}{1-a'}\right) + \frac{b'}{1-a'}\right) + b & \text{otherwise.} \end{cases}$$

The soundness of the primitive $range_{\mathcal{D}_\mathbb{R}}$ is established in Thm. 6 as follows:

Theorem 6. *For any* $vc \in \mathbb{N}$ *such that* $m_{vc} \leq vc \leq M_{vc}$, *we have:*

$$\gamma_{\mathcal{D}_\mathbb{R}}^{vc}(d) \subseteq range_{\mathcal{D}_\mathbb{R}}(d, [m_{vc}; M_{vc}]).$$

Proof. By studying the sign of $(u_{n+1} - u_n)$, for any $n \in \mathbb{N}$. $\qquad\square$

4.3 Representable Real Numbers

Until now, we have only used real numbers. In order to implement numerical abstract domains, we use a finite subset $\mathbb{F}$ of real numbers (such as the floating-point numbers) that contains the set of numbers $\{0, 1\}$ and that is closed under negation. The set $\overline{\mathbb{F}}$ is obtained by enriching the set $\mathbb{F}$ with two extra elements $+\infty$ and $-\infty$ that respectively describe the reals that are greater (resp. smaller) than the greatest (resp. smallest) element of $\mathbb{F}$. We denote the set $\{x \in \mathbb{F} \mid x \geq 0\}$ by $\mathbb{F}^+$ and the set $\mathbb{F}^+ \cup \{+\infty\}$ by $\overline{\mathbb{F}}^+$. The result of a computation on elements of $\overline{\mathbb{F}}$ may be not in $\overline{\mathbb{F}}$. So we suppose that we are given a function $\lceil \_ \rceil \in \mathbb{R} \to \overline{\mathbb{F}}$ such that $\lceil x \rceil \geq x$, for any $x \in \mathbb{R}$ and such that $\lceil x \rceil \leq 0$, for any $x \leq 0$. The domain $\overline{\mathbb{F}}$ is related to $\wp(\mathbb{R})$ via the concretization $\gamma_{\overline{\mathbb{F}}}$ that maps any representable number e into the set of the reals $r \in \mathbb{R}$ such that $|r| < e$, moreover we set $\gamma_{\overline{\mathbb{F}}}(+\infty) = \mathbb{R}$ and $\gamma_{\overline{\mathbb{F}}}(-\infty) = \emptyset$.

4.4 Representable Arithmetic-Geometric Constraints

We introduce the predomain $\mathcal{D}_{\mathbb{F}}$ as the set of the 5-tuples $(M, a, b, a', b') \in \left(\overline{\mathbb{F}}^+\right)^5$. The order $\sqsubseteq_{\mathcal{D}_{\mathbb{F}}}$, the concretizations $\gamma^{\text{vc}}_{\mathcal{D}_{\mathbb{F}}}$ (for any $\text{vc} \in \mathbb{N}$), the join operator $\sqcup_{\mathcal{D}_{\mathbb{F}}}$, and the clock tick primitive $\text{TICK}_{\mathcal{D}_{\mathbb{F}}}$ are respectively defined as restrictions of the order $\sqsubseteq_{\mathcal{D}_{\mathbb{R}}}$, the concretizations $\gamma^{\text{vc}}_{\mathcal{D}_{\mathbb{R}}}$, the join operator $\sqcup_{\mathcal{D}_{\mathbb{R}}}$, and the primitive $\text{TICK}_{\mathcal{D}_{\mathbb{R}}}$.

We now update the definition of the linear combination primitive $\textit{affine}_{\mathcal{D}_{\mathbb{F}}}$ and of the reduction primitive $\textit{range}_{\mathcal{D}_{\mathbb{F}}}$:

1. The primitive $\textit{affine}_{\mathcal{D}_{\mathbb{F}}}$ maps each pair $((\alpha_i, d_i), \beta)$ where $(\alpha_i) \in \mathbb{R}^n$ (where $n \in \mathbb{N}^*$ is a positive natural), $(d_i) = ((M_i, a_i, b_i, a'_i, b'_i)) \in \mathcal{D}^n_{\mathbb{F}}$, and $\beta \in \mathbb{R}$ to the element:

$$(g(M_i), \lceil a_\infty \times \alpha'_M \rceil, g(b_i), a'_\infty, g(b'_i))$$

   where:
   - $a_\infty = max\{|a_i| \mid 1 \leq i \leq n\}$, $a'_\infty = max\{|a'_i| \mid 1 \leq i \leq n\}$,
   - $s_n : \mathbb{R}^n \to \overline{\mathbb{F}}^+$ is defined by $s_0(()) = 0$ and $s_{n+1}((a_i)_{1 \leq i \leq n+1}) = \lceil s_n((a_i)_{1 \leq i \leq n}) + \lceil a_{n+1} \rceil \rceil$.
   - $\alpha'_m = -s_n((-|\alpha_i|)_{1 \leq i \leq n})$, $\alpha'_M = s_n((|\alpha_i|)_{1 \leq i \leq n})$,
   - $g : \mathbb{R}^n \to \overline{\mathbb{F}}^+$ maps each family (x_i) of real numbers into the real number that is defined by

$$min\left(max(\{|x_i| \mid 1 \leq i \leq n\}), \left\lceil s_n\left(\frac{\lceil |\alpha_i| \times |x_i| \rceil}{\alpha'_m}\right) + |\beta| \right\rceil\right).$$

Theorem 7. *For any clock value* $\text{vc} \in \mathbb{N}$, *we have:*

$$\left\{ \sum_{1 \leq i \leq n} \alpha_i \times X_i + \beta \;\middle|\; X_i \in \gamma^{\text{vc}}_{\mathcal{D}_{\mathbb{F}}}(d_i) \right\} \subseteq \gamma^{\text{vc}}_{\mathcal{D}_{\mathbb{F}}}\left(\textit{affine}_{\mathcal{D}_{\mathbb{F}}}((\alpha_i, d_i), \beta)\right).$$

Proof. By Lemma 5 and Thm. 4. $\qquad\square$

Remark 1. We define g as the minimum of two sound results. In the real field, the second one is more precise. However, it may become less precise when computing with rounding errors.

2. The interval $\textit{range}_{\mathcal{D}_{\mathbb{F}}}((M, a, b, a', b'), [m_{\text{vc}}; M_{\text{vc}}])$ is given by $[-l; l]$ where:
   - $l = max(u_{m_{\text{vc}}}, u_{M_{\text{vc}}})$;
   - $u_{\text{vc}} = \lceil \lceil a \times v_{\text{vc}} \rceil + b \rceil$;
   - $v_{\text{vc}} = \begin{cases} \lceil M + \lceil \text{vc} \times b' \rceil \rceil & \text{if } a' = 1, \\ \lceil c_1^+ + c_2^+ \rceil & \text{otherwise}; \end{cases}$
   - $\begin{cases} \exp_0^- = 1, \; \exp_{2 \times n}^- = -\lceil \exp_n^- \times (-\exp_n^-) \rceil, \\ \exp_{2 \times n+1}^- = -\lceil \lceil \exp_n^- \times (-\exp_n^-) \rceil \times a' \rceil; \end{cases}$
   - $\begin{cases} \exp_0^+ = 1, \; \exp_{2 \times n}^+ = \lceil \exp_n^+ \times \exp_n^+ \rceil, \\ \exp_{2 \times n+1}^+ = \lceil \lceil \exp_n^+ \times \exp_n^+ \rceil \times a' \rceil; \end{cases}$

$$- c_1^+ = \begin{cases} \lceil \exp_{vc}^+ \times \lceil M - c_2^- \rceil \rceil & \text{if } M \geq c_2^- \\ \lceil \exp_{vc}^- \times \lceil M - c_2^- \rceil \rceil & \text{otherwise;} \end{cases}$$

$$- c_2^- = -\left\lceil \frac{-b'}{\lceil 1 - a' \rceil} \right\rceil \text{ and } c_2^+ = \left\lceil \frac{-b'}{\lceil a' - 1 \rceil} \right\rceil.$$

Theorem 8. *For any clock value* $vc \in [m_{vc}; M_{vc}]$, *we have:*

$$\gamma_{\mathcal{D}_{\mathbb{F}}}^{vc}(d) \subseteq range_{\mathcal{D}_{\mathbb{F}}}(d, vc).$$

Proof. Because $\forall vc \in \mathbb{N}$, $\exp_{vc}^- \leq a'^{vc} \leq \exp_{vc}^+$, $c_1^+ \geq a'^{vc} \times \left(M - \frac{b'}{1-a'} \right)$ and $c_2^- \leq \frac{b'}{1-a'} \leq c_2^+$, and by applying Thm. 6. $\qquad \square$

Remark 2. In the implementation, we use memoization to avoid computing the same exponential twice.

4.5   Tuning the Extrapolation Strategy

Although $\overline{\mathbb{F}}$ is height-bounded, we introduce some extrapolation operators in order to accelerate the convergence of abstract iterations. A widening step consists in applying an extensive map to each unstable components of the 5-tuples. In order to let constraints stabilize, we only widen a component when it has been unstable a given number of times since its last widening. For that purpose, we associate each representable number in $\overline{\mathbb{F}}$ with a natural that denotes the number of times it has been unstable without being widened. We suppose that we are given a natural parameter n and an extensive function f over $\overline{\mathbb{F}}$. We first define the widening ∇_f^n of two annotated representable numbers $(x_1, n_1), (x_2, n_2) \in \overline{\mathbb{F}} \times \mathbb{N}$ by:

$$(x_1, n_1)\nabla_f^n(x_2, n_2) = \begin{cases} (x_1, n_1) & \text{if } x_1 \geq x_2 \\ (x_2, n_1 + 1) & \text{if } x_1 < x_2 \text{ and } n_1 < n \\ (f(x_2), 0) & \text{otherwise.} \end{cases}$$

A narrowing step refines an arithmetic-geometric constraint with another one if the last one is smaller component-wise (so that we are sure that this refinement does not locally lose accuracy). To avoid too long decreasing sequences, we count the number of times such a refinement has been applied with each constraint. Thus we associate each constraint with an extra counter.

We then introduce the predomain $\mathcal{D}_{\mathbb{F}}^{\mathcal{L}} = \left(\overline{\mathbb{F}}^+ \times \mathbb{N} \right)^5 \times \mathbb{N}$ of annotated constraints. The function *annotate* maps each element $d = (M, a, b, a', b') \in \mathcal{D}_{\mathbb{F}}$ to the annotated element that is defined by $(((M, 0), (a, 0), (b, 0), (a', 0), (b', 0)), 0) \in \mathcal{D}_{\mathbb{F}}^{\mathcal{L}}$, where all counters are initialized with the value 0. Conversely the function *remove* maps each element $(((M, n_M), (a, n_a), (b, n_b), (a', n_{a'}), (b', n_{b'})), n) \in \mathcal{D}_{\mathbb{F}}^{\mathcal{L}}$ to the annotation-free element $(M, a, b, a', b') \in \mathcal{D}_{\mathbb{F}}$. We can define the preorder $\sqsubseteq_{\mathcal{D}_{\mathbb{F}}^{\mathcal{L}}}$ by $a \sqsubseteq_{\mathcal{D}_{\mathbb{F}}^{\mathcal{L}}} b \iff remove(a) \sqsubseteq_{\mathcal{D}_{\mathbb{F}}} remove(b)$. The monotonic concretization $\gamma_{\mathcal{D}_{\mathbb{F}}^{\mathcal{L}}}$ is defined as the composition $\gamma_{\mathcal{D}_{\mathbb{F}}} \circ remove$.

Extrapolation operators store information about the history of the extrapolation process into the counters of their left argument, whereas the other primitives reset these counters: we define the union $a \sqcup_{\mathcal{D}_{\mathbb{F}}^{\mathcal{L}}} b$ by $annotate((remove(a)) \sqcup_{\mathcal{D}_{\mathbb{F}}}$ $(remove(b)))$, the affine combination $affine_{\mathcal{D}_{\mathbb{F}}^{\mathcal{L}}}((\alpha_i, d_i), \beta)$ by the abstract element $annotate(affine_{\mathcal{D}_{\mathbb{F}}}((\alpha_i, remove(d_i)), \beta))$, the abstract clock tick primitive $\text{TICK}_{\mathcal{D}_{\mathbb{F}}^{\mathcal{L}}}$ by the map $annotate \circ \text{TICK}_{\mathcal{D}_{\mathbb{F}}} \circ remove$, and the interval constraints $range_{\mathcal{D}_{\mathbb{F}}^{\mathcal{L}}}(d, I)$ by the interval map $range_{\mathcal{D}_{\mathbb{F}}}(remove(d), I)$.

We define extrapolation operators. Let f_a, f_b, and f_M be extensive functions over the set $\mathbb{F}$; let n_a, n_b, n_M, and n be some naturals. The functions f_a, f_b, and f_M and the naturals n_a, n_b, n_M, and n are left as parameters of our extrapolation strategy. The widening $((M_1, a_1, b_1, a_1', b_1'), n_1) \nabla_{\mathcal{D}_{\mathbb{F}}^{\mathcal{L}}} ((M_2, a_2, b_2, a_2', b_2'), n_2)$ is defined by $((M_1 \nabla_{f_M}^{n_M} M_2, a_1 \nabla_{f_a}^{n_a} a_2, b_1 \nabla_{f_b}^{n_b} b_2, a_1' \nabla_{f_a}^{n_a} a_2', b_1' \nabla_{f_b}^{n_b} b_2'), 0)$. The narrowing $(t_1, n_1) \triangle_{\mathcal{D}_{\mathbb{F}}^{\mathcal{L}}} (t_2, n_2)$ is then defined by $(t_2, n_1 + 1)$ in the case when $n_1 < n$ and $(t_2, n_2) \sqsubseteq_{\mathcal{D}_{\mathbb{F}}^{\mathcal{L}}} (t_1, n_1)$, and by (t_1, n_1) otherwise.

5   Refining an Existing Abstraction

We now show how we can extend an existing abstraction defined as in Def. 1 so that it can also deal with arithmetic-geometric constraints.

5.1   Domain Extension

Let $(Env_0^{\#}, \gamma_0, \sqcup_0, \text{ASSIGN}_0, \text{GUARD}_0, \text{TICK}_0, \perp_0, \nabla_0, \triangle_0, \text{RANGE}_0, \text{ABS}_0, \text{REDUCE}_0)$ be an abstraction which is called the underlying domain. We build the abstraction $Env^{\#}$ as the Cartesian product $Env_0^{\#} \times (\mathcal{V} \to \mathcal{D}_{\mathbb{F}}^{\mathcal{L}} \cup \{\top\})$. The element $\top \notin \mathcal{D}_{\mathbb{F}}^{\mathcal{L}}$ denotes the absence of constraint. The concretization $\gamma : Env^{\#} \to \wp(Env)$ maps each pair (e, f) to the following set of environments:

$$\gamma_0(e) \cap \left\{ \rho \in Env \ \middle| \ \forall X \in \mathcal{V} \text{ such that } f(X) \neq \top, \ \rho(X) \in \gamma_{\mathcal{D}_{\mathbb{F}}^{\mathcal{L}}}^{\rho(\text{clock})}(f(X)) \right\}.$$

Moreover, abstract iterations start with the element $\perp = (\perp_0, [X \mapsto \top])$.

5.2   Refinement Operators

The underlying domain and the arithmetic-geometric domain refine each other when the computation of an abstract primitive requires it. We introduce here some operators that describe these refinement steps.

The operator $r^{\leftarrow}$ uses the arithmetic-geometric constraints to refine the underlying domain. Given an abstract element $(e, f) \in Env^{\#}$ and a subset $V \subseteq \mathcal{V}$ of variables, we define $r^{\leftarrow}((e, f), V)$ by $(\text{REDUCE}_0(g, e), f)$ where $g(X)$ is given by:

$$\begin{cases} range_{\mathcal{D}_{\mathbb{F}}^{\mathcal{L}}}(f(X), \text{RANGE}_0(e)(\text{clock})) & \text{if } X \in V \text{ and } f(X) \neq \top, \\ \mathbb{R} & \text{otherwise.} \end{cases}$$

Conversely, we use the underlying domain to build new arithmetic-geometric constraints or to refine existing arithmetic-geometric constraints. Let $X \in \mathcal{V}$

be a variable, let a, $b \in \mathbb{F}^+$ be two non negative real parameters, and let $e \in Env_0^\sharp$ be an abstract element of the underlying domain. The variable X can soundly be associated with the arithmetic-geometric constraint $g_e(X, (a, b))$, where $g_e(X, (a, b))$ is given by:

$$
\begin{cases}
annotate\left(\left(\left\lceil \frac{max(0, \lceil l-b\rceil)}{a}\right\rceil, a, b, 1, 0\right)\right) & \text{if } a \neq 0, \\
annotate\left((a, b, 1, 0, l)\right) & \text{otherwise,}
\end{cases}
$$

where $l \in \overline{\mathbb{F}}$ is the least upper bound (in $\overline{\mathbb{F}}$) of the set $\{|x| \mid x \in \text{RANGE}_0(e)(X)\}$.

We now define the operator $r^\rightarrow$ which refines arithmetic-geometric constraints over a set of variables by weakening the range constraints that can be extracted from the underlying domain. Given an abstract element $(e, f) \in Env^\sharp$, a subset $A \subseteq \mathcal{V}$, and a map $\Gamma \in A \rightarrow \mathbb{F}^+ \times \mathbb{F}^+$, we define $r^\rightarrow((e, f), A, \Gamma)$ by (e, f') where $f'(X)$ is defined by:

$$
\begin{cases}
g_e(X, \Gamma(X)) & \text{if } X \in A \text{ and either } f(X) = \top, \text{ or } g_e(X, \Gamma(X)) \sqsubseteq_{\mathcal{D}_{\mathbb{F}}^{\mathcal{L}}} f(X), \\
f(X) & \text{otherwise.}
\end{cases}
$$

5.3   Primitives

Binary operators are all defined in the same way. Let $\circledast$ be an operator in $\{\sqcup, \triangle, \triangledown\}$ and let $(e_1, f_1), (e_2, f_2)$ be two abstract elements of $Env^\sharp$. Before applying a binary operator, we refine arithmetic-geometric constraints so that both arguments constrain the same set of variables: we set for any $i \in \{1, 2\}$, $(e_i', f_i') = (r^\rightarrow((e_i, f_i), V_{3-i} \setminus V_i, \Gamma_{3-i}))$, where for any $i \in \{1; 2\}$, $V_i = \{X \mid f_i(X) \neq \top\}$ and $\Gamma_i(X) = (a, b)$ when $f_i(X)$ matches (M, a, b, a', b'). We then apply $\circledast$ componentwise: we set $e'' = e_1' \circledast_0 e_2'$; we set $f''(X) = f_1'(X) \circledast_{\mathcal{D}_{\mathbb{F}}^{\mathcal{L}}} f_2'(X)$ for any $X \in V_1 \cup V_2$; we set $f''(X) = \top$ for any $X \in \mathcal{V} \setminus (V_1 \cup V_2)$. After applying a binary operator, we use the arithmetic-geometric constraints to refine the underlying domain: we define $(e_1, f_1) \circledast (e_2, f_2)$ by $r^\leftarrow((e'', f''), \mathcal{V})$.

We use a heuristics to drive the abstraction of assignments. This heuristics weakens the precondition to simplify the assigned expression: it takes some variable ranges, some arithmetic-geometric constraints and an expression; it replaces in the expression some variables with their range. The choice of the variables that are replaced is left as a parameter of the abstraction. Thus, the heuristics $heu \in ((\mathcal{V} \cup \{\texttt{clock}\} \rightarrow \mathcal{I}) \times (\mathcal{V} \rightarrow \mathcal{D}_{\mathbb{F}}^{\mathcal{L}} \cup \{\top\})) \times \mathcal{E} \rightarrow ((\mathbb{R} \setminus \{0\} \times \mathcal{V})^* \times \mathbb{R})$ maps each pair $((\rho^\sharp, f), E)$ to a pair $((\alpha_i, V_i)_{1 \leq i \leq n}, \beta)$ that satisfies:

$$
\gamma(\lfloor E \rfloor) \subseteq \left\{ \beta + \sum_{1 \leq i \leq n} \alpha_i \times \rho(V_i) \;\middle|\;
\begin{array}{l}
\forall \rho \in Env \text{ such that:} \\
\forall X \in \mathcal{V}, \rho(X) \in \rho^\sharp(X) \cap \gamma_{\mathcal{D}_{\mathbb{F}}^{\mathcal{L}}}^{\rho(\texttt{clock})}(f(X)) \\
\text{and } \rho(\texttt{clock}) \in \rho^\sharp(\texttt{clock})
\end{array}
\right\}.
$$

Let $(e, f) \in Env^\sharp$ be an abstract element. We consider several cases when abstracting an assignment $X = E$:

1. When computing an assignment $X = Y$ with $Y \in \mathcal{V}$, we associate the variable X with any constraint about Y. Thus we set:

$$\text{ASSIGN}(X = Y, (e, f)) = (\text{ASSIGN}_0(X = Y, e), f[X \mapsto f(Y)]);$$

2. When computing an assignment $X = E$ where $E \notin \mathcal{V}$ such that the pair $heu((\text{RANGE}_0(e), f), E)$ matches $((), \beta)$, we remove any arithmetic-geometric constraints about X. Thus we set:

$$\text{ASSIGN}(X = E, (e, f)) = (\text{ASSIGN}_0(X = E, e), f[X \mapsto \top]);$$

3. Otherwise, we denote by $((\alpha_i, V_i)_{1 \leq i \leq n}, \beta) = heu((\text{RANGE}_0(e), f), E)$ the approximation of E by the heuristics. Before the assignment, we use the underlying domain to refine information about the variables (V_i) that occur in the simplified expression. When such a variable is tied with no arithmetic-geometric constraint, we build one with arbitrary coefficients for the affine transformations. We also refine existing constraints without modifying the coefficients of the affine transformations. Thus we define the element (e', f') by $r^{\rightarrow}((e, f), \{V_i \mid 1 \leq i \leq n\}, \Gamma)$ where for any $i \in \mathbb{N}$ such that $1 \leq i \leq n$, we have $\Gamma(V_i) = (1, 0)$ if $f(V_i) = \top$ (*missing constraints*) and $\Gamma(V_i) = (a, b)$ if $f(V_i) = (M, a, b, a', b')$ (*existing constraints*). Then we apply the assignment component-wise: we define (e'', f'') by $(\text{ASSIGN}_0(X = E, e'), f[X \mapsto affine_{\mathcal{D}_{\mathbb{F}}^{\mathcal{L}}}((\alpha_i, f'(V_i)), \beta)])$. At last, we refine the underlying domain by the new computed constraint: we set $\text{ASSIGN}(X = E, (e, f)) = r^{\leftarrow}((e'', f''), \{X\})$.

The abstraction of a clock tick $\text{TICK}(e, f)$ is defined component-wise by $(\text{TICK}_0(e), f')$ where $f'(X) = \text{TICK}_{\mathcal{D}_{\mathbb{F}}^{\mathcal{L}}}(f(X))$ if $f(X) \neq \top$ and $f'(X) = \top$ otherwise. We do not deal directly with guards in the arithmetic-geometric domain. Nevertheless, if after applying a guard, we can prove in the underlying domain that the absolute value that is associated with a variable is less than the absolute value that is associated with another variable, we use this information to refine arithmetic-geometric constraints. So we define the primitive r^{ABS} that refines arithmetic-geometric constraints, according to absolute value constraints. Given a relation $\mathcal{R} \subseteq \mathcal{V}^2$ and a map $f \in \mathcal{V} \rightarrow \mathcal{D}_{\mathbb{F}}^{\mathcal{L}} \cup \{\top\}$, the map $r^{\text{ABS}}(\mathcal{R}, f) \in \mathcal{V} \rightarrow \mathcal{D}_{\mathbb{F}}^{\mathcal{L}} \cup \{\top\}$ associates any variable X with a minimal element (for $\sqsubseteq_{\mathcal{D}_{\mathbb{F}}^{\mathcal{L}}}$) of the set $(\{f(X)\} \cup \{f(Y) \mid (X, Y) \in \mathcal{R}\}) \setminus \{\top\}$ if this set is not empty, or with the element $\top$ otherwise. Then the abstract element $\text{GUARD}(X, I, (a, f))$ is defined by $(\text{GUARD}_0(X, I, a), r^{\text{ABS}}(\text{ABS}_0(\text{GUARD}_0(X, I, a)), f))$.

In order not to break the extrapolation process, we never refine arithmetic-geometric constraints after applying an extrapolation operator. Thus we define $\text{REDUCE}(\rho^{\sharp}, (e, f))$ by $(\text{REDUCE}_0(\rho^{\sharp}, e), f)$. Moreover, the domain $\mathcal{D}_{\mathbb{F}}^{\mathcal{L}}$ cannot help in comparing the absolute value of variables, so we set $\text{ABS}(e, f) = \text{ABS}_0(e)$. Nevertheless, the domain $\mathcal{D}_{\mathbb{F}}^{\mathcal{L}}$ can refine variable range: we set $\text{RANGE}(e, f)(X)$ by $\text{RANGE}_0(e)(X) \cap range_{\mathcal{D}_{\mathbb{F}}^{\mathcal{L}}}(f(X), \text{RANGE}_0(e)(\texttt{clock}))$.

Theorem 9. $(Env^{\sharp}, \gamma, \sqcup, \text{ASSIGN}, \text{GUARD}, \text{TICK}, \bot, \nabla, \triangle, \text{RANGE}, \text{ABS}, \text{REDUCE})$ *is an abstraction.*

Proof. We sketch the proof of Th. 9: all soundness requirements come from the soundness of both the underlying domain and the arithmetic-geometric pre-domain. During an extrapolation iteration (ascending or descending), the set of arithmetic-geometric constraints (i.e., the set of the variables that are not mapped into $\top$) is ultimately stationary (since the number of constraints is increasing, whereas $\mathcal{V}$ is finite); then each arithmetic-geometric constraint sequence is ultimately stationary; once the information that refines the underlying domain is fixed, the underlying domain termination criteria in Def. 1.(8-9) apply. $\square$

6 Dealing with Buffers

The definition of the primitive $\mathrm{TICK}_{\mathcal{D}_\mathbb{F}}$ in Sect. 4.4 implicitly supposes that the affine transformations that must be captured are fully computed between two clock ticks. For instance, Ex. 2 can be analyzed accurately because the multiplication and the division are computed in the same loop iteration. We first slightly modify Ex. 2 so that this atomicity assumption is not satisfied. Then we refine the primitive $\mathrm{TICK}_{\mathcal{D}_\mathbb{F}}$ to handle more complex cases precisely.

6.1 Motivating Example

Example 3. This example iterates a loop where a floating point is first divided by a coefficient $\alpha > 2$ and then multiplied by the coefficient α. Unlike Ex. 2, the division and the multiplication are not computed in the same iteration of the loop. At each iteration, the current value of X is multiplied by α and the result is stored in a buffer (denoted by the variable BUFFER). The next value for X is obtained by dividing the value that was in the buffer at the beginning of the iteration (while the current value of X is stored in a temporary variable TMP). For the sake of simplicity, we have removed reinitialization branches.

$$V = \mathbb{R};\ X = I;\ \mathrm{TMP} = 0;\ \mathrm{BUFFER} = I;$$
$$\textbf{while } (V \geq 0)\ \{$$
$$V = \mathbb{R};$$
$$\mathrm{TMP} = X;$$
$$X = [\tfrac{1}{\alpha} - \varepsilon_1; \tfrac{1}{\alpha} + \varepsilon_1] \times \mathrm{BUFFER} + [-\varepsilon_2; \varepsilon_2];$$
$$\mathrm{BUFFER} = [\alpha - \varepsilon_3; \alpha + \varepsilon_3] \times \mathrm{TMP} + [-\varepsilon_4; \varepsilon_4];$$
$$\textbf{tick}\}$$

where $0 < \varepsilon_i < 1$, for any $i \in \{1; 2; 3; 4\}$, $\alpha > 2$, and $I \in \mathcal{I}$.

Moreover, initialization values range in the intervals I. The parameter α is a coefficient in the example. The parameters ε_1 and ε_3 encode relative rounding errors, and the parameters ε_2 and ε_4 encode absolute rounding errors. The variable V allows stopping the loop iteration.

At the first abstract iteration, before the first clock tick, the variable BUFFER is associated with the 5-tuple $(M_1, a_1, b_1, 1, 0)$ where M_I is the least upper bound of the set $\{|x| \mid x \in I\}$, $a_1 = \lceil \alpha + \varepsilon_3 \rceil$ and $b_1 = \lceil \varepsilon_4 \rceil$. After the first clock tick, it is associated with $(M_1, 1, 0, a_1, b_1)$. At the second abstract iteration, before the clock tick, the variable X is associated with the 5-tuple $(M_1, a_2, b_2, a_1, b_1)$ where $a_2 = \lceil \frac{1}{\alpha} + \varepsilon_1 \rceil$ and $b_2 = \lceil \varepsilon_2 \rceil$. After the second clock tick, the variable X is associated with the 5-tuple $(M_1, 1, 0, a_1, max(b_1, b_2))$. We notice that the arithmetic-geometric domain cannot help in bounding the range of the variable X because of the computation of the exponential (since we have $a_1 > 2$). All information has been lost when computing the first clock tick in the abstract.

6.2   Refining the Domain

To refine the domain, we have to decide at each clock tick which affine computations are finished. For that purpose, we introduce two parameters $\beta_m, \beta_M \in \mathbb{F}^+$ very close to 1 and such that $\beta_m < 1 < \beta_M$. We then consider that an affine transformation $[X \mapsto a \times X + b]$ denotes a finished computation if and only if $\beta_m < a < \beta_M$. In fact, in the case when $a > \beta_M$ the arithmetic-geometric progression domain will provide useless range and in the case when $a < \beta_m$ the interval domain can provide accurate range by using widening and narrowing. Thus, we redefine the element $\text{TICK}_{\mathcal{D}_{\mathbb{F}}}(M, a, b, a', b')$ by $(M, a, 0, a', max\{b, b'\})$ in the case when both $a \notin [\beta_m; \beta_M]$ and $a' \geq 1$, and by $(M, 1, 0, max\{a, a'\}, max\{b, b'\})$ otherwise. This definition still satisfies Thm. 5.

In Ex. 3, after the first clock tick and provided that $a_1 < \beta_m$, the variable BUFFER is now associated with $(M_1, a_1, 0, 1, b_1)$. At the second abstract iteration, before the clock tick the variable X is associated with the 5-tuple $(M_1, a_3, b_3, 1, b_1)$ where $a_3 = \lceil \lceil \alpha + \varepsilon_3 \rceil \times a_1 \rceil$ and $b_3 = \varepsilon_3$. Then after the second clock tick and provided that $a_3 < \beta_M$, the variable X is associated with $(M_1, 1, 0, a_3, max(b_1, b_3))$. This constraint is stable and allows the computation of an accurate range for the variable X.

7   Benchmarks

We tested our framework with three programs of a same family of critical embedded software written in C. For each program we tested the ASTRÉE [2] analyzer with the classical domains (intervals [4], octagons [8], decision trees, and expanded digital filter domains [6]) and without/with the new arithmetic-geometric domain. For each of these analyses, we report in Fig. 4 the analyzed program size, the number of global variables, the number of arithmetic-geometric constraints that are captured by the analysis, the analysis time, the number of iterations for the main loop, and the number of warnings (in polyvariant function calls). These results have been obtained on a AMD Opteron 248, with 8 Gb of RAM. In two of the three programs, the arithmetic-geometric progression domain solve all the remaining false alarms which gives a proof of absence of run-time errors.

8   Conclusion

We have proposed a new numerical domain which relates the value of each variable to a clock counter. It approximates each value by an expression of the form $[X \mapsto \alpha \times X + \beta]^{(n)}(M)$, where (M, α, β) are discovered automatically and n is

lines of C	70,000		216,000		379,000	
global variables	13,400		7,500		9,000	
ari-geo progressions	disabled	enabled	disabled	enabled	disabled	enabled
ari-geo constraints		257		458		634
iterations	53	47	228	64	238	67
average time per iteration	1mn30s	1mn47s	5mn40s	6mn07s	10mn17s	11mn35s
analysis time	1h20mn	1h24mn	21h32mn	6h33mn	40h58mn	12h55mn
warnings	24	0	80	1	189	0

Fig. 4. Some statistics.

the maximum value of the clock counter. This approximation is proved correct and allows us to bound the value of some floating-point variables by using the program execution time. These bounds cannot be discovered either by ignoring the clock counter or by just bounding the difference between variable values and the clock value (c.f. [1]). Our framework allows the full certification of huge critical embedded softwares. The accuracy gain significantly reduces the exploration space which leads to an analysis speed-up in some of our examples.

Acknowledgments. We deeply thank the anonymous referees. We also thank Francesco Logozzo, Enea Zaffanella, and each member of the magic team: Bruno Blanchet, Patrick Cousot, Radhia Cousot, Laurent Mauborgne, Antoine Miné, David Monniaux, and Xavier Rival.

References

1. B. Blanchet, P. Cousot, R. Cousot, J. Feret, L. Mauborgne, A. Miné, D. Monniaux, and X. Rival. Design and implementation of a special-purpose static program analyzer for safety-critical real-time embedded software. In *The Essence of Computation: Complexity, Analysis, Transformation.*, LNCS 2566. Springer-Verlag, 2002.
2. B. Blanchet, P. Cousot, R. Cousot, J. Feret, L. Mauborgne, A. Miné, D. Monniaux, and X. Rival. A static analyzer for large safety-critical software. In *Proc. PLDI'03*. ACM Press, 2003.
3. P. Cousot. *Méthodes itératives de construction et d'approximation de points fixes d'opérateurs monotones sur un treillis, analyse sémantique des programmes.* PhD thesis, Université Scientifique et Médicale de Grenoble, 1978.
4. P. Cousot and R. Cousot. Abstract interpretation: a unified lattice model for static analysis of programs by construction or approximation of fixpoints. In *Proc. POPL'77*. ACM Press, 1977.
5. P. Cousot and R. Cousot. Abstract interpretation frameworks. *Journal of logic and computation*, 2(4), August 1992.
6. J. Feret. Static analysis of digital filters. In *European Symposium on Programming (ESOP'04)*, number 2986 in LNCS. Springer-Verlag, 2004.
7. X. Leroy, D. Doligez, J. Garrigue, D. Rémy, and J. Vouillon. The Objective Caml system, documentation and user's manual. Technical report, INRIA, 2002.
8. A. Miné. The octagon abstract domain. In *Proc. WCRE'01(AST'01)*, IEEE, 2001.
9. A. Miné. Relational abstract domains for the detection of floating-point run-time errors. In *Proc. ESOP'04*, LNCS. Springer, 2004.

An Overview of Semantics
for the Validation of Numerical Programs

Matthieu Martel

CEA – Recherche Technologique
LIST-DTSI-SOL
CEA F91191 Gif-Sur-Yvette Cedex, France
matthieu.martel@cea.fr

Abstract. In this article, we introduce a simple formal semantics for floating-point numbers with errors which is expressive enough to be formally compared to the other methods. Next, we define formal semantics for interval, stochastic, automatic differentiation and error series methods. This enables us to formally compare the properties calculated in each semantics to our reference, simple semantics. Most of these methods having been developed to verify numerical intensive codes, we also discuss their adequacy to the formal validation of softwares and to static analysis. Finally, this study is completed by experimental results.

1 Introduction

Interval computations, stochastic arithmetics, automatic differentiation, etc.: much work is currently done to estimate and to improve the numerical accuracy of programs. Beside the verification of numerical intensive codes, which is the historical applicative domain of these methods, a new problematic is growing that concerns the formal validation of the accuracy of numerical calculations in critical embedded systems.

Despite the large amount of work in this area, few comparative studies have been carried out. This is partly due to the fact that the numerical properties calculated by different methods are difficult to relate. For example, how to compare results coming from interval arithmetics to the ones obtained by automatic differentiation?

This article attempts to clarify the links between the most commonly used methods among the above-mentioned ones. First, we introduce a simple formal semantics for floating-point numbers with errors which is expressive enough to be formally compared to the other methods. This semantics is a special instance of a familly of semantics introduced recently [22]. Next, we define formal semantics for interval, stochastic, automatic differentiation and error series methods which are usually expressed in other, less semantical, settings. This enables us to compare the properties calculated by each semantics to our reference semantics and to oversee how different methods could be coupled to obtain more accurate results.

Most of these methods having been developed to verify numerical intensive codes, we discuss their adequacy to the formal validation of critical systems.

R. Cousot (Ed.): VMCAI 2005, LNCS 3385, pp. 59–77, 2005.

From our point of view, a method is well suited for the validation of embedded applications if it enables the user to detect errors in an application that uses standard, non-instrumented, floating-point numbers, once embedded. In addition, we discuss the adequacy of the different semantics to static analysis. We complete our study by conducting some experiments. The methods described in this article are applied to simple examples, to show their ability and limits to detect numerical errors in C codes.

We limit our study to the semantics dealing with numerical precision. This excludes other interesting related works that also contribute to the validation of the numerical accuracy of softwares, like formal proof techniques of numerical properties over the floating-point numbers (e.g. [5, 10, 19]), or constraints solvers over the floating-point numbers which are used for structural test case generation [24]. It also excludes alternative arithmetics enabling to improve the accuracy of the float operations like multiple precision arithmetics [18, 29] or exact arithmetics [28]. These alternative arithmetics are more accurate than the standard floating-point arithmetics but they do not provide information on the precision of the results.

This article is organized as follows. Section 2 briefly presents some aspects of the IEEE 754 Standard. In Section 3, we introduce a simple semantics attaching to each floating-point number an error term measuring the distance to the exact real number which has been approximated. Next, this semantics is compared to other semantics, based on interval arithmetics (Section 4), stochastic arithmetics (Section 5), automatic differentiation (Section 6) and error series (Section 7). In Section 8, we discuss the adequacy of each method to static analysis and finally, in Section 9, we present experimental results illustrating how the techniques described in this article work on simple examples. Section 10 concludes.

2   Floating-Point Numbers

The IEEE 754 Standard specifies the representation of floating-point numbers as well as the behavior of the elementary operations [2, 11]. It is now implemented in almost all modern processors and, consequently, it provides a precise semantics, used as a basis in this article, for the basic operations occurring in high-level programming languages. A floating-point number x in base β is defined by

$$x = s \cdot (d_0.d_1 \ldots d_{p-1}) \cdot \beta^e = s \cdot m \cdot \beta^{e-p+1} \qquad (1)$$

where $s \in \{-1, 1\}$ is the sign, $m = d_0 d_1 \ldots d_{p-1}$ is the mantissa with digits $0 \leq d_i < \beta$ [1], $0 \leq i \leq p-1$, p is the precision and e is the exponent, $e_{min} \leq e \leq e_{max}$. The IEEE Standard 754 specifies a few values for p, e_{min} and e_{max}. For example, simple precision numbers are defined by $\beta = 2$, $p = 23$, $e_{min} = -126$ and $e_{max} = +127$. the standard also defines special values like NAN (not a number) or $\pm\infty$. In this article, the notation $\mathbb{F}$ indifferently refers to the set of simple or double precision numbers, since our assumptions conform to both types. $\mathbb{R}$ denotes the set of real numbers.

---

[1] $d_0 \neq 0$ but for denormalized numbers.

The standard defines four rounding modes for elementary operations between floating-point numbers. These modes are towards $-\infty$, towards $+\infty$, towards zero and to the nearest. We write them $\circ_{-\infty}$, $\circ_{+\infty}$, $\circ_0$ and $\circ_\sim$ respectively. Let $\uparrow_\circ : \mathbb{R} \to \mathbb{F}$ be the function which returns the roundoff of a real number following the rounding mode $\circ \in \{\circ_{-\infty}, \circ_{+\infty}, \circ_0, \circ_\sim\}$. $\uparrow_\circ$ is fully specified by the norm. The standard specifies the behavior of the elementary operations $\Diamond \in \{+, -, \times, \div\}$ between floating-point numbers by

$$f_1 \,\Diamond_{\mathbb{F},\circ}\, f_2 \;=\; \uparrow_\circ (f_1 \,\Diamond_{\mathbb{R}}\, f_2) \tag{2}$$

In this article, we also use the function $\downarrow_\circ : \mathbb{R} \to \mathbb{R}$ which returns the roundoff error. We have $\downarrow_\circ (r) = r - \uparrow_\circ (r)$.

Many reasons may lead to an important loss of accuracy in a float computation. For example, a catastrophic cancellation arises when subtracting close approximate numbers x and y [11]. An absorption arises when adding two number of different magnitude $x \ll y$; in this case $x +_\mathbb{F} y = y$ with $x \neq 0$.

The error due to the roundoff of an initial datum or resulting from the roundoff of the result of an operation is called a first order error. When errors are multiplied together, we obtain higher order errors. For example $(x + \epsilon_x) \times (y + \epsilon_y) = xy + x\epsilon_y + y\epsilon_x + \epsilon_x\epsilon_y$. Here, $x\epsilon_y + y\epsilon_x$ is the new first order error and $\epsilon_x\epsilon_y$ is a second order error.

The errors arising during a float computation can be estimated in different ways. Let $g_\mathbb{R} : \mathbb{R} \to \mathbb{R}$ be a function of the reals and $g_\mathbb{F} : \mathbb{F} \to \mathbb{F}$ its implementation in the floating-point numbers. The forward error estimates, for a given input x the distance $d(g_\mathbb{R}(x), g_\mathbb{F}(x))$. The backward error $B(x)$ determines whether the approximated solution $g_\mathbb{F}(x)$ is the exact solution to a problem close to the original one [8]: $B(x) = \inf\{d(x,y) : y = g_\mathbb{R}^{-1}(g_\mathbb{F}(x))\}$. Most of the existing automatic methods (and all the methods used in this article) compute forward errors.

3 Global Error

In this section, we introduce the semantics $[\![.]\!]_E$ which is used as a reference in the rest of this article. $[\![.]\!]_E$ computes the floating-point number resulting from a calculation on a IEEE 754 compliant computer as well as the error arising during the execution. In other words, this semantics calculates the forward error, as defined in Section 2, between the exact result of a problem in the reals and the approximated solution returned by a program. To calculate the exact errors, $[\![.]\!]_E$ uses real numbers and, consequently, it remains a theoretical tool. This semantics corresponds to the semantics $\mathcal{S}^{\mathcal{L}^0}$ introduced in [22].

Formally, in $[\![.]\!]_E$, a value v is denoted by a two-dimensional vector $v = f\varepsilon_f + e\varepsilon_e$. $f \in \mathbb{F}$ denotes the float used by the machine and $e \in \mathbb{R}$ denotes the exact error attached to f. ε_f and ε_e are formal variables used to identify the float and error components of v. For example, in simple precision, using the functions $\uparrow_\circ$ and $\downarrow_\circ$ introduced in Section 2, the real number $\frac{1}{3}$ is represented

$$x_1 = f_1 \varepsilon_f + e_1 \varepsilon_e \quad \text{and} \quad x_2 = f_2 \varepsilon_f + e_2 \varepsilon_e \tag{3}$$

$$x_1 + x_2 = \uparrow_\circ (f_1 + f_2)\varepsilon_f + [e_1 + e_2 + \downarrow_\circ (f_1 + f_2)]\, \varepsilon_e \tag{4}$$

$$x_1 - x_2 = \uparrow_\circ (f_1 - f_2)\varepsilon_f + [e_1 - e_2 + \downarrow_\circ (f_1 - f_2)]\, \varepsilon_e \tag{5}$$

$$x_1 \times x_2 = \uparrow_\circ (f_1 \times f_2)\varepsilon_f + [e_1 f_2 + e_2 f_1 + e_1 e_2 + \downarrow_\circ (f_1 \times f_2)]\, \varepsilon_e \tag{6}$$

$$\frac{1}{x_1} = \uparrow_\circ \left(\frac{1}{f}\right)\varepsilon_f + \left[\downarrow_\circ \left(\frac{1}{f}\right) + \sum_{n \geq 1}(-1)^n \frac{e^n}{f^{n+1}}\right]\varepsilon_e \tag{7}$$

Fig. 1. The semantics $[\![.]\!]_{\mathrm{E}}$.

by the value $v = \uparrow_\circ (\frac{1}{3})\varepsilon_f + \downarrow_\circ (\frac{1}{3})\varepsilon_e = 0.333333\varepsilon_f + (\frac{1}{3} - 0.333333)\varepsilon_e$. The semantics interprets a constant d as follows:

$$[\![d]\!]_{\mathrm{E}} = \uparrow_\circ (d)\varepsilon_f + \downarrow_\circ (d)\varepsilon_e \tag{8}$$

The semantics of elementary operations is defined in Figure 1, the operands x_1 and x_2 being given in Equation (3). Equations (4–6) are immediate. For Equation (7), recall that $\frac{1}{1+x} = \sum_{n \geq 0}(-1)^n x^n$ for all x such that $-1 \leq x \leq 1$. We have:

$$\frac{1}{f + e} = \frac{1}{f} \times \frac{1}{1 + \frac{e}{f}} = \frac{1}{f} \times \sum_{n \geq 0}(-1)^n \frac{e^n}{f^n}$$

The power series development is valid for $-1 \leq \frac{e}{f} \leq 1$ or, equivalently, while $|e| \leq |f|$, i.e. as long as the error is less than the float in absolute value. The semantics of the square root function is obtained like for division but the other elementary functions (e.g. the trigonometric ones) are more difficult to handle, due to the fact that the IEEE 754 Standard does not specify how they are rounded. $[\![.]\!]_{\mathrm{E}}$ calculates the floating-point numbers returned by a program and the exact difference between the float and real results, as outlined by the following proposition.

Proposition 1 *Let a be an arithmetic expression. Then if $[\![a]\!]_{\mathrm{E}} = f\varepsilon_f + e\varepsilon_e$ then $[\![a]\!]_{\mathrm{F}} = f$ and $[\![a]\!]_{\mathrm{R}} = f + e$.*

By relating $[\![.]\!]_{\mathrm{E}}$ to the semantics $[\![.]\!]_{\mathrm{R}}$ of real numbers and to the semantics $[\![.]\!]_{\mathrm{F}}$ of floating-point numbers, Proposition 1 provides a correctness criterion for $[\![.]\!]_{\mathrm{E}}$.

$[\![.]\!]_{\mathrm{E}}$ is well suited for the formal validation of critical systems because it exactly gives the floating-point numbers f used by the non-instrumented embedded code running on a IEEE 754 compliant computer as well as the error e arising when f is used instead of the exact value $f + e$. However, this semantics remains a theoretical tool since it uses real numbers and the function $\downarrow_\circ$ which cannot be exactly calculated by a computer in general. In the next sections, we use it as a reference in the study of other, approximate, semantics. We will compare the other methods in their ability to estimates the quantities f and e that define the values $f\varepsilon_f + e\varepsilon_e$ of $[\![.]\!]_{\mathrm{E}}$. The link between $[\![.]\!]_{\mathrm{E}}$ and the other methods is summed up by propositions 2, 3, 4 and 5.

4 Intervals

The classical semantics of intervals $[\![.]\!]_I$ aims at bounding the real result of a calculation by a lower and an upper float value [27]. Obviously, the semantics of a constant d is

$$[\![d]\!]_I = [\uparrow_{-\infty} (d), \uparrow_{+\infty} (d)] \tag{9}$$

Similarly, let $x_1 = [\underline{x_1}, \overline{x_1}]$ and $x_2 = [\underline{x_2}, \overline{x_2}]$ be two float intervals, let $\Diamond$ be an elementary operation, and let $i = [\underline{i}, \overline{i}]$ be the interval with real bounds defined by $i = x_1 \Diamond x_2$. $[\![x_1 \Diamond x_2]\!]_I$ is defined by:

$$[\![x_1 \Diamond x_2]\!]_I = [\uparrow_{-\infty} (\underline{i}), \uparrow_{+\infty} (\overline{i})] \tag{10}$$

Basically, an interval computation bounds a real number by two floating-point numbers, the maximal float smaller or equal to the real and the minimal float greater or equal the real. In other terms, using the formalism of Section 3, an interval computation approximates from below and from above the sum $f + e$ corresponding to the float f and to the exact error e calculated by $[\![.]\!]_E$. This is summed up in the following proposition.

Proposition 2 *Let a be an arithmetic expression such that $[\![a]\!]_E = f\varepsilon_f + e\varepsilon_e$ and $[\![a]\!]_I = [\underline{x}, \overline{x}]$. Then we have $[\![f + e]\!]_I \subseteq [\underline{x}, \overline{x}]$.*

Note that if the interval bounds are expressed with the same precision as in the original program, as in the semantics defined by equations (9) and (10), then the result $[\underline{x}, \overline{x}]$ output by the interval method bounds both the float result f and the real result $f + e$. Otherwise, if the interval bounds are expressed with a greater precision than in the non-instrumented code then the interval method bounds the real result $f + e$ but not necessary the float result f. In this latter case, the method does not enable one to predict how a program behaves when using standard floating-point numbers.

Because $[\![.]\!]_I$ always adds the error terms to the floating-point numbers, an interval computation does not distinguish two different kinds of errors:

1. Sensivity errors, due to the fact that a small variation of the inputs may yield a large variation of the outputs, even with real numbers.
2. Numerical errors, due to the fact that a float calculation may diverge from a real calculation.

For example, numerical errors arise in the following program which uses simple precision floating-point numbers:

```
float x=1.0;
float y=1.0e-8;
for(int i=0;i<1e8;i++) { x=x-y; }
```

The value 10^{-8} being subtracted 10^8 times to 1, the exact result in the reals is $x_{\mathbb{R}} = 0$. But 10^{-8} is less than the least significant digit of the float 1.0 and, consequently, an absorption occurs: $1.0 - 10^{-8} = 1.0$ in the floating-point numbers. So, at the end of the iteration $x_F = 1.0$. The interval semantics defined by equations (9) and (10) returns an interval $x_I \supseteq [0, 1]$, indicating that the exact result is between 0 and 1. In $[\![.]\!]_E$, $x_E = 1.0\varepsilon_f - 1.0\varepsilon_e$ which means that the float value of x is 1 and that the exact forward error on x is -1.

As illustrated by our example, $[\![.]\!]_I$ provides less information than the semantics of global errors because no distinction is made between the float and error terms. Nevertheless, when the interval resulting from a calculation is small, we may conclude that the error term also is small. In this case, an interval method can validate a calculation. In addition, intervals can be used to implement the theoretical semantics $[\![.]\!]_E$, yielding a new semantics $[\![.]\!]_{EI}$. A value $v = f\varepsilon_f + [\underline{x}, \overline{x}]\varepsilon_e$ of $[\![.]\!]_{EI}$ is made of a float f and an interval of error $[\underline{x}, \overline{x}]$. The elementary operations are defined by the rules of Figure 1, in which the computations on error terms are carried out in $[\![.]\!]_I$.

Examples of interval arithmetic libraries are Boost [6] and MPFI [30], the latter being based on the multiple precision library MPFR [18]. Implementations of multiple precision interval libraries are compared in [17].

5 Stochastic Arithmetics

Stochastic arithmetics consists of running a few times the same program, the roundoff errors being, at each run, randomly propagated. The common digits of the results of all the executions are assumed exact [9, 31]. The stochastic arithmetic semantics $[\![.]\!]_S$, introduces the random roundoff function $\uparrow_? : \mathbb{F} \to \mathbb{F}$ defined by:

$$\uparrow_? (d) = \begin{cases} \text{either } \uparrow_{-\infty} (d) \\ \text{or } \uparrow_{+\infty} (d) \end{cases} \text{ with probability } \frac{1}{2} \tag{11}$$

In stochastic arithmetics, the n executions of a program are usually carried out synchronously, to cope with control flow problems, like ensuring that all the executions take the same branches. So, a stochastic value is a n-tuple containing the n values assigned to a number. A constant d is interpreted by:

$$[\![d]\!]_S = (\uparrow_? (d), \dots, \uparrow_? (d)) \tag{12}$$

and, for any elementary operation $\Diamond$, we have:

$$[\![x \Diamond x']\!]_S = (\uparrow_? (x_1 \Diamond x'_1), \dots, \uparrow_? (x_n \Diamond x'_n)) \tag{13}$$

$[\![.]\!]_S$ uses the fact that roundoff errors usually cancel each other. This enables the user to obtain less pessimistic results than, e.g., with interval arithmetics. More precisely, the mean $\overline{x}$ of the result $x = (x_1, \dots, x_n)$ of the n runs approximates the real result $x_\mathbb{R}$ of the calculation. Let $C(x, x_\mathbb{R})$ denote the number of digits common to $\overline{x}$ and $x_\mathbb{R}$. Using Student's test, the method makes it possible to compute $C(x, x_\mathbb{R})$ with probability P [9].

Proposition 3 *Let a be an expression such that $[\![a]\!]_S = (x_1, \dots, x_n)$ and $[\![a]\!]_E = f\varepsilon_f + e\varepsilon_e$. Then, with probability P, $\overline{x}$ and $f + e$ have $C(\overline{x}, f + e)$ common digits, where $C(\overline{x}, f + e) = \log_{10} \left(\frac{\sqrt{n}|\overline{x}|}{\sigma \tau_P} \right)$ and $\sigma^2 = \frac{1}{n-1} \sum_{i=1}^{n} (x_i - \overline{x})^2$.*

For $n = 3$ and $P = 0.95$, $\tau_P = 4,303$. However, Proposition 3 is based on the hypothesis that the roundoff errors are uniform and independent, the latter meaning that the errors arising at each step of a calculation are not correlated with each other. This is not always the case, mainly for loops. For example, in the program of Section 4, the same roundoff error is made at each iteration. In addition, Proposition 3 assumes that higher order errors are negligible with respect to the first order errors. In Section 6, we introduce an example for which this assumption does not hold.

Because $[\![.]\!]_S$ approximates, with probability P, the exact result of a program p in the reals, it does not enable the user to ensure that no precision loss arises in the non-instrumented execution of p which uses standard floating-point numbers. However, even if this method is mainly taylored to detect stability problems in the algorithms used in a program, it can assert the validity of a floating-point calculation when (1) $C(\overline{x}, x_\mathbb{R})$ is high and (2) $\overline{x}$ is close to the float result f.

An issue to improve a stochastic arithmetics for validation would be to define a new semantics $[\![.]\!]_{ES}$ based on $[\![.]\!]_E$. In this new semantics, the exact error terms of $[\![.]\!]_E$ would be computed in $[\![.]\!]_S$. A value $v = f\varepsilon_f + e\varepsilon_e$ of $[\![.]\!]_{ES}$ would be made of a float f and an error e which would be a stochastic number of $[\![.]\!]_S$. However, the hypotheses and the correctness proofs of $[\![.]\!]_S$ must be revisited. The CADNA library implements stochastic arithmetics [7].

6   Automatic Differentiation

In this section we introduce a simple semantics performing an automatic differentiation of programs. More elaborated techniques are described in the references mentioned later on. In automatic differentiation [3, 15], one considers that a program p calculates a function g of the data for which we are going to evaluate, at the same time as g, the numerical values of the derivatives. If $d_1, \ldots, d_n$ denote the data used in p, then the program computes the results $v_1, \ldots, v_m$ such that:

$$\begin{pmatrix} v_1 \\ \vdots \\ v_m \end{pmatrix} = \begin{pmatrix} g_1(d_1, \ldots, d_n) \\ \vdots \\ g_m(d_1, \ldots, d_n) \end{pmatrix} \tag{14}$$

$v_1, \ldots, v_m$ are the final results of the program, at the end of the execution. For each $1 \leq i \leq m$, v_i is a function g_i of the data $d_1, \ldots, d_n$. Automatic differentiation aims at numerically calculating, in addition to the terms v_i, the partial derivatives $\frac{\partial g_i}{\partial d_j}(d_1, \ldots, d_n)$ for all $1 \leq j \leq n$. By determining whether a slight modification of the initial value d_j implies a large modification of the result v_i, the partial derivative $\frac{\partial g_i}{\partial d_j}(d_1, \ldots, d_n)$ indicates the sensitivity of v_i to the variations of d_j. If $\frac{\partial g_i}{\partial d_j}(d_1, \ldots, d_n) \approx 0$, v_i is not much sensitive to a variation of d_j. If $\frac{\partial g_i}{\partial d_j}(d_1, \ldots, d_n) > 1$ then the error on d_j is magnified in v_i by a factor approximately equal to $\frac{\partial g_i}{\partial d_j}(d_1, \ldots, d_n)$.

The most intuitive way to calculate the derivatives is to achieve a linear approximation of order one by means of the well-known formula: $g'(x) \approx$

$$v_1 = (f_1, \delta_1, \ldots, \delta_n) \quad \text{and} \quad v_2 = (f_2, \eta_1, \ldots, \eta_n) \tag{15}$$

$$[\![v_1 + v_2]\!]_D = (f_1 + f_2, \delta_1 + \eta_1, \delta_2 + \eta_2, \ldots, \delta_n + \eta_n) \tag{16}$$

$$[\![v_1 - v_2]\!]_D = (f_1 - f_2, \delta_1 - \eta_1, \delta_2 - \eta_2, \ldots, \delta_n - \eta_n) \tag{17}$$

$$[\![v_1 \times v_2]\!]_D = (f_1 \times f_2, f_1\eta_1 + f_2\delta_1, f_1\eta_2 + f_2\delta_2, \ldots, f_1\eta_n + f_2\delta_n) \tag{18}$$

$$[\![\frac{v_1}{v_2}]\!]_D = \left(\frac{f_1}{f_2}, \frac{f_2\delta_1 - f_1\eta_1}{f_2^2}, \frac{f_2\delta_2 - f_1\eta_2}{f_2^2}, \ldots, \frac{f_2\delta_n - f_1\eta_n}{f_2^2} \right) \tag{19}$$

Fig. 2. The semantics $[\![.]\!]_D$ for automatic differentiation.

$\frac{g(x+\Delta x) - g(x)}{\Delta x}$. However this method yields imprecise results, due to the fact that Δx is usually small. Instead, automatic derivation techniques calculate the derivatives by composing elementary functions, according to the chain rule: $(f \circ g)'(x) = \left[f(g(x))\right]' = g'(x) \times f'(g(x))$. Each function g_i is viewed as a chain of elementary functions such as additions, products, trigonometric functions, etc. The derivatives $\frac{\partial g_i}{\partial d_j}(d_0, \ldots, d_n)$ are calculated by the chain rule.

The semantics $[\![.]\!]_D$ of Figure 2 achieves a sensitivity analysis to the data of a program p, by automatic differentiation. For a constant d_i, we have

$$[\![d_i]\!]_D = (d_i, \delta_1 = 0, \ldots, \delta_i = 1, \ldots, \delta_n = 0) \tag{20}$$

A numerical value v of $[\![.]\!]_D$ is a $(n+1)$-tuple $(f, \delta_1, \ldots, \delta_n)$. Intuitively, at some stage of the execution of p, v is the result of an intermediate calculation. In other terms, for a certain function g, the program p has calculated $h_1(d_1, \ldots, d_n)$ such that $g((d_1, \ldots, d_n)) = h_2 \circ h_1(d_1, \ldots, d_n)$ for some function h_2 and the current value v of $[\![.]\!]_D$ represents

$$v = (f, \delta_1, \ldots, \delta_n) = \left(h_1(d_1, \ldots, d_n), \frac{\partial h_1}{\partial d_1}(d_1, \ldots, d_n), \ldots, \frac{\partial h_1}{\partial d_n}(d_1, \ldots, d_n) \right) \tag{21}$$

Automatic differentiation can be viewed as a way to approximately calculate the error term $e\varepsilon_e$ of the semantics $[\![.]\!]_E$. Given a program that implements a function g, $[\![.]\!]_E$ calculates $[\![g(d_1, \ldots, d_n)]\!]_E = x_r = f_r\varepsilon_f + e_r\varepsilon_e$. In the simplest case $m = n = 1$, i.e. for a program p calculating a function g of a single datum d_1, we can estimate the error term e_r from the numerical values $g(d_1)$ and $\frac{\partial g}{\partial d_1}(d_1)$ returned by $[\![g(d_1)]\!]_D$. Let e_{d_1} denote the initial error on the argument d_1 of g. By linear approximation, we have

$$x_r \approx g(d_1)\varepsilon_f + \left(e_{d_1} \times \frac{\partial g}{\partial d_1}(d_1) \right) \varepsilon_e \tag{22}$$

In Equation (22), the exact error term e_r is approximated by $e_{d_1} \times \frac{\partial g}{\partial d_1}(d_1)$. In the general case, i.e. if $m \geq 1$ and $n \geq 1$, we have the following property.

Proposition 4 *Let $e_1, \ldots, e_n$ be the initial errors attached to data $d_1, \ldots, d_n$ and let $v_1, \ldots, v_m$ be the results of a computation as defined in Equation (14). If in the semantics $[\![.]\!]_E$, for all $1 \leq i \leq m$, $v_i = [\![g_i(d_1, \ldots, d_n)]\!]_E = x_i\varepsilon_f + e_{r_i}\varepsilon_e$*

then, in $[\![.]\!]_D$, $v_i = [\![g_i(d_1, \ldots, d_n)]\!]_D = (y_i, \delta_{i,1}, \ldots, \delta_{i,n})$ *such that* $x_i = y_i$ *and such that the error term* e_{r_i} *on the final result* v_i *is linearly approximated by:*

$$e_{r_i} \approx \sum_{1 \leq j \leq n} e_j \times \delta_{i,j} \qquad (23)$$

The main drawback of automatic differentiation stems from the linear approximation made in Equation (22), which may under-estimate the errors (or over-estimate them, though it is usually less critical for validation). For example, let us consider the function:

```
float g(float x,int n) {
  y=x;
  for (int i=0;i<n;i++) { y=y*x; };
  return y; }
```

In this function, if the parameter $x = f\varepsilon_f + e\varepsilon_e$ is such that $f < 1$ and $f + e > 1$ then, in the floating-point numbers, $g(x) \to 0$ as $n \to \infty$, while in the reals, $g(x) = g(f + e) \to \infty$ as $n \to \infty$. In $[\![.]\!]_D$, the value returned by g(x,n) is (f^{n+1}, nf^n), where the component nf^n gives the sensitivity of g to the parameter x. If $f < 1$ then $nf^n \to 0$ as $n \to \infty$ and the approximation of Equation (23) may become irrelevant. For instance, if $x = 0.95\varepsilon_f + 0.1\varepsilon_e$ then on one hand we have $[\![g(x,n)]\!]_E \to 0\varepsilon_f + \infty\varepsilon_e$ as $n \to \infty$ while, on the other hand $[\![g(x,n)]\!]_D \to (0,0)$ as $n \to \infty$ In this example, Equation (23) leads to the erroneous conclusion that for $x = 0.95\varepsilon_f + 0.1\varepsilon_e$, $e_x \approx 0$.

In addition, automatic differentiation only takes care of the errors on the initial data, neglecting the errors introduced by the operations, during the calculation. For example, from Equation (4), the semantics $[\![.]\!]_E$ of an addition is:

$$x_1 + x_2 = \uparrow_\circ (f_1 + f_2)\varepsilon_f + [e_1 + e_2 + \downarrow_\circ (f_1 + f_2)]\,\varepsilon_e$$

$[\![.]\!]_D$ makes it possible to estimate the terms e_1 and e_2 but neglects the error introduced by the addition itself, namely $\downarrow_\circ (f_1 + f_2)$. Finally, the higher-order error terms also are neglected. For example, the term $e_1 e_2$ occuring in the result of the product of Equation (6) is ignored.

Bischof et al. have recently published an overview of the implementations of automatic differentiation libraries [3]. In certain cases, automatic differentiation can also be used to improve the precision of a calculation, by adding correcting terms to the floating-point numbers computed by the machine [20, 21]. In this case, roundoff errors introduced by the elementary operations are not neglected and one can guarantee the precision of the final result.

7   Error Series

In this section, we introduce the semantics $[\![.]\!]_W$ of error series [13, 22]. The semantics $[\![.]\!]_E$ of Section 3 globally computes the difference between the float and the real result of a calculation. However, when this error term is large, no hint is given to the programmer concerning its source. $[\![.]\!]_W$ is a generalization of

$$r_1 +^{\ell_i} r_2 \overset{\text{def}}{=} \uparrow_\circ (f_1 + f_2)\varepsilon + \sum_{\ell \in \mathcal{L}^+} (\omega_1^\ell + \omega_2^\ell)\varepsilon_\ell + \downarrow_\circ (f_1 + f_2)\varepsilon_{\ell_i} \qquad (26)$$

$$r_1 -^{\ell_i} r_2 \overset{\text{def}}{=} \uparrow_\circ (f_1 - f_2)\varepsilon + \sum_{\ell \in \mathcal{L}^+} (\omega_1^\ell - \omega_2^\ell)\varepsilon_\ell + \downarrow_\circ (f_1 - f_2)\varepsilon_{\ell_i} \qquad (27)$$

$$r_1 \times^{\ell_i} r_2 \overset{\text{def}}{=} \uparrow_\circ (f_1 f_2)\varepsilon + \sum_{\substack{\ell_1 \in \mathcal{L}, \, \ell_2 \in \mathcal{L} \\ \ell_1 \cdot \ell_2 \neq \nu}} \omega_1^{\ell_1} \omega_2^{\ell_2} \varepsilon_{\ell_1 \cdot \ell_2} + \downarrow_\circ (f_1 f_2)\varepsilon_{\ell_i} \qquad (28)$$

$$(r_1)^{-1^{\ell_i}} \overset{\text{def}}{=} \uparrow_\circ (f_1^{-1})\varepsilon - \frac{1}{f_1} \sum_{\ell \in \mathcal{L}} \frac{\omega^\ell}{f_1} \varepsilon_\ell + \frac{1}{f_1} \sum_{n \geq 2} (-1)^n \left(\sum_{\ell \in \mathcal{L}} \frac{\omega^\ell}{f_1} \right)^n \varepsilon_{hi} + \downarrow_\circ (f_1^{-1})\varepsilon_{\ell_i} \qquad (29)$$

$$r_1 \div^{\ell_i} r_2 \overset{\text{def}}{=} r_1 \times^{\ell_i} (r_2)^{-1^{\ell_i}} \qquad (30)$$

Fig. 3. Elementary operations for floating-point numbers with errors.

$[\![.]\!]_E$ in which the roundoff errors arising at any stage of a calculation are traced, in order to detect which of them mainly contribute to the global error.

$[\![.]\!]_W$ assumes that the control points of the program are annotated by unique labels $\ell \in \mathcal{L}$. A value of $[\![.]\!]_W$ is a series

$$r = f\varepsilon + \sum_{\ell \in \mathcal{L}} \omega^\ell \varepsilon_\ell \qquad (24)$$

Error series generalize the values of $[\![.]\!]_E$. In Equation (24), f is the float approximating the value of r. f is always attached to the formal variable ε whose index is the empty word. A term $\omega^\ell \varepsilon_\ell$ denotes the contribution to the global error of the first-order error introduced by the operation labeled ℓ during the evaluation of r. $\omega^\ell \in \mathbb{R}$ is the scalar value of this error term and ε_ℓ is a formal variable. A special label hi which corresponds to no particular control point is used to identify the higher order errors. This comes from previous work [22] which introduces more general semantics for error series. Error terms of order n correspond to words of length n and the empty word ν is related to the term for the floating-point number. The multiplication of terms of order m and n yields a new term of order $m + n$ denoted by a word of length $m + n$. In this article, hi identifies all the words of length greater that one and the product of formal variables is defined by Equation (25).

$$\varepsilon_u \times \varepsilon_v = \begin{cases} \varepsilon_{uv} & \text{if length}(uv) \leq 1 \\ \varepsilon_{hi} & \text{otherwise} \end{cases} \qquad (25)$$

The elementary operations are defined in Figure 3 for $r_1 = f_1\varepsilon_1 + \sum_{\ell \in \mathcal{L}^+} \omega_1^\ell \varepsilon_\ell$ and $r_2 = f_2\varepsilon_2 + \sum_{\ell \in \mathcal{L}^+} \omega_2^\ell \varepsilon_\ell$. $\mathcal{L}^+$ denotes the set $\mathcal{L}$ without the empty word. In addition, the symbols f and ω are used interchangeably to denote the coefficient of the variable ε. The formal series $\sum_{\ell \in \mathcal{L}} \omega^\ell \varepsilon_\ell$ related to the result of an operation $\Diamond^{\ell_i}$ contains the combination of the errors on the operands plus a new error term $\downarrow_\circ (f_1 \Diamond f_2)\varepsilon_{\ell_i}$ corresponding to the error introduced by the operation $\Diamond$ occurring at point ℓ_i. The rules for addition and subtraction are natural. The elementary errors are added or subtracted componentwise in the formal series and the new error due to point ℓ_i corresponds to the roundoff of the result.

Multiplication requires more care because it introduces higher-order errors due to the multiplication of the first-order errors. For instance, let us consider the product at point ℓ_3 of two data $r_1^{\ell_1} = (f_1\varepsilon + \omega_1^{\ell_1}\varepsilon_{\ell_1})$ and $r_2^{\ell_2} = (f_2\varepsilon + \omega_2^{\ell_2}\varepsilon_{\ell_2})$:

$$r_1^{\ell_1} \times^{\ell_3} r_2^{\ell_2} = \uparrow_\circ (f_1 f_2)\varepsilon + f_2\omega_1^{\ell_1}\varepsilon_{\ell_1} + f_1\omega_2^{\ell_2}\varepsilon_{\ell_2} + \omega_1^{\ell_1}\omega_2^{\ell_2}\varepsilon_{hi} + \downarrow_\circ (f_1 f_2)\varepsilon_{\ell_3} \quad (31)$$

As shown in Equation (31), the floating-point number computed by this multiplication is $\uparrow_\circ (f_1 f_2)$. The initial first-order errors $\omega_1^{\ell_1}\varepsilon_{\ell_1}$ and $\omega_2^{\ell_2}\varepsilon_{\ell_2}$ are multiplied by f_2 and f_1 respectively. ν denotes the empty word. In addition, the multiplication introduces a new first-order error $\downarrow_\circ (f_1 f_2)$ which is attached to the formal variable ε_{ℓ_3} in order to indicate that this error is due to the product occurring at the control point ℓ_3. Finally, this operation also introduces a second-order error that we attach to the formal variable ε_{hi}. In Figure 3, Equation (28) is a generalization of Equation (31). The term for division is obtained by means of a power series development.

This semantics details the contribution to the global error of the first-order error terms and globally computes the higher-order error arising during the calculation. In practice, higher-order errors are often negligible. So, this semantics allows us to determine the sources of imprecision due to first order errors while checking that the higher-order errors are actually globally negligible. With respect to the semantics $[\![.]\!]_{\mathrm{E}}$, we have the following result.

Proposition 5 *Let a be an arithmetic expression such that $[\![a]\!]_{\mathrm{E}} = f\varepsilon_f + e\varepsilon_e$ and $[\![a]\!]_{\mathrm{W}} = \omega\varepsilon + \sum_{\ell \in \mathcal{L}} \omega^\ell \varepsilon_\ell$. Then $\omega = f$ and $\sum_{\ell \in \mathcal{L}} \omega^\ell = e$.*

Like $[\![.]\!]_{\mathrm{E}}$, $[\![.]\!]_{\mathrm{W}}$ is not directly implementable since it uses real numbers and the function $\downarrow_\circ : \mathbb{R} \to \mathbb{R}$. However, $[\![.]\!]_{\mathrm{W}}$ can also be approximated in the same way than $[\![.]\!]_{\mathrm{E}}$. The error terms can be calculated for instance with intervals or stochastic numbers, yielding new semantics $[\![.]\!]_{\mathrm{WI}}$ and $[\![.]\!]_{\mathrm{WS}}$.

In addition, the first order error terms of $[\![.]\!]_{\mathrm{W}}$ can be related to the partial derivatives computed by $[\![.]\!]_{\mathrm{D}}$. Let d_i be a datum identified by the control point ℓ of a program p such that p computes a function $g(d_1, \ldots, d_n)$. Then the term $\downarrow_\circ (d_i) \times \frac{\partial g}{\partial d_i}(d_1, \ldots, d_n)$ linearly approximates the error term $\omega^\ell \varepsilon_\ell$ of $[\![.]\!]_{\mathrm{W}}$. With respect to the exact semantics $[\![.]\!]_{\mathrm{W}}$, $[\![.]\!]_{\mathrm{D}}$ neglects the higher order error term $\omega^{hi}\varepsilon_{hi}$ as well as any error term $\omega^\ell \varepsilon_\ell$ such that ℓ is not related to an initial datum, i.e. such that ℓ is related to an operation.

Higher order errors often are negligible and are, in practice, neglected by most methods (but $[\![.]\!]_{\mathrm{W}}$ and $[\![.]\!]_{\mathrm{I}}$). The program of Section 6 is a case in which, for some inputs, first order errors are negligible while higher order errors are not: If the parameter $x = f\varepsilon + \omega\varepsilon_x$ is such that $f < 1$ and $f + \omega > 1$ then, in the floating-point numbers, $g(x) \to 0$ as $n \to \infty$, while in the reals, $g(x + \omega) \to \infty$ as $n \to \infty$. The global error tends towards infinity but it can be shown that all the first order error terms tend to 0. Since only the higher order errors are significant, a method neglecting them should not detect any problem in this computation.

8   Static Analysis

Numerical computations are increasingly used in critical embedded systems like planes or nuclear power plants. In this area, the designers used to use fixed-point numbers for two reasons: first, the embedded processors did not have floating-point units and, secondly, the calculations were rather simple. Nowadays, floating-point numbers are more and more used in these systems, due to the increasing complexity of the calculations and because floating-point units are integrated in most processors.

Concerning numerical computations, the validation of a critical embedded system requires at least to prove that the precision of a variable is always acceptable. Executions can be instrumented with an automatic differentiation or a stochastic semantics. However, these methods do not enable one to have a full covering of the possible configurations and representative data sets are specially difficult to define since very close inputs may yield very different results in terms of precision. In addition, for the same execution path, the precision may greatly differ, for different data sets. Static analysis addresses these problems by enabling to validate in a single time a code for a large class of inputs usually defined by ranges for all the parameters. In this article, we focus on validation of floating-point calculations but most results are similar for fixed point calculations. Basically, in the latter case, the function $\downarrow_\circ$ must be redefined. We detail below how the methods of sections 3 to 7 can be used for static analysis.

Many static analyzers implement an interval analysis (e.g. [4]). The main drawback of this approach was already outlined for the dynamic semantics: as discussed in Section 4, when an interval is large, one cannot assert that the precision of the results is acceptable. In addition, the intervals given to a static analyzer usually are larger than these used to simulate a single run. As a consequence, a static analyzer based on $[\![.]\!]_I$ often is too pessimistic to assert the accuracy of a floating-point computation.

To our knowledge, no static analysis based on stochastic arithmetics as been defined nor experimented yet. However, as suggested in [13], we can expect interesting results from static analyses combining $[\![.]\!]_S$ or $[\![.]\!]_{WS}$ and recent work on static analysis of probabilistic semantics [25, 26].

Automatic differentiation seems a good candidate to static analysis even if the classical semantics $[\![.]\!]_D$ has some limitations: some error terms are neglected and, for the others, there is a linear approximation. A semantics $[\![.]\!]_{WD}$ was recently proposed that performs automatic differentiation behind the semantics $[\![.]\!]_W$ of error series [23]. In $[\![.]\!]_{WD}$, no error term is neglected but the linear approximation remains. For loops, a static stability test based on the calculation of abstract Lyapunov exponents [1] can be used [23]. It allows one to iterate just enough to prove that the iterates of a function related to the body of a loop are stable.

Finally, concerning error series, a static analyzer named Fluctuat and based on $[\![.]\!]_{WI}$ has been implemented [14]. For a value $f\varepsilon + \sum_{\ell \in \mathcal{L}} \omega^\ell \varepsilon_\ell$, the float f is abstracted by a float interval and the error terms ω^ℓ are abstracted by intervals of multiple precision numbers. Fluctuat analyzes C programs and is currently experimented in an industrial context, for the validation of large-size avionic embedded softwares.

9   Experimental Results

In this section, we present some experimental results obtained using the methods described earlier. The tools and libraries that we use for interval arithmetics, stochastic arithmetics, automatic differentiation and error series respectively are MPFI [30], CADNA [9], ADOL-C [16] and Fluctuat [14]. Each example, written in C, was designed to illustrate how a certain method behaves in a particular case (mostly to show their limitations even if they all behave well on many other examples) but, in the following, we test all the methods for each case. Depending on the cases, Fluctuat either is asked to unroll the loops or to work as a static analyzer. When unrolling the loops, the tool exactly implements the semantics $[\![.]\!]_{WI}$ discussed in Section 7. Otherwise, additionnal approximations are performed by the static analysis. The results are given in the tables of figures 4, 5, 6 and 7. In each table, the *comment* column contains information on how the methods are configured and the *interpretation* column says what we can conclude from the experiment, assuming that we know nothing on the program but the result of the current method. So, if a method fails to detect a problem, the corresponding conclusion in the *interpretation* column is erroneous.

Our first example is the program already introduced in Section 4 to show how difficult it is to distinguish a purely numerical error from a sensitivity error, mainly with an interval method. This example was inspired by the well-known Patriot case (see, e.g. [13]) but, here, the solutions in $\mathbb{R}$ and $\mathbb{F}$ are finite.

```
float x = 1.0; float y = 1.0e-8;
for (int i=0;i<1e8;i++) { x = x-y; }
```

Our experimental results are given in Figure 4. As discussed in Section 4, the result returned by the interval method includes the interval [0, 1] if MPFI is asked to simulate single precision numbers. One can conclude that both the real and float solution belong to this interval, but we cannot conclude on the nature of the inaccuracy. If MPFI is asked to use multiple precision numbers, it outputs a small interval around 0. We can conclude that the real solution is close to 0, but no hint is given about the error arising in the non-instrumented code.

Concerning the other methods, CADNA computes that the real solution is close to -0.38, which is rather imprecise. As outlined in Section 5, this probably stems from the fact that the errors arising at each iteration are not independent, as supposed by the method. ADOL-C returns the float result and indicates that it is very sensitive to the value of y. The pitfall is detected by the automatic differentiation library as one could expect, since the computed function is linear. Finally, Fluctuat finds the exact floating-point result and states that the error is possibly large. The error is not bounded accurately because in static analysis mode, Fluctuat does not fully unroll the loop.

	Result	Comment	Interpretation
$[\![.]\!]_E$	x=1.0ε_f − 1.0ε_e	$[\![.]\!]_E$ is the theoretical, non implementable semantics.	An absorption arises at each iteration. The float result is 1.0 and the error w.r.t. to the real solution exactly is −1.0.
MPFI	x=[-1.244141e1,1.000000]	x is initialized by mpfi_init2 (x,24) to simulate the IEEE 754 Standard simple precision mode.	The real solution as well as the float solution belong to the given interval. The error may be as large as the interval width, i.e. 11.44141.
MPFI	x=[-4.11312855843084e-9, 3.28835822230294e-9]	x is initialized by mpfi_init_set_d to obtain a highly accurate result.	The real solution is very close to zero. There is no unstability in this example.
CADNA	x=-0.3808, cestac= 4	x and y are declared as single_st numbers.	With high probability, the real solution is x = −0.3808 and the first four significant digits seem correct.
ADOL-C	x = 1.0, $\frac{\partial x}{\partial y}$ = −1.0e8	Since ADOL only has double precision numbers, this test has been carried out using adouble numbers and y = 1.0e − 22. Results have been transposed to our example.	The float result is 1.0 but the sensitivity to y is high. By linear approximation, the real solution is 1.0 + $\frac{\partial x}{\partial y}$ × Δy where Δy is the initial error on y.
Fluctuat	x=1.0ε_f + [−∞,-1.0e-8]ε_e	No instrumentation of the code. Fluctuat does not unroll the loop (5 iterations are carried out).	Fluctuat detects that there is possibly (but not surely) a large negative error on the result.

Fig. 4. Experimental results for the program iterating x=x-1.0e-8.

Contrarily to the first example, our second test program, taken from [13], is an unstable numerical scheme computing the nth power u_n of the golden number $u_1 = \frac{\sqrt{5}-1}{2} \approx 0.618034$ using the property $u_{n+2} = u_n - u_{n+1}$.

```
double x = 1.0; double y = 0.618034;
for (i=0;i<=100;i++) {
   z=x; x=y; y=z-y; }
```

Our experimental results are given in Figure 5. With MPFI, y is initialized to the small interval [0.618034, 0, 618035]. MPFI returns a large interval and we can conclude that the scheme is unstable. When Fluctuat is initialized with y=[0.618034, 0, 618035]ε_f + 0ε_e, which means that the initial float is an exact value belonging to the given interval, Fluctuat states that the result belongs to a wide interval but that the error term is small. So this computation is unstable but it is not much perturbed by the roundoff of the operations arising in the loop. When Fluctuat is initialized with y = 0.618034ε_f + [0, 0.02]ε_e, which means that the initial float exactly is 0, 618034 and that a roundoff error is attached to it, the tool detects a large sensitivity to y. Concerning the other methods, CADNA does not detect the instability while ADOL-C does (this scheme is linear).

ADOL-C caught the numerical problems arising in the first two examples involving linear calculations. However, as discussed in Section 6, automatic differentiation methods may fail to detect such numerical errors, e.g. in the non-linear calculation introduced in Section 6 and repeated below:

	Result	Comment	Interpretation
MPFI	y=[-9.37805732496113e14, -1.04330402763639e13]	y initialized with mpfi_interv_d.	The real solution belong to the given interval. The error may be as large as the interval width, i.e. approximatively 9.27e14. The computation is unstable.
CADNA	y= -0.474119386437716e+15, cestac=15	x, y, z have double_st type. y was initialized to the median value of the interval.	With high probability, the real solution is y≈-0.47e+15 and the first fifteen significant digits are correct. This computation seems stable.
ADOL-C	y=-4.74119e+14, grad(y)=-3.54225e+20	x, y, z have adouble type. y is initialized to the median value of the interval.	The gradient indicates that this computation is unstable.
Fluctuat	y=[-9.37805732496110e14, -1.04330402763639e13]ε_f +[-25363.4,25363.4]ε_e	An assertion is used to initialize y to [0.618034,0.618035]ε_f+ 0ε_e. Fluctuat is asked to unroll the loop.	The results belong to a large interval but the errors never are greater than 25363.4. If the initial error on y is null, the computation is unstable but roundoff errors are negligible.
Fluctuat	y=[-1.04330402763639e13, -1.04330402763639e13]ε_f +[-9.27373e+14, -0.00149523]ε_e	An assertion is used to initialize y to 0.618034ε_f+[0,0,0]ε_e. Fluctuat is asked to unroll the loop.	This program is very sensitive to the initial value of y.

Fig. 5. Experimental results for the computation of the nth power of the golden number.

```
x = 1.0;  y = 0.99;
for (int i=0;i<1000;i++) { x = x*y; }
```

The experimental results obtained for this example are given in Figure 6. ADOL-C numerically computes the derivative given in Section 6 and does not detect the sensitivity of this code to the value of y. CADNA also indicates that this computation does not seem to be sensitive to its input values, possibly because the dominant error is non-linear. Using an assertion stating that initially y= $0.99\varepsilon_f + [0, 0.02]\varepsilon_e$, Fluctuat states that the float computed by a non-instrumented version of the program goes to 0 while the error with respect to the real result is increasingly large.

We end this section with a case study taken from [22] and concerning the validation of a class of executions of a simple numerical program implementating Jacobi's iterative method to solve a system of linear equations. As discussed in Section 8, in order to validate a class of executions for this program, we aim at showing that the errors arising during any execution performed with parameters taken in a certain set remain acceptable. We consider the systems:

$$(S_1) \ : \ \begin{cases} 2x + y = \frac{5}{3} \\ x + 3y = \frac{5}{2} \end{cases} \qquad (S_2) \ : \ \begin{cases} x_{n+1} = \frac{5}{6} - \frac{1}{2}y_n \\ y_{n+1} = \frac{5}{6} - \frac{1}{3}x_n \end{cases}$$

$$(S_3) \ : \ \begin{cases} x_{n+1} = [0.80, 0.85] - [0.4, 0.6]y_n \\ y_{n+1} = [0.80, 0.85] - [0.30, 0.35]x_n \end{cases}$$

To solve (S_1) by Jacobi's method [12], the sequence (S_2) is computed. (S_3) defines a class of systems including (S_2). Any system taken in the ranges given

	Result	Comment	Interpretation
$[\![.]\!]_{\mathbb{E}}$	x= 0.43e-4ε_f − $\omega\varepsilon_e$	ω is small if initially y = 0.99ε_f + $\omega'\varepsilon_e$ with ω' < 0.01. ω is large otherwise.	This computation is sensitive to y.
MPFI	x=[4.31712474106544e-5, 4.31712474106612e-5]	x and y initialized by mpfi_init. set_d.	The float solution is close to the real one since the interval width is small.
CADNA	x=0.43171247410657e-4, cestac =14	x and y are declared as double_st numbers.	With high probability, the real solution is x ≈ 0.43e−4 and the first fourteen significant digits are correct.
ADOL-C	x=4.31712e-5, $\frac{\partial x}{\partial y}$=0.0436073	The experiment has been carried out using adouble numbers.	The derivative is small. This computation seems to be not much sensitive to y.
Fluctuat	x=4.31712474106578e-5ε_f+[8.22526e-21,6.17629e-20]ε_e	No instrumentation of the code. Fluctuat is asked to fully unroll the loop.	Assuming that initially y is exact, no numerical error arises in this execution.
Fluctuat	x=4.31712474106578e-5ε_f+[-1.42622e-12,20959.2]ε_e	An assertion states that initially y = 0.99ε_f+[0.0, 0.02]ε_e. Fluctuat is asked to fully unroll the loop. The tool states that the dominant error is a higher order error.	The sensitivity to y is detected.

Fig. 6. Experimental results for the non-linear computation of Section 6.

in (S_3) is stable. The program implementing (S_2) is given below. The initial values are $x_0 = y_0 = [2.0, 3.0]$.

```
int i; double x1,y1;
double a = [0.8,0.85];    double b = [0.4,0.6];
double c = [0.8,0.85];    double d = [0.3,0.35];
double x2 = [2.0,3.0];    double y2 = [2.0,3.0];
for(i=0;i<1000;i++) {
  x1 = x2; y1 = y2;
  x2 = a-b*y1; y2 = c-d*x1; }
```

Our results are given in Figure 7. MPFI outputs small intervals enabling to assess the stability of the class of executions: the errors on x and y never exceed 0.26 and 0.15, respectively. Fluctuat finds intervals for x and y comparable to these of MPFI and, additionally, states that for any execution, the errors on x and y never exceed 2.0e-16, approximatively. For a particular execution achieved using the median values of the intervals, CADNA and ADOL-C also claim that the computation is stable. However, this does not enable us to conclude on the stability of the whole class of executions. It is interesting to note that, in this test, all the methods output comparable values: the real number output by CADNA belongs to MPFI and Fluctuat intervals which are almost identical. The error term of Fluctuat (≈1e-16) is in adequacy with CADNA result (cestac=15).

10   Conclusion

The validation of the numerical quality of programs is a difficult research topic. Independently of any tool or method, that is independently of *how* the validation can be carried out, the properties that must be proven, i.e. *what* must

	Result	Comment	Interpretation
MPFI	x=[3.53658536585365e-1, 6.16279069767442e-1], y=[5.84302325581395e-1, 7.43902439024391e-1]	x and y initialized by mpfi_interv_d.	The real solution as well as the float solution belong to the given intervals. The errors never are larger than the interval widths, i.e. about 0.26 for x and 0.15 for y.
CADNA	x=0.49253731343283, cestac=15; y=0.664925373134328, cestac=15	a, b, c, d, x2 and y2 are initialized to the median values of the intervals using the double_st type.	The large number of common digits indicates that the program, executed with the chosen parameters, is stable, with high probability.
ADOL-C	x=0.492537, $grad(x)$=0.0971263, y=0.664925, $grad(y)$=0.475897	a, b, c, d, x2 and y2 are initialized to the median values of the intervals using the adouble type.	The gradients indicate that this computation is stable in the neighborhood of the chosen parameters.
Fluctuat	x=[3.53658536585366e-1, 6.16279069767442e-1]ε_f +[-1.58101e-16,1.58101e-16]ε_e y=[5.84302325581395e-1, 7.43902439024390e-1]ε_f +[-1.24724e-16, 1.24724e-16]ε_e	Assertions are used to initialize the identifiers. Fluctuat is asked to unroll the loop.	Fluctuat states that the errors on x and y never are larger than, approximatively, $1.0e-16$ for any execution.

Fig. 7. Experimental results for the program implementing Jacobi's Method.

be verified, breads many discussions. In addition to the accuracy losses introduced by floating-point numbers, other sources of imprecision are introduced by modeling, by the choice of algorithms, etc. For instance, should an unstable numerical scheme such as the golden number example of Section 9 be considered as acceptable? On one hand the errors introduced by floating-point numbers are negligible and the program mimicks closely what happens in the reals. On the other hand the sensitivity to the possibly approximative initial value is high and, consequently, incompatible with the approximation introduced by floating-point arithmetics.

In this article, we attempted to clarify what properties some techniques exactly compute and what we can conclude from these properties about the numerical quality of the tested programs. The differences can be subtle: for instance, as discussed in sections 4 and 9, an interval method working with the same precision as the non-instrumented code does not just compute less accurately the same properties as an interval method using a higher precision. By examining closely what is computed by each technique, we do not provide sufficient conditions for the validation of numerical codes in general, as asked in the previous paragraph, but we clearly define which aspects of the whole validation can be addressed by each method.

Synthetically, we can classify the arithmetics presented in this article in two categories. First, the stochastic and multiple precision interval arithmetics are well-suited to approximate the exact result that a program would compute in the real numbers. These methods also perform less computations than the others and run faster. They are adapted to improve the quality of numerical intensive codes but give few hints on the approximations introduced by the floating-point arithmetics and on the sources of approximation. Second, automatic differentiation and error series compute the same floating-point values as the program and, additionnally, determine which roundoff errors will significantly modify the result of a calculation. They are well-suited to program verification and debugging.

We believe that future work should address two kinds of problems: to improve the dynamic semantics described in this article and to design new static analyses based on them. Concerning the dynamic semantics, we believe that many improvements could result from mixed methods: $[.]_{ES}$ would treat the higher order errors neglected by $[.]_S$, $[.]_{WS}$ and $[.]_{WD}$ would be less pessimistic than $[.]_{WI}$, etc. Next, we believe that interesting static analyses can be derived from all the methods presented in this article. These static analyses are of first interest to assert the numerical quality of programs: for example, test methods have few opportunities to detect the cancellation and absorption phenomena described in Section 2 that concern very particular data with no influence on the control flow of programs.

References

1. K. T. Alligood, T. D. Sauer, and J. A. Yorke. *Chaos, an Introduction to Dynamical Systems*. Springer-Verlag, 1996.
2. ANSI/IEEE. *IEEE Standard for Binary Floating Point Arithmetic*, Std 754 edition, 1985.
3. Christian Bischof, Paul D. Hovland, and Boyana Norris. Implementation of automatic differentiation tools. In *Partial Evaluation and Semantics-Based Program Transformations, PEPM'02*. ACM Press, 2002.
4. B. Blanchet, P. Cousot, R. Cousot, J. Feret, L. Mauborgne, A. Miné, D. Monniaux, and X. Rival. A static analyzer for large safety-critical software. In *Programming Language Design and Implementation, PLDI'03*. ACM Press, 2003.
5. S. Boldo and M. Daumas. Representable correcting terms for possibly underflowing floating point operations. In J.-C. Bajard and M. Schulte, editors, *Symposium on Computer Arithmetic*. IEEE Press, 2003.
6. H. Bronnimann and G. Melquiond. The boost interval arithmetic library. In *Real Numbers and Computers Conference, RNC'5*, 2003.
7. CADNA for C/C++ source codes User's Guide.
   http://www-anp.lip6.fr/cadna/Documentation/Accueil.php.
8. F. Chaitin-Chatelin and V. Frayssé. *Lectures on Finite Precision Computations*. SIAM, 1996.
9. J.-M. Chesneaux. L'arithmétique stochastique et le logiciel CADNA. Habilitation à diriger des recherches, Université Pierre et Marie Curie, Paris, 1995.
10. M. Daumas, Rideau L., and L Théry. A generic library for floating-point numbers and its application to exact computing. In *Theorem Proving and Higher Order Logics, TPHOLs'01*, number 2152 in LNCS. Springer-Verlag, 2001.
11. D. Goldberg. What every computer scientist should know about floating-point arithmetic. *ACM Computing Surveys*, 23(1), 1991.
12. G. H. Golub and C. F. Van Loan. *Matrix Computations*. The Johns Hopkins University Press, 2d edition, 1990.
13. E. Goubault. Static analyses of the precision of floating-point operations. In *Static Analysis Symposium, SAS'01*, number 2126 in LNCS. Springer-Verlag, 2001.

14. E. Goubault, M. Martel, and S. Putot. Asserting the precision of floating-point computations: a simple abstract interpreter. In *European Symposium on Programming, ESOP'02*, number 2305 in LNCS. Springer-Verlag, 2002.
15. A. Griewank. *Evaluating Derivatives: Principles and Techniques of Algorithmic Differentiation*. Frontiers in Applied Mathematics. SIAM, 2000.
16. A. Griewank, D. Juedes, and J. Utke. ADOL-C, a package for the automatic differentiation of algorithms written in c/c++. *ACM Trans. Math. Software*, 22:131–167, 1996.
17. M. Grimmer, K. Petras, and N. Revol. Multiple precision interval packages: Comparing different approaches. In *Dagstuhl Seminar on Numerical Software with Result Verification*, number 2991 in LNCS. Springer-Verlag, 2003.
18. G. Hanrot, V. Lefevre, Rouillier F., and P. Zimmermann. The MPFR library. Institut de Recherche en Informatique et Automatique, 2001.
19. J. Harrison. A machine-checked theory of floating point arithmetic. In *Theorem Proving and Higher Order Logics, TPHOLs'99*, number 1690 in LNCS. Springer-Verlag, 1999.
20. P. Langlois. Automatic linear correction of rounding errors. *BIT, Numerical Mathematics*, 41(3):515–539, 2001.
21. P. Langlois and F. Nativel. Improving automatic reduction of round-off errors. In *IMACS World Congress on Scientific Computation, Modelling and Applied Mathematics*, volume 2, 1997.
22. M. Martel. Propagation of roundoff errors in finite precision computations: a semantics approach. In *European Symposium on Programming, ESOP'02*, number 2305 in LNCS. Springer-Verlag, 2002.
23. M. Martel. Static analysis of the numerical stability of loops. In *Static Analysis Symposium, SAS'02*, number 2477 in LNCS. Springer-Verlag, 2002.
24. C. Michel, M. Rueher, and Y. Lebbah. Solving constraints over floating-point numbers. In *Principles and Practice of Constraint Programming, CP'01*, number 2239 in LNCS. Springer-Verlag, 2001.
25. D. Monniaux. Abstract interpretation of probabilistic semantics. In *Static Analysis Symposium, SAS'00*, number 1824 in LNCS. Springer-Verlag, 2000.
26. D. Monniaux. An abstract Monte-Carlo method for the analysis of probabilistic programs. In *Principles of Programming Languages, POPL'01*. ACM Press, 2001.
27. R. E. Moore. *Methods and Applications of Interval Analysis*. SIAM, 1979.
28. P. J. Potts, A. Edalat, and H. M. Escardó. Semantics of exact real arithmetic. In *Procs of Logic in Computer Science*. IEEE Computer Society Press, 1997.
29. M. Priest. Algorithms for arbitrary precision floating point arithmetic. In P. Kornerup and D. Matula, editors, *Symposium on Computer Arithmetic*, pages 132–144. IEEE Computer Society Press, 1991.
30. N. Revol and F. Rouillier. Motivations for an arbitrary precision interval arithmetic and the MPFI library. Technical Report RR-200227, Laboratoire de l'Informatique du Parallélisme, ENS-Lyon, France, 2002.
31. J. Vignes. A stochastic arithmetic for reliable scientific computation. *Mathematics and Computers in Simulation*, 35(3):233–261, 1993.

The Verifying Compiler, a Grand Challenge for Computing Research

C.A.R. Hoare

Microsoft Research Ltd., Cambridge, UK

The ideas of program verification date back to Turing and von Neumann, who introduced the concept of an assertion as the specification of an interface between parts of a program. The idea of mechanical theorem proving dates back to Leibniz; it has been explored in practice on modern computers by McCarthy, Milner, and many others since. A proposal for 'a program verifier', combining these two technologies, was the subject of a Doctoral dissertation by James C. King, submitted at the Carnegie Institute of Technology in 1969.

Early attempts at automatic program verification were premature. But much progress has been made in the last thirty five years, both in hardware capacity and in the software technologies for verification. I suggest that the renewed challenge of an automatic verifying compiler could provide a focus for interaction, cross-fertilisation, advancement and experimental evaluation of all the technologies of interest in this conference.

Perhaps by concerted international effort, we may be able to meet this challenge, only fifty years after it was proposed by Jim King. We only have fifteen years left to do it.

R. Cousot (Ed.): VMCAI 2005, LNCS 3385, p. 78, 2005.
© Springer-Verlag Berlin Heidelberg 2005

Checking Herbrand Equalities and Beyond

Markus Müller-Olm[1], Oliver Rüthing[1], and Helmut Seidl[2]

[1] Universität Dortmund, FB 4, LS V, 44221 Dortmund, Germany
{mmo,ruething}@ls5.cs.uni-dortmund.de
[2] TU München, Informatik, I2, 85748 Garching, Germany
seidl@in.tum.de

Abstract. A Herbrand equality between expressions in a program is an equality which holds relative to the Herbrand interpretation of operators. We show that the problem of *checking* validity of positive Boolean combinations of Herbrand equalities at a given program point is decidable – even in presence of disequality guards. This result vastly extends the reach of classical methods for global value numbering which cannot deal with disjunctions and are always based on an abstraction of conditional branching with non-deterministic choice. In order to introduce our analysis technique in a simpler scenario we also give an alternative proof that in the classic setting, where all guards are ignored, conjunctions of Herbrand equalities can be checked in polynomial time. As an application of our method, we show how to derive all valid Herbrand constants in programs with disequality guards. Finally, we present a PSPACE lower bound and show that in presence of equality guards instead of disequality guards, it is undecidable to check whether a given Herbrand equality holds or not.

1 Introduction

Analyses for finding definite equalities between variables or variables and expressions in a program have been used in program optimization for a long time where this information can be used for performing and enhancing powerful transformations like (partial) redundancy elimination including loop invariant code motion [19, 21, 12], strength reduction [22], constant propagation and branch elimination [3, 7].

Since determining whether two variables always have the same value at a program point is an undecidable problem even without interpreting conditionals [18], analyses are usually restricted to detect only a subset, i.e., a safe approximation, of all equivalences. Analyses based on Herbrand interpretation of operators consider two values equal only if they are constructed by the same operator applications. Cocke and Schwartz [4] presented the earliest such technique for finding equalities inside basic blocks. Since their technique operates by assigning hash values to computations, the detection of (Herbrand-)equivalences is often also referred to as *value numbering*. In his seminal paper [11], Kildall presents a technique for *global value numbering* that extends Cocke's and Schwartz's technique to flow graphs with loops. In contrast to a number of algorithms focusing more on efficiency than on precision [18, 1, 3, 20, 7, 9], Kildall's algorithm detects all Herbrand equalities in a program. However, the representation of equalities can be of exponential size in terms of the argument program.

R. Cousot (Ed.): VMCAI 2005, LNCS 3385, pp. 79–96, 2005.

This deficiency is still present in the algorithm for partial redundancy elimination of Steffen et al. [21] which employs a variant of Kildall's algorithm using a compact representation of Herbrand equivalences in terms of *structured partition DAGs (SPDAGs)*. Recently, Gulwani and Necula proposed a polynomial time variant of this algorithm exploiting the fact that SPDAGs can be pruned, if only equalities of bounded size are searched for [8].

The analyses based on Herbrand interpretation mentioned above ignore guards in programs[1]. In this paper, we present an analysis that fully interprets besides the assignments in the program also all the disequality guards with respect to Herbrand interpretation. We also consider a larger class of properties: positive Boolean combinations of Herbrand equalities. More specifically, we show that the problem of *checking* the validity of positive Boolean combinations of Herbrand equalities at a given program point is decidable – even in presence of non-equality guards. (A Herbrand equality between expressions in a program is an equality which holds relative to Herbrand interpretation of operators; a positive Boolean combination of Herbrand equalities is a formula constructed from Herbrand equalities by means of disjunction and conjunction.) We also present a PSPACE lower bound for this problem. Our analysis vastly extends the reach of the classical value numbering methods which cannot deal with disjunctions and are always based on an abstraction of conditional branching with non-deterministic choice. Unlike the classical methods our analysis checks given properties instead of deriving all valid properties of the considered class. Indeed we do not know how to derive all valid properties in our scenario. Note, however, that an iterated application of our checking procedure still allows us to determine all properties of bounded size. We also show how to derive all valid Herbrand constants in programs with non-equality guards.

In order to show the decidability result, we rely on effective weakest precondition computations using a certain lattice of assertions. While we have used the idea of effective weakest precondition computations before [13, 14, 17, 16], the type of assertions and the kind of results exploited is quite different here. In [13, 14, 17, 16] assertions are represented by bases of vector spaces or polynomial ideals and results from polynomial and linear algebra are exploited. Here we use equivalence classes of certain types of formulas as assertions and substitution-based techniques as used in automatic theorem proving. In order to introduce our technique in a simpler scenario and as a second application we show that in the classic setting where all guards are ignored, conjunctions of Herbrand equalities can be checked in polynomial time. While this follows also from the results in [8], our proof technique is different and illustrates the technique by which we obtain the new results presented in Section 5.

The considerations of this paper belong to a line of research in which we try to identify classes of (abstractions of) programs and analysis problems for which complete analyses are possible. Here, we abstract from the equality guards – and rely on Herbrand interpretation. There are two reasons why we must ignore equality guards. The first reason is that we cannot hope for a complete treatment of equality guards;

---

[1] The branch sensitive methods [3, 7, 2] based on the work of Click and Cooper [3] unify value numbering with constant propagation and elimination of dead branches. However, the value numbering component of these methods is based on the work of Alpern, Wegman and Zadeck [1] which is restricted to the detection of a small fragment of Herbrand equalities only.

c.f. Section 6, Theorem 6. The second reason is even more devastating: using Herbrand interpretation of programs with equality guards for inferring definite equalities w.r.t. another interpretation – which is what we are up to when we use Herbrand interpretation in program analysis – is unsound. The reason is that an equality might be invalid w.r.t. Herbrand interpretation but valid w.r.t. the "real" interpretation. Thus, it can happen that a Herbrand interpretation based execution would not pass an equality guard while executions based on the real semantics would do so. In this case, the Herbrand interpretation based analysis would consider too few executions, making it unsound. Note that this problem does not occur for disequality guards, because, whenever an equality is invalid w.r.t. the "real" interpretation it is also invalid w.r.t. Herbrand interpretation.

In Section 2 we introduce *Herbrand programs* as an abstract model of programs for which our analyses are complete. Moreover, we analyze the requirements a lattice of assertions must satisfy in order to allow weakest precondition computations. In Section 4 we introduce our technique by developing an analysis that checks conjunctions of Herbrand equalities in Herbrand programs *without* disequality guards in polynomial time. This analysis is extended in Section 5 to the analysis that checks arbitrary positive Boolean combinations of Herbrand equalities in Herbrand programs *with* disequality guards. For this analysis we can show termination but we do not have an upper bound for its running time. In Section 6 we show that there are no effective and complete analysis procedures for Herbrand programs with equality instead of disequality guards. Also we provide a PSPACE lower bound for the problem of checking Herbrand equalities in Herbrand programs with disequality guards.

2   Herbrand Programs

Terms and States. Let $\mathbf{X} = \{\mathbf{x}_1, \ldots, \mathbf{x}_k\}$ be the set of variables the program operates on. We assume that the variables take values which are constructed from variables and constants by means of operator application. Let Ω denote a signature consisting of a set Ω_0 of constant symbols and sets $\Omega_r, r > 0$, of operator symbols of rank r. In examples, we will omit brackets around the arguments of unary operators and often write binary operators *infix*. Let T_Ω be the set of all formal terms built up from Ω. For simplicity, we assume that the set Ω_0 is non-empty and that there is at least one operator. Given this, the set T_Ω is *infinite*. Let $T_\Omega(\mathbf{X})$ denote the set of all terms with constants and operators from Ω which additionally may contain occurrences of variables from $\mathbf{X}$. In the present context, we will not interpret constants and operators. Thus, a *state* assigning values to the variables is conveniently modeled by a *ground substitution* $\sigma : \mathbf{X} \to T_\Omega$.

Herbrand Programs. We assume that the basic statements in a Herbrand program are either assignments of the form $\mathbf{x}_j := t$, where $t \in T_\Omega(\mathbf{X})$, or nondeterministic assignments $\mathbf{x}_j :=?$. While we assume that branching is non-deterministic in general, we allow control statements that are *disequality guards* of the form $t_1 \neq t_2$. Note that positive Boolean combinations of disequality guards can be coded by small flow graphs as shown in Fig. 2 for $(t_1 \neq t_1' \wedge t_2 \neq t_2') \vee t_3 \neq t_3'$. Let Stmt be the set of assignments and disequality guards. Now, a *Herbrand program* is given by a *control flow graph* $G = (N, E, \mathsf{st})$ that consists of a set N of *program points*; a set of edges

$E \subseteq N \times \mathsf{Stmt} \times N$; and a special *entry (or start) point* $\mathsf{st} \in N$. An example of a Herbrand program is shown in Fig. 1.

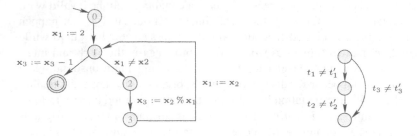

Fig. 1. An example Herbrand program.   **Fig. 2.** Boolean combinations of guards.

Herbrand programs serve as an abstraction of real programs. Non-deterministic assignments $x_j :=?$ can be used to abstract, e.g., input statements which return unknown values. Assignments $\mathbf{x}_j := \mathbf{x}_j$ that have no effect on the program state can be used as skip statements and for abstraction of guards that are not disequality guards. Our analyses are sound and complete for Herbrand programs. They are sound for abstracted programs in the sense that equalities found to be valid on the Herbrand program abstraction are also valid on the abstracted program.

Collecting Semantics. As common in flow analysis, we use the program's collecting semantics as primary semantic reference point. In order to prepare for the definition, we define the transformation on sets of states, $[\![s]\!]$, induced by a statement s first:

$$[\![\mathbf{x}_j := t]\!] \, S = \{\sigma[\mathbf{x}_j \mapsto \sigma(t)] \mid \sigma \in S\},$$
$$[\![\mathbf{x}_j :=?]\!] \, S = \{\sigma[\mathbf{x}_j \mapsto t'] \mid \sigma \in S, t' \in T_\Omega\}, \text{ and}$$
$$[\![t_1 \neq t_2]\!] \, S = \{\sigma \in S \mid \sigma(t_1) \neq \sigma(t_2)\}.$$

Here $\sigma(t)$ is the term obtained from t by replacing each occurrence of a variable $\mathbf{x}_i$ by $\sigma(\mathbf{x}_i)$ and $\sigma[\mathbf{x}_j \mapsto t']$ is the ground substitution that maps $\mathbf{x}_j$ to $t' \in T_\Omega$ and variables $\mathbf{x}_i \neq \mathbf{x}_j$ to $\sigma(\mathbf{x}_i)$. Note that for $s \equiv \mathbf{x}_j :=?$, the variable $\mathbf{x}_j$ may receive *any* value.

For a given set of initial states S, the collecting semantics assigns to each program point $u \in N$ the set of all those states that occur at u in some execution of the program from a state in S. It can be characterized as the least solution of the following constraint system, $\mathbf{V}_S$, on sets of states, i.e., sets of ground substitutions:

[V1] $\mathbf{V}_S[\mathsf{st}] \supseteq S$

[V2] $\mathbf{V}_S[v] \supseteq [\![s]\!](\mathbf{V}_S[u])$, for each $(u, s, v) \in E$.

By abuse of notation we denote the components of the least solution of the constraint system $\mathbf{V}_S$ (which exists by Knaster-Tarski fixpoint theorem) by $\mathbf{V}_S[v]$, $v \in N$. Often if we have no knowledge about possible initial states we choose $S = (\mathbf{X} \to T_\Omega)$. We call a program point $v \in N$ *dynamically reachable* if $\mathbf{V}_{(\mathbf{X} \to T_\Omega)}[v] \neq \emptyset$ and *dynamically unreachable* if $\mathbf{V}_{(\mathbf{X} \to T_\Omega)}[v] = \emptyset$.

Validity of Equations. An equation $t_1 = t_2$ is *valid* for a *substitution* $\sigma : \mathbf{X} \to \mathcal{T}_\Omega(\mathbf{X})$ iff $\sigma(t_1) = \sigma(t_2)$; $t_1 = t_2$ is valid at a program point v from a set S of initial states iff it is valid for all $\sigma \in \mathbf{V}_S[v]$. It is called valid at a program point v if it is valid at v from $(\mathbf{X} \to \mathcal{T}_\Omega)$. These definitions are straightforwardly extended to predicate-logical formulas over equations as atomic formulas. We write $\sigma \models \phi$ if ϕ is valid for a substitution σ. We call two formulas ϕ_1, ϕ_2 *equivalent* (and write $\phi_1 \Leftrightarrow \phi_2$) if they are valid for the same substitutions. We write $\phi_1 \Rightarrow \phi_2$ if $\sigma \models \phi_1$ implies $\sigma \models \phi_2$.

3 Weakest Preconditions

For every assignment or disequality guard s, we consider the corresponding *weakest precondition transformer* $[\![s]\!]^t$ which takes a formula ϕ and returns the weakest precondition of ϕ which must hold before execution of s such that ϕ holds after s. This transformation is given by the well-known rules:

$$[\![\mathbf{x}_j := t]\!]^t \phi = \phi[t/\mathbf{x}_j]\,, \;\; [\![\mathbf{x}_j :=?]\!]^t \phi = \forall\, \mathbf{x}_j.\,\phi\,, \;\text{and}\; [\![t_1 \neq t_2]\!]^t\, \phi \;=\; (t_1 = t_2) \vee \phi\,.$$

Here $\phi[t/\mathbf{x}_j]$ denotes the formula obtained from ϕ by substituting t for $\mathbf{x}_j$. The key property which summarizes the relationship between the transformation $[\![s]\!]$ and the weakest precondition transformation $[\![s]\!]^t$ is given in the following lemma.

Lemma 1. *Let* $S \subseteq \mathbf{X} \to \mathcal{T}_\Omega$ *be a set of ground substitutions and* ϕ *be any formula. Then:* $(\forall \sigma \in [\![s]\!]\, S : \sigma \models \phi)$ *iff* $(\forall \tau \in S : \tau \models [\![s]\!]^t\phi)$. $\qquad\square$

We identify the following desirable properties of a language L of formulas to be used for weakest precondition computations. First, it must be (semantically) closed under $[\![s]\!]^t$, i.e., under substitution, universal quantification, and, if we want to handle dise-quality guards, disjunction. More precisely, this means that L must contain formulas equivalent to $\phi[t/\mathbf{x}_i]$, $\forall\, \mathbf{x}_i.\phi$, and $\phi \vee \phi'$, respectively, for all $\phi, \phi' \in L$. Moreover, we want the fixpoint computation for characterizing the weakest pre-conditions at every program point to terminate. Therefore, we secondly demand that L is closed under fi-nite conjunctions, i.e., that it contains a formula equivalent to true as well as a formula equivalent to $\phi \wedge \phi'$ for all $\phi, \phi' \in L$, and that L is *compact*, i.e., for every sequence $\phi_0, \phi_1, \ldots$ of formulas, $\bigwedge_{i \geq 0} \phi_i \Leftrightarrow \bigwedge_{i=0}^{m} \phi_i$ for some $m \geq 0$.

In order to construct a lattice of properties from L we consider *equivalence classes of formulas*, which, however, will always be represented by one of their members. Let $\mathbb{L}$ denote the set of all equivalence classes of formulas. Then this set is partially ordered w.r.t. "$\Rightarrow$" (on the representatives) and the pairwise lower bound always exists and is given by "$\wedge$". By compactness, all descending chains in this lattice are ultimately stable. Therefore, not only finite but also infinite subsets $X \subseteq \mathbb{L}$ have a greatest lower bound. This implies that $\mathbb{L}$ is a complete lattice.

Assume that we want to check whether a formula ϕ holds at a specific program point v_t. Then we put up the following constraint system, **WP**, over $\mathbb{L}$:

$$[E1] \quad \mathbf{WP}[v_t] \Rightarrow \phi$$

$$[E2] \quad \mathbf{WP}[u] \Rightarrow [\![s]\!]^t(\mathbf{WP}[v])\,, \;\text{for each}\; (u, s, v) \in E\,.$$

Since $\mathbb{L}$ is a complete lattice, a greatest solution of the constraint system exists, again by Knaster-Tarski fixpoint theorem. This solution is denoted by $\mathbf{WP}[v]$, $v \in N$, as well.

Intuitively, the constraint system specifies that for each program point $v \in N$, $\mathbf{WP}[v]$ is a condition strong enough to guarantee that ϕ holds whenever an execution starting in v from a state s with $s \models \mathbf{WP}[v]$ reaches v_t. Accordingly, the greatest solution (i.e., the one with the weakest conditions) is the one looked for. We have:

Lemma 2. *Suppose ϕ_0 is a pre-condition, i.e., a formula describing initial states. Let $S_0 = \{\sigma : \mathbf{X} \to \mathcal{T}_\Omega \mid \sigma \models \phi_0\}$ be the corresponding set of initial states. Then:*

$$(\forall \sigma \in \mathbf{V}_{S_0}[v_t] : \sigma \models \phi) \quad \textit{iff} \quad \phi_0 \Rightarrow \mathbf{WP}[\mathsf{st}],$$

i.e., formula ϕ is valid at program point v_t from S_0 if and only if $\phi_0 \Rightarrow \mathbf{WP}[\mathsf{st}]$.

Proof. Consider a single program execution path $\pi \in \mathsf{Stmt}^*$. Define the collecting semantics $[\![\pi]\!] S$ of π relative to S by: $[\![\epsilon]\!] S = S$ and $[\![\pi's]\!] S = [\![s]\!] ([\![\pi']\!] S)$. Accordingly, define the weakest precondition $[\![\pi]\!]^\mathsf{t}$ of ϕ along π by: $[\![\epsilon]\!]^\mathsf{t} \phi = \phi$ and $[\![\pi's]\!]^\mathsf{t} \phi = [\![\pi']\!]^\mathsf{t} ([\![s]\!]^\mathsf{t} \phi)$.

Claim 1: For every path π, set of states S and formula ϕ, $\sigma \models \phi$ for all $\sigma \in [\![\pi]\!] S$ iff $\tau \models [\![\pi]\!]^\mathsf{t} \phi$ for all $\tau \in S$.

For a proof of Claim 1, we proceed by induction on the length of π. Obviously, the claim is true for $\pi = \epsilon$. Otherwise, $\pi = \pi's$ for some shorter path π' and a statement s. Define $S' = [\![\pi']\!] S$ and $\phi' = [\![s]\!]^\mathsf{t} \phi$. By Lemma 1, $\sigma \models \phi$ for all $\sigma \in [\![s]\!] S'$ iff $\sigma' \models \phi'$ for all $\sigma' \in S'$. By inductive hypothesis for π' and ϕ', however, the latter statement is equivalent to $\tau \models [\![\pi']\!]^\mathsf{t} \phi'$ for all $\tau \in S$, Since by definition, $[\![s]\!] S' = [\![\pi]\!] S$ and $[\![\pi']\!]^\mathsf{t} \phi' = [\![\pi]\!] \phi$, the assertion follows.   □

Claim 2: Let Π denote the set of paths from st to v_t. Then

1. $\mathbf{V}_S[v_t] = \bigcup \{[\![\pi]\!] S \mid \pi \in \Pi\}$;
2. $\mathbf{WP}[\mathsf{st}] = \bigwedge \{[\![\pi]\!]^\mathsf{t} \phi \mid \pi \in \Pi\}$.

Note that the second statement of Claim 2 is in fact well-defined as $\mathbb{L}$ is a complete lattice. Claim 2 follows from Kam and Ullman's classic MOP=MFP theorem [10] since both the transfer functions $[\![s]\!]$ of the constraint system for the collecting semantics as well as the transfer functions $[\![s]\!]^\mathsf{t}$ of the constraint system for the weakest precondition distribute over union and conjunction, respectively.   □

By Claim 2(1), ϕ is valid at v_t from S_0 iff $\sigma \models \phi$ for all $\pi \in \Pi$, $\sigma \in [\![\pi]\!] S_0$. By claim 1, this is the case iff $\tau \models [\![\pi]\!]^\mathsf{t} \phi$ for all $\pi \in \Pi$, $\tau \in S_0$. By Claim 2(2), this is true iff $\tau \models \mathbf{WP}[\mathsf{st}]$ for all $\tau \in S_0$. The latter is true iff $\phi \Rightarrow \mathbf{WP}[\mathsf{st}]$.   □

4   Conjunctions

In order to introduce our substitution-based technique in a simpler scenario, we first consider conjunctions of equalities as language of assertions for weakest precondition computations, i.e., the members of $E = \{s_1 = t_1 \wedge \ldots \wedge s_m = t_m \mid m \geq 0, s_i, t_i \in \mathcal{T}_\Omega(\mathbf{X})\}$. Clearly, conjunctions of equalities are not closed under "$\vee$". Hence, this assertion language is not able to handle disjunctions and thus disequality guards precisely. Therefore, we consider Herbrand programs *without disequality guards* in this section.

The Lattice. As explained in Section 3 we compute with equivalence classes of assertions (up to $\Leftrightarrow$). So let $\mathbb{E}$ be the set of all equivalence classes of finite conjunctions of equalities $s = t$, $s, t \in \mathcal{T}_\Omega(\mathbf{X})$. We call a conjunction $c \in E$ *satisfiable* iff $\sigma \models c$ for at least one σ. Otherwise, i.e., if c is unsatisfiable, c is equivalent to false (the Boolean value 'false'). Thus, we write false to denote the equivalence class of unsatisfiable conjunctions, which is the bottom value of our lattice $\mathbb{E}$. The greatest value is given by the *empty* conjunction which is always true and therefore also denoted by true. In preparing the discussion how satisfiable conjunctions are represented in the analysis algorithm, we recall the notion of most-general unifiers known from automatic theorem proving.

Most-General Unifiers. Whenever a conjunction $c \in E$ is satisfiable, then there is a *most general* satisfying substitution σ, i.e., $\sigma \models c$ and for every other substitution τ with $\tau \models c$ there is a substitution τ_1 with $\tau = \tau_1 \circ \sigma$. Such a substitution σ is also called *most general unifier* of the equations in c [5]. Recall that most general unifiers σ can be chosen *idempotent*, which means that $\sigma = \sigma \circ \sigma$ or, equivalently, that no variable $\mathbf{x}_i$ with $\sigma(\mathbf{x}_i) \not\equiv \mathbf{x}_i$ occurs in the image $\sigma(\mathbf{x}_j)$ of any variable $\mathbf{x}_j$.

Representation of Conjunctions and Compactness. We use compact representations of trees. In particular, we assume that identical subterms are represented only once. Therefore, we define the *size* of a term t as the number of distinct subtrees of t. Thus, e.g., the size of $t = a(b\mathbf{x}_1, bc)$ equals 5 whereas the size of $t' = a(bc, bc)$ equals 3. The size of a term t is also denoted by $|t|$. According to this definition, the size of $t[s/\mathbf{x}_i]$ is always less than $|t| + |s|$. A conjunction c is *reduced* iff c equals $\mathbf{x}_{i_1} = t_1 \wedge \ldots \wedge \mathbf{x}_{i_m} = t_m$ for distinct variables $\mathbf{x}_{i_1}, \ldots, \mathbf{x}_{i_m}$ such that $t_j \not\equiv \mathbf{x}_{i_j}$ for all j. Let the size $|c|$ of a finite conjunction c be the maximum of 1 and the maximal size of a term occurring in c. We show that every finite conjunction of equalities is equivalent to a reduced conjunction of at most the same size:

Lemma 3. *Every satisfiable conjunction c is equivalent to a reduced conjunction c' with $|c'| \leq |c|$. The conjunction c' can be constructed in polynomial time.*

Proof. It is not hard to show that a reduced conjunction equivalent to c is obtained by taking a most general unifier σ of c and returning the conjunction of equalities $\mathbf{x}_i = \sigma(\mathbf{x}_i)$ for the variables $\mathbf{x}_i$ with $\mathbf{x}_i \neq \sigma(\mathbf{x}_i)$. This reduced conjunction, however, may not satisfy the condition on sizes. The equation $a(\mathbf{x}_1, bbb\mathbf{x}_1) = a(bbc, \mathbf{x}_2)$, for example, has size 5. The most general unifier is the substitution $\sigma = \{\mathbf{x}_1 \mapsto bbc, \mathbf{x}_2 \mapsto bbbbbc\}$. The corresponding reduced equation system therefore would have size 6 – which does not conform to the assertion of the lemma. The reason is that most general unifiers typically are *idempotent*. If we drop this assumption, we may instead consider the substitution $\tau = \{\mathbf{x}_1 \mapsto bbc, \mathbf{x}_2 \mapsto bbb\mathbf{x}_1\}$ – which is neither idempotent nor a most general unifier, but yields the most general unifier after two iterations, namely, $\sigma = \tau \circ \tau$. The reduced system corresponding to τ has size 4 and therefore is small enough. Our construction of the reduced system thus is based on the construction of a substitution τ such that k-fold composition of τ results in the most general unifier of c. (Recall k is the number of variables.) Let σ denote an idempotent most general unifier of c. We introduce an equivalence relation $\equiv_\sigma$ on the set of variables $\mathbf{X}$ and subterms of

c by $s_1 \equiv_\sigma s_2$ iff $\sigma(s_1) = \sigma(s_2)$. Then there is a partial ordering "$\leq$" on the variables $\mathbf{X}$ such that whenever $\mathbf{x}_j \equiv_\sigma t$ for some subterm $t \notin \mathbf{X}$ of c, then $\mathbf{x}_i < \mathbf{x}_j$ for all variables $\mathbf{x}_i$ occurring in t. Moreover, for every variable $\mathbf{x}_j$:

- if $\sigma(\mathbf{x}_j) \in \mathbf{X}$ then $t \in \mathbf{X}$ for every t with $\mathbf{x}_j \equiv_\sigma t$.
- if $\sigma(\mathbf{x}_j) \notin \mathbf{X}$, then $\mathbf{x}_j \equiv_\sigma t$ for some subterm $t \notin \mathbf{X}$ of c.

Let us w.l.o.g. assume that $i < j$ implies $\mathbf{x}_i < \mathbf{x}_j$. Then we define substitutions $\tau_1, \ldots, \tau_k$ by $\tau_1 = \sigma$, and for $i > 1$,

$$\tau_i(\mathbf{x}_j) = \begin{cases} t_i & \text{if } i = j \\ \tau_{i-1}(\mathbf{x}_j) & \text{if } i \neq j, \end{cases}$$

where $t_i = \sigma(\mathbf{x}_i)$ if $\sigma(\mathbf{x}_i) \in \mathbf{X}$. Otherwise, we choose $t_i = t$ for any $t \notin \mathbf{X}$ with $\mathbf{x}_i \equiv_\sigma t$. By induction on i, we then verify that $\tau_i^i = \sigma$. We conclude that $c' \equiv \bigwedge \{ \mathbf{x}_i = \tau_k(\mathbf{x}_i) \mid \tau_k(\mathbf{x}_i) \neq \mathbf{x}_i \}$ is a conjunction which is equivalent to c whose non-variable right-hand sides all are sub-terms of right-hand sides of c. Since a most general unifier can be constructed in polynomial (even linear) time, the assertion follows.   □

Lemma 3 allows us to use reduced conjunctions to represent all equivalence classes of assertions except of false when we compute the greatest fixpoint of **WP**. The next lemma shows us that we can perform the necessary updates during the fixpoint computation in this representation in polynomial time as well.

Lemma 4. *If* $c \Rightarrow c_1$ *where* c *is satisfiable and* c_1 *is reduced, then* c *is equivalent to a reduced conjunction* $c_1 \wedge c'$. *In particular,* c' *can be computed in polynomial time.*

Proof. Let σ, σ_1 denote idempotent most general unifiers of c and c_1, respectively. Since $c \Rightarrow c_1$, $\sigma = \sigma' \circ \sigma_1$ for some σ', which can be chosen idempotent as well, where the domains of σ_1 and σ' are disjoint. Then we simply choose c' as the reduced conjunction constructed from σ' along the same lines as in Lemma 3.   □

As a corollary, we obtain:

Corollary 1. *For every sequence* $c_0 \Leftarrow \ldots \Leftarrow c_m$ *of pairwise inequivalent conjunctions* c_j, $m \leq k + 1$.   □

Corollary 1 implies compactness of the language of conjunctions of equalities.

Closure Properties. It remains to consider the closure properties of E. Clearly, it is closed under conjunctions and substitutions. For closure under universal quantification, we find the following equivalence for a single equality of the form $\mathbf{x}_i = s$:

$$\forall \mathbf{x}_j . \mathbf{x}_i = s \iff \begin{cases} \mathbf{x}_i = s & \text{if } i \neq j \text{ and } \mathbf{x}_j \text{ does not occur in } s \\ \text{true} & \text{if } i = j \text{ and } s \equiv \mathbf{x}_j \\ \text{false} & \text{otherwise}. \end{cases}$$

Since, by Lemma 3, satisfiable conjunctions can be written as reduced conjunctions and $\forall \mathbf{x}_i . (e_1 \wedge \ldots \wedge e_m) \iff (\forall \mathbf{x}_i . e_1) \wedge \ldots \wedge (\forall \mathbf{x}_i . e_m)$, conjunctions are closed under universal quantification. Thus, in absence of disequality guards, the weakest precondition of a conjunction w.r.t. a statement always is again a conjunction – or false.

The Algorithm. In order to check validity of a conjunction c at a program point v_t, we choose $\mathbb{L} = \mathbb{E}$, compute the greatest solution of constraint system $\mathbf{WP}$ by fixpoint iteration, and check, if $\mathbf{WP}[\mathsf{st}]$ is equivalent to true. The latter is equivalent to validity of c at v_t by Lemma 2. Let us estimate the running time of the fixpoint computation. By Corollary 1, each variable in the constraint system may be updated at most $k + 1$ times. The application of a transformer $[\![s]\!]^t$ as well as conjunction can be executed in time polynomial in their inputs. In order to obtain a polynomial time algorithm for computing the values $\mathbf{WP}[v]$, it therefore remains to prove that all conjunctions which are intermediately constructed during fixpoint iteration have polynomial sizes. For this, we recall the following two facts. First, a standard worklist algorithm for computing the least fixpoint will perform $\mathcal{O}(n \cdot k)$ evaluations of right-hand sides of constraints. Assuming that w.l.o.g. all right-hand sides in the program have constant size, each evaluation of a right-hand side may increase the maximal size of an equation at most by a constant. Since the greatest lower bound operation does not increase the maximal size, we conclude that all equalities occurring during fixpoint iteration, are bounded in size by $\mathcal{O}(n \cdot k + m)$ if m is the size of the initial equation c. Summarizing, we obtain:

Theorem 1. *Assume p is a Herbrand program without disequality guards, v_t is a program point and c is a conjunction of equalities. Then it can be decided in polynomial time whether or not c is valid in p at v_t.*   □

In practice, we can stop the fixpoint iteration for $\mathbf{WP}$ as soon as we find the value false at some reachable program point or change the value stored for the start point st since this implies that $\mathbf{WP}[\mathsf{st}]$ cannot be true. A worklist algorithm that integrates this test can be seen as a demand-driven backwards search for a reason why c fails at v_t.

As an example, consider the program from Section 2. Since we use conjunctions of equalities only, we must ignore the disequality guard. The weakest pre-conditions computed for the equality $x_3 = x_2 \% 2$ at program point 3 then are shown in Figure 3. Since the weakest pre-condition for the start node 0 is different from true, we cannot conclude that the equality $x_3 = x_2 \% 2$ holds at program point 3.

As a second application of wp-computations with the lattice $\mathbb{E}$ we obtain:

Theorem 2. *Assume p is a Herbrand program without disequality guards and v_t is a program point of p. Then it can be determined in polynomial time whether or not a*

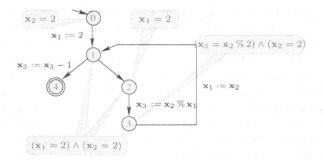

Fig. 3. The pre-conditions computed for $x_3 = x_2 \% 2$ at program point 3.

variable $\mathbf{x}_i$ *is constant at* v_t, *i.e., has always the same value* $c \in \mathcal{T}_\Omega$ *when program execution reaches* v_t.

Proof. We introduce the equality $\mathbf{x}_i = \mathbf{y}$ for some fresh variable $\mathbf{y}$. Then $\mathbf{x}_i$ is constant at program point v_t iff the weakest precondition $\mathbf{WP}[\mathbf{st}]$ of this equality at program entry is implied by $\mathbf{y} = c$ for some ground term $c \in \mathcal{T}_\Omega$. In this case $\mathbf{WP}[\mathbf{st}]$ either is equivalent to true – implying that v_t is dynamically unreachable – or equivalent to $\mathbf{y} = c$. In the latter case, the value c constitutes the constant value of $\mathbf{x}_i$ at program point v_t. Since $\mathbf{WP}[\mathbf{st}]$ for the given equality can be computed in polynomial time, we conclude that all program constants can be computed in polynomial time as well. $\square$

Theorems 1 and 2 also follow from results recently presented by Gulwani and Necula [8]. However, while Gulwani and Necula rely on a classic forward propagation of valid facts, we use a symbolic weakest precondition computation here with a backwards propagation of assertions. This backwards propagation technique is crucial for the next section in which we present the main novel results of this paper. We do not know how to achieve these results by means of forward propagation algorithms.

5 Disjunctions

In this section, we consider finite disjunctions of finite conjunctions of equalities which we call *DC-formulas*. Note that every positive Boolean combination of equalities, i.e. each formula which is built up from equalities by means of conjunctions and disjunctions can be written as a DC-formula by the usual distributivity laws. Clearly, the language of DC-formulas is closed under substitution and disjunction and, again by distributivity, also under conjunction. First, we convince ourselves that it is indeed also closed under universal quantification.

Lemma 5. *Assume that* $\mathcal{T}_\Omega$ *is infinite. Then we have:*

1. *For every conjunction c of equalities,* $\forall \mathbf{x}_j.\ c \iff c[t_1/\mathbf{x}_j] \wedge c[t_2/\mathbf{x}_j]$ *for any ground terms* $t_1, t_2 \in \mathcal{T}_\Omega$ *with* $t_1 \neq t_2$.
2. *For every disjunction* $\phi \equiv c_1 \vee \ldots \vee c_m$ *of conjunctions* c_i *of equalities,*

$$\forall \mathbf{x}_j.\ \phi \iff (\forall \mathbf{x}_j.\ c_1) \vee \ldots \vee (\forall \mathbf{x}_j.\ c_m).$$

Proof. Obviously, it suffices to verify assertion 1 only for a single equality $c \equiv \mathbf{x}_i = s$ for $\mathbf{x}_i \in \mathbf{X}$ and $s \in \mathcal{T}_\Omega(\mathbf{X})$, where s is syntactically different from $\mathbf{x}_i$. If c holds for all values of $\mathbf{x}_j$, then it also holds for particular values t_1, t_2 for $\mathbf{x}_j$. Therefore, it remains to prove the reverse implication. We distinguish two cases. First assume that the equation c does not contain an occurrence of $\mathbf{x}_j$. Then for $k = 1, 2$, $c[t_k/\mathbf{x}_j] \equiv c$, and validity of c also implies validity of $\forall \mathbf{x}_j.\ c$. Therefore in this case, assertion 1 holds. Now assume that c contains an occurrence of $\mathbf{x}_j$. We claim that then $c[t_1/\mathbf{x}_j] \wedge c[t_2/\mathbf{x}_j]$ is unsatisfiable. Under this assumption, $\forall \mathbf{x}_j.\ c$ is trivially implied and the assertion follows. Therefore, it remains to prove the claim. For a contradiction, assume that $c[t_1/\mathbf{x}_j] \wedge c[t_2/\mathbf{x}_j]$ is satisfiable and thus has a most general unifier $\sigma : (\mathbf{X} \backslash \{\mathbf{x}_j\}) \to \mathcal{T}_\Omega(\mathbf{X} \backslash \{\mathbf{x}_j\})$. If the variable $\mathbf{x}_i$ of the left-hand side of the equation c is given by $\mathbf{x}_j$, then $t_1 = \sigma(s) = t_2 -$

in contradiction to our choice of t_1, t_2. If on the other hand, $\mathbf{x}_j$ occurs in s, then $\sigma(\mathbf{x}_i) = \sigma(s[t_1/\mathbf{x}_j]) = \sigma(s[t_2/\mathbf{x}_j])$. Note that $\sigma(s[t_k/\mathbf{x}_j]) = \sigma(s)[t_k/\mathbf{x}_j]$ for $k = 1, 2$, since the t_k are ground. By induction on the size of a term s' containing the variable $\mathbf{x}_j$, we verify that the mapping $t \mapsto s'[t/\mathbf{x}_j]$ is injective, i.e., different t produce different results. Here, substituting t_1, t_2 into $\sigma(s)$ results in the same term $\sigma(\mathbf{x}_i)$. We conclude that therefore, t_1 must equal t_2 – in contradiction to our assumption. This completes the proof of assertion 1.

Assertion 2 follows from assertion 1 by means of infinite version of the pigeon-hole principle. Consider a disjunction $\phi \equiv c_1 \vee \ldots \vee c_m$ for conjunctions c_i, and assume that $\forall \mathbf{x}_j . \phi$ holds for some substitution σ. Thus, $\sigma \models \phi[t/\mathbf{x}_j]$ for every $t \in \mathcal{T}_\Omega$. Since $\mathcal{T}_\Omega$ is infinite, we conclude that there exists some i such that $\sigma \models c_i[t/\mathbf{x}_j]$ for infinitely many t. In particular, $\sigma \models c_i[t_1/\mathbf{x}_j] \wedge c_i[t_2/\mathbf{x}_j]$ for ground terms $t_1 \neq t_2$. Thus by assertion 1, $\sigma \models \forall \mathbf{x}_j . c_i$ and therefore also, $\sigma \models (\forall \mathbf{x}_j . c_1) \vee \ldots \vee (\forall \mathbf{x}_j . c_m)$, which proves one implication of assertion 2. The reverse implication is trivial. $\qquad\Box$

A DC-formula d need no longer have a single most general unifier. The disjunction $a\,\mathbf{x}_1 = a\,b \vee a\,c = a\,\mathbf{x}_1$, for example, has two maximally general unifiers $\{\mathbf{x}_1 \mapsto b\}$ and $\{\mathbf{x}_1 \mapsto c\}$. By Lemma 3, however, each conjunction in a DC-formula d can be brought into reduced form. Let us call the resulting formula a *reduced DC-formula*. Our further considerations are based on the following fundamental theorem.

Theorem 3. *Let $d_j, j \geq 0$, be a sequence of DC-formulas such that $d_j \Leftarrow d_{j+1}$ for all $j \geq 0$. Then this sequence is ultimately stable, i.e., there is some $m \in \mathbb{N}$ such that for all $m' \geq m$, $d_m \Leftrightarrow d_{m'}$.*

Proof. If any of the d_j is unsatisfiable, i.e., equivalent to false, then all positive Boolean combinations of greater index also must be unsatisfiable, and the assertion of the theorem follows. Therefore let us assume that all d_j are satisfiable. W.l.o.g. all d_j are reduced. We successively construct a sequence $\Gamma_j, j \geq 0$, where $\Gamma_0 = d_0$ and Γ_{j+1} is a reduced DC-formula equivalent to $\Gamma_j \wedge d_{j+1}$ for $j \geq 0$. Since $d_j \Leftarrow d_{j+1}$ for all j, Γ_j is equivalent to d_j. For a reduced DC-formula Γ, we maintain a vector $v[\Gamma] \in \mathbb{N}^k$ where the i-th component of $v[\Gamma]$ counts the number of conjunctions in Γ with exactly i equalities. On $\mathbb{N}^k$ we consider the lexicographical ordering "$\leq$" which is given by: $(n_1, \ldots, n_k) \leq (n'_1, \ldots, n'_k)$ iff either $n_l = n'_l$ for all l, or there is some $1 \leq i \leq k$ such that $n_l = n'_l$ for all $l < i$, and $n_i < n'_i$. Recall that this ordering is a *well-ordering*, i.e., it does not admit infinite strictly decreasing sequences.

Now assume that Γ_j equals $c_1 \vee \ldots \vee c_m$ for reduced conjunctions c_i. Assume that d_{j+1} equals $c'_1 \vee \ldots \vee c'_n$ for reduced conjunctions c'_l. Then by distributivity, $\Gamma_j \wedge d_{j+1}$ is equivalent to $\bigvee_{i=1}^m c_i \wedge (c'_1 \vee \ldots \vee c'_n)$. First, assume that for a given i, $c_i \wedge c'_l$ is equivalent to c_i for some l. Then also $c_i \wedge (c'_1 \vee \ldots \vee c'_n)$ is equivalent to c_i. Let V denote the subset of all i with this property. Thus for all $i \notin V$, c_i is *not* equivalent to any of the conjunctions $c_i \wedge c'_l$. Let $J[i]$ denote the set of all l such that $c_i \wedge c'_l$ is satisfiable. Then by Lemma 3, we can construct for every $l \in J[i]$, a non-empty conjunction c_{il} such that $c_i \wedge c_{il}$ is reduced and equivalent to $c_i \wedge c'_l$. Summarizing, we construct the reduced DC-formula Γ_{j+1} equivalent to $\Gamma_j \wedge d_{j+1}$ as:

$$\left(\bigvee_{i \in V} c_i \right) \vee \left(\bigvee_{i \notin V} \bigvee_{l \in J[i]} c_i \wedge c_{il} \right).$$

According to this construction, $v[\Gamma_j] = v[\Gamma_{j+1}]$ implies that $V = \{1,\ldots,k\}$ and therefore that Γ_j is equivalent to Γ_{j+1}. Moreover, if Γ_j is not equivalent to Γ_{j+1}, then $v[\Gamma_j] > v[\Gamma_{j+1}]$. Accordingly, if the sequence $\Gamma_j, j \geq 0$, is not ultimately stable, we obtain an infinite sequence of strictly decreasing vectors – contradiction.   □

In particular, Theorem 3 implies that compactness holds for DC-formulas as well. Note that if we consider not just positive Boolean combinations but additionally allow negation, then the compactness property is immediately lost. To see this, consider an infinite sequence $t_1, t_2, \ldots$ of pairwise distinct ground terms. Then obviously, all conjunctions $\bigwedge_{i=1}^{m}(\mathbf{x}_1 \neq t_i)$, $m \geq 0$, are pairwise inequivalent.

In order to perform effective fixpoint computations, we need an effective test for stability.

Lemma 6. *It is decidable for DC formulas d, d' whether or not $d \Rightarrow d'$.*

Proof. Assume $d \equiv c_1 \vee \ldots \vee c_r$ and $d' \equiv c'_1 \vee \ldots \vee c'_s$ for conjunctions c_i, c'_j. W.l.o.g. we assume that all conjunctions c_i are satisfiable and thus have a most general unifier σ_i. Then $d \Rightarrow d'$ iff $\sigma \models d$ implies $\sigma \models d'$ for all substitutions σ. The latter is the case iff for every i we can find some j such that $\sigma_i \models c'_j$. Since it is decidable whether or not a substitution satisfies a conjunction of equalities, the assertion follows. Note that this decision procedure for implications requires polynomial time.   □

We now extend the lattice $\mathbb{E}$ to a lattice $\mathbb{D}$ of equivalence classes of DC-formulas. Again, the ordering is given by implication "$\Rightarrow$" where the binary greatest lower bound operation is "$\wedge$". By Theorem 3, all descending chains in $\mathbb{D}$ are ultimately stable. Similar to $\mathbb{E}$, we deduce that $\mathbb{D}$ is in fact a *complete* lattice and therefore amenable to fixpoint computations. Note however that, in contrast to the complete lattice $\mathbb{E}$, the new lattice $\mathbb{D}$ has infinite strictly ascending chains. An example is the ascending chain defined by $\phi_0 = \mathsf{false}$ and $\phi_{i+1} = \phi_i \vee \mathbf{x}_1 = t_i$, where $t_0, t_1, \ldots$ is a sequence of pairwisely distinct ground terms. This implies that $\mathbb{D}$ does not have finite height and that there exist strictly descending chains of arbitrary lengths. This more general lattice allows us to treat also disjunctions and hence also Herbrand programs which, besides assignments, contain disequality guards $t_1 \neq t_2$. As weakest precondition computations generate descending chains at each program point, they must become stable eventually and by Lemma 6, we can detect when stability has been reached. In contrast, in a forward propagation of valid facts, we would generate ascending chains such that we could not guarantee termination. We obtain the main result of this section:

Theorem 4. *Assume p is a Herbrand program, possibly with disequality guards. For every program point v_t of p and every positive Boolean combination of equalities d, it is decidable whether or not d is valid at v_t.*   □

Consider again the example program from Section 2. Assuming that we want to check whether $\mathbf{x}_3 = \mathbf{x}_2 \% 2$ holds at program point 3, we compute the weakest pre-conditions for the program points $0, \ldots, 3$ as shown in Figure 4. Indeed, the pre-condition for the start node 0 is true implying that the equality to be checked is valid at program point 3.

Generalizing the idea from Section 4 for constant propagation, we obtain:

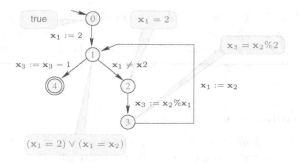

Fig. 4. The pre-conditions computed for $x_3 = x_2 \% 2$ at program point 3.

Theorem 5. *For a Herbrand program p possibly with disequality guards let $\mathbf{WP}[\mathrm{st}]$ denote the weakest precondition of $x_i = y$ at the program point v_t. Then we have:*

1. *v_t is dynamically unreachable iff $\mathbf{WP}[\mathrm{st}]$ is equivalent to* true.
2. *Suppose v_t is dynamically reachable and let $c \in \mathcal{T}_\Omega$, Then $x_i = c$ holds at v_t iff $\forall x_1. \ldots .x_k. \mathbf{WP}[\mathrm{st}]$ is equivalent to $y = c$.*

In particular, it can be decided whether x_i is constant at v_t.

Proof. We only prove the second assertion. Let $\phi \equiv (\forall x_1. \ldots .x_k. \mathbf{WP}[\mathrm{st}])$. We first show that for any given ground term $c \in \mathcal{T}_\Omega$, the following equivalence holds:

$$x_i = c \text{ holds at } v_t \quad \text{iff} \quad \phi[c/y] \text{ is equivalent to true}. \tag{1}$$

For proving this equivalence, consider for a given ground term $c \in \mathcal{T}_\Omega$ a modified program p_c which first performs the assignments $y := c; x_1 :=?; \ldots; x_k :=?$ and then behaves like p. As y is not used anywhere in the program p and the variables $x_1, \ldots, x_k$ have unknown initial values anyhow, $x_i = c$ holds at program point v_t in p if and only if it holds at v_t in p_c. This is the case iff $x_i = y$ holds at v_t in p_c because y is assigned c by the first assignment in p_c and is never modified. It follows from Lemma 2 that $x_i = y$ holds at v_t in p_c iff the weakest precondition for validity of $x_i = y$ at v_t in p_c is equivalent to true. If we compute this weakest precondition, we obtain at the start node of p_c a formula equivalent to $\phi[c/y]$ by the definition of weakest preconditions for statements. Equivalence (1) follows.

If ϕ is equivalent to true, $\mathbf{WP}[\mathrm{st}]$ is equivalent to true as well. In this case v_t is dynamically unreachable by assertion 1; assertion 2 follows for trivial reasons. If ϕ is equivalent to false, Equivalence (1) yields that there is no $c \in \mathcal{T}_\Omega$ such that $x_i = c$ holds at v_t; thus in this case both sides of the equivalence claimed in assertion 2 are dissatisfied.

Finally, if ϕ is equivalent to neither true nor false, it can be written as a non-empty disjunction of reduced, pairwisely inequivalent conjunctions by Lemma 5 and Lemma 3. As only y appears free in ϕ this disjunction takes the form $y = c_1 \vee \cdots \vee y = c_l$ with $l \geq 1$ and pairwisely distinct ground terms $c_1, \ldots, c_l \in \mathcal{T}_\Omega$. Then, $\phi[c/y]$ is equivalent to true iff $c \in \{c_1, \ldots, c_l\}$. By (1) this means that $x_i = c$ holds at v_t iff

$c \in \{c_1, \ldots, c_l\}$. For $l = 1$, both sides of the equivalence claimed in assertion 2 are satisfied. For $l > 1$, on the other hand, both $x_i = c_1$ and $x_i = c_2$ hold at v_t. As $c_1 \neq c_2$ this implies that v_t is dynamically unreachable and assertion 2 follows for trivial reasons. (Note, that in this case by assertion 1 **WP**[st] and thus ϕ is equivalent to true. Thus, actually the case $l > 1$ cannot appear.) $\square$

6   Limitations and Lower Bounds

In [15], we showed for *affine* programs, i.e., programs where the standard arithmetic operators except division are treated precisely, that equality guards allow us to encode Post's correspondence problem. In fact, multiplication with powers of 2 and addition of constants was used to simulate the concatenation with a given string. For Herbrand programs, we simply may encode letters by unary operators. Thus, we obtain:

Theorem 6. *It is undecidable whether a given equality holds at some program point in a Herbrand program with equality guards of the form* $\mathbf{x}_i = \mathbf{x}_j$. $\square$

We conclude that completeness cannot be achieved if we do not ignore equality guards. As explained in the introduction, Herbrand interpretation based analyses of equality guards are also questionable for soundness reasons. Turning to our algorithm for checking disjunctions, we recall that termination of the fixpoint algorithm is based on the well-foundedness of the lexicographical ordering. This argument does not provide any clue to derive an explicit complexity bound for the algorithm. We can show, however, that it is unlikely that an algorithm with polynomial worst case running time exits.

Theorem 7. *It is at least PSPACE-hard to decide in a Herbrand program with disequality guards whether a given Herbrand equality is true or not.*

We prove Theorem 7 by means of a reduction from the language-universality problem of non-deterministic finite automata (NFA), a well-known PSPACE-complete problem. The details can be found in Appendix A.

7   Conclusion

We presented an algorithm for checking validity of equalities in Herbrand programs. In absence of disequality guards, our algorithm runs in polynomial time. We generalized this base algorithm to an algorithm that checks positive Boolean combinations of equalities and deals with programs containing disequality guards. We also showed that our techniques are sufficient to find all Herbrand constants in such programs.

Many challenging problems remain. First, termination of the generalized algorithm is based on well-founded orderings. We succeeded in establishing a PSPACE lower bound to the complexity of our analysis. This lower bound, however, did not exploit the full strength of Herbrand programs – thus leaving room for, perhaps, larger lower bounds. On the other hand, a more constructive termination proof could help to derive explicit upper complexity bounds. Finally, note that any algorithm that checks validity can be used to *infer* all valid assertions up to a given size. Clearly, a more practical inference algorithm would be highly desirable. Also, it is still unknown how to decide whether or not *any* finite disjunction of Herbrand equalities exists which holds at a given program point.

Acknowledgments

We thank the anonymous referees for their detailed comments that helped us to improve readability of the paper.

References

1. B. Alpern, M. Wegman, and F. K. Zadeck. Detecting Equality of Variables in Programs. In *15th ACM Symp. on Principles of Programming Languages (POPL)*, 1–11, 1988.
2. P. Briggs, K. D. Cooper, and L. T. Simpson. Value Numbering. *Software- Practice and Experience*, 27(6):701–724, 1997.
3. C. Click and K. D. Cooper. Combining Analyses, Combining Optimizations. *ACM Transactions on Programming Languages and Systems*, 17(2):181–196, 1995.
4. J. Cocke and J. T. Schwartz. Programming Languages and Their Compilers. Courant Institute of Mathematical Sciences, NY, 1970.
5. D. Duffy. *Principles of Automated Theorem Proving*. Wiley, 1991.
6. M. R. Garey and D. S. Johnson. *Computers and Intractability: A Guide to the Theory of NP-Completeness*. W. H. Freeman and Company, 1978.
7. K. Gargi. A Sparse Algorithm for Predicated Global Value Numbering. In *ACM Conf. on Programming Language Design and Implementation (PLDI)*, 45–56, 2002.
8. S. Gulwani and G. C. Necula. A Polynomial-time Algorithm for Global Value Numbering. In *11th Int. Static Analysis Symposium (SAS)*,. Springer Verlag, 2004.
9. S. Gulwani and G. C. Necula. Global Value Numbering Using Random Interpretation. In *31st ACM Symp. on Principles of Programming Languages (POPL)*, 342–352, 2004.
10. J. B. Kam and J. D. Ullman. Monotone data flow analysis frameworks. Technical Report 169, Department of Electrical Engineering, Princeton University, Princeton, NJ, 1975.
11. G. A. Kildall. A Unified Approach to Global Program Optimization. In *First ACM Symp. on Principles of Programming Languages (POPL)*, 194–206, 1973.
12. J. Knoop, O. Rüthing, and B. Steffen. Code Motion and Code Placement: Just Synonyms? In *6th ESOP*, LNCS 1381, 154–196. Springer-Verlag, 1998.
13. M. Müller-Olm and O. Rüthing. The Complexity of Constant Propagation. In *10th European Symposium on Programming (ESOP)*, 190–205. LNCS 2028, Springer-Verlag, 2001.
14. M. Müller-Olm and H. Seidl. Polynomial Constants are Decidable. In *9th Static Analysis Symposium (SAS)*, 4–19. LNCS 2477, Springer-Verlag, 2002.
15. M. Müller-Olm and H. Seidl. A Note on Karr's Algorithm. In *31st Int. Coll. on Automata, Languages and Programming (ICALP)*, 1016–1028. Springer Verlag, LNCS 3142, 2004.
16. M. Müller-Olm and H. Seidl. Computing Polynomial Program Invariants. *Information Processing Letters (IPL)*, 91(5):233–244, 2004.
17. M. Müller-Olm and H. Seidl. Precise Interprocedural Analysis through Linear Algebra. In *31st ACM Symp. on Principles of Programming Languages (POPL)*, 330–341, 2004.
18. J. H. Reif and R. Lewis. Symbolic Evaluation and the Gobal Value Graph. In *4th ACM Symp. on Principles of Programming Languages (POPL)*, 104–118, 1977.
19. B. K. Rosen, M. N. Wegman, and F. K. Zadeck. Global Value Numbers and Redundant Computations. In *15th ACM Symp. on Principles of Programming Languages (POPL)*, 12–27, 1988.
20. O. Rüthing, J. Knoop, and B. Steffen. Detecting Equalities of Variables: Combining Efficiency with Precision. In *6th Int. Static Analysis Symposium (SAS)*, LNCS 1694, 232–247. Springer-Verlag, 1999.

21. B. Steffen, J. Knoop, and O. Rüthing. The Value Flow Graph: A Program Representation for Optimal Program Transformations. In *Third ESOP*, LNCS 432, 389–405. Springer-Verlag, 1990.
22. B. Steffen, J. Knoop, and O. Rüthing. Efficient Code Motion and an Adaption to Strength Reduction. In *4th Int. Joint Conf. on the Theory and Practice of Software Development (TAPSOFT)*, LNCS 494, 394–415. Springer-Verlag, 1991.

A   Proof of Theorem 7

As mentioned, we prove Theorem 7 by means of a polynomial-time reduction from the language-universality problem of non-deterministic finite automata (NFA). This is known to be a PSPACE-complete problem (cf. the remark to Problem AL1 in [6]). An instance of the problem is given by an NFA $\mathcal{A}$ over an alphabet Σ. The problem is to decide whether $\mathcal{A}$ accepts the universal language, i.e., whether $L(\mathcal{A}) = \Sigma^*$.

Without loss of generality, we may assume that $\Sigma = \{0, 1\}$. So suppose given an NFA $\mathcal{A} = (\Sigma, S, \delta, s_1, F)$, where $\Sigma = \{0, 1\}$ is the underlying alphabet, $S = \{s_1, \ldots, s_k\}$ is the set of states, $\delta \subseteq S \times \Sigma \times S$ is the transition relation, s_1 is the start state, and $F \subseteq S$ is the set of accepting states. From this NFA, $\mathcal{A}$, we construct a Herbrand program π which uses k variables $x_1, \ldots, x_k$ that correspond to the states of the automaton and another set $y_1, \ldots, y_k$ of auxiliary variables. These variables hold the values 0 or 1 only in executions of π. Consider first the programs π_σ^i for $\sigma \in \Sigma$, $i \in \{1, \ldots, k\}$ pictured in Fig. 5 that are used as building blocks in the construction of π. As mentioned in Sect. 2, the finite disjunctions and conjunctions of disequality guards used in π_σ^i (and later in π) can be coded by simple disequality guards. It is not hard to see that the following is valid:

Lemma 7. *For each initial state, in which the variables $x_1 \ldots, x_k$ hold only the values 0 and 1, π_σ^i has a unique execution. This execution sets y_i to 1 if and only if x_j holds 1 for some σ-predecessor s_j of s_i. Otherwise, it sets y_i to 0.*   □

$$\bigwedge \{x_j \neq 1 \mid (s_j, \sigma, s_i) \in \delta\} \qquad \bigvee \{x_j \neq 0 \mid (s_j, \sigma, s_i) \in \delta\}$$

$$y_i := 0 \qquad y_i := 1$$

Fig. 5. The program π_σ^i.

Consider now the program π shown in Fig. 6. Intuitively, each path from the initial program point 0, to the program point 2 corresponds to a word $w \in \Sigma^*$ and vice versa. Execution of the initializing assignments on the direct path from 0 to 2 corresponds to the empty word, ε. Each execution of the loop body amounts to a prolongation of the corresponding word by one letter. If the left branch is taken in the loop body (the one via program point 3) then the word is extended by the letter 0; if the right branch is

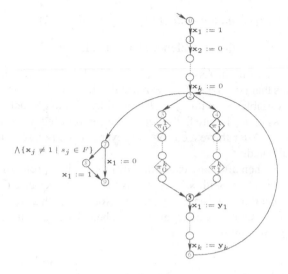

Fig. 6. The program π.

taken (the one via program point 4), the word is extended by the letter 1. Let p_w be the path from program node 0 to node 2 that corresponds to the word w. We prove:

Lemma 8. *After execution of p_w variable x_i (for $i = 1, \ldots, k$) holds the value 1 if state s_i is reachable in the automaton under the word w. Otherwise, x_i holds 0.*

Proof. We prove Lemma 8 by induction on the length of w.

Base Case: Under the empty word, just the initial state s_1 is reachable in $\mathcal{A}$. As the initialization sets x_1 to 1 and the variables $x_2, \ldots, x_k$ to 0, the property claimed in the lemma is valid for the empty word.

Induction Step: Suppose $w = w'0$ with $w' \in \Sigma^*$; the case $w = w'1$ is similar. Let p be the cycle-free path from 2 to itself via 3. Then $p_w = p_{w'}p$.

Assume s_i is reachable under the word w in $\mathcal{A}$. Then, clearly, there is a 0-predecessor s_j of s_i in $\mathcal{A}$ that is reachable under w'. Thus, by the induction hypothesis, x_j holds 1 after execution of $p_{w'}$. Consider executing p. The programs $\pi_0^1, \ldots, \pi_0^{i-1}$ do not change x_j. Thus, by Lemma 7, the program π_0^i sets y_i to 1 and this value is copied to x_i in the i-th assignment after program point 5 because the programs $\pi_0^{i+1}, \ldots, \pi_0^k$ do not change y_i.

Finally, assume that s_i is not reachable under the word w in $\mathcal{A}$. Then, clearly, no σ-predecessor s_j of s_i in $\mathcal{A}$ is reachable under w'. Thus, by the induction hypothesis, for all 0-predecessors s_j of s_i, x_j holds 0 after execution of $p_{w'}$. The programs $\pi_0^1, \ldots, \pi_0^{i-1}$ do not change these values. Thus, by Lemma 7, the program π_0^i sets y_i to 0 and this value is copied to x_i in the i-th assignment after program point 5 because the programs $\pi_0^{i+1}, \ldots, \pi_0^k$ do not change y_i. $\square$

It is not hard to see from this property that there is an execution of π that passes the guard at the edge between the nodes 7 and 8 if and only if $L(\mathcal{A}) \neq \Sigma^*$. This implies:

Lemma 9. *The relation* $x_1 = 0$ *is valid at node* 9 *of program* π *iff* $L(\mathcal{A}) = \Sigma^*$.

Proof. We prove both directions of the equivalence claimed in Lemma 9 separately:

"⇒": The proof is by contraposition. Assume $L(\mathcal{A}) \neq \Sigma^*$. Let $w \in \Sigma^*$ such that $w \notin L(\mathcal{A})$. This implies that no state $s_j \in F$ is reachable in $\mathcal{A}$ under w. Therefore, after executing p_w all variables x_j with $s_j \in F$ hold 0 by Lemma 8 such that the condition $\bigwedge \{x_j \neq 1 \mid s_j \in F\}$ is satisfied. Hence, we can proceed this execution via the nodes 7, 8, and 9. After this execution, however, x_1 holds 1 such that the relation $x_1 = 0$ is invalidated.

"⇐": Assume $L(\mathcal{A}) = \Sigma^*$. Then after any execution from the initial program node 0 to node 2 one of the variables x_j with $s_j \in F$ holds the value 1 because the word corresponding to this execution is accepted by $\mathcal{A}$. Therefore, the path 2, 7, 8, 9 is not executable, such that x_1 is set of 0 whenever 9 is reached. Therefore, the relation $x_1 = 0$ is valid at program point 9.   □

Note that our PSPACE-hardness proof does not exploit the full power of Herbrand programs and Herbrand equalities. We just use constant assignments of the form $x := 0$ and $x := 1$, copying assignments of the form $x := y$, and disequality guards of the form $x \neq 0$ and $x \neq 1$, where 0 and 1 are two different constants. Moreover, we just need to check whether a relation of the form $x = 0$ is valid at a given program point.

Static Analysis by Abstract Interpretation of the Quasi-synchronous Composition of Synchronous Programs

Julien Bertrane

Computer Science Department, École normale supérieure, Paris, France
bertrane@di.ens.fr

Abstract. We present a framework to graphically describe and analyze embedded systems which are built on asynchronously wired synchronous subsystems. Our syntax is close to electronic diagrams. In particular, it uses logic and arithmetic gates, connected by wires, and models synchronous subsystems as boxes containing these gates.

In our approach, we introduce a continuous-time semantics, connecting each point of the diagram to a value, at **any** moment. We then describe an analysis derived from the abstract interpretation framework enabling to statically and automatically prove temporal properties of the diagrams we defined. We can prove, for example, that the output of a diagram cannot be equal to a given value in a given interval of time.

1 Introduction

Embedded systems are often built on synchronous subsystems. Several tools help programmers to such a design, like SCADE^{TM}[2]/LUSTRE[5] or SIMULINK. For safety matters, these synchronous subsystems must however be redundant. This is the origin of several issues.

First, in case of disagreement between these redundant synchronous subsystems, the system has to *choose* which subsystem should be trusted. Then, it appears that the former problem will happen very frequently, because of the *de-synchronization* of the clocks of these subsystems: two physical clocks, even started simultaneously, cannot stay synchronized. This phenomenon is unavoidable as soon as we consider real embedded system with long use duration. In this case, the different synchronous subsystems compute in a de-synchronized way on different inputs and consequently always disagree!

This is why, without complementary hypothesis, asynchronous composition won't satisfy many safety properties. We therefore assume that the synchronous subsystems are always quasi-synchronous, which means that the duration of the cycles of these subsystems are very close to each other. Provided with this hypothesis, we may prove safety properties of some fault-tolerant systems.

Synchronous systems may have a discrete semantics. On the other hand, quasi-synchronous systems must be connected to a semantics that considers the time as continuous. Considering the quasi-synchronous hypothesis may indeed

R. Cousot (Ed.): VMCAI 2005, LNCS 3385, pp. 97–112, 2005.

drive us to suppose that one cycle starts for example between time t_1 and time t_2, which is a continuous-time property.

We present a framework that enables a graphical description of such processes. We then propose a tool to prove temporal safety properties of such complex compositions of programs. This tool is based on several analyses, derived from the abstract interpretation theory.

Previous works. P. Caspi and R. Salem presented in [6] a system *with fault tolerance without synchronization* between synchronous subsystems. They managed to prove by hand the robustness properties of the procedures they wrote. In [1] were introduced the LTTA, enabling, under some hypotheses, synchronous systems with non-perfect clocks to communicate in a secure way. S. Thompson and A. Mycroft, on the other side, proposed in [12] several abstractions to study *asynchronous circuits* that convinced us of the high simplification that could be achieved through abstraction. Their methods, however, could not be directly used to reach our goal, because their abstractions partially discard the time. Last, we widely used the theory and we inspired by the applications developed by P. Cousot, R. Cousot and their team ([4, 3, 8, 7, 11, 9]).

We introduce in Section 2 a new syntax and a continuous-time semantics. We then present in Section 3 an abstract domain based on constraints. Section 4 defines abstract operators. We then present our first analysis and an example in Section 5. Lastly, we propose in Section 6 another improved analysis.

2   Syntax and Semantics

The semantics developed in order to give a meaning to the asynchronous composition of synchronous programs often relies on a translation into a synchronous environment. However, it implies to check all the possible interleavings of the events of the synchronous subsystems. In our case, it appears that the number of interleavings is by far too big to be exhaustingly explored. That's why it seams reasonable to introduce a continuous-time semantics.

2.1   Syntax

We chose an easily representable syntax, inspired by electronic diagrams, with gates (arithmetic, logic,...), wires connecting the gates, and boxes isolating parts of the diagrams. The advantage of this graphic representation is that it reminds us that the elements of the syntax are continuous, like in a real electronic diagram, where each point is connected to a voltage at each time.

2.1.1   Calculus Units: Gates. The calculus of our programs are described by gates:

- $+$, $-$, $\times$, with two inputs and one output
- OR, XOR, AND, with two inputs and one output
- NOT, with one input and one output

 – CONST_α, with no input and one output
 – TRASH, with one input and no output
 – $\text{DELAY}[\alpha, \beta]$, with one input and one output

The meaning of the three first types of gates is obvious. The gate CONST_α is meant to generate a constant value, TRASH simply absorbates the value it is given, and $\text{DELAY}[\alpha, \beta]$ postpones the input values by a real delay which can vary between α and β.

2.1.2 Replacing Variables: Internal Wires. The previous gates are connected by wires, which simply transmit values arriving at their inputs. We also allow splitting wires, which transmit values identicaly and simultaneously to several gates.

 With the previous objects, we can already build diagrams like the one on Fig. 1.

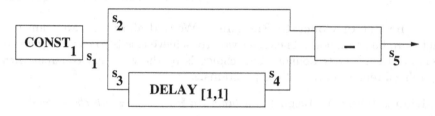

Fig. 1. A simple diagram

Definition 1 (control point). *A control point is any input or output of a gate or of a wire.*

We often collapse the two control points of the same wire. We call V the set of *control points* of a diagram.

2.1.3 Synchronous Units: Boxes. A box is meant to represent a whole synchronous program, i. e. gates and wires, executed quasi-synchrously. As a consequence, it has to be isolated from the rest of the diagram, which represents other programs and wires between them. A synchronous program is executed in a cyclic way. Each cycle is supposed to last between α and β. We therefore connect each box to an *execution duration interval* $[\alpha, \beta]$. For example, the box in Fig. 2 is assumed to be executed in constant time 1, since its execution duration interval is $[1, 1]$. Lastly, a box has the same inputs and outputs as the ones of the diagram it is built on. For example, the box in Fig. 2 has no input and one output.

2.1.4 Communication Units: External Wires. External wires connect an output of a box to an input of a box, in an oriented non-instantaneous way. They are tagged with a time interval, and therefore represented on diagrams as a DELAY gate, as depicted on the left diagram of Fig. 3.

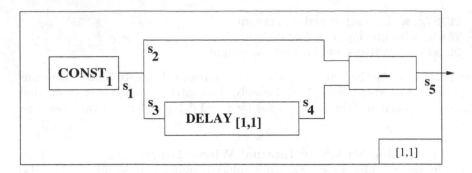

Fig. 2. A simple box

2.2   Continuous-Time Semantics

We write $\mathbb{R}$ for the set of reals, $\mathbb{R}^*_-$ for the negative reals, and $\mathbb{B}$ for the booleans.

2.2.1   The Set of Concrete Elements. We said above that we want our semantics to be continuous. The easier way to achieve this is to chose *signals* as elements of the concrete domain. This choice is by the way very coherent with the graphical representation of the programs.

Definition 2 (signal). *A* signal *is a function* $\mathbb{R} \mapsto \mathbb{B}$ *or* $\mathbb{R}$ *which is equal to 0 or* false *on* $\mathbb{R}^*_-$.

Definition 3 (concrete elements). *The set of* concrete elements *is* $V \rightarrow \mathcal{P}(\mathcal{S})$. *This set is ordered by the usual pointwise inclusion of sets.*

2.2.2   Two New Gates: The Sampler and the SHIFT. These gates won't be used when designing diagrams. They aim at translating the discrete properties of synchronous programs into our continuous model. They thus take a set of *clocks* as parameter, and have one input and one output. A *clock* is any strictly increasing function $c : \mathbb{N} \mapsto \mathbb{R}$, such that $c(0) = 0$. At this point, we do not discard Zeno's paradox. However, the semantics of the three time-sensitive gates (sampler, SHIFT, and DELAY$[\mu, \nu]$) prevents it to appear by requiring $\mu > 0$.

The *sampler* is represented on diagrams as $|||[\mu, \nu]$ and the SHIFT as SHIFT$_{[\mu,\nu]}$, where μ and ν are parameters restricting the clocks that may affect the input signal. They must satisfy: $\nu \geqslant \mu > 0$.

2.2.3   Equations Generated by the Gates

- The semantics of a OR gate with two input control points E_1 and E_2 and an output S_1 is noted $[\![(E_1, E_2), \text{OR}, S_1]\!]$ and is the equation:

$$\forall t \in \mathbb{R}, S_1(t) = True \ \textbf{iff} \ \ E_1(t) = True \ \textbf{or} \ E_2(t) = True$$

The other logic and arithmetic gates have a similar semantics.

– $[\![E_1, \text{DELAY}[\alpha, \beta], S_1]\!]$ is the equation:

$$\exists \delta : \mathbb{R} \to \mathbb{R}^+, \text{increasing, } \textbf{such that}$$

$$\forall t \in \mathbb{R}, \delta(t) - t \in [\alpha, \beta] \textbf{ and } \forall t \in \mathbb{R}, S_1(\delta(t)) = E_1(t).$$

– The semantics of a sampler $|||[\mu, \nu]$ is $[\![E_1, |||[\mu, \nu], S_1]\!]$, defined as:

$$\exists c \text{ clock}, \forall n \in \mathbb{N}, c(n+1) - c(n) \in [\mu, \nu], \text{ and}$$

$$\forall t \in [c(n), c(n+1)[, S(t) = S(c(n))$$

– The semantics of a SHIFT $\text{SHIFT}[\mu, \nu]$ is $[\![E_1, \text{SHIFT}[\mu, \nu], S_1]\!]$, defined as[1]:

$$\exists c \text{ clock}, \forall n \in \mathbb{N}, c(n+1) - c(n) \in [\mu, \nu], \text{ and}$$

$$\forall t \in [c(n), c(n+1)[, S(t) = S(c(n)^-)$$

– Lastly, the equations generated by wires are simple equalities.

You can notice that all the gates are considered as instantaneous, except $\text{DELAY}[\alpha, \beta]$, $\text{SHIFT}_{[\mu,\nu]}$, and $|||[\mu, \nu]$. The definition of $\text{DELAY}[\alpha, \beta]$ implies that it keeps the order between the values on the signal. It thus represents a *serial* transmission.

2.2.4 The Concrete Semantics

A preliminary transformation: We would like to consider the *function* connecting the control points to a set of signals which, at these points, satisfy the equations generated by a diagram as the semantics of the diagram. But this definition faces the existence of boxes. That's why we define a function Φ which connects a diagram S to another one $\Phi(S)$ such that, at each box B with an execution duration interval $[\alpha_B, \beta_B]$:

– we add at each input of B a gate $|||[\alpha_B, \beta_B]$.
– we add at each output of B a gate:
  • $\text{DELAY}[\alpha_B, \beta_B]$ if the box contains no DELAY gate.
  • $\text{SHIFT}[\alpha_B, \beta_B]$ if the box contains at least one DELAY gate.
– we remove the box!

Semantics.

Definition 4 (Semantics). *The equational semantics of a diagram is the function* $f : V \to \mathcal{P}(\mathcal{S})$, *such that for each* $v \in V$, $f(v)$ *is the set of signals* u *such that for each* $w \in V \setminus \{v\} = \{w_1, ..., w_{\#V-1}\}$ *exists a signal* s_w, *such that* $(u, s_{w_1}, ..., s_{w_{\#V-1}})$ *satisfies all the equations in the semantics of the elements of the diagram.*

We note $[\![D]\!]$ for the semantics of the diagram D.

---

[1] We define $f(x^-) \triangleq \lim\limits_{\substack{y \to x \\ y < x}} f(y)$

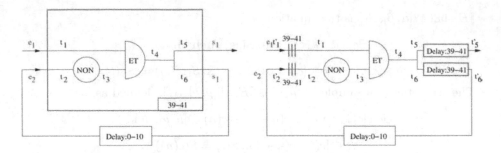

Fig. 3. Transforming a simple diagram

An example. let us consider the semantics[2] of the diagram on Fig. 2:

$$(,\mathrm{CONST}_1, s_1) \qquad (s_1, \mathrm{DUPL}, (s_2, s_3)) \; (s_3, \mathrm{DELAY}_{[1,1]}, s_4) \; ((s_2, s_4), -, s_5)$$

$$
\begin{array}{llll}
s_1 \mapsto & s_2, s_3 \mapsto & s_4 \mapsto & s_5 \mapsto \\
\{\lambda t.\mathbf{if}\ t < 0 & \{\lambda t.\mathbf{if}\ t < 0 & \{\lambda t.\mathbf{if}\ t < 1 & \{\lambda t.\mathbf{if}\ 0 \leqslant t < 1 \\
\mathbf{then}\ 0\ \mathbf{else}\ 1\} & \mathbf{then}\ 0\ \mathbf{else}\ 1\} & \mathbf{then}\ 0\ \mathbf{else}\ 1\} & \mathbf{then}\ 1\ \mathbf{else}\ 0\}
\end{array}
$$

2.3   Concrete Operators

The equational semantics is unfortunately quite difficult to handle. If, for example, we have an information on one control point of a diagram, it has consequences on the control points on the other side of any gate connected to this control point. But we still cannot easily control the propagation of the information. We choose to *orientate* this propagation *backwards*. To propagate the information backwards without loosing too much precision, we just define operators that compute the weakest precondition implying the postcondition we already have as hypothesis.

2.3.1   Operator DELAY[α, β]. We define $\Psi_{\mathrm{DELAY}[\alpha,\beta]}(A)$ as:

$$
\left\{ a \text{ such that } \exists \delta \; \middle| \; \begin{array}{c} \delta : \mathbb{R} \to \mathbb{R} \\ \forall t, \delta(t) - t \in [\alpha, \beta] \\ \lambda t. a(\delta(t)) \in A \end{array} \right\}.
$$

If we assume that (E_1, S_1) satisfies $[\![e_1, \mathrm{DELAY}[\alpha, \beta], s_1]\!]$, then $E_1 \subseteq \Psi_{\mathrm{DELAY}[\alpha,\beta]}(S_1)$.

---

[2] We here use Church's lambda calculus notation: $\lambda x.e$ is the function mapping x to the expression e

2.3.2 Operator DUPL

$$\Psi_{\text{DUPL}}(A, B) \triangleq A \cap B$$

Again, if $(E_1, (S_1, S_2))$ satisfies $[\![e_1, \text{DUPL}, (s_1, s_2)]\!]$, then $E_1 \subseteq \Psi_{\text{DUPL}}(S_1)$.

2.3.3 Logic Operators. Let us define:

$$\Psi_{\text{AND}}(A) \triangleq \{(x, y) | \exists a \in A, \forall t, x(t) \wedge y(t) = a(t)\}$$

Again, if $((E_1, E_2), S_1)$ satisfies $[\![(e_1, e_2)\text{AND}s_1]\!]$, then $(E_1, E_2) \subseteq^2 \Psi_{\text{AND}}(S_1)$. We define the same way $\Psi_{\text{OP}}(A)$ for the other logic gates, as well as for the arithmetic gates.

2.3.4 Operator $|||[\mu, \nu]$

$$\Psi_{|||[\mu,\nu]}(A) \triangleq \left\{ x \left| \begin{array}{c} \exists a \in A \\ \exists C \in \mathbb{N} \to \mathbb{R} \text{ str.} \nearrow \end{array} \right| \begin{array}{c} \forall n, C(n+1) - C(n) \in [\mu, v] \\ \forall t \in [C(n), C(n+1)[\\ a(t) = x(C(n)) \end{array} \right\}$$

If (E_1, S_1) satisfies $[\![e_1, |||[\mu, \nu], s_1]\!]$, then $E_1 \subseteq \Psi_{|||[\mu,\nu]}(S_1)$

2.3.5 Operator SHIFT.
In the following, we won't consider any longer the SHIFT operator. It can, however be connected to concrete operator and, later, to an abstract one. $\text{SHIFT}_{[\mu,\nu]}$ is indeed equivalent to a $\text{DELAY}_{[\varepsilon,\varepsilon]}$ followed by a $|||[\mu, \nu]$, where ε is very small compared to all the delays present in the box it comes from. Once divided into two gates, it may be transformed into two operators, either concrete or abstract ones.

2.3.6 Coding the Diagram into Operators.
We are now able to connect any diagram S to an operator Ψ_S coding its wiring. For example, Ψ connects the diagram on the right to the table on the left. We let T denote the semantics of the diagram on the right, and it thus is a function. We write $\Psi_{\text{OP}} \circ p_i(T)$ for $\Psi_{\text{OP}} \circ T(i)$, and $p_i(T) \circ \Psi_{\text{OP}}$ for the i-th coordinate of the result of Ψ_{OP}. As T is the semantics of the diagram, for any control point t, $T(t) \subseteq p_t \circ \Psi_{\text{OP}_t} \circ p'_t(T)$, where OP_t is the gate after t, p_t and p'_t represent the wiring with that gate.

$$T \subseteq \begin{pmatrix} \Psi_{|||[39,41]} \circ p_1 \\ \Psi_{|||[39,41]} \circ p_2 \\ p_1 \circ \Psi_{\text{AND}} \circ p_4 \\ \Psi_{\text{NOT}} \circ p_3 \\ p_2 \circ \Psi_{\text{AND}} \circ p_4 \\ \Psi_{\text{DUPL}} \circ (p_5, p_6) \\ \Psi_{\text{DELAY}[39-41]} \circ p_{5'} \\ \Psi_{\text{DELAY}[39-41]} \circ p_{6'} \\ \lambda x.\mathcal{S} \\ \Psi_{\text{DELAY}[0-10]} \circ p_{2'} \end{pmatrix} \quad (T)$$

The advantage of such a notation is that it is very easy to be translated into any abstract domain: we replace any concrete operator Ψ_{OP} by an abstract $\Psi_{OP}^{\#}$. These new abstract operators must however be *linked* to the concrete ones, so that the abstract properties possibly proved thanks to these abstract operators can be translated back into the concrete domain.

2.3.7 Expressing Concrete Properties with Concrete Operators and Fixpoints.

We said above that we have an operator Ψ_S built on all the operators Ψ_{OP}, satisfying the property: if T is the semantics of a diagram S, then $T \subseteq \Psi_S(T)$.

Let us try to express this property in a fixpoint form.

Let suppose we want to prove a property P on the signals in the semantics of a diagram S. Let $Z_{\neg P} : V \to \mathcal{P}(\mathcal{S})$ such that if $s_{v_1}, ..., s_{v_n} \in Z_{\neg P}(v_1), ..., Z_{\neg P}(v_n)$ then $s_{v_1}, ..., s_{v_n}$ doesn't satisfy P. We thus would like to prove the assertion $A \triangleq [\![S]\!] \cap Z_{\neg P} = \emptyset$. Now, since $A \subseteq [\![S]\!]$, $A \subseteq \Psi(A)$. Then $A = (\Psi \cap Id)(A)$, so that, by Tarski's fixpoint theorem,

$$A \subseteq \mathtt{gfp}_{Z_{\neg P}}(\Psi \cap Id)$$

Let us now try to prove that this fixpoint is empty. Introducing the operators, we solved the difficulty of controlling the propagation of the information. We now would like to take advantage of a better way to handle this information contained in the sets of signals. In particular, it should be easily handled by a computer program. We therefore design a new abstract domain.

3   A Non-relationnal Abstract Domain: The Constraints

3.1   The Constraints

We define three types of constraints:

- A constraint denoted by $[a; b] : x$, meaning that any signal takes the value x at least once during the interval $[a; b]$.
- A constraint denoted by $\langle a; b \rangle : x$, meaning that any signal takes the value x during the whole interval $[a; b]$.
- A constraint $\mathtt{Abs\_contr}$, which denotes the absence of constraint.

We let $\mathcal{Z}$ denote the set of all constraints.

3.2   Abstract Domain

The abstract domain is $V \to \mathcal{P}(\mathcal{P}(\mathcal{Z}))$. Each element is a disjunction of conjunctions of constraints, described in a disjunctive normal form. They represent the properties of the signals. At this point, we allow infinite conjunctions and disjunctions. However, we will see in Sec. 6 that we can avoid them, so that a computer is able to handle such elements.

3.3 Concretization Map

The set of signals that satisfy an abstract property $P^\#$ is given by $\gamma(P^\#)$, where γ is the concretization map, defined as follows.

Definition 5 (Concretization map).

$$
\begin{pmatrix}
V \to \mathcal{P}(\mathcal{P}(\mathcal{Z})) & \to & V \to \mathcal{P}(\mathcal{S}) \\[2ex]
\lambda v.\{f_{i,v}, i \in I\} & \mapsto & \lambda v. \bigcap_{i \in I} \begin{pmatrix} \bigcup_{([a,b]:y) \in f_{i,v}} \{x, \exists t \in [a,b], x(t) = y\} \\ \cup \left(\bigcup_{(\langle a;b\rangle:y) \in f_{i,v}} \{x, \forall t \in [a,b], x(t) = y\} \right) \end{pmatrix}
\end{pmatrix}
$$

Thus, for example:

- $\gamma(\{\emptyset\}) = \mathcal{S}$
- $\gamma(\{\{([0,1] : 1) \wedge ([1,2] : 0) \wedge \langle 2;3\rangle : 1\} \vee \{([0,1] : 0) \wedge ([1,2] : 1) \wedge \langle 2;3\rangle : 1\}\})$
  $\subseteq \{f \mid f$ switches from 0 to 1 or from 1 to 0 between 0 and 2, but is equal to 1 between 2 and 3$\}$

3.4 Pre-order, Union, Intersection

The abstract domain is pre-ordered by $\subseteq^\#$ defined by:

$$ f^\# \subseteq^\# g^\# \Leftrightarrow \gamma(f^\#) \subseteq \gamma(g^\#) $$

We use a pre-order because a set of signals may be described by several unrelated abstract elements. This change doesn't affect our analysis, and will be discussed later. Indeed, some of the equivalent notations representing the same abstract element are easier to manipulate and we will try to favour them.

We also define $\cap^\#$ and $\cup^\#$, as usually on disjunctive normal forms.

4 Abstract Operators

The abstract domain defined above isn't much simpler than the concrete one until we define abstract operators, enabling the translation of the fixpoint-based concrete properties into fixpoint-based abstract properties. We can now define abstract operators, either constraint by constraint, or directly. We thus define, for any operator OP, except $|||_{[\mu,\nu]}$ and DUPL:

$$ \Psi_{\mathtt{OP}}^\#(A^\#) = \left\{ \left\{ \dot{\Psi}_{\mathtt{OP}}^\#(C) \,\Big|\, C \in A_i^\# \right\} \Big| A_i^\# \in A^\# \right\} $$

with

$$ \Psi_{\mathtt{DUPL}}^\#(A^\#, B^\#) = A^\# \cap^\# B^\# $$

$$ \dot{\Psi}_{\mathtt{DELAY}[\alpha,\beta]}^\#(([a,b] : x)) = ([a - \beta, b - \alpha] : x) $$

$$ \dot{\Psi}_{\mathtt{DELAY}[\alpha,\beta]}^\#((\langle a;b\rangle : x)) = (\langle a - \alpha; b - \beta\rangle : x) $$

$$\dot{\Psi}^{\#}_{\mathrm{ET}}((I : True)) = (I : True, I : True)$$

$$\dot{\Psi}^{\#}_{\mathrm{OU}}((I : False)) = (I : False, I : False)$$

$$\dot{\Psi}^{\#}_{\mathrm{NON}}((I : x)) \qquad = \qquad (I : \neg x)$$

Now, we recursively define:

$$\dot{\Psi}^{\#}_{|||_{[\mu,\nu]}}(([a,b] : x)) = ([a - \nu, b] : x)$$

and

$$\Psi^{\#}_{|||_{[\mu,\nu]}}(A_1, ..., A_{k-1}, \{C_1, ..., C_{k-1}, (\langle a, b\rangle : x), C_k, ..., C_n\}, A_{k+1}, ..., A_n)$$
$$\triangleq \Psi^{\#}_{|||_{[\mu,\nu]}}(A_1, ..., A_{k-1}, \{C_i, i \in [1, n]\} \cup \{([t, t] : x), t \in [a, b]\}, A_{k+1}, ..., A_n)$$

5   Link Between Concrete and Abstract Properties

5.1   From Concrete Properties to Abstract Properties

We use the next theorem to link concrete properties and abstract properties:

Theorem 1. *For any Ψ defined above, $\Psi \circ \gamma \subseteq \gamma \circ \Psi^{\#}$*

It is easy to prove, considering each possible Ψ. We then are able to use the next theorem:

Theorem 2. [3] *If:*

- *F and $F^{\#}$ are continuous.*
- *$F \circ \gamma \subseteq \gamma \circ F^{\#}$*
- *$A^{\#}$ is an abstract element such that $F(\gamma(A^{\#})) \subseteq \gamma(A^{\#})$ and $F^{\#}(A^{\#}) \subseteq A^{\#}$*

then:

$$\mathrm{gfp}_{\gamma(A^{\#})} F \subseteq \gamma(\mathrm{gfp}_{A^{\#}} F^{\#})$$

Now, if, on the other hand, $Z_{\neg P} = \gamma(A^{\#})$ and $\gamma(\mathrm{gfp}_{A^{\#}}(\Psi_S \cap Id)^{\#}) = \emptyset$ then it entails that $\mathrm{gfp}_{Z_{\neg P}}(\Psi_S \cap Id) = \emptyset$ so that the wanted property P is true.

5.2   Example

Let us consider the diagram on Fig. 4, and try to prove $P = \nexists \delta \in \mathbb{R}, \forall t \in [\delta, \delta + 100], t'_5(t)$ is true. As we said above, we thus consider $\neg P$, and therefore try to propagate an hypothesis constraint $A^{\#} = \langle \delta, \delta + 100\rangle : True$ in this diagram, for any δ.

---

[3] Variant of Proposition 25, [9]

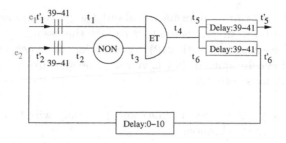

Fig. 4.

Step	Constraint function (control point → constraints)
1	$t_5' \rightarrow \langle \delta, \delta + 100 \rangle : True$
2	$t_5 \rightarrow \langle \delta - 39, \delta + 59 \rangle : True$
3	$t_4 \rightarrow \langle \delta - 39, \delta + 59 \rangle : True$
4	$t_1 \rightarrow \langle \delta - 39, \delta + 59 \rangle : True$ $t_3 \rightarrow \langle \delta - 39, \delta + 59 \rangle : True$
5	$t_1' \rightarrow \bigwedge_{t \in [\delta - 39, \delta + 59]} ([t - 41, t] : True)$ $t_2 \rightarrow \langle \delta - 39, \delta + 59 \rangle : False$
6	$t_2' \rightarrow \bigwedge_{t \in [\delta - 39, \delta + 59]} ([t - 41, t] : False)$
7	$t_6' \rightarrow \bigwedge_{t \in [\delta - 39, \delta + 59]} ([t - 51, t] : False)$
8	$t_6 \rightarrow \bigwedge_{t \in [\delta - 39, \delta + 59]} ([t - 82, t - 39] : False)$
9	$t_4 \rightarrow \bigwedge_{t \in [\delta - 39, \delta + 59]} ([t - 82, t - 39] : False)$

The result is that the control point t_4 must satisfy two contradictory constraints, $\langle \delta - 39, \delta + 59 \rangle : True$ and $\bigwedge_{t \in [\delta - 39, \delta + 59]} ([t - 82, t - 39] : False)$. Indeed, $\mathbf{gfp}_{Z_{\neg P}} (\Psi \cap Id)^{\#} \subseteq^{\#} (\Psi)^{\#^3} (Z_{\neg P}) \cap^{\#} (\Psi)^{\#^9} (Z_{\neg P}) \subseteq^{\#} \emptyset^{\#}$. As a consequence, $\mathbf{gfp}_{Z_{\neg P}} (\Psi \cap Id) = \emptyset$. We then proved that $P = \not\exists \delta, \forall t \in [\delta, \delta + 100], t_5'(t)$ is true.

Here, the contradiction appeared after only nine steps, but we can imagine a much later convergence, or even a convergence after an infinity of steps. In that case, we would have to use a *widening* operator [10].

6 Improvements to the Analysis

6.1 A Transformation of Diagrams

The main loss of information in our previous analysis is due to the imprecision of our abstract operators. The only way to solve this is to provide the operator representing a gate with more information about the gates around it. We now apply a transformation to diagrams in order to face this issue.

First, we label each gate P with $\sigma(P)$ representing its synchronicity group. Two gates are said synchronous if they have the same synchronicity group. This synchronicity group must satisfy:

- If P and P′ are any gates (except DELAY and |||) only wired to inputs of the same box, they are synchronous.
- If P and P′ are any gates (except DELAY and |||) only wired to synchronous inputs, they are synchronous.

Once this is done, let us define the *minimal stability*, denoted τ of control points. This *minimal stability* represents the minimum delay between two changes of the value of any signal at this control point:

- Any input of the diagram is connected to $\tau = 0$.
- Any output S of a sampler $||||[\mu, \nu]$, of input E, is connected to $\tau(S) = \mu$.
- Any output S of a gate DELAY$[\alpha, \beta]$, of input E, is connected to $\tau(S) = \tau(E) - (\beta - \alpha)$.
- Any output S of a gate DUPL or NON, of input E, is connected to $\tau(S) = \tau(E)$.
- Any output S of a gate ET, OR *or* XOR, of **synchronous** inputs E, is connected to $\tau(S) = \tau(E_1) = \tau(E_2)$.
- Any output S of a gate ET, OR *or* XOR, of **non synchronous** inputs E, is connected to $\tau(S) = 0$.
- Any output S of a gate CONST$_\alpha$, of input E, is connected to $\tau(S) = \infty$.

For example, this new transformation, applied to Fig. 4, gives the result shown on figure Fig. 5. In this diagram, the gates NOT, DUPL et AND are synchronous, and labeled "A". The control points are followed by their minimal stability.

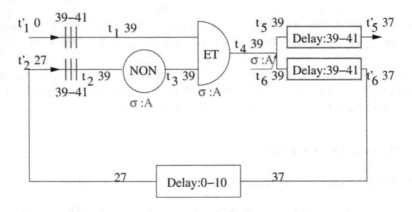

Fig. 5. Fig. 4, modified

6.2 Modification of the Operators $\Psi^\#$

The operators, as formerly defined, cannot be easily programmed. Indeed, the operator $\Psi^\#_{|||_{[\mu,\nu]}}$, applied to $\langle a,b\rangle : x$ generates $\bigwedge_{t\in[a,b]} \dot\Psi^\#_{|||_{[\mu,\nu]}}(([t,t]:x))$, which cannot be easily handled by a computer.

$\Psi^\#_{|||_{[\mu,\nu]}}$, instead of being computed on:

$$\Gamma_1 \vee ... \vee \quad (C_1 \wedge ... \wedge C_i \wedge (\langle a;b\rangle : x) \wedge ... \wedge C_k) \quad \vee ... \vee \Gamma_n$$

should now compute $\Psi^\#_{|||_{[\mu,\nu]}}$ of

$$\Gamma_1 \vee ...\vee$$
$$\left(C_1 \wedge ... \wedge C_i \wedge ([a,a]:x) \wedge ... \wedge \left(\left[a+\left\lfloor\frac{(b-a)}{\eta}\right\rfloor\eta, a+\left\lfloor\frac{(b-a)}{\eta}\right\rfloor\eta\right]:x\right) \wedge ... \wedge C_k \right)$$
$$\vee ... \vee \Gamma_n$$

This enables for example the equality:

$$\Psi^\#_{|||_{[\mu,\nu]}}\{\{(\langle a,b\rangle : x)\}\} = \bigcap_{j\in\left[0;\left\lfloor\frac{(b-a)}{\eta}\right\rfloor\right]} \Psi^\#_{|||_{[\mu,\nu]}}(\{\{([a+j\eta, a+j\eta]:x)\}\})$$

where $\eta = \frac{\mu}{k}$, is a parameter, with k an integer. This change is correct with respect to the theorem 1 of the Sec. 5.1, since it simply forgets some constraints. On the other hand, it appears that there won't be too much loss of information, since the former and the new constraint are equivalent (for $\subseteq^\#$), as far as the signals are restricted to those with a minimal stability superior or equal to μ.

6.3 Modification of the Abstract Domain

The abstract domain of Sec. 3 was non-relational. This means that the constraints on the different control points are independant. This is an issue if, for example one try to find which constraints on the inputs of a gate AND implies that its output satisfies $\langle a;b\rangle : false$. A *relational* abstract domain should therefore be defined.

Definition: The relational abstract domain is the disjunctive completion of the domain of Sec. 3, that is the set $\mathcal{Z}^{\vee\wedge} = \mathcal{P}(\mathcal{P}(V \to \mathcal{Z}))$, representing the disjunctions of the conjunctions of *functions* connecting control points to *one* constraint. We link the both abstract domains with two functions, that were implemented in ocaml.

Link with the non-relational domain
Let us consider: List_tab : $U \mapsto$ (W list)$-> $(U $\mapsto$ W) list, returning the list of the functions such that the n-th element of this list connects any element u of U to the n-th element of the list connected to u. In the following example, U is the set of integers and a function from U is represented as an array ($1 \mapsto x, 2 \mapsto y=[|x;y|]$):

$$\text{List\_tab}([|[1;3;5];[2;4;6]|]) = [[|1;2|];[|3;4|];[|5;6|]]$$

Let us consider $\texttt{Tab\_list} : (\texttt{U} \mapsto \texttt{W})~\texttt{list}-> \texttt{U} \mapsto (\texttt{W}~\texttt{list})$, returning a function connecting each u of U to to all the elements connected to u by a function of the list in argument. For example, with the same conventions as before:

$$\texttt{Tab\_list}([[|1;2|];[|3;4|];[|5;6|]]) = [|[1;3;5];[2;4;6]|]$$

Let $\texttt{map f l}$ be the function returning the list of the results of $\texttt{f}$ applied to each element of $\texttt{l}$. Then, let

$$\alpha = \texttt{Tab\_list} \circ (\texttt{map Tab\_list})$$

and

$$\gamma = (\texttt{map List\_tab}) \circ \texttt{List\_tab}$$

(α, γ) is a Galois connection. We can thus define for any operator OP.

$$\Psi_{\text{OP}}^{\text{relational}} = \gamma \circ \Psi_{\text{OP}}^{\text{non-relational}} \circ \alpha$$

These new operator are thus very close to the former ones, and won't improve precision. We therefore now refine some of them.

Improving the operators let $\ddot{\Psi}^{\#}_{(\sigma_1,\sigma_2,\text{ET},\sigma_3)}$ connects:

$$\begin{pmatrix} s_1 \rightarrow & d_1 \\ \vdots & \\ \sigma_3 \rightarrow & [a,b] : false \\ \vdots & \\ s_p \rightarrow & d_p \end{pmatrix}$$

to

$$\left\{ \begin{pmatrix} s_1 \rightarrow & d_1 \\ \vdots & \\ \sigma_2 \rightarrow & [a,b]: \\ & false \\ \vdots & \\ \sigma_1 \rightarrow & [a,b]: \\ & false \\ \vdots & \\ s_p \rightarrow & d_p \end{pmatrix}, \begin{pmatrix} s_1 \rightarrow & d_1 \\ \vdots & \\ \sigma_2 \rightarrow & [a,b]: \\ & true \\ \vdots & \\ \sigma_1 \rightarrow & [a,b]: \\ & false \\ \vdots & \\ s_p \rightarrow & d_p \end{pmatrix}, \begin{pmatrix} s_1 \rightarrow & d_1 \\ \vdots & \\ \sigma_2 \rightarrow & [a,b]: \\ & false \\ \vdots & \\ \sigma_1 \rightarrow & [a,b]: \\ & true \\ \vdots & \\ s_p \rightarrow & d_p \end{pmatrix} \right\}$$

As for the universal constraint $\langle a;b \rangle : false$, it is transformed into a set of existential constraints $\{[a+k\eta; a+k\eta] : x,~k \in [0; \lfloor \frac{(b-a)}{\eta} \rfloor]\}$. We already did such an operation in section 6.2. We then define $\dot{\Psi}^{\#}_{(\sigma_1,\sigma_2,\text{ET},\sigma_3)}$ such that:

$$\dot{\Psi}^{\#}_{(\sigma_1,\sigma_2,\text{ET},\sigma_3)}(\Gamma_1,...,\Gamma_k) = \left\{ a \wedge b, \begin{array}{l} a \in \ddot{\Psi}^{\#}_{(\sigma_1,\sigma_2,\text{ET},\sigma_3)}(\Gamma_1) \\ b \in \dot{\Psi}^{\#}_{(\sigma_1,\sigma_2,\text{ET},\sigma_3)}(\Gamma_2,...,\Gamma_n) \end{array} \right\}$$

Lastly,

$$\Psi^{\#}_{(\sigma_1,\sigma_2,\text{ET},\sigma_3)}(\Gamma_1, ..., \Gamma_n) = (\dot{\Psi}^{\#}_{(\sigma_1,\sigma_2,\text{ET},\sigma_3)}(\Gamma_1), ..., \dot{\Psi}^{\#}_{(\sigma_1,\sigma_2,\text{ET},\sigma_3)}(\Gamma_n))$$

A similar transformation is of course also applied to $\Psi^{\#}_{\text{OR}}$ and $\Psi^{\#}_{\text{XOR}}$. These new operators face the former problem of the loss of all information on some constraints by these operators.

7 Conclusion

The analyses we presented were easily implemented in the ocaml language, enabling to prove, the same way we did it for the example presented section 5.2, temporal properties of several diagrams, containing more than 20 gates. The continuous-time semantics we used solved many difficulties often met when analyzing these systems, in particular the exhaustive exploration of all the interleavings. We choosed, in order to prove these properties, a very simple abstract domain, which enabled all the same to prove the properties we submitted to our analyzer.

References

1. Albert Benveniste, Paul Caspi, Paul Le Guernic, Hervé Marchand, Jean-Pierre Talpin, and Stavros Tripakis. A protocol for loosely time-triggered architectures. *LNCS, Proceedings of the Second International Conference on Embedded Software, p. : 252 - 265*, 2002.
2. G. Berry. *The Constructive Semantics of Pure Esterel.* 1999.
3. B. Blanchet, P. Cousot, R. Cousot, J. Feret, L. Mauborgne, A. Miné, D. Monniaux, and X. Rival. Design and implementation of a special-purpose static program analyzer for safety-critical real-time embedded software. *The Essence of Computation: Complexity, Analysis, Transformation. Essays Dedicated to Neil D. Jones, LNCS 2566, 85-108. Springer*, 2002.
4. B. Blanchet, P. Cousot, R. Cousot, J. Feret, L. Mauborgne, A. Miné, D. Monniaux, and X. Rival. A static analyzer for large safety-critical software. *Proc. ACM SIGPLAN 2003 Conf. PLDI, 196-207, San Diego, CA, USA, . ACM Press*, 7-14 juin 2003.
5. Paul Caspi, Daniel Pilaud, Nicolas Halbwachs, and John Plaice. Lustre: A declarative language for programming synchronous systems. *Proceedings of the 14th ACM symposium on Principles of programming languages, POPL'87*, 1987.
6. Paul Caspi and Rym Salem. Threshold and bounded-delay voting in critical control systems. *Vol. 1926 of Lecture Notes in Computer Science*, September 2000.
7. P. Cousot and R. Cousot. Abstract interpretation: a unified lattice model for static analysis of programs by construction or approximation of fixpoints. *ACM SIGPLAN-SIGACT Symposium on Principles of Programming Languages, pages 238—252, Los Angeles, California*, 1977.
8. P. Cousot and R. Cousot. Constructive versions of tarski's fixed point theorems. *Pacific Journal of Mathematics, Vol. 82, No. 1,pp. 43—57*, 1979.

9. P. Cousot and R. Cousot. Abstract interpretation and application to logic programs. *Journal of Logic Programming, 13(2–3):103—179*, 1992.
10. P. Cousot and R. Cousot. Comparing the Galois connection and widening/narrowing approaches to abstract interpretation, invited paper. pages 269–295, 1992.
11. Patrick Cousot and Radhia Cousot. Abstract interpretation frameworks. *Journal of Logic and Computation, 2(4):511—547*, August 1992.
12. S. Thompson and A. Mycroft. Abstract interpretation of asynchronous circuits. *SAS, Verona, Italy*, August 2004.

Termination of Polynomial Programs[*]

Aaron R. Bradley, Zohar Manna, and Henny B. Sipma

Computer Science Department
Stanford University
Stanford, CA 94305-9045
{arbrad,zm,sipma}@theory.stanford.edu

Abstract. We present a technique to prove termination of multipath polynomial programs, an expressive class of loops that enables practical code abstraction and analysis. The technique is based on finite differences of expressions over transition systems. Although no complete method exists for determining termination for this class of loops, we show that our technique is useful in practice. We demonstrate that our prototype implementation for C source code readily scales to large software projects, proving termination for a high percentage of targeted loops.

1 Introduction

Guaranteed termination of program loops is necessary for many applications, especially those for which unexpected behavior can be catastrophic. Even for applications that are not considered "safety critical," applying automatic methods for proving loop termination would certainly do no harm. Additionally, proving general temporal properties of infinite state programs requires termination proofs, for which automatic methods are welcome [4, 7, 10].

We present a method of *nonlinear* termination analysis for imperative loops with multiple paths, polynomial guards, and polynomial assignments. The method is nonlinear, first, because the guards and assignments need not be linear and, second, because it can prove the termination of terminating loops that do not have linear ranking functions. The method is sound, but not complete. Indeed, we show that no complete method for this class of programs exists. In practical programs, however, our method proves termination of a high percentage of the targeted loops at low computation cost, and hence is useful.

Recent work on automatic proofs of termination for linear imperative loops has mostly focused on the synthesis of *linear ranking functions*. A ranking function for a loop maps the values of the loop variables to a well-founded domain; further, it decreases value on each iteration. A linear ranking function is a ranking function that is a linear combination of the loop variables and a constant. Colón

---

[*] This research was supported in part by NSF grants CCR-01-21403, CCR-02-20134 and CCR-02-09237, by ARO grant DAAD19-01-1-0723, by ARPA/AF contracts F33615-00-C-1693 and F33615-99-C-3014, by NAVY/ONR contract N00014-03-1-0939. The first author was additionally supported by a Sang Samuel Wang Stanford Graduate Fellowship.

R. Cousot (Ed.): VMCAI 2005, LNCS 3385, pp. 113–129, 2005.

and Sipma first address the synthesis of linear ranking functions in a deductive manner [2]. They present a method based on the manipulation of *polyhedral cones*, extending these results to loops with multiple paths and nested loops in [3]. In [11], Podelski and Rybalchenko specialize the analysis to a less expressive class of single-path imperative loops, providing an efficient and complete synthesis method based on linear programming. Departing from linear ranking function synthesis, Tiwari proves that the termination of a class of single-path loops with linear guards and assignments is decidable, providing a decision procedure via constructive proofs [13].

In the functional programming community, the *size-change principle* has recently been proposed for termination analysis of functional programs [6]. This effort is largely orthogonal to efforts for imperative loops. The principle focuses on structural properties of functional programs, given that particular expressions decrease or do not increase. While imperative loops, and in particular our abstractions of such loops, may be translated to tail-recursive functional programs, nothing is gained. Finding the proper *size measure* to show termination based on the size-change principle is equivalent to proving termination in the imperative setting. However, it is possible that our work may be applied as a size measure for the termination analysis of some functional programs or recursive functions in imperative programs, thus combining the strengths of each approach.

Our method extends termination analysis to *multipath polynomial programs* (MPPs). We show that this class is sufficiently expressive to serve as a sound abstraction for a large class of loops appearing in ordinary C code. We implemented our method and, via CIL [8], applied it to several large open-source C programs, with size up to 75K lines of code. The timing results clearly demonstrate the practicality of the analysis.

Unlike other recent work, we analyze loops via finite differences. Finite differences have a long history in program analysis (*e.g.*, [14, 5, 1]). These methods construct and solve difference equations and inequations, producing loop invariants, running times, and termination proofs. While the equations and inequations are often difficult to solve, we observe that, for termination analysis anyway, explicit solutions are unnecessary. Rather, our method analyzes loops for qualitative behavior – specifically, that certain expressions *eventually* only decrease by at least some positive amount, yet are bounded from below. We address the challenge of characterizing such behavior in loops with multiple paths and nonlinear assignments and guards.

The rest of the paper is ordered as follows. Section 2 introduces MPPs, while Section 3 develops the mathematical foundations for our analysis. Section 4 then formalizes the termination analysis of MPPs, additionally suggesting an alternate abstraction and analysis based on sets of guarded commands. Section 5 describes our prototype implementation and empirical results, and Section 6 concludes.

2   Preliminaries

Definition 1 (Multipath Polynomial Program) For real variables $\mathbf{x} = (x_1, \ldots, x_n)$, a *multipath polynomial program* (MPP) with m paths has the form shown in Figure 1(a), where $\mathbf{P}_i$ and P_{ij} are a vector and a matrix, respectively, of polynomials in $\mathbf{x}$. θ expresses the initial condition on $\mathbf{x}$.

This abstraction of loops is convenient. Multiple paths and arbitrary Boolean combinations of guard expressions are essential for a straightforward abstraction of real code. Moreover, the initial condition, θ, is useful for expressing invariants of variables unaffected by the loop. Such variables may appear in constant expressions in our analysis.

initially θ
while $\bigvee_i \bigwedge_j P_{ij}(\mathbf{x})\ \{\geq, >\}\ 0$ **do**
    $\tau_1:\ \mathbf{x} := \mathbf{P}_1(\mathbf{x})$
    or
    $\vdots$
    or
    $\tau_m:\ \mathbf{x} := \mathbf{P}_m(\mathbf{x})$
od

      (a)

while $x \geq y$ **do**
    $\tau_1:\ (x,\ y) := (x+1,\ y+x)$
    or
    $\tau_2:\ (x,\ y,\ z) := (x-z,\ y+z^2,\ z-1)$
od

      (b)

Fig. 1. (a) Form of multipath polynomial programs. (b) Multipath polynomial program CHASE.

Example 1. Consider the MPP CHASE in Figure 1(b). x and y may each increase or decrease, depending on current values. Further, while they both *eventually* increase, termination relies on y increasing more rapidly than x.

Theorem 1. (No Complete Method) *Termination of MPPs is not semi-decidable; that is, there is no complete method for determining termination of MPPs.*

Proof. We construct a reduction from Hilbert's 10th problem, the existence of a nonnegative integer root of an arbitrary Diophantine equation, which is undecidable. First, we note that the existence of such a root is semi-decidable, via a proper enumeration of vectors of integers: if a root exists, the enumeration terminates with an affirmative answer. Thus, the nonexistence of nonnegative integer roots is not semi-decidable. Now, we reduce from the question of *nonexistence* of roots.

Instance: Given Diophantine equation $P(\mathbf{x}) = 0$ in variables $\mathbf{x} = (x_1, \ldots, x_n)$, determine if there does not exist a nonnegative integer solution.

Reduction: Construct the multipath polynomial program with the following variables: (1) one variable corresponding to each x_i, called x_i; (2) counter variable c; and (3) upper limit variable N. The program has the following form:

$$\textbf{initially } c = 1 \wedge \bigwedge_{i=1}^{n} x_i = 0$$
$$\textbf{while } c \leq N \textbf{ do}$$
$$\{x_1, c\} := \{x_1 + 1,\ 2 \cdot P(\mathbf{x})^2 \cdot c\}$$
$$\textbf{or}$$
$$\vdots$$
$$\textbf{or}$$
$$\{x_n, c\} := \{x_n + 1,\ 2 \cdot P(\mathbf{x})^2 \cdot c\}$$
$$\textbf{od}$$

The program is a multipath polynomial program, as the loop condition and assignment statements involve only polynomials. Computations in which always $P(\mathbf{x}) \neq 0$ are terminating, as c is initially 1 and at least doubles on each iteration, while N remains constant. If $P(\mathbf{x}) = 0$ does occur in a computation, then c is assigned 0 on the subsequent iteration, and thus for every future iteration. When such a computation is possible, there exist values for N as the upper bound on c so that the computation does not terminate before $P(\mathbf{x}) = 0$; afterward, c remains 0, so the computation does not terminate. Since the program always terminates if and only if there is no solution to the Diophantine equation, we conclude that termination of multipath polynomial programs is neither decidable nor even semi-decidable.

Given this fundamental negative result, this paper focuses on a sound and computationally inexpensive method for concluding termination of multipath polynomial programs. The approach essentially looks for expressions that evolve with polynomial behavior, independently of the order in which transitions are taken. A polynomially behaved expression must eventually only increase, only decrease, or – in a degenerate case – remain unchanged, even if its initial behavior varies. The method that we present soundly classifies expressions that eventually only decrease (or eventually only increase). An expression that eventually only decreases, yet is bounded from below within the loop, indicates termination.

3   Finite Difference Trees

To classify polynomial expressions as eventually only decreasing with respect to a transition system, we use finite differences over transitions. We first recall the definition of a finite difference, placing finite differences in the context of transition systems.

Definition 2 (Finite Difference) The *finite difference* of an expression $E(\mathbf{x})$ in $\mathbf{x}$ over assignment transition τ is

$$\Delta_\tau E(\mathbf{x}) \stackrel{\text{def}}{=} E(\mathbf{x}') - E(\mathbf{x}),$$

where τ provides the value of $\mathbf{x}'$ in terms of $\mathbf{x}$. Thus, $\Delta_\tau E(\mathbf{x})$ is also an expression in $\mathbf{x}$. For convenience, we denote a chain of finite differences $\Delta_{\tau_{i_n}} \cdots \Delta_{\tau_{i_1}} E(\mathbf{x})$ by $\Delta_{\tau_{i_1}, \ldots, \tau_{i_n}} E(\mathbf{x})$ or more simply by $\Delta_{i_1, \ldots, i_n} E(\mathbf{x})$ (note the reversal of the list).

If $\tau_{i_n} = \cdots = \tau_{i_1}$, we denote the chain by $\Delta_{\tau_{i_1}}^n E(\mathbf{x})$ or more simply by $\Delta_{i_1}^n E(\mathbf{x})$. For list of transitions T with length n, we say that $\Delta_T E(\mathbf{x})$ is an nth *order* finite difference.

Example 2. For program CHASE, the first, second, and third order finite differences of $x - y$ over transition τ_1 are the following:

$$\Delta_1(x - y) = (x + 1) - (y + x) - (x - y) = 1 - x$$
$$\Delta_1^2(x - y) = \Delta_1(\Delta_1(x - y)) = \Delta_1(1 - x) = 1 - (x + 1) - (1 - x) = -1$$
$$\Delta_1^3(x - y) = \Delta_1(\Delta_1^2(x - y)) = \Delta_1(-1) = (-1) - (-1) = 0.$$

Consider also the first and second order finite differences

$$\Delta_2(x - y) = (x - z) - (y + z^2) - (x - y) = -(z^2 + z)$$
$$\Delta_{2,1}(x - y) = \Delta_1(\Delta_2(x - y)) = -(z^2 + z) + (z^2 + z) = 0.$$

Finite differences with respect to transitions in different orders can be represented in a *finite difference tree*.

Definition 3 (Finite Difference Tree) The *finite difference tree* (FDT) of an expression $E(\mathbf{x})$ with respect to transitions $T = \{\tau_1, \ldots, \tau_m\}$ has root $E(\mathbf{x})$ and branching factor m. Each node, indexed by its position with respect to the root, represents an expression over $\mathbf{x}$; specifically, the node indexed I represents finite difference $\Delta_I E(\mathbf{x})$. The *leaves* of an FDT are nodes with only 0-children (child nodes with value 0). Thus, each leaf is a constant expression with respect to T. The *height* of an FDT is the longest path to a leaf. A *finite FDT* is a finite difference tree with finite height.

For notational convenience, we sometimes refer to FDT nodes by their finite difference expressions; *i.e.*, $\Delta_T E(\mathbf{x})$ is the node indexed by T, where T is the list of transitions that lead from the root to the node.

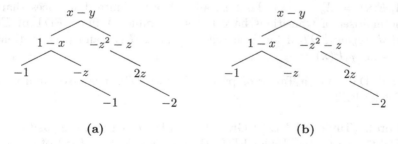

(a)   (b)

Fig. 2. (a) Finite difference tree for CHASE of $x-y$ with respect to $\{\tau_1, \tau_2\}$. (b) Taylored finite difference tree.

Example 3. The FDT of $x-y$ with respect to $\{\tau_1, \tau_2\}$ is shown in Figure 2(a). 0-nodes are not shown. The left node labeled with -1 is indexed (τ_1, τ_1), reflecting that it is the result of twice taking the finite difference with respect to τ_1.

The finite FDT t of an expression $E(\mathbf{x})$ succinctly describes the evolution of $E(\mathbf{x})$. Given computation $\pi = \tau_{i_0}\tau_{i_1}\tau_{i_2}\ldots$ with initial values $\mathbf{x}_0$, t has initial value t_0. Its subsequent values are found by applying each transition in turn, where an application of a transition τ_i to t increases each node by the value of its τ_i child (simultaneously, or starting from the root). The value of $E(\mathbf{x})$ depends not only on the number of times each transition is taken, but also on the *order* that transitions are taken.

Example 4. Suppose x, y, and z of CHASE have initial values x_0, y_0, and z_0, respectively. After taking transition τ_1, the root node of Figure 2(a) has value $x_0 - y_0 + 1 - x_0 = 1 - y_0$, node (τ_1) has value $-x_0$, and the other nodes remain unchanged. After then taking transition τ_2, the root and (τ_1) nodes have values $1 - y_0 - z_0^2 - z_0$ and $-x_0 - z_0$, respectively. The other nodes are similarly updated.

Note that an expression may not have a finite FDT with respect to some sets of transitions. Such cases arise when the transitions have exponential behavior (*e.g.*, $x := 2x$); conversely, finite cases arise when transitions have qualitatively polynomial behavior. Intuitively, the height of a finite FDT parallels the degree (*i.e.*, linear, quadratic, *etc.*) of the polynomial behavior. In this paper, we address only the finite case – expressions in loops that evolve with qualitatively polynomial behavior.

To facilitate the analysis we define *Taylor FDTs* and *partial Taylor FDTs*, which eliminate the dependence on the order in which the transitions are taken. We then show how every finite FDT can be conservatively approximated by a partial Taylor FDT.

Definition 4 (Critical Leaves) The set of *critical leaves* $\Delta_T E(\mathbf{x})$ of a finite FDT are those nodes such that for all permutations σ, $\Delta_{\sigma(T)} E(\mathbf{x})$ has value 0 or is a leaf, and for at least one permutation σ, $\Delta_{\sigma(T)} E(\mathbf{x})$ is a leaf.

Definition 5 (Taylor FDT and Partial Taylor FDT) A finite FDT of $E(\mathbf{x})$ is a *Taylor FDT* if for each sequence of transitions T and every permutation σ of T, $\Delta_T E(\mathbf{x}) = \Delta_{\sigma(T)} E(\mathbf{x})$. That is, all n^{th} order finite differences sharing the same multiset of transitions have the same value. A finite FDT of $E(\mathbf{x})$ is a *partial Taylor FDT* if for each critical leaf $\Delta_T E(\mathbf{x})$ and permutation σ, $\Delta_T E(\mathbf{x}) = \Delta_{\sigma(T)} E(\mathbf{x})$.

Even if an FDT is not a Taylor or partial Taylor FDT, it is associated with a partial Taylor FDT.

Definition 6 (Taylored FDT) Given finite FDT t of $E(\mathbf{x})$, the *positive Taylored FDT* t^+ is a partial Taylor FDT. Each critical leaf $\Delta_T E(\mathbf{x})$ of t is given value $\max_\sigma \Delta_{\sigma(T)} E(\mathbf{x})$ in t^+; the rest of t^+ is identical to t. The *negative Taylored FDT* t^- is similar, except that each critical leaf's value is given by $\min_\sigma \Delta_{\sigma(T)} E(\mathbf{x})$.

The definition of a positive Taylored FDT t^+ implies that the value of a node in t^+ is at least that of its counterpart in t. The opposite relation holds between t^-

and t. Consequently, given a computation $\pi = \tau_{i_0}\tau_{i_1}\tau_{i_2}\ldots$, $t^- \leq t \leq t^+$ always holds, where $\leq$ expresses nodewise comparison, and thus $E(\mathbf{x})^- \leq E(\mathbf{x}) \leq E(\mathbf{x})^+$.

Example 5. The Taylored FDT of x is shown in Figure 2(**b**). Node (τ_1, τ_2, τ_2) becomes 0 because

$$\max\{\Delta_{1,2,2}(x-y), \Delta_{2,1,2}(x-y), \Delta_{2,2,1}(x-y)\} = \max\{-1, 0, 0\} = 0.$$

For conceptual clarity, we extend the definition of a Taylored FDT so that the result is a Taylor FDT; however, the extension can only be computed with respect to the initial values of a computation.

Definition 7 (Fully Taylored FDT) Given finite FDT t of $E(\mathbf{x})$ and initial value $\mathbf{x}_0$, the *positive fully Taylored FDT* t_f^+ is a Taylor FDT. Each node n at index T in t_f^+ has value $\max_\sigma(\Delta_{\sigma(T)}E(\mathbf{x})[\mathbf{x} \mapsto \mathbf{x}_0])$. The *negative Taylored FDT* t_f^- is similar, except that each leaf's value is given by $\min_\sigma(\Delta_{\sigma(T)}E(\mathbf{x})[\mathbf{x} \mapsto \mathbf{x}_0])$.

We note that for a given initial state and computation π, always $t_f^- \leq t^- \leq t \leq t^+ \leq t_f^+$. Because the negative (fully) Taylored FDT of an expression is equivalent to the positive (fully) Taylored FDT of the negated expression, we will only consider the positive form henceforth and drop the qualifier "positive."

A fully Taylored FDT has the property that for any multiset of transitions T, all finite difference nodes $\Delta_{\sigma(T)}E(\mathbf{x})$ have the same value. Consequently, the FDT may be analyzed in a way parallel to the analysis of polynomials of multiple variables that vary continuously with time. Specifically, we look at the Taylor expansion around "time" 0 – the beginning of the computation. Since the behavior is polynomial, the Taylor expansion is exact.

Consider, for a moment, a fully Taylored FDT as expressing derivatives of $E(\mathbf{x})$ with respect to time. Then given the initial value of the computation, the Taylor series expansion is simply given by the FDT itself; *i.e.*,

$$\sum_{\Delta_T E(\mathbf{x}) \in t} \frac{\prod_{\tau \in T} x_\tau}{|T|!}\Delta_T E(\mathbf{x})[\mathbf{x} \mapsto \mathbf{x}_0],$$

viewing the Ts as lists or multisets. In the discrete context, the expansion is slightly different; however, the dominant terms are the same for the continuous and discrete expansions. Moreover, the coefficients of the dominant terms are those of the critical leaves, which are either constants or constant expressions. In some cases, constant expressions may be soundly approximated by constants, taking care that if a constant expression can possibly be 0, other terms in the expansion dominate. Then for a partial Taylor FDT, the dominant terms comprise the *dominant Taylor expression*.

Definition 8 (Dominant Taylor Expression) Given finite partial Taylor FDT t, its *dominant Taylor expression* is

$$\sum_{\Delta_T E(\mathbf{x}) \in critical\_leaves(t)} \frac{\prod_{\tau \in T} x_\tau}{|T|!}\Delta_T E(\mathbf{x}),$$

where one variable x_τ is introduced per transition τ, representing the number of times the transition has been taken.

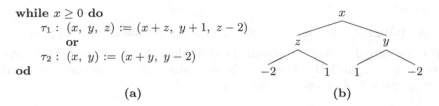

$$
\begin{aligned}
&\textbf{while } x \geq 0 \textbf{ do} \\
&\quad \tau_1 : \ (x, y, z) := (x + z, \ y + 1, \ z - 2) \\
&\quad\quad \textbf{or} \\
&\quad \tau_2 : \ (x, y) := (x + y, \ y - 2) \\
&\textbf{od}
\end{aligned}
$$

(a)   (b)

Fig. 3. (a) MPP INTERACTION. **(b)** Taylored FDT.

Example 6. For CHASE, the dominant Taylor expression of the Taylored FDT for the expression $x - y$ is

$$
-1\frac{x_1^2}{2!} - 2\frac{x_2^3}{3!} = \frac{-x_1^2}{2} - \frac{x_2^3}{3},
$$

where x_1 and x_2 express the number of times that transitions τ_1 and τ_2 are taken, respectively. Conceptually, we may consider a new MPP in which the nonnegativity of the dominant Taylor expression is the guard, x_i are the variables, and each transition τ_i in the original MPP corresponds to a transition $x_i := x_i + 1$ in the new MPP. Clearly, the value of the new guard at any point in a computation depends only on the number of times each transition has been taken.

Example 7. Consider MPP INTERACTION in Figure 3(a) and the Taylored FDT for x with respect to $\{\tau_1, \tau_2\}$ in Figure 3(b). The dominant Taylor expression of the Taylored FDT for the expression x is

$$
-2 \cdot \frac{1}{2!}x_1 x_1 + \frac{1}{2!}x_1 x_2 + \frac{1}{2!}x_2 x_1 - 2 \cdot \frac{1}{2!}x_2 x_2 = -x_1^2 + x_1 x_2 - x_2^2.
$$

Note the nonnegative term $x_1 x_2$, indicating the adverse interaction of τ_1 and τ_2.

Combining the result $t_f^- \leq t^- \leq t \leq t^+ \leq t_f^+$ with the dominant Taylor expression admits analysis of the evolution of $E(\mathbf{x})$. In the next section, we show how to use the dominant Taylor expression of t^+ to discover if $E(\mathbf{x})$ eventually decreases beyond any bound on all computations, which leads naturally into proofs of termination.

4   FDTs and Termination

In the last section, we developed a theory of finite differences for transition systems involving polynomial expressions and assignments. The conclusion hinted at the intuition for a termination analysis. If the dominant Taylor expression of the Taylored FDT of $E(\mathbf{x})$ with respect to the transitions $\mathcal{T}$ decreases without bound on all computations then, first, $E(\mathbf{x})_f^+$ from the fully Taylored FDT must decrease without bound so, second, as $E(\mathbf{x}) \leq E(\mathbf{x})^+ \leq E(\mathbf{x})_f^+$, $E(\mathbf{x})$ must also decrease without bound. If continuation of the loop depends on $E(\mathbf{x})$ $\{\geq, >\}$ 0, then the loop must terminate on all input. In this section, we formalize this description and analyze several conditions on a MPP guard's FDTs that ensure termination.

4.1 Single Loop Condition

For the case of one loop condition $P(\mathbf{x})$ $\{\geq, >\}$ 0, we consider the FDT of $P(\mathbf{x})$ with respect to the loop's assignment transitions $\mathcal{T}$.

Proposition 1. (Taylor Condition) *Suppose that for each nonempty $\mathcal{T}' \subseteq \mathcal{T}$,*

1. *the FDT t of $P(\mathbf{x})$ with respect to $\mathcal{T}'$ is finite;*
2. *the dominant Taylor expression of the Taylored FDT t^+ decreases without bound as the length of the computation increases.*

Then the loop terminates on all input.

Proof. Each subset $\mathcal{T}'$ represents a possible set of transitions that are taken infinitely often. Consider one such set. Suppose the dominant Taylor expression of t^+ with respect to $\mathcal{T}'$ decreases without bound as the length of the computation increases. For all initial values, the dominant Taylor expression dominates the Taylor expansion of the root of the fully Taylored FDT; therefore, $P(\mathbf{x})_f^+$ decreases without bound. But $P(\mathbf{x})_f^+ \geq P(\mathbf{x})^+ \geq P(\mathbf{x})$, so $P(\mathbf{x})$ also decreases without bound. Since this conclusion holds for all $\mathcal{T}'$, the loop must terminate. $\square$

Since the FDTs we consider have finite depth, if a dominant Taylor expression eventually only decreases, then it eventually decreases without bound. We refer to polynomials that satisfy the assumption of the proposition as *decreasing* with respect to $\mathcal{T}$.

Example 8. For CHASE, the dominant Taylor expressions for x with respect to $\{\tau_1\}$, $\{\tau_2\}$, and $\{\tau_1, \tau_2\}$ are the following, respectively:

$$\frac{-x_1^2}{2}, \quad \frac{-x_2^3}{3}, \quad \text{and} \quad \frac{-x_1^2}{2} - \frac{x_2^3}{3}.$$

The last expression was calculated in Example 6. All three expressions clearly decrease without bound as the length of the computation increases. Thus, CHASE terminates on all input.

The following example introduces a technique for showing that a more complicated dominant Taylor expression is decreasing. Changing to polar coordinates allows the length of a computation to appear explicitly in the dominant Taylor expression.

Example 9. Recall that the dominant Taylor expression for x with respect to $\{\tau_1, \tau_2\}$ in INTERACTION is $-x_1^2 + x_1 x_2 - x_2^2$. Call the expression $\sqrt{x_1^2 + x_2^2}$ the *absolute length* of a computation (in which both transitions are taken infinitely often). Since x_1 and x_2 express the number of times τ_1 and τ_2 have been taken, the absolute length is initially 0 and grows with each iteration. If the dominant Taylor expression decreases without bound as the absolute length of the computation increases, then the assumption of the Taylor condition is satisfied for each of τ_1 and τ_2 occurring infinitely often.

Let $x_1 = r\cos\theta$ and $x_2 = r\sin\theta$. r corresponds to the absolute length, while $\theta \in [0, \frac{\pi}{2}]$ expresses the ratio of x_2 to x_1. Then after a change of variables,

$$-x_1^2 + x_1 x_2 - x_2^2 = -r^2\cos^2\theta + r^2\cos\theta\sin\theta - r^2\sin^2\theta = r^2(\cos\theta\sin\theta - 1).$$

Call this expression $Q(r, \theta)$. Differentiating, we find

$$\frac{\partial Q}{\partial r} = 2r(\cos\theta\sin\theta - 1) \quad \text{and} \quad \frac{\partial^2 Q}{\partial r^2} = 2(\cos\theta\sin\theta - 1).$$

The relevant domain of θ is $[0, \frac{\pi}{2}]$, over which the maximum of $\frac{\partial^2 Q}{\partial r^2}$ is -1, occurring at $\theta = \frac{\pi}{4}$. Therefore, independent of θ, as r increases, $Q(r, \theta)$ eventually decreases without bound; therefore, the dominant Taylor expression also eventually decreases without bound.

Finally, considering the case where only τ_1 (τ_2) is taken after a certain point, we note that the dominant Taylor expression is $-x_1^2$ ($-x_2^2$), which decreases without bound. Thus, INTERACTION terminates on all input.

We can apply the trick of using the absolute length and changing to polar coordinates in general, via the usual extension of polar coordinates to higher dimensions. For m transitions and expression $Q(r, \theta_1, \ldots, \theta_{m-1})$, we check if $\frac{\partial^n Q}{\partial r^n}$ is everywhere at most some negative constant over $\theta_i \in [0, \frac{\pi}{2}]$, $i \in [1..m-1]$, where $\frac{\partial^n Q}{\partial r^n}$ is the first derivative with respect to r that is constant with respect to r.

In many cases, a weaker condition on the structure of the single FDT with respect to all transitions $\mathcal{T}$ is sufficient for proving termination, precluding an expensive analysis of the dominant Taylor expression for each subset of transitions. The condition follows from the Taylor condition, although it is intuitive by itself.

Proposition 2. (Standard Condition) *If every leaf of the FDT t of $P(\mathbf{x})$ with respect to $\mathcal{T}$ is negative, and the root of t has $|\mathcal{T}|$ children, then the loop terminates on all input.*

Example 10. The Taylored FDT for CHASE in Figure 2(b) meets this condition, proving termination, while the Taylored FDT for INTERACTION in Figure 3(b) does not.

4.2   General Loop Condition

Consider now the loop condition $\bigwedge_j P_j(\mathbf{x}) \{\geq, >\} 0$. Clearly, one simple condition is that at least one conjunct's FDT decreases without bounds; however, a stronger condition based on a lexical ordering is possible. The following definition will be useful for specifying the condition.

Definition 9 (Neutral Transitions) A set of transitions $\mathcal{T}_n \subseteq \mathcal{T}$ is *neutral* toward an expression $E(\mathbf{x})$ decreasing with respect to transitions $\mathcal{T} \backslash \mathcal{T}_n$ if $E(\mathbf{x})$ is decreasing with respect to $\mathcal{T}$, except possibly when only transitions in $\mathcal{T}_n$ are taken infinitely often.

Checking if a set of transitions is neutral merely requires excluding certain subsets of transitions (those that contain only transitions that need only be neutral) when analyzing termination. For the standard condition, if transition τ_i is neutral, the root need not have a τ_i child.

$$\begin{aligned}
&\textbf{while } x \geq 0 \wedge z^3 \geq y \textbf{ do} \\
&\qquad \tau_1 : \ (x, \ y) := (x - 1, \ y - 1) \\
&\qquad\qquad \textbf{or} \\
&\qquad \tau_2 : \ (y, \ z) := (y - 1, \ z + y) \\
&\textbf{od}
\end{aligned}$$

Fig. 4. Program CONJUNCT.

Example 11. Consider program CONJUNCT in Figure 4. The FDT of x with respect to $\{\tau_1, \tau_2\}$ is shown in Figure 5(a). Transition $\{\tau_2\}$ is neutral toward x, which decreases with respect to $\{\tau_1\}$. Its dominant Taylor expression is $-x_1$, which decreases without bound unless τ_1 is not taken after a certain iteration, regardless of how frequently τ_2 is taken.

Proposition 3. (Conjunction Condition) *Consider the loop with transitions $\mathcal{T}$, a conjunction of n loop conditions $P_j(\mathbf{x}) \{\geq, >\} 0$, and a map $\mu : \mathcal{T} \mapsto [1..n]$ mapping transitions to conjuncts. Then the loop terminates on all input if for each j, the set $\{\tau \mid \mu(\tau) > j\}$ is neutral toward $P_j(\mathbf{x})$, which decreases with respect to $\{\tau \mid \mu(\tau) = j\}$.*

Proof. Suppose the assumption holds, yet the computation σ is nonterminating. Let $\mathcal{T}_\infty$ be the set of transitions occurring infinitely often and $\mathcal{T}_{\min} = \{\tau \in \mathcal{T}_\infty \mid \mu(\tau) = \min_{\tau' \in \mathcal{T}_\infty} \mu(\tau')\}$ be the set of $\mathcal{T}_\infty$-transitions mapping to the loop condition with the lowest index, j. Following the assumption, $P_j(\mathbf{x})$ is decreasing with respect to $\mathcal{T}_{\min}$, while $\mathcal{T}_\infty \backslash \mathcal{T}_{\min}$ is neutral toward $P_j(\mathbf{x})$. Thus, $P_j(\mathbf{x})$ is decreasing with respect to $\mathcal{T}_\infty$, and $P_j(\mathbf{x}) \{\geq, >\} 0$ is violated in a finite number of steps, a contradiction.

For the most general loop condition $\bigvee_i \bigwedge_j P_{ij}(\mathbf{x}) \{\geq, >\} 0$, each disjunct must satisfy the conjunction condition. Of course, either the Taylor condition or the standard condition may be used to determine whether an expression is decreasing with respect to a certain set of transitions or if a set of transitions is neutral toward an expression.

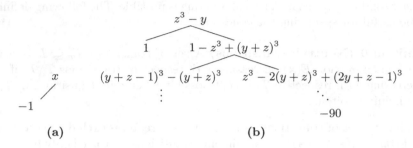

(a)   (b)

Fig. 5. FDTs of **(a)** x and **(b)** $z^3 - y$ with respect to the transitions of program CONJUNCT.

Example 12. Consider program CONJUNCT with index order $P_1(x, y, z) = x$, $P_2(x, y, z) = z^3 - y$, and map μ such that $\mu(\tau_1) = 1$, $\mu(\tau_2) = 2$. τ_2 is neutral toward x, while τ_1 is not neutral toward $z^3 - y$, as suggested by the FDT for $z^3 - y$ in Figure 5(**b**). Nonetheless, the conjunction condition holds, so CONJUNCT terminates on all input.

Specifically, for $P_1(x, y, z) = x$, we need only consider the subsets $\{\tau_1, \tau_2\}$ and $\{\tau_1\}$, each of which result in the decreasing dominant Taylor expression $-x_1$. For $P_2(x, y, z) = z^3 - y$, only the subset $\{\tau_2\}$ must be considered, for which the dominant Taylor expression $-\frac{90}{6!}x_2^6$ is decreasing.

Using the standard condition, we merely note that the FDT for x with respect to $\{\tau_1, \tau_2\}$ shows that $\{\tau_2\}$ is neutral toward x (no τ_2 child of the root), while x decreases with respect to $\{\tau_1\}$ (-1 leaf). Further, the rightmost branch in Figure 5(**b**), which is the FDT of $z^3 - y$ with respect to $\{\tau_2\}$, terminates with -90, also satisfying the standard condition.

4.3   Guarded Commands

Instead of an MPP, consider a set of *polynomial guarded commands* $\mathcal{C} = \{G_1 \rightarrow S_1, \ldots, G_n \rightarrow S_n\}$, for which the G_i are conjunctions of polynomial inequations and the S_i are polynomial assignments. An initial condition θ may be associated with the set of guarded commands.

Proposition 4. (Guarded Commands Condition) *Consider the set of guarded commands* $\mathcal{C} = \{G_1 \rightarrow S_1, \ldots, G_n \rightarrow S_n\}$. $\mathcal{C}$ *always terminates if there exists a permutation* σ *such that for each* i, *there exists a conjunct* ($e \{\geq, >\} 0$) *of* G_i *such that* e *is decreasing with respect to* $\{S_i\}$ *and to which* $\{S_j \mid \sigma(j) > \sigma(i)\}$ *is neutral.*

Briefly, the first guarded command given by σ can only be executed a finite number of times before its guard is violated; as the remaining commands are neutral toward G_1, it is henceforth violated. The same reasoning applies to the second command once the first command is disabled. The disabling of the remaining commands follows by induction.

The language of sets of polynomial guarded commands is more expressive than the language of MPPs – indeed, our practical experience (see Section 5) supports the guarded command abstraction as the more useful. However, the relationship between the general loop condition of Section 4.2 and Proposition 4 is incomparable. Given an MPP and its natural translation to a set of polynomial guarded commands, if Proposition 4 proves termination, then applying Proposition 3 to each disjunct of the MPP's guard also proves termination (extract the lexicographic orders for the latter from the single lexicographic order of the former). However, if, for example, the MPP has two disjuncts requiring opposite orders for Proposition 3, then no interpolation produces a suitable order for Proposition 4. Of course, Proposition 4 is more applicable, in some sense, because of the extra expressiveness of the guarded command abstraction. Allowing disjunction in the guards of the guarded commands makes the resulting guarded command abstraction and the natural termination condition strictly more powerful, but we have not found this additional power useful.

5 Experimental Results

To test the applicability of our termination analysis, we implemented a C loop abstracter in CIL [8] and the termination analysis in Mathematica [15]. The purpose of the loop abstracter is to extract a set of polynomial guarded commands from a C loop with arbitrary control flow, including embedded loops. The analysis then applies to the extracted guarded commands a version of Proposition 4 that exploits the standard condition. The implementation is weaker than Proposition 4, in that it requires for each i that all other assignments $S_j \neq S_i$ are neutral toward the expression e from G_i, rather than allowing a lexicographic ordering. The analysis is sound up to alias analysis, modification of variables by called functions, and unsigned casts. We chose to ignore these factors in our experimentation, as they have no bearing on the scalability of the actual termination analysis. Handling unsigned casts, for example, would require proving invariants about signed integers; a complete program analysis package would contain this functionality.

Given a loop, the abstraction first creates a *number abstraction* by slicing on the number typed variables that receive values within the loop from polynomial expressions. Division is allowed for floats, but not for integers; further, an integer cast of an expression with a floating point value excludes the expression from consideration. Nondeterministic choice replaces disallowed expressions. Next, the abstraction constructs all possible top-level guarded paths; variables that are modified by embedded loops are set nondeterministically (a heavy-handed version of summarizing embedded loops). The construction of a guarded path proceeds by the usual composition of assignments, so that the final guarded path consists of a conjunction of guard expressions and a single concurrent update to a set of variables. The result is a set of guarded commands, as described in Section 4.3. Our Mathematica implementation of the standard condition then analyzes this set, failing if an FDT reaches a predetermined maximum depth during construction.

```
while(i < a.n || j < b.n) {
  if (i >= a.n)
    c.e[c.n++] = b.e[j++];
  else if (j >= b.n)
    c.e[c.n++] = a.e[i++];
  else if (a.e[i] <= b.e[j])
    c.e[c.n++] = a.e[i++];
  else
    c.e[c.n++] = b.e[j++];
}
```

$$j < b.n \land i < a.n \;\rightarrow\; (c.n, j) := (c.n + 1, j + 1)$$
$$j < b.n \land i < a.n \;\rightarrow\; (c.n, i) := (c.n + 1, i + 1)$$
$$j \geq b.n \land i < a.n \;\rightarrow\; (c.n, i) := (c.n + 1, i + 1)$$
$$j < b.n \land i \geq a.n \;\rightarrow\; (c.n, j) := (c.n + 1, j + 1)$$

(a)   (b)

Fig. 6. (a) Imperative loop in C and (b) the corresponding set of polynomial guarded commands.

Example 13. The loop in Figure 6(a) merges two lists. The abstracted set of guarded commands is shown in Figure 6(b); four guarded commands with false guards were pruned. The analysis proves that the loop terminates.

5.1 Empirical Results

We applied the analysis to several open-source projects from Netlib [9] and Sourceforge [12]. The results of the analyses are summarized in Table 1. These programs span a range of applications: for example, **f2c** converts FORTRAN source to C source; **spin** is a model checker; and **meschach** is a package of numerical algorithms.

5.2 Analysis

A glance over the loops in the programs suggests that when the number abstraction of a C loop is proved terminating, the reason is probably because of a counter. In some sense, this observation is disappointing: of what value is our analysis when the reasons are trivial? Three points come to mind. First, applying any analysis at all is useful. Programmers regularly write loops with complicated control structure that span several editor pages. Verifying manually that all paths increment a counter (and the right counter) is thus tedious and ineffective. An automated analysis filters out correct cases, while remaining loops warrant a second look.

Second, our analysis scales well to triviality: the FDTs are shallow (of depth one for the counter case), thus requiring an insignificant amount of time. Compare the minimal computation required for the standard condition on a shallow FDT to the manipulation of polyhedra [2, 3], the solving of linear programs [11],

Table 1. Results of analysis. Legend: **LOC**: lines of code *of files successfully parsed and containing loops*, as measured by `wc`; **# L**: total number of analyzed loops; **# A**: number of loops successfully abstracted; **# P**: number of (abstracted) loops proved terminating; **% P/A**: percentage of abstracted loops proved terminating; **% P/L**: percentage of total loops proved terminating; **Time**: total time in seconds required to analyze the program. `small1` requires a maximum FDT height of 4; data for all others are for a maximum height of 1.

Name	LOC	# L	# A	# P	% P/A	% P/L	Time (s)
small1	310	8	6	4	66	50	4
vector	361	13	13	12	92	92	3
serv	457	9	6	5	83	55	4
dcg	1K	55	53	53	100	96	4
bcc	4K	70	18	18	100	25	6
sarg	7K	122	26	25	96	20	102
spin	19K	652	132	119	90	18	29
meschach	28K	896	803	770	95	85	40
f2c	30K	434	114	96	84	22	41
ffmpeg/libavformat	33K	453	270	214	79	47	45
gnuplot	50K	825	329	298	90	36	106
gaim	57K	605	60	52	86	8	97
ffmpeg/libavcodec	75K	2216	1945	1856	95	83	112

or the analysis of matrix-like transitions [13] (assuming that the latter two approaches can scale to multiple paths). However, the extra power of the nonlinear analysis is available when needed.

Finally, compared to a naive syntactic analysis, our approach has two advantages. First, a naive syntactic analysis would be sensitive to the presentation of the loop. For example, a syntactic analysis may well stumble on a `while` loop that terminates using `break` or `goto` statements. Our abstraction and analysis approach not only is insensitive to such presentations of loops, it may also identify other loop guards than the one explicitly provided by the `for` or `while` statement. Second, even trivial termination behavior is not always completely trivial. For example, the `meschach` source contains loops with terminating behavior similar to that in Figure 6. Our analysis easily handles such cases. Additionally, despite the prototype-related overheads of our implementation, the timing results indicate acceptable performance.

Reasons for failed proofs are numerous. A failure to abstract a nontrivial guarded set may indicate nontermination (especially if, say, all transitions but one increment a counter), but usually arises because the termination behavior is not number-related. Even "successful" abstractions may present only incidental information; termination may rest on other criteria. In several cases, we noted that the lack of an initial condition weakens the abstraction. Other cases played on the weaknesses of the analysis, including the following: (1) expressions evolve with exponential behavior, resulting in infinite FDTs; (2) variables are modified by inner loops, often in a way that trivially suggests an inequality relation.

The number abstraction may be extended beyond pure numbers. Many loops are based on iterating through collection data structures, such as linked lists and heaps. A sophisticated analysis tool would allow the user to input information about such data structures, allowing a number abstraction of iteration. The resulting termination analysis would be sound relative to the correctness of the data structure. Widely used implementations of data structures, such as those provided by the STL, are candidates for automatic analysis.

6   Conclusion

Multipath polynomial programs and polynomial guarded commands provide an expressive language for abstracting real code. Although termination for this class of loops is not even semi-decidable, we provide a sound analysis that is effective in practice. This analysis is notable for two reasons. First, it is applicable to polynomial, rather than just linear, expressions and assignments. Second, our analysis naturally scales to the difficulty of the problem, which enables our prototype implementation to analyze tens of thousands of lines of C in seconds.

The analysis can be strengthened in several ways. First, *head* and *tail loops*, or embedded loops that precede or follow, respectively, all assignments in the top-level loop, may be abstracted to form a set of paths to include as *neutral* top level paths. Second, analysis of the code preceding loop entry, or even invariant generation, can supply initial conditions. Third, embedded loops that modify some variables may sometimes be abstracted as transition relations with inequations. Extending both the abstraction and the analysis to handle such inequations would increase our method's applicability. Fourth, the analysis may be extended to handle FDTs with infinite or large finite height by arbitrarily curtailing FDT construction and using invariant analysis to provide useful bounds on the resulting leaves. Fifth, the abstraction may be extended to iterating over data structures. Finally, we plan to employ the analysis within a larger C analysis that exploits alias information, thus providing a path toward a sound implementation.

Acknowledgments

We thank the reviewers for their insightful comments and suggestions. Additionally, we gratefully acknowledge the contribution of George Necula and the other developers of CIL to the software analysis community.

References

1. COHEN, J. Computer-assisted microanalysis of programs. *Comm. ACM 25*, 10 (1982).
2. COLÓN, M., AND SIPMA, H. Synthesis of linear ranking functions. In *TACAS* (2001).
3. COLÓN, M., AND SIPMA, H. Practical methods for proving program termination. In *CAV* (2002).

4. H. B. SIPMA, T. E. URIBE, AND Z. MANNA. Deductive model checking. In *CAV* (1996).
5. KATZ, S., AND MANNA, Z. Logical analysis of programs. *Comm. ACM 19*, 4 (1976).
6. LEE, C. S., JONES, N. D., AND BEN-AMRAM, A. M. The size-change principle for program termination. In *POPL* (2001).
7. MANNA, Z., BROWNE, A., SIPMA, H., AND URIBE, T. E. Visual abstractions for temporal verification. In *Algebraic Methodology and Software Technology* (1998).
8. NECULA, G. C., MCPEAK, S., RAHUL, S. P., AND WEIMER, W. CIL: Intermediate language and tools for analysis and transformation of C programs. In *Proceedings of Conf. on Compiler Construction* (2002).
9. *Netlib Repository*, 2004. (http://www.netlib.org).
10. PODELSKI, A., AND RYBALCHENKO, A. Software model checking of liveness properties via transition invariants. Technical Report, MPI für Informatik, 2003.
11. PODELSKI, A., AND RYBALCHENKO, A. A complete method for the synthesis of linear ranking functions. In *VMCAI* (2004).
12. *SourceForge*, 2004. (http://sourceforge.net).
13. TIWARI, A. Termination of linear programs. In *CAV* (2004).
14. WEGBREIT, B. Mechanical program analysis. *Comm. ACM 18*, 9 (1975).
15. WOLFRAM RESEARCH, INC. *Mathematica, Version 5.0.* Champaign, IL, 2004.

Verifying Safety
of a Token Coherence Implementation
by Parametric Compositional Refinement*

Sebastian Burckhardt, Rajeev Alur, and Milo M.K. Martin

Department of Computer Science
University of Pennsylvania
{sburckha,alur,milom}@cis.upenn.edu

Abstract. We combine compositional reasoning and reachability analysis to formally verify the safety of a recent cache coherence protocol. The protocol is a detailed implementation of *token coherence*, an approach that decouples correctness and performance. First, we present a formal and abstract specification that captures the safety substrate of token coherence, and highlights the symmetry in states of the cache controllers and contents of the messages they exchange. Then, we prove that this abstract specification is coherent, and check whether the implementation proposed by the protocol designers is a refinement of the abstract specification. Our refinement proof is parametric in the number of cache controllers, and is compositional as it reduces the refinement checks to individual controllers using a specialized form of assume-guarantee reasoning. The individual refinement obligations are discharged using refinement maps and reachability analysis. While the formal proof justifies the intuitive claim by the designers about the ease of verifiability of token coherence, we report on several bugs in the implementation, and accompanying modifications, that were missed by extensive prior simulations.

1 Introduction

Shared memory multiprocessors have become the most important architecture used for commercial and scientific workloads. Such systems use hardware cache coherence protocols to create the illusion of a single, shared memory without caches. These protocols are important factors of the overall system performance, and numerous optimizations contribute to their complexity. Since hard-to-cover race conditions elude simulations of the protocols, formal methods are often employed to verify their correctness.

Token Coherence is a new approach to cache coherence protocols that decouples correctness requirements from performance choices, claiming to improve both performance and verifiability [22]. Separate correctness mechanisms ensure safety and liveness. *Safety* is achieved by token counting: per memory location,

---

* This research was partially supported by the NSF award CCR0306382, and a donation from Intel Corporation.

R. Cousot (Ed.): VMCAI 2005, LNCS 3385, pp. 130–145, 2005.

the number of tokens in the system is a global invariant. By requiring at least one token for read access and all tokens for write access, the protocol directly enforces a single-writer, multiple-reader policy. On the other hand, *Liveness* is achieved by persistent requests. This reliable, but slower protocol is used when the regular requests do not succeed within a timeout period. Persistent requests are required because the regular requests, while likely to complete quickly, do not guarantee eventual success.

In this work, we combine compositional verification and model checking to verify the safety of a detailed implementation of a token coherence protocol for an arbitrary number of caches. Our method takes advantage of the opportunities offered by the token coherence design. It proceeds in four steps.

1. We present a formal specification of the safety substrate of token coherence. This abstract protocol is based on rewrite rules and multisets, and expresses the symmetry between components and messages. It applies to arbitrary network topologies, cache numbers, and even cache hierarchies.
2. We prove manually that the abstract protocol is safe (i.e. coherent). The verification problem is thus reduced to checking that the implementation correctly refines the abstract protocol.
3. We prove that the refinement can be verified for each component individually, by replacing its context with an abstraction. We prove that this decomposition into local refinement obligations is sound, using a variant of assume-guarantee reasoning based on *contextual refinement*, and performing an induction on the number of caches.
4. We discharge the local refinement obligations with the conventional model checker Murφ [12, 11]. To obtain the models, we manually translate, abstract and annotate the implementation code. This procedure reduces the refinement checking to a reachability problem, which Murφ solves by enumerative state space search.

Even though the protocol implementation had been extensively simulated prior to this work, we discovered a few bugs, and were able to fix them quickly with the help of counterexamples produced by the model checker. The compositional refinement method proved to be effective in avoiding the state space explosion problem [16] which is commonly encountered in system-level models [28].

Because of the page limit, we had to omit most proofs. A more complete version of this article can be found online [7].

1.1   Related Work

Prior work on formal verification of cache coherence varies in (1) the protocol complexity and level of detail (2) the coverage achieved (safety, liveness, parametric systems) (3) the underlying tools (enumerative or symbolic model checkers, decision procedures, theorem provers), (4) reduction techniques (symmetry, abstraction, compositional verification), and (5) degree of automation.

We refer to Pong and Dubois [28] for a general survey, and to various illustrative efforts [23, 27, 14, 3].

Our proof methodology modifies and combines a variety of ideas in the formal verification literature. These include assume-guarantee reasoning for compositional verification (c.f. [1, 8, 2, 25]), structural induction for proving properties for arbitrary number of processes (c.f. [19, 9, 15, 13, 10, 4]), data abstraction (c.f. [32, 17]), use of term rewrite systems for hardware verification [5], and proving refinement using reachability analysis (c.f. [18]).

2   Process Model

In this section, we define the process model and introduce our assume-guarantee proof rules. We chose to define the process model from scratch, so to keep it concise and self-contained, and to obtain the desired combination of features. Except for the specialized definition of *contextual refinement*, all concepts (traces, composition, refinement) are standard and appear in many variations and combinations in the process algebra literature [29].

A process is defined as the set of its traces, which are finite words over an alphabet Σ of events. Σ is considered fixed and common to all processes. We further partition $\Sigma = \Sigma_e \cup \Sigma_c$ into disjoint subclasses: Σ_e contains events that are visible to external observers of the system only, while Σ_c describes synchronous communication events. Matching events in Σ_c (e.g. sending and receiving of a message) are denoted σ and $\overline{\sigma}$.

Definition 2.1. *A process P over Σ is a non-empty prefix-closed language; i.e. $P \subset \Sigma^*$, $P \neq \emptyset$ and for all $u, v \in \Sigma^* : uv \in P \Rightarrow u \in P$. A process P refines a process Q, written $P \preccurlyeq Q$, iff $P \subset Q$. A process P is* closed *if $P \subset \Sigma_e^*$.*

The refinement relation $\preccurlyeq$ is a complete partial order on the processes. The bottom (silent) process $\{\epsilon\}$ has but one trace: the empty string. The top (universal) process Σ^* includes all possible traces.

When composing processes, we merge their traces by interleaving their events and hiding mutual communication.

Definition 2.2. *Let $u, v, w \in \Sigma^*$ be traces. We define the relation $u \mid v \vdash w$ (speak: u, v can combine to form w) by the following inference rules:*

$$\frac{}{\epsilon \mid \epsilon \vdash \epsilon} \text{ (EPSILON)} \qquad \frac{u \mid v \vdash w \qquad \sigma \in \Sigma_c}{u\sigma \mid v\overline{\sigma} \vdash w} \text{ (COMMUNICATION)}$$

$$\frac{u \mid v \vdash w \qquad \sigma \in \Sigma}{u\sigma \mid v \vdash w\sigma} \text{ (L-EVENT)} \qquad \frac{u \mid v \vdash w \qquad \sigma \in \Sigma}{u \mid v\sigma \vdash w\sigma} \text{ (R-EVENT)}$$

Example 2.3. Let $\Sigma_e = \{a, b, c, d\}$ and $\Sigma_c = \{e, \overline{e}\}$. Then we have

$$ab \mid cd \vdash acbd \qquad ab \mid cd \vdash abcd \qquad ae \mid \overline{e}b \vdash ab \qquad ae \mid \overline{e}b \vdash ae\overline{e}b$$

but not $ae \mid \overline{e}b \vdash ba$.

Definition 2.4. *Let P, Q be processes. Then $P \mid Q \doteq \{w \in \Sigma^* \mid \exists u \in P : \exists v \in Q : u \mid v \vdash w\}$.*

Composition is commutative and associative. Composition does not restrict its components: for processes P, Q we always have $P \preccurlyeq P \mid Q$. This same style of communication is used by CCS [26].

Refinement is preserved by composition: if $P' \preccurlyeq P$, then $P' \mid Q \preccurlyeq P \mid Q$. We can use this fact to prove that a system implementation refines its specification

$$P' \mid Q' \preccurlyeq P \mid Q \tag{1}$$

from the simpler, local refinement conditions

$$P' \preccurlyeq P \quad \text{and} \quad Q' \preccurlyeq Q . \tag{2}$$

However, this method is not very powerful, because the refinements (2) do often not hold because of implicit assumptions on the context. Assume-guarantee reasoning remedies this shortcoming. We provide the context as an explicit subscript to the refinement relation, enabling us to conclude (1) from

$$P' \preccurlyeq_Q P \quad \text{and} \quad Q' \preccurlyeq_P Q . \tag{3}$$

Most process models used for compositional refinement of hardware [2, 24] can express the contextual refinement $P' \preccurlyeq_Q P$ directly as $P' \parallel Q \preccurlyeq P$ (using synchronous parallel composition). The same does not work in our context (as exemplified by the observation 5 below), so we use a direct definition instead.

Definition 2.5 (Contextual refinement). *Let P, P', C be processes. Then P' is said to refine P in context C, written $P' \preccurlyeq_C P$, iff for all traces $u \in P'$ the following condition holds: if there is a trace $v \in C$ such that $u \uparrow \Sigma_c = v \uparrow \Sigma_c$ (i.e. the communication events in u, v match up), then $u \in P$.*

Intuitively, we require that all behaviors of P' that are actually possible within an environment that adheres to C are allowed by P.

The following observations provide insight about contextual refinement.

1. For any process C, $\preccurlyeq_C$ is a pre-order on processes.
2. If $P' \preccurlyeq_C P$, and $C' \preccurlyeq C$, then $P' \preccurlyeq_{C'} P$.
3. Refinement in a universal context corresponds to regular refinement:
   $P' \preccurlyeq_{\Sigma^*} P \Leftrightarrow P' \preccurlyeq P$.
4. Refinement in a silent context corresponds to refinement of closed processes:
   $P' \preccurlyeq_{\{\epsilon\}} P \Leftrightarrow (P' \cap \Sigma_e^*) \preccurlyeq (P \cap \Sigma_e^*)$
5. The refinement $P' \mid C \preccurlyeq_{\{\epsilon\}} P \mid C$ does not imply $P' \preccurlyeq_C P$, because the traces of $P' \mid C$ do not indicate what mutual communication takes place. However, the converse always holds.

To avoid circularity in the assume-guarantee reasoning, we conservatively require that the specification processes can always engage in a subset of communication events $\Sigma_r \subset \Sigma_c$ that is sufficiently large, i.e. $\Sigma_r \cup \overline{\Sigma_r} = \Sigma_c$; in our case, we will take care of this requirement by having specification processes accept any message at any time[1]. We use the following definition to formalize this property of processes.

Definition 2.6. *Let P be a process over Σ, and $\Sigma_r \subset \Sigma$ be an event subset. P is called Σ_r-enabled iff $\forall u \in P : \forall \sigma \in \Sigma_r : u\sigma \in P$.*

We now give the two proof rules for compositional refinement. The first rule is simpler, but restricted to two components. The second rule is a generalization suited for induction.

Theorem 2.7. *Let P, P', Q, Q', C be processes over $\Sigma = \Sigma_e \cup \Sigma_c$. Let $\Sigma_r \subset \Sigma_c$ such that $\Sigma_r \cup \overline{\Sigma_r} = \Sigma_c$. Then the following proof rules are sound:*

$$\frac{P' \preccurlyeq_Q P \qquad P, Q \text{ are } \Sigma_r\text{-enabled} \qquad Q' \preccurlyeq_P Q}{P' \mid Q' \preccurlyeq_{\{\epsilon\}} P \mid Q}$$

$$\frac{P' \preccurlyeq_{Q\mid C} P \qquad P, Q \text{ are } \Sigma_r\text{-enabled} \qquad Q' \preccurlyeq_{P\mid C} Q}{P' \mid Q' \preccurlyeq_C P \mid Q}$$

For example, consider again the local refinement obligations (3). Suppose that the specification processes P, Q can receive messages at any time. We can then apply the first proof rule to conclude that $P' \mid Q'$ refines $P \mid Q$, if there is no external communication, i.e., there are no other components in the system.

3   Token Coherence

In this section, we introduce a formal specification of the safety substrate of token coherence. This abstract protocol is a generalization of the MOESI token counting rules in Martin's dissertation [20]. We then justify it's use as a specification, by proving that it is coherent, and with it any implementation that refines it.

3.1   Background: Cache Coherence

Cache coherence describes the contract between the memory system and the processor in a shared-memory multiprocessor. It is typically established at the granularity of a cache block. A memory system is cache coherent if for each block, writes are serialized, and reads get the value of the last write.

Definition 3.1. *Let V be the set of values of a fixed cache block, and $v_0 \in V$ the initial value. Let $\Sigma_{rw} = \{rd(v), wr(v) \mid v \in V\}$ be the alphabet of events,*

---

[1] If this is not true by default, we could extend the specification to generate a special error event if it receives an unexpected message.

describing accesses to the block by some processor. Then the coherent traces of the system are given by the following regular language over Σ_{rw} :

$$Coh = rd(v_0)^* \left(\bigcup_{v \in V} wr(v) \, rd(v)^* \right)^*$$

Token coherence, like many contemporary coherence protocols such as the popular MOESI protocol family [31], provides this strong form of coherence by enforcing a "single writer, multiple reader" policy[2].

3.2   The Abstract Protocol

In our abstract protocol, system components and messages are of the same type and treated completely symmetrically: both are represented by token bags. Token bags are finite multisets (or bags) over some set T of tokens, and may be required to satisfy some additional constraints (well-formedness). The tokens in the bag constitute the state of the component, or the contents of the message.

The state of the entire system is represented as yet another bag that encloses the token bags of the individual components and messages. The sending of a message is modeled as a division, where a bag separates into two bags, dividing its tokens. The receipt of a message, symmetrically, is modeled as a fusion of token bags. Change is expressed by local reactions: tokens within a bag can be consumed, produced or modified according to rewrite rules.

We give two preliminary definitions before proceeding to the definition of the abstract protocol.

Definition 3.2 (Multisets). *Let T be a set. Two words $u, v \in T^*$ are equivalent if one is a permutation of the other. The induced equivalence classes $\{[u] \mid u \in T^*\}$ are called finite multisets over T, or T-bags. Multiset union is defined as concatenation $[u] \smile [v] \doteq [uv]$. The set of all T-bags is denoted $\mathcal{M}(T)$. For $x \in \mathcal{M}(T)$, let $|x|$ denote the set of elements of T that occur in x.*

For example, for any $t_1, t_2 \in T$, all of the following denote the same T-bag: $[\, t_1^2 \, t_2 \,] = [\, t_1 \, t_1 \, t_2 \,] = \{t_1 t_1 t_2, t_1 t_2 t_1, t_2 t_1 t_1\}$. The exponent is a convenient notation for repeated symbols, and often used with regular languages.

Definition 3.3 (Token Transition System). *A TTS is a tuple (T, B, I, Σ_e, W) where T is a set of tokens, $B \subset \mathcal{M}(T)$ defines the set of well-formed T-bags, $I \in \mathcal{M}(B)$ is the initial configuration, Σ_e is a set of local events, and $W \subset \Sigma_e \times \mathcal{M}(T) \times 2^T \times \mathcal{M}(T)$ is a set of rewrite rules.*

A rewrite rule $(a, x, H, y) \in W$ is denoted $a\colon x \underset{H}{\Longrightarrow} y$. It describes a reaction labeled a that can occur whenever all the tokens in x are together in a bag, and

---

[2] We are considering only the interface between the memory system and the processor here. Independently, the contract between the processor and the programmer may use weaker forms of coherence that involve temporal reordering of events, as specified by the memory model.

the bag does not contain any of the inhibiting tokens listed in H. When the reaction fires, the tokens x are replaced by the tokens y. If H is empty, we omit it from the notation.

A TTS defines a process over the alphabet $\Sigma = \Sigma_e \cup \Sigma_c$, with $\Sigma_c = \{snd(b), rcv(b) \mid b \in B\}$, with the traces $\{u \in \Sigma^* \mid \exists C \in \mathcal{M}(B) : I \xrightarrow{u} C\}$, where we define the transition relation $C \xrightarrow{u} C'$ with the inference rules[3] below.

$$\frac{}{C \xrightarrow{\epsilon} C} \text{(STUTTER)} \qquad \frac{C \xrightarrow{u} C' \quad C' \xrightarrow{v} C''}{C \xrightarrow{uv} C''} \text{(TRANS)}$$

$$\frac{x \smallsmile y \in B}{[\,C\,x\,y\,] \xrightarrow{\epsilon} [\,C\,x \smallsmile y\,]} \text{(FUSION)} \qquad \frac{}{[\,C\,x \smallsmile y\,] \xrightarrow{\epsilon} [\,C\,x\,y\,]} \text{(DIVISION)}$$

$$\frac{a: x \underset{H}{\Longrightarrow} y \quad |z| \cap H = \emptyset \quad y \smallsmile z \in B}{[\,C\,x \smallsmile z\,] \xrightarrow{a} [\,C\,y \smallsmile z\,]} \text{(REACTION)}$$

$$\frac{}{[\,C\,x\,] \xrightarrow{snd(x)} [\,C\,]} \text{(SEND)} \qquad \frac{}{[\,C\,] \xrightarrow{rcv(x)} [\,C\,x\,]} \text{(RECEIVE)}$$

Token transition systems have a feel of concurrency much like a biological system where reactive substances are contained in cells that can undergo fusion and division. Chemical abstract machines [6] capture the same idea (with molecules, membranes, and solutions instead of tokens, bags, and configurations), but are also different in many ways (for example, they do not have fusion or division).

Definition 3.4 (The abstract protocol). *The safety substrate T_m (where m is the number of tokens, a fixed parameter) is a TTS (T, B, I, Σ_e, W) where*

- *T contains the following tokens:*
  R is a regular token as used by token coherence.
  $O(s)$ is a owner token in one of two states $s \in \{C, D\}$ (clean or dirty).
  $D(v)$ is an instance of the data, with value $v \in V$.
  $M(v)$ is a memory cell containing the value $v \in V$.
- *B is defined by imposing two conditions on a token bag $x \in \mathcal{M}(T)$:*
  - *if x contains data $D(v)$, then it must contain at least one regular token R or an owner token $O(s)$.*
  - *if x contains a dirty owner token $O(D)$, then it must contain data $D(v)$.*
- *$I \doteq [\,[\,R^{m-1}\,O(C)\,M(v_0)\,]\,]$.*
- *$\Sigma_e \doteq \{rd(v), wr(v), memread, memwrite, copy, drop \mid v \in V\}$.*
- *W consists of the rewrite rules shown in Table 1.*

Table 2 shows an example trajectory of the abstract protocol. Next, we explain the reaction rules and their interaction in some more detail.

---

[3] The variables in the rule templates range over the following domains: $u, v, w \in \Sigma^*$, $x, y, z \in B$, and $C, C', C'' \in \mathcal{M}(B)$. Furthermore, as a syntactic shortcut, we allow C, C', C'' to match several positions in a multiset of token bags: for example, $[\,C\,z\,]$ can match $[\,x\,y\,z\,]$ by setting $C = [\,x\,y\,]$.

Table 1. The reaction rules of the abstract protocol.

$$rd(v): \qquad\qquad [\, D(v)\,] \implies [\, D(v)\,]$$

$$wr(w): \qquad [\, R^{m-1}\, O(s)\, D(v)\,] \underset{\{D(v)\}}{\implies} [\, R^{m-1}\, O(D)\, D(w)\,]$$

$$memread: \qquad [\, M(v)\, O(C)\,] \implies [\, M(v)\, O(C)\, D(v)\,]$$

$$memwrite: \qquad [\, M(v)\, O(D)\, D(w)\,] \implies [\, M(w)\, O(C)\, D(w)\,]$$

$$copy: \qquad\qquad [\, D(v)\,] \implies [\, D(v)\, D(v)\,]$$

$$drop: \qquad\qquad [\, D(v)\,] \implies [\;]$$

Table 2. A short example trajectory of the abstract protocol, representing a system with a memory D and two caches C_1 and C_2. For clarification, token bags carry subscripts indicating the component that they represent. Those subscripts are *not* part of the abstract protocol.

Description	System trajectory
initial state	$[\,[\, M(v_0)\, O(C)\, R^{m-1}\,]_D\, [\;]_{C_1}\, [\;]_{C_2}\,]$
C_1 requests M	(requests are abstracted away)
D responds	
— read memory data	$\xrightarrow{memread} [\,[\, M(v_0)\, D(v_0)\, O(C)\, R^{m-1}\,]_D\, [\;]_{C_1}\, [\;]_{C_2}\,]$
— send data w/ tokens	$\xrightarrow{\epsilon} [\,[\, M(v_0)\,]_D\, [\, D(v_0)\, O(C)\, R^{m-1}\,]\, [\;]_{C_1}\, [\;]_{C_2}\,]$
C_1 receives response	$\xrightarrow{\epsilon} [\,[\, M(v_0)\,]_D\, [\, D(v_0)\, O(C)\, R^{m-1}\,]_{C_1}\, [\;]_{C_2}\,]$
C_1 writes value v_1	$\xrightarrow{wr(v_1)} [\,[\, M(v_0)\,]_D\, [\, D(v_1)\, O(D)\, R^{m-1}\,]_{C_1}\, [\;]_{C_2}\,]$
C_2 requests S	(requests are abstracted away)
C_1 responds	
— copy data	$\xrightarrow{copy} [\,[\, M(v_0)\,]_D\, [\, D(v_1)\, D(v_1)\, O(D)\, R^{m-1}\,]_{C_1}\, [\;]_{C_2}\,]$
— send data w/ token	$\xrightarrow{\epsilon} [\,[\, M(v_0)\,]_D\, [\, D(v_1)\, O(D)\, R^{m-2}\,]_{C_1}\, [\, D(v_1)\, R\,]\, [\;]_{C_2}\,]$

$rd(v)$ reads a value from a data instance (it can be applied at any time, and does not modify the state). $wr(w)$ modifies a data token, and can only be applied if all m tokens (one owner token and $m-1$ regular tokens) are present, and no other data copies are in the same bag (which guarantees that the data token being modified is the only one in the system).

To guarantee proper writebacks of modified data, a special owner token is used. The owner token records the clean/dirty state, i.e. whether the memory value is stale. When modifying data, the owner token is set to dirty. When the memory writes back the data (*memwrite*), the owner token is cleaned. *memread* loads data from the memory only if there is a clean owner token, and thereby avoids reading stale data.

The rules *copy* and *drop* imply that data instances $D(v)$ can be freely copied or destroyed, subject only to the restriction enforced by B that all bags are well-formed – for example, whoever has the dirty owner token must keep at least one data instance.

We can now prove that the abstract protocol is coherent.

Theorem 3.5. *The closed system* $T_m \cap \Sigma_e^*$ *is coherent:*

$$(T_m \cap \Sigma_e^*) \uparrow \Sigma_{rw} \subset Coh$$

To prove this, verify that (1) all of the following invariants hold in the initial state I and (2) prove (by induction on derivations) that if the invariants hold for a state C, they hold for any state C' such that $C \xrightarrow{u} C'$ for some $u \in \Sigma_e^*$.

1. The number of regular tokens R in the system is $m - 1$.
2. There is always exactly one owner token $O(s)$.
3. There is always exactly one memory cell $M(v)$.
4. All data instances $D(v)$ have the same values.
5. If the owner token is clean, any data instances present have the same value as the memory cell.
6. If there is a data token, it contains the value of the last write. Otherwise, the memory does.

Together, these invariants guarantee that all data instances $D(v)$ are always up-to-date; therefore, reads get the correct value which implies coherence.

All state is modeled by tokens, and there is no distinction between components and messages. This symmetry points out interesting design directions. For example, we consider the memory cell $M(v)$ to be stationary. However, the formal token rules do not impose this restriction and and could be used as an implementation guideline for a system with home migration.

4   Implementation

In this section, we describe how we verified the safety of a detailed implementation of token coherence for an arbitrary number of caches. We describe how we used compositional verification to deal with the parametric character, and how we employed abstraction to handle the fine level of detail. We conclude with a list of discovered bugs.

4.1   The Protocol Implementation

The protocol implementation was developed by Martin et al. for architecture research on token coherence [20], and was extensively simulated prior to this

	Request-Excl.	Request-Shared	Lockdown	Unlockdown	Data Owner	Data Shared	Ack	Ack Owner	Exclusive Compl.	Owned Compl.	Shared Compl.
O	d b j /NO	d j /NO	dd 1 /L			f q k	f q k		v i	w i	x i
NO	a b j	c j	a l /L		m f p k /O	f q k	f q k	n f p k /O	v i	w i	x i
L	j	j	1	1 / NO	r k	r k	r k	s k	v i	w i	x i

Fig. 1. The SLICC table for the memory controller. Rows show controller states, columns show events, and cells show transitions. For example, consider the upper left box. It states that if a Request-Exclusive message arrives while the controller is in state O, the actions d, b and j are executed in sequence, and the controller transitions to the NO state. Shaded cells indicate that an event is not expected to occur in the given state.

work. It consists of finite state machines (FSM) for the cache and memory controllers, augmented with message passing capabilities. The FSMs are specified using the domain-specific language SLICC (Specification Language for Implementing Cache Coherence) developed by Martin et al.

The FSMs include all necessary transient states that arise due to the asynchronous nature of the protocol. The memory and cache controller amount to 600 and 1800 lines of SLICC code, respectively, a scale on which purely manual analysis methods are impractical, in particular because these low-level specifications are usually changed over time.

The SLICC compiler generates (1) executables for the simulation environment and (2) summary tables containing the control states, events and transitions in a human-readable table format[4].

Fig. 1 shows the summary table for the memory controller, with its 3 states and 11 events. Note that some parts of the state, such as the number of tokens, or the actual data values, are stored in variables that are not visible in the summary table.

Due to lack of space, we can not reproduce the summary table for the cache controller (17 states and 20 events), and we can not explain further the meaning of the states and events. The complete SLICC code and interactive HTML-tables are online [21], along with implementations of three other cache coherence protocols.

4.2   Parametric Compositional Refinement Proof

Consider the system S'_n consisting of n caches C', a directory controller D' (which is attached to the memory, and sometimes called memory controller), and

---

[4] More about the table format can be found in Sorin et al. [30].

a interconnection network N'. We consistently use primes for implementation processes to distinguish them from specification processes:

$$S_n' \doteq \underbrace{C' \mid C' \mid \cdots \mid C'}_{n} \mid N' \mid D' \tag{4}$$

In the beginning, the memory holds all tokens. We define local specification processes as token transition systems:

$$D \doteq T_m = (T, B, I, \Sigma_e, W)$$
$$C \doteq (T, B, [\,[\ ]\,], \Sigma_e, W)$$
$$N \doteq (T, B, [\,[\ ]\,], \Sigma_e, W)$$

Since a token transition system already models all possible distributions of the state, no new behavior arises when it is composed:

$$C \mid D = D \qquad C \mid C = C$$

We now state the central result which (together with Theorem 3.5) allows us to verify the implementation components D', C' and N' individually, each within an abstracted context rather than a fully instantiated system.

Theorem 4.1. *If the implementation processes satisfy the local refinement obligations*

$$D' \preccurlyeq_C D \qquad C' \preccurlyeq_D C \qquad N' \preccurlyeq_D C$$

then for all $n \in \mathbb{N}$, we have $S_n' \preccurlyeq_{\{\epsilon\}} T_m$, i.e., the system refines the formal token coherence protocol.

The proof uses induction and the proof rules (Theorem 2.7).

4.3   Discharging the Obligations

To discharge the remaining obligations, we used manual translation, abstraction, and annotation, and the explicit model checker Murφ [12, 11]. The following steps give an overview of the method.

1. *Obtain models D', C' for the memory and cache controller implementations.* This step involves translating the SLICC code to Murφ, instrumenting it with the read/write events relevant for coherence, and abstracting both the state space and the message format. Fig. 2 shows snippets of translated code. The SLICC instructions that fell prey to the abstraction are in `slanted` face. For example, only a single cache block is modeled, therefore the code dealing with addresses is abstracted away. Also, message source and destination fields are irrelevant due to the deep symmetry of formal token coherence. Furthermore, two data values are sufficient[5].

---

[5] Restricting the set of values is justified by the *data-independence* [32], which implies that we can freely substitute values in the traces.

2. *Obtain good encodings for the specification/environment processes D, C.* We can take advantage (1) of the global system invariants established earlier and (2) of the fact that fusion and division are not observable. For example, the flattening map $[\ b_1\ b_2\ \ldots\ b_k\ ] \mapsto b_1 \smile b_2 \ldots \smile b_k$ provides a canonical representative state. This means that *a single T-bag, rather than a multiset of T-bags, is sufficient to model the context.* The models we obtain this way are compact and contribute much to the state-space economy of our approach.

3. *Annotate the transitions of the implementation with matching specification transitions, and provide refinement maps.* For each transition of the implementation process, the annotations specify a sequence of transitions of the specification process. Fig. 2 shows such annotations in uppercase. The refinement maps are functions that map a controller state to its corresponding token bag.

4. *Run the model checker Murφ separately for the two relevant obligations[6] $D' \preccurlyeq_C D$ and $C' \preccurlyeq_D C$.*

   Proposition 4.3 listed below describes how the contextual refinement is discharged. The state enumeration performed by the model checker effectively constructs and verifies the relation R, which describes the reachable states of the implementation process I within the abstract context C. The annotations provided by the user eliminate the need for existential quantification. The model checker also validates the assertions present in the implementation code.

Definition 4.2. *For a labeled transition system $(Q, q0, \Sigma \cup \{\epsilon\}, \delta)$, states $q_1, q_2 \in Q$ and a word $v \in \Sigma^*$ we define: $q \stackrel{v}{\Longrightarrow} q'$ iff there exists a $k \geq 0$ and a sequence of transitions $q_0 \stackrel{v_1}{\longrightarrow} q_1 \stackrel{v_2}{\longrightarrow} \ldots \stackrel{v_k}{\longrightarrow} q_k$ such that $q_0 = q$, $q_k = q'$ and $v_1 v_2 \ldots v_k = v$ (where $v_1 v_2 \ldots v_k = \epsilon$ for $k = 0$).*

Proposition 4.3. *Let I, S and C be processes defined by the trace sets of the labeled transition systems $L_i \doteq (Q_i, q0_i, \Sigma \cup \{\epsilon\}, \delta_i)$ with $i \in \{I, S, C\}$. Let $\phi : Q_I \to Q_S$ be a function (the refinement map). If $R \subset Q_I \times Q_C$ is a relation with the properties (R1)–(R4) listed below, then $I \preccurlyeq_C S$.*

(R1) $(q0_I, q0_C) \in R$, *and* $\phi(q0_I) = q0_S$

(R2)   *If $(q_I, q_C) \in R$ and $q_C \stackrel{u}{\to} q'_C$ for some $u \in \Sigma_e \cup \{\epsilon\}$, then $(q_I, q'_C) \in R$.*

(R3)   *If $(q_I, q_C) \in R$ and $q_I \stackrel{u}{\to} q'_I$ for some $u \in \Sigma_e \cup \{\epsilon\}$, then $(q'_I, q_C) \in R$ and $\phi(q_I) \stackrel{u}{\Longrightarrow} \phi(q'_I)$.*

(R4)   *If $(q_I, q_C) \in R$ and $q_I \stackrel{\sigma}{\to} q'_I$ and $q_C \stackrel{\bar{\sigma}}{\to} q'_C$ for some $\sigma \in \Sigma_c$, then $(q'_I, q'_C) \in R$ and $\phi(q_I) \stackrel{\sigma}{\Longrightarrow} \phi(q'_I)$.*

The full Murφ code is available online [7].

---

[6] Theorem 4.1 lists three obligations, but we skip $N' \preccurlyeq_D C$ because it reduces to checking the reliablity of the network, which is trivial at the given abstraction level.

```
rule "get Request-Excl in O state"
  (I_DirectoryState = state_O)
==>
begin
    d_sendDataWithAllTokens();
    I_DirectoryState := state_NO;
endrule;

procedure d_sendDataWithAllTokens();
var
  out_msg: I_message;
begin
  out_msg.RType := DATA_OWNER;
  if !(I_Tokens > 0) then
    error "d: assertion failed. ";
  endif;
  out_msg.Tokens := I_Tokens;
  out_msg.DataBlk := I_DataBlk;
  out_msg.Dirty := false;
  I_Tokens := 0;
  EVENT_MEMLOAD();
  EVENT_SEND(out_msg);
  EVENT_DROP();
end;
```

```
transition(O, RequestExcl, NO) {
  d_sendDataWithAllTokens;
  b_forwardToSharers;
  j_popIncomingRequestQueue;
}

action(d_sendDataWithAllTokens, "d") {
  peek(requestNetwork_in, RequestMsg) {
    enqueue(responseNetwork_out, ResponseMsg) {
      out_msg.Address := address;
      out_msg.Type := CoherenceResponseType:DATA_OWNER;
      out_msg.Sender := id;
      out_msg.SenderMachine := MachineType:Directory;
      out_msg.Destination.add(in_msg.Requestor);
      out_msg.DestMachine := MachineType:L1Cache;
      assert(directory[address].Tokens > 0);
      out_msg.Tokens := directory[in_msg.Address].Tokens;
      out_msg.DataBlk := directory[in_msg.Address].DataBlk;
      out_msg.Dirty := false;
      out_msg.MessageSize := MessageSizeType:Response_Data;
    }
  }
  directory[address].Tokens := 0;
}
```

Fig. 2. The murphi code (top) is obtained from the SLICC code (bottom).

4.4   Results

The translation required about two days of work. This estimate assumes familiarity with token coherence, and some knowledge of the implementation. We found several bugs of varying severity, all of which were missed by prior random simulation tests similar to those described by Wood et. al. [33]. Seven changes were needed to eliminate all failures (not counting mistakes in the verification model):

1. The implementation included assertions that do not hold in the general system. Although they were mostly accompanied by a disclaimer like "remove this for general implementation", the latter was missing in one case.
2. The implementation was incorrect for the case where a node has only one token remaining and answers a Request-Shared. This situation was not encountered by simulation, probably because the number of tokens always exceeded the number of simulated nodes. We fixed the implementation, which involved adding another state to the finite state control.
3. Persistent-Request-Shared messages (which are issued if the regular Request-Shared is not answered within a timeout period) suffered from the same problem, and we applied the same fix.
4. The implementation copied the dirty bit from incoming messages even if they did not contain the owner token. Although this does not compromise coherence, it can lead to suboptimal performance due to superfluous writebacks. This performance bug would have gone undetected had we only checked for coherence, rather than for refinement of the abstract protocol.
5. After fixing bug 4, a previously masked bug surfaced: the dirty bit was no longer being updated if a node with data received a dirty owner token.
6. Two shaded boxes (i.e. transitions that are specified to be unreachable) were actually reachable. This turned out to be yet another instance of the same kind of problem as in bug 2.
7. Finally, another (last) instance of bug 2 was found and fixed.

As expected, the compositional approach heavily reduced the number of searched states. This kept computational requirements low, in particular considering that the results are valid for an arbitrary number of caches. The measurements in Fig. 3 were carried out on a 300MHz Pentium III ThinkPad.

5   Conclusions and Future Work

We make three main contributions. First, we formally verified the safety of a system-level implementation of token coherence, for an arbitrary number of

# tokens	component	# states	# transitions	time
4	memory controller	92	1692	0.3s
8	memory controller	188	5876	0.6s
32	memory controller	764	83396	7.49s
4	cache controller	700	23454	1.4s
8	cache controller	1308	76446	4.6s
32	cache controller	4956	1012638	65.2s

Fig. 3. Computational requirements for the model checking.

caches. Second, we developed a general and formal specification of the safety substrate of token coherence, and prove its correctness. Third, we demonstrated that token coherence's "design for verification" approach indeed facilitates the verification as claimed.

Future work may address the following open issues. First, the methodology does not currently address liveness. Second, other protocols or concurrent computations may benefit from the high-level abstraction expressed by token transition systems, and offer opportunities for compositional refinement along the same lines. Third, much room for automation remains: for example, we could attempt to integrate theorem provers with the SLICC compiler.

References

1. M. Abadi and L. Lamport. Conjoining specifications. *ACM Transactions on Programming Languages and Systems*, 17(3):507–535, May 1995.
2. R. Alur and T. A. Henzinger. Reactive modules. In *Proceedings of the 11th Annual IEEE Symposium on Logic in Computer Science*, page 207. IEEE Computer Society, 1996.
3. R. Alur and B. Wang. Verifying network protocol implementations by symbolic refinement checking. In *Proceedings of the 13th International Conference on Computer-Aided Verification*, 2001.
4. T. Arons, A. Pnueli, S. Ruah, J. Xu, and L. D. Zuck. Parameterized verification with automatically computed inductive assertions. In *Computer Aided Verification*, pages 221–234, 2001.
5. Arvind and X. W. Shen. Using term rewriting systems to design and verify processors. *IEEE Micro*, 19(3):36–46, /1999.
6. G. Berry and G. Boudol. The chemical abstract machine. *Theoretical Computer Science*, 96(1):217–248, 1992.
7. S. Burckhardt et al. Verifying safety of a token coherence implementation by parametric compositional refinement: Extended version. http://www.seas.upenn.edu/~sburckha/token/, 2004.
8. K. M. Chandy and J. Misra. *Parallel program design: a foundation*. Addison-Wesley Longman Publishing Co., Inc., 1988.
9. E. M. Clarke, O. Grumberg, and S. Jha. Verifying parameterized networks. *ACM Trans. Program. Lang. Syst.*, 19(5):726–750, 1997.
10. G. Delzanno. Automatic verification of parameterized cache coherence protocols. In *Computer Aided Verification*, pages 53–68, 2000.
11. D. L. Dill. The murphi verification system. In *Proceedings of the 8th International Conference on Computer Aided Verification*, pages 390–393. Springer-Verlag, 1996.
12. D. L. Dill, A. J. Drexler, A. J. Hu, and C. H. Yang. Protocol verification as a hardware design aid. In *International Conference on Computer Design*, pages 522–525, 1992.
13. E. A. Emerson and V. Kahlon. Reducing model checking of the many to the few. In *Conference on Automated Deduction*, pages 236–254, 2000.
14. S. M. German. Formal design of cache memory protocols in IBM. *Formal Methods in System Design*, 22(2):133–141, 2003.
15. S. M. German and A. P. Sistla. Reasoning about systems with many processes. *J. ACM*, 39(3):675–735, 1992.

16. G. J. Holzmann. Algorithms for automated protocol verification. *AT&T Tech. J.*, Jan./Feb. 1990.
17. Y. Kesten and A. Pnueli. Control and data abstraction: The cornerstones of practical formal verification. *International Journal on Software Tools for Technology Transfer*, 2(4):328–342, 2000.
18. R. P. Kurshan. *Computer-aided verification of coordinating processes: the automata-theoretic approach.* Princeton University Press, 1994.
19. R. P. Kurshan and K. McMillan. A structural induction theorem for processes. In *Proceedings of the Eighth Annual ACM Symposium on Principles of Distributed Computing*, pages 239–247. ACM Press, 1989.
20. M. M. K. Martin. *Token Coherence.* PhD thesis, University of Wisconsin-Madison, 2003.
21. M. M. K. Martin et al. Protocol specifications and tables for four comparable MOESI coherence protocols: Token coherence, directory, snooping, and hammer. http://www.cs.wisc.edu/multifacet/theses/milo_martin_phd/, 2003.
22. M. M. K. Martin, M. D. Hill, and D. A. Wood. Token coherence: decoupling performance and correctness. In *Proceedings of the 30th Annual International Symposium on Computer Architecture*, pages 182–193. ACM Press, 2003.
23. K. McMillan and J. Schwalbe. Formal verification of the Encore Gigamax cache consistency protocol. In *Proceedings of the International Symposium on Shared Memory Multiprocessing*, pages 242–51, Tokyo, Japan, 1991.
24. K. L. McMillan. A compositional rule for hardware design refinement. In *Proceedings of the 9th International Conference on Computer-Aided Verification*, pages 24–35, June 1997.
25. K. L. McMillan. Verification of an implementation of tomasulo's algorithm by compositional model checking. In A. J. Hu and M. Y. Vardi, editors, *Computer Aided Verification*, volume 1427 of *Lecture Notes in Computer Science*, pages 110–121. Springer, 1998.
26. R. Milner. *Communicating and Mobile Systems: the π-Calculus.* Cambridge University Press, 1999.
27. S. Park and D. L. Dill. Verification of FLASH cache coherence protocol by aggregation of distributed transactions. In *Proceedings of the Eighth Annual ACM Symposium on Parallel Algorithms and Architectures*, pages 288–296. ACM Press, 1996.
28. F. Pong and M. Dubois. Verification techniques for cache coherence protocols. *ACM Computing Surveys*, 29(1):82–126, 1997.
29. A. Ponse, S. A. Smolka, and J. A. Bergstra. *Handbook of Process Algebra.* Elsevier Science Inc., 2001.
30. D. J. Sorin, M. Plakal, A. E. Condon, M. D. Hill, M. M. K. Martin, and D. A. Wood. Specifying and verifying a broadcast and a multicast snooping cache coherence protocol. *IEEE Transactions on Parallel and Distributed Systems*, 13(6):556–578, 2002.
31. P. Sweazey and A. J. Smith. A class of compatible cache consistency protocols and their support by the IEEE futurebus. In *Proceedings of the 13th Annual International Symposium on Computer Architecture*, pages 414–423. IEEE Computer Society Press, 1986.
32. P. Wolper. Expressing interesting properties of programs in propositional temporal logic. In *Proceedings of the 13th ACM SIGACT-SIGPLAN Symposium on Principles of Programming Languages*, pages 184–193. ACM Press, 1986.
33. D. A. Wood, G. A. Gibson, and R. H. Katz. Verifying a multiprocessor cache controller using random test generation. *IEEE Design & Test*, 7(4):13–25, 1990.

Abstraction for Liveness*

Amir Pnueli[1,2]

[1] New York University, New York
amir@cs.nyu.edu
[2] Weizmann Institute of Science

Abstract. Unlike model checking which is restricted to finite-state systems, there are two methods which can be applied for the verification of arbitrary infinite-state systems. These are the methods of *deductive verification* and *finitary abstraction* (FA). Finitary abstraction is the process which provides an abstraction mapping, mapping a potentially infinite-state system into a finite-state one. After obtaining the finite-state abstraction, we may apply model checking in order to verify the property.

In the talk, we will explore some of the relations between the methods of finitary abstraction and deductive verification. One important connection is the recent proof that finitary abstraction is as powerful as deductive verification, thus establishing the completeness (and universality) of the finitary abstraction method. In order to obtain this result, it was necessary to extend the procedure by allowing augmentation of the verified system with auxiliary variables prior to the application of abstraction. With this extension, it is possible to transform the phenomenon of well-founded descent which is essential for proofs of liveness properties into fairness properties of the finite abstracted system.

Since the proof of completeness of the FA method builds upon the proof of completeness of deductive verification, one may get the false impression that, while being as powerful as deductive verification, FA is not much easier to apply. The focus of the talk is aimed at dispelling this false impression, in particular for the case of liveness properties.

We consider first the case of *predicate abstraction*, which is a special case of FA. We can view predicate abstraction as an effort to find an inductive assertion, where the user does not know the full form of the assertion but can identify a set of atomic formulas under the conjecture that there exists a useful inductive assertion which is some boolean combination of these atomic formulas. In this case, we let the model checker find for us the correct (and best) boolean combination that yields an inductive assertion. In analogy with this view, we will consider the "augmented finitary abstraction" approach as a situation that the user finds it difficult to formulate a full ranking function, as required by deductive verification, but can identify some components of such a ranking function. In that case, we let the model checker arrange and combine these components into a full liveness proof. In both cases, the method relies on the superior ability of model checkers to exhaustively analyze all the combinations of a finite (but possibly large) set of components.

This is work is based on collaboration with Ittai Balaban, Yonit Kesten, and Lenore Zuck.

---

* This research was supported in part by NSF grant CCR-0205571 and ONR grant N00014-99-1-0131

Abstract Interpretation with Alien Expressions and Heap Structures

Bor-Yuh Evan Chang[1, ★] and K. Rustan M. Leino[2]

[1] University of California, Berkeley, California, USA
bec@cs.berkeley.edu
[2] Microsoft Research, Redmond, Washington, USA
leino@microsoft.com

Abstract. The technique of abstract interpretation analyzes a computer program to infer various properties about the program. The particular properties inferred depend on the particular abstract domains used in the analysis. Roughly speaking, the properties representable by an abstract domain follow a domain-specific schema of relations among variables. This paper introduces the congruence-closure abstract domain, which in effect extends the properties representable by a given abstract domain to schemas over arbitrary terms, not just variables. Also, this paper introduces the heap succession abstract domain, which when used as a base domain for the congruence-closure domain, allows given abstract domains to infer properties in a program's heap. This combination of abstract domains has applications, for example, to the analysis of object-oriented programs.

1 Introduction

The automatic reasoning about computer programs from their program text is called *static analysis*. It has applications in, for example, compiler optimizations and program verification. An important form of static analysis is *abstract interpretation* [6, 7], which systematically computes over-approximations of sets of reachable program states. The over-approximations are represented as elements of some given lattice, called an *abstract domain*. The elements of the abstract domain can be viewed as constraints on a set of variables, typically the variables of the program. For example, the polyhedra abstract domain [8] can represent linear-arithmetic constraints like $x + y \leqslant z$.

Often, the constraints of interest involve function and relation symbols that are not all supported by any single abstract domain. For example, a constraint of possible interest in the analysis of a Java or C# program is $\mathsf{sel}(H, o, \mathsf{x}) + k \leqslant \mathsf{length}(a)$ where H denotes the current heap, $\mathsf{sel}(H, o, \mathsf{x})$ represents the value of the x field of an object o in the heap H (written $o.x$ in Java and C#), and $\mathsf{length}(a)$ gives the length of an array a. A constraint like this cannot be

---

★ This work was performed while Bor-Yuh Evan Chang was a research intern at Microsoft Research.

R. Cousot (Ed.): VMCAI 2005, LNCS 3385, pp. 147–163, 2005.
© Springer-Verlag Berlin Heidelberg 2005

if $0 \leqslant x$ then	if $0 \leqslant o.x$ then	$x := 0$; $y := 0$;	$o.x := 0$; $p.y := 0$;
$y := x$	$y := o.x$	while $x < N$ do	while $o.x < N$ do
else	else	$y := y + x$;	$p.y := p.y + o.x$;
$y := -x$	$y := -o.x$	$x := x + 1$	$o.x := o.x + 1$
end	end	end	end
(a)	(b)	(c)	(d)

Fig. 1. Two pairs of simple programs demonstrating the difference in what can be inferred without and with the congruence-closure and the heap succession abstract domains.

represented directly in the polyhedra domain because the polyhedra domain does not support the functions sel and length. Consequently, the polyhedra abstract domain would very coarsely over-approximate this constraint as true – the lattice element that conveys no information. This example conveys a general problem for many abstract domains: the abstract domain only understands constraints consisting of variables and its supported function and relation symbols. If a given constraint mentions other, *alien*, function or relation symbols, it is ignored (that is, it is very coarsely over-approximated) by the abstract domain.

Rather than building in special treatment of such alien symbols in each abstract domain, we propose a coordinating *congruence-closure abstract domain*, parameterized by any set of given abstract domains that we shall refer to as *base domains*. The congruence-closure abstract domain introduces variables to stand for subexpressions that are alien to a base domain, presenting the base domain with the illusion that these expressions are just variables. For example, by itself, the polyhedra domain can infer that $0 \leqslant y$ holds after the program in Fig. 1(a), but it can only infer true after the program in Fig. 1(b). In contrast, the congruence-closure domain using the polyhedra domain as a base domain can also infer that $0 \leqslant y$ holds after the program in Fig. 1(b).

In this paper, we introduce the congruence-closure abstract domain and detail its operations. The congruence-closure abstract domain gets its name from the fact that it stores congruence-closed equivalence classes of terms. It is these equivalence classes that are represented as variables in the base domains. Equivalence classes may be dissolved as the variables of the program change. So as not to lose too much information, the congruence-closure domain consults its base domains during such updates.

We also introduce a particular base domain, the *heap succession abstract domain*, that is useful in analyzing programs with a heap, such as object-oriented programs (but also applies more generally to arrays and records). The benefit of this domain is demonstrated by the programs in Fig. 1 where program (d) involves updates to the heap. The polyhedra domain can infer that $0 \leqslant x \wedge 0 \leqslant y$ holds after the program in Fig. 1(c), but it can only infer true after the program in Fig. 1(d), even when the polyhedra domain is used as a single base domain of the congruence-closure domain. However, if one additionally uses the heap succession domain as a base domain, one can infer that $0 \leqslant o.x \wedge 0 \leqslant p.y$ holds after the program in Fig. 1(d).

2   Abstract Interpretation

In this section, we introduce the basic interface of each abstract domain. In an extended version of this paper [5], we briefly review abstract interpretation [6] and illustrate the use of our abstract-domain interface to infer properties of programs written in a toy imperative language.

Expressions. We assume expressions of interest to be variables and functions applied to expressions:

expressions	Expr	e, p	$::=$	$x \mid f(\vec{e})$
variables	Var	$x, y, \dots$		
function symbols	FunSym	f		
expression sequences	Expr[]	$\vec{e}$	$::=$	$e_0, e_1, \dots, e_{n-1}$

In programs and examples, we take the liberty of deviating from this particular syntax, instead using standard notation for constants and operators. For example, we write 8 instead of 8() and write $x + y$ instead of $+(x, y)$. A *constraint* is any boolean-valued expression.

Abstract Domains. The basic abstract domain interface is shown in Fig. 2. Each abstract domain provides a type Elt, representing the elements of the abstract domain lattice. Each lattice element corresponds to a constraint on variables. This constraint is returned by the `ToPredicate` operation. Conversely, `ToElt`(p) yields the most precise representation for constraint p in the lattice, which may have to lose some information. We do not need to compute `ToElt`, so we have omitted it from the abstract domain interface. In the literature [6], the functions corresponding to `ToElt` and `ToPredicate` are often written as α (abstraction) and γ (concretization), respectively.

```
interface AbstractDomain {
    type Elt ;
    ToPredicate : Elt → Expr ;
    Top : Elt ;
    Bottom : Elt ;
    AtMost : Elt × Elt → bool ;
    Constrain : Elt × Expr → Elt ;
    Eliminate : Elt × Var → Elt ;
    Rename : Elt × Var × Var → Elt ;
    Join : Elt × Elt → Elt ;
    Widen : Elt × Elt → Elt ;
}
```

Fig. 2. Abstract domains.

An abstract domain is required to define a partial ordering on the lattice elements (`AtMost`), `Top` and `Bottom` elements (required to correspond to true and false, respectively), and `Join` and `Widen` operations. Furthermore, an abstract domain must define operations to add a constraint to an element (`Constrain`), existentially quantify a variable (`Eliminate`), and rename a free variable (`Rename`), all of which may be conservative. See the extended version [5] for a more detailed description of these operations.

In the extended version [5], we also fix a particular imperative language and review how to apply the abstract domain operations to compute over-approximations of reachable states to infer properties about the program. This ends our general discussion of abstract interpretation. Next, we describe the congruence-closure abstract domain.

3   Congruences and Alien Expressions

The congruence-closure abstract domain $\mathcal{C}$ is parameterized by a list of base domains $\vec{\mathcal{B}}$. A lattice element of the congruence-closure domain is either $\perp$, representing $\texttt{Bottom}_{\mathcal{C}}$, or has the form $\langle G, \vec{B} \rangle$, where G is an equivalence graph (*e-graph*) that keeps track of the names given to alien expressions and $\vec{B}$ is a list containing one non-$\texttt{Bottom}_{\mathcal{B}_i}$ lattice element from each base domain $\mathcal{B}_i$. The names introduced by the congruence-closure domain to stand for alien expressions appear as variables to the base domains. To distinguish these from the variables used by the client of the congruence-closure domain, we call the newly introduced variables *symbolic values*. Intuitively, a symbolic value represents the value to which a client expression evaluates. Alternatively, one can think of the symbolic value as identifying an equivalence class in the e-graph. Throughout, we use Roman letters to range over client variables and Greek letters to range over symbolic values. The e-graph consists of a set of mappings:

mappings	Mapping	m	$::=$	$t \mapsto \alpha$
terms	Term	t	$::=$	$x \mid f(\vec{\alpha})$
symbolic values	SymVal	$\alpha, \beta, \ldots$		

In addition to providing the service of mapping alien expressions to symbolic values, the e-graph keeps track of equalities between terms. It represents an equality between terms by mapping these terms to the same symbolic value. For example, the constraint $w = f(x) \wedge g(x, y) = f(y) \wedge w = h(w)$ is represented by the e-graph

$$w \mapsto \alpha \quad x \mapsto \beta \quad f(\beta) \mapsto \alpha \quad y \mapsto \gamma \quad g(\beta, \gamma) \mapsto \delta \quad f(\gamma) \mapsto \delta \quad h(\alpha) \mapsto \alpha \quad \text{(Ex. 1)}$$

The e-graph maintains the invariant that the equalities it represents are congruence-closed. That is, if the e-graph represents the terms $f(x)$ and $f(y)$ and the equality $x = y$, then it also represents the equality $f(x) = f(y)$. For instance, if the e-graph in Ex. 1 is further constrained by $x = y$, then β and γ are unified, which in turn leads to the unification of α and δ, after which the e-graph becomes

$$w \mapsto \alpha \quad x \mapsto \beta \quad f(\beta) \mapsto \alpha \quad y \mapsto \beta \quad g(\beta, \beta) \mapsto \alpha \quad h(\alpha) \mapsto \alpha$$

A supplementary description of how these mappings can be viewed as a graph is given in Appendix A.

To compute $\texttt{ToPredicate}_{\mathcal{C}}(\langle G, \vec{B} \rangle)$, the congruence-closure domain first obtains a predicate from each base domain $\mathcal{B}_i$ by calling $\texttt{ToPredicate}_{\mathcal{B}_i}(B_i)$. Since the base domains represent constraints among the symbolic values, these predicates will be in terms of symbolic values. The congruence-closure domain then replaces each such symbolic value α with a client expression e, such that recursively mapping the subexpressions of e to symbolic values yields α. In Sec. 3.3, we explain how we ensure that such an e exists for each α. Finally, the congruence-closure domain conjoins these predicates with a predicate expressing the equalities represented by the e-graph. For example, if the congruence-closure domain uses a single base domain $\mathcal{B}_0$ for which $\texttt{ToPredicate}_{\mathcal{B}_0}(B_0)$ returns $\alpha \leqslant \gamma$, then the congruence-closure domain may compute $\texttt{ToPredicate}_{\mathcal{C}}(\langle(\text{Ex. 1}), \vec{B}\rangle)$ as $w = \mathsf{f}(x) \wedge \mathsf{g}(x, y) = \mathsf{f}(y) \wedge w = \mathsf{h}(w) \wedge w \leqslant y$.

In the remainder of this section, we detail the other abstract domain operations for the congruence-closure domain.

3.1   Constrain

The operation $\texttt{Constrain}_{\mathcal{C}}(\langle G, \vec{B}\rangle, p)$ may introduce some new symbolic values and constraints in G and then calls $\texttt{Constrain}_{\mathcal{B}_i}(B_i, p_i)$ on each base domain $\mathcal{B}_i$, where p_i is p with expressions alien to $\mathcal{B}_i$ replaced by the corresponding symbolic value. If any $\texttt{Constrain}_{\mathcal{B}_i}$ operation returns $\texttt{Bottom}_{\mathcal{B}_i}$, then $\texttt{Constrain}_{\mathcal{C}}$ returns $\perp$. Additionally, if the constraint p is an equality, then the congruence-closure domain will make note of it in the e-graph by calling $\texttt{Union}$ (discussed below).

In order for the congruence-closure domain to know which subexpressions of p to replace by symbolic values, we extend the interface of abstract domains with the following operation:

$\quad\texttt{Understands}: \mathsf{FunSym} \times \mathsf{Expr}[\,] \rightarrow \mathbf{bool}$

which indicates whether the abstract domain understands the given function symbol in the given context (*i.e.*, the arguments to the function in question). An abstract domain may choose to indicate it "understands" a function symbol even when it only partially interprets it.

To translate the client expression to an expression understandable to a base domain, the congruence-closure domain traverses top-down the abstract syntax tree of the client expression calling $\texttt{Understands}$ on the base domain for each function symbol. If the base domain understands the function symbol, then $\mathcal{C}$ leaves it as is. If not, then $\mathcal{C}$ replaces the alien subexpression with a symbolic value and adds this mapping to the e-graph. Hopeful that it will help in the development of good reduction strategies (see Sec. 6), we also let $\mathcal{C}$ continue to call $\texttt{Understands}$ on subexpressions of alien expressions and assert equalities with the symbolic value for any subexpression that is understood by the base domain. In fact, this is done whenever a new client expression is introduced into the e-graph as part of the $\texttt{Find}$ operation (discussed below).

To illustrate the $\texttt{Constrain}_{\mathcal{C}}$ operation, suppose the congruence-closure domain is given the following constraint:

$\quad\texttt{Constrain}_{\mathcal{C}}(\langle G, \vec{B}\rangle,\ 2 \cdot x + \mathsf{sel}(H, o, \mathsf{f}) \leqslant |y - z|)$

If a base domain $\mathcal{B}_i$ is the polyhedra domain, which understands linear arithmetic ($+$, $-$, $\cdot$, 2, $\leqslant$ in this example), then the congruence-closure domain makes the following calls on the polyhedra domain $\mathcal{B}_i$:

$\quad\texttt{Constrain}_{\mathcal{B}_i}(\texttt{Constrain}_{\mathcal{B}_i}(B_i,\ \gamma = \upsilon - \zeta),\ 2 \cdot \chi + \alpha \leqslant \beta)$

and the e-graph is updated to contain the following mappings:

$$
\begin{array}{lll}
x \mapsto \chi & H \mapsto \sigma & \mathsf{sel}(\sigma, \omega, \phi) \mapsto \alpha \\
y \mapsto \upsilon & o \mapsto \omega & |\gamma| \mapsto \beta \\
z \mapsto \zeta & \mathsf{f} \mapsto \phi & \upsilon - \zeta \mapsto \gamma
\end{array}
$$

We now define the union-find operations on the e-graph. The Union operation merges two equivalence classes. It does so by unifying two symbolic values and then merging other equivalence classes to keep the equivalences congruence-closed. Unlike the standard union operation, but akin to the union operation in the Nelson-Oppen congruence closure algorithm that combines decision procedures in a theorem prover [15], doing the unification involves updating the base domains.

The Find operation returns the name of the equivalence class of a given client expression, that is, its symbolic value. If the e-graph does not already represent the given expression, the Find operation has a side effect of adding the representation to the e-graph. Like Union, this operation differs from the standard find operation in that it involves updating the base domains. As noted above, to avoid loss of information by the congruence-closure domain, additional equality constraints between understandable subexpressions and their symbolic values (like $\gamma = \upsilon - \zeta$ in the example above) are given to the base domains. Detailed pseudo-code for $\mathtt{Constrain}_{\mathcal{C}}$ along with both Union and Find are given in the extended version [5].

3.2   Rename and Eliminate

Since the base domains never see client variables, the congruence-closure domain can implement $\mathtt{Rename}_{\mathcal{C}}$ without needing to call the base domains. The congruence-closure domain need only update its e-graph to map the new variable to the symbolic value mapped by the old variable (and remove the mapping of the old variable).

Similar to $\mathtt{Rename}_{\mathcal{C}}$, we implement $\mathtt{Eliminate}_{\mathcal{C}}$ by simply removing the mapping of the given variable (without calling the base domains). This means that base domains may have constraints on symbolic values that are no longer representable in terms of client variables. We postpone eliminating such "garbage values" from the base domains until necessary, as we describe in the next subsection. Pseudo-code for $\mathtt{Rename}_{\mathcal{C}}$ and $\mathtt{Eliminate}_{\mathcal{C}}$ are also given in the extended version [5].

3.3   Cleaning up Garbage Values

Garbage values – symbolic values that do not map to any client expressions – can be generated by $\mathtt{Eliminate}_{\mathcal{C}}$, $\mathtt{Join}_{\mathcal{C}}$, and $\mathtt{Widen}_{\mathcal{C}}$. The garbage values would be a problem for $\mathtt{ToPredicate}_{\mathcal{C}}$. Therefore, at strategic times, including at the start of the $\mathtt{ToPredicate}_{\mathcal{C}}$ operation, the congruence-closure domain performs a garbage collection. Roughly speaking, Eliminate with garbage collection is a lazy quantifier elimination operation.

To garbage collect, we use a "mark-and-sweep" algorithm that determines which terms and symbolic values are *reachable* in the e-graph from a client expression; a symbolic value that is not reachable is a garbage value. We define "reachable (from a client expression)" as the smallest relation such that: (a) any client variable is reachable, (b) any function application term whose arguments are all reachable is reachable, and (c) if the left-hand side of a mapping in the e-graph is reachable, then so is the right-hand side of the mapping.

There may be terms in the e-graph that depend on unreachable symbolic values (*i.e.*, that take unreachable symbolic values as arguments). Dropping these may lead to an undesirable loss of information, as we demonstrate in Sec. 4. However, the base domains may have additional information that would allow us to rewrite the term to not use the garbage value. To harvest such information, we extend the abstract domain interface with the following operation:

$$\texttt{EquivalentExpr: Elt} \times \texttt{Queryable} \times \texttt{Expr} \times \texttt{Var} \rightarrow \texttt{Expr option}$$

Operation $\texttt{EquivalentExpr}(B, Q, t, \alpha)$ returns an expression that is equivalent to t but does not mention α (if possible). The Queryable parameter Q provides the base domain an interface to broadcast queries to all other abstract domains about certain predicates, which it might need to yield an equivalent expression.

After marking, the garbage collector picks a candidate garbage value (say α), if any. Then, for every mapping $t \mapsto \beta$ where t mentions α, each base domain is asked for an equivalent expression for t that does not mention α; if one is obtained, then the t in the mapping is replaced by the equivalent expression. The marking algorithm is then resumed there, in case an equivalent expression may have given rise to more reachable terms and symbolic values. After that, if α is still unreachable, all remaining mappings that mention α are removed from the e-graph and $\texttt{Eliminate}_{\mathcal{B}_i}(B_i, \alpha)$ is called on every base domain $\mathcal{B}_i$. At this time, α has either been determined to be reachable after all, or it has been eliminated completely from the e-graph and all base domains. The garbage collector then repeats this process for the next candidate garbage value, if any.

3.4   Congruence-Closure Lattice

Mathematically, we view the congruence-closure domain $\mathcal{C}$ as the Cartesian product lattice [7] over an *equivalences lattice* $\mathcal{E}$ and the base domain lattices. We consider the equivalences lattice $\mathcal{E}$ as the lattice over (empty, finite, and infinite) conjunctions of equality constraints between expressions ordered by logical implication. Elementary lattice theory gives us that both $\mathcal{E}$ and $\mathcal{C}$ are indeed lattices (assuming the base domain lattices are indeed lattices) [4].

However, as with other "standard" e-graph data structures, the e-graph described in previous sections represents only an empty or finite conjunction of ground equalities plus implied congruences, that is, only a proper subset of $\mathcal{E}$. To define the set of equalities implied by an e-graph, we define the evaluation judgment $G \vdash e \Downarrow \alpha$, which says that the e-graph G evaluates the client expression e to the symbolic value α:

$$\boxed{G \vdash e \Downarrow \alpha}$$

$$\frac{G(x) = \alpha}{G \vdash x \Downarrow \alpha} \text{ var} \qquad \frac{G \vdash e_0 \Downarrow \alpha_0 \quad \cdots \quad G \vdash e_{n-1} \Downarrow \alpha_{n-1} \quad G(f(\alpha_0, \alpha_1, \ldots, \alpha_{n-1})) = \alpha}{G \vdash f(e_0, e_1, \ldots, e_{n-1}) \Downarrow \alpha} \text{ fun}$$

This corresponds to intuition that an expression belongs to the equivalence class of expressions labeled by the symbolic value to which it evaluates. We define the equalities implied by an e-graph by introducing the following judgment:

$$\boxed{G \Vdash e_0 = e_1}$$

$$\frac{G \vdash e_0 \Downarrow \alpha \quad G \vdash e_1 \Downarrow \alpha}{G \Vdash e_0 = e_1} \text{ eval} \qquad \frac{G \Vdash e_0 = e_1}{G \Vdash f(e_0) = f(e_1)} \text{ cong}$$

$$\frac{}{G \Vdash e = e} \text{ refl} \qquad \frac{G \Vdash e_1 = e_0}{G \Vdash e_0 = e_1} \text{ symm} \qquad \frac{G \Vdash e_0 = e_1 \quad G \Vdash e_1 = e_2}{G \Vdash e_0 = e_2} \text{ trans}$$

An equality is implied by the e-graph if either both sides evaluate to the same symbolic value, it is a congruence implied by the e-graph, or it is implied by the axioms of equality.

We let $\mathcal{G}$ denote the poset of e-graphs ordered with the partial order from $\mathcal{E}$ (*i.e.*, logical implication). All the operations already described above have the property that given an element representable by an e-graph, the resulting element can be represented by an e-graph. However, $\text{Join}_\mathcal{G}$ cannot have this property, which is demonstrated by the following example given by Gulwani *et al.* [9]:

$$(x = y) \sqcup_\mathcal{E} (\text{g}(x) = \text{g}(y) \wedge x = \text{f}(x) \wedge y = \text{f}(y)) = \bigwedge_{i:\ i \geqslant 0} \text{g}(\text{f}^i(x)) = \text{g}(\text{f}^i(y)) \quad \text{(Ex. 2)}$$

where we write $\sqcup_\mathcal{E}$ for the join in the lattice $\mathcal{E}$ and $\text{f}^i(x)$ for i applications of f. This example shows that $\mathcal{G}$ is not a lattice, since for any k, $\bigwedge_{i:\ 0 \leqslant i \leqslant k} \text{g}(\text{f}^i(x)) = \text{g}(\text{f}^i(y))$ can be represented by an e-graph, but not the infinite conjunction. Thus, $\text{Join}_\mathcal{E}$ may have to conservatively return an e-graph that is less precise (*i.e.*, higher) than the join in $\mathcal{E}$. These issues are discussed further in Sec. 3.5.

AtMost. Aside from the trivial cases where one or both of the inputs are $\text{Top}_\mathcal{E}$ or $\text{Bottom}_\mathcal{E}$, $\text{AtMost}_\mathcal{E}(\langle G_0, \vec{B}_0 \rangle, \langle G_1, \vec{B}_1 \rangle)$ holds if and only if $G_1 \Vdash e_0 = e_1$ implies $G_0 \Vdash e_0 = e_1$ for all e_0, e_1 and $\text{AtMost}_{\vec{\mathcal{B}}}(\vec{B}_0, \vec{B}_1)$. For the e-graphs, we determine if all equalities implied by G_1 are implied by G_0 by considering all "ground" equalities in G_1 (given by two mappings to the same symbolic value) and seeing if a $\textsf{Find}$ on both sides in G_0 yield the same symbolic value (since the e-graph is congruence-closed).

3.5 Join

The primary concern is how to compute the join of two e-graphs, since the overall join for elements of the congruence-closure domain is simply the join of the e-graphs and the join for the base domains (which is obtained by calling $\text{Join}_{\vec{B}}$ on the base domains). Some may find the graphical view of the e-graph described in Appendix A more intuitive for understanding this algorithm, though it is not necessary. Intuitively, there is a potential symbolic value (*i.e.*, node) in the result e-graph for every pair of symbolic values in the input e-graphs (one from each). Let us denote a symbolic value in the resulting e-graph with the pair of symbolic values from the input e-graphs, though we actually assign a new symbolic value to each unique pair of symbolic values. Then, the resulting e-graph $G = \text{Join}_\mathcal{G}(G_0, G_1)$ consists of the following mappings:

$$
\begin{aligned}
x &\mapsto \langle \alpha', \beta' \rangle & \text{if } G_0(x) = \alpha' \text{ and } G_1(x) = \beta' \\
f(\langle \vec{\alpha}, \vec{\beta} \rangle) &\mapsto \langle \alpha', \beta' \rangle & \text{if } G_0(f(\vec{\alpha})) = \alpha' \text{ and } G_1(f(\vec{\beta})) = \beta'
\end{aligned}
$$

In Fig. 3, we give the algorithm that computes this join of e-graphs, introduces the new symbolic values in the base domains, and then computes $\text{Join}_\mathcal{C}$ as the Cartesian product of the various joins. As we create new symbolic values in the result e-graph, we need to remember the corresponding pair of symbolic values in the input graphs. This is given by two partial mappings M_0 and M_1 that map symbolic values in the resulting e-graph to symbolic values in G_0 and G_1, respectively. *Visited*$_0$ and *Visited*$_1$ track the symbolic values that have already been considered in G_0 and G_1, respectively.

The workset W gets initialized to the variables and 0-ary functions that are in common between the input graphs (along with where they map in the input graphs) (line 5, Fig. 3). One can consider the workset as containing terms (*i.e.*, edges) that will be in the resulting e-graph but do not yet have a symbolic value to map to (*i.e.*, a destination node).

Then, until the workset is empty, we choose some term to determine what symbolic value it should map to in the resulting e-graph. For a $\langle t, \alpha_0, \alpha_1 \rangle \in W$, if the pair $\langle \alpha_0, \alpha_1 \rangle$ is one where we have already assigned a symbolic value γ in the resulting e-graph G, then map t to γ in G (line 9). Otherwise, it is a new pair, and we create a new symbolic value (*i.e.*, node) ρ in G, update M_0 and M_1 accordingly, consider α_0 and α_1 visited, and map t to ρ in G (lines 11–15). So that information is not lost unnecessarily (unless chosen to by the base domains), we assert equalities between the symbolic values in the input graphs with the corresponding symbolic values in the result graph (line 12) before taking the join of the base domains. Finally, we find each function in common between G_0 and G_1 from α_0 and α_1, respectively, where all arguments have now been visited (α_0 and α_1 being the last ones). We add each such function to the workset but with the arguments being in terms of the symbolic values of the resulting e-graph (line 16).

We can make a few small optimizations when creating a new symbolic value in the result graph. First, if we have a global invariant that symbolic values are never reused, then α can be used for the symbolic value in the resulting e-graph corresponding to the pair $\langle \alpha, \alpha \rangle$ in the input graphs (rather than getting a fresh symbolic value). Second, for the first symbolic value ρ in the resulting e-graph that maps to α_0 in the input graph G_0, rather than calling

```
0: fun Joinₑ(⟨G₀, B⃗₀⟩ : Elt, ⟨G₁, B⃗₁⟩ : Elt) : Elt =
1:    let G : EGraph in
2:    let B'₀, B'₁ : Elt[] = B₀, B₁ in
3:    let M₀, M₁ : SymVal → SymVal in
4:    let Visited₀, Visited₁ : set of SymVal in
5:    let W : set of Term × SymVal × SymVal =
         {⟨x, G₀(x), G₁(x)⟩ | x ∈ domain(G₀) ∧ x ∈ domain(G₁)}
         ∪ {⟨f(), G₀(f()), G₁(f())⟩ | f() ∈ domain(G₀) ∧ f() ∈ domain(G₁)}
      in
6:    while W is not empty do
7:       pick and remove (t, α₀, α₁) ∈ W ;
8:       if M₀⁻¹(α₀) ∩ M₁⁻¹(α₁) = {γ} then
9:          add t ↦ γ to G
10:      else
11:         let ρ : SymVal = fresh SymVal in
12:         B⃗'₀ := Constrain_B⃗(B⃗'₀, α₀ = ρ); B⃗'₁ := Constrain_B⃗(B⃗'₁, α₁ = ρ);
13:         add ρ ↦ α₀ to M₀ and ρ ↦ α₁ to M₁ ;
14:         add t ↦ ρ to G ;
15:         add α₀ to Visited₀ and α₁ to Visited₁ ;
16:         find each f(β⃗₀) ∈ domain(G₀) and f(β⃗₁) ∈ domain(G₁) such that
            β⃗₀ ⊆ Visited₀ ∧ α₀ ∈ β⃗₀ ∧ β⃗₁ ⊆ Visited₁ ∧ α₁ ∈ β⃗₁
            and add each ⟨f(β⃗), G₀(f(β⃗₀)), G₁(f(β⃗₁))⟩ to W such that
            M₀(β⃗) = β⃗₀ ∧ M₁(β⃗) = β⃗₁ ∧ ρ ∈ β⃗
17:      end if
18:   end while;
19:   ⟨G, Join_B⃗(B⃗'₀, B⃗'₁)⟩
20: end fun
```

Fig. 3. The join for the congruence-closure abstract domain.

$\mathtt{Constrain}_{\vec{B}}(\vec{B}'_0, \alpha_0 = \rho)$, we can call $\mathtt{Rename}_{\vec{B}}(\vec{B}'_0, \alpha_0, \rho)$ since α_0 will not be a symbolic value in the result e-graph (and similarly for G_1).

Soundness. We show that the above join algorithm indeed gives an upper bound. Note that since the $\mathtt{Constrain}_{\vec{B}}$ calls on the base domain simply give multiple names to existing variables, the soundness of $\mathtt{Join}_e$ reduces to soundness of the join of the e-graphs (assuming the joins of the base domains are sound). We write $Join_{\mathcal{G}}$ for the algorithm described in Fig. 3 ignoring the base domains. Informally, $Join_{\mathcal{G}}$ is sound if for any equality implied by the resulting e-graph, it is implied by both input e-graphs. The formal statement of the soundness theorem is given below, while its proof is given in our extended paper [5].

Theorem 1 (Soundness of $Join_{\mathcal{G}}$) *Let* $G = Join_{\mathcal{G}}(G_0, G_1)$. *If* $G \Vdash e_0 = e_1$, *then* $G_0 \Vdash e_0 = e_1$ *and* $G_1 \Vdash e_0 = e_1$.

Completeness. Note that different e-graphs can represent the same lattice element. For example, consider the following e-graphs

$$x \mapsto \alpha \quad y \mapsto \alpha \qquad \text{(Ex. 3a)} \qquad x \mapsto \alpha \quad y \mapsto \alpha \quad \mathsf{f}(\alpha) \mapsto \beta \quad \text{(Ex. 3b)}$$

that both represent the constraint $x = y$ (and any implied congruences). For the previous operations, the element that is represented by the result was the same regardless of the form of the e-graph in the input; however, the precision of the join algorithm is actually sensitive to the particular e-graph given as input. For example, the join of the e-graphs shown in Ex. 3a and Ex. 3b with an e-graph representing the constraint $\mathsf{f}(x) = \mathsf{f}(y)$ yields elements true and $\mathsf{f}(x) = \mathsf{f}(y)$, respectively, as shown below:

$$\mathsf{Join}_{\mathcal{G}}(\{x \mapsto \alpha, y \mapsto \alpha\}, \{x \mapsto \gamma, y \mapsto \delta, \mathsf{f}(\gamma) \mapsto \varepsilon, \mathsf{f}(\delta) \mapsto \varepsilon\}) = \{x \mapsto \rho, y \mapsto \sigma\}$$
$$\mathsf{Join}_{\mathcal{G}}(\{x \mapsto \alpha, y \mapsto \alpha, \mathsf{f}(\alpha) \mapsto \beta\}, \{x \mapsto \gamma, y \mapsto \delta, \mathsf{f}(\gamma) \mapsto \varepsilon, \mathsf{f}(\delta) \mapsto \varepsilon\})$$
$$= \{x \mapsto \rho, y \mapsto \sigma, \mathsf{f}(\rho) \mapsto \tau, \mathsf{f}(\sigma) \mapsto \tau\}$$

A naïve idea might be to extend e-graph (Ex. 3a) to (Ex. 3b) in the join algorithm as necessary; however, the algorithm no longer terminates if the join in the lattice $\mathcal{E}$ is not representable as a finite conjunction of equality constraints plus their implied congruences. Recall that Ex. 2 shows that such a non-representable join is possible.

Ex. 2 does, however, suggest that $\mathsf{Join}_{\mathcal{G}}$ can be made arbitrarily precise though not absolutely precise. In fact, the precision is controlled exactly by what terms are represented in the e-graph. If an equality is represented in both input e-graphs to $\mathsf{Join}_{\mathcal{G}}$, then that equality will be implied by the result e-graph. In fact, a slightly stronger statement holds that says that the equality will also be represented in the result e-graph. Thus, the precision of the join can be controlled by the client by introducing expressions it cares about in the initial e-graph. We state the completeness theorem formally below, while its proof is given in the extended version [5].

Theorem 2 (Relative Completeness of $\mathsf{Join}_{\mathcal{G}}$) *Let* $G = \mathsf{Join}_{\mathcal{G}}(G_0, G_1)$. *If* $G_0 \vdash e_0 \Downarrow \alpha_0$, $G_0 \vdash e_1 \Downarrow \alpha_0$, $G_1 \vdash e_0 \Downarrow \alpha_1$, *and* $G_1 \vdash e_1 \Downarrow \alpha_1$, *then* $G \Vdash e_0 = e_1$.

This theorem, however, does not directly indicate anything about the precision of the entire join $\mathsf{Join}_{\mathcal{E}}$. While without the calls to $\mathsf{Constrain}_{\vec{\mathcal{B}}}$, much information would be lost, it is not clear if as much as possible is preserved. Gulwani *et al.* [9] give the following challenge for obtaining precise combinations of join algorithms. Let $E_0 \stackrel{\text{def}}{=} a = a' \wedge b = b'$ and $E_1 \stackrel{\text{def}}{=} a = b' \wedge b = a'$, then

$$E_0 \sqcup_{\mathcal{E}} E_1 \equiv \text{true} \qquad\qquad E_0 \sqcup_{\mathcal{P}} E_1 \equiv a + b = a' + b'$$
$$E_0 \sqcup_{\mathcal{E},\mathcal{P}} E_1 \sqsubseteq_{\mathcal{E},\mathcal{P}} \bigwedge_{i:\, i \geqslant 0} f^i(a) + f^i(b) = f^i(a') + f^i(b')$$

where $\mathcal{P}$ is the polyhedra abstract domain and $\mathcal{E}, \mathcal{P}$ is a hypothetical combination of equalities of uninterpreted functions and linear arithmetic. Note that the combined join also yields an infinite conjunction of equalities not representable by our e-graph. Thus, we cannot achieve absolute completeness using the congruence-closure domain with the polyhedra domain as a base domain;

however, we do achieve an analogous relative completeness where we obtain all conjuncts where the terms are represented in the input e-graphs. In the table below, we show the e-graphs for E_0 and E_1 with one application of f to each variable explicitly represented and the join of these e-graphs. Consider the input elements for the polyhedra domain to be $\mathrm{Top}_\mathcal{P}$. We show the elements after the calls to $\mathrm{Constrain}_\mathcal{P}$ during $\mathrm{Join}_\mathcal{E}$ and the final result after the polyhedra join.

	C_0		C_1		$\mathrm{Join}_\mathcal{E}(C_0, C_1)$	
E-Graph	$a \mapsto \alpha_0$	$b \mapsto \beta_0$	$a \mapsto \alpha_1$	$b \mapsto \beta_1$	$a \mapsto \rho$	$b \mapsto \tau$
	$a' \mapsto \alpha_0$	$b' \mapsto \beta_0$	$b' \mapsto \alpha_1$	$a' \mapsto \beta_1$	$a' \mapsto \sigma$	$b' \mapsto \upsilon$
	$\mathsf{f}(\alpha_0) \mapsto \gamma_0$	$\mathsf{f}(\beta_0) \mapsto \delta_0$	$\mathsf{f}(\alpha_1) \mapsto \gamma_1$	$\mathsf{f}(\beta_1) \mapsto \delta_1$	$\mathsf{f}(\rho) \mapsto \phi$	$\mathsf{f}(\tau) \mapsto \psi$
					$\mathsf{f}(\sigma) \mapsto \chi$	$\mathsf{f}(\upsilon) \mapsto \omega$
Polyhedra	$\alpha_0 = \rho = \sigma$	$\beta_0 = \tau = \upsilon$	$\alpha_1 = \rho = \upsilon$	$\beta_1 = \tau = \sigma$	$\rho + \tau = \sigma + \upsilon$	
(after $\mathrm{Constrains}$)	$\gamma_0 = \phi = \chi$	$\delta_0 = \psi = \omega$	$\gamma_1 = \phi = \omega$	$\delta_1 = \psi = \chi$	$\phi + \psi = \chi + \omega$	

$\mathrm{ToPredicate}_\mathcal{E}$ on the result yields $a + b = a' + b' \wedge \mathsf{f}(a) + \mathsf{f}(b) = \mathsf{f}(a') + \mathsf{f}(b')$, as desired. (Gulwani and Tiwari have indicated that they have a similar solution for this example.) Note that there are no equality constraints in the resulting e-graph; these equalities are only reflected in the base domain. This example suggests that such equalities inferred by a base domain should be propagated back to the e-graph in case those terms exist in the e-graph for another base domain where such a term is alien (akin to equality sharing of Nelson-Oppen [15]).

3.6 Widen

Unfortunately, the above join operation successively applied to an ascending chain of elements may not stabilize (even without consideration of the base domains), as can be demonstrated by the following example. Let G_i (for $i \geqslant 0$) be an ascending chain of e-graphs representing $x = \mathsf{f}^{2^i}(x)$. Then,

$$G_0' = G_0 \quad G_1' = \mathrm{Join}_\mathcal{G}(G_0', G_1) = G_1 \quad G_2' = \mathrm{Join}_\mathcal{G}(G_1', G_2) = G_2 \quad \cdots$$

does not reach a fixed point. The above sequence does not converge because a cycle in the e-graph yields an infinite number of client expressions that evaluate to a symbolic value (by following the loop several times). Thus, a non-stabilizing chain can be constructed by joining with a chain that successively rules out terms that follow the loop less than k times (as given above). The same would be true for acyclic graphs with the join algorithm that adds additional terms to the e-graph as necessary to be complete. Therefore, we can define $\mathrm{Widen}_\mathcal{E}$ by following the join algorithm described in Fig. 3 except fixing a finite limit on the number of times a cycle can be followed in G_0 (and calling $\mathrm{Widen}_{\vec{\mathcal{B}}}$ on the base domains rather than $\mathrm{Join}_{\vec{\mathcal{B}}}$). Once the e-graph part stabilizes, since the set of symbolic values are fixed up to renaming, the base domains will also stabilize by the stabilizing property of $\mathrm{Widen}_{\vec{\mathcal{B}}}$.

4 Heap Structures

In this section, we specifically consider programs with heaps, such as object-oriented programs. We view a heap as an array indexed by heap locations. Therefore, what we say here more generally applies also to arrays and records.

4.1 Heap-Aware Programs

We consider an imperative programming language with expressions to read object fields ($o.x$) and statements to update object fields ($o.x := e$). To analyze these programs, we explicitly represent the heap by a program variable H. The heap is an array indexed by heap locations $\langle o, \mathsf{x} \rangle$, where o denotes an object identity and x is a field name.

A field read expression $o.x$ in the language is treated simply as a shorthand for $\mathsf{sel}(H, o, \mathsf{x})$. Intuitively, this function retrieves the value of H at location $\langle o, \mathsf{x} \rangle$. Thus, from what we have already said, the congruence-closure domain allows us to infer properties of programs that read fields. For example, using the polyhedra domain as a base domain on the program in Fig. 1(b), we infer arithmetic properties like $y = \mathsf{sel}(H, o, \mathsf{x}) \land 0 \leqslant \mathsf{sel}(H, o, \mathsf{x})$ after the statement in the true-branch and $0 \leqslant y$ after the entire program.

The semantics of the field update statement $o.x := e$ is usually defined as an assignment $H := \mathsf{upd}(H, o, x, e)$ (*cf.* [10, 11, 16]), where upd is a function with the following axiomatization:

$$\mathsf{sel}(\mathsf{upd}(H, o, x, e), o', x') = e \qquad \text{if } o = o' \text{ and } x = x'$$
$$\mathsf{sel}(\mathsf{upd}(H, o, x, e), o', x') = \mathsf{sel}(H, o', x') \qquad \text{if } o \neq o' \text{ or } x \neq x'$$

We choose a slightly different formulation introducing the *heap succession* predicate $H \equiv_{o.x} H'$, which means H' is an updated heap equivalent to H everywhere except possibly at $o.x$. We thus regard the field update statement $o.x := e$ as the following assignment:

$$H := H' \quad \text{where } H' \text{ is such that } H \equiv_{o.x} H' \text{ and } \mathsf{sel}(H', o, x) = e$$

A more precise semantics is given in the extended version [5].

Unfortunately, this is not enough to be useful in the analysis of heap structured programs. Consider the program in Fig. 1(d). Applying the congruence-closure domain with, say, the polyhedra domain as a single base domain gives the disappointingly weak predicate **true** after the entire program. The problem is that an analysis of the field update statement will effect a call to the operation $\mathtt{Eliminate}_{\mathcal{C}}(\langle G, \vec{B} \rangle, H)$ on the congruence-closure domain, which has the effect of losing all the information that syntactically depends on H. This is because no base domain $\mathcal{B}_i$ is able to return an expression in response to the congruence-closure domain's call to $\mathtt{EquivalentExpr}_{\mathcal{B}_i}(B_i, Q, \mathsf{sel}(H, o, \mathsf{x}), H)$ (or more precisely, with expression $\mathsf{sel}(\sigma, \phi, \chi)$ and variable σ that are the corresponding symbolic values).

To remedy the situation, we develop an abstract domain that tracks heap updates. Simply including this abstract domain as a base domain in our congruence-closure abstract domain solves this problem.

4.2   Heap Succession Abstract Domain

A lattice element in the *heap succession abstract domain* S represents false or a conjunction of heap succession predicates

$$(\exists \ldots \bullet H_0 \equiv_{o_0.x_0} H_1 \wedge H_1 \equiv_{o_1.x_1} H_2 \wedge \cdots \wedge H_{n-1} \equiv_{o_{n-1}.x_{n-1}} H_n)$$

for some $n \geqslant 0$, where the H_i, o_i, and x_i are variables, some of which may be existentially bound, and where no H_i is repeated.

The heap succession domain, like any other base domain, works only with variables and implements the abstract domain interface. However, of primary importance is that it can often return useful results to `EquivalentExpr` calls. Specifically, it substitutes newer heap variables for older heap variables in expressions when it is sound to do so, which is exactly what we need. The operation `EquivalentExpr`$_S(S, Q, t, H)$ returns nothing unless t has the form $\mathsf{sel}(H, o, x)$ and element S contains a successor of heap H. If there is a heap successor H' of H, that is, if S contains a predicate $H \equiv_{p.y} H'$, then S first determines whether $o \neq p \vee x \neq y$ (*i.e.*, whether the references o and p are known to be unaliased or the fields are distinct). If it finds that $o \neq p \vee x \neq y$ and H' is not existentially bound, then the operation returns the expression $\mathsf{sel}(H', o, x)$; otherwise, the operation iterates, this time looking for a heap successor of H'. If x and y denote two different fields (which are represented as 0-ary functions), the condition is easy to determine. If not, the heap succession domain may need to query the other abstract domains via Q to find out if any other abstract domain knows that $o \neq p$.

4.3   Preserving Information Across Heap Updates

We give an example to illustrate how the heap succession domain can allow information to be preserved across heap updates. Consider a heap update statement $o.x := z$ and suppose that before the update, the abstract domains have the information that $p.y = 8$ (*i.e.*, $\mathsf{sel}(H, p, y) = 8$). After the update to $o.x$, we hope to preserve this information, since the update is to a different field name. Consider the relevant mappings in the e-graph after the update:

$$
\begin{array}{cccc}
& H \mapsto \sigma' & \mathsf{sel}(\sigma, \psi, \upsilon) \mapsto \alpha & \mathsf{sel}(\sigma', \phi, \chi) \mapsto \zeta \\
p \mapsto \psi & o \mapsto \phi & 8 \mapsto \alpha & z \mapsto \zeta \\
y \mapsto \upsilon & x \mapsto \chi & &
\end{array}
$$

while the heap succession domain has the following constraint: $\sigma \equiv_{\phi.\chi} \sigma'$. The old heap σ is now a garbage value. Recall that during garbage collection before σ is eliminated from the base domain, the congruence-closure domain will call `EquivalentExpr`$_{B_i}$ to ask each base domain B_i whether it can give an equivalent expression for $\mathsf{sel}(\sigma, \psi, \upsilon)$ without σ. In this case, the heap succession domain can return $\mathsf{sel}(\sigma', \psi, \upsilon)$ because field name constants x and y are distinct. Thus, the information that $\mathsf{sel}(H, p, y) = 8$ is preserved. In the same way, the congruence-closure domain with heap succession and polyhedra as base domains computes $0 \leqslant o.x \wedge N \leqslant o.x \wedge 0 \leqslant p.y$ after the program in Fig. 1(d).

5   Related Work

Gulwani *et al.* [9] describe several join algorithms for both special cases of the theory of uninterpreted functions and in general. The representation of equality constraints they consider, called an *abstract congruence closure* [1, 2], is a convergent set of rewrite rules of the form $f(c_0, c_1, \ldots, c_{n-1}) \rightarrow c$ or $c_0 \rightarrow c$ for fresh constants $c, c_0, c_1, \ldots, c_{n-1}$. If the latter form is excluded, then we obtain something analogous to our e-graph where the fresh constants are our symbolic values. In fact, because the latter form can lead to many different sets of rewrite rules for the same set of equality constraints, Gulwani *et al.* quickly define a *fully reduced* abstract congruence closure that precisely excludes the latter form and then only work with fully reduced abstract congruence closures. Our work goes further by introducing the concept of base domains and recognizing that symbolic values can be used to hide alien expressions. Gulwani *et al.* discuss an item of future work to combine their join algorithm for the theory of uninterpreted functions with some other join algorithm (*e.g.*, for linear arithmetic) and a challenge for such a combination. Using the congruence-closure abstract domain with polyhedra as a base domain, we seem to stand up to the challenge (see Sec. 3.5).

Previous research in the area of abstract interpretation and dynamic data structures has centered around *shape analysis* [14], which determines patterns of connectivity between pointers in the heap. Using transitive closure, shape analysis can reason about reachability in the heap and abstracts many heap objects into so-called summary nodes. Our technique of combining abstract domains does not specifically attempt to abstract objects into summary nodes, though it would be interesting to consider the possibility of using such a shape analyzer as a base domain in our technique. In shape analysis, properties of nodes can be encoded as specially interpreted predicates (*cf.* [17, 12]). Our technique differs in that it extends the representable properties of nodes by simply plugging in, as base domains, classic abstract domains that reason only with relations among variables. This feature allows our analysis to obtain properties like $o.f \leqslant p.g$ with an "off-the-shelf" polyhedra implementation.

Logozzo uses abstract interpretation to infer object invariants with several objects but with some restrictions on the possible aliasing among object references [13]. The abstract domains described in this paper might be able to be used as building blocks for another method for inferring object invariants.

6   Conclusion

We have described a technique to extend any abstract domain to handle constraints over arbitrary terms, not just variables, via a coordinating abstract domain of congruences. Moreover, this technique is designed so that abstract domains can be used mostly unmodified and oblivious to its extended reasoning. To implement the congruence-closure domain, we have given a sound and relatively complete algorithm to join e-graphs.

Additionally, we have described the heap succession domain, which allows our framework to handle heap updates. This domain need only be a base domain and thus fits modularly into our framework. Lastly, the handling of heap updates can be improved modularly through other base domains that yield better alias (or rather, unaliased) information.

We have a prototype implementation of our technique in the abstract interpretation engine of the Spec# program verifier, which is part of the Spec# programming system [3], and are in the process of obtaining experience with it.

Our work is perhaps a step toward having a uniform way to combine abstract domains, analogous to the Nelson-Oppen algorithm for cooperating decision procedures [15]. For example, continuing to assign symbolic values to subexpressions of alien expressions, as well as notifying base domains of additional understandable subexpressions suggests some kind of potential sharing of information between abstract domains. The structure of our framework that uses a coordinating abstract domain of congruences is perhaps also reminiscent of Nelson-Oppen. While equality information flows from the congruence-closure domain to the base domains, to achieve cooperating abstract domains, we need to add a way for each base domain to propagate information, like equalities that it discovers, to the congruence-closure domain and other base domains. We believe exploring this connection would be an exciting line of research.

Acknowledgments. We thank Simon Ou and River Sun for helpful discussions about the e-graph join algorithm. Francesco Logozzo provided extensive comments on an early version of some work leading to the present paper. Rob Klapper participated in a preliminary study of applying abstract interpretation to object-oriented programs. Sumit Gulwani and the anonymous referees provided useful comments on earlier drafts. Finally, we thank the rest of the Spec# team at Microsoft Research for various discussions.

References

1. Leo Bachmair and Ashish Tiwari. Abstract congruence closure and specializations. In David McAllester, editor, *Conference on Automated Deduction (CADE 2000)*, volume 1831 of *LNAI*, pages 64–78, June 2000.
2. Leo Bachmair, Ashish Tiwari, and Laurent Vigneron. Abstract congruence closure. *Journal of Automated Reasoning*, 31(2):129–168, 2003.
3. Mike Barnett, K. Rustan M. Leino, and Wolfram Schulte. The Spec# programming system: An overview. In *Construction and Analysis of Safe, Secure and Interoperable Smart devices (CASSIS)*, LNCS. Springer, 2004. To appear.
4. Garrett Birkhoff. *Lattice Theory*, volume XXV of *Colloquium Publications*. American Mathematical Society, 1940.
5. Bor-Yuh Evan Chang and K. Rustan M. Leino. Abstract interpretation with alien expressions and heap structures. Technical Report MSR-TR-2004-115, Microsoft Research, November 2004.
6. Patrick Cousot and Radhia Cousot. Abstract interpretation: a unified lattice model for static analysis of programs by construction or approximation of fixpoints. In *Fourth POPL*, pages 238–252, January 1977.

7. Patrick Cousot and Radhia Cousot. Systematic design of program analysis frameworks. In *Sixth POPL*, pages 269–282, January 1979.
8. Patrick Cousot and Nicolas Halbwachs. Automatic discovery of linear restraints among variables of a program. In *Fifth POPL*, pages 84–96, January 1978.
9. Sumit Gulwani, Ashish Tiwari, and George C. Necula. Join algorithms for the theory of uninterpreted functions. In *24th Conference on Foundations of Software Technology and Theoretical Computer Science (FSTTCS 2004)*, December 2004.
10. C. A. R. Hoare and N. Wirth. An axiomatic definition of the programming language PASCAL. *Acta Informatica*, 2(4):335–355, 1973.
11. K. Rustan M. Leino. *Toward Reliable Modular Programs*. PhD thesis, California Institute of Technology, 1995. Available as Technical Report Caltech-CS-TR-95-03.
12. Tal Lev-Ami, Thomas Reps, Mooly Sagiv, and Reinhard Wilhelm. Putting static analysis to work for verification: A case study. In *International Symposium on Software Testing and Analysis (ISSTA 2000)*, pages 26–38, 2000.
13. Francesco Logozzo. Separate compositional analysis of class-based object-oriented languages. In *10th International Conference on Algebraic Methodology And Software Technology (AMAST'2004)*, volume 3116 of *LNCS*, pages 332–346. Springer, July 2004.
14. Steven S. Muchnick and Neil D. Jones. Flow analysis and optimization of Lisp-like structures. In Steven S. Muchnick and Neil D. Jones, editors, *Program Flow Analysis: Theory and Applications*, chapter 4, pages 102–131. Prentice-Hall, 1981.
15. Greg Nelson and Derek C. Oppen. Simplification by cooperating decision procedures. *ACM Transactions on Programming Languages and Systems*, 1(2):245–257, October 1979.
16. Arnd Poetzsch-Heffter. Specification and verification of object-oriented programs. Habilitationsschrift, Technische Universität München, 1997.
17. Mooly Sagiv, Thomas W. Reps, and Reinhard Wilhelm. Parametric shape analysis via 3-valued logic. *ACM Transactions on Programming Languages and Systems*, 24(3):217–298, 2002.

A   Graphical View of the E-Graph

We can view the e-graph as a rooted directed graph where the vertices are the symbolic values (plus a distinguished root node) and the edges are the terms. Variables and 0-ary functions are labeled edges from the root node to the symbolic value to which they map. The n-ary functions are multi-edges with the (ordered) source nodes being the arguments of the function and the destination node being the symbolic value to which they map labeled with the function symbol. More precisely, let G be a mapping in Sec. 3, then the corresponding graph is defined as follows:

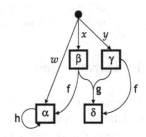

Fig. 4. An e-graph.

$$\text{vertices}(G) = \text{range}(G) \cup \{\bullet\}$$
$$\text{edges}(G) = \left\{ \bullet \xrightarrow{x} G(x) \;\middle|\; x \in \text{domain}(G) \right\} \cup \left\{ \vec{\alpha} \xrightarrow{f} G(f(\vec{\alpha})) \;\middle|\; f(\vec{\alpha}) \in \text{domain}(G) \right\}$$

where $\bullet$ stands for the distinguished root node, as well as the empty sequence. Fig. 4 gives the graph for Ex. 1.

Shape Analysis by Predicate Abstraction*

Ittai Balaban[1], Amir Pnueli[1], and Lenore D. Zuck[2]

[1] New York University, New York
{balaban,amir}@cs.nyu.edu
[2] University of Illinois at Chicago
lenore@cs.uic.edu

Abstract. The paper presents an approach for shape analysis based on predicate abstraction. Using a predicate base that involves reachability relations between program variables pointing into the heap, we are able to analyze functional properties of programs with destructive heap updates, such as list reversal and various in-place list sorts. The approach allows verification of both safety and liveness properties. The abstraction we use does not require any abstract representation of the heap nodes (e.g. abstract shapes), only reachability relations between the program variables.

The computation of the abstract transition relation is precise and automatic yet does not require the use of a theorem prover. Instead, we use a small model theorem to identify a truncated (small) finite-state version of the program whose abstraction is identical to the abstraction of the unbounded-heap version of the same program. The abstraction of the finite-state version is then computed by BDD techniques.

For proving liveness properties, we augment the original system by a well-founded ranking function, which is abstracted together with the system. Well-foundedness is then abstracted into strong fairness (compassion). We show that, for a restricted class of programs that still includes many interesting cases, the small model theorem can be applied to this joint abstraction.

Independently of the application to shape-analysis examples, we demonstrate the utility of the ranking abstraction method and its advantages over the direct use of ranking functions in a deductive verification of the same property.

1 Introduction

The goal of *shape analysis* is to analyze properties of programs that perform destructive updating on dynamically allocated storage (heaps) [11]. Programs manipulating heap structures can be viewed as *parameterized* in the number of heap nodes, or, alternatively, the memory size.

This paper presents an approach for shape analysis based on *predicate abstraction* that allows for analyses of functional properties such as safety and liveness. The abstraction used does *not* require any abstract representation of the heap nodes (e.g. abstract shapes), but rather, requires only reachability relations between the program variables.

---

* This research was supported in part by NSF grant CCR-0205571 and ONR grant N00014-99-1-0131

R. Cousot (Ed.): VMCAI 2005, LNCS 3385, pp. 164–180, 2005.

States are abstracted using a predicate base that contains reachability relations among program variables pointing into the heap. The computation of the abstract states and transition relation is precise and automatic and does not require the use of a theorem prover. Rather, we use a small model theorem to identify a truncated (small) finite-state version of the program whose abstraction is identical to the abstraction of the unbounded-heap version of the same program. The abstraction of the finite-state version is then computed by BDD techniques.

For proving liveness properties, we augment the original system by a well-founded ranking function, which is then abstracted together with the system. Well-foundedness is abstracted into strong fairness (compassion). We show that, for a restricted class of programs (that still includes numerous interesting cases), the small model theorem can be applied to this joint abstraction.

We demonstrate the power of the ranking abstraction method and its advantages over direct use of ranking functions in a deductive verification of the same property, independent of its application to shape-analysis examples.

The method is illustrated on two examples, both using (singly) linked lists: List reversal and in-place sort. We show how various predicate abstractions can be used to establish various safety properties, and how, for each program, one of the abstractions can be augmented with a progress monitor to establish termination.

The paper is organized as follows. Section 2 describes the formal model of *fair transitions systems* and their finite heap version, *finite heap systems*. Section 3 has an overview of finitary abstraction and predicate abstraction. Section 4 deals with the symbolic computation of abstractions. It states and proves the small model property, and describes how to apply it to obtain abstract finite heap systems. Section 5 deals with proving liveness of heap systems. Sections 2–5 use a list reversal program as a running example. Section 6 presents a more involved example of a nested loop bubble sort, and shows its formal verification using the new method.

Related Work

The work in [16] presents a parametric framework for shape analysis that deals with the specification language of the shape analysis framework and the construction of the shape analyzer from the specification. A 2-value logic is used to represent concrete stores, and a 3-valued logic is used to represent abstract stores. Properties are specified by first-order formulae with transitive closure; these also describe the transitions of the system. The shape analyzer computes a fixed point of the set of equations that are generated from the analysis specification. The systems considered in [16] are more general than ours, e.g., we allow at most one "next pointer" for each node. Due to the restricted systems and properties we consider, we do not have to abstract the heap structure itself, and therefore our computation of the transition relation is precise. Moreover, their work does not handle liveness properties.

In [7], Dams and Namjoshi study shape analysis using predicate abstraction and model checking. Starting with shape predicates and a property, the method iteratively computes weakest preconditions to find more predicates and constructs abstract programs that are then model checked. As in the [16] framework, the abstraction computed in not precise. Some manual intervention is required to apply widening-like techniques and guide the system into convergence. This work, too, does not handle liveness.

There are several works studying logics for shape analysis. E.g., [5] present a decidable logic for reasoning about heap structures. No treatment of liveness is described.

Some related but less relevant works are [9, 8] that study concurrent garbage collection using predicate abstraction, [10] that study loop invariants using predicate abstraction, and [13] that calculates weakest preconditions for reachability. All these works do not apply shape analysis or use shape predicates.

2   The Formal Framework

In this section we present our computation model.

2.1   Fair Discrete Systems

As our computational model, we take a *fair discrete system* (FDS) $S = \langle V, \Theta, \rho, \mathcal{J}, \mathcal{C} \rangle$, where

- V — A set of *system variables*. A *state* of S provides a type-consistent interpretation of the variables V. For a state s and a system variable $v \in V$, we denote by $s[v]$ the value assigned to v by the state s. Let Σ denote the set of all states over V.
- Θ — The *initial condition*: An assertion (state formula) characterizing the initial states.
- $\rho(V, V')$ — The *transition relation*: An assertion, relating the values V of the variables in state $s \in \Sigma$ to the values V' in an S-successor state $s' \in \Sigma$.
- $\mathcal{J}$ — A set of *justice (weak fairness)* requirements (assertions); A computation must include infinitely many states satisfying each of the justice requirements.
- $\mathcal{C}$ — A set of *compassion (strong fairness)* requirements: Each compassion requirement is a pair $\langle p, q \rangle$ of state assertions; A computation should include either only finitely many p-states, or infinitely many q-states.

For an assertion ψ, we say that $s \in \Sigma$ is a ψ-state if $s \models \psi$.

A *computation* of an FDS S is an infinite sequence of states $\sigma : s_0, s_1, s_2, ...$, satisfying the requirements:

- *Initiality* — s_0 is initial, i.e., $s_0 \models \Theta$.
- *Consecution* — For each $\ell = 0, 1, ...$, the state $s_{\ell+1}$ is an S-successor of s_ℓ. That is, $\langle s_\ell, s_{\ell+1} \rangle \models \rho(V, V')$ where, for each $v \in V$, we interpret v as $s_\ell[v]$ and v' as $s_{\ell+1}[v]$.
- *Justice* — for every $J \in \mathcal{J}$, σ contains infinitely many occurrences of J-states.
- *Compassion* – for every $\langle p, q \rangle \in \mathcal{C}$, either σ contains only finitely many occurrences of p-states, or σ contains infinitely many occurrences of q-states.

2.2   Finite Heap Systems

To allow the automatic computation of abstractions, we place further restrictions on the systems we study, leading to the model of *finite heap systems* (FHS), that is essentially the model of bounded discrete systems of [2] specialized to the case of heap programs.

For brevity, we describe here a simplified two-type model; the extension for the general multi-type case is straightforward.

We allow the following data types parameterized by the positive integer h, intended to specify the heap size:

1. **bool**: boolean and finite-range scalars; With no loss of generality, we assume that all finite domain values are encoded as booleans.
2. **index**: $[0..h]$;
3. Arrays of the types **index** $\mapsto$ **bool** (**bool** array) and **index** $\mapsto$ **index** (**index** array).

We assume a signature of variables of all of these types. Constants are introduced as variables with reserved names. Thus, we admit the boolean constants $\mathbf{0}$ and $\mathbf{1}$, and the **index** constant nil. An additional reserved-name variable is H : **index** whose value is always h.

We often refer to an element of type **index** as a *node*. If the interpretation of an **index** variable x in a state s is ℓ, then we say that in s, x *points to the node* ℓ. An **index** *term* is an **index** variable or an expression $Z[y]$, where Z is an **index** array and y is an **index** variable.

Atomic formulas are defined as follows:

- If x is a boolean variable, B is a **index** $\mapsto$ **bool** array, and y is an **index** variable, then x and $B[y]$ are atomic formulas.
- If t_1 and t_2 are **index** terms, then $t_1 = t_2$ is an atomic formula.
- A *Transitive closure* formula *(tcf)* of the form $Z^*(x_1, x_2)$, denoting that x_2 is Z-reachable from x_1, where x_1 and x_2 are **index** variables and Z is an **index** array.

A *restricted A-assertion* is a formula of the form $\forall \vec{y}.\psi(\vec{x}, \vec{y})$, where $\vec{y}$ is a list of **index** variables that do not include nil, and $\psi(\vec{x}, \vec{y})$ is a boolean combination of atomic formulas such that the only atomic formulas referring to a universally quantified y are of the forms $B[y]$, $y = u$, or $Z_1[y] = Z_2[y]$ under positive polarity. In particular, note that in restricted A-assertions, universally quantified variables may *not* occur in tcf's. As the initial condition Θ, the transition relation ρ, as well as the fairness requirements, we only allow restricted A-assertions.

The definition of restricted A-assertions allows for programs that manipulate heap elements strictly via a constant set of *reference* variables, which is in accordance with most programming languages. The set of operations that are allowed is however greatly restricted. For example, arithmetic operations are not allowed. While the present definition doesn't allow inequalities, it is not hard to extend it to support them.

Example 1 (List Reversal). Consider program LIST-REVERSAL in Fig. 1, which is a simple list reversal program. The array Nxt describes the pointer structure. We ignore the actual data values, but they can easily be added as **bool** type variables.

Fig. 2 describes the FHS corresponding to program LIST-REVERSAL. The expression $pres(V_1)$ is an abbreviation for $\bigwedge_{v \in V_1}(v' = v)$, i.e., $pres(V_1)$ means that all the variables in V_1 are not changed by the transition. The expression $pres\text{-}array(Nxt, U)$ is an abbreviation for $\forall u \in \textbf{index}.u \notin U \rightarrow (Nxt'[u] = Nxt[u])$. Note that all the clauses in Fig. 2 are restricted assertions. The justice requirement states that as long as the program has not terminated, its execution continues.

$$
\boxed{
\begin{array}{l}
H \quad : \textbf{integer where } H = h \\
x, y \; : [0..h] \textbf{ init } y = nil \\
\quad Nxt \; : \textbf{array } [0..h] \textbf{ of } [0..h] \\
\left[
\begin{array}{ll}
1 : \textbf{while } x \neq nil \textbf{ do} \\
2 : \quad\quad (x, y, Nxt[x]) := (Nxt[x], x, y) \\
\quad\quad \textbf{end} \\
3 :
\end{array}
\right]
\end{array}
}
$$

Fig. 1. Program LIST-REVERSAL

$$
V : \left\{
\begin{array}{l}
H : \quad \textbf{integer} \\
x, y : [0..h] \\
Nxt : \textbf{array } [0..h] \textbf{ of } [0..h] \\
\pi : \quad [1..3]
\end{array}
\right.
$$

$\Theta : H = h \;\wedge\; \pi = 1 \;\wedge\; y = nil$

$$
\rho : \left[
\begin{array}{l}
\quad \pi = 1 \;\wedge\; x = nil \;\wedge\; \pi' = 3 \;\wedge\; pres(\{H, x, y\}) \;\wedge\; \textit{pres-array}(Nxt, \emptyset) \\
\vee \;\; \pi = 1 \;\wedge\; x \neq nil \;\wedge\; \pi' = 2 \;\wedge\; pres(\{H, x, y\}) \;\wedge\; \textit{pres-array}(Nxt, \emptyset) \\
\vee \;\; \pi = 2 \;\wedge\; x' = Nxt[x] \;\wedge\; y' = x \;\wedge\; Nxt'[x] = y \;\wedge\; \pi' = 1 \;\wedge \\
\quad pres(\{H\}) \;\wedge\; \textit{pres-array}(Nxt, \{x\}) \\
\vee \;\; \pi = 3 \;\wedge\; \pi' = 3 \;\wedge\; pres(\{H, x, y, \pi\}) \;\wedge\; \textit{pres-array}(Nxt, \emptyset)
\end{array}
\right]
$$

$\mathcal{J} : \{\pi \neq 1, \pi \neq 2\}$

$\mathcal{C} : \emptyset$

Fig. 2. FHS for Program LIST-REVERSAL

3   Abstraction

We fix an FHS $S = \langle V, \Theta, \rho, \mathcal{J}, \mathcal{C} \rangle$ whose set of states is Σ for this section.

3.1   Finitary Abstraction

The material here is an overview of (a somewhat simplified version of) [12]. See there for details.

An *abstraction* is a mapping $\alpha : \Sigma \to \Sigma_A$ for some set Σ_A of *abstract states*. The abstraction α is *finitary* if the set of abstract states Σ_A is finite. We focus on abstractions that can be represented by a set of equations of the form $u_i = E_i(V)$, $i = 1, \ldots, n$, where the E_i's are assertions over the concrete variables (V) and $\{u_1, \ldots, u_n\}$ is the set of *abstract variables*, denoted by V_A. Alternatively, such α can be expressed by:

$$
V_A = \mathcal{E}_\alpha(V)
$$

For an assertion $p(V)$, we define its abstraction by:

$$
\alpha(p) : \quad \exists V.(V_A = \mathcal{E}_A(V) \;\wedge\; p(V))
$$

The semantics of $\alpha(p)$ is $\|\alpha(p)\| = \{\alpha(s) \mid s \in \|p\|\}$. Note that $\|\alpha(p)\|$ is, in general, an over-approximation – an abstract state is in $\|\alpha(p)\|$ iff *there exists* some concrete

p-state that is abstracted into it. An assertion $p(V, V')$ over both primed and unprimed variables is abstracted by:

$$\alpha(p): \quad \exists V, V'.(V_A = \mathcal{E}_A(V) \wedge V'_A = \mathcal{E}_A(V') \wedge p(V, V'))$$

The assertion p is said to be *precise with respect to the abstraction* α if $\|p\| = \alpha^{-1}(\|\alpha(p)\|)$, i.e., if two concrete states are abstracted into the same abstract state, they are either both p-states, or they are both $\neg p$-states. For a temporal formula ψ in positive normal form (where negation is applied only to state assertions), ψ^{α} is the formula obtained by replacing every maximal state sub-formula p in ψ by $\alpha(p)$. The formula ψ is said to be *precise with respect to* α if each of its maximal state sub-formulas are precise with respect to α.

In all cases discussed in this paper, the formulae are precise with respect to the relevant abstractions. Hence, we can restrict to the over-approximation semantics.

The α-*abstracted version of* S is the system

$$S^{\alpha} = \langle V_A, \alpha(\Theta), \alpha(\rho), \bigcup_{J \in \mathcal{J}} \alpha(J), \bigcup_{(p,q) \in \mathcal{C}} (\alpha(p), \alpha(q)) \rangle$$

From [12] we derive the soundness of finitary abstraction:

Theorem 1. *For a system S, abstraction α, and a positive normal form temporal formula ψ:*

$$S^{\alpha} \models \psi^{\alpha} \quad \Longrightarrow \quad S \models \psi$$

Thus, if an abstract system satisfies an abstract property, then the concrete system satisfies the concrete property.

3.2 Predicate Abstraction

Predicate abstraction is an instance of finitary abstraction where the abstract variables are boolean. Following [15], an initial predicate abstraction is chosen as follows: Let $\mathcal{P}$ be the (finite) set of atomic state formulas occurring in ρ, Θ, $\mathcal{J}$, $\mathcal{C}$ and the concrete formula ψ that refer to non-control and non-primed variables. Then the abstraction α is the set of equations $\{B_p = p : p \in \mathcal{P}\}$. The formula ψ^{α} is then checked over S^{α} producing either a confirmation that $S^{\alpha} \models \psi^{\alpha}$ or a counterexample. In the former case, the process terminates concluding that $S \models \psi$. Else, the counterexample produced is concreticized and checked whether it is indeed a feasible S-trace. If so, the process terminates concluding that $S \not\models \psi$. Otherwise, the concrete trace implies a refinement α' of α under which the abstract error trace is infeasible. The process repeats (with a') until it succeeds – ψ is proven to be valid or invalid – or the refinement reaches a fixpoint, in which case the process fails. See [6,3,4] for discussion of the iterated abstraction refinement method.

We close this section by demonstrating the process of predicate abstraction on program LIST-REVERSAL. In the next section we show how to automatically compute the abstraction.

Example 2 (List Reversal Abstraction). Consider program LIST-REVERSAL of Example 1. One of the safety properties one wishes to prove is that no elements are removed from the list, i.e., that every element initially reachable from x is reachable from y upon termination. This property can be expressed by:

$$\forall t.(\pi = 1 \wedge t \neq nil \wedge Nxt^*(x, t)) \rightarrow \Box(\pi = 3 \rightarrow Nxt^*(y, t)) \tag{1}$$

We augment the program with a generic variable t, which is a variable whose initial value is unconstrained and remains fixed henceforth. Then validity of Formula (1) reduces to the validity of:

$$(\pi = 1 \wedge t \neq nil \wedge Nxt^*(x, t)) \rightarrow \Box(\pi = 3 \rightarrow Nxt^*(y, t)) \tag{2}$$

Following the above discussion, to prove the safety property of Formula (2), the set $\mathcal{P}$ consists of $x = nil$, $t = nil$, $Nxt^*(x, t)$, and $Nxt^*(y, t)$, which we denote as the abstract variables x_nil, t_nil, r_xt, and r_yt respectively.

The abstract program is ABSTRACT-LIST-REVERSAL, shown in Fig. 3, and the abstract property corresponding to Formula (2) is:

$$\psi^\alpha : (\Pi = 1 \wedge \neg t\_nil \wedge r\_xt) \rightarrow \Box(\Pi = 3 \rightarrow r\_yt)$$

where Π is the program counter of the abstract program.

$$
\begin{array}{l}
\quad\quad x\_nil, t\_nil, r\_xt, r\_yt : \textbf{bool} \\
\quad\quad \textbf{init } x\_nil = t\_nil = 0, r\_xt = 1, r\_yt = t\_nil \\
\left[
\begin{array}{l}
1 : \textbf{while } \neg x\_nil \textbf{ do} \\
\quad \left[
\begin{array}{l}
(r\_xt, r\_yt) := \textbf{case} \\
\quad\quad \neg r\_xt \wedge \neg r\_yt : (\mathbf{0}, \mathbf{0}) \\
\quad\quad \neg r\_xt \wedge r\_yt \;\; : \{(\mathbf{0}, \mathbf{1}), (\mathbf{1}, \mathbf{1})\} \\
\quad\quad \textbf{otherwise} \quad\quad : \{(\mathbf{0}, \mathbf{1}), (\mathbf{1}, \mathbf{0}), (\mathbf{1}, \mathbf{1})\} \\
\quad \textbf{esac} \\
x\_nil := \textbf{if } r\_xt \textbf{ then } \mathbf{0} \textbf{ else } \{\mathbf{0}, \mathbf{1}\}
\end{array}
\right] \\
\quad \textbf{end} \\
3 :
\end{array}
\right.
\end{array}
$$

2 :

Fig. 3. Program ABSTRACT-LIST-REVERSAL

It is now left to check whether $S^\alpha \models \psi^\alpha$, which can be done, e.g., using a model checker. Here, the initial abstraction is precise enough, and program ABSTRACT-LIST-REVERSAL satisfies ψ^α. In Section 6 we present a more challenging example requiring several iterations of refinement.

4   Symbolic Computation of Abstractions

This section describes a methodology for symbolically computing an abstraction of an FHS. The methodology is based on a small model property, that establishes that satisfiability of a restricted assertion can be checked on small instantiation of a system.

Let $\mathcal{V}$ be a *vocabulary* of typed variables, whose types are taken from the restricted type system allowed in an FHS. A *model* M for $\mathcal{V}$ consists of the following elements:

- A positive integer $h > 0$.
- For each boolean variable $b \in \mathcal{V}$, a boolean value $M[b] \in \{\mathbf{0}, \mathbf{1}\}$. It is required that $M[\mathbf{0}] = \mathbf{0}$ and $M[\mathbf{1}] = \mathbf{1}$.
- For each **index** variable $x \in \mathcal{V}$, a natural value $M[x] \in [0..h]$. It is required that $M[nil] = 0$ and $M[H] = h$.
- For each boolean array $B \in \mathcal{V}$, a boolean function $M[B] : [0..h] \mapsto \{\mathbf{0}, \mathbf{1}\}$.
- For each **index** array $Z \in \mathcal{V}$, a function $M[Z] : [0..h] \mapsto [0..h]$.

We define the *size* of model M to be $h + 1$. Let $\varphi = \forall \vec{y}. \psi(\vec{x}, \vec{y})$ be a restricted A-assertion, where $\vec{x}$ is the set of free variables appearing in φ. For a given $\vec{x}$-model M, we can evaluate the formula φ over the model M. Model M is called a *satisfying model* for φ if $M \models \varphi$. An **index** term $t \in \{x, Z[x]\}$ is called a *free term* in φ. Let $\mathcal{T}_\varphi$ denote the set consisting of the term nil and all free terms which occur in formula φ.

A model M is called a *Z-uniform model* (*uniform model* for short), if for every $k \in [0..h]$ and every **index** arrays Z_1 and Z_2 such that $M[Z_1](k) = k_1$ and $M[Z_2](k) = k_2$ for $k_1 \neq k_2$, then k and at least one of k_1 or k_2 are M-interpretations of a free term belonging to $\mathcal{T}_\varphi$. A restricted A-assertion is called a *Z-uniform assertion* (uniform assertion for short) if all its models are Z-uniform. For example, assertion ρ of Fig. 2 is uniform where Z_1 and Z_2 are the arrays Nxt and Nxt'. From now on, we will restrict our attention to uniform assertions and their models. This restriction is justified since in all programs we are studying here, every pointer that is being updated is assigned a value of a variable or a free term, e.g., $Nxt'[x] = y$ or $Nxt'[y] = Nxt[yn]$ (though the value of the pointer before the assignment is not necessarily pointed to by any variable).

The following theorem states that if φ has a satisfying model, then it has a small satisfying model. The theorem is a variant of a similar one stated originally in [14].

Theorem 2 (Small model property). *Let* $\varphi : \forall \vec{y}. \psi$ *be a uniform restricted A-assertion and* $\mathcal{T}$ *be a set of free terms containing* $\mathcal{T}_\varphi$. *Then* φ *has a satisfying model iff it has a satisfying model of size not exceeding* $|\mathcal{T}| + 1$.

Proof. Let M be a satisfying model of size exceeding $|\mathcal{T}| + 1$. We will show that M can be reduced to a smaller satisfying model $\overline{M}$ whose size does not exceed $|\mathcal{T}| + 1$.

Let $0 = n_0 < \cdots < n_m$ be all the distinct values that model M assigns to the terms in $\mathcal{T}$. Obviously, $m < |\mathcal{T}|$. Let d be the minimal value in $[0..h]$ which is different from each of the n_i's. Define a mapping $\gamma \colon [0..h] \to [0..m]$ as follows:

$$\gamma(u) = \begin{cases} i & \text{if } u = n_i \\ m+1 & \text{otherwise} \end{cases}$$

We define the model $\overline{M}$ as follows:

- $\overline{h} = m+1$.
- $\overline{M}[x] = M[x]$ for each boolean variable $x \in \mathcal{T}$.
- $\overline{M}[u] = \gamma(M[u])$, for each free **index** variable $u \in \mathcal{T}$.

- $\overline{M}[B] = \lambda i.\textbf{if } i \leq m \textbf{ then } M[B](n_i) \textbf{ else } M[B](d)$, for each boolean array $B \in \mathcal{T}$.
- Finally consider an **index** array $Z \in \mathcal{T}$. We let $\overline{M}[Z](m+1) = m+1$. For $i \leq m$ let $v = M[Z](n_i)$. If some $n \in \{n_0, \ldots, n_m\}$ is Z-reachable from v in M, let n_j, $j \leq m$, be the "Z-closest" to v, and then $\overline{M}[Z](i) = j$. Otherwise, $\overline{M}[Z](i) = m+1$.

Concerning the last clause in the definition, note that if n_j is "Z_1-closest" to v then, due to uniformity, it is also the "Z_2-closest" to v, for every Z_2.

It remains to show that $\overline{M} \models \varphi$ under the assumption that $M \models \varphi$. The proof of this claim is presented in Appendix A. $\square$

For example, consider a formula φ and a set $\mathcal{T} = \{nil, v_1, v_2, v_3\}$ that includes $\mathcal{T}_\varphi$. Let M be a uniform model with $h = 7$; $M[v_1] = 1$; $M[v_2] = 3$, $M[v_3] = 5$, $M[Nxt] = [6, 6, 7, 5, 5, 5, 7]$. Then, according to the construction, $\overline{h} = 4$; $\overline{M}[nil] = 0$; $\overline{M}[v_1] = 1$; $\overline{M}[v_2] = 2$; $\overline{M}[v_3] = 3$; $\overline{M}[Nxt] = [3, 4, 3, 4]$.

Given a restricted A-assertion φ and a positive integer h_0, we define the h_0-*bounded* version of φ, denoted $\lfloor \varphi \rfloor_{h_0}$, to be the conjunction $\varphi \wedge (H \leq h_0)$. Theorem 2 can be interpreted as stating that φ is satisfiable iff $\lfloor \varphi \rfloor_{|\mathcal{T}|}$ is satisfiable.

Next, we would like to extend the small model theory to the computation of abstractions. Consider first the case of a restricted A-assertion φ which only refers to unprimed variables. As explained in Subsection 3.1, the abstraction of φ is given by $\alpha(\varphi) = \exists V(V_A = \mathcal{E}_A(V) \wedge \varphi(V))$. Assume that the set of (finitely many combinations of) values of the abstract system variables V_A is $\{U_1, \ldots, U_k\}$. Let $sat(\varphi)$ be the subset of indices $i \in [1..k]$, such that $U_i = \mathcal{E}_\alpha(V) \wedge \varphi(V)$ is satisfiable. Then, it is obvious that the abstraction $\alpha(\varphi)$ can be expanded into

$$\alpha(\varphi)(V_A) = \bigvee_{i \in sat(\varphi)} (V_A = U_i) \tag{3}$$

Next, let us consider the abstraction of $\lfloor \varphi \rfloor_{|\mathcal{T}|}$, where $\mathcal{T}$ consists of all free terms in φ and $\mathcal{E}_\alpha(V)$ and the variable H, i.e. all the free terms in the assertion $U_i = \mathcal{E}_\alpha(V) \wedge \varphi(V) \wedge (H \leq h_0)$. Our reinterpretation of Theorem 2 implies that $sat(\lfloor \varphi \rfloor_{|\mathcal{T}|}) = sat(\varphi)$ which leads to the following theorem:

Theorem 3. *Let φ be an assertion which only refers to unprimed variables, $\alpha : V_A = \mathcal{E}_A(V)$ be an abstraction mapping, $\mathcal{T}$ be the set of free terms in the formula $(U_i = \mathcal{E}_A(V)) \wedge \varphi(V) \wedge (H \leq h_0)$, and $h_0 = |\mathcal{T}|$. Then*

$$\alpha(\varphi)(V_A) \quad \sim \quad \alpha(\lfloor \varphi \rfloor_{h_0})(V_A)$$

Theorem 3 deals with assertions that do not refer to primed variables. It can be extended to the abstraction of an assertion such as the transition relation ρ. Recall that the abstraction of such an assertion involves a double application of the abstraction mapping, an unprimed version and a primed version. Thus, we need to consider the set of free terms in the formula $(U_i = \mathcal{E}_A(V)) \wedge U_j = \mathcal{E}_A(V') \wedge \rho(V, V')$ plus the variable H.

Next we generalize these results to entire systems. For an FHS $S = \langle V, \Theta, \rho, \mathcal{J}, \mathcal{C} \rangle$ and positive integer h_0, we define the h_0-bounded version of S, denoted $\lfloor S \rfloor_{h_0}$, as

$\langle V \cup \{H\}, \lfloor \rho \rfloor_{h_0}, \lfloor \mathcal{J} \rfloor_{h_0}, \lfloor \mathcal{C} \rfloor_{h_0} \rangle$, where $\lfloor \mathcal{J} \rfloor_{h_0} = \{\lfloor J \rfloor_{h_0} \mid J \in \mathcal{J}\}$ and $\lfloor \mathcal{C} \rfloor_{h_0} = \{(\lfloor p \rfloor_{h_0}, \lfloor q \rfloor_{h_0}) \mid (p, q) \in \mathcal{C}\}$. Let h_0 be the maximum size of the sets of free terms for all the abstraction formulas necessary for computing the abstraction of all the components of S. Then we have the following theorem:

Theorem 4. *Let S be an* FHS, *α be an abstraction mapping, and h_0 the maximal size of the relevant sets of free terms as described above. Then the abstract system S^α is equivalent to the abstract system $\lfloor S \rfloor_{h_0}^\alpha$.*

We use TLV [1] to compute the abstract system $\lfloor S \rfloor_{h_0}^\alpha$. The only manual step in the process is the choice of the state predicates. As discussed in Section 3, the initial choice is usually straightforward. One of the attractive advantages of using a model checker for the abstraction is that it can be invisible – thus, the abstraction, and checking of the (abstract) property over it, can be done completely automatically, and the user need not see the abstract program, giving rise to the *method of invisible abstraction*. However, because of the need for refinement, the user may actually prefer to view the abstract program.

Example 3. Consider again program LIST-REVERSAL of Example 1. In Example 2 (of Section 3) we described its abstraction, which was manually derived. In order to obtain an automatic abstraction for the system whose set of free terms is $\mathcal{T} = \{nil, H, x, y, t, x', y', Nxt'[x]\}$, we bounded the system by $h_0 = 8$.

We compute the abstraction in TLV by initially preparing an input file describing the concrete truncated system. We then use TLV's capabilities for dynamically constructing and updating a model to construct the abstract system by separately computing the abstraction of the concrete initial condition, transition relation, and fairness requirements.

Having computed the abstract system, we check the safety property ψ^α, which, of course, holds. All code is in *http://www.cs.nyu.edu/acsys/shape-analysis*.

5   Liveness

5.1   Transition Abstraction

State abstraction often does not suffice to verify liveness properties and needs to be augmented with *transition abstraction*. Let $(\mathcal{D}, \succ)$ be a partially ordered well founded domain, and assume a *ranking function* $\delta \colon \Sigma \to \mathcal{D}$. Define a function *decrease* by:

$$decrease = \begin{cases} 1 & \delta \succ \delta' \\ 0 & \delta = \delta' \\ -1 & \text{otherwise} \end{cases}$$

Transition abstraction can be incorporated into a system by (synchronously) composing the system with a *progress monitor* [12], shown in Fig. 4. The compassion requirement corresponds to the well-foundedness of $(\mathcal{D}, \succ)$: the ranking cannot decrease infinitely many times without increasing infinitely many times. To incorporate this in a state abstraction α, we add the defining equation $dec_A = dec$ to α.

$$\begin{array}{l}
dec : \{\textbf{-1}, 0, 1\} \\
\textbf{compassion } (dec = 1, dec = -1) \\
\left[\begin{array}{l}
\textbf{loop forever do} \\
\quad 1 : \; dec := decrease
\end{array}\right]
\end{array}$$

Fig. 4. Progress Monitor $M(\delta)$ for a Ranking δ

Example 4 (List Reversal Termination). Consider program LIST-REVERSAL and the termination property $\Diamond(\pi = 3)$. The loop condition $x \neq nil$ in line 1 implies that the set of nodes starting with x is a measure of progress. This suggests the ranking $\delta = \{i \mid Nxt^*(x, i)\}$ over the well founded domain $(2^N, \supset)$. That is, the rank of a state is the set of all nodes which are currently reachable from x. As the computation progresses, this set loses more and more of its members until it becomes empty. Using a sufficiently precise state abstraction, one can model check that the abstract property $\Diamond(\Pi = 3)$ indeed holds over the program.

Just like the case of predicate abstraction, we lose nothing (except efficiency) by adding potentially redundant rankings. The main advantage here over direct use of ranking functions within deductive verification is that one may contribute as many elementary ranking functions as one wishes. Assuming a finitary abstraction, it is then left to the model-checker to sort out their interaction and relevance. To illustrate this, consider the program NESTED-LOOPS in Fig. 5. The statements $x := ?, y := ?$ in lines 0 and 2 denote assignments of a random natural to x and y. Due to this unbounded non-determinism, a deductive termination proof of this program needs to use a ranking function ranging over lexicographic triplets, whose core is $(\pi = 0, x, y)$. With augmentation, however, one need only provide the rankings $\delta_1 : x$ and $\delta_2 : y$.

5.2 Computing the Augmented Abstraction

We aim to apply symbolic abstraction computation of Section 4 to systems augmented with progress monitors. However, since progress monitors are not limited to restricted A-assertions, such systems are not necessarily FHS's. Thus, for any ranking function δ, one must show that Theorem 4 is applicable to such an extended form of FHS's. Since all assertions in the definition of an augmented system, with the exception of the transition relation, are restricted A-assertions, we need only consider the augmented transition relation $\rho \wedge \rho_\delta$, where ρ is the unaugmented transition relation and ρ_δ is defined as $dec' = decrease$. Let T be a set consisting of all free terms in the assertions $\rho \wedge \rho_\delta$,

$$\begin{array}{l}
\qquad x, y : \mathbb{N} \\
\left[\begin{array}{l}
0 : x := ? \\
1 : \textbf{while } x > 0 \textbf{ do} \\
\quad \left[\begin{array}{l}
2 : y := ? \\
3 : \textbf{while } y > 0 \textbf{ do} \\
\quad \left[\begin{array}{l}
4 : y := y - 1 \\
5 : \textbf{skip}
\end{array}\right] \\
6 : x := x - 1 \\
7 : \textbf{skip}
\end{array}\right] \\
8 :
\end{array}\right]
\end{array}$$

Fig. 5. Program NESTED-LOOPS

$\mathcal{E}_\alpha(V)$, and $\mathcal{E}_\alpha(V')$, as well as the variable H. Then Theorem 4 holds if it is the case that

$$sat(\lfloor \rho \wedge \rho_\delta \rfloor_{|\mathcal{T}|}) = sat(\rho \wedge \rho_\delta) \tag{4}$$

Since proving Formula (4) for an arbitrary ranking is potentially a significant manual effort, we specifically consider the following commonly used ranking functions over the well founded domain $(2^{\mathbb{N}}, \supset)$:

$$\delta_1(x) = \{i \mid Nxt^*(x, i)\} \tag{5}$$
$$\delta_2(x, y) = \{i \mid Nxt^*(x, i) \wedge Nxt^*(i, y)\} \tag{6}$$

In the above, x, y are **index** variables, and Nxt is an **index** array. Ranking δ_1 is used to measure the progress of a forward moving pointer x, while ranking δ_2 is used to measure the progress of pointers x and y toward each other. Throughout the rest of this section we assume that the variables x and y appearing in δ_1 or δ_2 are free terms in the unaugmented transition relation.

In order to extend the small model property to cover transition relations of the form ρ_δ we impose stronger conditions on the set of terms $\mathcal{T}$. A term set $\mathcal{T}$ is said to be *history closed* if for every term of the form $Nxt[x]$, $Nxt'[x] \in \mathcal{T}$ only if $Nxt[x] \in \mathcal{T}$. From now on, we restrict to history-closed term sets. Note that history closure implies a stronger notion of uniformity as follows: For any model M and nodes k, k_1, k_2, if $M[Nxt](k) = k_1 \neq k_2 = M[Nxt'](k)$, then all of k, k_1, k_2 are pointed to by terms in $\mathcal{T}$.

The following theorem, whose proof is in Appendix B, establishes the soundness of our method for proving liveness for the two ranking functions we consider.

Theorem 5. *Let S be an unaugmented* FHS *with transition relation ρ, δ_i be a ranking with $i \in \{1, 2\}$, M be a uniform model satisfying $\rho \wedge \rho_\delta$, $\mathcal{T}$ be a history-closed term set containing the variable H and the free **index** terms in the assertions $\rho \wedge \rho_\delta$, $\mathcal{E}_\alpha(V)$, and $\mathcal{E}_\alpha(V')$, and $\overline{M}$ be the appropriate reduced model of size $h_0 = |\mathcal{T}|$.*
Then $\overline{M} \models \rho_{\delta_i}$ only if $M \models \rho_{\delta_i}$.

Example 5 (List Reversal Termination, concluded). In Example 4 we propose the ranking δ_1 to verify termination of program LIST-REVERSAL. From the Theorem 5 it follows that there is a small model property for the augmented program. The bound of the truncated system, according to Theorem 4, is

$$h_0 = |\mathcal{T}| = |\{H, nil, x, y, x', y', Nxt'[x], Nxt[x]\}| = 8$$

We have computed the abstraction, and proved termination of LIST-REVERSAL using TLV.

6   Bubble Sort

We present our experience in verifying a bubble sort algorithm on acyclic, singly-linked lists. The program is given in Fig. 6. The requirement of acyclicity is expressed in the initial condition $Nxt^*(x, nil)$ on the array Nxt. In Subsection 6.1 we summarize the proof of some safety properties. In Subsection 6.2 we discuss issues of computational efficiency, and in Subsection 6.3 we present a ranking abstraction for proving termination.

$$
\begin{array}{ll}
H & : \textbf{integer where } H = h \\
x, y, yn, prev, last & : [0..h] \\
Nxt & : \textbf{array } [0..h] \textbf{ of } [0..h] \textbf{ where } Nxt^*(x, nil) \\
D & : \textbf{array } [0..h] \textbf{ of bool}
\end{array}
$$

```
 0 :  (prev, y, yn, last) := (nil, x, Nxt[x], nil);
 1 :  while last ≠ Nxt[x] do
        ⎡ 2 : while yn ≠ last do
        ⎢      ⎡ 3 : if (D[y] > D[yn]) then
        ⎢      ⎢      ⎡ 4 : (Nxt[y], Nxt[yn]) := (Nxt[yn], y);
        ⎢      ⎢      ⎢ 5 : if (prev = nil) then
        ⎢      ⎢      ⎢        6 : x := yn
        ⎢      ⎢      ⎢      else
        ⎢      ⎢      ⎢        7 : Nxt[prev] := yn;
        ⎢      ⎢      ⎣ 8 : (prev, yn) := (yn, Nxt[y])
        ⎢      ⎢      else
        ⎣      ⎣ 9 : (prev, y, yn) := (y, yn, Nxt[y])
10 : (prev, y, yn, last) := (nil, x, Nxt[x], y);
11 :
```

Fig. 6. Program BUBBLE SORT

6.1 Safety

Two safety properties of interest are preservation and sortedness, expressed as follows:

$$\forall t.(\pi = nil \ \wedge \ t \neq nil \ \wedge \ Nxt^*(x,t)) \rightarrow \Box(Nxt^*(x,t)) \tag{7}$$

$$\forall t, s.(\pi = 11 \ \wedge \ Nxt^*(x,t) \ \wedge \ Nxt^*(t,s)) \Rightarrow D[t] \leq D[s] \tag{8}$$

As in Example 2 we augment the program with a generic variable for each universal variable. The initial abstraction consists of predicates collected from atomic formulas in properties (7) and (8) and from conditions in the program. These predicates are

$$last = Nxt[x], \ yn = last, \ D[y] > D[yn], \ prev = nil, \ t = nil,$$
$$Nxt^*(x, nil), \ Nxt^*(x,t), \ Nxt^*(t,s), \ D[t] \leq D[s]$$

This abstraction is too coarse for either property, requiring several iterations of refinement. Since we presently have no heuristic for refinement, new predicates must be derived manually from concretized counterexamples. In shape analysis typical candidates for refinement are reachability properties among program variables that are not expressible in the current abstraction. For example, the initial abstraction cannot express any nontrivial relation among the variables $x, last, y, yn$, and $prev$. Indeed, our final abstraction includes, among others, the predicates $Nxt^*(x, prev)$ and $Nxt^*(yn, last)$. In the case of $prev, y$, and yn, it is sufficient to use 1-step reachability, which is more efficiently computed. Hence we have the predicates $Nxt[prev] = y$ and $Nxt[y] = yn$.

6.2 Optimizing the Computation

When abstracting BUBBLE SORT, one difficulty, in terms of time and memory, is in computing the BDD representation of the abstraction mapping. This becomes apparent as the abstraction is refined with new graph reachability predicates. Naturally, computing the abstract program is also a major bottleneck.

One optimization technique used is to compute a series of increasingly more refined (and complex) abstractions $\alpha_1, \ldots, \alpha_n$, with α_n being the desired abstraction.

For each $i = 1, \ldots, n - 1$, we abstract the program using α_i and compute the set of abstract reachable states. Let φ_i be the concretization of this set, which represents the strongest invariant expressible by the predicates in α_i. We then proceed to compute the abstraction according to α_{i+1}, while using the invariant φ_i to limit the state space. This technique has been invaluable in limiting state explosion, almost doubling the size of models we have been able to handle.

6.3 Liveness

Proving termination of BUBBLE SORT is more challenging than that of LIST-REVERSAL due to the nested loop. While a deductive framework would require constructing a global ranking function, the current framework requires only to identify individual rankings of each loop. Therefore we examine both loops independently, specifically their exit conditions.

The outer loop condition ($last \neq Nxt[x]$) implies that "nearness" of $last$ to x is a measure of progress. We conjecture that after initialization, subsequent assignments advance $last$ "backward" toward x. This suggests the ranking δ_2 defined in Subsection 5.2. As for the inner loop, it iterates while $yn \neq last$. We conjecture that yn generally progresses "forward" toward the list tail. This suggests the ranking δ_1 from Subsection 5.2.

We use δ_1 and δ_2 as a ranking augmentation, as well as a version of state abstraction described in Subsection 6.1 that omits predicates related to generic variables.

7   Conclusion

We have shown an approach for combining augmentation and predicate abstraction with model-checking, for the purpose of performing shape analysis without explicit representation of heap shapes. Using a small model property as a theoretical basis, we are able to use the model-checker in a role traditionally relegated to external decision procedures. Consequently, the complete process, from abstraction to verification, is automatic and fully encapsulated in the model-checker. We have shown successful application of the method to two programs that perform destructive heap updates – a list reversal algorithm and a bubble sort algorithm on linked lists.

In the immediate future we plan to focus on optimization of the abstraction computation. One such direction is to integrate with a SAT-solver. Another natural direction is to generalize the model from singly-linked structures to trees and finite DAG's.

Acknowledgement

We would like to thank Scott Stoller who suggested to us that small model properties can be used for shape analysis.

References

1. A. Pnueli and E. Shahar. A platform combining deductive with algorithmic verification. In Rajeev Alur and Thomas A. Henzinger, editors, *Proceedings of the Eighth International Conference on Computer Aided Verification CAV*, volume 1102, page 184, New Brunswick, NJ, USA, / 1996. Springer Verlag.

2. T. Arons, A. Pnueli, S. Ruah, J. Xu, and L. Zuck. Parameterized verification with automatically computed inductive assertions. In CAV'01, pages 221–234. LNCS 2102, 2001.
3. T. Ball, A. Podelski, and S. K. Rajamani. Relative completeness of abstraction refinement for software model checking. In *Tools and Algorithms for Construction and Analysis of Systems*, pages 158–172, 2002.
4. T. Ball and S. K. Rajamani. Automatically validating temporal safety properties of interfaces. *Lecture Notes in Computer Science*, 2057:103+, 2001.
5. M. Benedikt, T. W. Reps, and S. Sagiv. A decidable logic for describing linked data structures. In *European Symposium on Programming*, pages 2–19, 1999.
6. E. M. Clarke, O. Grumberg, S. Jha, Y. Lu, and H. Veith. Counterexample-guided abstraction refinement. In *Computer Aided Verification*, pages 154–169, 2000.
7. D. Dams and K. S. Namjoshi. Shape analysis through predicate abstraction and model checking. In *Proceedings of the 4th International Conference on Verification, Model Checking, and Abstract Interpretation*, pages 310–324. Springer-Verlag, 2003.
8. S. Das and D. L. Dill. Successive approximation of abstract transition relations. In *Proceedings of the 16th Annual IEEE Symposium on Logic in Computer Science*, page 51. IEEE Computer Society, 2001.
9. S. Das, D. L. Dill, and S. Park. Experience with predicate abstraction. In *Proceedings of the 11th International Conference on Computer Aided Verification*, pages 160–171. Springer-Verlag, 1999.
10. C. Flanagan and S. Qadeer. Predicate abstraction for software verification. In *Proceedings of the 29th ACM SIGPLAN-SIGACT symposium on Principles of programming languages*, pages 191–202. ACM Press, 2002.
11. N. Jones and S. Muchnick. Flow analysis and optimization of Lisp-like structures. In S. Muchnick and N. Jones, editors, *Program Flow Analysis: Theory and Applications*, chapter 4, pages 102–131. Prentice-Hall, Englewood Cliffs, NJ, 1981.
12. Y. Kesten and A. Pnueli. Verification by augmented finitary abstraction. *Information and Computation*, 163(1):203–243, 2000.
13. G. Nelson. Verifying Reachability Invariants of Linked Structures. In *Proc. 10th ACM Symp. Princ. of Prog. Lang.*, pages 38–47, 1983.
14. A. Pnueli, S. Ruah, and L. Zuck. Automatic deductive verification with invisible invariants. In TACAS'01, pages 82–97. LNCS 2031, 2001.
15. S. Graf and H. Saidi. Construction of abstract state graphs with PVS. In O. Grumberg, editor, *Proc. 9th INternational Conference on Computer Aided Verification (CAV'97)*, volume 1254, pages 72–83. Springer Verlag, 1997.
16. M. Sagiv, T. Reps, and R. Wilhelm. Parametric shape analysis via 3-valued logic. *ACM Trans. Program. Lang. Syst.*, 24(3):217–298, 2002.

A   Proof of Claim in Theorem 2

To complete the proof of Theorem 2, we show that, with the given construction of $\overline{M}$, $\overline{M} \models \varphi$ under the assumption that $M \models \varphi$.

To interpret the formula φ over $\overline{M}$, we consider an arbitrary assignment $\overline{\eta}$ to the quantified variables $\vec{y}$ which assigns to each variable y a value $\overline{\eta}[y] \in [0..m+1]$. For compatibility, we pick an assignment η, which assigns an M-value to variable y, given by $\eta(y) = \text{if } \overline{\eta}(y) = i \text{ then } n_i \text{ else } d$. It remains to prove that $(\overline{M}, \overline{\eta}) \models \psi$ under the assumption that $(M, \eta) \models \psi$. For simplicity, we denote by M_η the joint interpretation (M, η) which interprets all quantified variables according to η and all other terms according to M. Similarly, let $\overline{M}_\eta$ denote the joint interpretation $(\overline{M}, \overline{\eta})$.

We list below several properties of the extended model $\overline{M}_\eta$

P1. For every boolean variable b, $\overline{M}_\eta[b] = M_\eta[b]$.
P2. For every boolean array B and variable $u \in \vec{x} \cup \vec{y}$, $\overline{M}_\eta[B[u]] = M_\eta[B[u]]$.
P3. If t is a free term, then $M_\eta[t] \in \{n_0, \dots, n_m\}$ and $\overline{M}_\eta[t] = i$ iff $M_\eta[t] = n_i$.
P4. If t is a non-free term, such that $M_\eta[t] = n_i$ for some $i \leq m$, then $\overline{M}_\eta[t] = i$.
P5. If x_1 and x_2 are free variables then $\overline{M}_\eta \models Z^*(x_1, x_2)$ iff $M_\eta \models Z^*(x_1, x_2)$

Properties **P1–P3** are direct consequences of the definition of $\overline{M}_\eta$. Let us consider Property **P4**. For the case that $t = y$, then $M_\eta[y] = n_i$ iff $\eta[y] = n_i$ iff $\overline{\eta}[y] = i$ iff $\overline{M}_\eta[y] = i$. The other case is that $t = Z[y]$. By considering separately the cases that $M_\eta[y] = n_j$ and $M_\eta[y] = d$, we can show that $\overline{M}_\eta[Z[y]] = i$.

Property **P5** follows from the definition of $\overline{M}[Z]$ and the fact that $\overline{M}[Z](m+1) = m+1$, so that no spurious Z-chains through $m+1$ are generated by $\overline{M}$.

To prove $\overline{M} \models \varphi$, it is sufficient to show that each free atomic formula (i.e., a formula not referring to any of the $\vec{y}$ variables) is true in $\overline{M}_\eta$ iff it is true in M_η and, for each non-free atomic formula p, if $M_\eta \models p$ then $\overline{M}_\eta \models p$. The relaxation in the requirements about non-free atomic formulas stems from the fact that they always appear under positive polarity in φ. We consider in turn each type of an atomic formula p that may occur in ψ.

For the case that p is a boolean variable b or a boolean term $B[u]$, the claim follows from properties **P1**, **P2**.

Next, consider the case that p is the formula $t_1 = t_2$, where t_1 and t_2 are free **index** terms. According to Property **P3**, the values of t_1 and t_2 are equal in $\overline{M}_\eta$ iff they are equal in M_η.

Turning to the case that p is the formula $y = u$, where y is a quantified variable, the correspondence between the assignments $\overline{\eta}$ and η, guarantee that this equality holds in $\overline{M}_\eta$ iff it holds in M_η.

Finally, let us consider the non-free atomic formula $Z_1[y] = Z_2[y]$, and the case that $M_\eta \models Z_1[y] = Z_2[y]$. For the case that $M_\eta[y] = d$, the equality holds in $\overline{M}_\eta$ since $\overline{M}_\eta[Z_1](m+1) = \overline{M}_\eta[Z_2](m+1) = m+1$. Otherwise, let $M_\eta[y] = n_i$, and let $n = M_\eta[Z_1](n_i) = M_\eta[Z_2](n_i)$. If $n = n_j$ then $\overline{M}_\eta[Z_1(y)] = \overline{M}_\eta[Z_2(y)] = j$. Otherwise, $\overline{M}_\eta[Z_1(y)]$ and $\overline{M}_\eta[Z_2(y)]$ are both equal to j, where n_j is the closest n_k which is Z_1-reachable (equivalently, Z_2-reachable) from n, if there exist one. If no such n_k is Z_1-reachable from n, then $\overline{M}_\eta[Z_1(y)] = \overline{M}_\eta[Z_2(y)] = m+1$.

The case of atomic formulas of the form $Z^*(x_1, x_2)$ follows from Property **P5**. $\square$

B Proof of Theorem 5

Theorem 5 claims that $M \models \rho_{\delta_i}$ implies $\overline{M} \models \rho_{\delta_i}$, where ρ_{δ_i} is defined as $dec' = decrease$. We prove the claim for a ranking δ_1 of the form $\delta_1(x) = \{i \mid Nxt^*(x, i)\}$ specified in equation (5). The case of δ_2 is justified by similar arguments.

The evaluation of δ_1 in M, written $M[\delta_1]$, is the set $\{i \mid M[Nxt^*](M[x], i)\}$, i.e, the set of all M-nodes which are reachable from $M[x]$ by $M[Nxt]$-links. The evaluation of δ_1 in $\overline{M}$ and of δ_1' in M and $\overline{M}$ are defined similarly.

First note the following property of terms in $\mathcal{T}$: It follows directly from Property **P5** of Theorem 2 that, for any term t in $\mathcal{T}$ and $\delta \in \{\delta_1, \delta_1'\}$, $M[t] \in M[\delta]$ iff $\overline{M}[t] \in \overline{M}[\delta]$.

To prove the claim it is enough to show that both properties $\delta_1 \supset \delta_1'$ and $\delta_1 = \delta_1'$ are satisfied by M iff they are satisfied by $\overline{M}$. First assume $M \models \delta_1 \supset \delta_1'$. It is easy to show that $\delta_1 \supseteq \delta_1'$ is satisfied in $\overline{M}$. This is true since by construction, any node $i \in [0 \dots N]$ is pointed to in $\overline{M}$ by a term in $\mathcal{T}$, and membership in δ_1, δ_1' is preserved for such terms.

It is left to show that $\delta_1 \neq \delta_1'$ is satisfied in $\overline{M}$. We do this by identifying a term in $\mathcal{T}$ that M interprets as a node in $M[\delta_1] - M[\delta_1']$. Such a term must point to a node in $\overline{M}$ that is a member of $\overline{M}[\delta_1] - \overline{M}[\delta_1']$. To perform this identification, let ℓ be a node in $M[\delta_1] - M[\delta_1']$. Let $M[x] = r_1, \dots, r_q = \ell$ denote the shortest Nxt-path in M from the node $M[x]$ to ℓ, i.e., for $i = 1, \dots, q-1$, $M[Nxt](r_i) = r_{i+1}$. Let j be the maximal index in $[1..q]$ such that $r_j \in \{n_0, \dots, n_m\}$, i.e., r_j is the M-image of some term $t \in \mathcal{T}$. If $r_j \notin M[\delta_1']$, our identification is complete.

Assume therefore that $r_j \in M[\delta_1']$. According to our construction, there exists an $M[Nxt]$-chain connecting r_j to ℓ, proceeding along $r_{j+1}, r_{j+2}, \dots, \ell$. Consider the chain of $M[Nxt']$-links starting from r_j. At one of the intermediate nodes: $r_j, \dots, \ell$, the $M[Nxt]$-chain and the $M[Nxt']$-chain must diverge, otherwise ℓ would also belong to $M[\delta_1']$. Assume that the two chains diverge at r_k, for some $j \leq k < q$. Then, according to strong uniformity (implied by history closure), $r_{k+1} \in \{n_0, \dots, n_m\}$, contradicting the assumed maximality of j.

In the other direction, assume that $\overline{M}$ satisfies $\delta_1 \supset \delta_1'$. We first show that M satisfies $\delta_1 \supseteq \delta_1'$. Let n be a node in $M[\delta_1']$, and consider a Nxt'-path from $M[x']$ to n in M. Let m be the ancestor nearest to n that is pointed to by a term in $\mathcal{T}$. From Theorem 2 it follows that $m \in M[\delta_1]$. The fact $n \in M[\delta_1]$ follows by induction on path length from m to n and by uniformity of M and $\overline{M}$. Therefore $M[\delta_1] \supseteq M[\delta_1']$. We now show that M satisfies $\delta_1 \supset \delta_1'$. Let j be a node such that $j \in \overline{M}[\delta_1] - \overline{M}[\delta_1']$. By construction, j is pointed to in $\overline{M}$ by a term t or $j = m+1$. In the first case, t points to a node n_j in M, such that $n_j \in M[\delta_1] - M[\delta_1']$, and we are done. In the latter case, from construction we have $\overline{M}[Nxt](m+1) = \overline{M}[Nxt'](m+1) = m+1$. Therefore, if $m+1$ is not Nxt'-reachable from $\overline{M}[x']$, there must exist a node i in $\overline{M}[\delta_1] - \overline{M}[\delta_1']$ such that $\overline{M}[Nxt](i) \neq \overline{M}[Nxt'](i)$. By uniformity, i must be pointed to in $\overline{M}$ by a term in $\mathcal{T}$. From Theorem 2 there exists a corresponding node in M.

It is left to show that $M \models (\delta_1 = \delta_1')$ iff $\overline{M} \models (\delta_1 = \delta_1')$. This is done by similar arguments.

The case of δ_2, while not presented here, is shown by generalization: While δ_1 involves nodes reachable from a single distinguished pointer x, δ_2 involves nodes on a path between x and a pointer y. Thus, given node ℓ satisfying some combination of properties of membership in δ_2, δ_2', we identify a node satisfying the same properties, that is also pointed to by a term in $\mathcal{T}$. Here, however, we consider not only distant ancestors of ℓ on the path from x, but also distant successors on the path to y.   □

Predicate Abstraction and Canonical Abstraction
for Singly-Linked Lists

Roman Manevich[1,*], E. Yahav[2], G. Ramalingam[2], and Mooly Sagiv[1]

[1] Tel Aviv University
{rumster,msagiv}@tau.ac.il
[2] IBM T.J. Watson Research Center
{eyahav,rama}@watson.ibm.com

Abstract. Predicate abstraction and canonical abstraction are two finitary abstractions used to prove properties of programs. We study the relationship between these two abstractions by considering a very limited case: abstraction of (potentially cyclic) singly-linked lists.

We provide a new and rather precise family of abstractions for potentially cyclic singly-linked lists. The main observation behind this family of abstractions is that the number of shared nodes in linked lists can be statically bounded. Therefore, the number of possible "heap shapes" is also bounded. We present the new abstraction in both predicate abstraction form as well as in canonical abstraction form.

As we illustrate in the paper, given any canonical abstraction, it is possible to define a predicate abstraction that is equivalent to the canonical abstraction. However, with this straightforward simulation, the number of predicates used for the predicate abstraction is exponential in the number of predicates used by the canonical abstraction.

An important feature of the family of abstractions we present in this paper is that the predicate abstraction representation we define is far more practical as it uses a number of predicates that is quadratic in the number of predicates used by the corresponding canonical abstraction representation. In particular, for the most abstract abstraction in this family, the number of predicates used by the canonical abstraction is linear in the number of program variables, while the number of predicates used by the predicate abstraction is quadratic in the number of program variables.

We have encoded this particular predicate abstraction and corresponding transformers in TVLA, and used this implementation to successfully verify safety properties of several list manipulating programs, including programs that were not previously verified using predicate abstraction or canonical abstraction.

1 Introduction

Abstraction and abstract interpretation [7] are essential techniques for automatically proving properties of programs. The main challenge in abstract interpretation is to develop abstractions that are precise enough to prove the required property and efficient enough to be applicable to realistic applications.

---

* Partially supported by the Israeli Academy of Science.

Predicate abstraction [11] abstracts the program into a Boolean program which conservatively simulates all potential executions. Every safety property which holds for the Boolean program is guaranteed to hold for the original program. Furthermore, abstraction refinement [6, 2] can be used to refine the abstraction when the analysis produces a "false alarm". When the process terminates, it yields a concrete error trace in which the property is violated, or successfully verifies the property. In principle, the whole process can be fully mechanized given a sufficiently powerful theorem prover. This process was successfully used in SLAM [19] and BLAST [12] to prove safety properties of device drivers.

Canonical abstraction [23] is a finitary abstraction that was specially developed to model properties of unbounded memory locations (inspired by [16]). This abstraction has been implemented in TVLA [17], and successfully used to prove various properties of heap-manipulating programs (e.g., [21, 25, 24]).

1.1 Main Results

In this paper, we study the utility of predicate abstraction to prove properties of programs operating on singly-linked lists. We also compare the expressive power of predicate abstraction and canonical abstraction.

The results in this paper can be summarized as follows:

- We show that current state-of-the-art iterative refinement techniques fail to prove interesting properties of singly-linked lists such as pointer equalities and absence of null dereferences in a fully automatic manner. This means that on many simple programs the process of refinement will diverge when the program is correct. This result is inline with the experience of Blanchet et al. [4].
- We show that predicate abstraction can simulate arbitrary finitary abstractions and, in particular, canonical abstraction. This trivial result is not immediately useful because of the number of predicates used. The number of predicates required to simulate canonical abstraction is, in the worst case, exponential in the number of predicates used by the canonical abstraction (usually, this means exponential in the number of program variables).
- We develop a new family of abstractions for heaps containing (potentially cyclic) singly-linked lists. The main idea is to summarize list elements on unshared list segments not pointed-to by local variables. For programs manipulating singly-linked lists, this abstraction is finitary since the number of shared list elements reachable from program variables is bounded. Abstractions in this family vary in their level of precision, which is controlled by the level of sharing-relationships recorded.
- We show that the abstraction recording only one-level sharing relationships (i.e., the least precise member of the family that records sharing) is sufficient for successfully verifying all our example programs, including programs that were not verified earlier using predicate abstraction or canonical abstraction.
- We show how to code the one-level-sharing abstraction using both canonical abstraction (with a linear number of unary predicates) and predicate abstraction (with a quadratic number of nullary predicates).

```
      //head points to the first element of an acyclic list
      //tail points to the last element of the same list
1     curr = head;
2     while (curr != tail) {
3         assert (curr != null);
4         curr = curr.n;
5     }
```

Fig. 1. A simple program on which counterexample-guided refinement diverges

1.2 Motivating Examples

Fig. 1 shows a program that traverses a singly-linked list with a head-pointer `head` and a tail-pointer `tail`. This is a trivial program since it only uses an acyclic linked list, and does not contain destructive pointer updates. When counterexample-guided iterative refinement is applied to this program to assure that the assertion at line 3 is never violated, it will diverge. At the i-th iteration it will generate an assertion of the form $\text{curr}(.\text{n})^i! = \text{null}$. However, no finite value of i will suffice. Indeed, the problem of proving the absence of null-dereferences is undecidable even in programs manipulating singly-linked lists and even under the (non-realistic) assumption that all control flow paths are executable [5].

In contrast, the TVLA abstract interpreter [17] proves the absence of null dereferences in this program in 2 seconds, consuming 0.6MB of memory. TVLA uses canonical abstraction which generalizes predicate abstraction by allowing first-order predicates (relation symbols) that can have arguments. Thus, nullary (0-arity) predicates correspond to predicates in the program and in predicate abstractions. Unary predicates (1-arity) are used to denote sets of unbounded locations and binary (2-arity) predicates are used to denote relationships between unbounded locations.

A curious reader may ask herself: *Are there program properties that can be verified with canonical abstractions but not with predicate abstractions?*

It is not hard to see that the answer is negative, since any finitary abstraction can be simulated by a suitable predicate abstraction. For example, consider an abstraction mapping $\alpha : C \rightarrow A$, from a concrete domain C to a finite abstract domain of indexed elements $A = \{1, \ldots, n\}$. Define the predicate $\text{BIT}[j]$ to hold for the set of concrete states $\{c \mid \text{the } j\text{th bit of } \alpha(c), \text{ in its binary representation, is } 1\}$. Now, the set of predicates $\{\text{BIT}[j]\}_{j=1}^{\lceil \log n \rceil}$ yields a predicate abstraction that simulates A. This simulation is usually not realistic, since it contains too many predicates. The number of predicates required by predicate abstraction to simulate canonical abstraction can be exponential in the number of predicates used by the canonical abstraction.

Fortunately, the only nullary predicate crucial to prove the absence of null dereferences in this program is the fact that `tail` is reachable from `curr` by a path of n selectors (of some length). Similar observations were suggested independently in [15, 3, 14]. In this paper, we define a quadratic set of nullary predicates that captures the invariants in many programs manipulating (potentially cyclic) singly-linked lists.

Fig. 2 shows a simple program removing a contiguous segment from a cyclic singly-linked list pointed-to by x. For this example program, we would like to verify that the resulting structure pointed-to by x remains a cyclic singly-linked list. Unfortunately,

```
      // x points to a cyclic singly-linked list
      // low and high are two integer values, low < high
1     t = null;
2     y = x;
3     while (t != x && y.data < low) {
4         t = y.n; y = t;
5     }
6     z = y;
7     while (z != x && z.data < high) {
8         t = z.n; z = t;
9     }
10    t = null;
11    if (y != z) {
12        y.n = null;
13        y.n = z;
14    }
```

Fig. 2. A simple program that removes the segment between low and high from a linked list

using TVLA's canonical abstraction with the standard set of predicates turns out to be insufficient. The problem stems from the fact that canonical abstraction with the standard set of predicates loses the ordering between the 3 reference variables that point to that cyclic singly-linked list (this is further explained in the next section).

In this paper, we provide two abstractions – a predicate abstraction, and a canonical abstraction – that are able to correctly determine that the result of this program is indeed a cyclic singly-linked list.

The rest of this paper is organized as follows: Sec. 2 provides background on the basic concrete semantics we are using, canonical abstraction, and predicate abstraction. Sec. 3 presents an instrumented concrete semantics that records list interruptions. Sec. 4 shows a quite precise predicate abstraction for singly-linked lists. Sec. 5 shows a quite precise canonical abstraction of singly-linked lists. In Sec. 6, we show that the predicate abstraction of Sec. 4 and the canonical abstraction of Sec. 5 are equivalent. Sec. 7 describes our experimental results.

Proofs of claims and additional technical details can be found in [18].

2   Background

In this section, we provide basic definitions that we will use throughout the paper. In particular, we define canonical abstraction and predicate abstraction.

2.1   Concrete Program States

We represent the state of a program using a first-order logical structure in which each individual corresponds to a heap-allocated object and predicates of the structure correspond to properties of heap-allocated objects.

Definition 1. *A* 2-valued logical structure *over a vocabulary (set of predicates)* $\mathcal{P}$ *is a pair* $S = \langle U, \iota \rangle$ *where* U *is the universe of the 2-valued structure, and* ι *is the interpretation function mapping predicates to their truth-value in the structure: for every predicate* $p \in \mathcal{P}$ *of arity* k, $\iota(p) : U^k \to \{0, 1\}$.

We denote the set of all 2-valued logical structures over a set of predicates $\mathcal{P}$ by 2-STRUCT$_\mathcal{P}$. In the sequel, we assume that the vocabulary $\mathcal{P}$ is fixed, and abbreviate 2-STRUCT$_\mathcal{P}$ to 2-STRUCT.

Table 1. Predicates used for representing concrete program states

Predicates	Intended Meaning
$eq(v_1, v_2)$	v_1 is equal to v_2
$\{x(v) : x \in PVar\}$	reference variable x points to the object v
$n(v_1, v_2)$	next field of the object v_1 points to the object v_2

Table 1 shows the predicates we use to record properties of individuals. A unary predicate $x(v)$ holds when the object v is pointed-to by the reference variable x. We assume that the set of predicates includes a unary predicate for every reference variable in a program. We use *PVar* to denote the set of all reference variables in a program. A binary predicate $n(v_1, v_2)$ records the value of the reference field n.

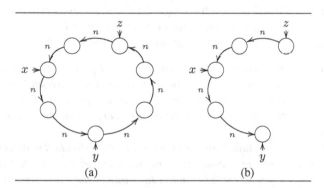

(a)   (b)

Fig. 3. The effect of the statement `y.n=null` in the concrete semantics. (a) a possible state of the program of Fig. 2 at line 12; (b) the result of applying `y.n=null` to (a)

Concrete Semantics. Program statements are modelled by *actions* that specify how statements transform an incoming logical structure into an outgoing logical structure. This is done primarily by defining the values of the predicates in the outgoing structure using formulae of first-order logic with transitive closure over the incoming structure [23]. The update formulae for heap-manipulating statements are shown in Table 2. For brevity, we omit the treatment of the allocation statement `new T()`, the interested reader may find the details in [23].

To simplify update formulae, we assume that every assignment to the n field of an object is preceded by first assigning null to it. Therefore, the statement at line 12 of the example program of Fig. 2 assigns null to `y.n` before the next statement assigns it the new value z.

Table 2. Predicate-update formulae that define the semantics of heap-manipulating statements

Statement	Update formulae
x = null	$x'(v) = 0$
x = t	$x'(v) = t(v)$
x = t.n	$x'(v) = \exists v_1 : t(v_1) \wedge n(v_1, v)$
x.n = null	$n'(v_1, v_2) = n(v_1, v_2) \wedge \neg x(v_1)$
x.n = t (assuming x.n == null)	$n'(v_1, v_2) = n(v_1, v_2) \vee (x(v_1) \wedge t(v_2))$

Example 1. Applying the action y.n = null to the concrete structure of Fig. 3(a), results with the concrete structure of Fig. 3(b). Throughout this paper we assume that all heaps are garbage-free, i.e., every element is reachable from some program variable, and that the concrete program semantics reclaims garbage elements immediately after executing program statements. Thus, the two objects between y and z are collected when y.n is set to null, as they become unreachable.

2.2 Canonical Abstraction

The goal of an abstraction is to create a finite representation of a potentially unbounded set of 2-valued structures (representing heaps) of potentially unbounded size. The abstractions we use are based on 3-valued logic [23], which extends boolean logic by introducing a third value $1/2$ denoting values that may be 0 or 1.

We represent an abstract state of a program using a 3-valued first-order structure.

Definition 2. *A* 3-*valued logical structure over a set of predicates* $\mathcal{P}$ *is a pair* $S = \langle U, \iota \rangle$ *where* U *is the universe of the* 3-*valued structure (an individual in* U *may represent multiple heap-allocated objects), and* ι *is the interpretation function mapping predicates to their truth-value in the structure: for every predicate* $p \in \mathcal{P}$ *of arity* k, $\iota(p) : U^k \to \{0, 1, 1/2\}$.

An abstract state may include summary nodes, *i.e., an individual which corresponds to one or more individuals in a concrete state represented by that abstract state. A summary node* u *has* $eq(u, u) = 1/2$, *indicating that it may represent more than a single individual.*

Embedding. We now formally define how states are represented using abstract states. The idea is that each individual from the (concrete) state is mapped into an individual in the abstract state. More generally, it is possible to map individuals from an abstract state into an individual in another, less precise, abstract state.

Formally, let $S = \langle U, \iota \rangle$ and $S' = \langle U', \iota' \rangle$ be abstract states. A function $f : U \to U'$ such that f is surjective is said to *embed* S *into* S' if for each predicate p of arity k, and for each $u_1, \ldots, u_k \in U$, one of the following holds:

$$\iota(p(u_1, \ldots, u_k)) = \iota'(p(f(u_1), \ldots, f(u_k))) \quad \text{or} \quad \iota'(p(f(u_1), \ldots, f(u_k))) = 1/2$$

We say that S' *represents* S when there exists such an embedding f.

One way of creating an embedding function f is by using *canonical abstraction.* Canonical abstraction maps concrete individuals to an abstract individual based on the values of the individuals' unary predicates. All individuals having the same values for unary predicate symbols are mapped by f to the same abstract individual.

Table 3. Predicates used for the canonical abstraction in Fig. 4, and their meaning

Predicates	Intended Meaning	Defining formulae
$\{x(v) : x \in PVar\}$	reference variable x points to v	
$n(u, v)$	next field of u points to v	
$\{r_x(v) : x \in PVar\}$	v is reachable from x by dereferencing n fields	$\exists v_x. x(v_x) \wedge n^*(v_x, v)$
$c_n(v)$	v resides on a cycle of n fields	$n^+(v, v)$
$is(v)$	v is heap-shared	$\exists v_1, v_2. n(v_1, v) \wedge n(v_2, v) \wedge (v_1 \neq v_2)$

Table 3 presents the set of predicates used in [23] to abstract singly-linked lists. The predicates $r_x(v)$, $c_n(v)$, and $is(v)$, referred to in [23] as *instrumentation predicates*, record derived information and are used to refine the abstraction.

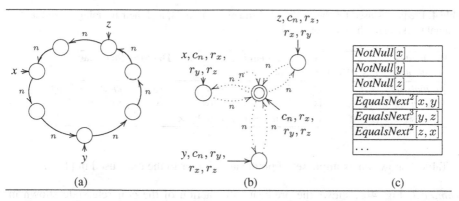

(a)   (b)   (c)

Fig. 4. (a) a concrete possible state of the program of Fig. 2 at line 12, (b) its canonical abstraction in TVLA, (c) its predicate abstraction with the set of predicates in Table 4

This set of predicates has been used for successfully verifying many programs manipulating singly-linked lists, but is insufficient for verifying that the output of the example program of Fig. 2 is a cyclic singly-linked list pointed-to by x.

Example 2. Fig. 4(b) shows the canonical abstraction of the concrete state of Fig. 4(a), using the predicates of Table 3. The node with double-line boundaries is a *summary node*, possibly representing more than a single concrete node. The dashed edges are $1/2$ edges, a dashed edge exists between v_1 and v_2 when $n(v_1, v_2) = 1/2$. The abstract state of Fig. 4(b) records the fact that x,y, and z point to a cyclic list (using the $c_n(v)$ predicate), and that all list elements are reachable from all 3 reference variables (using the $r_x(v)$, $r_y(v)$, and $r_z(v)$ predicates). This abstract state, however, does not record the order between the reference variables. In particular, it does not record that x does not reside between y and z (the segment that is about to be removed by the program statement at line 12). As a result, applying the abstract effect of y.n=z to this abstract state results with a possible abstract state in which the cyclic list is broken.

2.3 Predicate Abstraction

Predicate abstraction abstracts a concrete state into a truth-assignment for a finite set of propositional (nullary) predicates.

A predicate abstraction is defined by a vocabulary $P^A = \{P_1, \dots, P_m\}$, where each P_i is associated with a defining formula φ_i that can be evaluated over concrete states. An abstract state is a truth assignment to the predicates in P^A. Given an abstract state A, we denote the value of P_i in A by A_i.

A concrete state S over a vocabulary P^C, is mapped to an abstract state A by an abstraction mapping $\beta \colon 2\text{-STRUCT}[P^C] \to 2\text{-STRUCT}[P^A]$. The abstraction mapping evaluates the defining formulae of the predicates in P^A over S and sets the appropriate values to the respective predicates in A. Formally, for every $1 \leq i \leq m$, $A_i = [\![\varphi_i]\!]_2^S$.

Table 4. Predicates used for the predicate abstraction in Fig. 4, and their meaning. Note that the maximal tracked length K is fixed a priori

Predicates	Intended meaning	Defining formulae
$\{NotNull[x] : x \in PVar\}$	x is not null	$\exists v_x.x(v_x)$
$\{EqualsNext^k[x,y]$	the node pointed-to by y	$\exists v_0, \dots, v_k.x(v_0) \wedge y(v_k) \wedge$
$: x, y \in PVar,$	is reachable by k n fields	$\bigwedge_{0 \leq i < k} n(v_i, v_{i+1})$
$0 \leq k \leq K\}$	from the node pointed-to by x	

Table 4 shows an example set of predicates similar to the ones used in [1, 8].

Example 3. Fig. 4(c) shows the predicate abstraction of the concrete state shown in Fig. 4(a) using the predicates of Table 4. A predicate of the form *NotNull*[x] records the fact that x is not null. In Fig. 4(c), all three variables x,y,and z are not null. A predicate of the form *EqualsNext*^{k}[x, y] records that the node pointed-to by y is reachable by k steps over the n fields from the node pointed-to by x (Note that K, the maximal tracked length, is fixed a priori). For example, in Fig. 4(c), the list element pointed-to by y is reachable from the list element pointed-to by x in 2 steps over the n field, and therefore *EqualsNext*^{2}[x, y] holds.

3 Recording List Interruptions

In this section, we instrument the concrete semantics to record a designated set of nodes, called *interruptions*, in singly-linked lists. The instrumented concrete semantics presented in this section serves as the basis for the predicate abstraction and the canonical abstraction presented in the following sections.

3.1   The Intuition

The intuition behind our instrumented concrete is that a garbage-free heap, containing only singly-linked lists, is characterized by two factors: (i) the "shape" of the heap, i.e., the connectivity relations between a set of designated nodes (interruptions); and (ii) the length of "simple" list segments connecting interruptions, but not containing interruptions themselves. This intuition is similar to proofs of small model properties (e.g., [22]).

Considering this characterization, we observe that the number of shapes that are equivalent, up to lengths of simple list segments, is bounded. We therefore instrument our concrete semantics to record interruptions, which are an essential ingredient of the sharing patterns.

The abstractions presented in the next sections, abstract the lengths of simple list segments into a fixed set of abstract lengths (thereby obtaining a finite representation). These abstractions retain the general shape of the heap but lose any correlations between the actual lengths of different simple list segments. Our experience indicates that the correctness of program properties usually depends on the shape of heap, rather than on the lengths of simple list segments.

In the rest of this section, we formally define the notions of interruptions and simple list segments, and formally define the information recorded by our instrumented concrete semantics.

3.2   Basic Definitions

We say that a list node v is an *interrupting node*, or simply an *interruption*, if it is pointed-to by a program variable or it is heap-shared. Fig. 5 shows a heap with 4 interruptions: (i) the node pointed-to by x, (ii) the node pointed-to by y, (iii) the node pointed-to by $x_{s,1}$ and $y_{s,1}$, and (iv) the node pointed-to by $x_{s,2}$ and $y_{s,2}$.

Definition 3 (Uninterrupted Lists). *We say that there is an* uninterrupted list *between list node u and list node v, denoted by UList(u, v), when there is a non-empty path between them, such that, every node on the path between them (i.e., not including u and v) is non-interrupting.*

We also say that there is an uninterrupted list between list node v and null, denoted by UListNULL(v), when there is a non-empty path from v to null, such that, every node on the path, except possibly v, is non-interrupting.

Table 5 formulates UList(u, v) and UListNULL(v) as formulae in FO^{TC}.

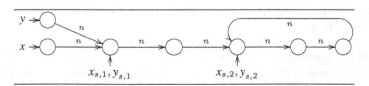

Fig. 5. Two lists sharing the same tail, and their representation in the instrumented concrete semantics

Table 5. Shorthand notations used throughout this paper

Shorthand	Meaning	Formula
$HeapShared(v)$	v is heap-shared	$\exists a, b.n(a, v) \wedge n(b, v) \wedge (a \neq b)$
$PtByVar(v)$	v is pointed-to by some variable	$\bigvee_{var \in PVar} var(v)$
$Interruption(v)$	v is an interrupting list node	$HeapShared(v) \vee PtByVar(v)$
$UList_1(u, v)$	there is an uninterrupted list of length 1 from u to v	$n(u, v)$
$UList_2(u, v)$	there is an uninterrupted list of length 2 from u to v	$\exists m.\neg Interruption(m) \wedge$ $n(u, m) \wedge n(m, v)$
$UList_{>2}(u, v)$	there is an uninterrupted list of length > 2 from u to v	$\exists m_1, m_2 : n(u, m_1) \wedge n(m_2, v) \wedge$ $(TC\ a, b : n(a, b) \wedge \neg Interruption(a) \wedge$ $\neg Interruption(b))(m_1, m_2)$
$UList(u, v)$	there is an uninterrupted list of some length from u to v	$UList_1(u, v) \vee UList_2(u, v) \vee$ $UList_{>2}(u, v)$
$UListNULL_1(v)$	there is an uninterrupted list of length 1 from v to null	$\forall w.\neg n(v, w)$
$UListNULL_2(v)$	there is an uninterrupted list of length 2 from v to null	$\exists m.n(v, m) \wedge \neg Interruption(m) \wedge$ $UListNULL_1(m)$
$UListNULL_{>2}(v)$	there is an uninterrupted list of length > 2 from v to null	$\exists m_1, m_2 : n(v, m_1) \wedge UListNULL_1(m_2)$ $(TC\ a, b : n(a, b) \wedge \neg Interruption(a) \wedge$ $\neg Interruption(b))(m_1, m_2)$
$UListNULL(v)$	there is a list of some length from v to null	$UListNULL_1(v) \vee UListNULL_2(v) \vee$ $UListNULL_{>2}(v)$

Given a heap, we are actually interested in a subset of its uninterrupted lists. We say that an uninterrupted list is *maximal* when it is not contained in a longer uninterrupted list.

The heap in Fig. 5 contains 4 maximal uninterrupted lists: (i) from the node pointed-to by x and the node pointed-to by $x_{s,1}$ and $y_{s,1}$, (ii) from the node pointed-to by y and the node pointed-to by $x_{s,1}$ and $y_{s,1}$, (iii) from the node pointed-to by $x_{s,1}$ and $y_{s,1}$ to the node pointed-to by $x_{s,2}$ and $y_{s,2}$, and (iv) from the node pointed-to by $x_{s,2}$ and $y_{s,2}$ to itself.

3.3 Statically Naming Heap-Shared Nodes

We now explain how to use a quadratic number of auxiliary variables to statically name all heap-shared nodes. This will allow us to name all maximal uninterrupted lists using nullary predicates for the predicate abstraction, and using unary predicates for the canonical abstraction.

Proposition 1. *A garbage-free heap, consisting of only singly-linked lists with n program variables, contains at most n heap-shared nodes and at most $2n$ interruptions.*

Corollary 1. *In a garbage-free heap, consisting of only singly-linked lists with n program variables, list node v is reachable from list node u if and only if it is reachable by* *a sequence of $k < n$ uninterrupted lists. Similarly, there is a path from node v to null if and only if there is a path from v to null by a sequence of $k < n$ uninterrupted lists.*

Proof. By Proposition 1, every simple path (from u to v or from v to null) contains at most n interruptions, and, therefore, at most $n - 1$ maximal uninterrupted lists.

For every program variable x, we define a set of auxiliary variables $\{x_{s,k} | k = 1 \ldots n - 1\}$. Auxiliary variable $x_{s,k}$ points to a heap-shared node u when there exists a simple path consisting of k maximal uninterrupted lists from the node pointed by x-to to u, such that all of the interrupting nodes on the path are not pointed-to by program variables (i.e., they are heap-shared). Formally, we define the set of auxiliary variables derived for program variable x by using the following set of formulae in FO^{TC}.

$$x_{s,1}(v) \equiv \exists v_x.x(v_x) \wedge UList(v_x, v) \wedge HeapShared(v) \wedge \neg PtByVar(v),$$
$$\ldots$$
$$x_{s,k+1}(v) \equiv \exists v_k.x_{s,k}(v_k) \wedge UList(v_k, v) \wedge HeapShared(v) \wedge$$
$$\neg PtByVar(v) \wedge \neg(\textstyle\bigvee_{m=1\ldots k} x_{s,m}(v)) \ .$$

We denote the set of auxiliary variables by *AuxVar* and the set of all (program and auxiliary) variables by $Var = PVar \cup AuxVar$.

Proposition 2. *Every heap-shared node is pointed-to by a variable in Var. Also, $x_{s,k}(v)$ holds for at most one node, for every reference variable x and k.*

3.4 Parameterizing the Concrete Semantics

Let n denote the number of (regular) program variables. Notice that $|AuxVar| = O(n^2)$. In the following sections, we will see that using the full set of auxiliary variables yields a canonical abstraction with a quadratic ($O(n^2)$) number of unary predicates, and a predicate abstraction with a bi-quadratic ($O(n^4)$) number of predicates.

We use a parameter k to define different subsets of *Var* as follows: $Var_k = PVar \cup \{x_{s,i}(v) | x \in PVar, i \leq k\}$. By varying the "heap-shared depth" parameter k, we are able to distinguish between different sets of heap-shared nodes. We discovered that, in practice, heap-shared nodes with depth > 1 rarely exist (they never appear in our examples), and, therefore, restricting k to 1 is usually enough to capture all maximal uninterrupted lists. Using Var_1 as the set of variables to record, we obtain a canonical abstraction with a linear number of unary predicates ($O(n)$) and a predicate abstraction with a quadratic ($O(n^2)$) number of variables.

Fig. 5 shows a heap containing a heap-shared node of depth 2 (pointed by $x_{s,2}$ and $y_{s,2}$). By setting the heap-shared depth parameter k to 1, we are able to record the following facts about this heap: (i) there is a list of length 1 from the node pointed-to by x to a heap-shared node, (ii) there is a list of length 1 from the node pointed-to by y to a heap-shared node, (iii) the heap-shared node mentioned in (i) and (ii) is the same (we record aliasing between variables), and (iv) there is a partially cyclic list (i.e., a non-cyclic list connected to a cyclic list) from the heap-shared node mentioned in (iii). We know that the list from the first heap-shared node does not reach null (since we record lists from interruptions to null) and it is not a cycle from the first-heap shared node to itself (otherwise there would be no second heap-shared node and the cycle would be recorded). The information lost, due to the fact that $x_{s,2}$ and $y_{s,2}$ are not recorded, is that the list from the first heap-shared node to second has length 2 and the cycle from the second heap-shard node to itself is also of length 2.

The Instrumented Concrete Semantics. The instrumented concrete semantics operates by using the update formulae presented in Table 2 and then using the defining formulae of the auxiliary variables to update their values.

4   A Predicate Abstraction for Singly-Linked Lists

We now describe the abstraction used to create a finite (bounded) representation of a potentially unbounded set of 2-valued structures (representing heaps) of potentially unbounded size.

4.1   The Abstraction

We start by defining a vocabulary P^A of nullary predicates, which we use in our abstraction. The predicates are shown in Table 6.

Table 6. Predicates used for the predicate abstraction and their meaning

Predicates	Defining formulae and intended meaning
$\{\,Aliased[x,y] : x,y \in Var\,\}$	$\exists v : x(v) \wedge y(v)$
	variables x and y point to the same object
$\{\,UList_1[x,y] : x,y \in Var\,\}$	$\exists v_x, v_y : x(v_x) \wedge y(v_y) \wedge n(v_x, v_y)$
	the n field of the object pointed-to by x and the variable y point to the same object
$\{\,UList_2[x,y] : x,y \in Var\,\}$	$\exists v_x, v_y : x(v_x) \wedge y(v_y) \wedge UList_2(v_x, v_y)$
	there is an uninterrupted list of length 2 from the object pointed-to by x to the object pointed-to by y
$\{\,UList[x,y] : x,y \in Var\,\}$	$\exists v_x, v_y : x(v_x) \wedge y(v_y) \wedge UList(v_x, v_y)$
	there is an uninterrupted list of length 1 or more from the object pointed-to by x to the object pointed-to by y
$\{\,UList_1[x,\text{null}] : x \in Var\,\}$	$\exists v_x : x(v_x) \wedge UListNULL_1(v_x)$
	there n field of the object pointed-to by x points to null
$\{\,UList_2[x,\text{null}] : x \in Var\,\}$	$\exists v_x.x(v_x) \wedge UListNULL_2(v_x)$
	there is an uninterrupted list of length 2 from the object pointed-to by x to null
$\{\,UList[x,\text{null}] : x \in Var\,\}$	$\exists v_x.x(v_x) \wedge UListNULL(v_x)$
	there is an uninterrupted list of length 1 or more from the object pointed-to by x to null

Intuitively, the heap is partitioned into a linear number of uninterrupted list segments and each list segment is delimited by some variables. The predicates in Table 6 abstract the path length of list segments into one of the following abstract lengths: 0 (via the *Aliased*$[x, y]$ predicates), 1 (via the *UList*$_1$$[x, y]$ predicates), 2 (via the *UList*$_2$$[x, y]$ predicates), or any length ≥ 1 (via the *UList*$[x, y]$ predicates), and infinity (i.e., there is no uninterrupted path and thus all of the previously mentioned predicates are 0).

The abstraction function $\beta_{PredAbs} : 2\text{-STRUCT}[P^C] \rightarrow 2\text{-STRUCT}[P^A]$ operates as described Sec. 2.3 where P^A is the set of predicates in Table 6.

Aliased$[x, x]$, *Aliased*$[y, y]$, *Aliased*$[z, z]$
UList$_2$$[x, y]$, *UList*$_2$$[z, x]$
UList$[x, y]$, *UList*$[y, z]$, *UList*$[z, x]$

(a)

Aliased$[x, x]$, *Aliased*$[y, y]$, *Aliased*$[z, z]$
UList$_1$$[y, \text{null}]$
UList$_2$$[x, y]$, *UList*$_2$$[z, x]$
UList$[x, y]$, *UList*$[z, x]$, *UList*$[y, \text{null}]$

(b)

Fig. 6. The abstract effect of y.n=null under predicate abstraction. (a) predicate abstraction of the state of Fig. 3(a); (b) result of applying the abstract transformer of y.n=null to (a)

Example 4. Fig. 6(a) shows an abstract state abstracting the concrete state of Fig. 3(a). The predicates *Aliased*$[x, x]$,*Aliased*$[y, y]$, *Aliased*$[z, z]$ represent the fact that the reference variables x, y, and z are not null. The predicate *UList*$_2$$[x, y]$ represents the fact that there is an uninterrupted list of length exactly 2 from the object pointed-to by x to the object pointed-to by y. This adds on the information recorded by the predicate *UList*$[x, y]$, which represents the existence of a list of length 1 or more. Similarly, the predicate *UList*$_2$$[z, x]$ records the fact that a list of exactly length 2 exists from z to x. Note that the uninterrupted list between y and z is of length 3, a length that is abstracted away and recorded as a uninterrupted list of an arbitrary length by *UList*$[y, z]$.

4.2   Abstract Semantics

Rabin [20] showed that monadic second-order logic of theories with one function symbol is decidable. This immediately implies that first-order logic with transitive closure of singly-linked lists is decidable, and thus the best transformer can be computed as suggested in [22]. Moreover, Rabin also proved that every satisfiable formula has a small model of limited size, which can be employed by the abstraction. For simplicity and efficiency, we directly define the abstractions and the abstract transformer. The reader is referred to [13] which shows that reasonable extensions of this logic become undecidable. We believe that our techniques can be employed even for undecidable logics but the precision may vary. In particular, the transformer we provide here is the *best transformer* and operates in polynomial time.

Example 5. In order to simplify the definition of the transformer for y.n = null, we split it to 5 different cases (shown in [18]) based on classification of the next list interruption. The abstract state of Fig. 6(a) falls into the case in which the next list interruption is a node pointed-to by some regular variable (z in this case) and not heap-shared (case 3). The update formulae for this case are the following:

$$ULlist_1[z_1, z_2]' = ULlist_1[z_1, z_2] \wedge \neg Aliased[z_1, y]$$
$$ULlist_1[z_1, \text{null}]' = ULlist_1[z_1, \text{null}] \vee Aliased[z_1, y]$$
$$ULlist_2[z_1, z_2]' = ULlist_2[z_1, z_2] \wedge \neg Aliased[z_1, y]$$
$$ULlist[z_1, z_2]' = ULlist[z_1, z_2] \wedge \neg Aliased[z_1, y]$$
$$ULlist[z_1, \text{null}]' = ULlist[z_1, \text{null}] \vee Aliased[z_1, y]$$

Applying this update to the abstract state of Fig. 6(a) yields the abstract state of Fig. 6(b).

In [18], we show that these formulae are produced by manual construction of the best transformer.

5 Canonical Abstraction for Singly-Linked Lists

In this section, we show how canonical abstraction, with an appropriate set of predicates, provides a rather precise abstraction for (potentially cyclic) singly-linked lists.

5.1 The Abstraction

As in Sec. 4, the idea is to partition the heap into a linear number of uninterrupted list segments, where each segment is delimited by a pair of variables (possibly including auxiliary variables). The predicates we use for canonical abstraction are shown in Table 7. The predicates of the form $cul[x](v)$, for $x \in Var$, record uninterrupted lists starting from the node pointed-to by x.

Table 7. Predicates used for the canonical abstraction and their meaning. We use the shorthand $ULlist(u, v)$ as defined in Def. 3

Predicates	Intended Meaning	Defining Formulae
$\{ x(v) : x \in Var \}$	object v is pointed-to by x	
$\{ cul[x](v) : x \in Var \}$	there exists an uninterrupted list to v, starting from the node pointed-to by x	$\exists v_x : x(v_x) \wedge ULlist(v_x, v)$

Example 6. Fig. 7(a) shows an abstract state abstracting the concrete state of Fig. 3(a). The predicates $cul[x](v), cul[y](v)$, and $cul[z](v)$ record uninterrupted list segments. Note that, in contrast to the abstract state of Fig. 4(b) (which uses the standard TVLA predicates), the abstract configuration of Fig. 7(a) records the order between the reference variables, and is therefore able to observe that x is not pointing to an object on the list from y to z.

6 Discussion

Equivalence of the Canonical Abstraction and the Predicate Abstraction. We first show that the two abstractions – the predicate abstraction of Sec. 4, and the canonical abstraction of Sec. 5 – are equivalent. That is, both observe the same set of distinctions between concrete heaps.

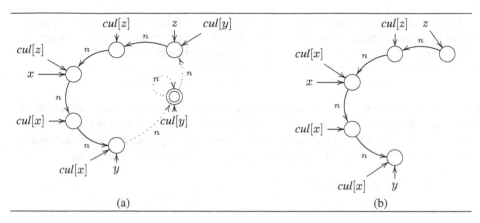

Fig. 7. The abstract effect of y.n=null under canonical abstraction. (a) canonical abstraction of the state of Fig. 3(a); (b) result of applying the abstract transformer of y.n=null to (a)

Theorem 1. *The abstractions presented in Section 4 and in Section 5 are equivalent.*

Proof (Sketch). We prove the equivalence of the two abstractions by showing that, for any two concrete heaps C_1 and C_2 (2-valued structures), we have $\beta_{PredAbs}(C_1) = \beta_{PredAbs}(C_2)$ if and only if $\beta_{Canonic}(C_1) = \beta_{Canonic}(C_2)$.

Denote the result of applying the predicate abstraction to the concrete heaps by $A_1^P = \beta_{PredAbs}(C_1)$ and $A_2^P = \beta_{PredAbs}(C_2)$, and the result of applying the canonical abstraction to the concrete heaps by $A_1^C = \beta_{Canonic}(C_1)$ and $A_2^C = \beta_{Canonic}(C_2)$.

When A_1^P and A_2^P have different values for some predicate in P^A, we show that: (i) there exists an individual v_1 in A_1^C that does not exist in A_2^C (i.e., there is no individual in A_2^C with the same values for all unary predicates as v_1 has in A_1^C), or (ii) there exist corresponding pairs of individuals (i.e., with same values for all unary predicates) in A_1^C and A_2^C such that the value of n between them is different for A_1^C and A_2^C. This is done by considering every predicate from P^A in turn.

Finally, when all predicates in P^A have the same values for both A_1^P and A_2^P, we show that there is a bijection between the universe of A_1^C and the universe of A_2^C that preserves the values of all predicates.

The Number of Predicates Used by the Abstractions. In general, the number of predicates needed by a predicate abstraction to simulate a given canonical abstraction is exponential in the number of unary predicates used by the canonical abstraction. It is interesting to note that, in this case, we were able to simulate the canonical abstraction using a sub-exponential number of nullary predicates.

We note that there exist predicate abstractions and canonical abstractions that are equivalent to the most precise member of the family of abstractions presented in the previous sections (i.e., with the full set of auxiliary variables) but require less predicates. We give the intuition to the principles underlying those abstractions and refer the reader to [18] for the technical details.

In heaps that do not contain cycles, the predicates in Table 3 are sufficient for keeping different uninterrupted lists from being merged. We can "reduce" general heaps to heaps without cycles by considering only interruptions that occur on cycles:

$$Interruption_c(v) \equiv Interruption(v) \wedge OnCycle(v) \;,$$

and use these interruptions to break cycles by redefining the formulae for uninterrupted lists to use $Interruption_c$ instead of $Interruption$. Now, a linear number of auxiliary variables can be used to syntactically capture those interruptions. For every reference variable x, we add an auxiliary variable x_c, which is captured by the formula

$$x_c(v) \equiv x(v) \wedge OnCycle(v) \vee$$
$$\exists v_1, v_2. x(v_1) \wedge n^*(v_1, v_2) \wedge \neg OnCycle(v_2) \wedge n(v_2, v) \;.$$

The set of all variables is defined by $Var' = PVar \cup \{x_c \mid x \in PVar\}$, and the predicates in Table 8 define the new canonical abstraction.

Table 8. Predicates used for the new canonical abstraction with linear number of predicates. The shorthand $UList_c$ denotes an uninterrupted list where interruptions are defined by $Interruption_c$

Predicates	Intended Meaning	Defining Formulae
$\{ x(v) : x \in Var' \}$	object v is pointed-to by x	
$\{ cul_c[x](v) : x \in Var' \}$	there exists an uninterrupted list to v, starting from the node pointed-to by x	$\exists v_x : x(v_x) \wedge UList_c(v_x, v)$
$is(v)$	u is heap-shared	$HeapShared(v)$

Recording Numerical Relationships. We believe that our abstractions can be generalized along the lines suggested by Deutsch in [9], by capturing numerical relationships between list lengths. This will allow us to prove properties of programs which traverse correlated linked lists, while maintaining the ability to conduct strong updates, which could not be handled by Deutsch. Indeed, in [10] numerical and canonical abstractions were combined in order to handle such programs.

7   Experimental Results

We implemented in TVLA the analysis based on the predicates and abstract transformers described in Section 2.3. We applied it to verify various specifications of programs operating on lists, described in Table 9. For all examples, we checked the absence of null dereferences. For the running example and reverse_cyclic we also verified that the output list is cyclic and partially cyclic, respectively.

The experiments were conducted using TVLA version 2, running with SUN's JRE 1.4, on a laptop computer with a 796 MHZ Intel Pentium Processor with 256 MB RAM.

The results of the analysis are shown in Table 9. In all of the examples, the analysis produced no false alarms. In contrast, TVLA, with the abstraction predicates in Table 1, is unable to prove that the output of reverse_cyclic is a partially cyclic list and that the output of removeSegment is a cyclic list.

The dominating factor in the running times and memory consumption is the loading phase, in which the predicates and update formulae are created (and explicitly represented). For example, the time and space consumed during the chaotic iteration of the `merge` example is 8 seconds and 7.4 MB, respectively.

Table 9. Time, space and number of errors measurements. Rep. Err. is the number of errors reported by the analysis, and Act. Err. is the number of real errors

Benchmark	Description	Time (sec)	Space (MB)	Rep. Err./ Act. Err.
create	Dynamically allocates a new linked list	3	1.8	0/0
delete	Removes an element from a list	7	9.1	0/0
deleteAll	Deallocates a list	3	2.7	0/0
getLast	Retrieves the last element in a list	4	4	0/0
insert	Inserts an element into a sorted list	9	13.5	0/0
merge	Merges two sorted lists into a single list	15	29.6	0/0
removeSegment	The running example	7	8.4	0/0
reverse	Reverses an acyclic list in-place	5	6	0/0
reverse_cyclic	reverse, applied to a partially cyclic list	2	7.1	0/0
rotate	Moves the first element after the last element	6	7.9	0/0
search	Searches for an element with a specified value	3	2.1	0/0
search_nullderef	Erroneous implementation of search that dereferences a null pointer	3	2.4	1/1
swap	Swaps the first two elements in a list	6	8.8	0/0

Acknowledgements

The authors wish to thank Alexey Loginov, Thomas Reps, and Noam Rinetzky for their contribution to this paper.

References

1. T. Ball, R. Majumdar, T. Millstein, and S. Rajamani. Automatic predicate abstraction of C programs. In *Proc. Conf. on Prog. Lang. Design and Impl.*, pages 203–213, June 2001.
2. T. Ball and S. Rajamani. Generating abstract explanations of spurious counterexamples in c programs. Report MSR-TR-2002-09, Microsoft Research, Microsoft Redmond, Jan. 2002. http://research.microsoft.com/slam/.
3. M. Benedikt, T. Reps, and M. Sagiv. A decidable logic for describing linked data structures. In *Proceedings of the 1999 European Symposium On Programming*, pages 2–19, Mar. 1999.
4. B. Blanchet, P. Cousot, R. Cousot, J. Feret, L. Mauborgne, M. Mine, D. Monniaux, and X. Rival. A static analyzer for large safety-critical software. In J. J. B. Fenwick and C. Norris, editors, *Proceedings of the ACM SIGPLAN 2003 Conference on Programming Language Design and Implementation (PLDI-03)*, volume 38, 5 of *ACM SIGPLAN Notices*, pages 196–207, New York, June 9–11 2003. ACM Press.
5. V. T. Chakaravarthy. New results on the computability and complexity of points–to analysis. In *Proceedings of the 30th ACM SIGPLAN-SIGACT symposium on Principles of programming languages*, pages 115–125. ACM Press, 2003.

6. E. Clarke, O. Grumberg, S. Jha, Y. Lu, and H. Veith. Counterexample-guided abstraction refinement. In *Proc. Computer Aided Verification*, pages 154–169, 2000.
7. P. Cousot and R. Cousot. Systematic design of program analysis frameworks. In *Proc. Symp. on Principles of Prog. Languages*, pages 269–282, New York, NY, 1979. ACM Press.
8. D. Dams and K. S. Namjoshi. Shape analysis through predicate abstraction and model checking. In *Proceedings of the 4th International Conference on Verification, Model Checking, and Abstract Interpretation*, pages 310–324. Springer-Verlag, 2003.
9. A. Deutsch. Interprocedural may-alias analysis for pointers: Beyond k-limiting. In *Proc. Conf. on Prog. Lang. Design and Impl.*, pages 230–241, New York, NY, 1994. ACM Press.
10. D. Gopan, F. DiMaio, N.Dor, T. Reps, and M. Sagiv. Numeric domains with summarized dimensions. In *Tools and Algs. for the Construct. and Anal. of Syst.*, pages 512–529, 2004.
11. S. Graf and H. Saidi. Construction of abstract state graphs with PVS. *LNCS*, 1254:72–83, 1997.
12. T. Henzinger, R. Jhala, R. Majumdar, and G. Sutre. Lazy abstraction. In *Symposium on Principles of Programming Languages*, pages 58–70, 2002.
13. N. Immerman, A. Rabinovich, T. Reps, M. Sagiv, and G. Yorsh. The boundary between decidability and undecidability for transitive closure logics. *Proc. Computer Science Logic*, 2004. to appear.
14. S. S. Ishtiaq and P. W. O'Hearn. BI as an assertion language for mutable data structures. *ACM SIGPLAN Notices*, 36(3):14–26, Mar. 2001.
15. J. Jensen, M. Joergensen, N.Klarlund, and M. Schwartzbach. Automatic verification of pointer programs using monadic second-order logic. In *Proc. Conf. on Prog. Lang. Design and Impl.*, 1997.
16. N. Jones and S. Muchnick. Flow analysis and optimization of Lisp-like structures. In S. Muchnick and N. Jones, editors, *Program Flow Analysis: Theory and Applications*, chapter 4, pages 102–131. Prentice-Hall, Englewood Cliffs, NJ, 1981.
17. T. Lev-Ami and M. Sagiv. TVLA: A framework for Kleene based static analysis. In *Proc. Static Analysis Symp.*, volume 1824 of *LNCS*, pages 280–301. Springer-Verlag, 2000.
18. R. Manevich, E. Yahav, G. Ramalingam, and M. Sagiv. Predicate abstraction and canonical abstraction for singly-linked lists. Technical Report TR-2005-01-191212, Tel Aviv University, 2005.
19. Microsoft Research. The SLAM project. http://research.microsoft.com/slam/, 2001.
20. M. Rabin. Decidability of second-order theories and automata on infinite trees. *Trans. Amer. Math. Soc*, 141(1):1–35, 1969.
21. G. Ramalingam, A. Warshavsky, J. Field, D. Goyal, and M. Sagiv. Deriving specialized program analyses for certifying component-client conformance. In *Proc. Conf. on Prog. Lang. Design and Impl.*, volume 37, 5, pages 83–94, June 2002.
22. T. Reps, M. Sagiv, and G. Yorsh. Symbolic implementation of the best transformer. In *Proc. Verification, Model Checking, and Abstract Interpretation*, pages 252–266. Springer-Verlag, 2004.
23. M. Sagiv, T. Reps, and R. Wilhelm. Parametric shape analysis via 3-valued logic. *ACM Transactions on Programming Languages and Systems (TOPLAS)*, 24(3):217–298, 2002.
24. R. Shaham, E. Yahav, E. K. Kolodner, and M. Sagiv. Establishing local temporal heap safety properties with applications to compile-time memory management. In *Proc. of the 10th International Static Analysis Symposium, SAS 2003*, volume 2694 of *LNCS*, June 2003.
25. E. Yahav and G. Ramalingam. Verifying safety properties using separation and heterogeneous abstractions. In *Proceedings of the ACM SIGPLAN 2004 conference on Programming language design and implementation*, pages 25–34. ACM Press, 2004.

Purity and Side Effect Analysis
for Java Programs

Alexandru Sălcianu and Martin Rinard

Massachusetts Institute of Technology
{salcianu,rinard}@csail.mit.edu

Abstract. We present a new purity and side effect analysis for Java programs. A method is pure if it does not mutate any location that exists in the program state right before the invocation of the method. Our analysis is built on top of a combined pointer and escape analysis, and is able to determine that methods are pure even when the methods mutate the heap, provided they mutate only new objects.

Our analysis provides useful information even for impure methods. In particular, it can recognize *read-only* parameters (a parameter is read-only if the method does not mutate any objects transitively reachable from the parameter) and *safe* parameters (a parameter is safe if it is read-only and the method does not create any new externally visible heap paths to objects transitively reachable from the parameter). The analysis can also generate regular expressions that characterize the externally visible heap locations that the method mutates.

We have implemented our analysis and used it to analyze several applications. Our results show that our analysis effectively recognizes a variety of pure methods, including pure methods that allocate and mutate complex auxiliary data structures.

1 Introduction

Accurate side effect information has several important applications. For example, many program analyses need to understand how the execution of invoked methods may affect the information that the analysis maintains [14,15,18]. In program understanding and documentation, the knowledge that a method is *pure,* or has no externally visible side effects, is especially useful because it guarantees that invocations of the method do not inadvertently interfere with other computations. Pure methods can safely be used in program assertions and specifications [3,21]. As a final example, when model checking Java programs [11,12,32,34], the model checker can reduce the search space by ignoring irrelevant interleavings between pure methods, or, more generally, between methods that access disjoint parts of the heap.

This paper presents a new method purity analysis for Java programs. This analysis is built on top of a combined pointer and escape analysis that accurately extracts a representation of the region of the heap that each method may access. We use an updated version of the Whaley and Rinard pointer analysis [35].

R. Cousot (Ed.): VMCAI 2005, LNCS 3385, pp. 199–215, 2005.

The updated analysis retains many ideas from the original analysis, but has been completely redesigned in order to allow the analysis correctness proof from [29]. Our analysis conservatively tracks object creation, updates to the local variables and updates to the object fields. This information enables our analysis to distinguish objects allocated within the execution of a method from objects that existed before the method was invoked.

Therefore, our analysis can check that a method is pure, in the sense that it does not mutate any object that exists in the prestate, i.e., the program state right before the method invocation; this is also the definition of purity adopted in the Java Modeling Language (JML) [21]. This definition allows a pure method to perform mutation on temporary objects (e.g., iterators) and/or construct complex object structures and return them as a result.

Our analysis applies a more flexible purity criterion than previously implemented purity analyses, e.g., [8,20], that consider a method to be pure only if it does not perform any writes on heap locations at all, and does not invoke any impure method.

Other researchers have used different pointer analyses to infer side effects [9, 16,25,28]. While our pointer analysis is not the only choice for the basis of a side effect analysis, it has several advantages that recommend it for this task. First, the analysis abstraction distinguishes between prestate objects and newly allocated objects, enabling the support of a more general purity property. Second, the additional information that the analysis computes can identify other useful side effect information (see below). Third, our underlying pointer analysis has already been proved correct [29], implemented, and used for a variety of tasks, including optimizations like stack allocation and synchronization removal [35], and modular reasoning about aspect oriented programs [27].

Purity Generalizations. Even when a method is not pure, it may have some useful generalized purity properties. For example, our analysis can recognize *read-only* parameters; a parameter is read-only if the method does not mutate any object reachable from the parameter. It can also recognize *safe* parameters; a parameter is safe if it is read-only and the method does not create any new externally visible heap paths to objects reachable from the parameter.

For compositionality reasons, our analysis examines each method once, under the assumption that objects from the calling context are maximally unaliased. The intraprocedural analysis computes a single parameterized result for each method; the interprocedural analysis instantiates this result to take into account the aliasing at each call site. Similarly, the clients of the analysis should use the read-only/safe parameter information in the context of the aliasing information at each call site[1]. For example, to infer that a call to an impure method does not mutate a specific object, one needs to check that the object is unreachable from parameters that are not read-only. This is the common approach in detecting and specifying read-only annotations for Java [2].

---

[1] Our underlying pointer analysis already provides such aliasing information.

Here is an example scenario for using the safe parameter information: a typestate checker, e.g., [14], is a tool that tracks the state of objects and usually checks the correct usage of finite state machine-like protocols. The typestate checker can precisely track only the state of the objects for which all aliasing is statically known. Consider the case of a method invocation that uses a tracked object in the place of a safe parameter. As the typestate checker knows all aliasing to the tracked object, it can check whether the tracked object is not aliased with objects transitively reachable from non-safe arguments at the call site. In that case, the typestate checker can rely on the fact that the method call does not change the state of the object, and that it does not introduce new aliasing to the object.

Finally, our analysis is capable of generating regular expressions that completely characterize the externally visible heap locations that a method mutates. These regular expressions identify paths in the heap that start with a parameter or static class field and end with a potentially mutated object field.

The side effect information that our analysis computes for impure methods – read-only/safe parameters and the aforementioned regular expressions – can provide many of the same benefits as the purity information because it enables other program analyses and developers to bound the potential effects of an impure method.

Contributions:

- **Purity Analysis:** We present a new analysis for finding pure methods in unannotated Java programs. Unlike previously implemented purity analyses, we track variable and field updates, and allow pure methods to mutate newly allocated data structures. Our analysis therefore supports the use of important programming constructs such as iterators in pure methods.
- **Experience:** We present our experience using our analysis to find pure methods in a number of benchmark programs. We found that our analysis was able to recognize the purity of methods that 1) were known to be pure, but 2) were beyond the reach of previously implemented purity analyses because they allocate and mutate complex internal data structures.
- **Beyond Purity:** Our analysis detects *read-only* and *safe* parameters. In addition, our analysis generates regular expressions that conservatively approximate all externally visible locations that an impure method mutates.

Paper Structure: Section 2 introduces our analysis through an example. Section 3 presents our analysis, and Section 4 shows how to interpret the raw analysis results to infer useful side effect information. Section 5 presents experimental results, Section 6 discusses related work, and Section 7 concludes.

2   Example

Figure 1 presents a sample Java program that manipulates singly linked lists. Class List implements a list using cells of class Cell, and supports two operations: add(e) adds object e to a list, and iterator() returns an iterator over the list elements[2]. We also define a class `Point` for bidimensional points, and two static methods that process lists of `Points`: `Main.sumX(list)` returns the sum of the x coordinates of all points from `list`, and `Main.flipAll(list)` flips the x and y coordinates of all points from `list`.

```
1   class List {                          39   class Point {
2     Cell head = null;                   40     Point(float x, float y) {
3     void add(Object e) {                41       this.x = x; this.y = y;
4       head = new Cell(e, head);         42     }
5     }                                   43     float x, y;
6     Iterator iterator() {               44     void flip() {
7       return new ListItr(head);         45       float t = x; x = y; y = t;
8     }                                   46     }
9   }                                     47   }
10                                        48
11  class Cell {                          49   class Main {
12    Cell(Object d, Cell n) {            50     static float sumX(List list) {
13      data = d; next = n;               51       float s = 0;
14    }                                   52       Iterator it = list.iterator();
15    Object data;                        53       while(it.hasNext()) {
16    Cell   next;                        54         Point p = (Point) it.next();
17  }                                     55         s += p.x;
18                                        56       }
19  interface Iterator {                  57       return s;
20    boolean hasNext();                  58     }
21    Object next();                      59
22  }                                     60     static void flipAll(List list) {
23                                        61       Iterator it = list.iterator();
24  class ListItr implements Iterator {   62       while(it.hasNext()) {
25    ListItr(Cell head) {                63         Point p = (Point) it.next();
26      cell = head;                      64         p.flip();
27    }                                   65       }
28    Cell cell;                          66     }
29    public boolean hasNext() {          67
30      return cell != null;              68     public static void main(String args[]) {
31    }                                   69       List list = new List();
32    public Object next() {              70       list.add(new Point(1,2));
33      Object result = cell.data;        71       list.add(new Point(2,3));
34      cell = cell.next;                 72       sumX(list);
35      return result;                    73       flipAll(list);
36    }                                   74     }
37  }                                     75   }
```

Fig. 1. Sample Code for Section 2.

Method `sumX` iterates over the list elements by repeatedly invoking the `next()` method of the list iterator. The method `next()` is impure, because it mutates the state of the iterator; in our implementation, it mutates the field `cell` of the iterator. However, the iterator is an auxiliary object that did not exist at the beginning of `sumX`. Our analysis is able to infer that `sumX` is pure, in spite of the mutation on the iterator. Our analysis is also able to infer that the impure method `flipAll` mutates only locations that are accessible in the prestate[3] along paths that match the regular expression `list.head.next*.data.(x|y)`.

---

[2] In real code, the classes `Cell` and `ListItr` would be implemented as inner classes of `List`; we use a flat format for simplicity.

[3] I.e., the state of the program right before the execution of an invoked method.

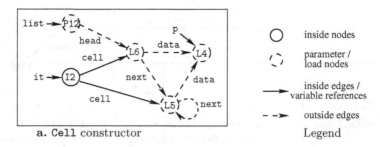

a. Cell constructor   Legend

Fig. 2. Points-To Graph for the end of Main.sumX(List).

2.1   Analysis Overview

For each method m and for each program point inside m, the analysis computes a points-to graph that models the part of the heap that the method m accesses up to that program point. During the analysis of method m, the analysis scope contains m and its transitive callees. Figure 2 presents the points-to graph for the end of Main.sumX(List).

The nodes from the points-to graphs model heap objects. The *inside nodes* model the objects created by the analyzed method; there is one inside node for each allocation site; this node models all objects allocated at that site during the current execution of the analyzed method. The *parameter nodes* model the objects passed as arguments; there is one parameter node for each formal parameter of object type (i.e., not an int, boolean, etc.). The *load nodes* model the objects read from outside the method; there is at most one load node for each load instruction. In Fig. 2, the parameter node P12 models the List object pointed by the formal parameter list, the inside node I2 models the iterator allocated to iterate over the list, and the load node L6 represents the first list cell (read from P12 by the invoked method List.iterator, at line 7). For each analyzed program, the number of nodes is bounded, ensuring the termination of our fixed-point computations.

The edges from the points-to graphs model heap references; each edge is labeled with the field it corresponds to. We write $\langle n_1, f, n_2 \rangle$ to denote an edge from n_1 to n_2, labeled with the field f; intuitively, this edge models a reference from an object that n_1 models to a node that n_2 models, along field f. The analysis uses two kinds of edges: the *inside edges* model the heap references created by the analyzed method, while the *outside edges* model the heap references read by the analyzed method from escaped objects. An object *escapes* if it is reachable from outside the analyzed method (e.g., from one of the parameters); otherwise, the object is *captured*. An outside edge always ends in a load node. In Fig. 2, the outside edge $\langle P12, \text{head}, L6 \rangle$ models a reference read from the escaped node P12; the inside edges $\langle I2, \text{cell}, L6 \rangle$ and $\langle I2, \text{cell}, L5 \rangle$ model the references created by sumX[4] from the iterator I2 to the first, respectively to the next list cells. "Loop"

---

[4] Indirectly, through the iterator-related methods it invokes.

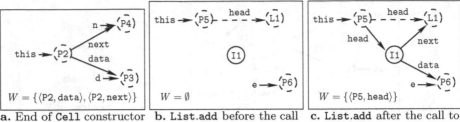

a. End of `Cell` constructor b. `List.add` before the call c. `List.add` after the call to
                                to the `Cell` constructor   the `Cell` constructor

Fig. 3. Analysis results for several simple methods. We use the conventions from Fig. 2.

edges like ⟨L5, next, L5⟩ are typical for methods that manipulate recursive data structures.

For each method m, the analysis also computes a set W_m containing the modified abstract fields that are externally visible (the term will become clear later in this section). An abstract field is a field of a specific node, i.e., a pair of the form ⟨n, f⟩. There are no externally visible modified fields for `Main.sumX`.

The analysis examines methods starting with the leaves of the call graph. The analysis examines each method m without knowing m's calling context. Instead, the analysis uses parameter/load nodes to abstract over unknown nodes, and computes a single parameterized result for m. This result is later instantiated for the aliasing relation at each call site that may invoke m; the interprocedural analysis contains an algorithm that disambiguates parameter/load nodes. Normally, the analysis processes each method once; still, recursive methods may require several analysis passes in order to reach a fixed point.

2.2   Analysis of the Example

Figure 3.a presents the analysis results for the end of the constructor of class `Cell`. The analysis uses the parameter nodes P2, P3, and P4 to model the objects that the three parameters – `this`[5], d, and n – point to. The analysis uses inside edges to model the references that the `Cell` constructor creates from P2 to P3 and P4. The constructor of `Cell` mutates the fields `data` and `next` of the parameter node P2.

Parts b and c of Fig. 3 present the analysis results at different points inside the method `List.add`. The analysis of method `List.add` uses the parameter node P5 to model the `this` object (the list we add to), and the parameter node P6 to model the object to add to the list. The method reads the field `this.head`. The analysis does not know what `this.head` points to in the calling context. Instead, the analysis uses the load node L1 to model the loaded object and adds the outside edge ⟨P5, head, L1⟩. Next, the method allocates a new `Cell`, that we model with the inside node I1 (see Fig. 3.b), and calls the `Cell` constructor with the arguments I1, P6, and L1. Based on the points-to graph before the call, and

---

[5] For each non-static Java method, the parameter `this` points to the receiver object.

the points-to graph for the invoked constructor (Fig. 3.a), the analysis maps each parameter node from the Cell constructor to one or more corresponding nodes from the calling context. In this case, P2 maps to (i.e., stands for) I1, P3 maps to P6, and P4 maps to L1. The analysis uses the node mapping to incorporate information from the points-to graph of the Cell constructor: the inside edge ⟨P2, data, P3⟩ translates into the inside edge ⟨I1, data, P6⟩. Similarly, we have the inside edge ⟨I1, next, L1⟩. As P2 stands for I1, the analysis knows that the fields data and next of I1 are mutated. However, I1 represents a new object, that did not exist in the prestate; hence, we can ignore the mutation of I1. This illustrates two features of our analysis: 1) the analysis propagates mutations interprocedurally, using the mappings for the callee nodes and 2) the analysis ignores mutations on inside nodes. Finally, the analysis of List.add adds the inside edge ⟨P5, head, I1⟩, and records the mutation on the field head of P5. Figure 3.c presents the result for the end of the method.

The analysis of the rest of the program proceeds in a similar fashion (see [30, Section 2] for the full details). Figure 2 presents the points-to graph for the end of Main.sumX (the set of modified abstract fields is empty). The results for Main.flipAll are similar to those for Main.sumX, with the important difference that the method flipAll mutates the fields x and y or node L4.

Analysis Results: For the method Main.sumX, the analysis does not detect any mutation on the prestate. Therefore, the method sumX is pure, and we can freely use it in assertions and specifications.

The analysis detects that the method Main.flipAll is not pure, due to the mutations on the node L4 that is transitively loaded from the parameter P12. Still, the analysis is able to conservatively describe the set of modified prestate locations: these are locations that are reachable from P12 (the only parameter), along paths of outside edges. These paths are generated by the regular expression head.next*.data. Hence, flipAll may modify only the prestate locations reachable along a path that matches list.head.next*.data.(x|y). We can still propagate information across calls to flipAll, as long as the information refers only to other locations. For example, as none of the list cells matches the aforementioned regular expression (by a simple type reasoning), the list spine itself is not affected, and we can propagate list non-emptiness of across calls to flipAll.

3   Analysis

This section continues the presentation of the analysis that we started in Sec. 2.1. Due to space constraints, we give an informal presentation of the analysis. A formal presentation is available in a companion technical report [30].

In addition to the points-to relation, each points-to graph records the nodes that *escape globally*, i.e., those nodes that are potentially accessed by unknown code: nodes passed as arguments to native methods and nodes pointed from static fields; in addition, any node that is transitively reachable from these nodes along inside/outside edges escapes globally too. The analysis has to be very conservative about these nodes: in particular, they can be mutated by unknown code. We use the additional special node n_{GBL} as a placeholder for other unknown globally escaping nodes: nodes loaded from a static field and nodes returned from an unanalyzable/native method.

3.1 Intraprocedural Analysis

At the start of each method, each object-type parameter (i.e., not an `int`, `boolean`, etc.) points to the corresponding parameter node. Next, our analysis propagates information along the control flow edges, using transfer functions to abstractly interpret statements from the analyzed program. At control flow join points, the analysis merges the incoming points-to graphs: e.g., the resulting points-to graph contains any edge that exists in one or more of the incoming points-to graphs. The analysis iterates over loops until it reaches a fixed point.

As a general rule, we perform strong updates on variables, i.e., assigning something to a variable removes its previous values, and weak updates on node fields, i.e., the analysis of a store statement that creates a new edge from $n_1.f$ leaves the previous edges in place. Because n_1 may represent multiple objects, all of these edges may be required to correctly represent all of the references that may exist in the heap.

A copy statement "$v_1 = v_2$" makes v_1 point to all nodes that v_2 points to. A new statement "$v = $ **new** C" makes v point to the inside node attached to that statement. For a store statement "$v_1.f = v_2$", the analysis introduces an f-labeled inside edge from each node to which v_1 points to each node to which v_2 points.

The case of a load statement "$v_1 = v_2.f$" is more complex. First, after the load, v_1 points to all the nodes that were pointed by an inside edge from $v_2.f$. If one of the nodes that v_2 points to, say n_2, escapes, a parallel thread or an unanalyzed method may create new edges from $n_2.f$, edges that point to objects created outside the analysis domain. The analysis represents these objects using the load node n_L attached to this load statement. The analysis sets v_1 to point to n_L too, and introduces an outside edge from n_2 to n_L. The interprocedural analysis uses this outside edge to find nodes from the calling context that may have been loaded at this load statement.

3.2 Interprocedural Analysis

For each call statement "$v_R = v_0.s(v_1, \ldots, v_j)$", the analysis uses the points-to graph G before the call and the points-to graph G_{callee} from the end of the invoked method *callee* to compute a points-to graph for the program point after the call. If there are multiple possible callees (this may happen because of dynamic dispatch), the analysis considers all of them and merges the resulting set of points-to graphs.

The interprocedural analysis operates in two steps. First, the analysis computes a node mapping that maps the parameter and load nodes from the callee

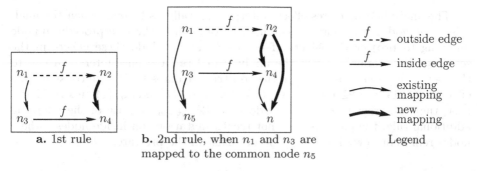

a. 1st rule   **b.** 2nd rule, when n_1 and n_3 are   Legend

mapped to the common node n_5

Fig. 4. Rules for the construction of the interprocedural node mapping.

to the nodes they may represent. Next, the analysis uses the node mapping to project G_{callee} and merge it with the points-to graph from before the call.

Due to space constraints, we describe only the construction of the node mapping, and we refer the reader to [30] for an in-depth description of the second step. Intuitively, the second step involves projecting the callee graph through the node mapping, and next merging the result with the graph before the call.

Initially, the analysis maps each parameter node to the nodes to which the corresponding actual argument points. It then repeatedly applies the two rules from Fig. 4 to match outside edges (from read operations) against inside edges (from corresponding write operations) and discover additional node mappings, until a fixed point is reached. The first rule matches outside edges from the callee against inside edges from the caller. This rule handles the case when the callee reads data from the calling context. If node n_1 maps to node n_2, we map each outside edge $\langle n_1, f, n_3 \rangle$ from G_{callee} against each inside edge $\langle n_2, f, n_4 \rangle$ from G, and add a mapping from n_3 to n_4. The second rule maps outside and inside edges from the callee. This rule handles the unknown aliasing introduced at the calling context. If nodes n_1 and n_2 have a common mapping, or one of them is mapped to the other one, they may represent the same location. This potential aliasing was unknown during the analysis of the callee, and we have to handle it now. Therefore, we match each callee outside edge $\langle n_1, f, n_3 \rangle$ from G_{callee} against each callee inside edge $\langle n_2, f, n_4 \rangle$ and map n_3 to n_4, and to all nodes that n_4 maps to.

3.3 Effect Analysis

We piggy-back the side-effect analysis on top of the pointer analysis described in the previous two sections. For each analyzed method m, the analysis maintains a set W_m containing the abstract fields (pairs of nodes and fields) that m mutates. The set W_m is initialized to the empty set. Each time the analysis of m encounters an instruction that writes a heap field, it records into W_m the relevant field and node(s). For example, the analysis of the Cell constructor records the mutations of $\langle P2, data \rangle$ and $\langle P2, next \rangle$.

The analysis propagates effects interprocedurally as follows: when the analysis of method m encounters a call instruction, it uses the interprocedural node mapping to project the effects of the callee and include these effects in the set W_m. For example, when the analysis of List.add encounters the call to the Cell constructor, as P2 from the constructor maps to I1, the constructor's effects $\{\langle \text{P2}, \text{data} \rangle, \langle \text{P2}, \text{next} \rangle\}$ are projected into $\{\langle \text{I1}, \text{data} \rangle, \langle \text{I1}, \text{next} \rangle\}$. However, these abstract fields are not added to $W_{\text{List.add}}$ because of the following additional rule: the analysis does not record mutations on inside nodes – these nodes represent new objects that do not exist in the prestate.

4 Inferring the Side Effect Information

After the analysis terminates, for each analyzable method m, we can use the points-to graph G for the end of m, and the set W_m of modified abstract fields to infer method purity, read-only parameters, safe parameters, and write effects. We explain each such application in the next paragraphs.

Method Purity. To check whether m is pure, we compute the set A of nodes that are reachable in G from parameter nodes, along outside edges. These nodes represent prestate objects read by the method. The method m is pure iff $\forall n \in A$, 1) n does not escape globally, and 2) no field of n is mutated, i.e., $\forall f.\langle n, f \rangle \notin W_m$.

For constructors, we can follow the JML convention of allowing a pure constructor to mutate fields of the "this" object: it suffices to ignore all modified abstract fields for the parameter node $n_{m,0}^P$ that models the "this" object.

Read-Only Parameters. A parameter p is *read-only* iff none of the locations transitively reachable from p is mutated. To check this, consider the corresponding parameter node n_p, and let S_1 be the set that contains n_p and all the load nodes reachable from n_p along outside edges. Parameter p is read-only iff 1) there is no abstract field $\langle n, f \rangle \in W_m$ such that $n \in S_1$, and 2) no node from S_1 escapes globally.

Safe Parameters. A parameter is *safe* if it is read-only and the method m does not create any new externally visible heap paths to an object transitively reachable from the parameter. To detect whether a read-only parameter p is safe, we compute, as before, the set S_1 that contains the corresponding parameter node n_p and all the load nodes reachable from n_p along outside edges. We also compute the set S_2 of nodes reachable from the parameter nodes and/or from the returned nodes, along inside/outside edges; S_2 contains all nodes from G that may be reachable from the caller after the end of m. To check the absence of a new externally visible path to an object reachable from p, it suffices to check the absence of any inside edges from nodes in S_2 to nodes in S_1.

Write Effects. We can infer regular expressions that describe all the prestate locations modified by m as follows: we construct a finite state automaton F with the following states: 1) all the nodes from the points-to graph G, 2) an initial state s, and 3) an accepting state t. Each outside edge from G generates a transition in F, labeled with the field that labels the outside edge. For each parameter p of m, we create a transition from s to the corresponding parameter node, and label it with the parameter p. For each mutated abstract field $\langle n, f \rangle$, we add a transition from n to the accepting state t, and label it with the field f. In addition, for each globally lost node n, we add a transition from n to t, and label it with the special field REACH. The heap path P.PATH matches all objects that are transitively reachable from an object that matches P.

The regular expression that corresponds to the constructed automaton F describes all modified prestate locations. We can use automaton-minimization algorithms to try to reduce the size of the generated regular expression.

Note: The generated regular expression is valid if G does not contain an inside edge and a load edge with the same label. This condition guarantees that the heap references modeled by the outside edges exist in the prestate (the regular expressions are supposed to be interpreted in the prestate). An interesting example that exhibits this problem is presented in [31]. If this "bad" situation occurs, we conservatively generate a regular expression that covers all nodes reachable from all parameters, with the help of the REACH field. In practice, we found that most of the methods do not read and mutate the same field.

5   Experience

We implemented our analysis in the MIT Flex compiler infrastructure [1], a static compiler for Java bytecode. To increase the analysis precision (e.g., by reducing the number of nodes that are mistakenly reported as globally escaped and therefore mutated) we manually provide the points-to graphs for several common native methods. Also, we attach type information to nodes, in order to prevent type-incorrect edges, and avoid inter-procedural mappings between nodes of conflicting types.

5.1   Checking Purity of Data Structure Consistency Predicates

We ran our analysis on several benchmarks borrowed from the Korat project [3, 24]. Korat is a tool that generates non-isomorphic test cases up to a finite bound. Korat's input consists of 1) a type declaration of a data structure, 2) a finitization (e.g., at most 10 objects of type A and 5 objects of type B), and 3) repOk, a pure boolean predicate written in Java that checks the consistency of the internal representation of the data structure. Given these inputs, Korat generates all non-isomorphic data structures that satisfy the repOk predicate. Korat does so efficiently, by monitoring the execution of the repOk predicate and back-tracking only over those parts of the data structure that repOk actually reads.

Korat relies on the purity of the repOk predicates but cannot statically check this. Writing repOk-like predicates is considered good software engineering practice; during the development of the data structure, programmers can write assertions that use repOk to check the data structure consistency. Programmers do not want assertions to change the semantics of the program, other than aborting the program when it violates an assertion. The use of repOk in assertions provides additional motivation for checking the purity of repOk methods.

We analyzed the repOk methods for the following data structures:

BinarySearchTree - Binary tree that implements a set of comparable keys.

DisjSet - Array-based implementation of the fast union-find data structure, using path compression and rank estimation heuristics to improve efficiency of find operations.

HeapArray - Array-based implementation of heaps (priority queues).

BinomialHeap and FibonacciHeap - Alternative heap implementations.

LinkedList - Doubly-linked lists from the the Java Collections Framework.

TreeMap - Implementation of the Map interface using red-black trees.

HashSet - Implementation of the Set interface, backed by a hash table.

LinkedList, TreeMap, and HashSet are from the standard Java Library. The only change the Korat developers performed was to add the corresponding repOk methods. The repOk methods use complex auxiliary data structures: sets, linked lists, wrapper objects, etc. (see [30, Appendix A] for an example). Checking the purity of these methods is beyond the reach of simple purity checkers that prohibit pure methods to call impure methods, or to do any heap mutation.

The first problem we faced while analyzing the data structures is that our analysis is a whole-program analysis that operates under a closed world assumption: in particular, it needs to know the entire class hierarchy in order to infer the call graph. Therefore, we should either 1) give the analysis a whole program (clearly impossible in this case), or 2) describe the rest of the world to the analysis. In our case, we need to describe to the analysis the objects that can be put in the data structures. The methods that our data structure implementations invoke on the data structure elements are overriders of the following methods: java.lang.Object.equals, java.lang.Object.hashCode, java.util.Comparable.compareTo, and java.lang.Object.toString.

We call these methods, and all methods that override them, *special* methods. We specified to the analysis that these methods are pure and all their parameters are safe[6]. Therefore, these methods do not mutate their parameters and do not introduce new externally visible aliasing. Hence, the analysis can simply ignore calls to these methods (even dynamically dispatched calls)[7].

We ran the analysis and analyzed the repOk methods for all the data structures, and all the methods transitively called from these methods. The analysis was able to verify that all repOk methods mutate only new objects, and are

---

[6] These assumptions correspond to the common intuition about the special methods. E.g., we do not expect equals to change the objects it compares.

[7] Additional processing is required to model the result of the toString special methods: as Strings are supposed to be values, each call to toString is treated as an object creation site. The other special methods return primitive values.

Table 1. Java Olden benchmark applications.

Application	Description
BH	Barnes-Hut N-body solver
BiSort	Bitonic Sort
Em3d	Simulation of electromagnetic waves
Health	Health-care system simulation
MST	Bentley's algorithm for minimum spanning tree in a graph
Perimeter	Computes region perimeters in an image represented as a quad-tree
Power	Maximizes the economic efficiency of a community of power consumers
TSP	Randomized alg. for the traveling salesman problem
TreeAdd	Recursive depth-first traversal of a tree to sum the node values
Voronoi	Voronoi diagram for random set of points

therefore pure. On a Pentium 4 @ 2.8Ghz with 1Gb RAM, our analysis took between 3 and 9 seconds for each analyzed data structure.

Of course, our results are valid only if our assumptions about the special methods are true. Our tool tries to verify our assumptions for all the special methods that the analysis encountered. Unfortunately, some of these methods use caches for performance reasons, and are not pure. For example, several classes cache their hashcode; other classes cache more complex data, e.g., java.util.AbstractMap caches its set of keys and entries (these caches are nullified each time a map update is performed).

Fortunately, our analysis can tell us which memory locations the mutation affects. We manually examined the output of the analysis, and checked that all the fields mutated by impure special methods correspond to caching.

Discussion. In order to analyze complex data structures that use the real Java library, we had to sacrifice soundness. More specifically, we had to trust that the caching mechanism used by several classes from the Java library has only a performance impact, and is otherwise semantically preserving. We believe that making reasonable assumptions about the unknown code in order to check complex known code is a good tradeoff. As our experience shows, knowing why exactly a method is impure is useful in practice: this feature allows us to identify (and ignore) benign mutation related to caching.

5.2   Pure Methods in the Java Olden Benchmark Suite

We also ran the purity analysis on the applications from the Java Olden benchmark suite [6, 7]. Table 1 presents a short description of the Java Olden applications. On a Pentium 4 @ 2.8Ghz with 1Gb RAM, the analysis time ranges from 3.4 seconds for TreeAdd to 7.2 seconds for Voronoi. In each case, the analysis processed all methods, user and library, that may be transitively invoked from the main method.

Table 2. Percentage of Pure Methods in the Java Olden benchmarks.

Application	All Methods		User Methods	
	count	% pure	count	% pure
BH	264	55%	59	47%
BiSort	214	57%	13	38%
Em3d	228	55%	20	40%
Health	231	57%	27	48%
MST	230	58%	31	54%
Perimeter	236	63%	37	89%
Power	224	53%	29	31%
TSP	220	56%	14	35%
TreeAdd	203	58%	5	40%
Voronoi	308	62%	70	71%

Table 2 presents the results of our purity analysis. For each application, we counted the total number of methods (user and library), and the total number of user methods. For each category, we present the percentage of pure methods, as detected by our analysis. Following the JML convention, we consider that constructors that mutate only fields of the "this" objects are pure. As the data from Table 2 shows, our analysis is able to find large numbers of pure methods in Java applications. Most of the applications have similar percentages of pure methods, because most of them use the same library methods. The variation is much larger for the user methods, ranging from 31% for Power to 89% for Perimeter.

6   Related Work

Modern research on effect inference stems from the seminal work of Gifford et al on type and effect systems [17, 23] for mostly functional languages. More recent research on effects is usually done in the context of program specification and verification. JML is a behavioral specification language for Java [5] that allows annotations containing invocations of pure methods. JML also allows the user to specify "assignable" locations, i.e., locations that a method can mutate [26]. Currently, the purity and assignable clauses are either not checked or are checked using very conservative analyses: e.g., a method is pure iff 1) it does not do I/O, 2) it does not write any heap field, and 3) it does not invoke impure methods [20]. ESC/Java is a tool for statically checking JML-like annotations of Java programs. ESC/Java uses a theorem prover to do modular checking of the provided annotations. A major source of unsoundness in ESC/Java is the fact that the tool uses purity and modifies annotations, but does not check them.

Several approaches to solve this problem rely on user-provided annotations; we mention here the work on data groups from [19, 22], and the use of region types [13, 33] and/or ownership types [4, 10] for specifying effects at the granularity of regions/ownership boundaries. In general, annotation based approaches are well suited for modular checking; they also provide abstraction mechanisms to hide representation details.

Analysis-based approaches like ours are appealing because they do not require additional user annotations. Even in situations where annotations are desired (e.g., to facilitate modular checking), static analysis can still be used to give the user a hint of what the annotations should look like. We briefly discuss several related analyses.

ChAsE [8] is a syntactic tool for modular checking of JML `assignable` clauses. For each method, the tool traverses the method code and collects write effects; for method invocation, ChAsE uses the `assignable` clauses from the callee specification. Although lightweight and useful in many practical situations, ChAsE is an *unsound* syntactic tool; in particular, unlike our analysis, it does not keep track of the values / points-to relation of variables and fields, and ignores all aliasing. Some of these problems are discussed in [31]. [31] contains compelling evidence that a static analysis for this purpose should propagate not only the set of mutated locations, but also information about the new values stored in those locations; otherwise, the analysis results are either unsound or overly-conservative. Our analysis uses the set of inside edges to keep track of the new value of pointer fields. Unfortunately, we are unaware of an implementation of the analysis proposed in [31].

Other researchers [9, 16, 25, 28], have already considered the use of pointer analysis while inferring side effects. Unlike these previous analyses, our analysis uses a separate abstraction (the inside nodes) for the objects allocated by the current invocation of the analyzed method. Therefore, our analysis focuses on prestate mutation and supports pure methods that mutate newly allocated objects. [28] offers evidence that almost all pure methods can be detected using a very simple pointer analysis. However, the method purity definition used in [28] is more rigid than ours; for example, pure methods from [28] are not allowed to construct and return new objects.

Fugue [14] is a tool that tracks the correct usage of finite state machine-like protocols. Fugue requires annotations that specify the state of the tracked objects on method entry/exit. All aliasing to the tracked objects must be statically known. Many library methods 1) do not do anything relevant to the checked protocol, and 2) are too tedious to annotate. Hence, Fugue tries to find "[NonEscaping]" parameters that are equivalent to our safe parameters. The current analysis/type checking algorithm from Fugue is very conservative as it does not allow a reference to a "[NonEscaping]" object to be stored in fields of locally captured objects (e.g., iterators).

Javari [2] is an extension to Java that allows the programmer to specify `const` (i.e., read-only) parameters and fields. A type checker checks the programmer annotations. To cope with caches in real applications, Javari allows the programmer to declare `mutable` fields; such fields can be mutated even when they belong to a `const` object. Of course, the `mutable` annotation must be used with extreme caution. Our solution is to expose the mutation on caches to the programmer, and let the programmer judge whether the mutation is allowed or not. Our tool could complement Javari by inferring read-only parameters for legacy code.

7   Conclusions

Recognizing method purity is important for a variety of program analysis and understanding tasks. We present the first implemented method purity analysis for Java that is capable of recognizing pure methods that mutate newly allocated objects. Because this analysis produces a precise characterization of the accessed region of the heap, it can also recognize generalized purity properties such as read-only and safe parameters. Our experience using our implemented analysis indicates that it can effectively recognize many pure methods. It therefore provides a useful tool that can support a range of important program analysis and software engineering tasks.

Acknowledgements

We thank Darko Marinov and Suhabe Bugrara for their help. This research was supported by the DARPA Cooperative Agreement FA 8750-04-2-0254, DARPA Contract 33615-00-C-1692, the Singapore-MIT Alliance, and the NSF Grants CCR-0341620, CCR-0325283, and CCR-0086154.

References

1. C. S. Ananian. MIT FLEX compiler infrastructure for Java. Available from http://www.flex-compiler.lcs.mit.edu, 1998-2004.
2. A. Birka. Compiler-enforced immutability for the Java language. Technical Report MIT-LCS-TR-908, MIT Laboratory for Computer Science, June 2003. Revision of Master's thesis.
3. C. Boyapati, S. Khurshid, and D. Marinov. Korat: Automated testing based on Java predicates. In *Proc. ISSTA*, 2002.
4. C. Boyapati and M. C. Rinard. A parameterized type system for race-free Java programs. In *Proc. 16th OOPSLA*, 2001.
5. L. Burdy, Y. Cheon, D. Cok, M. D. Ernst, J. Kiniry, G. T. Leavens, K. R. M. Leino, and E. Poll. An overview of JML tools and applications. Technical Report NII-R0309, Computing Science Institute, Univ. of Nijmegen, 2003.
6. B. Cahoon and K. S. McKinley. Data flow analysis for software prefetching linked data structures in Java. In *Proc. 10th International Conference on Parallel Architectures and Compilation Techniques*, 2001.
7. M. C. Carlisle and A. Rogers. Software caching and computation migration in Olden. In *Proc. 5th PPoPP*, 1995.
8. N. Cataño and M. Huismann. ChAsE: a static checker for JML's assignable clause. In *Proc. 4th VMCAI*, 2003.
9. J.-D. Choi, M. Burke, and P. Carini. Efficient flow-sensitive interprocedural computation of pointer-induced aliases and side effects. In *Proc. 20th POPL*, 1993.
10. D. Clarke and S. Drossopoulou. Ownership, encapsulation and the disjointness of type and effect. In *Proc. 17th OOPSLA*, 2002.
11. J. Corbett, M. Dwyer, J. Hatcliff, C. Pasareanu, Robby, S. Laubach, and H. Zheng. Bandera: Extracting finite-state models from Java source code. In *Proc. 22nd ICSE*, 2000.

12. J. C. Corbett. Using shape analysis to reduce finite-state models of concurrent java programs. *Software Engineering and Methodology*, 9(1), 2000.
13. K. Crary, D. Walker, and G. Morrisett. Typed memory management in a calculus of capabilities. In *Proc. 26th POPL*, 1999.
14. R. DeLine and M. Fähndrich. Typestates for objects. In *Proc. 18th ECOOP*, 2004.
15. C. Flanagan, K. R. M. Leino, M. Lilibridge, G. Nelson, J. B. Saxe, and R. Stata. Extended Static Checking for Java. In *Proc. PLDI*, 2002.
16. M. Hind and A. Pioli. Which pointer analysis should I use? In *Proc. ISSTA*, 2000.
17. P. Jouvelot and D. K. Gifford. Algebraic reconstruction of types and effects. In *Proc. 18th POPL*, 1991.
18. V. Kuncak, P. Lam, and M. Rinard. Role analysis. In *Proc. 29th POPL*, 2002.
19. V. Kuncak and K. R. M. Leino. In-place refinement for effect checking. In *2nd Intl. Workshop on Automated Verification of Infinite-State Systems*, 2003.
20. G. T. Leavens. Advances and issues in JML. Presentation at the Java Verification Workshop, 2002.
21. G. T. Leavens, A. L. Baker, and C. Ruby. Preliminary design of JML. Technical Report 96-06p, Iowa State University, 2001.
22. K. R. M. Leino, A. Poetzsch-Heffter, and Y. Zhou. Using data groups to specify and check side effects. In *Proc. PLDI*, 2002.
23. J. M. Lucassen and D. K. Gifford. Polymorphic effect systems. In *Proc. 15th POPL*, 1988.
24. D. Marinov, A. Andoni, D. Daniliuc, S. Khurshid, and M. Rinard. An evaluation of exhaustive testing for data structures. Technical Report MIT-LCS-TR-921, MIT CSAIL, Cambridge, MA, 2003.
25. A. Milanova, A. Rountev, and B. G. Ryder. Parameterized object sensitivity for points-to and side-effect analyses for Java. In *Proc. ISSTA*, 2002.
26. P. Mueller, A. Poetzsch-Heffter, and G. T. Leavens. Modular specification of frame properties in JML. Technical Report TR 02-02, Iowa State University, 2002.
27. M. Rinard, A. Sălcianu, and S. Bugrara. A classification system and analysis for aspect-oriented programs. In *Proc. 12th FSE*, 2004.
28. A. Rountev. Precise identification of side-effect-free methods in Java. In *IEEE International Conference on Software Maintenance*, 2004.
29. A. Salcianu. Pointer analysis and its applications to Java programs. Master's thesis, MIT Laboratory for Computer Science, 2001.
30. A. Salcianu and M. Rinard. A combined pointer and purity analysis for Java programs. Technical Report MIT-CSAIL-TR-949, MIT CSAIL, 2004.
31. F. Spoto and E. Poll. Static analysis for JML's **assignable** clauses. In *Proc. 10th FOOL*, 2003.
32. O. Tkachuk and M. B. Dwyer. Adapting side effects analysis for modular program model checking. In *Proc. 11th FSE*, 2003.
33. M. Tofte and L. Birkedal. A region inference algorithm. *Transactions on Programming Languages and Systems*, 20(4), 1998.
34. W. Visser, K. Havelund, G. Brat, and S. Park. Model checking programs. In *Proc. 15th ASE*, 2000.
35. J. Whaley and M. Rinard. Compositional pointer and escape analysis for Java programs. In *Proc. 14th OOPSLA*, 1999.

Automata as Abstractions

Dennis Dams and Kedar S. Namjoshi

Bell Labs, Lucent Technologies, 600 Mountain Ave., Murray Hill, NJ 07974
{dennis,kedar}@research.bell-labs.com

Abstract. We propose the use of tree automata as abstractions in the verification of branching time properties, and show several benefits. In this setting, soundness and completeness are trivial. It unifies the abundance of frameworks in the literature, and clarifies the role of concepts therein in terms of the well-studied field of automata theory. Moreover, using automata as models simplifies and generalizes results on maximal model theorems.

1 Introduction

Program verification, and in particular the model checking [3, 27] approach that we consider here, usually takes the form of property checking: Given a program model M and a property φ, does M satisfy φ ($M \models \varphi$)? The answer obtained should be *true* or *false*; otherwise verification has failed. *Program analysis* [26], on the other hand, serves a somewhat different purpose, namely to collect information about a program. Thus, program analysis produces a set of properties that M satisfies. The more properties there are, the better: this enables more compiler optimizations, better diagnostic messages, etc.

Abstraction is fundamental to both verification and analysis. It extends model checking to programs with large state spaces, and program analyses can be described in a unified way in terms of Abstract Interpretation [5]. An *abstraction framework* includes the following components. The set C of *concrete objects* contains the structures whose properties we are principally interested in, such as programs. A is the set of *abstract objects* (or *abstractions*), which simplify concrete objects by ignoring aspects that are irrelevant to the properties to be checked (in verification) or collected (in analysis), thus rendering them amenable to automated techniques. An *abstraction relation* $\rho \subseteq C \times A$ specifies how each concrete object can be abstracted. Properties are expressed in a *logic L* and interpreted over concrete objects with $\models \ \subseteq C \times L$ and over abstract objects[1] with $\models^\alpha \ \subseteq A \times L$. A principal requirement for any abstraction framework is that it is *sound*: if $\rho(c, a)$ and $a \models^\alpha \varphi$, then $c \models \varphi$. This ensures that we can establish properties of concrete objects by inspecting suitable abstractions.

Abstraction for analysis and verification. In program analysis, depending on the kind of information that needs to be collected, a particular *abstract data domain* is chosen that provides *descriptions* of concrete data values. The abstract object

---

[1] One could choose different logics on the concrete and abstract sides, but this would unnecessarily complicate the discussion here.

R. Cousot (Ed.): VMCAI 2005, LNCS 3385, pp. 216–232, 2005.

is then, e.g., a non-standard collecting semantics, computed by "lifting" all program operations to the abstract domain. Soundness is ensured by showing that each lifted operation correctly mimics the effect of the corresponding concrete operation. Ideally, lifted operations are *optimal*, which means that the largest possible set of properties is computed relative to the chosen abstract domain. As this is not always possible, the *precision* of a lifted operation is of interest.

In Model Checking, the properties of interest go beyond the universal safety properties that are commonly the target of program analyses; they include liveness aspects and existential quantification over computations, as formalized by branching-time temporal logics. Under these circumstances, the usual recipe for lifting program transitions to abstract domains falls short: the abstract programs thus constructed are sound only for universal, but not for existential properties. This can be fixed by lifting a transition relation in two different ways, interpreting universal properties over one relation (called *may*), and existential ones over the other relation (called *must*) [22].

Given an abstract domain, optimal *may* and *must* relations can be defined [4, 7, 28]. But one may argue that for program verification, the notion of precision is overshadowed by the issue of choosing a suitable abstract domain. In verification, unlike in analysis, a partial answer is not acceptable: one wants to either prove or disprove a property. Hence, even an optimal abstraction on a given domain is useless if it does not help settle the verification question. In other words, the focus shifts from precision of operators to precision of domains. Tools for verification via abstraction will need to be able to construct modal transition systems over domains of varying precision, depending on the given program and property.

Is it, then, enough to consider a may-must transition system structure over arbitrarily precise abstract domains? *No*, suggest a number of research results [23, 25, 30, 6, 10]: modifying must transitions so as to allow multiple target states – a *must hyper-transition* – enables one to devise even more precise abstract objects, which satisfy more existential properties. Are there other missing ingredients? When have we added enough? To answer these questions, we first need to formulate a reasonable notion of "enough".

From precision to completeness. As we have argued earlier, precision is not really the key abstraction issue in the context of verification. Even within the limited setting where abstract objects are finite transition systems with only *may* transitions, it is always possible to render more universal properties true, by making a domain refinement. The implicit question in the above-mentioned papers is a different one, namely: is it always possible to find a *finite* abstract object that is precise enough to prove a property true of the concrete object? (The emphasis on finiteness is because the end goal is to apply model checking to the abstract object.) This is the issue of (in)completeness: An abstraction framework is *complete*[2] if for every concrete object $c \in C$ and every property

---

[2] A different notion of completeness is studied by Giacobazzi et. al. in [14]. Their notion of completeness requires that for every concrete object, there exists an abstraction of it that satisfies precisely all the properties as the concrete object, relative to a given logic. For example, in the context of CTL, this requires the concrete and abstract transition systems to be bisimilar, and thus there is not always a finite abstraction.

$\varphi \in L$ such that $c \models \varphi$, there exists a *finite* abstract object $a \in A$ such that $\rho(c, a)$ and $a \models \varphi$. For the case of linear-time properties, completeness was first addressed in [32, 20].

The quest for completeness for branching time, undertaken in [25, 6], has shown that without the addition of *must* hyper-transitions (obtained by so-called *focus* moves in [6]), modal transition systems are incomplete for existential safety properties. Furthermore, as already predicted by [32, 20], *fairness conditions* are needed to achieve completeness for liveness properties.

Contribution of this paper. Over the years, research in refinement and abstraction techniques for branching time properties on transition systems has produced a large and rather bewildering variety of structures: *Modal Transition Systems*, with *may* and *must* relations [22]; *Abstract Kripke structures* [9] and *partial* and *multi-valued Kripke structures* [1, 2], with 3-valued components; *Disjunctive Modal Transition Systems* [23], *Abstract transition structures* [10], and *Generalized Kripke Modal Transition Systems* [30], with *must* hyper-transitions; and *Focused Transition Systems*, with focus and defocus moves and acceptance conditions [6]. Having achieved completeness for full branching time logic with Focused Transition Systems, which put all essential features together, it may be time to step back to try and see the bigger picture in this abundance of concepts. Is there an encompassing notion in terms of which the key features of all of these can be understood?

In this paper we answer this question affirmatively: indeed, behind the various disguises lives the familiar face of *tree automata*. We start by showing how automata themselves can be employed as abstract objects, giving rise to remarkably simple soundness and completeness arguments. The technical development rests upon known results from automata theory. We view this as a strong positive: it shows that establishing the connection enables one to apply results from the well-developed field of automata theory in a theory of abstraction. Then, we connect automata to previously proposed notions of abstract objects, by showing how one of the existing frameworks can be embedded into the automaton framework.

A tree automaton, indeed, can be seen as just an ordinary (fair) transition system extended with an OR-choice (or "focus") capability. Remarkably, this simple extension turns out to be enough to guarantee completeness. Automata thus identify a minimal basis for a complete framework, showing that some of the concepts developed in modal/mixed/focused structures are not strictly necessary[3]. As a further illustration of the clean-up job achieved by our observation, we illustrate how the use of automata generalizes and simplifies known *maximal model theorems* [15, 21].

An appetizer. To demonstrate how the use of automata as abstractions simplifies matters, we consider the notions of soundness and completeness in an abstraction

---

[3] This conclusion applies only to the issue of completeness: in terms of size, for instance, focused transition systems may be exponentially more compact than ordinary automata, since they can exploit both 3-valuedness (in propositional labelings and in transitions) and alternation.

framework that uses automata (details follow in subsequent sections). For an automaton $\mathcal{A}$ considered as an abstract object, the set of concrete objects that it abstracts (its *concretization*) is taken to be its (tree[4]) language $\mathcal{L}(\mathcal{A})$.

The question is how to define the evaluation of temporal properties over tree automata such that soundness is ensured. Adopting the automata-theoretic view, we express also a property φ by an automaton, whose language consists of all models of φ. Clearly, the answer then is to define, for any automaton $\mathcal{A}$ and property $\mathcal{B}$, $\mathcal{A} \models \mathcal{B}$ as $\mathcal{L}(\mathcal{A}) \subseteq \mathcal{L}(\mathcal{B})$. Soundness then holds trivially: if $M \in \mathcal{L}(\mathcal{A})$ and $\mathcal{A} \models \mathcal{B}$, then $M \in \mathcal{L}(\mathcal{B})$. Furthermore, also completeness follows immediately: Given any, possibly infinite, M such that $M \models \mathcal{B}$, there exists a finite abstraction of M through which $\mathcal{B}$ can be demonstrated, namely $\mathcal{B}$ itself: clearly, $M \in \mathcal{L}(\mathcal{B})$ and $\mathcal{B} \models \mathcal{B}$. All this is trivial, and that is precisely the point: using automata, constructions that are otherwise rather involved now become straightforward.

In practice, the above set-up is less appealing, since checking a property over an abstraction requires deciding tree-language inclusion, which is EXPTIME-hard. In Section 3, we define a notion of simulation between tree automata. Deciding the existence of such a simulation has a lower complexity (in NP, and polynomial in the common case), yet it is a sufficient condition for language inclusion. We show that the approach remains sound and complete for this choice.

2   Background

In the introduction, we make an informal case that tree automata are more appropriate than transition systems as the objects of abstraction. Tree automata are usually defined (cf. [12]) over complete trees with binary, ordered branching (i.e., each node has a 0-successor and a 1-successor). This does not quite match with branching time logics: for example, the basic EX operator of the μ-calculus cannot distinguish between the order of successors, or between bisimilar nodes with different numbers of successors. In [18,19], Janin and Walukiewicz introduced a tree automaton type appropriately matched to the μ-calculus, calling it a μ-*automaton*. We use this automaton type in the paper.

Definition 1 (Transition System, Kripke Structure). *A transition system with state labels from* Lab *is a tuple* $\mathcal{S} = (S, \hat{S}, R, L)$ *where* S *is a nonempty, countable set of* states, $\hat{S} \subseteq S$ *is a set of* initial *states,* $R \subseteq S \times S$ *is a transition relation, and* $L : S \rightarrow Lab$ *is a labeling function.*

Fix $Prop$ *to be a finite set of propositions. A* Kripke Structure *is a transition system with state labels from* 2^{Prop}. □

From each initial state, a transition system can be "unfolded" into its computation tree. Formally, a *tree* is a transition system with state space isomorphic

---
[4] We focus on verification of branching-time properties, and consequently use tree automata as abstractions. But our suggestion to use automata as abstractions specializes to the case of linear-time properties and word automata, and indeed was inspired by it – see [20].

to a subset of strings over the naturals such that if $x.c$ is a state, so is x, and there is a transition from x to $x.c$. The state corresponding to the empty string is called the *root*. We refer to a state in a tree as a *node*.

Definition 2 (μ-Automaton [18]). *A μ-automaton[5] is a tuple $\mathcal{A} = (Q, B, \hat{Q},$ OR, BR, $L, \Omega)$ where:*

- *Q is a non-empty, countable set of states, called OR states,*
- *B is a countable set of states, disjoint from Q, called BRANCH states,*
- *$\hat{Q} \subseteq Q$ is a non-empty set of initial states,*
- *OR $\subseteq Q \times B$ is a choice relation, from OR states to BRANCH states,*
- *BR $\subseteq B \times Q$ is a transition relation, from BRANCH states to OR states,*
- *$L : B \rightarrow 2^{Prop}$ is a labeling function, mapping each BRANCH state to a subset of propositions,*
- *$\Omega : Q \rightarrow \mathbb{N}$ is an indexing function, used to define the acceptance condition.*

$\square$

We sometimes Curry relations: for instance, OR(q) is the set $\{b \mid (q, b) \in$ OR$\}$. The automaton is *finite* iff $Q \cup B$ is a finite set. Only finite automata are formulated in [18]; we allow automata to be infinite so that an infinite transition system can be viewed as a simple tree automaton. (Indeed, μ-automata generalize fair transition systems only in allowing non-trivial OR choice relations. This is made precise in Definition 5 of the next section.) In the rest of the paper, we use "automaton" to stand for "μ-automaton", unless mentioned otherwise.

Informal Semantics: Given an infinite tree, a run of an automaton on it proceeds as follows. The root of the tree is tagged with an initial automaton state; a pair consisting of a tree node and an automaton state is called a *configuration*. At a configuration (n, q), the automaton has several choices as given by OR(q); it chooses (non-deterministically) a BRANCH state b in OR(q) whose labeling matches that of n. The automaton tags the children of n with OR states in BR(b), such that every OR-state tags some child, and every child is tagged with some OR state. This results in a number of successor configurations, which are explored in turn, ad infinitum. Notice that there can be many runs of an automaton on a tree, based on the non-determinism in choosing BRANCH states in the automaton, and in the way children are tagged in the tree. An input tree is accepted if there is *some* run where every sequence of configurations produced on that run meets the automaton acceptance condition. To illustrate this process, Figure 1 shows a tree, an automaton for the CTL formula EFp ("a state labeled p is reachable"), and an accepting run of the automaton on the tree.

Definition 3 (Automaton Acceptance [18]). *Let $\mathcal{S} = (S, \{\epsilon\}, R, L_{\mathcal{S}})$ be a tree with labels from 2^{Prop}, and let $\mathcal{A} = (Q, B, \hat{Q}, $ OR, BR, $L_A, \Omega)$ be an automaton. For $\hat{q} \in \hat{Q}$, a $\hat{q}$-run of $\mathcal{A}$ on $\mathcal{S}$ is a tree $\mathcal{T}$ where each node is labeled with a configuration from $S \times (Q \cup B)$, satisfying the following conditions.*

---

[5] We have made some minor syntactic changes over the definition in [18]: making the role of the BRANCH states explicit, allowing multiple initial states, and eliminating transition labels.

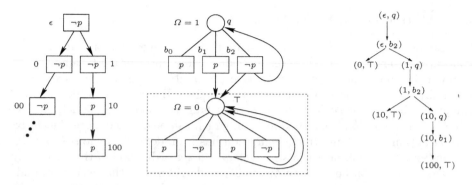

Fig. 1. Left: an input tree. Middle: μ-automaton for EFp, taking $Prop = \{p\}$. The state $\top$ accepts any subtree. Right: an accepting run.

1. *(Initial) The root of $\mathcal{T}$ is labeled with $(\epsilon, \hat{q})$.*
2. *(OR) Every node of $\mathcal{T}$ that is labeled with (n, q), where $q \in Q$, has a child labeled (n, b) for some $b \in \mathrm{OR}(q)$.*
3. *(BRANCH) For every node $x \in \mathcal{T}$ that is labeled with (n, b) where $b \in B$:*
   (a) $L_{\mathcal{S}}(n) = L_{\mathcal{A}}(b)$.
   (b) For every $n' \in R(n)$, there is a child of x labeled with (n', q'), for some $q' \in \mathrm{BR}(b)$.
   (c) For every $q' \in \mathrm{BR}(b)$, there is a child of x labeled with (n', q'), for some $n' \in R(n)$.

A $\hat{q}$-run $\mathcal{T}$ of $\mathcal{A}$ on $\mathcal{S}$ is accepting (by the so-called "parity condition") iff on every infinite path π in $\mathcal{T}$, the least value of $\Omega(q)$, for OR-states q that appear infinitely often on π, is even. The tree $\mathcal{S}$ is accepted by $\mathcal{A}$ iff for some $\hat{q} \in \hat{Q}$, there is a $\hat{q}$-run of $\mathcal{A}$ on $\mathcal{S}$ that is accepting. A Kripke Structure is accepted by $\mathcal{A}$ iff all trees in its unfolding are accepted by $\mathcal{A}$. The language $\mathcal{L}(\mathcal{A})$ of $\mathcal{A}$ is the set of all Kripke Structures that are accepted by $\mathcal{A}$. □

3   Abstraction with Automata

3.1   Abstraction with Language Inclusion

We now define the *abstraction framework based on automaton language inclusion* that was discussed at the end of the introduction. The concrete objects are Kripke Structures. The abstract objects are *finite* automata. The abstraction relation is language membership: i.e., a Kripke Structure $\mathcal{S}$ is abstracted by automaton $\mathcal{A}$ iff $\mathcal{S} \in \mathcal{L}(\mathcal{A})$. Finally, branching time temporal properties are given as *finite* automata, where a property $\mathcal{B}$ holds of a Kripke Structure $\mathcal{S}$ (i.e., a concrete object) iff $\mathcal{S} \in \mathcal{L}(\mathcal{B})$, and $\mathcal{B}$ holds of an automaton $\mathcal{A}$ (i.e., an abstract object) iff $\mathcal{L}(\mathcal{A}) \subseteq \mathcal{L}(\mathcal{B})$. In the introduction we showed the following.

Theorem 1. *The abstraction framework based on automaton language inclusion is sound and complete.*

3.2   Abstraction with Simulation

The simplicity of the framework presented above makes it attractive from a conceptual point of view. However, checking a temporal property amounts to deciding language inclusion between tree automata, which is quite expensive (EXPTIME-hard even for the finite tree case [29]). Hence, we consider below a framework based on a sufficient condition for language inclusion, namely the existence of a simulation between automata, which can be checked more efficiently.

For automata on finite trees, simulation has been defined previously, see e.g. [8], and our definition here is a straightforward generalization of that. Roughly speaking, simulation between automata $\mathcal{A}_1$ and $\mathcal{A}_2$ ensures that at corresponding OR states, any OR choice in $\mathcal{A}_1$ can be simulated by an OR choice in $\mathcal{A}_2$. As such, it follows the structure of the standard definition of simulation between transition systems [24]. At corresponding BRANCH states, however, the requirement is more reminiscent of the notion of *bisimulation*: any BRANCH transition from one automaton has a matching BRANCH transition from the other. In order to deal with the infinitary acceptance conditions, it is convenient to describe simulation checking as an infinite, two-player, game, as is done in [16] for fair simulation on Kripke Structures.

Definition 4 (Automaton Simulation). *Let $\mathcal{A}_1$ and $\mathcal{A}_2$ be automata. For initial states $\hat{q}_1 \in \hat{Q}_1$ and $\hat{q}_2 \in \hat{Q}_2$, we define the $(\hat{q}_1, \hat{q}_2)$-game as follows. Every play is a sequence of configurations as specified by the following rules. Each configuration consists of a pair of states of the same type (i.e., both are OR states or both are BRANCH states).*

1. *(Initial) The initial configuration is $(\hat{q}_1, \hat{q}_2)$.*
2. *(OR) In an "OR" configuration (q_1, q_2) (where $q_1 \in Q_1$ and $q_2 \in Q_2$), Player II chooses b_1 in $\mathrm{OR}(q_1)$; Player I has to respond with some b_2 in $\mathrm{OR}(q_2)$, and the play continues from configuration (b_1, b_2).*
3. *(BRANCH) In a "BRANCH" configuration (b_1, b_2) (where $b_1 \in B_1$ and $b_2 \in B_2$), each of the following are continuations of the play:*
   (a) *(Prop) In this continuation, the play ends and is a win for Player I if $L_1(b_1) = L_2(b_2)$, and it is a win for Player II otherwise.*
   (b) *(Bisim) Player II chooses a 'side' i in $\{1, 2\}$, and an OR-state q_i in $\mathrm{BR}_i(b_i)$; Player I must respond with an OR-state q_j in $\mathrm{BR}_j(b_j)$, from the other side j (i.e., $j \in \{1, 2\}; j \neq i$) and the play continues from configuration (q_1, q_2).*

If a finite play ends by rule 3a, the winner is as specified in that rule. For an infinite play π, and $i \in \{1, 2\}$, let $proj_i(\pi)$ be the infinite sequence from Q_i^ω obtained by projecting the OR configurations of π onto component i. Then π is a win for Player I iff either $proj_1(\pi)$ does not satisfy the acceptance condition for $\mathcal{A}_1$, or $proj_2(\pi)$ satisfies the acceptance condition for $\mathcal{A}_2$.

We say that $\mathcal{A}_1$ is simulated by $\mathcal{A}_2$, written $\mathcal{A}_1 \sqsubseteq \mathcal{A}_2$, if for every $\hat{q}_1 \in \hat{Q}_1$, there exists $\hat{q}_2 \in \hat{Q}_2$ such that player I has a winning strategy for the $(\hat{q}_1, \hat{q}_2)$-game.   □

Theorem 2. *If $\mathcal{A}_1 \sqsubseteq \mathcal{A}_2$ then $\mathcal{L}(\mathcal{A}_1) \subseteq \mathcal{L}(\mathcal{A}_2)$.*

Theorem 3. *Deciding the existence of a simulation relation between finite automata is in NP, and can be done by a deterministic algorithm that is polynomial in the size of the automata and exponential in the number of parity classes.*

Proof. (sketch) A winning strategy for Player I in the simulation game corresponds to a tree labeled with configurations where every path satisfies the winning condition. It is easy to construct a finite automaton that accepts such trees. The automaton remembers the current configuration and which player's turn it is, while the transitions of the automaton ensure that the successors in the tree are labeled with configurations that respect the constraints of the game (e.g., a node where player II takes a turn must have all possible successor configurations for a move by player II). This automaton is of size proportional to the product of the original automaton sizes. Its acceptance condition is that of the game. A parity condition can be written as either a Rabin or a Streett (complemented Rabin) condition, so the winning condition for the game, which has the shape $(\neg(parity) \vee parity)$, is a Rabin condition. Thus, the existence of a winning strategy reduces to the non-emptiness of a non-deterministic Rabin tree automaton. The complexity results then follow from the bounds given in [11] for this question. If the acceptance conditions are Büchi, the simulation check is in polynomial time.

The *simulation-based framework* is defined like the one based on language inclusion, except that a branching-time temporal property $\mathcal{B}$ is defined to hold of an automaton $\mathcal{A}$ (i.e., an abstract object) iff $\mathcal{A} \sqsubseteq \mathcal{B}$. Soundness and completeness are again easy to show.

Theorem 4. *The simulation based framework is sound and complete.*

Proof. (Soundness) Let $\mathcal{S}$ be a Kripke structure, and $\mathcal{B}$ an automaton property. Suppose that $\mathcal{A}$ is an abstraction of $\mathcal{S}$ ($\mathcal{S} \in \mathcal{L}(\mathcal{A})$) which satisfies property $\mathcal{B}$ ($\mathcal{A} \sqsubseteq \mathcal{B}$). By Theorem 2, it follows that $\mathcal{L}(\mathcal{A}) \subseteq \mathcal{L}(\mathcal{B})$. So it follows that $\mathcal{S} \in \mathcal{L}(\mathcal{B})$, i.e. $\mathcal{S}$ satisfies property $\mathcal{B}$.

(Completeness) Let $\mathcal{S}$ be a Kripke Structure that satisfies an automaton property $\mathcal{A}$ ($\mathcal{S} \in \mathcal{L}(\mathcal{A})$). So $\mathcal{A}$ itself is an abstraction of $\mathcal{S}$. Since it satisfies $\mathcal{A}$ ($\mathcal{A} \sqsubseteq \mathcal{A}$), completeness follows.

The abstraction relation in the framework based on simulation is still language membership: a Kripke Structure $\mathcal{S}$ is abstracted by automaton $\mathcal{A}$ iff $\mathcal{S} \in \mathcal{L}(\mathcal{A})$. However, this can be replaced by an equivalent definition in terms of simulation. For this, we need to be able to "lift" a Kripke Structure to an automaton. The structure states become BRANCH states of the automaton, and trivial OR states are inserted that each have only a single OR choice.

Definition 5. *Let $\mathcal{S} = (S, \hat{S}, R, L)$ be a Kripke Structure. The automaton associated with $\mathcal{S}$, $\mathcal{A}ut(\mathcal{S})$, is as follows. $\mathcal{A}ut(\mathcal{S})$ has OR states $\{q_s \mid s \in S\}$, BRANCH states $\{b_s \mid s \in S\}$, and initial states $\{q_{\hat{s}} \mid \hat{s} \in \hat{S}\}$. Each OR state q_s has b_s as its only OR choice. Each BRANCH state b_s has a BR transition to q_t for every t such* *that $R(s,t)$ in the Kripke Structure. The labeling of a* BRANCH *state b_s is the labeling of s in the Kripke Structure. The indexing function assigns 0 to every* OR *state.* □

It can be shown that $Aut(\mathcal{S})$ accepts precisely the bisimulation class of $\mathcal{S}$. We now have:

Lemma 1. $\mathcal{S} \in \pounds(\mathcal{A})$ *iff* $Aut(\mathcal{S}) \sqsubseteq \mathcal{A}$.

Proof. (sketch) The simulation game for $Aut(\mathcal{S}) \sqsubseteq \mathcal{A}$ is identical to an automaton run in this special case where the automaton on the left hand side is obtained from a Kripke Structure.

4 Translations: KMTS's to Automata

In the previous section, we gave a simple translation from Kripke Structures to automata. In this section we present a more elaborate translation from *Kripke Modal Transition Systems (KMTS's)* [17] to automata. This provides insight into their relation, and can be adapted to obtain translations from similar notions, such as the Disjunctive Modal Transition Systems [23]. KMTS's are based on 3-valued logic. Let $\mathbf{3} = \{true, maybe, false\}$, and define the *information ordering* $\leq$ by: $maybe \leq x$, $x \leq x$ for every $x \in \mathbf{3}$, and $x \not\leq y$ otherwise. $\leq$ is lifted in the standard way to functions into $\mathbf{3}$, and $\geq$ denotes the inverse of $\leq$. A proposition p in a state of a KMTS takes on values in $\mathbf{3}$. We formalize this by letting p be a 3-valued predicate that maps states to $\mathbf{3}$. The following definitions are adapted from [13].

Definition 6 ([13]). *A Kripke Modal Transition System is a tuple $M = (S, \hat{S}, \longrightarrow, \dashrightarrow, P)$, where S is a nonempty countable set of states, $\hat{S} \subseteq S$ is a subset of initial states, $\longrightarrow, \dashrightarrow \subseteq S \times S$ are the must and may transition relations resp., such that $\longrightarrow \subseteq \dashrightarrow$, and $P = \{pred_p \mid p \in Prop\}$, where for every $p \in Prop$, $pred_p : S \to \mathbf{3}$.* □

With $\longrightarrow = \dashrightarrow$ and P the 2-valued predicates $pred_p : S \to \{true, false\}$ we recover the Kripke Structures from Definition 1.

We usually just write p for $pred_p$. Finite state KMTS's have been suggested as abstract objects in a framework where the concrete objects of interest are Kripke Structures and the properties are phrased in branching-time temporal logic. The concretization of a KMTS M (the set of Kripke Structures that are abstracted by M) is called its *completion*, defined as follows.

Definition 7 ([13]). *The* completeness preorder $\succeq$ *between states of KMTS's $M_1 = (S_1, \hat{S}_1, \longrightarrow_1, \dashrightarrow_1, P_1)$ and $M_2 = (S_2, \hat{S}_2, \longrightarrow_2, \dashrightarrow_2, P_2)$ is the greatest relation $B \subseteq S_1 \times S_2$ such that $(s_1, s_2) \in B$ implies: (1) for every $p \in Prop$, $p(s_1) \geq p(s_2)$; (2) $\longrightarrow_1$ simulates $\longrightarrow_2$; and (3) $\dashrightarrow_1$ is simulated by $\dashrightarrow_2$. M_1 is* more complete *than M_2, denoted $M_1 \succeq M_2$, iff for every $\hat{s}_1 \in \hat{S}_1$ there exists $\hat{s}_2 \in \hat{S}_2$ with $\hat{s}_1 \succeq \hat{s}_2$. The* completion *$C(M)$ of M is the set of all Kripke Structures S such that $S \succeq M$.* □

The final component we need for a KMTS-based abstraction framework is an interpretation of branching-time properties over a KMTS. Also in this case, the setting is 3-valued. We consider here the so-called *thorough* semantics since it has a more direct connection to automata.

Definition 8 ([13]). *The* thorough semantics *assigns a truth value from* **3** *to a KMTS and a temporal formula, as follows:* $[M \models \varphi] = true$ *(false) if* $S \models \varphi$ *is true (resp. false) for all* $S \in C(M)$, *and* $[M \models \varphi] = maybe$ *otherwise*[6]. □

Note that the relations $\longrightarrow$ and $\dashrightarrow$ can together be seen as a 2-bit encoding of a single "3-valued transition relation", i.e. a predicate that maps every pair s, t of states into **3**: when $s \longrightarrow t$ and $s \dashrightarrow t$, this transition relation has value *true*; when neither $s \longrightarrow t$ nor $s \dashrightarrow t$, it has value *false*; and when only $s \dashrightarrow t$, it is *maybe*; note that the fourth combination is excluded by the requirement that $\longrightarrow \subseteq \dashrightarrow$. In terms of this 3-valued transition relation, the intuition behind a KMTS's transition structure can be explained as follows. View a state s of a KMTS as the set of all Kripke Structure states that it abstracts (i.e., $\{n \mid n \succeq s\}$). Consider the value of the transition between KMTS states s and t. If it is *true*, then all states in s have a transition to some state in t. If it is *false*, then *no* state in s has a transition to any state in t. If it is *maybe*, then some states in s do, and others do not, have a transition to some state in t.

We can "massage" a KMTS into an automaton by splitting its states so that all propositions and transitions become definite (*true* or *false*). What makes this possible[7] is the presence of OR states: Initially, trivial OR states (with single successors) are inserted into the KMTS – one OR state preceding every KMTS state – similar to the definition of the transformation $\mathcal{A}ut$ of Definition 5. Consider a state s and a proposition p that evaluates to *maybe* in s, see Figure 2(a). If we view s as its concretization some of its concrete states will evaluate p to *true*, and others to *false*. We split s so as to separate these states from one another, creating new abstract states s' and s'' in place of s, one where p is *true*, and another where it is *false*. All transitions from s are copied to both s' and s''. Similarly, a state s with an outgoing *maybe* transition (to OR state t, say) is replaced by two states, one with a *true* transition to t, the other with a *false* transition to t; see Figure 2(b).

This is done for every state s, every proposition that is *maybe* in s, and every outgoing *maybe* transition from s. This translation, called τ, will be defined more formally below. While it turns the completion of a KMTS into the language of the resulting automaton, i.e. $C(M) = \pounds(\tau(M))$, it does not follow that M and $\tau(M)$

---

[6] Compared to the definitions in [17] and [13], we have added initial states to KMTS's. In this case, a temporal property is defined to be *true* (*false*) for a KMTS if it is *true* (resp. *false*) in all initial states, and *maybe* otherwise.

[7] This is not possible in general if we stay within the framework of KMTS's, which can be seen by considering the KMTS that has a single state where the (single) proposition p is *maybe*, and which has *must* and *may* transitions back to itself. There exists no *finite* 2-valued KMTS that has the same completion – the set of all total trees labeled with subsets of $\{p\}$.

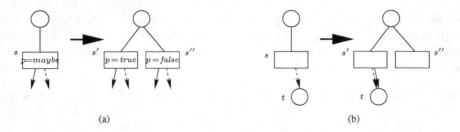

(a)   (b)

Fig. 2. Removing 3-valuedness from propositions (a) and transitions (b) by splitting states. Must and may transitions are depicted as solid and dashed arrows resp.

make the same properties true. For this, we need to generalize the semantics $\models^\alpha$ of branching-time properties, interpreted over automata, to be 3-valued as well.

Definition 9. *The 3-valued semantics $\models^\alpha$ maps an automaton and a branching-time property φ (expressed by an automaton $\mathcal{A}_\varphi$) to $\mathbf{3}$, as follows. $[\mathcal{A} \models^\alpha \mathcal{A}_\varphi] =$ true (false) if $\mathcal{L}(\mathcal{A}) \subseteq \mathcal{L}(\mathcal{A}_\varphi)$ (resp. $\mathcal{L}(\mathcal{A}) \subseteq \overline{\mathcal{L}(\mathcal{A}_\varphi)}$) and maybe otherwise.*   □

Theorem 5. *For every KMTS M and branching-time temporal property φ, $[M \models \varphi] = [\tau(M) \models^\alpha \mathcal{A}_\varphi]$.*

4.1   Modal Automata

The description of τ above can be seen as a two-step process. First, by inserting OR states, the KMTS is lifted into a special kind of automaton, namely one that allows 3-valued propositions and transitions. Then, this 3-valuedness is compiled away by splitting BRANCH states.

Definition 10. *A modal automaton $\mathcal{A}$ is a tuple $(Q, B, \hat{Q}, \mathrm{OR}, \longrightarrow, \dashrightarrow, P, \Omega)$ where Q, B, $\hat{Q}$, OR, Ω are as in Definition 2, and:*

- *$\longrightarrow, \dashrightarrow \subseteq B \times Q$ are must and may transition relations, resp., from BRANCH states to OR states, and*
- *$P = \{pred_p \mid p \in Prop\}$, where for every $p \in Prop$, $pred_p : B \to \mathbf{3}$.*   □

The notion of automaton simulation from Definition 4, $\sqsubseteq$, is extended to these modal automata.

Definition 11. *The simulation relation $\sqsubseteq$ on modal automata is defined as in Definition 4 where $\mathcal{A}_1$ and $\mathcal{A}_2$ are now modal automata, and rule 3 is replaced by the following:*

3. *(BRANCH) In a "BRANCH" configuration (b_1, b_2) (where $b_1 \in B_1$ and $b_2 \in B_2$), each of the following are continuations of the play:*
   (a) *(Prop) In this continuation, the play ends and is a win for Player I if for all $p \in Prop$, $p(b_1) \geq p(b_2)$, and it is a win for for Player II otherwise.*
   (b) *(may) Player II chooses an OR state q_1 such that $b_1 \dashrightarrow_1 q_1$; Player I must respond with an OR state q_2 such that $b_2 \dashrightarrow_2 q_2$, and the play continues from configuration (q_1, q_2).*

(c) (must) Player II chooses an OR *state* q_2 *such that* $b_2 \longrightarrow_2 q_2$; *Player I must respond with an* OR *state* q_1 *such that* $b_1 \longrightarrow_1 q_1$, *and the play continues from configuration* (q_1, q_2).

The language $\pounds(\mathcal{A})$ *of a modal automaton* $\mathcal{A}$ *is the set of all Kripke Structures* $\mathcal{S}$ *such that* $Aut(\mathcal{S}) \sqsubseteq \mathcal{A}$. □

τ is now defined as the composition of translations τ_1 and τ_2:

$$\tau: \quad \text{KMTS} \xrightarrow{\tau_1} \text{modal (i.e., 3-valued) automaton} \xrightarrow{\tau_2} \text{(2-valued) automaton}$$

The definition of τ_1 is a generalization of the embedding Aut of Def. 5.

Definition 12. *Let* $M = (S, \hat{S}, \longrightarrow, \dashrightarrow, P)$ *be a KMTS. The modal automaton associated with* M, $\tau_1(M)$, *is as follows:* $\tau_1(M)$ *has* OR *states* $\{q_s | s \in S\}$, BRANCH *states* $\{b_s \mid s \in S\}$, *and initial states* $\{q_{\hat{s}} \mid \hat{s} \in \hat{S}\}$. *Each* OR *state* q_s *has* b_s *as its only* OR *choice. Each* BRANCH *state* b_s *has a* $\longrightarrow$ $(\dashrightarrow)$ *transition to* q_t *for every* t *such that* $\longrightarrow (s,t)$ *(resp.* $\dashrightarrow (s,t)$) *in the KMTS. The predicates of* $\tau_1(M)$ *are the same as in the KMTS. The indexing function assigns 0 to every* OR *state.* □

Lemma 2. *Let* M *be a KMTS. Then* $C(M) = \pounds(\tau_1(M))$.

Proof. Similar to the proof of Lemma 1.

The translation τ_2, that compiles away 3-valued propositions and transitions from a modal automaton while preserving its language, is itself defined in two steps. The first step, τ_{2A}, removes 3-valuedness from the propositional labeling, yielding modal automata that have *must* and *may* transitions, but whose state predicates assign definite values to states.

Definition 13. *Let* $\mathcal{A} = (Q, B, \hat{Q}, \text{OR}, \longrightarrow, \dashrightarrow, P, \Omega)$ *be a modal automaton. For* $b \in B$, *define its associated* valuation $val(b) : Prop \to \mathbf{3}$ *to be* $\lambda\ p \in Prop\ .\ pred_p(b)$. *For a valuation* $v : Prop \to \mathbf{3}$, *define its* completion $Compl(v)$ *as* $\{w : Prop \to \mathbf{2} \mid w \geq v\}$. *With every state* $b \in B$ *we associate a fresh set* $C(b) = \{b_w \mid w \in Compl(val(b))\}$ *of states. The modal automaton* $\tau_{2A}(\mathcal{A})$ *is defined as follows.*

- *its set of* OR *states is* Q,
- *its set of* BRANCH *states is* $\bigcup_{b \in B} C(b)$,
- *its set of initial states is* $\hat{Q}$,
- *its choice relation is* $\{(q, b_w) \mid (q, b) \in \text{OR}, b_w \in C(b)\}$,
- *its must transition relation is* $\{(b_w, q) \mid b \longrightarrow q, b_w \in C(b)\}$,
- *its may transition relation is* $\{(b_w, q) \mid b \dashrightarrow q, b_w \in C(b)\}$,
- *for every* $p \in Prop$ *and* $b_w \in$ BRANCH, $pred_p(b_w) = w(p)$, *and*
- *its indexing function is* $\lambda\ q\ .\ 0$. □

Lemma 3. *Let* $\mathcal{A}$ *be a modal automaton. Then* $\pounds(\mathcal{A}) = \pounds(\tau_{2A}(\mathcal{A}))$.

The kind of automata targeted by τ_{2A} have actually been defined in [19], where it is also shown that they can be translated back to (non-modal) automata. We reuse their result here, to emphasize the close relationship between the use of 3-valuedness for abstraction in verification, and developments in the field of automata theory. In [19], the BRANCH transitions from a state t which has OR successors $q_1, \ldots, q_k$ are given as a first-order logic formula of the form $\exists n_1, \ldots, n_k. \ q_1(n_1) \wedge \cdots \wedge q_k(n_k) \ \wedge \ \forall z. \ \beta(z)$ which specifies when a tree node x is accepted from the automaton state t. The variables n_i and z range over the child nodes of x. The notation $q(n)$ means that (the tree rooted at) child n is accepted from state q, and $\beta(z)$ is a conjunction of disjunctions of formulas of the form $q(n)$. Thus, the formula says that for every $1 \le i \le k$, there exists a child n_i of x that is accepted from q_i, and in addition the constraint β must hold for all children of x. Note that the automata from Def. 2 are a special case where the β is of the form $\exists 1 \le i \le k. \ q_i(z)$. Furthermore, *must* and *may* transitions can be recovered as well. Let $Q_{must} = \{q'_1, \ldots, q'_l\}$ be a subset of $\{q_1, \ldots, q_k\}$. The formula $\exists n_1, \ldots, n_l. \ q'_1(n_1) \wedge \cdots \wedge q'_l(n_l) \ \wedge \ \forall z \ \exists 1 \le i \le k. \ q_i(z)$ then specifies that the states in Q_{must} act as *must* successors, while all q_i are *may* successors of t. Hence this special form of automaton is the same as a modal automaton with *must* and *may* transitions, but in which all propositional valuations are definite. In [19] it is shown that such automata can be translated back into the restricted form of Def. 2, i.e., calling the translation τ_{2B}, it is shown that $\mathcal{L}(\mathcal{A}) = \mathcal{L}(\tau_{2B}(\mathcal{A}))$. Together with Lemma 3, this implies the correctness of τ_2 which is defined as τ_{2A} followed by τ_{2B}.

Lemma 4. *Let $\mathcal{A}$ be a modal automaton. Then $\mathcal{L}(\mathcal{A}) = \mathcal{L}(\tau_2(\mathcal{A}))$.*

Finally, Theorem 5 follows easily from Lemma 2 and Lemma 4.

5   Maximal Model Theorems

In the previous sections we have proposed to use automata as the abstract objects in an abstraction framework for checking branching-time properties over transition systems. In the resulting framework, the concrete and abstract objects do not live in strictly separated worlds: through the embedding $\mathcal{A}ut$ from Definition 5, transition systems themselves are promoted to automata – be it possibly infinite ones. It follows from Lemma 1 that the transition system and its embedding satisfy the same branching time properties, regardless of whether these are evaluated using the language inclusion or the simulation based definition. Furthermore, Lemma 1 and Theorem 2 together show that the abstraction relation between the concrete and abstract domains can be embedded into the *abstraction order* $\sqsubseteq$ over the abstract domain.

Another area that can benefit from this view is the study of *maximal models*. There, we also consider objects ordered by an abstraction order which is such that more-abstract objects satisfy fewer properties, relative to a given logic of interest. A *maximal model* for a property is then a model for the property that is maximally abstract. In abstraction frameworks such as the ones above, where the concrete domain is embedded in the abstract domain, there is a close connection between maximal models and completeness, made explicit below.

Theorem 6. *If every property has a finite maximal model, then the abstraction framework is complete.*

Proof. Let M be a model of property ϕ, and let max_ϕ be a finite maximal model for ϕ. By definition of maximality, max_ϕ abstracts M. Thus, one can always pick max_ϕ as a finite abstraction for M, ensuring completeness.

The converse is not necessarily true.Grumberg and Long showed [15] how to construct finite, fair Kripke Structures that are maximal models for ACTL (the universal fragment of CTL) through tableaux constructions; this was extended to ACTL* by Kupferman and Vardi [21], using a combination of tableaux and automata-theoretic constructions. By the theorem above, it follows immediately that fair simulation abstraction yields a complete framework for ACTL, ACTL*, and linear-time temporal logic (which can be considered to be a sublogic of ACTL*). For the richer branching time logics that include existential path quantification, however, there cannot be such maximal models.

Theorem 7. *In abstraction frameworks for branching time logics that are based on Kripke Structures or Kripke Modal Transition Systems, not every property has a finite maximal model.*

Proof. This follows immediately from Theorem 6 and the result of [6] showing that these frameworks are incomplete for existential properties.

One can recover the guarantee of finite maximal models, however, by enlarging the class of structures to include automata[8]. A Kripke Structure M is now viewed as the automaton $\mathcal{A}ut(M)$.

Theorem 8. *In the automaton abstraction frameworks based either on language inclusion or on simulation, every property has a finite maximal model.*

Proof. Consider a property given as a finite automaton $\mathcal{B}$. Viewed as a structure, $\mathcal{B}$ satisfies the property $\mathcal{B}$ in either framework. For any other model M of $\mathcal{B}$, letting the satisfaction and simulation relations coincide for automata models, $\mathcal{B}$ is maximal in the abstraction order. Hence, $\mathcal{B}$ is a finite maximal model for property $\mathcal{B}$ in either framework.

We can use the connection made in Theorem 8 to re-derive the maximal model results for ACTL and ACTL*; in fact, we can extend these easily to the universal fragment of the mu-calculus, A_μ. It should be noted that A_μ is more expressive than even ACTL* (e.g., "every even-depth successor satisfies P" ($\nu Z : p \wedge \mathsf{AX}(\mathsf{AX}(Z))$) is expressible in A_μ but not in ACTL*). The idea is to (i) construct an equivalent finite automaton for a formula in this logic – this is using known techniques from automata theory –, (ii) view this automaton as a maximal model, following the theorem above, and then (iii) show that, due to its special structure, it can be transformed back to a Kripke Structure. The result is the following theorem. Its proof is omitted due to space constraints.

---

[8] This solution is similar to the introduction of complex numbers: enlarging the solution space from real to complex numbers ensures that every non-constant polynomial has a "zero".

Theorem 9. *The fair simulation abstraction framework on Kripke Structures is complete for A_μ.*

6   Discussion

We have proposed to use tree automata as abstractions of countable transition systems, in the verification of branching time properties. A tree automaton serves as an abstraction for any transition system in its language. Expressing also branching time properties as tree automata, the definition of when a property holds on an abstraction can be defined as language inclusion, or alternatively as simulation between automata. Both frameworks are trivially sound. The notion of simulation between automata on infinite trees is novel to the best of our knowledge. Like in the word case, it is easier to decide than language inclusion, and is a sufficient condition for it.

Also completeness follows directly in both frameworks. The completeness argument shows that, for a transition system S and a property A_φ that is true of it, the finite abstraction of S that can be used to demonstrate A_φ is A_φ itself. This highlights the essence of the more elaborate completeness arguments presented in [32, 20, 25, 6]. The use of Janin and Walukiewicz' μ-automata, whose languages are closed under bisimulation and therefore correspond naturally to the μ-calculus, further simplifies the technical presentation.

Section 4 demonstrated how Kripke Modal Transition Systems can be transformed into automata. Similar constructions can be carried out for the other transition notions, such as disjunctive modal transition systems. The insight gained from these transformations is that one can view the various proposals in the literature as being but variations on automaton syntax, some more compact than others. This point is implicit in our earlier paper [6], which demonstrates that *alternating* tree automata – the most compact automaton notation – correspond to Focused Transition Systems.

A key issue in the practice of verification via abstractions is how to automatically obtain suitable abstractions. By the embedding results of Section 4, any approach to the construction of abstractions (e.g. [30]) can be used in the automaton-based framework. While the problem is undecidable in general, the completeness result guarantees that a suitable automaton-as-abstraction always exists.

Going beyond the technical benefits of automata, we feel that viewing automata as abstract objects, and realizing that known notions are but automata in disguise, is a simple but profound shift of perspective that should enable many fruitful connections between abstraction and automata theory.

Acknowledgements

We thank Nils Klarlund for his contributions to several discussion on the topic of this paper, and for his comments on an earlier draft. This work is supported in part by NSF grant CCR-0341658.

References

1. G. Bruns and P. Godefroid. Model checking partial state spaces with 3-valued temporal logics. In *CAV*, volume 1633 of *LNCS*. Springer, 1999.
2. M. Chechik, S. Easterbrook, and V. Petrovykh. Model-Checking over Multi-valued Logics. In *FME*, volume 2021 of *LNCS*. Springer, 2001.
3. E.M. Clarke and E. A. Emerson. Design and synthesis of synchronization skeletons using branching time temporal logic. In *Workshop on Logics of Programs*, volume 131 of *LNCS*. Springer-Verlag, 1981.
4. R. Cleaveland, P. Iyer, and D. Yankelevich. Optimality in abstractions of model checking. In *SAS*, volume 983 of *LNCS*. Springer, 1995.
5. P. Cousot and R. Cousot. Abstract interpretation: A unified lattice model for static analysis of programs by construction or approximation of fixpoints. In *POPL*, 1977.
6. D. Dams and K.S. Namjoshi. The existence of finite abstractions for branching time model checking. In *LICS*, 2004.
7. D. Dams, R. Gerth, and O. Grumberg. Abstract interpretation of reactive systems. *ACM TOPLAS*, 19(2):253–291, 1997.
8. D. Dams, Y. Lakhnech, and M. Steffen. Iterating transducers. In *J. of Logic and Algebraic Programming*, 52–53:109–127. Elsevier, 2002.
9. D. Dams. *Abstract Interpretation and Partition Refinement for Model Checking*. PhD thesis, July 1996.
10. L. de Alfaro, P. Godefroid, and R. Jagadeesan. Three-valued abstractions of games: Uncertainty, but with precision. In *LICS*, 2004.
11. E.A. Emerson and C.S. Jutla. The complexity of tree automata and logics of programs (extended abstract). In *FOCS*, 1988. Full version in *SIAM Journal of Computing*, 29(1):132–158, 1999.
12. E.A. Emerson and C.S. Jutla. Tree automata, mu-calculus and determinacy (extended abstract). In *FOCS*, 1991.
13. P. Godefroid and R. Jagadeesan. On the expressiveness of 3-valued models. In *VMCAI*, volume 2575 of *LNCS*. Springer, 2003.
14. R. Giacobazzi, F. Ranzato, and F. Scozzari. Making abstract interpretations complete. *Journal of the ACM*, 47(2):361–416, 2000.
15. O. Grumberg and D.E. Long. Model checking and modular verification. In *ACM TOPLAS*, 1994.
16. T.A. Henzinger, O. Kupferman, and S. Rajamani. Fair simulation. In *CONCUR*, volume 1243 of *LNCS*. Springer, 1997.
17. M. Huth, R. Jagadeesan, and D. Schmidt. Modal transition systems: A foundation for three-valued program analysis. In *ESOP*, volume 2028 of *LNCS*. Springer, 2001.
18. D. Janin and I. Walukiewicz. Automata for the modal mu-calulus and related results. In *MFCS*, volume 969 of *LNCS*. Springer, 1995.
19. D. Janin and I. Walukiewicz. On the expressive completeness of the propositional mu-calculus with respect to monadic second order logic. In *CONCUR*, volume 1119 of *LNCS*. Springer, 1996.
20. Y. Kesten and A. Pnueli. Verification by augmented finitary abstraction. *Information and Computation*, 163(1):203-243. Elsevier, 2000.
21. O. Kupferman and M.Y. Vardi. Modular model checking. In *COMPOS*, volume 1536 of *LNCS*. Springer, 1997.
22. K.G. Larsen and B. Thomsen. A modal process logic. In *LICS*, 1988.
23. K.G. Larsen and L. Xinxin. Equation solving using modal transition systems. In *LICS*, 1990.

24. R. Milner. An algebraic definition of simulation between programs. In *2nd IJCAI*. William Kaufmann, 1971.
25. K.S. Namjoshi. Abstraction for branching time properties. In *CAV*, volume 2725 of *LNCS*. Springer, 2003.
26. F. Nielson, H. R. Nielson, and C. Hankin. *Principles of Program Analysis*. Springer, 1999.
27. J.P. Queille and J. Sifakis. Specification and verification of concurrent systems in CESAR. In *Proc. of the 5th Intl. Symp. on Programming*, volume 137 of *LNCS*. Springer-Verlag, 1982.
28. D. A. Schmidt. Closed and logical relations for over- and under-approximation of powersets. In *SAS*, volume 3148 of *LNCS*. Springer, 2004.
29. H. Seidl. Deciding equivalence of finite tree automata. *SIAM Journal of Computing*, 19:424–437, 1990.
30. S. Shoham and O. Grumberg. Monotonic abstraction-refinement for CTL. In *TACAS*, volume 2988 of *LNCS*. Springer, 2004.
31. R.S. Streett and E.A. Emerson. The propositional mu-calculus is elementary. In *ICALP*, volume 172 of *LNCS*, 1984. Full version in *Information and Computation* 81(3): 249-264, 1989.
32. T.E. Uribe. *Abstraction-Based Deductive-Algorithmic Verification of Reactive Systems*. PhD thesis, Stanford University, 1999.

Don't Know in the μ-Calculus

Orna Grumberg[1], Martin Lange[2], Martin Leucker[3], and Sharon Shoham[1]

[1] Computer Science Department, The Technion, Haifa, Israel
[2] Institut für Informatik, University of Munich, Germany
[3] Institut für Informatik, Technical University of Munich, Germany

Abstract. This work presents game-based model checking for abstract models with respect to specifications in μ-calculus, interpreted over a 3-valued semantics. If the model checking result is indefinite (*don't know*), the abstract model is refined, based on an analysis of the cause for this result. For finite concrete models our abstraction-refinement is fully automatic and guaranteed to terminate with a definite result *true* or *false*.

1 Introduction

This work presents a game-based [19] model checking approach for abstract models with respect to specifications in the μ-calculus, interpreted over a 3-valued semantics. In case the model checking result is indefinite (*don't know*), the abstract model is refined, based on an analysis of the cause for this result. If the concrete model is finite then our abstraction-refinement is fully automatic and guaranteed to terminate with a definite result (*true* or *false*).

Abstraction is one of the most successful techniques for fighting the state explosion problem in model checking [3]. Abstractions hide some of the details of the verified system, thus result in a smaller model. Usually, they are designed to be *conservative* for *true*, meaning that if a formula is true of the abstract model then it is also true of the concrete (precise) model of the system. However, if it is false in the abstract model then nothing can be deduced of the concrete one.

The *μ-calculus* [12] is a powerful formalism for expressing properties of transition systems using fixpoint operators. Many verification procedures can be solved by translating them into μ–calculus model checking [1]. Such problems include (fair) CTL model checking, LTL model checking, bisimulation equivalence and language containment of ω-regular automata.

In the context of abstraction, often only the universal fragment of μ-calculus is considered [14]. Over-approximated abstract models are used for verification of such formulae while under-approximated abstract models are used for their refutation.

Abstractions designed for full μ-calculus [6] have the advantage of handling both verification and refutation on the same abstract model. A greater advantage is obtained if μ-calculus is interpreted w.r.t the 3-valued semantics [11,10]. This semantics evaluates a formula to either *true*, *false* or *indefinite*. Abstract models can then be designed to be conservative for both *true* and *false*. Only if the value of a formula in the abstract model is indefinite, its value in the concrete

R. Cousot (Ed.): VMCAI 2005, LNCS 3385, pp. 233–249, 2005.
© Springer-Verlag Berlin Heidelberg 2005

model is unknown. Then, a refinement is needed in order to make the abstract model more precise. Previous works [13, 16, 17] suggested abstraction-refinement mechanisms for various branching time logics over *2-valued* semantics.

Many algorithms for μ-calculus model checking with respect to the 2-valued semantics have been suggested [8, 20, 22, 5, 15]. An elegant solution to this problem is the game-based approach [19], in which two players, the verifier (denoted $\exists$) and the refuter (denoted $\forall$), try to win a game. A formula φ is true in a model M iff the verifier has a winning strategy, meaning that she can win any play, no matter what the refuter does. The game is played on a *game graph*, consisting of configurations $s \vdash \psi$, where s is a state of the model M and ψ is a subformula of φ. The players make moves between configurations in which they try to verify or refute ψ in s. These games can also be studied as *parity games* [7] and we follow this approach as well.

In model checking games for the 2-valued semantics, exactly one of the players has a winning strategy, thus the model checking result is either true or false. For the 3-valued semantics, a third value should also be possible. Following [18], we change the definition of a game for μ-calculus so that a *tie* is also possible.

To determine the winner, if there is one, we adapt the recursive algorithm for solving parity games by Zielonka [23]. This algorithm recursively computes the set of configurations in which one of the players has a winning strategy. It then concludes that in all other configurations the other player has a winning strategy.

In our algorithm we need to compute recursively three sets, since there are also those configurations in which none of the players has a winning strategy. We prove that our algorithm always terminates and returns the correct result.

In case the model checking game results in a tie, we identify a cause for the tie and try to eliminate it by refining the abstract model. More specifically, we adapt the presented algorithm to keep track of why a vertex in the game is classified as a tie. We then exploit the information gathered by the algorithm for refinement. The refinement is applied only to parts of the model from which tie is possible. Vertices from which there is a winning strategy for one of the players are not changed. Thus, the refined abstract models do not grow unnecessarily. If the concrete model is finite then our abstraction-refinement is guaranteed to terminate with a definite result.

It is the refinement based on the algorithm which rules out the otherwise interesting approach taken for example in [11, 10] in which a 3-valued μ-calculus model checking problem is reduced to two 2-valued μ-calculus model checking problems.

Organization of the paper. The 3-valued μ-calculus is introduced in the next section. Then we describe the abstractions we have in mind. In Section 4, a 3-valued model-checking game for μ-calculus is shown. We give a model-checking algorithm for 3-valued games with a finite board in Section 5, and, explain how to refine the abstract model, in case of an indefinite answer in Section 6. We conclude in Section 7.

2 The 3-Valued μ-Calculus

Let $\mathcal{P}$ be a set of *propositional constants*, and $\mathcal{A}$ be a set of *action names*. Every $a \in \mathcal{A}$ is associated with a so-called *must*-action $a!$ and a *may*-action $a?$. Let $\mathcal{A}! = \{a! \mid a \in \mathcal{A}\}$ and $\mathcal{A}? = \{a? \mid a \in \mathcal{A}\}$. A *Kripke Modal Transition System* (KMTS) is a tuple $\mathcal{T} = (\mathcal{S}, \{\xrightarrow{x} \mid x \in \mathcal{A}! \cup \mathcal{A}?\}, L)$ where $\mathcal{S}$ is a set of states, and $\xrightarrow{x} \subseteq \mathcal{S} \times \mathcal{S}$ for each $x \in \mathcal{A}! \cup \mathcal{A}?$ is a binary relation on states, s.t. for all $a \in Act$: $\xrightarrow{a!} \subseteq \xrightarrow{a?}$.

Let $\mathbb{B}_3 = \{\bot, ?, \top\}$ be partially ordered by $\bot \leq ? \leq \top$. Then $L : \mathcal{S} \to \mathbb{B}_3^{\mathcal{P}}$, where $\mathbb{B}_3^{\mathcal{P}}$ is the set of functions from $\mathcal{P}$ to $\mathbb{B}_3$. We use $\top$ to denote that a proposition holds in a state, $\bot$ for not holding, and $?$ if it cannot be determined whether it holds or not.

A Kripke structure in the usual sense can be regarded as a KMTS by setting $\xrightarrow{a!} = \xrightarrow{a?}$ for all $a \in \mathcal{A}$ and not distinguishing them anymore. Furthermore, its states labelling is over $\{\bot, \top\}$.

Let $\mathcal{V}$ be a set of propositional variables. Formulae of the *3-valued modal μ-calculus* in *positive normal form* are given by

$$\varphi ::= q \mid \neg q \mid Z \mid \varphi \vee \varphi \mid \varphi \wedge \varphi \mid \langle a \rangle \varphi \mid [a]\varphi \mid \mu Z.\varphi \mid \nu Z.\varphi$$

where $q \in \mathcal{P}$, $a \in \mathcal{A}$, and $Z \in \mathcal{V}$. Let $3\text{-}\mathcal{L}_\mu$ denote the set of *closed* formulae generated by the above grammar, where the fixpoint quantifiers μ and ν are variable binders. We will also write η for either μ or ν. Furthermore we assume that formulae are well-named, i.e. no variable is bound more than once in any formula. Thus, every variable Z *identifies* a unique subformula $fp(Z) = \eta Z.\psi$ of φ, where the set $Sub(\varphi)$ of *subformulae* of φ is defined in the usual way.

Given variables Y, Z we write $Y \prec_\varphi Z$ if Z occurs freely in $fp(Y)$ in φ, and $Y <_\varphi Z$ if (Y, Z) is in the transitive closure of $\prec_\varphi$. The alternation depth $ad(\varphi)$ of φ is the length of a maximal $<_\varphi$-chain of variables in φ s.t. adjacent variables in this chain have different fixpoint types.

The semantics of a $3\text{-}\mathcal{L}_\mu$ formula is an element of $\mathbb{B}_3^{\mathcal{S}}$—the functions from $\mathcal{S}$ to $\mathbb{B}_3$—which forms a boolean lattice when equipped with the following partial order: let $f, g : \mathcal{S} \to \mathbb{B}_3$. $f \sqsubseteq g$ iff $\forall s \in \mathcal{S} : f(s) \leq g(s)$. Joins (meets) in this lattice are denoted by $f \sqcup g$ ($f \sqcap g$, resp.). The complement of f, written $\overline{f}$ is defined by $\overline{f}(s) := \overline{f(s)}$ for $s \in \mathcal{S}$ where $\bot$ and $\top$ are complementary to each other, and $\overline{?} =?$.

Then the *semantics* $\llbracket \varphi \rrbracket_\rho^{\mathcal{T}}$ of a $3\text{-}\mathcal{L}_\mu$ formula φ w.r.t. a KMTS $\mathcal{T} = (\mathcal{S}, \{\xrightarrow{x} \mid x \in \mathcal{A}! \cup \mathcal{A}?\}, L)$ and an *environment* $\rho : \mathcal{V} \to \mathbb{B}_3^{\mathcal{S}}$, which explains the meaning of free variables in φ, is an element of $\mathbb{B}_3^{\mathcal{S}}$. We assume $\mathcal{T}$ to be fixed and do not mention it explicitly anymore. With $\rho[Z \mapsto f]$ we denote the environment that maps Z to f and agrees with ρ on all other arguments. Later, when only closed formulae are considered, we will also drop the environment from the semantic brackets.

$$
\begin{aligned}
\llbracket q \rrbracket_\rho &:= \lambda s.L(s)(q) \\
\llbracket \neg q \rrbracket_\rho &:= \lambda s.\overline{L(s)(q)} \\
\llbracket Z \rrbracket_\rho &:= \rho(Z)
\end{aligned}
$$

$$[\![\varphi \vee \psi]\!]_\rho \quad := \quad [\![\varphi]\!]_\rho \sqcup [\![\psi]\!]_\rho$$
$$[\![\varphi \wedge \psi]\!]_\rho \quad := \quad [\![\varphi]\!]_\rho \sqcap [\![\psi]\!]_\rho$$

$$[\![\langle a \rangle \varphi]\!]_\rho \quad := \quad \lambda s. \begin{cases} \top \,, \text{ if } \exists t \in \mathcal{S}, \text{ s.t. } s \xrightarrow{a!} t \text{ and } [\![\varphi]\!]_\rho(t) = \top \\ \bot \,, \text{ if } \forall t \in \mathcal{S}, \text{ if } s \xrightarrow{a?} t \text{ then } [\![\varphi]\!]_\rho(t) = \bot \\ ? \,, \text{ otherwise} \end{cases}$$

$$[\![[a]\varphi]\!]_\rho \quad := \quad \lambda s. \begin{cases} \top \,, \text{ if } \forall t \in \mathcal{S}, \text{ if } s \xrightarrow{a?} t \text{ then } [\![\varphi]\!]_\rho(t) = \top \\ \bot \,, \text{ if } \exists t \in \mathcal{S}, \text{ s.t. } s \xrightarrow{a!} t \text{ and } [\![\varphi]\!]_\rho(t) = \bot \\ ? \,, \text{ otherwise} \end{cases}$$

$$[\![\mu Z.\varphi]\!]_\rho \quad := \quad \bigsqcap \{f \mid [\![\varphi]\!]_{\rho[Z \mapsto f]} \sqsubseteq f\}$$
$$[\![\nu Z.\varphi]\!]_\rho \quad := \quad \bigsqcup \{f \mid f \sqsubseteq [\![\varphi]\!]_{\rho[Z \mapsto f]}\}$$

Note that $s \xrightarrow{a!} t$ implies $s \xrightarrow{a?} t$.

The functionals $\lambda f.[\![\varphi]\!]_{\rho[Z \mapsto f]} : \mathbb{B}_3^{\mathcal{S}} \to \mathbb{B}_3^{\mathcal{S}}$ are monotone w.r.t. $\sqsubseteq$ for any Z, φ and $\mathcal{S}$. According to [21], least and greatest fixpoints of these functionals exist.

Approximants of 3-$\mathcal{L}_\mu$ formulae are defined in the usual way: if $fp(Z) = \mu Z.\varphi$ then $Z^0 := \lambda s.\bot$, $Z^{\alpha+1} := [\![\varphi]\!]_{\rho[Z \mapsto Z^\alpha]}$ for any ordinal α and any environment ρ, and $Z^\lambda := \bigsqcap_{\alpha < \lambda} Z^\alpha$ for a limit ordinal λ. Dually, if $fp(Z) = \nu Z.\varphi$ then $Z^0 := \lambda s.\top$, $Z^{\alpha+1} := [\![\varphi]\!]_{\rho[Z \mapsto Z^\alpha]}$, and $Z^\lambda := \bigsqcup_{\alpha < \lambda} Z^\alpha$.

Theorem 1. [21] *For all KMTS $\mathcal{T}$ with state set $\mathcal{S}$ there is an $\alpha \in \mathbb{O}rd$ s.t. for all $s \in \mathcal{S}$ we have: if $[\![\eta Z.\varphi]\!]_\rho(s) = x$ then $Z^\alpha(s) = x$.*

3   Abstraction

We use *Kripke Modal Transition Systems* [11, 9] as abstract models that preserve satisfaction and falsification of 3-$\mathcal{L}_\mu$ formulae.

Let $\mathcal{T}_C = (\mathcal{S}_C, \{\xrightarrow{a}_C \mid a \in \mathcal{A}\}, L_C)$ be a (concrete) Kripke structure. Let $\mathcal{S}_A$ be a set of *abstract states* and $\gamma : \mathcal{S}_A \to 2^{\mathcal{S}_C}$ a total *concretization function* that maps each abstract state to the set of concrete states it represents. An abstract model, a KMTS $\mathcal{T}_A = (\mathcal{S}_A, \{\xrightarrow{x}_A \mid x \in \mathcal{A}! \cup \mathcal{A}?\}, L_A)$, can then be defined as follows.

The labelling of an abstract state is defined in accordance with the labelling of all the concrete states it represents. For $p \in \mathcal{P} : L_A(s_a)(p) = \top \,(\bot)$ only if $\forall s_c \in \gamma(s_a) : L_C(s_c)(p) = \top \,(\bot)$. In the remaining cases $L_A(s_a)(p) = ?$.

The *may*-transitions in an abstract model are computed such that every concrete transition between two states is represented by them: For every action $a \in \mathcal{A}$, if $\exists s_c \in \gamma(s_a)$ and $\exists s_c' \in \gamma(s_a')$ such that $s_c \xrightarrow{a}_C s_c'$, then there exists a may transition $s_a \xrightarrow{a?}_A s_a'$. Note that it is possible that there are additional may transitions as well. The *must*-transitions, on the other hand, represent concrete transitions that are common to all the concrete states that are represented by the source abstract state: a *must*-transition $s_a \xrightarrow{a!}_A s_a'$ exists only if $\forall s_c \in \gamma(s_a)$ $\exists s_c' \in \gamma(s_a')$ such that $s_c \xrightarrow{a}_C s_c'$. Note that it is possible that there are less must transitions than allowed by this rule. That is, the may and must transitions do not have to be *exact*, as long as they maintain these conditions.

$$\frac{s \vdash \psi_0 \vee \psi_1}{s \vdash \psi_i} \; \exists : \; i \in \{0,1\} \qquad\qquad \frac{s \vdash \psi_0 \wedge \psi_1}{s \vdash \psi_i} \; \forall : \; i \in \{0,1\}$$

$$\frac{s \vdash \eta Z.\varphi}{s \vdash Z} \; \exists \qquad\qquad \frac{s \vdash Z}{s \vdash \varphi} \; \exists : \text{if } fp(Z) = \eta Z.\varphi$$

$$\frac{s \vdash \langle a \rangle \varphi}{t \vdash \varphi} \; \exists : \; s \xrightarrow{a!} t \text{ or } s \xrightarrow{a?} t \qquad\qquad \frac{s \vdash [a]\varphi}{s \vdash \varphi} \; \forall : \; s \xrightarrow{a!} t \text{ or } s \xrightarrow{a?} t$$

Fig. 1. The model checking game rules for 3-$\mathcal{L}_\mu$.

Theorem 2. [9] *Let $\mathcal{T}$ be a Kripke structure and let $\mathcal{T}'$ be a KMTS obtained from $\mathcal{T}$ with the abstraction process described above. Let s be a state of $\mathcal{T}$ and s' its corresponding abstract state in $\mathcal{T}'$. For all closed $\varphi \in$ 3-$\mathcal{L}_\mu$: $[\![\varphi]\!]^{\mathcal{T}'}(s') \neq ?$ implies $[\![\varphi]\!]^{\mathcal{T}}(s) = [\![\varphi]\!]^{\mathcal{T}'}(s')$.*

4 Model Checking Games for 3-$\mathcal{L}_\mu$

The *model checking game* $\Gamma_\mathcal{T}(s_0, \varphi_0)$ on a KMTS $\mathcal{T}$ with state set $\mathcal{S}$, initial state $s_0 \in \mathcal{S}$ and a 3-$\mathcal{L}_\mu$ formula φ_0 is played by players $\exists$ and $\forall$ in order to determine the truth value of φ_0 in s_0, cf. [19]. Configurations are elements of $\mathcal{C} \subseteq \mathcal{S} \times Sub(\varphi_0)$, and written $t \vdash \psi$. Each play of $\Gamma_\mathcal{T}(s_0, \varphi_0)$ is a maximal sequence of configurations that starts with $s_0 \vdash \varphi_0$. The game rules are presented in Figure 1. Each rule is marked by $\exists$ / $\forall$ to indicate which player makes the move. A rule is applied when the player is in configuration C_i, which is of the form of the upper part of the rule. C_{i+1} is then the configuration in the lower part of the rule. The rules shown in the first and third lines present a choice which the player can make. Since no choice is possible when applying the rules shown in the second line, we arbitrarily assign one player, let us say $\exists$, and call the rules *deterministic*. If no rule can be applied the play terminates.

Definition 1. *A play is called $\exists$-consistent, resp. $\forall$-consistent, if Player $\exists$, resp. Player $\forall$, never chooses a transition of type $\xrightarrow{a?}$ for some $a \in \mathcal{A}$.*
    Player $\exists$ wins an $\exists$-consistent play $C_0, C_1, \ldots$ iff

1. there is an $n \in \mathbb{N}$, s.t. $C_n = t \vdash q$ with $L(t)(q) = \top$ or $C_n = t \vdash \neg q$ with $L(t)(q) = \bot$, or
2. there is an $n \in \mathbb{N}$, s.t. $C_n = t \vdash [a]\psi$ and there is no $t' \in \mathcal{S}$ s.t. $t \xrightarrow{a?} t'$, or
3. the outermost variable that occurs infinitely often is of type ν.

Player $\forall$ *wins a $\forall$-consistent play $C_0, C_1 \ldots$ iff*

4. there is an $n \in \mathbb{N}$, s.t. $C_n = t \vdash q$ with $L(t)(q) = \bot$ or $C_n = t \vdash \neg q$ with $L(t)(q) = \top$, or
5. there is an $n \in \mathbb{N}$, s.t. $C_n = t \vdash \langle a \rangle \psi$ and there is no $t' \in \mathcal{S}$ s.t. $t \xrightarrow{a?} t'$, or
6. the outermost variable that occurs infinitely often is of type μ.

In all other cases, the result of the play is a *tie*.

Definition 2. *The* truth value *of a configuration* $t \vdash \psi$ *in the context of* ρ *is the value of* $[\![\psi]\!]_\rho(t)$. *The value* $\top$ *improves* both *? and* $\bot$, *while ? only improves* $\bot$. *On the other hand,* x *worsens* y *iff* y *improves* x.

An inspection of game rules and semantics shows: The deterministic rules preserve the truth value in a move from one configuration to another. Player $\exists$ cannot improve it but can preserve $\top$. Player $\forall$ cannot worsen it but can preserve $\bot$.

A *strategy* for player p is a partial function $\zeta : \mathcal{C} \to \mathcal{C}$, such that its domain is the set of configurations where player p moves. Player p plays a game according to a strategy ζ if all his choices agree with ζ. A strategy for player p is called a *winning strategy* if player p wins every play where he plays according to this strategy.

Theorem 3. *Given a KMTS* $\mathcal{T} = (\mathcal{S}, \{\overset{x}{\longrightarrow} \mid x \in \mathcal{A}! \cup Act?\}, L)$, *an* $s \in \mathcal{S}$, *and a closed* $\varphi \in 3\text{-}\mathcal{L}_\mu$, *we have:*

(a) $[\![\varphi]\!]^{\mathcal{T}}(s) = \top$ *iff Player* $\exists$ *has a winning strategy for* $\Gamma_{\mathcal{T}}(s, \varphi)$,

(b) $[\![\varphi]\!]^{\mathcal{T}}(s) = \bot$ *iff Player* $\forall$ *has a winning strategy for* $\Gamma_{\mathcal{T}}(s, \varphi)$,

(c) $[\![\varphi]\!]^{\mathcal{T}}(s) = ?$ *iff neither Player* $\exists$ *nor Player* $\forall$ *has a winning strategy for* $\Gamma_{\mathcal{T}}(s, \varphi)$.

Theorem 4. *Let* $\mathcal{T} = (\mathcal{S}, \{\overset{x}{\longrightarrow} \mid x \in \mathcal{A}\}, L)$ *be a Kripke structure with* $s \in \mathcal{S}$ *and* $\mathcal{T}' = (\mathcal{S}', \{\overset{x}{\longrightarrow} \mid x \in \mathcal{A}! \cup \mathcal{A}?\}, L')$ *be an abstraction of* $\mathcal{T}$ *with concretization function* γ. *Let* $s' \in \mathcal{S}'$ *with* $s \in \gamma(s')$.

(a) If Player $\exists$ *has a winning strategy for* $\Gamma_{\mathcal{T}'}(s', \varphi)$ *then* $\mathcal{T}, s \models \varphi$.

(b) If Player $\forall$ *has a winning strategy for* $\Gamma_{\mathcal{T}'}(s', \varphi)$ *then* $\mathcal{T}, s \not\models \varphi$.

5 Winning Model Checking Games for 3-$\mathcal{L}_\mu$

The previous section relates model checking games with the semantics of 3-$\mathcal{L}_\mu$. An algorithm estimating the winner of the game and a winning strategy is yet to be given. Note that the result of the previous section also holds for infinite-state systems. From now on, however, we restrict to finite KMTS.

For the sake of readability we will deal with parity games. Instead of Player $\exists$ and $\forall$, we talk of Player 0 and Player 1, resp., and use σ to denote Player 0 or 1 and $\bar{\sigma} = 1 - \sigma$ for the opponent[1].

Parity games are traditionally used to describe the model checking game for μ-calculus. In order to describe our game for the 3-$\mathcal{L}_\mu$, we need to generalize them in the following way: (1) we have two types of edges: must edges and may edges, where every must edge is also a may edge, (2) terminal configurations (dead-end) are classified as either winning for one player, or as tie-configurations, and (3) a consistency requirement is added to the winning conditions.

A *generalized parity game* $G = (A, \chi)$ has an *arena* $A = (V_0, V_1, V_{tie}, \overset{must}{\longrightarrow}, \overset{may}{\longrightarrow})$ for which every $v \in V_{tie}$ is a dead-end and $\overset{must}{\longrightarrow} \subseteq \overset{may}{\longrightarrow}$. The set of vertices is denoted

---

[1] The numbers 0 and 1 have parities and this is more intuitive for this notion of game.

by $V = V_0 \uplus V_1 \uplus V_{tie}$. $\chi : V \to \mathbb{N}$ is a *priority function* that maps each vertex $v \in V$ to a *priority*.

A play is a maximal sequence of vertices $v_0, \ldots$, where Player σ moves from v_i to v_{i+1} when $v_i \in V_\sigma$ and $(v_i, v_{i+1}) \in \xrightarrow{may}$. It is called σ-*consistent* iff Player σ chooses only moves that are (also) in $\xrightarrow{must}$. A σ-consistent play is *winning* for Player σ if

- it is finite and ends in V_σ, or
- it is infinite and the maximal priority occurring infinitely often is even when $\sigma = 0$ or odd when $\sigma = 1$.

All other plays are a *tie*.

A model checking game is a generalized parity game (see also [7]): Set V_0 to the configurations in which $\exists$ moves together with configurations in which the play terminates and $\exists$ wins. Set V_1 to the configurations in which $\forall$ moves, together with configurations in which the play terminates and $\forall$ wins. The remaining configurations, i.e. the ones of the form $t \vdash q$ or $t \vdash \neg q$ with $L(t)(q) = L(t)(\neg q) = ?$ are set to V_{tie}. $\xrightarrow{must}$ comprises the moves based on the rules shown in the first two lines in Figure 1 or when a $a!$-transition is taken while $\xrightarrow{may}$ comprises all possible moves. The priority of a vertex $t \vdash \varphi$ is only non-zero when φ is a fixpoint formula. Then, it is given by the alternation depth of φ, possibly plus 1 to assure that it is even iff the outermost fixpoint variable in φ is ν. It is easy to see that the notions of winning and winning strategies for both notions of games coincide.

We define an algorithm for solving generalized parity games. Our algorithm partitions V into three sets: W_0, W_1, W_{tie}, where for $\sigma \in \{0, 1\}$, the set W_σ consists of all the vertices from which Player σ has a winning strategy and the set W_{tie} consists of all the vertices from which none of the players has a winning strategy. When applied to model checking whether $s_0 \models \varphi_0$, we check when the algorithm terminates whether $v = s_0 \vdash \varphi_0$ is in W_0, W_1, or W_{tie} and conclude *true*, *false*, or *indefinite*, respectively.

We adapt the recursive algorithm for solving parity games by Zielonka [23]. Its recursive nature makes it easy to understand and analyze, allows simple correctness proofs, and can be used as basis for refinement.

The main idea of the algorithm presented in [23] is as follows. In each recursive call, σ denotes the parity of the maximal priority in the current game. The algorithm computes the set $W_{\bar\sigma}$ iteratively and the remaining vertices form W_σ. In our generalized game, we again compute $W_{\bar\sigma}$ iteratively, but we then add a phase where we also compute W_{tie} iteratively. Only then, we set W_σ to the remaining vertices.

We start with some definitions. For $X \subseteq V$, the subgraph of G induced by X, denoted by $G[X]$, is $(A|_X, \chi|_X)$ where $A|_X = (V_0', V_1', V_{tie} \cap X, \xrightarrow{must} \cap X \times X, \xrightarrow{may} \cap X \times X)$ and $\chi|_X$ is the restriction of χ to X. For $\sigma \in \{0, 1\}$, let B_σ denote the set of non-dead-end vertices that belong to V_σ in G, but become dead-ends in $G[X]$. Then, in $G[X]$, $V_\sigma' = ((V_\sigma \setminus B_\sigma) \cup B_{\bar\sigma}) \cap X$. That is, vertices that become dead-ends, move to the set of vertices of the other player.

$G[X]$ is a *subgame* of G w.r.t. σ, for $\sigma \in \{0,1\}$, if all non-dead-end vertices of V_σ in G remain non-dead-ends in $G[X]$. It is a *subgame* of G if it is a subgame w.r.t. to both players. That is, if $G[X]$ is a subgame, then every dead-end in it is also a dead-end in G.

For $\sigma \in \{0,1\}$ and $X \subseteq V$, we define the must-attractor set $\text{Attr!}_\sigma(G,X) \subseteq V$ and the may-attractor set $\text{Attr?}_\sigma(G,X) \subseteq V$ of Player σ in G.

The *must-attractor* $\text{Attr!}_\sigma(G,X) \subseteq V$ is the set of vertices from which Player σ has a strategy in the game G to attract the play to X or a dead-end in V_σ while maintaining consistency. The *may-attractor* $\text{Attr?}_\sigma(G,X) \subseteq V$ is the set of vertices from which Player σ has a strategy in G to either (1) attract the play to X or a dead-end in $V_\sigma \cup V_{tie}$, possibly without maintaining his own consistency or (2) to prevent $\bar{\sigma}$ from playing consistently. In other words, if $\bar{\sigma}$ plays consistently, σ can attract the play to one of the vertices described in (1).

Let D_0, D_1, D_{tie} denote the dead-end vertices of V_0, V_1, V_{tie} respectively (i.e., $D_{tie} = V_{tie}$). It can be shown that the following is an equivalent definition of the sets $\text{Attr!}_\sigma(G,X)$ and $\text{Attr?}_\sigma(G,X)$.

$$
\begin{aligned}
\text{Attr!}_\sigma^0(G,X) &= X \cup D_\sigma \\
\text{Attr!}_\sigma^{i+1}(G,X) &= \text{Attr!}_\sigma^i(G,X) \\
&\quad \cup \{v \in V_\sigma \setminus D_\sigma \mid \exists v'.v \xrightarrow{must} v' \wedge v' \in \text{Attr!}_\sigma^i(G,X)\} \\
&\quad \cup \{v \in V_{\bar\sigma} \setminus D_{\bar\sigma} \mid \forall v'.v \xrightarrow{may} v' \implies v' \in \text{Attr!}_\sigma^i(G,X)\} \\
\text{Attr!}_\sigma(G,X) &= \bigcup\{\text{Attr!}_\sigma^i(G,X) \mid i \geq 0\}
\end{aligned}
$$

$$
\begin{aligned}
\text{Attr?}_\sigma^0(G,X) &= X \cup D_\sigma \cup D_{tie} \\
\text{Attr?}_\sigma^{i+1}(G,X) &= \text{Attr?}_\sigma^i(G,X) \\
&\quad \cup \{v \in V_\sigma \setminus D_\sigma \mid \exists v'.v \xrightarrow{may} v' \wedge v' \in \text{Attr?}_\sigma^i(G,X)\} \\
&\quad \cup \{v \in V_{\bar\sigma} \setminus D_{\bar\sigma} \mid \forall v'.v \xrightarrow{must} v' \implies v' \in \text{Attr?}_\sigma^i(G,X)\} \\
\text{Attr?}_\sigma(G,X) &= \bigcup\{\text{Attr?}_\sigma^i(G,X) \mid i \geq 0\}
\end{aligned}
$$

The latter definition of the attractor sets provides a method for computing them. As i increases, we calculate $\text{Attr!}_\sigma^i(G,X)$ or $\text{Attr?}_\sigma^i(G,X)$ until it is the same as $\text{Attr!}_\sigma^{i-1}(G,X)$ or $\text{Attr?}_\sigma^{i-1}(G,X)$, respectively.

Note that $\text{Attr!}_\sigma^i(G,X) \subseteq \text{Attr?}_\sigma^i(G,X)$, and that for $X' = V \setminus \text{Attr?}_\sigma(G,X)$ we have $X' = \text{Attr!}_{\bar\sigma}(G,X')$. Thus, the corresponding must and may attractors partition V.

Solving the Game

We present a recursive algorithm $\texttt{SolveGame}(G)$ (see Algorithm 3) that computes the sets W_0, W_1, and W_{tie} for a parity game G. Let n be the maximum priority occurring in G.

$n = 0$:
$$
\begin{aligned}
W_1 &= \text{Attr!}_1(G,\emptyset) \\
W_0 &= V \setminus \text{Attr?}_1(G,\emptyset) \\
W_{tie} &= \text{Attr?}_1(G,\emptyset) \setminus \text{Attr!}_1(G,\emptyset)
\end{aligned}
$$

Since the maximum priority of G is 0, Player 1 can only win G on dead-ends in V_1 or vertices from which he can consistently attract the play to such

---

Algorithm 1 Winning vertices for the opponent: `ComputeOpponentWin`

---

1 **Function** ComputeOpponentWin(G, σ, n)
2    $W_{\bar{\sigma}} := \emptyset$.
3   **repeat**
4      $W'_{\bar{\sigma}} := W_{\bar{\sigma}}$
5      $X_{\bar{\sigma}} := \text{Attr!}_{\bar{\sigma}}(G, W_{\bar{\sigma}})$
6      $X_{\sigma} := V \setminus X_{\bar{\sigma}}$
7      $N := \{v \in X_{\sigma} \mid \chi(v) = n\}$
8      $Y := X_{\sigma} \setminus \text{Attr?}_{\sigma}(G[X_{\sigma}], N)$
9      $(Y_0, Y_1, Y_{tie}) := \text{SolveGame}(G[Y])$
10     $W_{\bar{\sigma}} := X_{\bar{\sigma}} \cup Y_{\bar{\sigma}}$
11   **until** $W'_{\bar{\sigma}} = W_{\bar{\sigma}}$
12   **return** $W_{\bar{\sigma}}$

---

a dead-end. This is exactly $\text{Attr!}_1(G, \emptyset)$. From the rest of the vertices Player 1 does not have a winning strategy. For vertices in $V \setminus \text{Attr?}_1(G, \emptyset)$, Player 0 can always avoid reaching dead-ends in $V_1 \cup V_{tie}$, while playing consistently. Since the maximum priority in this subgraph is 0, it is easy to see that she wins in such vertices. The remaining vertices in $\text{Attr?}_1(G, \emptyset) \setminus \text{Attr!}_1(G, \emptyset)$ are a subset of $\text{Attr?}_1(G, \emptyset)$, which is why Player 0 does not win from them (and neither does Player 1, as previously claimed). Therefore none of the players wins in $\text{Attr?}_1(G, \emptyset) \setminus \text{Attr!}_1(G, \emptyset)$.

$n \geq 1$: We assume that we can solve every game with maximum priority smaller than n. Let $\sigma = n \mod 2$ be the player that wins if the play visits infinitely often the maximum priority n.

We first compute $W_{\bar{\sigma}}$ in G. This is done by the function `ComputeOpponentWin` shown in Algorithm 1.

Intuitively, in each iteration we hold a subset of the winning region of Player $\bar{\sigma}$. We first extend it to $X_{\bar{\sigma}}$ by using the must-attractor set of Player $\bar{\sigma}$ (which ensures his consistency, line 5). From the remaining vertices, we disregard those from which Player σ can attract the play to a vertex with maximum priority n, perhaps by giving up his consistency. Left are the vertices in Y (line 8) and Player σ is basically trapped in it. He can only "escape" from it to $X_{\bar{\sigma}}$. Thus, we can add the winning region of Player $\bar{\sigma}$ in $G[Y]$ to his winning region in G. This way, each iteration results in a better (bigger) under approximation of the winning region of Player $\bar{\sigma}$ in G, until the full region is found (line 11). The correctness proof of the algorithm is sketched in the following.

Lemma 1. *1. For every X_{σ} as used in Algorithm 1, $G[X_{\sigma}]$ is a subgame w.r.t. σ.*

2. For every Y as used in Algorithm 1, $G[Y]$ is a subgame.

Moreover, the maximum priority in $G[Y]$ is smaller than n, which is why the recursion terminates.

Lemma 2. *At the beginning of each iteration in Algorithm 1, $W_{\bar{\sigma}}$ is a winning region for Player $\bar{\sigma}$ in G.*

Proof. The proof is by induction. The base case is when $W_{\bar{\sigma}} = \emptyset$ and the claim holds. Suppose that at the beginning of the ith iteration $W_{\bar{\sigma}}$ is a winning region for Player $\bar{\sigma}$ in G. We show that it continues to be so at the end of the iteration and therefore at the beginning of the $i + 1$ iteration.

Clearly, $X_{\bar{\sigma}} = \text{Attr}!_{\bar{\sigma}}(G, W_{\bar{\sigma}})$ is also a winning region for Player $\bar{\sigma}$ in G: by simply using his strategy to attract the play to $D_{\bar{\sigma}}$ or to $W_{\bar{\sigma}}$ (where he wins) while being consistent, and from there using the winning strategy of $W_{\bar{\sigma}}$ in G.

We now show that $Y_{\bar{\sigma}}$ is also a winning region of Player $\bar{\sigma}$ in G. We know that it is a winning region for him in $G[Y]$ (by the correctness of the algorithm SolveGame for games with a maximum priority smaller than n). As for G, for every vertex in $Y_{\bar{\sigma}}$, as long as the play remains in Y, Player $\bar{\sigma}$ can use his strategy for $G[Y]$. Since $G[Y]$ is a subgame, Player $\bar{\sigma}$ will always be able to stay within Y in his moves in G and if the play stays there, then he wins (since he uses his winning strategy). Clearly Player σ cannot move from Y to $X_{\sigma} \setminus Y = \text{Attr}?_{\sigma}(G[X_{\sigma}], N)$. Otherwise the vertex $v \in Y \subseteq X_{\sigma}$ where this is done belongs to $\text{Attr}?_{\sigma}(G[X_{\sigma}], \text{Attr}?_{\sigma}(G[X_{\sigma}], N))$ (because the same move is possible in $G[X_{\sigma}]$). Hence v belongs to $\text{Attr}?_{\sigma}(G[X_{\sigma}], N)$ as well, in contradiction to $v \in Y$. Finally, if Player σ moves to $V \setminus X_{\sigma} = X_{\bar{\sigma}}$, then Player $\bar{\sigma}$ will use his strategy for $X_{\bar{\sigma}}$ in G and also win.

We conclude that $X_{\bar{\sigma}} \cup Y_{\bar{\sigma}}$ is a winning region for Player $\bar{\sigma}$ in G. $\square$

This lemma ensures that the final result $W_{\bar{\sigma}}$ of ComputeOpponentWin is indeed a subset of the winning region of Player $\bar{\sigma}$ in G. It remains to show that this is actually an equality, i.e. that no winning vertices are missing.

Lemma 3. *When $W'_{\bar{\sigma}} = W_{\bar{\sigma}}$, then $V \setminus W_{\bar{\sigma}}$ is a non-winning region for Player $\bar{\sigma}$ in G.*

Proof. When $W'_{\bar{\sigma}} = W_{\bar{\sigma}}$, it must be the case that the last iteration of SolveGame ended with $Y_{\bar{\sigma}} = \emptyset$, and $W_{\bar{\sigma}} = X_{\bar{\sigma}}$. Therefore it suffices to show that $V \setminus X_{\bar{\sigma}} = X_{\sigma}$ is a non-winning region for Player $\bar{\sigma}$ in G.

Clearly, Player $\bar{\sigma}$ cannot move from X_{σ} to $X_{\bar{\sigma}}$ without compromising his consistency. Otherwise the vertex $v \in X_{\sigma}$ where this is done belongs to $\text{Attr}!_{\bar{\sigma}}(G, X_{\bar{\sigma}})$ and so to $X_{\bar{\sigma}}$ as well. This contradicts $v \in X_{\sigma}$. Hence, Player $\bar{\sigma}$ cannot win by moving to $X_{\bar{\sigma}}$. As $G[X_{\sigma}]$ is a subgame w.r.t. σ, Player σ is never obliged to move to $X_{\bar{\sigma}}$.

Consider the case where the play stays in X_{σ}. In order to prevent Player $\bar{\sigma}$ from winning, Player σ will play as follows. If the current configuration is in Y, then Player σ will use his strategy on $G[Y]$ for preventing Player $\bar{\sigma}$ from winning (such a strategy exists since $Y_{\bar{\sigma}} = \emptyset$). If the play visits a vertex $v \in N$, then Player σ will move to any successor v' inside X_{σ}. Such a successor must exist since vertices in N are never dead-ends in G. Furthermore, they belong to V_{σ}, thus since $G[X_{\sigma}]$ is a subgame w.r.t. σ (by Lemma 1.1), they remain non-dead-ends in $G[X_{\sigma}]$. If the play visits $\text{Attr}?_{\sigma}(G[X_{\sigma}], N) \setminus N$, then Player σ will use his strategy to either cause Player $\bar{\sigma}$ to be inconsistent, or to attract the play

---

Algorithm 2 Vertices in which no win is possible: `ComputeNoWin`

---

13 **Function** ComputeNoWin(G, σ, n,$W_{\bar{\sigma}}$)

14    $nowin := W_{\bar{\sigma}}$.

15   **repeat**

16      $nowin' := nowin$

17      $X_{\bar{\sigma}} :=$ Attr?$_{\bar{\sigma}}(G, nowin)$

18      $X_{\sigma} := V \setminus X_{\bar{\sigma}}$

19      $N := \{v \in X_{\sigma} \mid \chi(v) = n\}$

20      $Y := X_{\sigma} \setminus$ Attr!$_{\sigma}(G[X_{\sigma}], N)$

21      $(Y_0, Y_1, Y_{tie}) :=$ SolveGame($G[Y]$)

22      $nowin := X_{\bar{\sigma}} \cup Y_{\bar{\sigma}} \cup Y_{tie}$

23   **until** $nowin' = nowin$

24   **return** $nowin$

---

in a finite number of steps to N or $D'_{\sigma} \cup D_{tie}$ (such a strategy exists by the definition of a may-attractor set). We use D'_{σ} to denote the dead-end vertices of Player σ in $G[X_{\sigma}]$. Since $G[X_{\sigma}]$ is not necessarily a subgame w.r.t. $\bar{\sigma}$, D'_{σ} may contain non-dead-end vertices of Player $\bar{\sigma}$ from G that became dead-ends in $G[X_{\sigma}]$. However, this means that all their successors are in $X_{\bar{\sigma}}$, and as stated before Player $\bar{\sigma}$ cannot move consistently from X_{σ} to $X_{\bar{\sigma}}$, thus he cannot win in them in G as well.

It is easy to see that this strategy indeed prevents Player $\bar{\sigma}$ from winning. $\square$

Corollary 1. *The result of* `ComputeOpponentWin` *is the full winning region of Player* $\bar{\sigma}$ *in* G.

In the original algorithm in [23], given the set $W_{\bar{\sigma}}$, we could conclude that all the remaining vertices form the winning region of Player σ in G. Yet, this is not the case here. We now divide the remaining vertices into W_{tie} and W_{σ}. We first compute the set *nowin* of vertices in G from which Player σ does not have a winning strategy, i.e. Player $\bar{\sigma}$ has a strategy that prevents Player σ from winning. This is again done iteratively, by the function `ComputeNoWin`, given as Algorithm 2.

The algorithm `ComputeNoWin` resembles the algorithm `ComputeOpponentWin`. The initialization here is to $W_{\bar{\sigma}}$, since this is clearly a non-winning region of Player σ. Furthermore, in this case after the recursive call to `SolveGame`($G[Y]$), the set $X_{\bar{\sigma}}$ is extended not only by the winning region of Player $\bar{\sigma}$ in $G[Y]$, $Y_{\bar{\sigma}}$, but also by the tie-region Y_{tie} (line 22). Apart from those differences, one can see that the only difference is that the use of a must-attractor set is replaced by a may-attractor set and vice versa. This is because in the case of `ComputeOpponentWin` we are after a definite win of Player $\bar{\sigma}$, whereas in the case of `ComputeNoWin` we also allow a tie, therefore may edges take a different role. Namely, in this case, when we extend the current set *nowin* (line 17), we use a may-attractor set of Player $\bar{\sigma}$ because when our goal is to prevent Player σ from winning, we allow Player $\bar{\sigma}$ to be inconsistent. On the other hand, in the computation of Y we now remove from $X_{\bar{\sigma}}$ only the vertices from which Player σ can *consistently* attract the play to the maximum priority (using the must-attractor set, line 20). This is because only such vertices cannot contribute to the goal of preventing Player σ from winning. Other vertices where he can reach the maximum priority, but only at the expense of consistency can still be of use for this goal.

Lemma 4. *1. For every X_σ as used in Algorithm 2, $G[X_\sigma]$ is a subgame.*
2. For every Y as used in Algorithm 2, $G[Y]$ is a subgame.

Again, the maximum priority in $G[Y]$ is smaller than n, which is why the recursion terminates.

Lemma 5. *At the beginning of each iteration, the set nowin is a non-winning region for Player σ in G.*

This lemma that can be shown with a careful analysis ensures that the final result *nowin* of ComputeNoWin is indeed a subset of the non-winning region of Player σ in G. It remains to show that no non-winning vertices are missing.

Lemma 6. *When $nowin' = nowin$, then $V \setminus nowin$ is a winning region for Player σ in G.*

Proof. When $nowin' = nowin$, it must be the case that the last iteration of SolveGame ended with $Y_{\bar\sigma} = Y_{tie} = \emptyset$, and $nowin = X_{\bar\sigma}$. Therefore it suffices to show that $V \setminus X_{\bar\sigma} = X_\sigma$ is a winning region for Player σ in G.

Clearly, Player $\bar\sigma$ cannot move from X_σ to $X_{\bar\sigma}$. Otherwise the vertex $v \in X_\sigma$ where this is done belongs to $\text{Attr?}_{\bar\sigma}(G, X_{\bar\sigma})$ and therefore to $X_{\bar\sigma}$ as well. This contradicts $v \in X_\sigma$. Hence, Player $\bar\sigma$ is "trapped" in X_σ and as $G[X_\sigma]$ is a subgame, Player σ is never obliged to move to $X_{\bar\sigma}$.

Consider the case where the play stays in X_σ. In order to win, Player σ will play as follows. If the current configuration is in Y, then Player σ will use his winning strategy on $G[Y]$ (such a strategy exists since $Y_{\bar\sigma} = Y_{tie} = \emptyset$ and $Y_\sigma = Y$). If the play visits a vertex $v \in N$, then Player σ will move to a must successor v' inside X_σ. Such a successor exists because otherwise $v \in \text{Attr?}_{\bar\sigma}(G, X_{\bar\sigma})$ and hence also in $X_{\bar\sigma}$, in contradiction to $v \in N \subseteq X_\sigma$. If the play visits $\text{Attr!}_\sigma(G[X_\sigma], N) \setminus N$, then Player σ will attract it in a finite number of steps to N or D_σ, while being consistent.

This strategy ensures that Player σ is consistent and is indeed winning. $\quad\square$

Corollary 2. ComputeNoWin *returns the full non-winning region of Player σ in G.*

We can now conclude that the remaining vertices in $V \setminus nowin$ form the full winning region of Player σ in G, and the tie region in G is exactly $nowin \setminus W_{\bar\sigma}$. This is the set of vertices from which neither player wins.

Solving the game is now achieved by Function SolveGame shown in Algorithm 3.

We have suggested an algorithm for computing the winning (and non-winning) regions of the players. The correctness proofs also show how to define strategies for the players. Yet, we omit this discussion due to space limitations. The algorithm can also be used for checking a concrete system in which all may-edges are also must-edges and $V_{tie} = \emptyset$.

Algorithm 3 The main function: `SolveGame`

---

25 **Function** SolveGame(G)
26      $n := max\{\chi(v) \mid v \in V\}$
27   **if** $n = 0$ **then** // *return* (W_0, W_1, W_{tie})
28   **return** ($V \setminus \text{Attr?}_1(G, \emptyset)$, $\text{Attr!}_1(G, \emptyset)$, $\text{Attr?}_1(G, \emptyset) \setminus \text{Attr!}_1(G, \emptyset)$)
29   **else**
30          $\sigma := n \mod 2$
31          $W_{\bar{\sigma}} := \text{ComputeOpponentWin}(G, \sigma, n)$
32          $W_{\sigma} := V \setminus \text{ComputeNoWin}(G, \sigma, n, W_{\bar{\sigma}})$
33          $W_{tie} := V \setminus (W_{\bar{\sigma}} \cup W_{\sigma})$
34   **return** (W_0, W_1, W_{tie})

Remark 1. Let G be a parity game in which $V_{tie} = \emptyset$ and all edges are must. Then W_{tie} computed by the algorithm `SolveGame` is empty.

Complexity. Let l and m denote the number of vertices and edges of G. Let n be the maximum priority. A careful analysis shows that the algorithm is in $O((l + m)^{n+1})$.

Theorem 5. *Function* `SolveGame` *computes the winning regions* (W_0, W_1, W_{tie}) *for a given parity game in time exponential in the maximal priority. Additionally, it can be used to determine the winning strategy for the corresponding winner.*

We conclude that when applied to a model checking game $\Gamma_T(s_0, \varphi_0)$, the complexity of `SolveGame` is exponential in the alternation depth of φ_0.

6   Refinement of Generalized Parity Games

Assume we are interested to know whether a concrete state s_c satisfies a given formula φ. Let (W_0, W_1, W_{tie}) be the result of the previous algorithm for the parity game obtained by the model checking game. Assume the vertex $v = s_a \vdash \varphi$, where s_a is the abstract state of s_c, is in W_0 or W_1. Then the answer is clear: $s_c \models \varphi$ if $v \in W_0$ and $s_c \not\models \varphi$ if $v \in W_1$. Otherwise, the answer is indefinite and we have to refine the abstraction to get the answer.

As in most cases, our refinement consists of two parts. First, we choose a criterion telling us how to split abstract states. We then construct the refined abstract model using the refined abstract state space. In this section we study the first part.

Given that $v \in W_{tie}$, our goal in the refinement is to find and eliminate at least one of the causes of the indefinite result. Thus, the criterion for splitting the abstract states is obtained from a *failure vertex*. This is a vertex $v' = s'_a \vdash \varphi'$ s.t. (1) $v' \in W_{tie}$; (2) the classification of v' to W_{tie} *affects* the indefinite result of v; and (3) the indefinite classification of v' can be *changed* by splitting it. The latter requirement means that v' *itself* is responsible for introducing (some) uncertainty. The others demand that this uncertainty is relevant to the result in v.

The game solving algorithm is adapted to remember for each vertex in W_{tie} a failure vertex, and a failure reason. We distinguish between the case where $n = 0$ and the case where $n \geq 1$ in SolveGame.

$\boldsymbol{n = 0}$: In this case the set W_{tie} is computed by $\text{Attr?}_1(G, \emptyset) \setminus W_1$. Note that W_1 is already updated when the computation of $\text{Attr?}_1(G, \emptyset)$ starts. We now enrich the computation of $\text{Attr?}_1(G, \emptyset)$ to record failure information for vertices which are not in W_1 and thus will be in W_{tie}.

In the initialization we have two possibilities: (1) vertices in D_1, which are clearly not in W_{tie}, thus no additional information is needed; and (2) vertices in D_{tie}, for which the failure vertex and reason are the vertex itself [failDE].

As for the iteration, suppose we have $\text{Attr?}_1^i(G, \emptyset)$, with the additional information attached to every vertex in it which is not in W_1. We now compute the set $\text{Attr?}_1^{i+1}(G, \emptyset)$. Let v' be a vertex that is added to $\text{Attr?}_1^{i+1}(G, \emptyset)$. If $v' \in W_1$, then no information is needed. Otherwise, we do the following.

1. If $v' \in V_1$ and there exists a may edge $v' \xrightarrow{may} v''$ s.t. $v'' \in W_1$, then v' is a failure state, with this edge being the reason [failP1].
2. If $v' \in V_0$ and has a may edge $v' \xrightarrow{may} v''$ s.t. $v'' \notin \text{Attr?}_1^i(G, \emptyset)$, then v' is a failure state, with this edge being the reason [failP0].
3. Otherwise, there exists a may (that is possibly also a must) edge $v' \xrightarrow{may} v''$ s.t. $v'' \in \text{Attr?}_1^i(G, \emptyset) \setminus W_1$. The failure state and reason of v' are those of v''.

Note that the order of the "if" statements in the algorithm determines the failure state returned by the algorithm. Different heuristics can be applied regarding their order. A careful analysis shows the following.

Lemma 7. *The computation of failure vertices for $n = 0$ is well defined, meaning that all the possible cases are handled. Furthermore, if the failure reason computed by it is a may edge, then this edge is* not *a must edge.*

Intuitively, during each iteration of the computation, if the vertex $v' \in W_{tie}$ that is added to $\text{Attr?}_1^{i+1}(G, \emptyset)$ is not responsible for introducing the indefinite result (cases 1 and 2), then the computation greedily continues with a vertex in W_{tie} that *affects* its indefinite classification (case 3).

There are three possibilities where we say that the vertex itself is responsible for ? and consider it a failure vertex: failDE, failP1 and failP0. For a vertex in V_{tie} (case failDE), the failure reason is clear. Consider case failP1. In this case $v' \in V_1$ is considered a failure vertex, with the may edge to $v'' \in W_1$ being the failure reason. By Lemma 7 we have that it is *not* a must edge. The intuition for v' being a failure vertex is that if this edge was a must edge, it would change the classification of v' to W_1. If no such edge existed, then v' would not be added to $\text{Attr?}_1^{i+1}(G, \emptyset)$ and thus to W_{tie}. Finally, consider case failP0. In this case $v' \in V_0$ has a may edge to v'' which is still unclassified at the time v' is added to $\text{Attr?}_1(G, \emptyset)$. This edge is considered a failure reason because if it was a must edge rather than a may edge then v' would remain unclassified as well for at least one more iteration. Thus it would have a better chance to eventually remain outside the set $\text{Attr?}_1^i(G, \emptyset)$ until the fixpoint is reached, changing the classification of v' to W_0.

$n \geq 1$: In this case the set W_{tie} is computed by $V \setminus (W_{\bar{\sigma}} \cup W_\sigma)$. This equals
ComputeNoWin$(G, \sigma, n, W_{\bar{\sigma}}) \setminus W_{\bar{\sigma}}$, where $W_{\bar{\sigma}}$ is already updated when the computation of ComputeNoWin$(G, \sigma, n, W_{\bar{\sigma}})$ starts. Similarly to the previous case, we
enrich the computation of ComputeNoWin$(G, \sigma, n, W_{\bar{\sigma}})$, and remember a failure
vertex for each vertex which is not in $W_{\bar{\sigma}}$ and thus will be in W_{tie}.

In each iteration of ComputeNoWin the vertices added to the computed set
are of three types: $X_{\bar{\sigma}}$, $Y_{\bar{\sigma}}$ and Y_{tie}.

The set $X_{\bar{\sigma}}$ is computed by Attr?$_{\bar{\sigma}}(G, nowin)$. Thus in order to find failure
vertices for such vertices that are not in $W_{\bar{\sigma}}$ we use an enriched computation of
the may-attractor set, as described in the case of $n = 0$. This time the role of W_1
is replaced by $W_{\bar{\sigma}}$, 0 is replaced by σ and 1 by $\bar{\sigma}$. Furthermore, in the initialization
of the computation we now also have the set $nowin$ from the previous iteration,
for which we already have the required information.

Vertices in Y_{tie} already have a failure vertex and reason, recorded during the
computation of SolveGame$(G[Y])$.

We now explain how to handle vertices in $Y_{\bar{\sigma}}$. Such vertices have the property
that Player $\bar{\sigma}$ wins from them in $G[Y]$. Hence, as long as the play stays in $G[Y]$,
Player $\bar{\sigma}$ wins. Furthermore, Player $\bar{\sigma}$ can always stay in $G[Y]$ in his moves. Thus,
for a vertex v' in $Y_{\bar{\sigma}}$ that is *not* in $W_{\bar{\sigma}}$ it must be the case that Player σ can force
the play out of $G[Y]$ and into $(V \setminus Y) \setminus W_{\bar{\sigma}}$ (If the play reaches $W_{\bar{\sigma}}$ then Player $\bar{\sigma}$
can win after all). Thus, $v' \in$ Attr?$_\sigma(G, (V \setminus Y) \setminus W_{\bar{\sigma}})$. Let $\bar{Y} = V \setminus Y$ be the set of
vertices outside $G[Y]$. We get that $Y_{\bar{\sigma}} \setminus W_{\bar{\sigma}} = Y_{\bar{\sigma}} \cap$ Attr?$_\sigma(G, \bar{Y} \setminus W_{\bar{\sigma}})$. Therefore,
to find the failure reason in such vertices, we compute Attr?$_\sigma(G, \bar{Y} \setminus W_{\bar{\sigma}})$. During
this computation, for each vertex v' in $Y_{\bar{\sigma}}$ that is added to the attractor set (and
thus will be in W_{tie}) we choose the failure vertex and reason based on the
reason for v' being added to the set. This is because if the vertex was not in
Attr?$_\sigma(G, \bar{Y} \setminus W_{\bar{\sigma}})$, it would be in $W_{\bar{\sigma}}$ in G as well. The information is recorded
as follows.

In the initialization of the computation we have vertices in D_σ, D_{tie} or $\bar{Y} \setminus W_{\bar{\sigma}}$
which are clearly not in $Y_{\bar{\sigma}}$, thus no additional information is needed.

As for the iteration, suppose we have Attr?$_\sigma^i(G, \bar{Y} \setminus W_{\bar{\sigma}})$, with the additional
information attached to every vertex in it which is in $Y_{\bar{\sigma}}$ (by the above equality
such a vertex is not in $W_{\bar{\sigma}}$). We now compute the set Attr?$_\sigma^{i+1}(G, \bar{Y} \setminus W_{\bar{\sigma}})$. Let v'
be a vertex that is added to Attr?$_\sigma^{i+1}(G, \bar{Y} \setminus W_{\bar{\sigma}})$. If $v' \notin Y_{\bar{\sigma}}$, then no information
is needed. Otherwise, we do the following.

1. If $v' \in V_\sigma$ and there exists a may edge $v' \xrightarrow{may} v''$ which is *not* a must edge
   s.t. $v'' \in \bar{Y} \setminus W_{\bar{\sigma}}$, then v' is a failure state, with this edge being the reason.
2. If $v' \in V_\sigma$ and it has a must edge to $v'' \in X_{\bar{\sigma}} \setminus W_{\bar{\sigma}}$, then we set the failure
   vertex and reason of v' to be those of v'' (which are already computed).
3. Otherwise, v' has a may (possibly must) edge to a vertex $v'' \in$ Attr?$_\sigma^i(G, \bar{Y} \setminus W_{\bar{\sigma}}) \cap Y_{\bar{\sigma}}$. In this case the failure state and reason of v' are those of v''.

Lemma 8. *The computation of failure vertices for $n \geq 1$ is well defined, meaning that all the possible cases are handled.*

Intuitively, in case 1, v' is considered a failure state, with the may (not must)
edge to $v'' \in \bar{Y} \setminus W_{\bar{\sigma}}$ being the reason because if this edge did not exist, v' would

not be added to the may-attractor set, and thus would remain in $W_{\bar{\sigma}}$ in G. A careful analysis shows that the only possibility where there exists such a *must* edge to $v'' \in \bar{Y} \setminus W_{\bar{\sigma}}$ is when this edge is to $X_{\bar{\sigma}} \setminus W_{\bar{\sigma}}$. This is handled separately in case 2. The set $X_{\bar{\sigma}} \setminus W_{\bar{\sigma}}$ is a subset of W_{tie} for which the failure was already analyzed, and in case 2 we set the failure vertex and reason of v' to be those of $v'' \in X_{\bar{\sigma}} \setminus W_{\bar{\sigma}}$. This is because changing the classification of v'' to $W_{\bar{\sigma}}$ would make a step in the direction of changing the classification of $v' \in V_{\sigma}$ to $W_{\bar{\sigma}}$ as well. Similarly, since the edge from v' to v'' is a must edge, changing the classification of v'' to W_{σ} would change the classification of $v' \in V_{\sigma}$ to W_{σ}. In all other cases, the computation recursively continues with a vertex in $Y_{\bar{\sigma}}$ that was already added to the may-attractor set and that *affects* the addition of v' to it (case 3).

This concludes the description of how `SolveGame` records the failure information for each vertex in W_{tie}. A simple case analysis shows the following.

Theorem 6. *Let v_f be a vertex that is classified by `SolveGame` as a failure vertex. The failure reason can either be the fact that $v_f \in V_{tie}$, or it can be an edge $(v_f, v') \in \xrightarrow{may} \setminus \xrightarrow{must}$.*

Once we are given a failure vertex $v' = s'_a \vdash \varphi'$ and a corresponding reason for failure, we guide the refinement to discard the cause for failure in the hope for changing the model checking result to a definite one. This is done as in [18], where the failure information is used to determine how the set of concrete states represented by s'_a should be split in order to eliminate the failure reason. A criterion for splitting *all* abstract states can then be found by known techniques, depending on the abstraction used (e.g. [4,2]).

After refinement, one has to re-run the model checking algorithm on the game graph based on the refined KMTS to get a definite value for s_c and φ. However, we can restrict this process to the previous W_{tie}. When constructing the game graph based on the refined KMTS, every vertex $s_a^2 \vdash \varphi'$ for which a vertex $s_a \vdash \varphi'$ (where s_a^2 results from splitting s_a) exists in W_0 or W_1 in the previous game graph can be considered a dead end winning for Player 0 or Player 1, respectively. In this way we avoid unnecessary refinement.

7   Conclusion

This work presents a game-based model checking for abstract models with respect to specifications in μ-calculus, interpreted over a 3-valued semantics, together with automatic refinement, if the model checking result is indefinite.

The closest work to ours is [18], in which a game-based framework is suggested for abstraction-refinement for CTL with respect to a 3-valued semantics. While it is relatively simple to extend their approach to alternation-free μ-calculus, the extension to full μ-calculus is not trivial. This is because, in the game graph for alternation-free μ-calculus each strongly connected component can be uniquely identified by a single fixpoint. For full μ-calculus, this is not the case any more, thus a more complicated algorithm is needed in order to determine who has the winning strategy.

References

1. J. R. Burch, E. M. Clarke, K. L. McMillan, D. L. Dill, and L. J. Hwang. Symbolic model checking: 10^{20} states and beyond. *Information and Computation*, 98(2):142–170, June 1992.
2. E. Clarke, O. Grumberg, S. Jha, Y. Lu, and H. Veith. Counterexample-guided abstraction refinement. In *Computer Aided Verification (CAV), LNCS* 1855, 2000.
3. E. Clarke, O. Grumberg, and D. Peled. *Model Checking*. MIT press, Dec. 1999.
4. E. Clarke, A. Gupta, J. Kukula, and O. Strichman. SAT based abstraction-refinement using ILP and machine leraning techniques. In *CAV*, 2002.
5. R. Cleaveland. Tableau-based model checking in the propositional mu-calculus. *Acta Inf.*, 27:725–747, 1990.
6. D. Dams, R. Gerth, and O. Grumberg. Abstract interpretation of reactive systems. *ACM Transactions on Programming Languages and Systems*, 19(2), March 1997.
7. E. A. Emerson, and C. S. Jutla Tree automata, μ-calculus and determinacy. In *Proc. 32th Symp. on Foundations of Computer Science (FOCS'91)*, pp. 368–377, 1991, *IEEE Computer Society Press*.
8. E. A. Emerson and C.-L. Lei. Efficient model checking in fragments of the propositional mu-calculus. In *Logic in Computer Science (LICS)*, 1986.
9. P. Godefroid and R. Jagadeesan. Automatic abstraction using generalized model checking. In *Computer-Aided Verification (CAV), LNCS* 2404, pp. 137–150, 2002.
10. P. Godefroid and R. Jagadeesan. On the expressiveness of 3-valued models. In *VMCAI, LNCS* 2575, pp. 206–222, 2003.
11. M. Huth, R. Jagadeesan, and D. Schmidt. Modal transition systems: A foundation for three-valued program analysis. In *European Symposium on Programming (ESOP)*, LNCS 2028, pp. 155–169, 2001.
12. D. Kozen. Results on the Propositional μ-calculus. *TCS*, 27: 333–354, 1983.
13. W. Lee, A. Pardo, J.-Y. Jang, G. D. Hachtel, and F. Somenzi. Tearing based automatic abstraction for CTL model checking. In *ICCAD*, pp. 76–81, 1996.
14. C. Loiseaux, S. Graf, J. Sifakis, A. Bouajjani, and S. Bensalem. Property preserving abstractions for the verification of concurrent systems. *Formal Methods in System Design*, 6:11–45, 1995.
15. D. Long, A. Browne, E. Clark, S. Jha, and W. Marrero. An improved algorithm for the evaluation of fixpoint expressions. In *CAV, LNCS* 818, pp. 338–350, 1994.
16. A. Pardo and G. D. Hachtel. Automatic abstraction techniques for propositional mu-calculus model checking. In *Computer Aided Verification (CAV)*, 1997.
17. A. Pardo and G. D. Hachtel. Incremental CTL model checking using BDD subsetting. In *Design Automation Conference (DAC)*, pp. 457–462, 1998.
18. S. Shoham and O. Grumberg. A game-based framework for CTL counterexamples and 3-valued abstraction-refinemnet. In *Computer Aided Verification (CAV)*, LNCS 2725, pp. 275–287, 2003.
19. C. Stirling. Local model checking games. In *Concurrency Theory (CONCUR)*, LNCS 962, pp. 1–11, 1995.
20. C. Stirling and D. J. Walker. Local model checking in the modal mu-calculus. In *Theory and Practice of Software Development*, LNCS, 1989.
21. A. Tarski. A lattice-theoretical fixpoint theorem and its application. *Pacific J.Math.*, 5:285–309, 1955.
22. G. Winskel. Model checking in the modal ν-calculus. In *International Colloquium on Automata, Languages, and Programming (ICALP)*, 1989.
23. W. Zielonka. Infinite games on finitely coloured graphs with applications to automata on infinite trees. *Theoretical Computer Science*, 200(1–2):135–183, 1998.

Model Checking
of Systems Employing Commutative Functions*

A. Prasad Sistla, Min Zhou, and Xiaodong Wang

University of Illinois at Chicago
{sistla,mzhou,xwang1}@cs.uic.edu

Abstract. The paper presents methods for model checking a class of possibly infinite state concurrent programs using various types of bi-simulation reductions. The proposed methods work for the class of programs in which the functions that update the variables are mutually commutative. A number of bi-simulation relations are presented for such systems. Explicit state model checking methods that employ on-the-fly reductions with respect to these bi-simulations are given. Some of these methods have been implemented and have been used to verify some well known protocols that employ integer variables.

1 Introduction

Two of the bottlenecks that hinder wider applicability of model checking approach is the state explosion problem and its less effectiveness in handling infinite state systems. In this paper, we present an approach for model checking that works for certain classes of infinite state systems and that can also be used to contain the state explosion problem.

One standard model checking method, employed often, is to construct the reachability graph of the given program and then check the correctness property against this graph. One way of reducing the size of the explored graph is to employ a reduction with respect to a bi-simulation relation U on the states of the reachability graph. Such a relation U is either known a priori through an implicit representation or has been computed by other means.

In this paper, we give a method that does not require a priori computation of a bi-simulation relation. Instead, we give a sufficient condition on any two states to determine if they are bi-similar. This condition requires equivalence of certain predicates associated with the two states. In fact, we present a number of bi-simulation relations that can be used in on-the-fly model checking methods. Our approach works for certain classes of programs that employ commutative unary functions for updating variables. Since bi-similarity of two states is based on the future behavior from these states, in general, it is not possible to check their bi-similarity by looking only at the values of the variables in these states.

We assume that the concurrent program is given by a Transition Diagram (TD) [8] which is an edge labeled directed graph. Each edge label consists of

---

* This work is supported in part by the NSF grants CCR-9988884 and CCR-0205365

R. Cousot (Ed.): VMCAI 2005, LNCS 3385, pp. 250–266, 2005.
© Springer-Verlag Berlin Heidelberg 2005

a condition, called guard, and an action which is a concurrent assignment of values to variables. We consider a class of TDs, called simple TDs, in which an expression that is assigned to a variable x is either a constant, or a variable, or of the form $f(x)$ where f is a unary function. Further more, we require that the functions that are used be mutually commutative, that is, for any two functions f, g, $fg = gf$. (Note that such TDs are as powerful as Turing M/Cs).

Our approach works as follows. First we preprocess the TD and compute a set of *predicate templates* with respect to each node q in the TD. (A predicate template is a predicate together with a function that renames some of its variables). These sets of predicate templates are computed, using a terminating fix-point computation on the graph of the TD, from guards of the transitions of the TD and from predicates that appear in the correctness formula. In the second step, the reachability graph is constructed in a symbolic form. Each of its states consists of a node in the TD and other components that give the values of the variables in symbolic form. We define an equivalence relation, $\sim_0$, on the states by instantiating the predicate templates associated with the corresponding TD node. Two states are equivalent if they are at the same TD node and the instantiations of the predicate templates in both the states are equivalent. We show that this equivalence relation is a bi-simulation. In general checking equivalence of predicates may require a theorem prover. However, for certain types of programs, such as those that use integer variables and additions of constants as functions, this equivalence can be checked efficiently if the predicates only involve standard comparison operators such as $<, >$, etc.

The requirements for the bi-simulation $\sim_0$ can some times be too strong. In order for two symbolic states s, t at a node q to be related by $\sim_0$, we require that the instantiations, of each predicate template pt associated with q, in the states s and t be equivalent. Each such predicate template pt corresponds to a guard of a transition of the TD from some node r or to an atomic predicate in the correctness formula. Suppose that none of the guards of the transitions entering node r are ever satisfiable; then, we don't need to require equivalence of the instantiations of pt with respect to both s and t because r will be never reached from either s or t. As a consequence, we can relax the equivalence requirement as follows. Suppose e is a transition entering the node r; then we require equivalence of the instantiations of pt only if the transition e is enabled with respect to both the states s and t. Thus we require conditional equivalence of template instantiations. The above relaxation in the requirement is done with respect to all the transitions entering node r and for every such node. The resulting binary relation $\sim_1$ on symbolic states is also going to be a bi-simulation.

The above notion of relaxing the requirement with respect to edges entering each node can be generalized to paths of length i entering each node. When we do this, we get the relations $\sim_i$ for each $i > 0$. The relation $\sim_0$, defined earlier, can be considered to be the relation when we consider paths of length zero, i.e. null paths, entering a node. We show that each $\sim_i$ is a bi-simulation and that $\sim_i \subseteq \sim_{i+1}$ for each $i \geq 0$. Thus we get a chain of non-decreasing bi-simulations. For each i, we also show that there exists a TD for which $\sim_i$ is strictly contained in $\sim_{i+1}$. In fact, we can get a TD for which $\sim_i \subset \sim_{i+1}$ for every $i \geq 0$. It is to be noted that using $\sim_{i+1}$ gives us a smaller bi-simulation reduction, however there will be more conditional equivalence checks for $\sim_{i+1}$ than for $\sim_i$.

All the above bi-simulations preserve correctness under fairness also. We have implemented the above methods and applied them to examples such as the sliding window protocol, etc. Experimental results showing the effectiveness of our approach are presented.

The paper is organized as follows. Section 2 discusses applicability of the results of the paper and related work. Section 3 contains definitions and notation. Section 4 presents our method based on the bi-simulation relation $\sim_0$. Section 5 defines the bi-simulation relations with respect to paths of the TD, i.e. it defines the relations $\sim_i$ for $i > 0$ and presents results relating them. Section 6 presents experimental results. Section 7 contains conclusions.

2   Discussion and Related Work

The results of the paper are applicable to concurrent systems that can be modeled by simple TDs over any domain as described earlier. In particular, they can be applied to TDs over integer domains, i.e., where the variables range over integers and are updated by addition of constants and the predicates are of the form $e\rho c$ where e is a linear combination of variables, ρ is a comparison relation and c is a constant. One class of integer TDs for which $\sim_0$ gives a finite quotient of the reachability graph is where each expression appearing in the predicates has finite number of values in the reachability states, or each such expression is positive, i.e., all its coefficients are positive and all its variables are always incremented by positive constants. The exact characterization of systems for which each of the bi-simulations $\sim_i$ (for $i \geq 0$) gives a finite quotient needs to be explored as part of future research.

The work that is most closely related is that given in [9]. In this work the authors present a method that syntactically transforms a program with variables ranging over infinite domain to boolean programs. Their approach involves two steps. In the first step, they perform a fix point computation to generate a set of predicates. In the second step, a boolean program is constructed using binary variables to represent the generated predicates and this program is checked using any existing model checker. The first step in their approach may not terminate. They also give a completeness result showing that if the given program has finite quotient under the most general bi-simulation then there exists a constant k so that their fix point computation when terminated after k steps gives a boolean program that is bi-similar to the give concurrent program. However it is not clear how one knows the value of k in advance.

The first step of our method for computing the predicate templates always terminates and the computed predicate templates are different from those generated by [9]. Our second step involves constructing the reduced graph and may not terminate sometimes. Our methods are better suited for on-the-fly model checking; i.e., we can terminate with an error message when the first error state is encountered during the construction of the reduced graph. In case of the method of [9], the first step needs to be completed before actual model checking can begin, and the first step may not terminate sometimes. There are examples for which our system terminates but the method of [9] may not terminate. There are examples over integer domains where their system terminates but our does not; of course their approach is applicable to more general class of systems. Our system is amenable for on-the-fly model checking for the particular classes of TDs that we consider; this is achieved by checking the given property at the same time as the reduced reachability graph is constructed.

There have also been techniques that construct the bi-simulation reduction in an on-the-fly manner in [7]. The method given in [7] assumes symbolic representation of groups of states and requires efficient computation of certain operations on such representations. Our work is also different from the predicate abstraction methods used in [11, 12, 5] and also in [1] These works use predicates to abstract the concrete model, to get the abstract model and then perform model checking on it. This abstraction ensures that there is a simulation relation from the concrete model to the abstract model. They use ∀CTL for model checking. If the abstract model does not satisfy the correctness then they will have to refine the abstraction and try this process again. Since we use bi-simulation based approach, we do not need any further iterations for refinement.

It should be noted that the commutativity assumption of TDs is different from the commutativity assumption in partial reductions [10, 6]; our assumption requires commutativity of functions employed to update the variables, while in partial-order based methods commutativity of transitions is used which is more restrictive.

It is to be noted that our method based on the bi-simulation $\sim_0$ is itself a generalized method for [2] where a location based bisimulation is used. Our work is different from other works for handling large/infinite state systems such as the one in [3] where symbolic representation of periodic sets is employed.

The work given in [4] considers verification of systems with integer variables. Their method is based on computing invariants and employs approximation techniques based on widening operators. Our method is based on bi-simulation and can be employed for other domains also apart from systems with integer variables.

3 Definitions and Notation

3.1 Transition Diagram

We use *Transition Diagram* (TD) to model a concurrent system. Formally, a TD is a triple $G = (Q, X, E)$ such that Q denotes a set of nodes, X is a set of variables, and E is a set of transitions which are quadruples of the form $\langle q, C, \Lambda, q' \rangle$ where $q, q' \in Q$, C is a condition involving the variables in X and Λ is a set of assignments of the form $x := \rho$ where $x \in X$ and ρ is an expression involving the variables in X. For a transition $\langle q, C, \Lambda, q' \rangle$, we call C the condition part or *guard* of the transition and Λ the action part of the transition and we require that Λ contains at most one assignment for each variable. For any node q of G, we let $guards(q)$ denote the set of guards of transitions from the node q. We also let $guards(G)$ denote the set of guards of all transitions of G.

An evaluation h of a set of variables X is a function that assigns type-consistent values to each variable in X. A state of a TD $G = (Q, X, E)$ is a pair (q, h) where $q \in Q$ and h is an evaluation of X. We say that a transition $e = (q_1, C, \Lambda, q_2)$ is enabled in the state (q, h) if $q = q_1$ and the condition C is satisfied by h, i.e., the values of the variables given by h satisfy C. We say that a state (q', h') is obtained from (q, h) by executing the transition e if e is enabled in (q, h), $q' = q_2$ and the following property is satisfied: for each variable $x \in X$, if there is an assignment of the form $x := \rho$ in Λ then $h'(x) = h(\rho)$, otherwise $h'(x) = h(x)$.

A path in G from node q to node r is a sequence of transitions starting with a transition from q and ending with a transition leading to r such that each successive transition starts from the node where the preceding transition ends. Let $\pi = e_0, e_1, ..., e_{m-1}$ be a path in G from node q and let $s_0 = (q, h_0)$ be a state. We say that π is *feasible* from s_0 if there exists a sequence of states $s_1, ..., s_m$ such that for each i, $0 \le i < m$, the transition e_i is enabled in s_i and state s_{i+1} is obtained by executing e_i in the state s_i. In this case, i.e., when π is feasible from s_0, we say that s_m is the state obtained by executing the path π from s_0.

The left part of figure 1 shows a TD with node set $\{0, 1, 2\}$, variable set $\{a, b, x, y\}$ and transition set $\{t_1, t_2, t_3, t_4\}$. Notice that the transitions t_1 and t_2 both have empty guards meaning that they are always enabled. It is easy to see that the reachability graph from an initial state may be infinite since x, y can grow arbitrarily large.

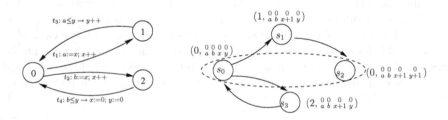

Fig. 1. Example of a TD and its reduced symbolic state graph

Commutativity Requirement

In this paper, we consider the TDs whose action parts only have assignments of the following forms: $x := c$ where c is a constant, or $x := f(x)$, or $x := y$ where y is another variable of the same type as x. We require all functions that are applied to variables of the same type to be commutative. We call such TDs as *simple* TDs. In the full paper, we show how the commutativity requirement can be further relaxed.

3.2 Kripke Structures, Bi-simulation, etc.

A labeled Kripke structure H over a set of atomic propositions AP and over a set of labels Σ is a triple (S, R, L) where S is a set of states, $R \subseteq S \times \Sigma \times S$ and $L : S \to 2^{AP}$ associates with each state a set of atomic propositions. The Kripke structure H is said to be deterministic if for every $s \in S$ and every $\alpha \in \Sigma$ there exists at most one $s' \in S$ such that $(s, \alpha, s') \in R$.

For the Kripke structure $H = (S, R, L)$, an execution σ is an infinite sequence $s_0, e_0, s_1, e_1, ..., s_i, e_i, ...$ of alternating states and labels in Σ such that for each $i \geq 0$, $(s_i, e_i, s_{i+1}) \in R$. A finite execution is a finite sequence of the above type ending in a label in Σ. Corresponding to the execution σ that is finite or infinite, let $trace(\sigma)$ denote the sequence $L(s_0), e_0, ..., L(s_i), e_i, ...$ A finite trace from state s is the sequence $trace(\sigma)$ corresponding to a finite execution from s. The length of a finite trace is the number of transitions in it. For any integer $k > 0$, let $Finite\_Traces_k(H, s)$ denote the set of finite traces of length k from s.

Let $H = (S, R, L)$ and $H' = (S', R', L')$ be two structures over the same set of atomic propositions AP and the same set Σ of labels. A relation $B \subseteq S \times S'$ is a bi-simulation between H and H' iff for all $s \in S$ and $s' \in S'$, if $(s, s') \in B$, then $L(s) = L(s')$ and the following conditions hold: (a) for every $(s, \alpha, s_1) \in R$, there exists a state $s_1' \in S'$ such that $(s', \alpha, s_1') \in R'$ and $(s_1, s_1') \in B$; (b) similarly, for every $(s', \alpha, s_1') \in R'$, there exists a state $s_1 \in S$ such that $(s, \alpha, s_1) \in R$ and $(s_1, s_1') \in B$.

Let $G = (Q, X, E)$ be a TD, u be a state of G and $Reach(G, u) = (S, R, L)$ denote the Kripke structure over the set of atomic propositions AP and the set of labels E defined as follows: S is the set of reachable states obtained by executing the TD G from u; R is the set of triples (s, e, s') such that the transition $e \in E$ is enabled in state s and s' is obtained by executing e in state s; for any $s \in S$, $L(s)$ is the set of atomic propositions in AP that are satisfied in s. It is not difficult to see that $Reach(G, u)$ is a deterministic structure.

Let B be a bi-simulation relation from $Reach(G, u)$ to itself. Instead of constructing $Reach(G, u)$, we can construct a smaller structure using the relation B. We incrementally construct the structure by executing G starting from u. Whenever we get a state w by executing a transition from an already reached state v, we check if there exists an already reached state w' such that (w, w') or (w', w) is in B; if so, we simply add an edge to w' or else we include w into the set of reached states and add an edge to w. This procedure is carried until no more new nodes can be added to the set of reached states. We call the resulting structure as the bi-simulation reduction of $Reach(G, u)$ with respect to B. This reduction has the property that no two states in it are related by B. The number of states in this reduction may not be unique and may depend on the the order of execution of the enabled transitions. However, if B is an equivalence relation then the number of states in the reduction is unique and equals the number of equivalence classes of S with respect to B.

Let G be a TD that captures the behavior of a concurrent program. The Kripke structure $Reach(G, u)$ is deterministic. An infinite execution σ is said to be weakly fair if every process which is enabled continuously from a certain point in σ is executed infinitely often. Let $Fair\_traces(s)$ denote the set of all $trace(\sigma)$ where σ is an infinite weakly fair execution s. For any bi-simulation B from $Reach(G, u)$ to itself, it is easy to show that for every $(s, t) \in B$, $Fair\_traces(s) = Fair\_traces(t)$. This condition holds for many other fairness conditions such as strong fairness, etc.

We use the temporal logic CTL* to specify properties of $Reach(G, u)$. Each atomic proposition in the formulas is a predicate involving variables in X or the special variable lc which refers to the nodes of G. We let AP be the set of predicates that appear in the temporal formula that we want to check. For any formula or predicate p, we let $var(p)$ denote the set of variables appearing in it.

If K is a reduction of $Reach(G, u)$ with respect to a bi-simulation relation then a state which is present in both $Reach(G, u)$ and K satisfies the same set of CTL* formulas in both structures even if we restrict the path quantifiers to fair paths. Also, any two states in $Reach(G, u)$ that are bi-similar to each other satisfy the same set of CTL* formulas.

We also use the following notation. If Φ represents an expression, then $\Phi\{\beta/\alpha\}$ is the expression obtained from Φ by substituting β for α.

3.3   Symbolic State Graph

Let $G = (Q, X, E)$ be a TD, $u = (q_0, h_0)$ be the initial state of G and AP be the set of predicates that appear in the temporal formula to be checked. We execute G symbolically starting with u, to obtain a structure $Sym\_Reach(G, u) = (S', R', L')$. We call the structure $Sym\_Reach(G, u)$ as the symbolic graph and the states of S' symbolic states since the variables are represented by expressions. (It should be noted that our use of the term symbolic state is different from the traditional use where it is meant to be some representation for sets of actual states). Each state s in S' is a triple of the form $(s.lc, s.val, s.exp)$ where $s.lc \in Q$, $s.val$ is an evaluation of the variables in X and $s.exp$ is a function that assigns each variable x an expression which involves only the variable x. Intuitively, $s.lc$ denotes the node in Q where the control is, $s.val(x)$ denotes the latest constant assigned to x and $s.exp(x)$ denotes the composition of functions that were applied to x since then. We associate each symbolic state s with a state $act\_state(s)$ of G defined as follows: $act\_state(s) = (q, h)$ where $q = s.lc$ and $h(x) = s.exp(x)\{s.val(x)/x\}$ for each $x \in X$; that is the value of a variable x is obtained by evaluating $s.exp(x)$ after substituting $s.val(x)$ for x in the expression. We say that a transition e is enabled in a symbolic state s if it is enabled in the corresponding actual state, i.e., it is enabled in $act\_state(s)$.

The successor states of a symbolic state s are the states obtained by enabled transitions in s. Assume that $e = (q, C, \Lambda, q')$ is enabled in s. The new symbolic state s' obtained by executing e from s is defined as follows: $s'.lc = q'$ and for each variable x, if there is no assignment to x in Λ then $s'.val(x) = s.val(x)$ and $s'.exp(x) = s.exp(x)$. If there is an assignment of the form $x := c$ where c is a constant then $s'.val(x) = c$ and $s'.exp(x) = x$. If there is an assignment of the form $x := \psi(x)$ in Λ then $s'.val(x) = s.val(x)$ and $s'.exp(x) = \psi(s.exp(x))$; that is the value remains unchanged and the new expression is obtained by applying the function ψ to the old expression. If there is an assignment of the form $x := y$ in Λ then $s'.val(x) = s.val(y)$ and $s'.exp(x) = s.exp(y)\{x/y\}$; that is the value of $s.val(y)$ is copied and the expression of y in s is also copied after replacing every y by x in the expression. If s' is obtained by executing an enabled transition e from a state s in S', then s' is a state in S' and $(s, e, s') \in R'$. Also for any $s \in S'$, $L'(s) = L(act\_state(s))$.

Consider the TD given in the left part of figure 1 with initial value $a = b = x = y = 0$. We represent each variable $v \in X$ as a pair $(v.val, v.exp)$. The actual value of v is $v.exp\{v.val/v\}$. For figure 1, the initial state s_0 is $(0, \begin{smallmatrix} 0 & 0 & 0 & 0 \\ a & b & x & y \end{smallmatrix})$, where the first 0 denotes the node, the vectors $(0, 0, 0, 0)$ and (a, b, x, y) represent the functions $s_0.val$ and $s_0.exp$ respectively. In s_0, transition t_1 and t_2 are enabled. Suppose we execute t_1 from s_0 and get state s_1. The node in s_1 is 1. For variable a, since x is assigned to it, we copy $x.val$ and $x.exp$ to $a.val$ and $a.exp$ respectively. For variable x, which is updated by a function of itself, we keep $x.val$ as before and change $x.exp$ from x to $x + 1$ according to the updating function. Since there is no assignment to b and y in t_1, their val and exp remain unchanged. So, s_1 is $(1, \begin{smallmatrix} 0 & 0 & 0 & 0 \\ a & b & x+1 & y \end{smallmatrix})$. We know t_3 is enabled in s_1 since the actual values of a, y satisfy the guard. We execute t_3 from s_1 and get $s_2 = (0, \begin{smallmatrix} 0 & 0 & 0 & 0 \\ a & b & x+1 & y+1 \end{smallmatrix})$ similarly. Similarly, executing t_2 from s_0 we get s_3. Executing t_4 from s_3 we get s_0; notice that since x is assigned 0, in the successor state s_0 we have $s.val(x) = 0$ and $s.exp(x) = x$ and same holds for variable y.

Lemma 1 *Let G be a TD, u be a state of G. Then the relation $\{(act\_state(s), s) : s$ is a symbolic state in $Sym\_Reach(G, u)\}$ is a bi-simulation between $Reach(G, u)$ and $Sym\_Reach(G, u)$.*

4   Our Method

4.1   Intuitive Description

Let $G = (Q, X, E)$ be a TD. Recall that AP is the set of predicates appearing in the temporal formula. We motivate our definition of the bi-simulation relation and give an intuitive explanation for the commutativity requirement. For ease of explanation, assume that all the assignments in the transitions of G are of the form $x := \psi(x)$. Also assume that all the predicates in $guards(G) \cup AP$ have at most one variable. It is not difficult to see that any two states $s = (q, h)$ and $t = (q, h')$ satisfying the following conditions are bisimilar in $Reach(G, u)$: (i) for every path π from node q, π is feasible in s iff it is feasible from t; (ii) for every path π from node q to any node r such that π is feasible from s, if s', t' are the states obtained by executing π from s, t respectively then s', t' satisfy the same predicates in $guards(r) \cup AP$. For any path π in G and variable $x \in X$, let $F_{\pi, x}$ denote the composition of the functions that update the variable x in the path π where the composition is taken in the order they appear on the path. Using the above observation, it can be seen that the following relation U over the states of $Reach(G, u)$ is a bi-simulation. U is the set of all pairs (s, t) of states where $s = (q, h)$, $t = (q, h')$ for some $q \in Q$ and some evaluations h, h' such that the following condition is satisfied: for every node r and for every path π from q to r in G, and for every predicate $p(x) \in guards(r) \cup AP$, the truth values $p(x)\{F_{\pi,x}(h(x))/x\}$ and $p(x)\{F_{\pi,x}(h'(x))/x\}$ are the same.

Analogous to the relation U, we can define a relation V over the states of the symbolic graph $Sym\_Reach(G, u)$ as follows. V is the set of all pairs (v, w) of symbolic states where $v.lc = w.lc = q$ for some $q \in Q$, $v.val(x) = w.val(x) = c$ for some constant c and for every node r to which there is a path in G from node q, and for every predicate $p(x) \in guards(r) \cup AP$ the following condition (A) is satisfied: (A) for every path π from q to r in G, the truth values $p(x)\{F_{\pi,x}(\rho_1(c))/x\}$ and $p(x)\{F_{\pi,x}(\rho_2(c))/x\}$ are the same where $\rho_1(x), \rho_2(x)$ are the expressions $v.exp(x)$, $w.exp(x)$ respectively. Note that $\rho_1(c)$ is the value of $\rho_1(x)$ when c is substituted for x. It is not difficult to see that V is also a bi-simulation over $Sym\_Reach(G, u)$. Due to the commutativity requirement on the functions that update variables, we can see that $F_{\pi,x}(\rho_1(c)) = \rho_1(F_{\pi,x}(c))$ and a similar equality holds for the state w. As a consequence, condition (A) can be rewritten as follows: (B) for every path π from q to r in G, the truth values $p(x)\{\rho_1(F_{\pi,x}(c))/x\}$ and $p(x)\{\rho_2(F_{\pi,x}(c))/x\}$ are equal. Now we see that condition (B) is automatically satisfied if the two predicates $p(x)\{\rho_1(x)/x\}$ and $p(x)\{\rho_2(x)/x\}$ are equivalent (this is seen by substituting the value $F_{\pi,x}(c)$ for x in these two predicates). As a consequence we can replace condition (A) by condition (C) which requires the equivalence of the above two predicates. Checking condition (A) requires considering every path from q to r which is not needed for checking (C). The above argument holds even if we have predicates with more than one free variable in $guards(G) \cup AP$. However, if we have other types of assignments to variables then we need to rename some of the variables to obtain the predicates whose equivalence needs to be checked. This is done by computing a set of predicate templates with respect to each node in G.

4.2   Predicate Templates

To define the bi-simulation, we associate a set of predicate templates, denoted $ptemplates(q)$, with each node q in the TD. Intuitively, $ptemplates(q)$ is the set of pairs of predicates and renaming functions on their variables; roughly speaking, our bi-simulation condition requires that the predicates, obtained by renaming the variables and substituting them by the corresponding expressions in two symbolic states, should be equivalent. Formally, a predicate template is a pair (p, f) where p is a predicate and f, called renaming function, is a total function from $var(p)$ to $X \cup \{*\}$.

First we need the following definition. Let π be a path in G. Each such path denotes a possible execution in G. With respect to π, we define a function $depends_\pi$ from X to $X \cup \{*\}$. Intuitively, if $depends_\pi(x)$ is a variable, say y, then this denotes that the value of x at the end of the execution of π depends on the value of y at the beginning of this execution; otherwise, i.e., $depends_\pi(x) = *$, the value of x at the end of π does not depend on the value of any variable at the beginning of π; for example, this happens if x is assigned a constant some where along π. We define $depends_\pi$ inductively on the length of π. If π is a single transition $\langle q, C, \Lambda, q' \rangle$ then $depends_\pi(x)$ is given as follows: if Λ has the assignment $x := y$ then $depends_\pi(x) = y$; if Λ has no assignment to x or has an assignment of the form $x := \psi(x)$ then $depends_\pi(x) = x$; when x is assigned a constant, $depends_\pi(x) = *$. If π is the path consisting of π_1 followed by π_2 then $depends_\pi$ is defined as follows: for each $x \in X$, if $depends_{\pi_2}(x)$ is a variable then $depends_\pi(x) = depends_{\pi_1}(depends_{\pi_2}(x))$, otherwise $depends_\pi(x) = *$. For the TD given in figure 1 and the path π given by the single transition from node 0 to 1, we see that $depends_\pi(a) = x$.

For a node q, $ptemplates(q) = \{(p, depends_\pi) : \pi$ is a path from node q to some node r and $p \in guards(r) \cup AP\}$. Although the number of paths from q can be infinite, the number of functions $depends_\pi$ and hence $ptemplates(q)$ is a bounded set. We can compute $ptemplates(q)$ without examining all the paths from q as follows.

For a template (p, f) and a set of assignments Λ, let $(p, f)_\Lambda$ be the template (p, f') where f' is given as follows: (note that (p, f') is different from the the the weakest precondition of p with respect to Λ)

- if $f(x) = *$, then $f'(x) = *$.
- if $f(x) = y$ where $y \in X$, then if the action part Λ has
  - no assignment for y or an assignment of the form $y := \psi(y)$, then $f'(x) = y = f(x)$.
  - an assignment of the form $y := z$, then $f'(x) = z$.
  - an assignment of the form $y := c$ where c is a constant, then $f'(x) = *$.

Let f_{id} be the identity function. For each node $q \in Q$, the set $ptemplates(q)$ is the least fix point solution for the variables $temp(q)$ in the following set of equations:

$$temp(q) = \{(p, f_{id}) | p \in AP \vee p \in guards(q)\} \cup$$
$$\{(p, f)_\Lambda | (p, f) \in temp(q') \wedge \exists(q, C, \Lambda, q') \in E\}$$

Consider the system given in figure 1. Suppose we want to check the formula $\forall \Box (x \geq y)$. Let p_0 denote $x \geq y$, p_1 denote $a \leq y$, p_2 denote $b \leq y$. Template (p_0, f_{id}) will appear in templates of each location since it is in AP. (p_1, f_{id}) will appear in $ptemplates(1)$ since p_1 is in $guards(1)$. In the remainder of our description, we will also represent a predicate template (p, f) where f maps v_1, v_2 to z_1, z_2 respectively by the tuple $(p, v_1 : z_1, v_2 : z_2)$. Suppose t is a transition, let Λ_t denote the action part of t. By definition, $(p_1, f_{id})_{\Lambda_{t_1}}$ will appear in $ptemplate(0)$. Since Λ_{t_1} contains the assignments $a := x$ and $x := x + 1$, the template $(p_1, f_{id})_{\Lambda_{t_1}}$ is given by $(p_1, a : x, y : y)$. Using transition t_4, we see that the template $(p_0, x : *, y : *)$ is in $ptemplates(2)$; note that in this template both the variables are mapped to $*$ since both these variables are assigned constant values in t_4. By doing this, eventually, we will have

$$ptemplates(1) = \{(p_0, f_{id}), (p_1, f_{id}),$$
$$\{(p_1, a : x, \ y : y), (p_2, b : x, \ y : y)\}$$

We have only given the templates associated with node 1 and even from this we omitted the templates whose renaming function maps all the variables to $*$. From the above definition, we see that $ptemplates(q)$ contains all the templates in $\{(p, f_{id})|p \in AP \cup guards(q)\}$.

We can use standard fix point algorithm to compute the set $ptemplates(q)$ for each $q \in Q$. It is easy to see that the algorithm terminates since the total number of predicate templates is bounded.

Let N_n, N_t, N_v be the number of nodes in G, number of transitions in G and the number of variables respectively. Similarly let N_p and N_a respectively be the number of predicates in $guards(G) \cup AP$ and the maximum number of variables appearing in any predicate. Since the maximum number of renaming functions is $(N_v+1)^{N_a}$, we see that the maximum number of predicate templates is $N_p \cdot (N_v + 1)^{N_a}$. Thus the number of the outer iterations of the fix point computations is at most $N_n \cdot N_p \cdot (N_v+1)^{N_a}$. The time complexity of the algorithm is $O(N_n \cdot N_p \cdot N_t \cdot (N_v + 1)^{N_a})$. Thus we see that the number of predicates is exponential in the number of variables that can appear in a predicate. In most cases we have unary or binary predicates and hence the complexity will not be a problem. Also this worst case complexity occurs when every variable is assigned to every other variable directly or indirectly. We believe that this is a rare case.

4.3   Definition of the Bi-simulation Relation

Now we define the instantiation of a predicate template in a symbolic state. Suppose s is a state of the symbolic state graph $Sym\_Reach(G, u)$, (p, f) is a predicate template and $x_1, x_2, \cdots, x_n$ are variables appearing in p. Let p' be the predicate obtained by replacing every occurrence of the variable x_i (for $1 \leq i \leq n$), for those x_i such that $f(x_i) \neq *$, by the expression $s.exp(y_i)\{x_i/y_i\}$ where y_i is the variable $f(x_i)$. Note that the variables x_i for which $f(x_i) = *$ are not replaced. We define $(p, f)[s]$ to be p' as given above.

For the system given in figure 1, it is easy to see that for the state s_1, $(p_1, a : x, \ y : y)[s_1]$ is $a + 1 \leq y$. Note that for those templates whose renaming function maps all the variables to $*$, the instantiation of them in any two symbolic states will be identical and thus they are trivially equivalent. We can just ignore such templates.

Definition 1. *Define relation $\sim_0$ as follows: For any two states s and t, $s \sim_0 t$ iff $s.lc = t.lc$, $s.val = t.val$ and for each $(p, f) \in ptemplates(s.lc)$, $(p, f)[s] \equiv (p, f)[t]$ is a valid formula.*

Theorem 1. $\sim_0$ *is a bi-simulation on the symbolic state graph Sym_Reach (G, u).*

It is possible that two symbolic states s, t correspond to the same actual state but $(s, t) \notin \sim_0$. To overcome this problem, we consider the relation $\sim_{equal} = \{(s, t) : s, t$ are symbolic states and $act\_state(s) = act\_state(t)\}$. Clearly, $\sim_{equal}$ is a bi-simulation on $Sym\_Reach(G, u)$. Given symbolic states s, t checking if $(s, t) \in \sim_{equal}$ is simple. We simply compute $act\_state(s)$ and $act\_state(t)$ and check if they are equal. Now, we consider the relation $\sim_0 \cup \sim_{equal}$. It is well known that the union of bi-simulation relations is also a bi-simulation. From this, we see that $\sim_0 \cup \sim_{equal}$ is a bi-simulation on $Sym\_Reach(G, u)$. The reduction of $Sym\_Reach(G, u)$ with respect to the bi-simulation $\sim_0 \cup \sim_{equal}$ has at most as many states as the number of states in $Reach(G, u)$.

Checking if $s \sim_0 t$ requires checking equivalence of predicates $(p, f)[s]$ and $(p, f)[t]$ for each template $(p, f) \in ptemplates(s.lc)$. This check can be done efficiently for cerain class of programs over integer domains. Details are left out due to lack of space.

5   Bi-simulation Relations
with Respect to the Paths in the TD

In section 4, we defined the bi-simulation relation $\sim_0$. Two symbolic states s, t are related by this relation, if $s.lc = t.lc$ and for every node r and for every $p \in guards(r) \cup AP$ and for every path π from $s.lc$ to r, the two predicates $(p, depends_\pi)[s]$ and $(p, depends_\pi)[t]$ are equivalent (note that $(p, depends_\pi)$ is a template in $ptemplates(s.lc)$). If none of the guards of transitions entering r is satisfiable then we don't need to require the equivalence of the above two predicates since r is never reached. We define a bi-simulation relation $\sim_1$ in which we relax the condition equivalence condition. Suppose e is a transition entering node r, then in the definition of $\sim_1$, we require the equivalence of $(p, depends_\pi)[s]$ and $(p, depends_\pi)[t]$ only for those cases when the transition e is enabled with respect to both s and t. Such a requirement will be made with respect to every transition entering r. This notion of relaxing the requirement can be generalized to paths of length k entering node r leading to bi-simulation relations $\sim_k$ for each $k > 0$. We describe this below.

First, we need the following definitions. Let π be a path in G and p be any predicate. We define the weakest precondition of p with respect to π, denoted by $WP(\pi, p)$, inductively on the length of π as follows. If π is of length zero, i.e., π is an empty path then $WP(\pi, p) = p$. If π is a single transition given by (r, C, Λ, r'), where Λ is the set of assignments $x_1 := \rho_1, ..., x_k := \rho_k$, then $WP(\pi, p)$ is the predicate $p\{\rho_1/x_1, ..., \rho_k/x_k\}$. If π has more than one transition and consists of the path π' followed by the single transition e then $WP(\pi, p) = WP(\pi', WP(e, p))$. The following lemma is proved by a simple induction on the length of π. (It is to be noted that our definition of the weakest precondition is slightly different from the traditional one; for example, the traditional weakest precondition is $C \supset WP(\pi, p)$ for the case when π is a single transition with guard C).

Lemma 2 *If path π of G is feasible from state s, and t is the state obtained by executing π from s, then t satisfies p iff s satisfies $WP(\pi, p)$.* $\square$

Let $\pi = e_0, e_1, ..., e_{k-1}$ be a path in G where, for $0 \le i < k$, C_i is the guard of the transition e_i. For each i, $0 < i \le k$, let $\pi(i)$ denote the prefix of π consisting of the first i transitions, i.e., the prefix up to e_{i-1}. Define $Cond(\pi)$ to be the predicate $C_0 \wedge \bigwedge_{0 < i < k} WP(\pi(i), C_i)$. The following lemma is proved using the property of the weakest preconditions given by the previous lemma.

Lemma 3 *A path π of G is feasible from state s iff s satisfies the predicate $Cond(\pi)$.* $\square$

Let $k > 0$ be an integer. Now for each node q of G, we define a set called *extended_templates(q, k)* as follows. The set *extended_templates(q, k)* is defined as a set of triples. These triples are of the form $(Cond(\pi''), WP(\pi'', p), depends_{\pi'})$ where π', π'' are paths such that $\pi'\pi''$ (i.e., π' followed by π'') is a path from q to some node r, the length of π'' is k and $p \in guards(r) \cup AP$. Consider the TD given in figure 2. By taking π' to be the empty path and π'' to be the single edge from q_0 to q_1, it is easy to see that the triple $(x_2 = 0, x_1 \geq 20, f_{id})$ is in *extended_templates$(q_0, 1)$*. Similarly the tuple $(x_1 = 0, x_2 \geq 20, f_{id})$ is also in this set. The only other significant tuples in the above set are $(true, x_1 = 0, f_{id})$ and $(true, x_2 = 0, f_{id})$. These tuples are obtained by respectively using the paths consisting of the self loop that increments x_1 and the edge to q_2, and a similar path containing the self loop that increments x_2 and the edge to q_1.

Now we define the binary relation $\sim_k$ on the states of $Sym\_Reach(G, u)$ as follows. $\sim_k$ is the set of all pairs (s, t) where s, t are states of $Sym\_Reach(G, u)$ such that (a) $s.lc = t.lc$ and $s.val = t.val$, (b) $Finite\_Traces_k(Sym\_Reach(G, u), s) = Finite\_Traces_k(Sym\_Reach(G, u), t)$ and (c) for every triple (p_1, p_2, f) in the set *extended_templates$(s.lc, k)$*, the formula $((p_1, f)[s] \wedge (p_1, f)[t]) \supset ((p_2, f)[s] \equiv (p_2, f)[t])$ is a valid formula. Observe that in the template (p_1, p_2, f), the predicate p_1 corresponds to a path π'' of length k in G, p_2 corresponds to a predicate p which is a member of AP or is a guard of some transition e from the last node in π''; roughly speaking condition (c) asserts an inductive hypothesis stating that if it is possible to reach from s, t states s', t' (respectively) so that that π'' is feasible from both s', t' and if state s'', t'' are reached by executing π'' from s', t' (respectively) then p has the same truth value in both s'' and t''. Thus (c) together with (b) ensure inductively that the same set of infinite traces are possible from both s and t.

Theorem 2. *For each $k > 0$, $\sim_k$ is a bi-simulation relation.* $\square$

The bi-simulation relation $\sim_k$ is defined using paths of length k. We can consider the relation $\sim_0$ defined in section 4 as $\sim_k$ for $k = 0$; in this case, we consider an empty path as a path of length zero. The following theorem states that $\sim_k$ is contained in $\sim_{k+1}$ for each $k \geq 0$ and that for for every k there exists a TD in which this containment is strict. Figure 2 gives a TD for which $\sim_0 \subset \sim_1$.

Theorem 3. *(1) For every $k \geq 0$, every TD G, and for every set AP of atomic predicates, $\sim_k \subseteq \sim_{k+1}$. (2) For every $k \geq 0$, there exists a TD G and a set of atomic predicates AP for which the above containment is strict, i.e. $\sim_k \subset \sim_{k+1}$.*

The set *extended_templates(q, k)* for any node q and for any $k > 0$ can be computed using a fix point computation just like the computation of *ptem-*

$plates(q)$. An efficient way to check condition (b) in the definition of $\sim_k$, i.e., to check $Finite\_Traces_k(Reach(G, u), s) = Finite\_Traces_k(Reach(G, u), s)$, is as follows. First check that s and t satisfy the same predicates from AP. For every transition e enabled from s, check that e is also enabled from t and vice versa; further, if s', t' are the states obtained by executing e from s, t respectively, then check if $Finite\_Traces_{k-1}(Reach(G, u), s') = Finite\_Traces_{k-1}(Reach(G, u), t')$ inductively. This method works because $Reach(G, u)$ is a deterministic structure.

It should be noted that for any $i < j$, checking if $(s, t) \in \sim_j$ is going to be more expensive than checking if $(s, t) \in \sim_i$. This is because checking condition (c) in the definition of $\sim_i$ is less expensive since it requires checking equivalence of fewer formulas since $extended\_templates(q, i)$ is a smaller set than $extended\_templates(q, i)$. Similarly, checking condition (b) is less expensive for $\sim_i$ since the number of traces of length i less than the number of traces of length j. However, the bi-simulation reduction with respect to $\sim_j$ will be smaller. Thus there is a trade off. We believe that, in general, it is practical to use $\sim_i$ for small values of i such as $i = 0, 1$, etc.

As in the section 4, for each $i > 0$, we can use the bi-simulation $\sim_i \cup \sim_{equal}$ on the $Sym\_Reach(G, u)$ to get a smaller bi-simulation reduction.

6   Experimental Results

We implemented the method given in the paper for checking invariance properties. This implementation uses the reduction with respect to the bi-simulation $\sim_0$.

Our implementation takes a concurrent program given as a transition system T. The syntax of the input language is similar to that of SMC [13]. The input variables can be either binary variables or integer variables. The implementation has two parts. The first part reads the description of T and converts it in to a TD G by executing the finite state part of it. All the parts in the conditions and actions that refer to integer variables in the transitions of T are transferred to guards and actions in the transitions of G. The second part of the implementation constructs the bi-simulation reduction of G given in section 4 and checks the invariance property on the fly.

We tested our implementation for a variety of examples. Our implementation terminated in all cases excepting for the example of an unbounded queue implementation. In those cases where it terminated, it gave the correct answer. One of our examples is the sliding window protocol with bounded channel. It is an infinite state system due to the sequence numbers. This protocol has a sender and receiver process communicating over a channel. The sender transmits messages tagged with sequence numbers and the receiver sends acknowledgments (also tagged with sequence numbers) after receiving a message. We checked the safety property that every message value received by the receiver was earlier transmitted by the sender. We tested this protocol with a bounded channel under different assumptions. The results are given in Table 2. The table shows the window sizes, the time in seconds, the number of states and edges in the

Table 1. Summary of the tests

Problem Instance	Property	t in sec	# of states
Ticket algorithm	$\forall\Box(\neg(pc_1 = C_1 \wedge pc_2 = C_2))$	0	9

ProducerConsumer size of buffer	Property	t in sec	# of states
30	$\forall\Box(0 \leq p_1 + p_2 - (c_1 + c_2) \leq s)$	0.01	31
100	$\forall\Box(0 \leq p_1 + p_2 - (c_1 + c_2) \leq s)$	0.09	101

Circular Queue size of queue	Property	t in sec	# of states
10	$\forall\Box(h \leq s \wedge t \leq s)$	0.24	121
	$\forall\Box(t \geq h \rightarrow p - c = t - h)$	0.12	121
	$\forall\Box(t \leq h \rightarrow p - c = s - (h - t) + 1)$	0.12	121
	$\forall\Box(0 \leq p - c \leq s)$	0.15	121
30	$\forall\Box(h \leq s \wedge t \leq s)$	16.4	961
	$\forall\Box(t \geq h \rightarrow p - c = t - h)$	2.8	961
	$\forall\Box(t \leq h \rightarrow p - c = s - (h - t) + 1)$	2.7	961
	$\forall\Box(0 \leq p - c \leq s)$	3.2	961

reduced graph and the environment for which the protocol is supposed to work (here "duplicates" means the channel can duplicate messages, "lost" means the channel can lose messages).

We also tested with three other examples taken from [4]. These are the Ticket algorithm for mutual exclusion, Producer-Consumer algorithm and Circular queue implementation. The detailed descriptions of these examples can be found in [4]. All these examples use integer variables as well as binary variables. The ticket algorithm is an algorithm similar to the bakery algorithm. We checked the mutual exclusion property for this algorithm. The Producer-Consumer algorithm consists of two producer and two consumer processes. The producer processes generate messages and place them in a bounded buffer which are retrieved by the consumer processes. In this algorithm, the actual content of the buffer is not modeled. The algorithm uses some binary variables, four integer variables p_1, p_2, c_1, c_2 and a parameter s denoting the size of the buffer. Here p_1, p_2 denote the total number of messages generated by each of the producers respectively; similarly, c_1, c_2 denote the number of messages consumed by the consumers. The circular queue example has the bounded variables h, t which are indexes into a finite array, positive integer variables p, c and a parameter s that denotes the size of the buffer. Here p, c respectively denote the number of messages that are enqueued and dequeued since the beginning. In all these examples, our method terminated and the results are shown in table 1. Time in the table is the time used to get the reduced symbolic state graph. Checking the property does not take that much time.

We have also implemented the method using the relation $\sim_1$. We run it on examples such as the one given in figure 2 and get a smaller bi-simulation reduction. More realistic examples need to be further examined.

Table 2. Experiment on sliding window protocol

Sender Window	Receiver Window	t[s]	# of states	# of edges	Environment
1	1	0.016	47	164	duplicate, lost
1	2	0.203	447	1076	duplicate
1	2	0.296	509	1731	duplicate, lost
2	1	0.860	1167	3832	duplicate
2	2	11.515	4555	11272	duplicate

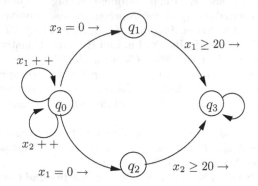

Fig. 2. Example of a TD for which $\sim_0 \subset \sim_1$

7 Conclusion

In this paper we gave methods for model checking of concurrent programs modeled by simple Transition Diagrams. We have given a chain of non-decreasing bi-simulation relations, $\sim_i$ for each $i \geq 0$, on these TDs. They are defined by using predicate templates and extended predicate templates that can be computed by performing a static analysis of the TD. Recall that $\sim_i$ is defined by using templates with respect paths of length i in the TD. Each of these bi-simulations require that the two related states be indistinguishable with respect to the corresponding templates. All these relations can be used to compute a reduced graph for model checking. We have also given how some of these bi-simulation conditions can be checked efficiently for certain types of programs. We have also shown how they can be used to show the decidability of the reachability problem of some simple hybrid automata when the time domain is discrete. We have also presented variants of the above approaches. We have implemented the model checking method using the bi-simulations $\sim_0, \sim_1$. We have given experimental results showing their effectiveness. To the best our knowledge, this is the first time such a comprehensive analysis of simple TDs has been done and the various types of bi-simulations have been defined and used.

Further work is needed on relaxing some of the assumptions such as the commutativity and also on weakening the equivalence condition. Further investigation is also needed on identifying classes of programs to which this approach can be applied.

References

1. T. Ball and S. K. Rajmani. The slam toolkit. In *CAV2001*, 2001.
2. G. Behrmann, E. Bouyer, P. Fleury, and K. G. Larsen. Static guard analysis in timed automata verification. In *TACAS*, pages 254–270, 2003.
3. B. Boigelot and P. Wolper. Symbolic verification with periodic sets. In D. L. Dill, editor, *CAV94, Stanford, California, USA, Proceedings*, volume 818 of *Lecture Notes in Computer Science*, pages 55–67. Springer, 1994.
4. T. Bultan, R. Gerber, and W. Pugh. Model-checking concurrent systems with unbounded integer variables: symbolic representations, approximations, and experimental results. *ACM Trans. Program. Lang. Syst.*, 21(4):747–789, 1999.
5. E. M. Clarke, O. Grumberg, S. Jha, Y. Lu, and H. Veith. Counter-example guided abstraction refinement. In *CAV 2000, Chicago, IL, USA, July 15-19, 2000, Proceedings*, volume 1855 of *Lecture Notes in Computer Science*. Springer, 2000.
6. P. Godefroid. *Partial-order methods for the verification of concurrent systems: an approach to the state-explosion problem*, volume 1032. Springer-Verlag Inc., New York, NY, USA, 1996.
7. D. Lee and M. Yannakakis. Online minimization of transition systems (extended abstract). In *Proceedings of the twenty-fourth annual ACM symposium on Theory of computing*, pages 264–274. ACM Press, 1992.
8. Z. Manna and A. Pnueli. *The Temporal Logic of Reactive and Concurrent Systems: Specification*. Springer-Verlag, Berlin, Jan. 1992.
9. K. S. Namjoshi and R. P. Kurshan. Syntactic program transformations for automatic abstraction. In *CAV2000*, pages 435–449, 2000.
10. D. Peled. All from one, one for all, on model-checking using representatives. In C. Courcoubetis, editor, *CAV 93, Elounda, Greece, Proceedings*, volume 697 of *Lecture Notes in Computer Science*, pages 409–423. Springer, 1993.
11. S. Graf and H. Saidi. Construction of abstract state graphs with PVS. In O. Grumberg, editor, *CAV97*, volume 1254, pages 72–83. Springer Verlag, 1997.
12. H. Saidi and N. Shankar. Abstract and model check while you prove. In N. Halbwachs and D. Peled, editors, *CAV99, Trento, Italy,Proceedings*, volume 1633 of *Lecture Notes in Computer Science*, pages 443–454. Springer, 1999.
13. A. P. Sistla, V. Gyuris, and E. A. Emerson. SMC: A symmetry based model checker for safety and liveness properties. *ACM Transactions on Software Engineering Methodologies*, 9(2):133–166, 2000.

Weak Automata for the Linear Time μ-Calculus

Martin Lange

Institut für Informatik, University of Munich, Germany

Abstract. This paper presents translations forth and back between formulas of the linear time μ-calculus and finite automata with a weak parity acceptance condition. This yields a normal form for these formulas, in fact showing that the linear time alternation hierarchy collapses at level 0 and not just at level 1 as known so far. The translation from formulas to automata can be optimised yielding automata whose size is only exponential in the alternation depth of the formula.

1 Introduction

One of the main reasons for the apparent success of automata theory within computer science is the tight connection that exists between automata and logics. Often, automata are the only tool for deriving (efficient) decision procedures for a logic.

Starting in the 60s, Büchi and Rabin have used automata to show that Monadic Second Order Logic (MSO) over infinite words and trees is decidable [5, 18]. Since then, automata have been found to be particularly useful for temporal logics which usually are fragments of MSO over words or trees. Their emptiness and membership problems are used to decide satisfiability and model checking for various logics, and often certain automata and logics have been shown to be equi-expressive. This characterises logics computationally and automata denotationally.

The type of automaton used – i.e. structures they work upon, rank of determinism, acceptance mode – depends on the type of logic one is interested in: linear time logics need automata over words [21], branching time logics need automata over trees [14]. In any case, alternating automata [16, 6] – i.e. those featuring nondeterministic as well as universal choices – have proved to be most beneficial for two reasons: (1) a temporal logic usually has disjunctions and conjunctions which can uniformly be translated into automata states. (2) Alternating automata are usually more succinct then (non-)deterministic automata, hence, they can lead to more efficient decision procedures.

The acceptance condition needs to match the temporal constructs featured in the logic. LTL for example is happy with a simple Büchi condition since it only has very simple temporal constructs. Logics with more complex temporal operators like extremal fixpoint quantifiers are best matched with more complex acceptance conditions like Rabin, Streett, or Muller conditions for example.

R. Cousot (Ed.): VMCAI 2005, LNCS 3385, pp. 267–281, 2005.

Best suited, however, for fixpoint logics with alternation[1] – the interleaved nesting of least and greatest fixpoint operators – are parity automata. Here, every state is assigned a priority, and acceptance means the parity of the least priority seen infinitely often in a run must be even. The match to fixpoint logics can be explained as follows: both least and greatest fixpoints are recursion mechanisms that get translated into automata states. A least fixpoint quantifier is a recursive program that is bound to terminate eventually. Its dual counterpart, a greatest fixpoint quantifier is a recursive program that is allowed to run ad infinitum. Thus, automata states obtained from least fixpoint quantifiers obtain odd priorities, those obtained from greatest fixpoint quantifiers obtain even priorities.

Fixpoint alternation means a least fixpoint recursion X can call a greatest fixpoint recursion Y which can in return call X, and vice versa. Then, the outermost program, i.e. the one that called the other first, determines whether or not infinite recursion is good or bad. Hence, for example seeing priority 17 infinitely often is alright, as long as priority 8 is also seen infinitely often.

The connection between parity tree automata, parity games – the evaluation of a run of an alternating parity automaton – and the modal μ-calculus is widely known, and much has been written about it [9, 8, 19, 7]. This immediately entails an equal connection between its pendant over infinite words, the linear time μ-calculus μTL [1, 20], and parity word automata. Just as the modal μ-calculus can be seen as a backbone for branching time logics, μTL is the backbone for linear time logics capable of defining at most regular properties.

Fixpoint alternation is what makes formulas hard to evaluate. Equally, the emptiness and word problems for parity automata are harder than those for simple Büchi automata and usually require algorithms that recurse over the number of priorities present in the automaton. It is fair to look for simpler acceptance conditions that still capture the essence of some logic's constructs. One possibility are weak automata. This concept was first introduced by Muller, Saoudi and Schupp [17] as a structural restriction on Büchi automata. Weakness refers to the fact that there are ω-regular languages that cannot be accepted by these automata.

Alternation, however, makes up for weakness [13]: every alternating Büchi automaton can be translated into a weak alternating Büchi automaton. The problem of having established the term "weak" but also knowing that these automata are not any weaker is solved by redefining weakness in terms of acceptance rather than the structure of an automaton's state space. Weak Büchi acceptance is looking for the occurrence of a final state rather than its infinite recurrence. Consequently, a weak parity automaton accepts if the least priority occurring at all is even.

---

[1] Note that the term *alternation* is overloaded. It describes the type of the transition function in an automaton as well as a structural property of formulas with fixpoint quantifiers. Each time we use the term alternation it should become clear from the context which type is meant. However, we will try to speak of *fixpoint alternation* in the latter case.

The advantage that weak parity automata have over normal parity automata is apparent: it is easy to keep track of the least priority seen in a run so far without worrying whether or not it would occur infinitely often. Consequently, emptiness or word problems for weak automata are easier to solve.

Here we present first of all a direct translation from formulas of the linear time μ-calculus into weak alternating parity automata. The novel part of this is the directness. It is known that this translation is possible via alternating parity automata, alternating Muller automata, and alternating Büchi automata. The complexity of this translation however is exponential in the size of the formula. We also show how to improve the direct translation in order to obtain weak automata that are exponentially large in the alternation depth of the formula only.

Then we present the converse translation from weak alternating parity automata back into μTL. This is based on ideas from [11] and [15]. The latter deals with the connection between weak alternating automata and MSO. The former considered automata models for μTL, obtaining an important result that does not hold true for the modal μ-calculus [4]: every ω-regular language can be defined by a μTL formula of alternation depth at most 1. A simple translation from ω-regular expressions into μTL – just meant to form an intuition about how μTL formulas express ω-regular properties – yields an alternative proof of this result. But the translation back from weak alternating parity automata into formulas of the linear time μ-calculus even improves this: the μTL alternation hierarchy indeed collapses at level 0.

This paper is organised as follows. Section 2 recalls notions about infinite words, alternating automata and the linear time μ-calculus. Section 3 presents the aforementioned translations. Their complexities and possible optimisations are discussed in Section 4. Finally, Section 5 concludes with a discussion about the usefulness of this automaton characterisation for ω-regular word languages.

2 Preliminaries

2.1 Infinite Words and ω-Regular Expressions

Let $\Sigma = \{a, b, \ldots\}$ be a finite set of symbols. As usual, Σ^ω denotes the set of infinite words over Σ. Given a $w \in \Sigma^\omega$ we write w^k for the k-th symbol in w, i.e. $w = w^0 w^1 w^2 \ldots$.

Σ^* denotes the set of finite words over Σ. For an $L_1 \subseteq \Sigma^*$ and an $L_2 \subseteq \Sigma^\omega$, their concatenation $L_1 L_2$ consists of all words $w \in \Sigma^\omega$ that can be decomposed into $w = w_1 w_2$ s.t. $w_1 \in L_1$ and $w_2 \in L_2$.

An ω-regular expression is of the form

$$\alpha \ := \ \epsilon \mid a \mid \alpha \cup \alpha \mid \alpha; \alpha \mid \alpha^* \mid \alpha^\omega$$

describing, resp. the language containing just the empty word, all words beginning with the letter a, the union and the concatenation of two languages, finite and infinite iteration of a language. We write $[\![\alpha]\!]$ for the language defined by α.

Theorem 1. [5] *For every ω-regular language L there is an ω-regular expression of the form $\delta = \bigcup_{i=1}^{n} \alpha_i; \beta_i^{\omega}$ for some $n \in \mathbb{N}$, s.t. $[\![\delta]\!] = L$. Additionally, for all $i = 1, \ldots, n$ we have: neither α_i nor β_i contains a subexpression of the form γ^{ω}, and $\epsilon \notin [\![\beta_i]\!]$.*

2.2   The Linear Time μ-Calculus μTL

Definition 1. Let $\Sigma = \{a, b, \ldots\}$ be a finite alphabet, and let $\mathcal{V} = \{X, Y, \ldots\}$ be a set of propositional variables. Formulas of the linear time μ-calculus μTL are defined by the following grammar.

$$\varphi \ ::= \ a \mid X \mid \varphi \vee \varphi \mid \varphi \wedge \varphi \mid \bigcirc\varphi \mid \mu X.\varphi \mid \nu X.\varphi$$

where $a \in \Sigma$ and $X \in \mathcal{V}$. With $\varphi\{\psi/\chi\}$ we denote the formula that is obtained from φ by replacing every occurrence of χ in it with ψ. We will write σ for either of the fixpoint quantifiers μ or ν.

The set of subformulas of a μTL formula is defined in the usual way, i.e. $Sub(\varphi \vee \psi) = \{\varphi \vee \psi\} \cup Sub(\varphi) \cup Sub(\psi)$ and $Sub(\sigma X.\varphi) = \{\sigma X.\varphi\} \cup Sub(\varphi)$ for example. Equally, $free(\varphi)$ is the usual set of variables occurring in φ which are not in the scope of a binding quantifier. We assume that formulas are well-named, i.e. a variable is not quantified more than once in a formula. Then for every closed φ there is a function $fp_{\varphi}() : \mathcal{V} \cap Sub(\varphi) \to Sub(\varphi)$ which maps each variable X to its unique defining fixpoint formula $\sigma X.\varphi$. We say that X has fixpoint type μ if $fp_{\varphi}(X) = \mu X.\psi$ for some ψ, otherwise it is ν.

Assuming that $1 < |\Sigma| < \infty$ it is easy to define the propositional constants true and false as $\mathbf{tt} := \bigvee_{a \in \Sigma} a$ and $\mathbf{ff} := a \wedge b$ for some $a, b \in \Sigma$ with $a \neq b$. If the assumption does not hold then one can also include $\mathbf{tt}$ and $\mathbf{ff}$ as primitives in the logic.

Formulas of μTL are interpreted over ω-words $w \in \Sigma^{\omega}$. Since the semantics is defined inductively, one needs to explain the meaning of open formulas. This is done using an *environment* which is a mapping $\rho : \mathcal{V} \to 2^{\mathbb{N}}$. With $\rho[X \mapsto M]$ we denote the function that maps X to M and behaves like ρ on all other arguments.

$$
\begin{aligned}
[\![a]\!]_{\rho}^{w} \quad &:= \quad \{i \in \mathbb{N} \mid w^i = a\} \\
[\![X]\!]_{\rho}^{w} \quad &:= \quad \rho(X) \\
[\![\varphi \vee \psi]\!]_{\rho}^{w} \quad &:= \quad [\![\varphi]\!]_{\rho}^{w} \cup [\![\psi]\!]_{\rho}^{w} \\
[\![\varphi \wedge \psi]\!]_{\rho}^{w} \quad &:= \quad [\![\varphi]\!]_{\rho}^{w} \cap [\![\psi]\!]_{\rho}^{w} \\
[\![\bigcirc\varphi]\!]_{\rho}^{w} \quad &:= \quad \{i \in \mathbb{N} \mid i+1 \in [\![\varphi]\!]_{\rho}^{w}\} \\
[\![\mu X.\varphi]\!]_{\rho}^{w} \quad &:= \quad \bigcap\{M \subseteq \mathbb{N} \mid [\![\varphi]\!]_{\rho[X \mapsto M]}^{w} \subseteq M\} \\
[\![\nu X.\varphi]\!]_{\rho}^{w} \quad &:= \quad \bigcup\{M \subseteq \mathbb{N} \mid M \subseteq [\![\varphi]\!]_{\rho[X \mapsto M]}^{w}\}
\end{aligned}
$$

We write $w \models_{\rho} \varphi$ iff $0 \in [\![\varphi]\!]_{\rho}^{w}$. If φ does not contain free variables we also drop ρ since in this case the positions in w satisfying φ do not depend on it. The set of all models of φ is denoted $L(\varphi) := \{w \in \Sigma^{\omega} \mid w \models \varphi\}$. Two formulas φ and ψ are equivalent, $\varphi \equiv \psi$, if $L(\varphi) = L(\psi)$.

Approximants of a formula $\mu X.\varphi$ are defined for all $k \in \mathbb{N}$ as

$$\mu^0 X.\varphi \; := \; \text{ff} \qquad\qquad \mu^{k+1} X.\varphi \; := \; \varphi\{\mu^k X.\varphi/X\}$$

Dually, approximants of a $\nu X.\varphi$ are defined as

$$\nu^0 X.\varphi \; := \; \text{tt} \qquad\qquad \nu^{k+1} X.\varphi \; := \; \varphi\{\nu^k X.\varphi/X\}$$

The next result is a standard result about approximants.

Lemma 1.
a) $w \models \mu X.\varphi$ iff there is a $k \in \mathbb{N}$ s.t. $w \models \mu^k X.\varphi$.
b) $w \models \nu X.\varphi$ iff for all $k \in \mathbb{N}$: $w \models \nu^k X.\varphi$.

The fixpoint depth $fpd(\varphi)$ of φ measures the maximal number of fixpoint quantifiers seen on any path in $\varphi's$ syntax tree. It is defined as

$$
\begin{aligned}
fpd(a) = fpd(X) &:= 0 \\
fpd(\varphi \vee \psi) = fpd(\varphi \wedge \psi) &:= \max\{fpd(\varphi), fpd(\psi)\} \\
fpd(\bigcirc\varphi) &:= fpd(\varphi) \\
fpd(\sigma X.\varphi) &:= 1 + fpd(\varphi)
\end{aligned}
$$

We say that X depends on Y in φ, written $Y \prec_\varphi X$, if $Y \in free(fp_\varphi(X))$. We write $<_\varphi$ for the transitive closure of $\prec_\varphi$. The nesting depth $nd(\varphi)$ of φ is the length n of a maximal chain $X_0 <_\varphi \ldots <_\varphi X_n$. The alternation depth $ad(\varphi)$ is the length of such a maximal chain in which adjacent variables have different fixpoint types. Note that for any φ we have $ad(\varphi) \leq nd(\varphi) \leq fpd(\varphi)$. Let $\mu\text{TL}^k := \{\varphi \in \mu\text{TL} \mid free(\varphi) = \emptyset \text{ and } ad(\varphi) \leq k+1\}$.

A formula φ is guarded if every occurrence of a variable $X \in Sub(\varphi)$ is in the scope of a $\bigcirc$ operator inside of $fp_\varphi(X)$. It is strictly guarded if every occurrence of a variable $X \in Sub(\varphi)$ is immediately preceeded by a $\bigcirc$ operator.

Lemma 2. *Every $\varphi \in \mu\text{TL}^k$ for any $k \in \mathbb{N}$ is equivalent to a strictly guarded $\varphi' \in \mu\text{TL}^k$.*

Proof. It is known from [12] or [22] for example that every formula of the modal μ-calculus can equivalently be translated into a guarded formula. There, guardedness means occurrence in the scope of either a $\langle a \rangle$ or a $[a]$. The alternation depth is not effected by this process. The construction for μTL formulas proceeds in just the same way.

Finally, strict guardedness can easily be achieved by pushing the next operator inwards using the equivalences $\bigcirc(\varphi \vee \psi) \equiv \bigcirc\varphi \vee \bigcirc\psi$ and $\bigcirc(\varphi \wedge \psi) \equiv \bigcirc\varphi \wedge \bigcirc\psi$. What remains to be seen is that the next operator also commutes with the fixpoint quantifiers. Take a formula of the form $\bigcirc\mu X.\varphi(X,Y)$. By induction hypothesis, X is already strictly guarded in it, but Y may not. Let $\varphi^{(\bigcirc X)}$ be the formula that results from $\bigcirc\varphi$ by pushing the $\bigcirc$ operators in as far as possible and removing it right in front of every occurrence of X. By hypothesis it exists. Now

$$\bigcirc \mu X.\varphi(X,Y) \; \equiv \; \bigcirc \bigvee_{i\in\mathbb{N}} \mu^i X.\varphi(X,Y)$$

$$\equiv \; \bigcirc \mathbf{ff} \vee \bigvee_{i\geq 1} \bigcirc \mu^i X.\varphi(X,Y)$$

$$\equiv \; \bigvee_{i\geq 1} \bigcirc \varphi(\mu^{i-1} X.\varphi(X,Y),Y)$$

$$\equiv \; \bigvee_{i\geq 1} \varphi^{(\bigcirc X)}(\bigcirc \mu^{i-1} X.\varphi(X,Y),Y)$$

$$\equiv \; \bigvee_{i\geq 1} \mu^i X.\varphi^{(\bigcirc X)}(X,Y)$$

$$\equiv \; \mu X.\varphi^{(\bigcirc X)}(X,Y)$$

The penultimate step requires a straight-forward induction on i. The temporary introduction of infinitary formulas is justified by Lemma 1. The case of a greatest fixpoint formula is analogous. $\square$

Just like the modal μ-calculus can define all (bisimulation-invariant) regular languages of infinite trees [10], μTL can define all ω-regular word languages. We will show this by giving a translation from ω-regular expressions into μTL.

Definition 2. For any ω-regular expression α we define $tr_X(\alpha) \in \mu$TL that describes the same ω-language over Σ. The inductive and uniform translation uses a free variable X that will eventually be bound by an $^\omega$-operator. This is essentially continuation-passing if the ω-regular expression is regarded as a computation.

$$
\begin{aligned}
tr_X(\epsilon) \; &:= \; X \\
tr_X(a) \; &:= \; a \wedge \bigcirc X \\
tr_X(\alpha_0 \cup \alpha_1) \; &:= \; tr_X(\alpha_0) \vee tr_X(\alpha_1) \\
tr_X(\alpha_0;\alpha_1) \; &:= \; tr_X(\alpha_0)\{tr_X(\alpha_1)/X\} \\
tr_X(\alpha^*) \; &:= \; \mu Y.X \vee tr_Y(\alpha) \\
tr_X(\alpha^\omega) \; &:= \; \nu X.tr_X(\alpha)
\end{aligned}
$$

This translation does not only give an automata-free proof of the fact that μTL can describe all ω-regular languages. It also yields an alternative way of showing that the alternation hierarchy in μTL collapses at level 1.

Theorem 2. *For every μTL formula φ there is a $\varphi' \in \mu$TL^1 s.t. $\varphi \equiv \varphi'$.*

Proof. It is well-known that a μTL formula can be regarded as an alternating parity automaton. These can be translated into alternating Muller automata, then into alternating Büchi automata, then into nondeterministic Büchi automata, and finally into ω-regular expressions – whilst preserving equivalence in each step. According to Theorem 1, the resulting expressions do not contain nested $^\omega$-operators. Using Definition 2 they can be translated into μTL formulas whose subformulas of the form $\mu X.\psi$ contain at most one free variable that is bound by a ν-operator. Hence, the alternation depth of the resulting formula is at most 1. $\qquad\square$

Not only can this result be improved in terms of the level at which the hierarchy collapses – see below. Such a translation is also of no practical relevance since it is at least double exponential in the size of the formula.

2.3 Positive Boolean Formulas

For a given set Q let $\mathbb{B}^+(Q)$ be the set of positive boolean formulas over Q. I.e. $\mathbb{B}^+(Q)$ is the least set that contains Q and fulfils: if $f, g \in \mathbb{B}^+(Q)$ then $f \vee g, f \wedge g \in \mathbb{B}^+(Q)$. We say that $P \subset Q$ is a model of f if f evaluates to tt when every $q \in P$ in it is replaced by tt and every $q \notin P$ in it is replaced by ff.

We write $f[q'/q]$ for the positive boolean formula that results from f by replacing every occurrence of q in it with q'.

Later we will use a simple operation $()^l$ that tags the elements of Q as q^l. This is extended to $\mathbb{B}^+(Q)$ in the obvious way: $(f \vee g)^l := (f)^l \vee (g)^l$, and $(f \wedge g)^l := (f)^l \wedge (g)^l$.

2.4 Alternating Automata

An alternating parity automaton (APA) is a tuple $\mathcal{A} = (Q, \Sigma, q_0, \delta, \Omega)$ where Q is a finite set of states, Σ a finite alphabet, and $q_0 \in Q$ the designated starting state, $\delta : Q \times \Sigma \to \mathbb{B}^+(Q)$ is the transition function. $\Omega : Q \to \mathbb{N}$ assigns to each state a priority.

A run r of $\mathcal{A}$ on a word $w \in \Sigma^\omega$ is an infinite tree rooted with q_0, s.t. for every node q_j on level i the set $\{p_1, \ldots, p_n\}$ of its children is a model of $\delta(q_j, w^i)$.

Let $\pi = q_0, q_1, \ldots$ be a path of a run r of $\mathcal{A}$ on w. Let

$$Occ(\pi) := \{q \mid \exists i \in \mathbb{N} \text{ s.t. } q_i = q\}$$
$$Inf(\pi) := \{q \mid \forall j \in \mathbb{N} : \exists i \geq j \text{ s.t. } q_i = q\}$$

A run r of an APA $\mathcal{A}$ on w is accepting iff for every path π of r: $\min\{\Omega(q) \mid q \in Inf(\pi)\}$ is even. $\mathcal{A}$ accepts w if there is an accepting run of $\mathcal{A}$ on w. The language $L(\mathcal{A})$ is the set of all words accepted by $\mathcal{A}$.

A weak alternating parity automaton (WAPA) is an APA $\mathcal{A}$ with a less demanding acceptance condition. A run r of a WAPA $\mathcal{A}$ on w is accepting if for all paths π of r: $\min\{\Omega(q) \mid q \in Occ(\pi)\}$ is even. $L(\mathcal{A})$ is defined in the same way.

An alternating Büchi automaton (ABA) is an APA $\mathcal{A} = (Q, \Sigma, q_0, \delta, \Omega)$ where $\Omega : Q \to \{0, 1\}$. We usually write an ABA as $(Q, \Sigma, q_0, \delta, F)$ with $F := \{q \in Q \mid$

$\Omega(q) = 0$}. Acceptance then boils down to a state in F being visited infinitely often.

A weak alternating Büchi automaton (WABA) could just be defined as a WAPA with two priorities only. However, for technical reasons we prefer the equivalent and original definition from [17]. A WABA is an ABA $\mathcal{A} = (Q, \Sigma, q_0, \delta, F)$ where Q can be partitioned into components $C_0, \ldots, C_n$ s.t.

- for all $q \in Q$, $i, j \in \{0, \ldots, n\}$, $a \in \Sigma$: if $q \in C_i$ and $q' \in C_j$ and $\delta(q, a) = f(\ldots, q', \ldots)$ for some f then $j \leq i$,
- for all $0 \leq i \leq n$: $C_i \subseteq F$ or $C_i \cap F = \emptyset$.

3   From μTL to WAPA and Back

Definition 3. A WAPA with a hole q is a $\mathcal{A} = (Q, \Sigma, q_0, \delta, \Omega)$ with $q \in Q$ s.t. $\delta(q, a) = \bot$ (undefined) for any $a \in \Sigma$, and $\Omega(q) = \bot$. Intuitively, a WAPA with a hole is a WAPA whose construction is not finished yet.

Let $\mathcal{A}$ be a WAPA with a hole q, $\mathcal{B}$ be another WAPA and $L \subseteq \Sigma^\omega$. We write $\mathcal{A}[q : \mathcal{B}]$ for the WAPA that results from $\mathcal{A}$ by replacing q in $\mathcal{A}$ with the starting state of $\mathcal{B}$. We also write $\mathcal{A}[q : L]$ instead of $\mathcal{A}[q : \mathcal{B}]$ for some $\mathcal{B}$ with $L(\mathcal{B}) = L$.

Let $\mathcal{A}_{\mathbf{ff}} = (\{\mathbf{ff}\}, \Sigma, \mathbf{ff}, \{(\mathbf{ff}, a) \mapsto \mathbf{ff} \mid a \in \Sigma\}, \{\mathbf{ff} \mapsto 1\})$ be a WAPA that accepts the empty language.

Theorem 3. *For every closed $\varphi \in \mu$TL there is a WAPA $\mathcal{A}_\varphi$ s.t. $L(\mathcal{A}_\varphi) = L(\varphi)$.*

Proof. The proof proceeds by induction on the structure of φ. According to Lemma 2, φ can be assumed to be strictly guarded.

Despite closeness of φ, we need to handle open subformulas. This will be done using WAPAs with holes. Furthermore, we need to strengthen the inductive hypothesis: for every φ we will construct a WAPA $\mathcal{A} = (Q, \Sigma, q_0, \delta, \Omega)$ with $\Omega(q_0) > \Omega(q)$ for all $q \neq q_0$.

Figure 1 shows the intuition behind some of the cases below.

Case $\varphi = a$. Let $\mathcal{A}_a = (\{a, \mathbf{tt}, \mathbf{ff}\}, \Sigma, a, \delta, \Omega)$ with $\delta(a, a) = \mathbf{tt}$, $\delta(a, b) = \mathbf{ff}$ for any $b \neq a$, $\delta(q, a) = q$ for any $a \in \Sigma, q \in \{\mathbf{tt}, \mathbf{ff}\}$ and $\Omega(a) = 2$, $\Omega(\mathbf{ff}) = 1$, $\Omega(\mathbf{tt}) = 0$. Then $L(\mathcal{A}_a) = \{a\}\Sigma^\omega = L(a)$.

Case $\varphi = X$. Let $\mathcal{A}_X$ be the WAPA that consists of the hole X only.

Case $\varphi = \bigcirc\psi$. By hypothesis there is a WAPA $\mathcal{A}_\psi = (Q, \Sigma, q_0, \delta, \Omega)$ with $L(\mathcal{A}_\psi) = L(\psi)$. Assume $\varphi \notin Q$, and let $p := 1 + \max\{\Omega(q) \mid q \in Q\}$. Define $\mathcal{A}_\varphi = (Q \cup \{\varphi\}, \Sigma, \varphi, \delta', \Omega')$ with $\delta' = \delta \cup \{(q, a) \mapsto q_0 \mid a \in \Sigma\}$, $\Omega' = \Omega \cup \{q \mapsto p\}$. Then $L(\mathcal{A}_\varphi) = \Sigma L(\mathcal{A}_\psi) = L(\bigcirc\psi)$. Note that every run of $\mathcal{A}_\varphi$ starts with φ but then contains only states with strictly smaller priorities. Thus, a word aw is accepted by $\mathcal{A}_\varphi$ iff w is accepted by $\mathcal{A}_\psi$.

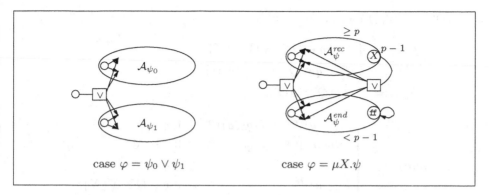

$$\geq p$$

case $\varphi = \psi_0 \vee \psi_1$ case $\varphi = \mu X.\psi$

Fig. 1. Illustrations of the translation from μTL to WAPA.

Case $\varphi = \psi_0 \vee \psi_2$. By hypothesis there are WAPAs $\mathcal{A}_{\psi_i} = (Q_i, \Sigma, q_{0,i}, \delta_i, \Omega_i)$ for $i \in \{0,1\}$ s.t. $L(\mathcal{A}_{\psi_i}) = L(\psi_i)$. We can assume Q_0 and Q_1 to be disjoint. Let $Q := Q_0 \cup Q_1 \cup \{\varphi\}$. This is where strict guardedness is needed. It ensures that inside each $\mathcal{A}_{\psi_i}$ there is a proper transition between the starting state and any hole. Define $\mathcal{A}_\varphi = (Q, \Sigma, \varphi, \delta, \Omega)$ where for any $a \in \Sigma$, $q \in Q$:

$$\delta(q,a) := \begin{cases} \delta_0(q_{0,0}, a) \vee \delta(q_{0,1}, a) & \text{if } q = \varphi \\ \delta_i(q,a) & \text{if } q \in Q_i, i \in \{0,1\} \end{cases}$$

$$\Omega(q) := \begin{cases} 1 + \max\{\Omega_i(q) \mid q \in Q_i, i \in \{0,1\}\} & \text{if } q = \varphi \\ \Omega_i(q) & \text{if } q \in Q_i, i \in \{0,1\} \end{cases}$$

A run of $\mathcal{A}_\varphi$ on any w is also a run of either $\mathcal{A}_{\psi_0}$ or $\mathcal{A}_{\psi_1}$ on w with the exception that the root of the run in $\mathcal{A}_\varphi$ has a higher priority. Hence, if $w \in L(\mathcal{A}_\varphi)$ then $w \in L(\mathcal{A}_{\psi_i})$ for some $i \in \{0,1\}$. For the converse direction we need the stronger hypothesis. Suppose $w \in L(\mathcal{A}_{\psi_i})$ for some $i \in \{0,1\}$. Thus, on any path the minimal priority that occurs is even. However, this cannot be the priority of the root since it is the greatest occurring at all. But then the corresponding run of $\mathcal{A}_\varphi$ accepts w, too.

Case $\varphi = \psi_0 \wedge \psi_1$. Analogous to the previous case. The automaton for φ is obtained as the disjoint union of the automata for the conjuncts with a new starting state which does the conjunction of the two components' starting states.

Case $\varphi = \mu X.\psi$. By hypothesis there is a WAPA $\mathcal{A}_\psi = (Q, \Sigma, q_0, \delta, \Omega)$. Let $p' := \max\{\Omega(q) \mid q \in Q\}$ and $p := p' + 2 + (p' \mod 2)$ a strict even upper bound on all the priorities occurring in $\mathcal{A}_\psi$.

Note that $\mu X.\psi \equiv \psi$ if $X \notin \mathit{free}(\psi)$. Thus, $\mathcal{A}_\psi$ can be assumed to contain a hole X. Note that one hole suffices since holes are states that clearly behave in the same way – namely not at all – and hence, can be collapsed.

$\mathcal{A}_\varphi$ will consist of two disjoint copies of $\mathcal{A}_\psi$: one that unfolds the fixpoint a finite number of times and one that puts a halt to the recursion. Technically, let

$\mathcal{A}_\varphi = (Q', \Sigma, \varphi, \delta', \Omega')$ where

$$
\begin{aligned}
Q^{rec} &:= \{q^{rec} \mid q \in Q \setminus \{X\}\} \cup \{X\} \\
Q^{end} &:= \{q^{end} \mid q \in Q \setminus \{X\}\} \cup \{\mathtt{ff}\} \\
Q' &:= \{\varphi\} \cup Q^{rec} \cup Q^{end}
\end{aligned}
$$

$$
\delta'(q,a) := \begin{cases}
(\delta(q_0,a))^{rec} \vee (\delta(q_0,a))^{end} & \text{if } q = \varphi \\
(\delta(q_0,a))^{rec} \vee (\delta(q_0,a))^{end} & \text{if } q = X \\
\mathtt{ff} & \text{if } q = \mathtt{ff} \\
(\delta(q,a))^{rec} & \text{if } q \in Q^{rec} \setminus \{X\} \\
(\delta(q,a))^{end}[\mathtt{ff}/X] & \text{if } q \in Q^{end} \setminus \{\mathtt{ff}\}
\end{cases}
$$

$$
\Omega'(q) := \begin{cases}
2 \cdot p - 1 & \text{if } q = \varphi \\
p - 1 & \text{if } q = X \\
1 & \text{if } q = \mathtt{ff} \\
\Omega(q) + p & \text{if } q \in Q^{rec} \setminus \{X\} \\
\Omega(q) & \text{if } q \in Q^{end} \setminus \{\mathtt{ff}\}
\end{cases}
$$

Let $\mathcal{A}_\psi^{end}$ and $\mathcal{A}_\psi^{rec}$ be the respective restrictions of $\mathcal{A}_\varphi$ to Q^{end} and Q^{rec}. Note the following facts:

- All the priorities in $\mathcal{A}_\psi^{end}$ are strictly smaller than those in $\mathcal{A}_\psi^{rec}$.
- In $\mathcal{A}_\psi^{rec}$, state X has the smallest priority which is odd.
- $\mathcal{A}_\psi^{end}$ is isomorphic to $\mathcal{A}_\psi[X : \emptyset]$.
- $\mathcal{A}_\psi^{rec}$ has the same structure as $\mathcal{A}_\psi$ except for state X which accepts either $L(\mathcal{A}_\psi^{end})$ or $L(\mathcal{A}_\psi^{rec})$.
- Every path in an accepting run of $\mathcal{A}_\varphi$ must not visit state X infinitely often, for otherwise the least priority seen on this path at all would be odd.

Thus, $L(\mathcal{A}_\varphi)$ is the least solution to the equation

$$
L = L(\mathcal{A}_\psi[X : \emptyset]) \cup L(\mathcal{A}_\psi[X : L])
$$

Using the hypothesis twice as well as the approximant characterisation of least fixpoints and Lemma 1 we get

$$
L(\mathcal{A}_\varphi) = \bigcup_{k \geq 1} L(\mu^k X.\psi) = \bigcup_{k \geq 0} L(\mu^k X.\psi) = L(\mu X.\psi) = L(\varphi)
$$

Case $\varphi = \nu X.\psi$. This is dual to the previous case. In order to adhere to Lemma 1, the starting state as well as the recursion state X conjunctively combine the transitions of q_0^{rec} and q_0^{end}. State X obtains an even priority. The whole X in the *end*-component is filled by a state $\mathtt{tt}$ which has priority 0 and loops back to itself with any alphabet symbol. $\qquad\square$

The next theorem is featured as an observation in [15] already. However, we include its proof here in order to have a complete and effective translation from WAPAs to μTL formulas. The result is also very similar to the theorem in [13] stating that ABAs can be translated into WABAs. Consequently, its proof proceeds along the same lines.

Theorem 4. [15, 13]   *For every WAPA $\mathcal{A}$ there is a WABA $\mathcal{A}'$ s.t. $L(\mathcal{A}') = L(\mathcal{A})$.*

Proof. Let $\mathcal{A} = (Q, \Sigma, q_0, \delta, \Omega)$ with $\Omega : Q \rightarrow \{0, \dots, p\}$. Define $\mathcal{A}' = (Q \times \{0, \dots, p\}, \Sigma, (q_0, \Omega(q_0)), \delta', F)$ where for all $q \in Q$, $a \in \Sigma$:

$$\delta'((q, k), a) := \langle \delta(q, a) \rangle^{\min\{k, \Omega(q)\}}$$

with $\langle f \vee g \rangle^k := \langle f \rangle^k \vee \langle f \rangle^k$, $\langle f \wedge g \rangle^k := \langle f \rangle^k \wedge \langle f \rangle^k$, and $\langle q \rangle^k := (q, k)$. Finally, let $F := \{ (q, k) \mid k \text{ is even} \}$.

First observe that $\mathcal{A}'$ is indeed a WABA. Let $C_i := \{(q, i) \mid q \in Q\}$. Then $C_0, \dots, C_p$ is a partition on $Q \times \{0, \dots, p\}$, transitions either stay inside a C_i or lead to a C_j with $j < i$. At last, for every C_i we either have $C_i \subseteq F$ or $C_i \cap F = \emptyset$.

Now suppose that $w \in L(\mathcal{A})$. A run r of $\mathcal{A}$ on w naturally induces a run r' of $\mathcal{A}'$ on w. Every node in this run carries an extra component which remembers the minimal priority seen on this path so far. Hence, if r is accepting, so is r' since every path will eventually be trapped in a component that remembers even priorities. The converse direction is proved in the same way. If every path of a run in $\mathcal{A}'$ visits infinitely many final states, then the corresponding run of $\mathcal{A}$ must have seen even priorities as the least on every path.   □

Theorem 5. *For every WABA $\mathcal{A}$ there is a μTL^0 formula $\varphi_{\mathcal{A}}$ s.t. $L(\varphi_{\mathcal{A}}) = L(\mathcal{A})$.*

Proof. Let $\mathcal{A} = (Q, \Sigma, q_0, \delta, F)$ with Q being disjointly partitioned into components $C_0, \dots, C_p$. W.l.o.g. we can assume for any $i \in \{0, \dots, p\}$ that $C_i \subseteq F$ if i is even, and $C_i \cap F = \emptyset$ if i is odd. Since transitions can at most lead into components with smaller indices we can also assume $q_0 \in C_p$.

Take such a component C_i and a state $q \in C_i$. For each component we use the same method as proposed in [11] in order to come up with a μTL formula. First, C_i is unfolded into a tree-like structure with root q that admits loops but no merging of paths. A state at the beginning of a loop is called a (q, i)-loop state. With C_i^q we denote this unfolding of C_i.

We will translate every unfolded C_i^q into a formula φ_i^q using auxiliary formulas that describe the local behaviour of state q in component i with root q':

$$\psi_{q',i}^q := \begin{cases} \sigma_i X_{q',i} . \bigwedge_{a \in \Sigma} a \rightarrow \bigcirc \| \delta(q', a) \|_i^q & \text{if } q' \text{ is a } (q, i) - \text{loop state} \\ \bigwedge_{a \in \Sigma} a \rightarrow \bigcirc \| \delta(q', a) \|_i^q & \text{o.w.} \end{cases}$$

where $\sigma_i = \mu$ if i is odd, $\sigma_i = \nu$ if it is even, and

$$\|f \vee g\|_i^q := \|f\|_i^q \vee \|g\|_i^q$$
$$\|f \wedge g\|_i^q := \|f\|_i^q \wedge \|g\|_i^q$$
$$\|q'\|_i^q := \begin{cases} X_{q',i} & \text{if } q' \text{ is a } (q,i) - \text{loop state} \\ \psi_{q',i} & \text{o.w.} \end{cases}$$

Finally, let $\varphi_i^q := \psi_{q,i}$.

Note that every connected component of $\mathcal{A}$ is translated into a formula without free variables that only uses closed formulas from components with lower indices. Furthermore, the formulas created from one component have a single fixpoint type only. Hence, the resulting formula is alternation-free.

The correctness of this construction can be shown using tableaux or games for μTL as it is done in [11]. $\qquad\square$

Corollary 1. *Every $\varphi \in \mu$TL is equivalent to a $\varphi' \in \mu$TL^0.*

Proof. By composition of Theorems 3, 4 and 5. $\qquad\square$

4   Optimising the Translations

Proposition 1. *For every $\varphi \in \mu$TL there is a WAPA $\mathcal{A}_\varphi$ with $L(\mathcal{A}_\varphi) = L(\varphi)$ s.t. $|\mathcal{A}| = O(|\varphi| \cdot 2^{fpd(\varphi)})$.*

Proof. Immediate from the proof of Theorem 3. All inductive constructions are linear, except those for fixpoint quantifiers. They double the size of the automata. $\qquad\square$

Proposition 2. *For every WAPA $\mathcal{A}$ there is a $\varphi_{\mathcal{A}} \in \mu$TL^0 with $L(\varphi_{\mathcal{A}}) = L(\mathcal{A})$ s.t. $|\varphi| = O(|\mathcal{A}|^4)$.*

Proof. Using Theorem 4, $\mathcal{A}$ can be transformed into a WABA of size $O(|\mathcal{A}|^2)$. Note that it is fair to assume that there are not more priorities than there are states. Furthermore, Theorem 5 constructs for every state, every component and every state in that component – i.e. every pair of states – a μTL formula of linear size. Composing these two constructions yields a formula of size $O(|\mathcal{A}|^4)$. $\qquad\square$

In the following we discuss how to improve the translation from μTL formulas into WAPAs. The main focus is on optimising the costly translation of fixpoint quantifiers. The first attempt reduces the size of the automaton by not duplicating automata for nested but closed fixpoint formulas.

Take a formula of the form $\varphi = \sigma_1 X_1.\psi_1(\sigma_2 X_2.\psi_2)$ s.t. $X_1 \notin free(\psi_2)$. Thus, X_2 does not depend on X_1 and $nd(\varphi) < fpd(\varphi)$. A clever algorithm for calculating the semantics of φ would calculate the semantics of $\sigma_2 X_2.\psi_2$ only once and reuse it in every iteration needed to calculate the semantics of φ. Note that the automaton constructed in the proof of Theorem 3 would include the automaton $\mathcal{A}_2$ for $\sigma_2 X_2.\psi_2$ twice. Since there is no path out of $\mathcal{A}_2$ it suffices to include a

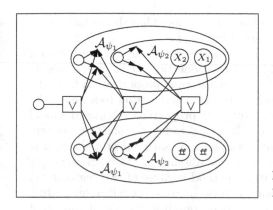

Fig. 2. Simultaneously translating fixpoint formulas into WAPAs.

single copy of $\mathcal{A}$. However, in the worst case $\mathcal{A}_2$ is a lot smaller than the automaton for ψ_1 and no asymptotic improvement compared to $O(|\varphi| \cdot 2^{fpd(\varphi)})$ is achieved.

The second attempt is based on Békič's Theorem. Let $\mu x.f$ denote the least fixpoint of an arbitrary function f that takes an argument x.

Theorem 6. [2] *Let $A \times B$ be a complete lattice and $F : A \times B \to A \times B$ a monotone function defined by $F(x,y) = (f_1(x,y), f_2(x,y))$. Then $\mu(x,y).F = (\mu x.f_1(x, \mu y.f_2(x,y)), \mu y.f_2(\mu x.f_1(x, \mu y.f_2(x,y)), y))$.*

The same holds for greatest fixpoints. Regarding formulas of μTL, Theorem 6 says that fixpoints of the same type can be computed simultaneously. We will show how to build automata that do so for two fixpoint formulas. It can easily be extended to formulas of arbitrary nesting depth as long as all variables are of the same type.

Take a formula $\varphi = \mu X_1.\psi_1(X_1, \mu X_2.\psi_2(X_1, X_2))$. Instead of building an automaton for $\mu X_2.\psi_2(X_1, X_2)$ and then one for φ we will construct an automaton for φ directly. By hypothesis we can assume that we already have automata $\mathcal{A}_{\psi_2}$ with two holes X_1 and X_2, as well as an automaton $\mathcal{A}_{\psi_1}$ with a hole for X_1 and another hole Z.

First let $\mathcal{A}' := \mathcal{A}_{\psi_1}[Z : \mathcal{A}_{\psi_2}]$. We can collapse holes and assume that $\mathcal{A}'$ only contains two holes X_1 and X_2. Then a WAPA $\mathcal{A}_\varphi$ for $L(\varphi)$ can be built by duplicating $\mathcal{A}'$ in the same way as it is done in the proof of Theorem 3. The two states X_1 and X_2 get odd priorities that lie between those in the *rec*-part and those in the *end*-part. Additionally, X_1 has transitions back to either of the beginnings of $\mathcal{A}_{\psi_1}$, X_2 has transitions back to either of the beginnings of $\mathcal{A}_{\psi_2}$. An illustration of this construction is given in Figure 2.

Proposition 3. *Every μTL formula φ can be translated into an equivalent WAPA of size $O(|\varphi| \cdot 2^{ad(\varphi)})$.*

5   Conclusion

We reinforced the importance of weak alternating automata in the algorithmics of ω-regular languages by giving direct translations from formulas of the linear time μ-calculus into these automata and back. Definition 2 has shown that every ω-regular expression can easily be translated into μTL.

Remember that – just as the modal μ-calculus can be used as a specification language for the verification of branching time properties – μTL is a straightforward temporal logic for the verification of linear time properties. In fact, the work presented here is part of the development of a verification tool under the term "bounded model checking for all ω-regular properties". Bounded model checking [3] only considers paths of finite length through a transition system, and uses SAT-solvers for finding counterexamples to unsatisfied properties. It is incomplete in the sense that it cannot show the absence of errors. However, it is very successful as a symbolic verification method because of two reasons: (1) often, errors occur "early", i.e. small boundedness parameters suffice for finding them. (2) In recent years, much effort has been put into the development of SAT-solvers that behave efficiently despite SAT's NP-hardness.

So far, bounded model checking is – to the best of our knowledge – only done for LTL, hence, is only suitable for the verification of star-free, resp. first-order definable properties. The work presented here yields a computational model for all regular, i.e. monadic second-order definable properties that is easy to handle algorithmically. It will be used in a bounded model checker that verifies regular properties. Weak alternating parity automata will serve as the link between a denotational specification language like μTL or ω-regular expressions on one hand, and the actual model checker that generates formulas of propositional logic on the other hand. These formulas then only need to describe the run of a WAPA on a finite word or a word of the form wv^ω. Weakness, i.e. checking for occurrence of priorities rather than infinite recurrence simplifies this process vastly.

We believe that the direct translation from μTL, resp. ω-regular properties to weak alternating automata can prove to be useful for other verification purposes as well.

References

1. H. Barringer, R. Kuiper, and A. Pnueli. A really abstract concurrent model and its temporal logic. In *Proc. 13th Annual ACM Symp. on Principles of Programming Languages*, pages 173–183. ACM, 1986.
2. H. Békič. *Programming Languages and Their Definition, Selected Papers*, volume 177 of *LNCS*. Springer, 1984.
3. A. Biere, A. Cimatti, E. M. Clarke, and Y. Zhu. Symbolic model checking without BDDs. In R. Cleaveland, editor, *Proc. 5th Int. Conf. on Tools and Algorithms for the Analysis and Construction of Systems, TACAS'99*, volume 1579 of *LNCS*, Amsterdam, NL, March 1999.
4. J. C. Bradfield. The modal μ-calculus alternation hierarchy is strict. In U. Montanari and V. Sassone, editors, *Proc. 7th Conf. on Concurrency Theory, CONCUR'96*, volume 1119 of *LNCS*, pages 233–246, Pisa, Italy, August 1996. Springer.
5. J. R. Büchi. On a decision method in restricted second order arithmetic. In *Proc. Congress on Logic, Method, and Philosophy of Science*, pages 1–12, Stanford, CA, USA, 1962. Stanford University Press.

6. A. K. Chandra, D. C. Kozen, and L. J. Stockmeyer. Alternation. *Journal of the ACM*, 28(1):114–133, January 1981.
7. S. Dziembowski, M. Jurdziński, and I. Walukiewicz. How much memory is needed to win infinite games? In *Proc. 12th Symp. on Logic in Computer Science, LICS'97*, pages 99–110, Warsaw, Poland, June 1997. IEEE.
8. E. A. Emerson. Model checking and the μ-calculus. In N. Immerman and P. G. Kolaitis, editors, *Descriptive Complexity and Finite Models*, volume 31 of *DIMACS: Series in Discrete Mathematics and Theoretical Computer Science*, chapter 6. AMS, 1997.
9. E. A. Emerson and C. S. Jutla. Tree automata, μ-calculus and determinacy. In *Proc. 32nd Symp. on Foundations of Computer Science*, pages 368–377, San Juan, Puerto Rico, October 1991. IEEE.
10. D. Janin and I. Walukiewicz. On the expressive completeness of the propositional μ-calculus with respect to monadic second order logic. In U. Montanari and V. Sassone, editors, *Proc. 7th Conf. on Concurrency Theory, CONCUR'96*, volume 1119 of *LNCS*, pages 263–277, Pisa, Italy, August 1996. Springer.
11. R. Kaivola. *Using Automata to Characterise Fixed Point Temporal Logics*. PhD thesis, LFCS, Division of Informatics, The University of Edinburgh, 1997. Tech. Rep. ECS-LFCS-97-356.
12. D. Kozen. Results on the propositional μ-calculus. *TCS*, 27:333–354, December 1983.
13. O. Kupferman and M. Y. Vardi. Weak alternating automata are not that weak. *ACM Transactions on Computational Logic*, 2(3):408–429, 2001.
14. O. Kupferman, M. Y. Vardi, and P. Wolper. An automata-theoretic approach to branching-time model checking. *Journal of the ACM*, 47(2):312–360, March 2000.
15. C. Löding and W. Thomas. Alternating automata and logics over infinite words. In *Proc. IFIP Int. Conf. on Theoretical Computer Science, IFIP TCS2000*, volume 1872 of *LNCS*, pages 521–535. Springer, August 2000.
16. D. Muller and P. Schupp. Alternating automata on infinite objects: determinacy and rabin's theorem. In M. Nivat and D. Perrin, editors, *Proc. Ecole de Printemps d'Informatique Théoretique on Automata on Infinite Words*, volume 192 of *LNCS*, pages 100–107, Le Mont Dore, France, May 1984. Springer.
17. D. E. Muller, A. Saoudi, and P. E. Schupp. Weak alternating automata give a simple explanation of why most temporal and dynamic logics are decidable in exponential time. In *Proc. 3rd Symp. on Logic in Computer Science, LICS'88*, pages 422–427, Edinburgh, Scotland, July 1988. IEEE.
18. M. O. Rabin. Decidability of second-order theories and automata on infinite trees. *Trans. of Amer. Math. Soc.*, 141:1–35, 1969.
19. C. Stirling. Local model checking games. In I. Lee and S. A. Smolka, editors, *Proc. 6th Conf. on Concurrency Theory, CONCUR'95*, volume 962 of *LNCS*, pages 1–11, Berlin, Germany, August 1995. Springer.
20. M. Y. Vardi. A temporal fixpoint calculus. In ACM, editor, *Proc. Conf. on Principles of Programming Languages, POPL'88*, pages 250–259, NY, USA, 1988. ACM Press.
21. M. Y. Vardi. *An Automata-Theoretic Approach to Linear Temporal Logic*, volume 1043 of *LNCS*, pages 238–266. Springer, New York, NY, USA, 1996.
22. I. Walukiewicz. Completeness of Kozen's axiomatization of the propositional μ-calculus. In *Proc. 10th Symp. on Logic in Computer Science, LICS'95*, pages 14–24, Los Alamitos, CA, 1995. IEEE.

Model Checking for Process Rewrite Systems and a Class of Action-Based Regular Properties

Laura Bozzelli

Dipartimento di Matematica e Applicazioni, Università di Napoli "Federico II"
Via Cintia, I-80126 Napoli, Italy
laura.bozzelli@dma.unina.it

Abstract. We consider the model checking problem for Process Rewrite Systems (*PRSs*), an infinite-state formalism (non Turing-powerful) which subsumes many common models such as Pushdown Processes and Petri Nets. *PRSs* can be adopted as formal models for programs with dynamic creation and synchronization of concurrent processes, and with recursive procedures. The model-checking problem for *PRSs* w.r.t. action-based linear temporal logic (*ALTL*) is undecidable. However, decidability for some interesting fragment of *ALTL* remains an open question. In this paper we state decidability results concerning generalized acceptance properties about infinite derivations (infinite term rewriting) in *PRSs*. As a consequence, we obtain decidability of the model-checking (restricted to infinite runs) for *PRSs* and a meaningful fragment of *ALTL*.

1 Introduction

Automatic verification of systems is nowadays one of the most investigated topics. A major difficulty to face when considering this problem is that reasoning about systems in general may require dealing with infinite–state models. Software systems may introduce infinite states both manipulating data ranging over infinite domains, and having unbounded control structures such as recursive procedure calls and/or dynamic creation of concurrent processes (e.g. multi–threading). Many different formalisms have been proposed for the description of infinite–state systems. Among the most popular are the well known formalisms of Context Free Processes, Pushdown Processes, Petri Nets, and Process Algebras. The first two are models of sequential computation, whereas Petri Nets and Process Algebra explicitly take into account concurrency. The model checking problem for these infinite–state formalisms have been studied in the literature. As far as Context Free Processes and Pushdown Processes are concerned, decidability of the modal μ–calculus, the most powerful of the modal and temporal logics used for verification, has been established (see [2, 5, 10, 14]). In [4, 8, 9], model checking for Petri nets has been studied. The branching temporal logic as well as the state-based linear temporal logic are undecidable even for restricted logics. Fortunately, the model checking for action-based linear temporal logic (*ALTL*) [8, 9] is decidable.

Verification of formalisms which accommodate both parallelism and recursion is a challenging problem. In order to formally study this kind of systems,

R. Cousot (Ed.): VMCAI 2005, LNCS 3385, pp. 282–297, 2005.

recently the formal framework of Process Rewrite Systems (*PRSs*) has been introduced [12, 13]. This framework (non Turing-powerful), which is based on term rewriting, subsumes many common infinite–states models such as Pushdown Processes and Petri Nets. *PRSs* can be adopted as formal models for programs with dynamic creation and (a restricted form of) synchronization of concurrent processes, and with recursive procedures. The decidability results already known in the literature for the general framework of *PRSs* concern the reachability problem between two fixed terms and the *reachable property* problem [12, 13]. This last is the problem of deciding whether there is a reachable term that satisfies certain properties that can be encoded as follows: some given rewrite rules are applicable and/or other given rewrite rules are *not* applicable. Decidability of this problem can be also used to decide the deadlock reachability problem. Recently, in [3], symbolic reachability analysis is investigated (i.e., the constructibility problem of the potentially infinite set of terms that are reachable from a given possibly infinite set of terms). However, the algorithm given in [3] can be applied only to a subclass of *PRSs* (strictly less expressive), i.e, the *synchronization–free* PRSs (the so–called PAD systems) which subsume Pushdown processes and the *synchronization–free* Petri nets. As concerns the *ALTL* model–checking problem, it is undecidable for the whole class of *PRSs* [1, 12, 13]. It remains undecidable even for restricted models such as PA processes [1] (these systems correspond to a subclass, strictly less expressive, of PAD systems). Fortunately, Bouajjani in [1] proved that for the complement of *simple ALTL*[1] (*simple ALTL* corresponds to Büchi ω-automata where there are only self–loop), model–checking PA processes is decidable. Anyway, decidability for some interesting fragment of *ALTL* and the general framework of *PRSs* remains an open question.

In this paper we prove decidability of the model–checking problem (restricted to infinite runs) for the whole class of *PRSs* w.r.t. a meaningful fragment of *ALTL* that captures, exactly, the class of regular properties invariant under permutation of atomic actions (along infinite runs). This fragment (closed under boolean connectives) is defined as follows:

$$\varphi ::= F\,\psi \mid GF\,\psi \mid \neg\varphi \mid \varphi \wedge \varphi \qquad (1)$$

where ψ is an *ALTL* propositional formula (i.e, a boolean combination of atomic actions). Within this fragment, class of properties useful in system verification can be expressed: some *safety properties* (e.g., $G\,\psi_1$), some *guarantee properties* (e.g., $F\,\psi_1$), some *obligation properties* (e.g., $F\,\psi_1 \rightarrow F\,\psi_2$, or $G\,\psi_1 \rightarrow G\,\psi_2$), some *recurrence properties* (e.g., $GF\,\psi_1$), some *persistence properties* (e.g., $FG\,\psi_1$), and finally some *reactivity properties* (e.g., $GF\,\psi_1 \rightarrow GF\,\psi_2$) [2].

---

[1] *Simple ALTL* is *not* closed under negation, and is defined as follows:

$$\varphi ::= \psi \mid \varphi \vee \varphi \mid \varphi \wedge \varphi \mid \langle a \rangle\varphi \mid G\,\psi \mid \psi U\,\varphi$$

where ψ is an *ALTL* propositional formula, a is an atomic action, and $<a>$, G, and U are the *next*, *always*, and *until* operators.

[2] ψ_1 and ψ_2 denote *ALTL* propositional formulae.

Notice that important classes of properties like invariants, as well as strong and weak fairness constraints, can be expressed. Moreover, notice that this fragment and *simple ALTL* are incomparable (in particular, strong fairness cannot be expressed by *simple ALTL*).

In order to prove our result, we introduce the notion of *Multi Büchi Rewrite System (MBRS)* that is, informally speaking, a *PRS* with a finite number of accepting components, where each component is a subset of the *PRS*. Then, we reduce our initial problem to that of verifying the existence of infinite derivations (infinite term rewriting) in *MBRS*s satisfying *generalized* acceptance properties (*a la* Büchi). Finally, we prove decidability of this last problem by a reduction to the *ALTL* model–checking problem for Petri nets and Pushdown processes (that is decidable). There are two main steps in the proof of decidability:

- First, we prove decidability of a problem concerning the existence of *finite* derivations leading to a given term and satisfying generalized acceptance properties. This problem is strictly more general than reachability problem and is not comparable with the reachable property problem of Mayr [12, 13]. Moreover, our approach is substantially different from that used by Mayr.
- The second step concerns reasoning about infinite derivations in *PRS*s which have not been investigated (to the best of our knowledge) in other papers on *PRS*s.

The framework of *MBRS*s, introduced in this paper, can be also used to suitably express other important class of regular properties, for example, the *ALTL* fragment given by *simple ALTL* without the *next* operator. Properties in this fragment can be translated in orderings of occurrences of rules belonging to the accepting components of the given *MBRS*. Actually, we are working on the satisfiability problem of the conjunction of this *ALTL* fragment with the fragment (1) w.r.t. *PRS*s (i.e., the problem about the existence of an infinite run in the given *PRS* satisfying a given formula), using a technique similar to that used in this paper. The result would be particularly interesting, since it is possible to prove (using a result of Emerson [7]) that the *positive* boolean combination of this fragment with the fragment (1) subsumes the relevant *ALTL* fragment (closed under boolean connectives) with the *always* and *eventually* operators (G and F) nested arbitrarily, i.e., (linear-time) Lamport logic[3]. This means that the main result of this paper is an intermediate but fundamental step for resolving the model–checking problem of *PRS*s against a full action-based temporal logic, i.e., (linear-time) Lamport logic.

Plan of the paper: In Section 2, we recall the framework of Process Rewrite Systems and *ALTL* logic. In Section 3, we introduce the notion of *Multi Büchi Rewrite System*, and show how our decidability result about generalized acceptance properties of infinite derivations in *PRS*s can be used in model-checking for the *ALTL* fragment (1). In Sections 4 and 5, we prove our decidability result.

---

[3] Since Lamport logic (as well as the fragment (1)) is closed under negation, decidability of the satisfiability problem implies decidability of the model–checking problem, and viceversa.

Finally, in Section 6, we conclude with some considerations about the complexity of the considered problem.

Several proofs are omitted for lack of space. They can be found in the longer version of this paper that can be requested to the author.

2 Preliminaries

2.1 Process Rewrite Systems

Let $Var = \{X, Y, \ldots\}$ be a finite set of *process variables*. The set T of *process terms* t over Var is defined by the following syntax:

$$t ::= \varepsilon \mid X \mid t.t \mid t \| t$$

where $X \in Var$, ε is the empty term, and "$\|$" (resp., ".") denotes parallel composition (resp., sequential composition). We always work with equivalences classes of process terms modulo commutativity and associativity of "$\|$", and modulo associativity of ".". Moreover, ε will act as the identity for both parallel and sequential composition.

Definition 1 ([13]). *A* Process Rewrite System (PRS *for short*) *over* Var *and an alphabet of atomic actions* Σ *is a* finite *set of rewrite rules of the form* $t \xrightarrow{a} t'$, *where* t $(\neq \varepsilon)$ *and* t' *are terms in* T, *and* $a \in \Sigma$.

A *PRS* $\Re$ induces a Labelled Transition System (LTS) with set of states T, and a transition relation $\rightarrow \subseteq T \times \Sigma \times T$ defined by the following inference rules:

$$\frac{(t \xrightarrow{a} t') \in \Re}{t \xrightarrow{a} t'} \qquad \frac{t_1 \xrightarrow{a} t_1'}{t_1 \| t \xrightarrow{a} t_1' \| t} \qquad \frac{t_1 \xrightarrow{a} t_1'}{t_1.t \xrightarrow{a} t_1'.t}$$

where t, t', t_1, t_1' are process terms and $a \in \Sigma$. In similar way we define for every rule $r \in \Re$ the notion of *one–step derivation* relation by r, denoted by $\xRightarrow{r}_{\Re}$.

A *path in* $\Re$ from $t \in T$ is a (finite or infinite) sequence $\pi = t_0 \xrightarrow{a_0} t_1 \xrightarrow{a_1} t_2 \ldots$ such that $t = t_0$ and every triple $t_i \xrightarrow{a_i} t_{i+1}$ is a LTS edge. We write π^i for the path $t_i \xrightarrow{a_i} t_{i+1} \xrightarrow{a_{i+1}} \ldots$. Let $firstact(\pi) := a_0$. A *run in* $\Re$ from t is a maximal path from t, i.e., a path that is either infinite, or terminates in a term without successors. We denote by $runs_{\Re}(t)$ (resp., $runs_{\Re,\infty}(t)$) the set of runs (resp., infinite runs) in $\Re$ from t, and by $runs(\Re)$ the set of all the runs in $\Re$.

Given a finite (resp., infinite) sequence $\sigma = r_1 r_2 \ldots$ of rules in $\Re$, a *finite* (resp., *infinite*) *derivation* in $\Re$ from a term t (through σ), is a finite (resp., infinite) sequence d of the form $t_0 \xRightarrow{r_1}_{\Re} t_1 \xRightarrow{r_2}_{\Re} t_2 \ldots$ such that $t_0 = t$ and every triple $t_i \xRightarrow{r_i}_{\Re} t_{i+1}$ is a one–step derivation. If d is finite and terminates in the term t', we say t' is *reachable* in $\Re$ from t (through derivation d). If σ is empty, we say d is a *null derivation*. For terms $t, t' \in T$ and a rule sequence σ, we write $t \xRightarrow{\sigma}_{\Re}$ (resp., $t \xRightarrow{\sigma}_{\Re} t'$) to mean that there exists a derivation (resp., a finite derivation terminating in t') from t through σ.

For technical reasons, we also consider *PRSs* in a restricted syntactical form called *normal form* [13]. A *PRS* $\Re$ is said to be in *normal form* if every rule $r \in \Re$ has one of the following forms:

PAR rules: $X_1 \| X_2 \ldots \| X_p \xrightarrow{a} Y_1 \| Y_2 \ldots \| Y_q$ where $p \in \mathbb{N} \setminus \{0\}$ and $q \in \mathbb{N}$.
SEQ rules: $X \xrightarrow{a} Y.Z$ or $X.Y \xrightarrow{a} Z$ or $X \xrightarrow{a} Y$ or $X \xrightarrow{a} \varepsilon$.

with $X, Y, Z, X_i, Y_j \in Var$. A *PRS* where all the rules are SEQ (resp., PAR) rules is called *sequential* (resp., *parallel*) *PRS*.

2.2 *ALTL* (Action–Based LTL) and *PRSs*

The set of *ALTL* formulae over a set Σ of atomic actions is defined as follows:

$$\varphi ::= true \mid \neg\varphi \mid \varphi \wedge \varphi \mid \langle a \rangle \varphi \mid \varphi U \varphi$$

where $a \in \Sigma$, $\langle a \rangle$ is the *next* operator, and U is the *until* operator. We also define $F\varphi := true \, U \, \varphi$ (*"eventually φ"*) and its dual $G\varphi := \neg F \neg\varphi$ (*"always φ"*). Given a *PRS* $\Re$ and an *ALTL* formula φ, the set of the runs in $\Re$ *satisfying* φ, in symbols $[[\varphi]]_\Re$, is defined inductively on the structure of φ as follows:

- $[[true]]_\Re = runs(\Re)$,
- $[[\neg\varphi]]_\Re = runs(\Re) \setminus [[\varphi]]_\Re$,
- $[[\varphi_1 \wedge \varphi_2]]_\Re = [[\varphi_1]]_\Re \cap [[\varphi_2]]_\Re$,
- $[[\langle a \rangle \varphi]]_\Re = \{\pi \in runs(\Re) \mid firstact(\pi) = a \text{ and } \pi^1 \in [[\varphi]]_\Re\}$,
- $[[\varphi_1 U \varphi_2]]_\Re = \{\pi \in runs(\Re) \mid \text{ for some } i \geq 0 : \pi^i \in [[\varphi_2]]_\Re \text{ and }$
  $\text{for all } j < i, \ \pi^j \in [[\varphi_1]]_\Re \}$.

For any term $t \in T$, we say t satisfies φ (resp., satisfies φ restricted to infinite runs) w.r.t. $\Re$, in symbols $t \models_\Re \varphi$ (resp., $t \models_{\Re,\infty} \varphi$), if $runs_\Re(t) \subseteq [[\varphi]]_\Re$ (resp., $runs_{\Re,\infty}(t) \subseteq [[\varphi]]_\Re$). The model-checking problem (resp., model–checking problem restricted to infinite runs) for *ALTL* w.r.t. *PRSs* is the problem of deciding whether, given a *PRS* $\Re$, an *ALTL* formula φ and a term $t \in T$, $t \models_\Re \varphi$ (resp., $t \models_{\Re,\infty} \varphi$). The following is a well–known result:

Proposition 1 (see [2, 8, 12]). *The model–checking problem for* ALTL *w.r.t. parallel (resp., sequential) PRSs, possibly restricted to infinite runs, is decidable.*

In this paper we are interested in the model-checking problem (restricted to infinite runs) for unrestricted *PRSs* against the following *ALTL* fragment:

$$\varphi ::= F\psi \mid GF\psi \mid \neg\varphi \mid \varphi \wedge \varphi \tag{1}$$

where ψ denotes an *ALTL propositional* formula defined by the following syntax:
$\psi ::= <a> true \mid \psi \wedge \psi \mid \neg\psi$ (where $a \in \Sigma$).

3 Multi Büchi Rewrite Systems

In order to prove the main result of this paper, i.e. the decidability of the model-checking problem (restricted to infinite runs) of *PRSs* against the *ALTL* fragment defined in Subsection 2.2, we introduce the framework of Multi Büchi Rewrite Systems.

Definition 2. *A* Multi Büchi Rewrite System (MBRS) *(with n accepting components) over Var and Σ is a tuple $M = \langle \Re, \langle \Re_1, \ldots, \Re_n \rangle \rangle$, where $\Re$ is a PRS over Var and Σ, and, for all $i = 1, \ldots, n$, $\Re_i \subseteq \Re$. $\Re$ is called the* support *of M.*

We say M is a *MBRS in normal form* (resp., *sequential MBRS, parallel MBRS*) if the support $\Re$ is in normal form (resp., sequential, parallel).

For a rule sequence σ in $\Re$ the *finite acceptance of σ w.r.t. M*, denoted by $\Upsilon_M^f(\sigma)$, is the set $\{i \in \{1, \ldots, n\} \mid \sigma$ contains some occurrence of rule in $\Re_i\}$. The *infinite acceptance of σ w.r.t. M*, denoted by $\Upsilon_M^\infty(\sigma)$, is the set $\{i \in \{1, \ldots, n\} \mid \sigma$ contains infinite occurrences of some rule in $\Re_i\}$. Given $K, K_\omega \subseteq \{1, \ldots, n\}$ and a derivation d of the form $t \overset{\sigma}{\Rightarrow}_\Re$, we say d is a $(K, K_\omega)-$ *accepting derivation* in M if $\Upsilon_M^f(\sigma) = K$ and $\Upsilon_M^\infty(\sigma) = K_\omega$. Moreover, we say d has *finite acceptance* (resp., *infinite acceptance*) K (resp., K_ω) in M. For all $n \in \mathbb{N} \setminus \{0\}$, let us denote by P_n the set $2^{\{1,\ldots,n\}}$ (i.e., the set of the subsets of $\{1, \ldots, n\}$).
Now, let us consider the following problem:

Fairness Problem: *Given a* MBRS *$M = \langle \Re, \langle \Re_1, \ldots, \Re_n \rangle \rangle$ over Var and Σ, a process term t, and two sets $K, K_\omega \in P_n$, is there a (K, K_ω)-accepting infinite derivation in M from t?*

Without loss of generality we can assume that the input term t in the Fairness Problem is a process variable. In fact, if $t \notin Var$, then we add a fresh variable X and a rule of the form $X \to t$ whose finite acceptance is the empty set.

As stated by the following Theorem, the Fairness Problem represents a suitable encoding of our initial problem in the framework of *MBRSs*.

Theorem 1. *Model–checking* PRSs *against the considered* ALTL *fragment, restricted to infinite runs, is polynomial-time reducible to the Fairness Problem.*

In the remainder of this paper we prove that the Fairness Problem is decidable. We proceed in two steps. First, in Section 4 we decide the problem for the class of *MBRSs* in normal form. Then, in Section 5 we extend the result to the whole class of *MBRSs*. For the proof we need some preliminary decidability results, stated by the following Propositions 2–4, concerning acceptance properties of derivations in parallel and sequential *MBRSs*. In particular, the problems in Propositions 2–3 (resp., in Proposition 4) are polynomial-time reducible to the *ALTL* model–checking problem for parallel (resp., sequential) *PRSs* that is decidable (see Proposition 1).

Proposition 2. *Given a parallel MBRS M_P over Var and with n accepting components, two variables $X, Y \in Var$ and $K \in P_n$, it is decidable whether* *there is a finite derivation in M_P of the form $X \overset{\sigma}{\Rightarrow} (resp., of the form $X \overset{\sigma}{\Rightarrow} Y$, of the form $X \overset{\sigma}{\Rightarrow} \varepsilon$, of the form $X \overset{\sigma}{\Rightarrow} t\|Y$ with $|\sigma| > 0$) such that $\Upsilon^f_{M_P}(\sigma) = K$.*

Proposition 3. *Let M_{P_1} and M_{P_2} be two parallel MBRSs over Var, with the same support $\Re_P$, and with n accepting components. Given $X \in Var$, $K, K_\omega \in P_n$, and a subset Λ of $\Re_P$, it is decidable whether: (1) there exists a (K, K_ω)-accepting infinite derivation in M_{P_1} from X; (2) there exists a derivation in $\Re_P$ of the form $X \overset{\sigma}{\Rightarrow}$ such that $\Upsilon^f_{M_{P_1}}(\sigma) = K$, $\Upsilon^\infty_{M_{P_1}}(\sigma) \cup \Upsilon^f_{M_{P_2}}(\sigma) = K_\omega$, and σ is either infinite or contains some occurrence of rule in Λ.*

Now, we give the notion of s-reachability in sequential *PRSs*.

Definition 3. *Given a sequential PRS $\Re_S$ over Var, and $X, Y \in Var$, Y is s-reachable from X in $\Re_S$ if there exists a term t of the form $Y.X_1.X_2.\dots.X_n$ (where $X_i \in Var$ for any $i = 1, \dots, n$, and $n \geq 0$) such that $X \Rightarrow t$.*

Proposition 4. *Given a sequential MBRS M_S over Var and with n accepting components, two variables $X, Y \in Var$, and two sets $K, K_\omega \in P_n$, it is decidable whether: (1) Y is s-reachable from X in M_S through a $(K, \emptyset)$-accepting derivation; (2) there is a (K, K_ω)-accepting infinite derivation in M_S from X.*

4 Decidability of the Fairness Problem for *MBRSs* in Normal Form

In this subsection we prove decidability of the Fairness Problem for the class of *MBRSs* in normal form. We fix a *MBRS* in normal form $M = \langle \Re, \langle \Re_1, \dots, \Re_n \rangle \rangle$ over Var and Σ, and two elements K and K_ω of P_n. Given $X \in Var$, we have to decide if there exists a (K, K_ω)-accepting infinite derivation in M from X.

Remark 1 Since M is in normal form (and in the following we only consider derivations starting from variables or terms in which no sequential composition occurs) we can limit ourselves to consider only *terms in normal form*, defined as $t ::= \varepsilon \mid X \mid t\|t \mid t.X$ (where $X \in Var$). In fact, given a term in normal form t, each term t' reachable from t in M is still in normal form.

There are two main steps for the decidability proof of the Fairness Problem.

Step 1 First, we prove decidability of the following problem:
   Problem 1 (Finite Derivations): Given $X, Y \in Var$ and $K' \in P_n$, is there a finite derivation in M of the form $X \overset{\sigma}{\Rightarrow} (resp., $X \overset{\sigma}{\Rightarrow} Y$) such that $\Upsilon^f_M(\sigma) = K'$?
Step 2 Using decidability of Problem **1**, we show that the Fairness Problem can be reduced to (a combination of) simpler and decidable problems regarding acceptance properties of derivations of parallel and sequential *MBRSs*.

Before illustrating our approach, we need additional notation.

In the following, $M_P = \langle \Re_P, \langle \Re_{P,1}, \ldots, \Re_{P,n} \rangle \rangle$ denotes the restriction of M to the PAR rules, i.e., $\Re_P$ (resp., $\Re_{P,i}$ for $i = 1, \ldots, n$) is the set $\Re$ (resp., $\Re_i$ for $i = 1, \ldots, n$) restricted to the PAR rules. Moreover, we shall use a fresh variable Z_F, and denote by T (resp., T_{PAR}, T_{SEQ}) the set of process terms in normal form (resp., in which no sequential composition occurs, in which no parallel composition occurs) over $Var \cup \{Z_F\}$.

Definition 4 (Subderivation). *Let* $\bar{t} \overset{\lambda}{\Rightarrow} t \| (s.X) \overset{\sigma}{\Rightarrow}$ *be a derivation[4] in* $\Re$ *from* $\bar{t} \in T$. *The set of the* subderivations d' *of* $d = (t \| (s.X) \overset{\sigma}{\Rightarrow})$ *from* s *is inductively defined as follows:*

1. *if d is a null derivation or $s = \varepsilon$ or d is of the form $t \| (Z.X) \overset{r}{\Rightarrow} t \| Y \overset{\sigma'}{\Rightarrow}$ (with $r = Z.X \overset{a}{\rightarrow} Y$ and $s = Z$), then d' is the null derivation from s;*

2. *if d is of the form $t \| (s.X) \overset{r}{\Rightarrow} t \| (s'.X) \overset{\sigma'}{\Rightarrow}$ (with $s \overset{r}{\Rightarrow} s'$ and $r \in \Re$) and $s' \overset{\mu'}{\Rightarrow}$ is a subderivation of $t \| (s'.X) \overset{\sigma'}{\Rightarrow}$ from s', then $s \overset{r}{\Rightarrow} s' \overset{\mu'}{\Rightarrow}$ is a subderivation of d from s;*

3. *if d is of the form $t \| (s.X) \overset{r}{\Rightarrow} t' \| (s.X) \overset{\sigma'}{\Rightarrow}$ (with $t \overset{r}{\Rightarrow} t'$ and $r \in \Re$), then every subderivation of $t' \| (s.X) \overset{\sigma'}{\Rightarrow}$ from s is also a subderivation of d from s.*

Moreover, we say that d' is a subderivation of $\bar{t} \overset{\lambda}{\Rightarrow} t \| (s.X) \overset{\sigma}{\Rightarrow}$.

Given a rule sequence σ in $\Re$, and a subsequence σ' of σ, $\sigma \setminus \sigma'$ denotes the rule sequence obtained by removing from σ all and only the occurrences of rules in σ'.

STEP 1   We prove decidability of Problem **1** by a reduction to a similar problem restricted to a parallel *MBRS* (that is decidable by Proposition 2). The main idea is to mimic finite derivations in M of the form $p \overset{\sigma}{\Rightarrow} t$ (preserving p, the finite acceptance of σ in M, and the final term t if $t \in T_{PAR}$) starting from terms in T_{PAR} by using only PAR rules belonging to an extension, denoted by M_{PAR} (and with support $\Re_{PAR}$), of the parallel *MBRS* M_P. In order to illustrate this, let us denote by $N_{SEQ}(\sigma)$ the number of occurrences in σ of SEQ rules of the form $X \overset{a}{\rightarrow} Z.Y$. We proceed by induction on $N_{SEQ}(\sigma)$. If $N_{SEQ}(\sigma) = 0$, since $p \in T_{PAR}$, we deduce that $p \overset{\sigma}{\Rightarrow} t$ is also a derivation in M_P (and so in M_{PAR}, since M_{PAR} is an extension of M_P). Now, let us assume that $N_{SEQ}(\sigma) > 0$. In this case $p \overset{\sigma}{\Rightarrow} t$ can be rewritten in the form $p \overset{\lambda}{\Rightarrow} \bar{p} \| X \overset{r}{\Rightarrow} \bar{p} \| (Z.Y) \overset{\nu}{\Rightarrow} t$ where $r = X \overset{a}{\rightarrow} Z.Y$, λ contains only occurrences of PAR rules in $\Re$, $\bar{p} \in T_{PAR}$ and $X, Y, Z \in Var$. Let $Z \overset{\rho}{\Rightarrow} t_1$ be a subderivation of $\bar{p} \| (Z.Y) \overset{\nu}{\Rightarrow} t$ from Z. By the definition of subderivation only one of the following three cases may occur:

---

[4] In the following, locutions of the kind 'the derivation $t \overset{\sigma}{\Rightarrow}$' mean that (there is a derivation of this form) and we are considering a specific derivation of the form $t \overset{\sigma}{\Rightarrow}$, and $t \overset{\sigma}{\Rightarrow}$ is used as a reference to this derivation.

A $t_1 \neq \varepsilon$, $\overline{p} \overset{\nu \backslash \rho}{\Rightarrow} t_2$, and $t = t_2 \| (t_1.Y)$.

B $t_1 = \varepsilon$ and $p \overset{\sigma}{\Rightarrow} t$ is of the form $p \overset{\lambda}{\Rightarrow} \overline{p} \| X \overset{r}{\Rightarrow} \overline{p} \| (Z.Y) \overset{\nu_1}{\Rightarrow} t_2 \| Y \overset{\nu_2}{\Rightarrow} t$, where ρ is a subsequence of ν_1 and $\overline{p} \overset{\nu_1 \backslash \rho}{\Rightarrow} t_2$.

C $t_1 = W \in Var$, and $p \overset{\sigma}{\Rightarrow}$ can be written as

$$p \overset{\lambda}{\Rightarrow} \overline{p} \| X \overset{r}{\Rightarrow} \overline{p} \| (Z.Y) \overset{\nu_1}{\Rightarrow} t_2 \| (W.Y) \overset{r'}{\Rightarrow} t_2 \| W' \overset{\nu_2}{\Rightarrow} t \tag{1}$$

where $r' = W.Y \overset{b}{\to} W'$, ρ is a subsequence of ν_1 and $\overline{p} \overset{\nu_1 \backslash \rho}{\Rightarrow} t_2$.

Cases **A**, **B** and **C** can be dealt in similar way, so that we examine only case **C**. Let us consider equation (1). By anticipating the application of the rules in $\rho r'$ before the application of the rules in $\nu_1 \backslash \rho$ we obtain the following derivation that has the same finite acceptance as (1): $p \overset{\lambda}{\Rightarrow} \overline{p} \| X \overset{r}{\Rightarrow} \overline{p} \| (Z.Y) \overset{\rho}{\Rightarrow} \overline{p} \| (W.Y) \overset{r'}{\Rightarrow} \overline{p} \| W' \overset{\gamma}{\Rightarrow} t$, where $\gamma = (\nu_1 \backslash \rho) \nu_2$. Since $Z \overset{\rho}{\Rightarrow} W$ with $Z, W \in Var$ and $N_{SEQ}(\rho) < N_{SEQ}(\sigma)$, by the induction hypothesis there will be a derivation in M_{PAR} having the form $Z \overset{\pi}{\Rightarrow}_{\Re_{PAR}} W$ with $\Upsilon^f_{M_{PAR}}(\pi) = \Upsilon^f_M(\rho)$. By Proposition 2 for each $K' \in P_n$ it is decidable whether there exists in M_{PAR} a finite derivation starting from variable Z and leading to variable W, having finite acceptance K' (in M_{PAR}). Then, the idea is to collapse the finite derivation $d = X \overset{r}{\Rightarrow} Z.Y \overset{\rho}{\Rightarrow} W.Y \overset{r'}{\Rightarrow} W'$ into a single PAR rule of the form $r'' = X \overset{K'}{\to} W'$ such that $K' = \Upsilon^f_M(rr')$ $\cup \Upsilon^f_{M_{PAR}}(\pi) = \Upsilon^f_M(rr'\rho)$ and $\Upsilon^f_{M_{PAR}}(r'') = K'$. So, rule r'' keeps track of the meaningful information of the derivation d, i.e., the starting term $X \in Var$, the final term $W' \in Var$, and the finite acceptance of $rr'\rho$ in M. Since the set of rules of the form $X \overset{K'}{\to} W'$ with $X, W' \in Var$ and $K' \in P_n$ is finite, M_{PAR} can be built effectively. After all, we have that $p \overset{\lambda r''}{\Rightarrow}_{\Re_{PAR}} \overline{p} \| W'$ and $\overline{p} \| W' \overset{\gamma}{\Rightarrow}_{\Re} t$ such that $\overline{p} \| W' \in T_{PAR}$, $\Upsilon^f_{M_{PAR}}(\lambda r'') = \Upsilon^f_M(\lambda rr'\rho)$ and $N_{SEQ}(\gamma) < N_{SEQ}(\sigma)$. Applying again the induction hypothesis we deduce that there exists a finite derivation in M_{PAR} of the form $p \overset{\xi}{\Rightarrow}_{\Re_{PAR}} p'$ such that $\Upsilon^f_{M_{PAR}}(\xi) = \Upsilon^f_M(\sigma)$, and $p' = t$ if $t \in T_{PAR}$. The fresh variable Z_F is used to manage case **A**, where the subderivation $Z \overset{\rho}{\Rightarrow} t_1$ does not influence the applicability of rules in $\nu \backslash \rho$ (i.e., $\overline{p} \overset{\nu \backslash \rho}{\Rightarrow} t_2$). In this case, in order to keep track of the derivation $X \overset{r}{\Rightarrow} Z.Y \overset{\rho}{\Rightarrow} t_1.Y$, it suffices to preserve the starting term X and the finite acceptance of $r\rho$. Therefore, we introduce a new rule of the form $r'' = X \overset{K'}{\to} Z_F$ such that $K' = \Upsilon^f_M(r\rho)$ and $\Upsilon^f_{M_{PAR}}(r'') = K'$. M_{PAR} is formally defined as follows.

Definition 5. *The MBRS* $M_{PAR} = \langle \Re_{PAR}, \langle \Re_{PAR,1}, \ldots, \Re_{PAR,n} \rangle \rangle$ *is the least parallel MBRS, over* $Var \cup \{Z_F\}$ *and the alphabet* $\Sigma \cup P_n$, *such that:*

1. $\Re_{PAR} \supseteq \Re_P$ *and* $\Re_{PAR,i} \supseteq \Re_{P,i}$ *for all* $i = 1, \ldots, n$.
2. *Let* $r = X \overset{a}{\to} Z.Y \in \Re$, $Z \overset{\sigma}{\Rightarrow}_{\Re_{PAR}} p$ *for some term* p *(resp.,* $Z \overset{\sigma}{\Rightarrow}_{\Re_{PAR}} \varepsilon$*), and* $K' = \Upsilon^f_M(r) \cup \Upsilon^f_{M_{PAR}}(\sigma)$. *Then* $r' = X \overset{K'}{\to} Z_F \in \Re_{PAR}$ *(resp.,* $r' = X \overset{K'}{\to} Y \in \Re_{PAR}$*) and* $\Upsilon^f_{M_{PAR}}(r') = K'$.

3. *Let $r = X \xrightarrow{a} Z.Y \in \Re$, $r' = W.Y \xrightarrow{b} W' \in \Re$, $Z \xRightarrow{\sigma}_{\Re_{PAR}} W$, and $K' = \Upsilon_M^f(rr')$*
$\cup \, \Upsilon_{M_{PAR}}^f(\sigma)$. *Then $r'' = X \xrightarrow{K'} W' \in \Re_{PAR}$ and $\Upsilon_{M_{PAR}}^f(r'') = K'$.*

Lemma 1. *The parallel MBRS M_{PAR} can be effectively constructed.*

Proof. Figure 1 reports the procedure BUILD-PARALLEL-MBRS(M) which builds M_{PAR}. The algorithm uses the routine $UPDATE(r', K')$ defined as:
$\Re_{PAR} := \Re_{PAR} \cup \{r'\}$;
for each $i \in K'$ **do** $\Re_{PAR,i} := \Re_{PAR,i} \cup \{r'\}$;
Notice that by Proposition 2, the conditions in each of the **if** statements in lines 7, 9 and 13 are decidable, therefore, the procedure is effective. Moreover, since the set of rules of the form $X \xrightarrow{K'} Y$ with $X \in Var$, $Y \in Var \cup \{Z_F\}$ and $K' \in P_n$ is finite, termination is guaranteed.

Algorithm BUILD–PARALLEL–MBRS(M)

1 $\Re_{PAR} := \Re_P$;
2 **for** $i = 1, \ldots, n$ **do** $\Re_{PAR,i} := \Re_{P,i}$;
3 **repeat**
4   *flag:=false;*
5   **for each** $r = X \xrightarrow{a} Z.Y \in \Re$ *and* $K_1 \in P_n$ **do**
6   *Set* $K' = K_1 \cup \Upsilon_M^f(r)$;
7   **if** $Z \xRightarrow{\sigma}_{\Re_{PAR}} p$ *for some p such that* $\Upsilon_{M_{PAR}}^f(\sigma) = K_1$ **then**
8   **if** $r' = X \xrightarrow{K'} Z_F \notin \Re_{PAR}$ **then** $UPDATE(r', K')$; *flag:=true;*
9   **if** $Z \xRightarrow{\sigma}_{\Re_{PAR}} \varepsilon$ *such that* $\Upsilon_{M_{PAR}}^f(\sigma) = K_1$ **then**
10   **if** $r' = X \xrightarrow{K'} Y \notin \Re_{PAR}$ **then** $UPDATE(r', K')$; *flag:=true;*
11   **for each** $r' = W.Y \xrightarrow{b} W' \in \Re$ **do**
12   *Set* $K' = K_1 \cup \Upsilon_M^f(rr')$;
13   **if** $Z \xRightarrow{\sigma}_{\Re_{PAR}} W$ *such that* $\Upsilon_{M_{PAR}}^f(\sigma) = K_1$ **then**
14   **if** $r'' = X \xrightarrow{K'} W' \notin \Re_{PAR}$ **then** $UPDATE(r'', K')$; *flag:=true;*
15 **until** *flag = false*

Fig. 1. Algorithm to build the parallel *MBRS M_{PAR}.*

The following two lemmata (whose proof is simple) establish the correctness of our construction.

Lemma 2. *Let $p \xRightarrow{\sigma}_{\Re} t \| p'$ with $p, p' \in T_{PAR}$. Then, there exists $s \in T_{PAR}$ such that $p \xRightarrow{\rho}_{\Re_{PAR}} s \| p'$, $\Upsilon_M^f(\sigma) = \Upsilon_{M_{PAR}}^f(\rho)$, $s = \varepsilon$ if $t = \varepsilon$, and $|\rho| > 0$ if $|\sigma| > 0$.*

Lemma 3. *Let $p \xRightarrow{\sigma}_{\Re_{PAR}} p' \| p''$ such that $p, p', p'' \in T_{PAR}$, p' does not contain occurrences of Z_F, and p'' does not contain occurrences of variables in Var. Then, there exists $t \in T$ such that $p \xRightarrow{\rho}_{\Re} p' \| t$, $\Upsilon_M^f(\rho) = \Upsilon_{M_{PAR}}^f(\sigma)$, $t = \varepsilon$ if $p'' = \varepsilon$, and $|\rho| > 0$ if $|\sigma| > 0$.*

These two results, together with Proposition 2, allow us to conclude that Problem 1 is decidable.

STEP 2   Let us go back to the Fairness Problem. We define a class of derivations, in symbols $\Pi(K, K_\omega)$, that is the set of derivations d in $\Re$ such that there is *not* a subderivation of d that is a (K, K_ω)-accepting infinite derivation in M. Now, we show that we can limit ourselves to consider only this class of derivations. Let d be a (K, K_ω)-accepting infinite derivation in M from a variable X. If d does *not* belong to $\Pi(K, K_\omega)$, then it can be written in the form $X \overset{\beta}{\Rightarrow} t\|W \overset{r}{\Rightarrow} t\|(Z.Y) \overset{\nu}{\Rightarrow}$, with $Z \in Var$ and $r = W \overset{a}{\to} Z.Y$, and such that there exists a subderivation of $t\|(Z.Y) \overset{\nu}{\Rightarrow}$ from Z that is a (K, K_ω)-accepting infinite derivation in M. Following this argument we can prove that there exist $m \in \mathbb{N} \setminus \{0\} \cup \{\infty\}$, a sequence of variables $(X_h)_{h=0}^{h=m}$ with $X_0 = X$, and a sequence of SEQ rules $(r_h)_{h=1}^{h=m}$ such that one of the following two conditions is satisfied:

1. m is finite, for each $h = 0, \ldots, m-1$ we have that $X_h \overset{\rho_h}{\Rightarrow} t_h\|Y_{h+1}$, $r_{h+1} = Y_{h+1} \overset{a_{h+1}}{\to} X_{h+1}.Z_{h+1}$, $\Upsilon_M^f(\rho_h r_{h+1}) \subseteq K$, and there exists a (K, K_ω)-accepting infinite derivation in M from X_m *belonging* to $\Pi(K, K_\omega)$.

2. (for $K = K_\omega$) m is infinite, and for all $h \in \mathbb{N}$ we have that $X_h \overset{\rho_h}{\Rightarrow} t_h\|Y_{h+1}$, $r_{h+1} = Y_{h+1} \overset{a_{h+1}}{\to} X_{h+1}.Z_{h+1}$, and $\Upsilon_M^f(\rho_0 r_1 \rho_1 r_2 \ldots) = \Upsilon_M^\infty(\rho_0 r_1 \rho_1 r_2 \ldots) = K_\omega$.

For each h let us consider the derivation $X_h \overset{\rho_h}{\Rightarrow} t_h\|Y_{h+1}$. By Lemma 2 there exists a finite derivation in M_{PAR} of the form $X_h \overset{\lambda_h}{\Rightarrow}_{\Re_{PAR}} p_h\|Y_{h+1}$ such that $\Upsilon_{M_{PAR}}^f(\lambda_h) = \Upsilon_M^f(\rho_h)$ and $p_h \in T_{PAR}$. By Proposition 2 for each $K' \in P_n$ it is decidable whether variable Y_{h+1} is partially reachable in M_{PAR} from X_h through a derivation having finite acceptance K'. The idea is to introduce a SEQ rule of the form $X_h \overset{K'}{\to} Y_{h+1}$ where $K' = \Upsilon_{M_{PAR}}^f(\lambda_h)$, and whose finite acceptance is K'. Let us denote by M_{SEQ} the sequential *MBRS* (with n accepting components) containing these new rules (whose number is finite) and all the SEQ rules of M having the form $X \overset{a}{\to} Z.Y$, and whose accepting components agree with the labels of the new rules. Then, case 2 above amounts to check the existence of a (K, K_ω)-accepting infinite derivation in M_{SEQ} from variable X. By Proposition 4 this is decidable. Case 1 amounts to check the existence of a variable $Y \in Var$ such that Y is s-reachable from X in M_{SEQ} through a derivation with finite acceptance (in M_{SEQ}) $K' \subseteq K$ (by Proposition 4 this is decidable), and there exists a (K, K_ω)-accepting infinite derivation in M from Y belonging to $\Pi(K, K_\omega)$. M_{SEQ} is formally defined as follows.

Definition 6. *By* $M_{SEQ} = \langle \Re_{SEQ}, \langle \Re_{SEQ,1}, \ldots, \Re_{SEQ,n} \rangle \rangle$ *we denote the sequential* MBRS *over* Var *and the alphabet* $\Sigma \cup P_n$ *defined as follows:*

$$- \Re_{SEQ} = \{X \overset{a}{\to} Z.Y \in \Re\} \cup$$
$$\{X \overset{K'}{\to} Y \mid X, Y \in Var, X \overset{\sigma}{\Rightarrow}_{\Re_{PAR}} p\|Y$$
$$\textit{for some } p \in T_{PAR}, |\sigma| > 0, \textit{ and } \Upsilon_{M_{PAR}}^f(\sigma) = K'\}$$
$$- \Re_{SEQ,i} = \{X \overset{a}{\to} Z.Y \in \Re_i\} \cup \{X \overset{K'}{\to} Y \in \Re_{SEQ} \mid i \in K'\} \textit{ for all } i = 1, \ldots, n.$$

By Proposition 2 we obtain the following result

Lemma 4. M_{SEQ} *can be built effectively.*

Thus, we obtain a first reduction of the Fairness Problem.

Lemma 5. *Given* $X \in Var$, *there exists a* (K, K_ω)-*accepting infinite derivation in* M *from* X *if, and only if, one of the following conditions is satisfied:*

1. *There exists a variable* $Y \in Var$ *s-reachable from* X *in* $\Re_{SEQ}$ *through a* $(K', \emptyset)$-*accepting derivation in* M_{SEQ} *with* $K' \subseteq K$, *and there exists a* (K, K_ω)-*accepting infinite derivation in* M *from* Y *belonging to* $\Pi(K, K_\omega)$.
2. *(Only when* $K = K_\omega$*) There exists a* (K, K_ω)-*accepting infinite derivation in* M_{SEQ} *from* X.

Therefore, it remains to manage the class $\Pi(K, K_\omega)$. We proceed by induction on $|K| + |K_\omega|$. Let $p \overset{\sigma}{\Rightarrow}$ be a (K, K_ω)-accepting infinite derivation in M from $p \in T_{PAR}$ belonging to $\Pi(K, K_\omega)$. If σ contains only occurrences of PAR rules, then $p \overset{\sigma}{\Rightarrow}$ is also a (K, K_ω)-accepting infinite derivation in M_{PAR}. Otherwise, it can be rewritten in the form $p \overset{\lambda}{\Rightarrow} \overline{p} \| W \overset{r}{\Rightarrow} \overline{p} \| (Z.Y) \overset{\nu}{\Rightarrow}$ where $r = W \overset{a}{\rightarrow} Z.Y$, λ contains only occurrences of PAR rules in $\Re$, $\overline{p} \in T_{PAR}$ and $W, Y, Z \in Var$. Let $Z \overset{\beta}{\Rightarrow}$ be a subderivation of $\overline{p} \| (Z.Y) \overset{\nu}{\Rightarrow}$ from Z. If $Z \overset{\beta}{\Rightarrow}$ is finite, as shown in *Step 1*, we can keep track of the finite derivation $W \overset{r}{\Rightarrow} Z.Y \overset{\beta}{\Rightarrow}$ (preserving acceptance properties) by using a PAR rule belonging to M_{PAR}. If $|K| + |K_\omega| = 0$ (i.e., $K = K_\omega = \emptyset$), since $p \overset{\sigma}{\Rightarrow}$ belongs to $\Pi(K, K_\omega)$ (and ρ is a subsequence of σ), then $Z \overset{\beta}{\Rightarrow}$ can be only finite. Therefore, all the subderivations of $p \overset{\sigma}{\Rightarrow}$ are finite. Then, by Step 1 we deduce that there must exist a $(\emptyset, \emptyset)$-accepting infinite derivation in M_{PAR} from p. Since $Var \subseteq T_{PAR}$, by Lemma 5 we obtain the following decidable (by Propositions 3–4) characterization for the existence of a $(\emptyset, \emptyset)$-accepting infinite derivation in M from a variable X:

– (when $K = K_\omega = \emptyset$) Either (1) there exists a $(\emptyset, \emptyset)$-accepting infinite derivation in M_{SEQ} from X, or (2) there exists a variable Y *s*-reachable from X in M_{SEQ} through a derivation having finite acceptance (in M_{SEQ}) $K = \emptyset$, and there exists a $(\emptyset, \emptyset)$-accepting infinite derivation in M_{PAR} from Y.

Now, let us assume that $|K| + |K_\omega| > 0$ and $Z \overset{\beta}{\Rightarrow}$ is infinite. Since $\overline{p} \| (Z.Y) \overset{\nu}{\Rightarrow}$ is also in $\Pi(K, K_\omega)$, by definition of subderivation we deduce that there is a derivation belonging to $\Pi(K, K_\omega)$ having the form $\overline{p} \overset{\nu \setminus \rho}{\Rightarrow}$. Since $p \overset{\sigma}{\Rightarrow}$ belongs to $\Pi(K, K_\omega)$, it follows that $\Upsilon_M^f(\rho) = \overline{K} \subseteq K$, $\Upsilon_M^\infty(\rho) = \overline{K}_\omega \subseteq K_\omega$, and $|\overline{K}| + |\overline{K}_\omega| < |K| + |K_\omega|$. By our assumptions (induction hypothesis) it is decidable whether there exists a $(\overline{K}, \overline{K}_\omega)$-accepting infinite derivation in M from variable Z. Then, we keep track of the infinite derivation $W \overset{r}{\Rightarrow}_\Re Z.Y \overset{\beta}{\Rightarrow}_\Re$ by adding a PAR rule of the form $r' = W \overset{K_1, \overline{K}_\omega}{\rightarrow} Z_F$ with $K_1 = \overline{K} \cup \Upsilon_M^f(r) \subseteq K$. So, the label of r' keeps track of the finite and infinite acceptance of $r\rho$ in M. Now, we can apply recursively the same argument to the derivation $\overline{p} \| Z_F \overset{\nu \setminus \rho}{\Rightarrow}$ in $\Re$ from $\overline{p} \| Z_F \in T_{PAR}$, which belongs to $\Pi(K, K_\omega)$ and whose finite (resp., infinite) acceptance in M is contained in K (resp., K_ω). In other words, all the subderivations of

$p \overset{\sigma}{\Rightarrow}$ are abstracted away by PAR rules non belonging to $\Re$, according to the intuitions given above. Formally, we define two extensions of M_{PAR} (with the same support) that will contain these new PAR rules $r' = W^{K_1, \overline{K}_\omega} \overset{}{\Rightarrow} Z_F$. The accepting components of the first (resp., the second) extension agree with the first component K_1 (resp., the second component $\overline{K}_\omega$) of the label of r' (that keep track of the finite acceptance – resp., the infinite acceptance – of the simulated infinite rule sequences in M).

Definition 7. By $M_{PAR}^{K, K_\omega} = \langle \Re_{PAR}^{K, K_\omega}, \langle \Re_{PAR,1}^{K, K_\omega}, \ldots, \Re_{PAR,n}^{K, K_\omega} \rangle \rangle$ and $M_{PAR,\infty}^{K, K_\omega} = \langle \Re_{PAR}^{K, K_\omega}, \langle \Re_{PAR,\infty,1}^{K, K_\omega}, \ldots, \Re_{PAR,\infty,n}^{K, K_\omega} \rangle \rangle$ we denote the parallel MBRSs over $Var \cup \{Z_F\}$ and the alphabet $\Sigma \cup P_n \cup P_n \times P_n$ (with the same support), defined as follows:

- $\Re_{PAR}^{K, K_\omega} = \Re_{PAR} \cup$
$$\{X \overset{\overline{K}, \overline{K}_\omega}{\to} Z_F \mid \overline{K} \subseteq K, \overline{K}_\omega \subseteq K_\omega, \text{ there exist } r = X \overset{a}{\to} Z.Y \in \Re$$
$$\text{and an infinite derivation } Z \overset{\sigma}{\Rightarrow}_\Re \text{ such that}$$
$$|\Upsilon_M^f(\sigma)| + |\Upsilon_M^\infty(\sigma)| < |K| + |K_\omega| \text{ and}$$
$$\Upsilon_M^f(\sigma) \cup \Upsilon_M^f(r) = \overline{K} \text{ and } \Upsilon_M^\infty(\sigma) = \overline{K}_\omega\}.$$

- $\Re_{PAR,i}^{K, K_\omega} = \Re_{PAR,i} \cup \{X \overset{\overline{K}, \overline{K}_\omega}{\to} Z_F \in \Re_{PAR}^{K, K_\omega} \mid i \in \overline{K}\}$ for all $i = 1, \ldots, n$.
- $\Re_{PAR,i,\infty}^{K, K_\omega} = \{X \overset{\overline{K}, \overline{K}_\omega}{\to} Z_F \in \Re_{PAR}^{K, K_\omega} \mid i \in \overline{K}_\omega\}$ for all $i = 1, \ldots, n$.

By the induction hypothesis on the decidability of the Fairness Problem for sets $\overline{K}, \overline{K}_\omega \in P_n$ such that $\overline{K} \subseteq K$, $\overline{K}_\omega \subseteq K_\omega$ and $|\overline{K}| + |\overline{K}_\omega| < |K| + |K_\omega|$, we have

Lemma 6. M_{PAR}^{K, K_ω} and $M_{PAR,\infty}^{K, K_\omega}$ can be built effectively.

The following two Lemmata establish the correctness of our construction.

Lemma 7. Let $p \overset{\sigma}{\Rightarrow}$ be a $(\overline{K}, \overline{K}_\omega)$-accepting derivation in M from $p \in T_{PAR}$ belonging to $\Pi(K, K_\omega)$, where $\overline{K} \subseteq K$ and $\overline{K}_\omega \subseteq K_\omega$. Then, there exists in $\Re_{PAR}^{K, K_\omega}$ a derivation of the form $p \overset{\rho}{\Rightarrow}$ such that $\Upsilon_{M_{PAR}^{K, K_\omega}}^f(\rho) = \overline{K}$, $\Upsilon_{M_{PAR}^{K, K_\omega}}^\infty(\rho) \cup \Upsilon_{M_{PAR,\infty}^{K, K_\omega}}^f(\rho) = \overline{K}_\omega$. Moreover, if σ is infinite, then either ρ is infinite or contains some occurrence of rule in $\Re_{PAR}^{K, K_\omega} \setminus \Re_{PAR}$.

Lemma 8. Let $p \overset{\sigma}{\Rightarrow}_{\Re_{PAR}^{K, K_\omega}}$ such that $p \in T_{PAR}$, and σ is either infinite or contains some occurrence of rule in $\Re_{PAR}^{K, K_\omega} \setminus \Re_{PAR}$. Then, there exists in $\Re$ an infinite derivation of the form $p \overset{\delta}{\Rightarrow}$ such that $\Upsilon_M^f(\delta) = \Upsilon_{M_{PAR}^{K, K_\omega}}^f(\sigma)$ and $\Upsilon_M^\infty(\delta) = \Upsilon_{M_{PAR}^{K, K_\omega}}^\infty(\sigma) \cup \Upsilon_{M_{PAR,\infty}^{K, K_\omega}}^f(\sigma)$.

Finally, we can prove the desired result

Theorem 2. The Fairness Problem is decidable for MBRSs in normal form.

Proof. We start constructing M_{PAR} and M_{SEQ} (they do not depend on K and K_ω). Then, we accumulate information about the existence of $(\overline{K}, \overline{K}_\omega)$-accepting infinite derivations in M from variables in Var, where $|\overline{K}| + |\overline{K}_\omega| \le |K| + |K_\omega|$ and $\overline{K} \subseteq K$ and $\overline{K}_\omega \subseteq K_\omega$, proceeding for crescent values of $|\overline{K}| + |\overline{K}_\omega|$. We have seen that this is decidable for $|\overline{K}| + |\overline{K}_\omega| = 0$. We keep track of this information by adding new PAR rules according to Definition 7. When $|\overline{K}| + |\overline{K}_\omega| > 0$ (assuming without loss of generality that $\overline{K} = K$ and $\overline{K}_\omega = K_\omega$), by Lemmata 5, 7, and 8 the problem for a variable $X \in Var$ is reduced to check that one of the following two conditions (that are decidable by Propositions 3–4) holds:

- There exists a variable $Y \in Var$ s-reachable from X in $\Re_{SEQ}$ through a $(K', \emptyset)$-accepting derivation in M_{SEQ} with $K' \subseteq K$, and there exists a derivation $Y \overset{\rho}{\Rightarrow}_{\Re_{PAR}^{K,K_\omega}}$ such that $\Upsilon^f_{M_{PAR}^{K,K_\omega}}(\rho) = K$ and $\Upsilon^\infty_{M_{PAR}^{K,K_\omega}}(\rho) \cup \Upsilon^f_{M_{PAR,\infty}^{K,K_\omega}}(\rho) = K_\omega$. Moreover, ρ is either infinite or contains some occurrence of rule in $\Re_{PAR}^{K,K_\omega} \setminus \Re_{PAR}$.
- (only when $K = K_\omega$). There exists a (K, K_ω)-accepting infinite derivation in M_{SEQ} from X.

5   Decidability of the Fairness Problem for Unrestricted *MBRS*s

In this section we extend the decidability result stated in the previous Section to the whole class of *MBRS*s, showing that the Fairness Problem for unrestricted *MBRS*s is reducible to the Fairness Problem for *MBRS*s in normal form. We use a construction very close to that used in [12, 13] to solve reachability for *PRS*s. We recall that we can assume that the input term in the Fairness Problem is a process variable. Let M be a *MBRS* over Var and Σ, and with n accepting components. Now, we describe a procedure that transforms M into a new *MBRS* M' with the same number of accepting components. Moreover, this procedure has as input also a finite set of rules $\Re_{AUX}$, and transforms it in $\Re'_{AUX}$. If M is not in normal form, then there exists some rule r in M (that we call *bad rule* [12]) that is neither a PAR rule nor a SEQ rule. There are five types of bad rules[5]:

1. $r = u \overset{a}{\rightarrow} u_1 \| u_2$. Let Z_1, Z_2, W be fresh variables. We get M' replacing the bad rule r with the rules $r' = u \rightarrow W$, $r_3 = W \rightarrow Z_1 \| Z_2$, $r_1 = Z_1 \rightarrow u_1$, $r_2 = Z_2 \rightarrow u_2$ such that $\Upsilon^f_{M'}(r') = \Upsilon^f_M(r)$, $\Upsilon^f_{M'}(r_1) = \Upsilon^f_{M'}(r_2) = \Upsilon^f_{M'}(r_3) = \emptyset$ [6]. If $r \in \Re_{AUX}$, then $\Re'_{AUX} = (\Re_{AUX} \setminus \{r\}) \cup \{r', r_1, r_2, r_3\}$, otherwise, $\Re'_{AUX} = \Re_{AUX}$.
2. $r = u_1 \| (u_2.u_3) \overset{a}{\rightarrow} u$. Let Z_1, Z_2 be fresh variables. We get M' replacing the bad rule r with the rules $r_1 = u_1 \rightarrow Z_1$, $r_2 = u_2.u_3 \rightarrow Z_2$, $r' = Z_1 \| Z_2 \rightarrow u$ such that $\Upsilon^f_{M'}(r') = \Upsilon^f_M(r)$, $\Upsilon^f_{M'}(r_1) = \Upsilon^f_{M'}(r_2) = \emptyset$. If $r \in \Re_{AUX}$, then $\Re'_{AUX} = (\Re_{AUX} \setminus \{r\}) \cup \{r', r_1, r_2\}$, otherwise, $\Re'_{AUX} = \Re_{AUX}$.

---

[5] We assume that sequential composition is left-associative. So, when we write $t_1.t_2$, then t_2 is either a single variable or a parallel composition of process terms.

[6] Note that we have not specified the label of the new rules, since it is not relevant.

3. $r = u \xrightarrow{a} u_1.u_2$ (resp., $r = u_1.u_2 \xrightarrow{a} u$) where u_2 is not a single variable. Let Z be a fresh variable. We get M' and $\Re'_{AUX}$ in two steps. First, we substitute Z for u_2 in (left-hand and right-hand sides of) all the rules of M and $\Re_{AUX}$. Then, we add the rules $r_1 = Z \to u_2$ and $r_2 = u_2 \to Z$ such that $\Upsilon^f_{M'}(r_1) = \Upsilon^f_{M'}(r_2) = \emptyset$.

4. $r = u_1 \xrightarrow{a} u_2.X$. Let Z, W be fresh variables. We get M' replacing the bad rule r with the rules $r' = u_1 \to W$, $r_1 = W \to Z.X$, $r_2 = Z \to u_2$ such that $\Upsilon^f_{M'}(r') = \Upsilon^f_M(r)$ and $\Upsilon^f_{M'}(r_1) = \Upsilon^f_{M'}(r_2) = \emptyset$. If $r \in \Re_{AUX}$, then $\Re'_{AUX} = (\Re_{AUX} \setminus \{r\}) \cup \{r', r_1, r_2\}$, otherwise, $\Re'_{AUX} = \Re_{AUX}$.

5. $r = u_1.X \xrightarrow{a} u_2$ where u_1 is not a single variable. Let Z be a fresh variable. We get M' replacing the bad rule r with the rules $r_1 = u_1 \to Z$, $r' = Z.X \to u_2$, such that $\Upsilon^f_{M'}(r') = \Upsilon^f_M(r)$ and $\Upsilon^f_{M'}(r_1) = \emptyset$. If $r \in \Re_{AUX}$, then $\Re'_{AUX} = (\Re_{AUX} \setminus \{r\}) \cup \{r', r_1\}$, otherwise, $\Re'_{AUX} = \Re_{AUX}$.

After a finite number of applications of this procedure, starting from $\Re_{AUX} = \emptyset$, we obtain a *MBRS* M' in normal form and a finite set of rules $\Re'_{AUX}$. Let $M' = \langle \Re', \langle \Re'_1, \ldots, \Re'_n \rangle \rangle$. Now, let us consider the *MBRS* in normal form with $n + 1$ accepting components given by $M_F = \langle \Re', \langle \Re'_1, \ldots, \Re'_n, \Re' \setminus \Re'_{AUX} \rangle \rangle$. We can prove that, given a variable $X \in Var$ and two sets $K, K_\omega \in P_n$, there exists a (K, K_ω)-accepting infinite derivation in M from X if, and only if, there exists a $(K \cup \{n+1\}, K_\omega \cup \{n+1\})$-accepting infinite derivation in M_F from X.

6   Complexity Issues

We conclude with some considerations about the complexity of the considered problem. Model–checking parallel *PRSs* (that are equivalent to Petri nets) w.r.t. the considered *ALTL* fragment, interpreted on infinite runs, is *EXPSPACE*-complete (also for a fixed formula) [11]. *ALTL* model–checking for sequential *PRSs* (that are equivalent to Pushdown processes) is less hard, since it is *EXP-TIME*-complete [2]. Therefore, model–checking the whole class of *PRSs* w.r.t. the considered *ALTL* fragment (restricted to infinite runs) is at least *EXPSPACE*-hard. We have reduced this problem (in polynomial time) to the Fairness Problem (see Theorem 1). Moreover, as seen in Section 5, we can limit ourselves (through a polynomial-time reduction) to consider only *MBRSs* in normal form. The algorithm presented in Section 4 to resolve the Fairness Problem for *MBRSs* in normal form is an exponential reduction (in the number n of accepting components) to the *ALTL* model–checking problem for Petri nets and Pushdown processes: we have to resolve an exponential number in n of instances of decision problems about acceptance properties of derivations of parallel and sequential *MBRSs*, whose size is exponential in n [7]. These last problems (see Propositions 2–4) are polynomial-time reducible to the *ALTL* model–checking problem for Petri nets and Pushdown processes. It was shown [8] that for Petri nets, and for

---

[7] Note that the number of new rules added in order to built M_{PAR}, M_{SEQ}, M^{K,K_ω}_{PAR}, and $M^{K,K_\omega}_{PAR,\infty}$ is exponential in n and polynomial in $|Var|$.

a fixed *ALTL* formula, model checking has the same complexity as reachability (that is *EXPSPACE*-hard, but the best known upper bound is not primitive recursive). Therefore, for n fixed (i.e., for a fixed formula of our *ALTL* fragment) the upper bound given by our algorithm is the same as reachability for Petri nets.

Acknowledgment

I thank Aldo De Luca, Salvatore La Torre, Margherita Napoli, and Adriano Peron for very helpful discussions.

References

1. A. Bouajjani and P. Habermehl. Constrained Properties, Semilinear Systems, and Petri Nets. In *Proc. of CONCUR'96*, Springer LNCS 1119, pp. 481–497, 1996.
2. A. Bouajjani, J. Esparza, and O. Maler. Reachability Analysis of Pushdown Automata: Application to Model-Checking. In *Proc. CONCUR'97*, Springer LNCS 1243, pp. 135–150, 1997.
3. A. Bouajjani and T. Touili. Reachability Analysis of Process Rewrite Systems. In *Proc. of FSTTCS'03*, Springer LNCS 2914, pp. 74–87, 2003.
4. O. Burkart, B. Steffen. Pushdown Processes: Parallel Composition and Model Checking. In *Proc. of CONCUR'94*, Springer LNCS 836, pp. 98–113, 1994.
5. O. Burkart, D. Caucal, F. Moller, and B. Steffen. Verification on Infinite Structures. In *Handbook of Process Algebra*, North-Holland, Amsterdam, pp. 545–623, 2001.
6. Martin D. Davis, Elaine J. Weyuker. *Computability, Complexity, and Languages.* pp. 47–49, Academic Press, 1983.
7. E. Allen Emerson, Joseph Y. Halpern. *"Sometimes" and "Not Never" Revisited: On Branching Versus Linear Time.* POPL 1983, pp. 127–140.
8. J. Esparza. On the Decidability of Model Checking for Several μ-calculi and Petri Nets. In *Trees in Algebra and Programming*, CAAP'94, vol. 787 of LNCS. Springer Verlag, pp. 115–129, 1994.
9. J. Esparza. Decidability of Model Checking for Infinite–State Concurrent Systems. In *Acta Informaticae*, 34(2), pp. 85–107, 1997.
10. J. Esparza, D. Hansel, P. Rossmanith, and S. Schwoon. Efficient Algorithms for Model Checking Pushdown Systems. In *Proc. Computer Aided Verification* (CAV'00), Springer LNCS 1855, pp. 232–247, 2000.
11. P. Habermehl. On the complexity of the linear-time mu-calculus for Petri nets. In *Proc. of the International Conference on Application and Theory of Petri Nets*, Springer LNCS 1248, pp. 102–116, 1997.
12. R. Mayr. Decidability and Complexity of Model Checking Problems for Infinite-State Systems. PhD. thesis, Techn. Univ. of Munich, 1998.
13. R. Mayr. Process Rewrite Systems. In *Information and Computation*, Vol. 156, 2000, pp. 264–286.
14. I. Walukiewicz. Pushdown processes: Games and Model Checking. In *Int. Conf. on Compter Aided Verification*, LNCS 1102, pages 62–74. Springer Verlag, 1996.

Minimizing Counterexample
with Unit Core Extraction and Incremental SAT

ShengYu Shen, Ying Qin, and SiKun Li

Office 607,School of Computer Science, National University of Defense Technology
410073 ChangSha, China
{syshen,qy123,skli}@nudt.edu.cn
http://www.nudt.edu.cn

Abstract. It is a hotly researching topic to eliminate irrelevant variables from counterexample, to make it easier to be understood. K Ravi proposes a two-stages counterexample minimization algorithm. This algorithm is the most effective one among all existing approaches, but time overhead of its second stage(called BFL) is very large due to one call to SAT solver per candidate variable to be eliminated. So we propose a faster counterexample minimization algorithm based on unit core extraction and incremental SAT. First, for every unsatisfiable instance of BFL, we perform unit core extraction algorithm to extract the set of variables that are sufficient to lead to conflict, all variables not belong to this set can be eliminated simultaneously. In this way, we can eliminate many variables with only one call to SAT solver. At the same time, we employ incremental SAT approach to share learned clauses between similar instances of BFL, to prevent overlapped state space from being searched repeatedly. Theoretic analysis and experiment result show that, our approach is 1 order of magnitude faster than K Ravi's algorithm, and still retains its ability to eliminate irrelevant variables.

1 Introduction

Model checking technology is widely employed to verify software and hardware system. One of its major advantages in comparison to such method as theorem proving is the production of a counterexample, which explains how the system violates some assertion.

However, it is a tedious task to understand the complex counterexamples generated by model checker. Therefore, how to automatically extract useful information to aid the understanding of counterexample, is an area of hotly research [5, 6, 13, 14].

A counterexample can be viewed as an assignment to a variable set $Free$, There must be a variables subset $R \subseteq Free$, which is sufficient to lead to counterexample. Then for variables in $Free - R$,no matter what value do they take on, they can't prevent the counterexample. Thus we call R as **minimization set**, and call the process that extract R as **counterexample minimization**.

Now we demonstrate the concept of counterexample minimization with following example:

R. Cousot (Ed.): VMCAI 2005, LNCS 3385, pp. 298–312, 2005.

For AND gate $z = a\&b$, assume the assertion is "z always equal to 1", then there are three counterexamples: $\{a \Leftarrow 0, b \Leftarrow 0, z \Leftarrow 0\}$, $\{a \Leftarrow 1, b \Leftarrow 0, z \Leftarrow 0\}$, and $\{a \Leftarrow 0, b \Leftarrow 1, z \Leftarrow 0\}$.

However, from an intuitive viewpoint, b is an irrelevant variable when a equal to 0. At the same time, a is also an irrelevant variable when b equals to 0. Then we can minimize above three counterexamples, and obtain 2 minimization sets: $\{a \Leftarrow 0, z \Leftarrow 0\}$ and $\{b \Leftarrow 0, z \Leftarrow 0\}$.

Thus, a minimized counterexample is much easier to be understood.

K Ravi[5] proposes a two-stage counterexample minimization algorithm. In the first stage, an Implication Graph Based Lifting(IGBF) algorithm is performed to quickly eliminate some irrelevant variables. In the second stage, a highly expensive Brute Force Lifting algorithm(BFL) is performed to further eliminate more irrelevant variables.

In BFL, free variables set contains input variables at all cycle and the initial state variables. "free" means that they can take on any value independent of others. For every free variable v, BFL constructs a SAT instance SAT(v), to determine if some assignment to v can prevent the counterexample. If SAT(v) is unsatisfiable, then v can't prevent the counterexample from happening , thus v is irrelevant to counterexample and can be eliminated.

K Ravi[5] compares his approach with other counterexample minimization approaches, and concludes that his approach is the most efficient one, it can often eliminates up to 70% free variables. However, the run time complexity of his approach is much higher than all other existing approaches. At the same time, run time overhead of BFL is 1 to 3 orders of magnitude larger than that of IGBF. So the key to speedup K Ravi's two-stage approach is to reduce time overhead of BFL.

The reasons of BFL's large time overhead are:

1. It needs to call SAT solver for every free variable. But there are often thousands of free variables in a counterexample. This means BFL needs to call SAT solver thousands of times, it is a huge overhead;
2. It can't share learned clause between similar SAT instances, so overlapped state space may be searched repeatedly.

Accordingly, the keys to reduce time overhead of BFL are:

1. Eliminate as many as possible variables after every call to SAT solver;
2. Share learned clauses between similar SAT instances, to avoid searching overlapped state space repeatedly.

So we propose a faster counterexample minimization algorithm based on unit core extraction and incremental SAT. First, for every unsatisfiable instance of BFL, we perform unit core extraction algorithm to extract the set of variables that are sufficient to lead to conflict, all variables not belong to this set can be eliminated simultaneously. In this way, we can eliminate many variables with only one call to SAT solver. At the same time, we employ incremental SAT approach to share learned clauses between similar instances of BFL, to prevent overlapped state space from being searched repeatedly.

We implement our algorithm based on zchaff[10] and NuSMV[9], and perform experiment on ISCAS89 benchmark suite[11]. Experiment result shows that, our approach is 1 order of magnitude faster than K Ravi's algorithm[5], and without any lost in its ability to eliminate irrelevant variables.

The remainder of this paper is organized as follows. Section 2 presents background material. Section 3 presents the counterexample minimization approach based on unit core extraction. Section 4 presents the incremental SAT approach. Section 5 presents experiment result of our approach and compares it to that of K Ravi's approach[5]. Section 6 reviews related works. Section 7 concludes with a note on future work.

2   Preliminaries

2.1   Satisfiability Solvers

Basic Notions of Satisfiability Solvers
Given a Boolean formula F, the SAT problem involves finding whether a satisfying assignment for F exists. A SAT solver typically computes a total satisfying assignment for F, if one exists, otherwise returns an UNSATISFIABLE answer. In a SAT solver a Boolean formula F is usually represented in CNF. For instance,

$$f = (a \lor b) \land (\neg c \lor d) \qquad (1)$$

A CNF formula is a conjunction of clauses. A clause is a disjunction of literals. A literal is a variable or its negation. As shown by equation (1), formula f contains two clauses:$(a \lor b)$ and $(\neg c \lor d)$. Clause $(\neg c \lor d)$ include two literals:$\neg c$ and d. $\neg c$ is a negative phase literal of variable c, and d is a positive phase literal of d.

A *total* satisfying assignment for f is $\{(a, 0), (b, 1), (c, 0), (d, 0)\}$. "total" means that it contains assignments to all variables. $\{(b, 1), (c, 0)\}$ is a *partial* satisfying assignment because it contains only assignments to a subset of variables.

It is also convenient to use literals to designate variable-value pairs. For example, the assignment $\{(a, 0), (b, 1), (c, 0), (d, 0)\}$ can be denoted by $\{\neg a, b, \neg c, \neg d\}$.

Implication Graph
According to *unit clause rule*, when a clause contains only one unassigned literal, and all other literals are rendered false, then the variable of this unassigned literal can take on its value according to its phase. This mechanism is called *implication*. For instance, for clause $(\neg c \lor d)$ and assignment $\{\neg d\}$, variable c must take on value 0 to make this clause true.

With this implication mechanism, we can construct an Implication Graph $G = (V, E)$. The nodes set V represents the literals of the assignments made by implications or decisions. Each directed hyperedge $E \subseteq 2^V \times V$ represents an implication, caused by an antecedent clause.

Conflict Learning

Conflict learning[8] can significantly boost performance of modern SAT solver.

While solving SAT instance, when a conflict arises, SAT solver will analyze implication graph to construct learned clauses, and insert these clauses into clause database. These clauses record the information of searched state space, to prevent them from being searched again.

So after SAT solver terminates,there are two types of clauses in clause database:

1. **Origin clauses** are those clauses inserted into clause database before SAT solver start running.
2. **Learned clauses** are those clauses generated by conflict analysis.

2.2   Bounded Model Checking

We first define the Kripke structure:

Definition 1 (Kripke structure). *Kripke structure is a tuple M=(S,I,T,L), with a finite set of states S, the set of initial states $I \subseteq S$, a transition relation between states $T \subseteq S \times S$, and the labeling of the states $L : S \rightarrow 2^{AP}$ with atomic propositions set AP.*

Bounded Model Checking (BMC)[7] is a model checking technology that consider only limited length path. We call this length k as the bound of path. Let S_i and S_{i+1} be the state of the i-th and (i+1)-th cycle, and $T(S_i, S_{i+1})$ represents the transition relation between them.

Assume q is a boolean proposition, and the safety assertion under verification is "$G\ q$", then the goal of BMC is to find a state S that violates q, that is to say, $\neg q \in L(S)$. In the remainder of this paper, $\neg q$ will be denoted by P, and we will not refer to q any more.

Let P_i be P at i-th cycle ,then BMC problem can be expressed as:

$$F := I(S_0) \wedge \bigwedge_{i=0}^{k-1} T(S_i, S_{i+1}) \wedge \bigwedge_{i=0}^{k-1} \neg P_i \wedge P_k$$

BMC always searches for shortest counterexample, so $\bigwedge_{i=0}^{k-1} \neg P_i$ always holds true. Thus, we can remove it from above equation, and obtain following equation:

$$F := I(S_0) \wedge \bigwedge_{i=0}^{k-1} T(S_i, S_{i+1}) \wedge P_k \tag{2}$$

Reduce equation (2) into propositional satisfiability problem, and solve it with SAT solver, then a counterexample can be found if it exists.

2.3   BFL Algorithm and Its Shortcoming

BFL algorithm proposed by K Ravi[5] can eliminate much more free variables than all existing algorithms, often up to 70% free variables can be eliminated.

Lets first define some terminology below:

Definition 2 (Assignment Clause). *Assume the value of variable v in counterexample is denoted by $Value(v) \in \{0, 1\}$, then the Assignment Clause of v is a unit clause which contain only one literal, which is defined as:*

$$Assign(v) := \begin{cases} \{v\} & \text{if } Value(v) == 1 \\ \{\neg v\} & \text{otherwise} \end{cases} \quad (3)$$

Definition 3 (Free Variables Set). *Assume the set of input variables is W, then input variables set of i-th cycle is denoted by W_i. Assume the set of state variables is X, then state variables set of i-th cycle is denoted by X_i.*

Assume the bound of counterexample is k, then the set of free variables is $Free := X_0 \cup \bigcup_{i=0}^{k} W_i$.

Obviously, *Free* includes input variables at all cycle and initial state variables. "Free" means that they can take on any value independent of others.

For a free variable $v \in Free$, v is an irrelevant variable if and only if the following statement holds true: "no matter what value do v take on, it can't prevent the counterexample from happening. That is to say, it can't prevent P_k of equation (2) from equal to 1". Formal definition of irrelevant variable is presented below:

Definition 4 (Irrelevant Variable). *for $v \in Free$, v is irrelevant variable iff:*

$$\neg \exists c \in \{0, 1\}.(\bigwedge_{i=0}^{k-1} T(S_i, S_{i+1}) \wedge (v \Leftarrow c) \wedge \bigwedge_{v' \in Free \backslash v} Assign(v') \wedge \neg P_k) \quad (4)$$

Convert $\bigwedge_{i=0}^{k-1} T(S_i, S_{i+1}) \wedge \bigwedge_{v' \in Free \backslash v} Assign(v') \wedge \neg P_k$ into SAT instance, then v is irrelevant variable iff this SAT instance is unsatisfiable.

Thus, the BFL algorithm that extracts minimization set from counterexample is shown below:

Algorithm 1: BFL Counterexample Minimization Algorithm

1. $F" = \bigwedge_{i=0}^{k-1} T(S_i, S_{i+1}) \wedge \neg P_k$
2. for each $v \in Free$
3. $F' = F" \wedge \bigwedge_{v' \in Free \backslash v} Assign(v')$
4.   if(SAT_Solve(F')==UNSATISFIABLE) $Free = Free \backslash v$
5. *Free* is the minimization set

We introduce 2 definitions here to make it easier to describe our algorithm:

Definition 5 (Model Clause Set). *In step 3 of algorithm 1, the clauses set generated from $F"$ is called Model Clause Set.*

Definition 6 (Assignment Clause Set). *In step 3 of algorithm 1, the clauses set generated from $\bigwedge_{v' \in Free \backslash v} Assign(v')$ is called Assignment Clause Set.*

We call $F"$ *Model Clause Set* because it represents inverted model checking problem of equation (2). We call $\bigwedge_{v' \in Free \backslash v} Assign(v')$ *Assignment Clause Set* because it is used to assign to all variables their value in counterexample, except v. SAT solver will assign these values to them by performing BCP.

3   Counterexample Minimization with Unit Core Extraction

As stated before, the key to reduce time overhead of BFL is to eliminate multiple variables after every call to SAT solver. So we present our key ideas below:

> In algorithm 1, when SAT instance F' is unsatisfiable, a variables set R that is sufficient to lead to conflict can be extracted from it by unit core extraction. Then $F'' \wedge \bigwedge_{v' \in R} Assign(v')$ is an unsatisfiable clause subset of F'. Thus $Free - R$ can be eliminated immediately. In this way, we can achieve our goal of eliminating multiple variables simultaneously.

In this section, we first describe the overall algorithm flow in subsection 3.1, and then describe the most important part– unit core extraction algorithm in subsection 3.2. We will prove its correctness in subsection 3.3. At last, we will analyze the complexity of this algorithm in subsection 3.4.

3.1   Overall Algorithm Flow

Run time overhead of BFL is very large due to one call to SAT solver per candidate variable to be eliminated. Therefore, it is very important to reduce the number of calls to SAT solver.

Overall flow of our algorithm is shown by algorithm 2:

Algorithm 2 BFL with unit core extraction

1. $F'' = \bigwedge_{i=0}^{k-1} T(S_i, S_{i+1}) \wedge \neg P_k$
2. for each $v \in Free$
3. $F' = F'' \wedge \bigwedge_{v' \in Free \setminus v} Assign(v')$
4.   if(SAT_Solve(F')==UNSATISFIABLE)
5.   **R=Unit_Core(v)**
6.   **Free = Free ∩ R**
7. $Free$ is the minimization set

Compare it to algorithm 1, step 5 and 6 of algorithm 2 are newly inserted steps, which are highlighted with bold font. In step 5, we perform unit core extraction to extract the variables set R that lead to UNSATISFIABLE. And then in step 6, we eliminate all variables not belong to R, then we don't need to call SAT solver for them any more. Thus, the number of calls to SAT solver is significantly decreased in our approach compared to BFL.

3.2   Unit Core Extraction Algorithm

As stated by last subsection, we perform unit core extraction algorithm to extract the variable set R that lead to UNSATISFIABLE. Main idea of our unit core extraction algorithm are presented below:

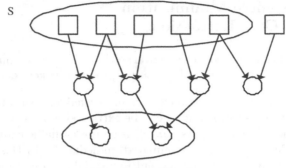

all literal of conflict clause c

Fig. 1. Implication graph starting from the unit clauses at the leaves and ending with the conflict clause c at the root.

For SAT instance F', let $F"$ be its model clause set, and A be its assignment clause set. After SAT solver finished running, let C be its learned clause set.

Refer to last paragraph of section 2.2 of L.Zhang's famous paper about unsatisfiable core extraction [16],we have the following theorem 1.

Theorem 1. *If F' is unsatisfiable, then there must be a conflict clause at decision level 0, we denote it by c. Because the decision level is 0, so there are no decided variables, any variables can only take on their value by implication.*

According to this theorem,there must be an implication graph starting from the unit clauses at the leaves and ending with the conflict clause c at the root. We show this implication graph in figure 1.Every rectangle is an unit clause, and S is the set of unit clauses that make all literals of conflict clause c to be false. Staring from clause c, we can traverse the implicate graph in reverse direction, to obtain the set of unit clauses S that lead to conflict. We denote the assignment clauses in S by $S \cap A$, then the variables set that lead to conflict is $R = \{v | Assign(v) \in S \cap A\}$. This is the key idea of Unit Core Extraction.

Now we present the unit core extraction algorithm below.

Algorithm 3 Unit Core Extraction Unit_Core(v)

1. set $S = \phi$;
2. queue $Q = \phi$;
3. for each literal $l \in c$
4.   push antecedent clause of l into Q
5.   mark antecedent clause of l as visited
6. while(Q is not empty)
7. cls=pop first clause from Q
8.   if(cls is unit clause)
9. $S = S + \{cls\}$
10.   if(cls is a learned unit clause) return $R = Free \setminus v$

11.   else
12.   for each literal $l \in cls$
13.   assume $ante(l)$ is antecedent clause of l
14.   if($ante(l)$ has not being visited before)
15.   push $ante(l)$ into Q
16.   mark $ante(l)$ as visited
17. return $R = \{v | Assign(v) \in S \cap A\}$

There is a special case in step 10 of algorithm 3. When cls is a learned clause with only one literal, we can't backtrack further because the SAT solver has not record the clauses involved in resolution to generate learned clause cls. In this case, we abandon the effort to extract unit core, and just return $R = Free \setminus v$. This means that we can eliminate only one variable v in this case.

Fortunately, we has not met with this special case in our experiments. But we just can't prove its absence in theory. Currently, I think it is because of the 1UIP conflict learning mechanism of zchaff, which may never generate learning clause with only one literal.

The unsatisfiable core extraction approaches[16,17] do provide a mechanism to record the clauses involved in resolution to generate learned clause. This mechanism do help to eliminate more irrelevant variables, but it imposes very large time overhead, which will outweigh the benefit of unit core extraction.

3.3   Correctness of Algorithm

Theorem 2. $F" \wedge \bigwedge_{cls \in S} cls$ is an unsatisfiable clause subset of F'

Proof. It is obvious that $F" \wedge \bigwedge_{cls \in S} cls$ is a clause subset of F', so we only need to prove that $F" \wedge \bigwedge_{cls \in S} cls$ is unsatisfiable.

Assume $C' \subseteq C$ is the set of conflict clauses met with by algorithm 3 while traverse the implication graph. Then according to algorithm 3 and figure 1, $F" \wedge \bigwedge_{cls \in S} cls \wedge \bigwedge_{cls \in C'} cls$ is unsatisfiable. Then if we can remove $\bigwedge_{cls \in C'} cls$ from it, and still retain its unsatisfiability?

For every learned clause $cls \in C'$, assume $NU(cls)$ and $U(cls)$ are non-unit clauses set and unit clauses set that involved in resolution to construct cls. Then it is obvious that $F" \wedge \bigwedge_{cls \in S} cls \wedge \bigwedge_{cls \in C'} (\bigwedge_{cls' \in U(cls)} cls' \wedge \bigwedge_{cls' \in NU(cls)} cls')$ is unsatisfiable.

It is obvious that $NU(cls) \subseteq F"$. And according to [8], unit clauses never involve in resolution, so $U(cls)$ is empty set. Thus we can remove $\bigwedge_{cls \in C'} (\bigwedge_{cls' \in U(cls)} cls' \wedge \bigwedge_{cls' \in NU(cls)} cls')$ from $F" \wedge \bigwedge_{cls \in S} cls \wedge \bigwedge_{cls \in C'} (\bigwedge_{cls' \in U(cls)} cls' \wedge \bigwedge_{cls' \in NU(cls)} cls')$, and still reatin its unsatisfiability.

So $F" \wedge \bigwedge_{cls \in S} cls$ is unsatisfiable.

Thus this theorem is proven.

Theorem 3. $F" \wedge \bigwedge_{v' \in R} Assign(v')$ is an unsatisfiable clause subset of F'

Proof. It is obvious that $R \in Free \setminus v$, so $F" \wedge \bigwedge_{v' \in R} Assign(v')$ is clause subset of $F' = F" \wedge \bigwedge_{v' \in Free \setminus v} Assign(v')$.

So we only need to prove that $F" \wedge \bigwedge_{v' \in R} Assign(v')$ is unsatisfiable.

According to step 17 of algorithm 3, $\bigwedge_{v' \in R} Assign(v')$ is equal to $\bigwedge_{cls \in S \cap A} cls$.

So we only need to prove that $F" \wedge \bigwedge_{cls \in S \cap A} cls$ is unsatisfiable.

According to theorem 2, $F" \wedge \bigwedge_{cls \in S} cls$ is unsatisfiable, and it can be rewritten as $F" \wedge \bigwedge_{cls \in S \cap A} cls \wedge \bigwedge_{cls \in S - A - F"} cls$.

We discuss it in 2 aspects:

1. if $S - A - F"$ is an empty set, then $F" \wedge \bigwedge_{cls \in S} cls$ and $F" \wedge \bigwedge_{cls \in S \cap A} cls$ are of the same, then $F" \wedge \bigwedge_{cls \in S \cap A} cls$ is unsatisfiable.

2. otherwise, $S - A - F"$ isn't an empty set. In this case, algorithm 3 will meet with a learning clause with only one literal. According to step 10 of algorithm 3,it will abandon the effort to extract unit core, and eliminate only one variable v. According to step 3 of algorithm 2, it is obvious that $F" \wedge \bigwedge_{v' \in R} Assign(v')$ is unsatisfiable.

Thus this theorem is proven.

According to theorem 3, Assigning to all variables in R their value in counterexample can make F' unsatisfiable. Thus according to definition 3, variables in $Free - R$ are all irrelevant variables. No matter what value do they take on, they can't prevent the counterexample. Thus, we can eliminate $Free - R$ simultaneously in step 6 of algorithm 2.

3.4   Complexity Analysis

Because our algorithm depends heavily on SAT solver, so we don't analyze its complexity directly. Instead, we compare our algorithm with SAT solver.

We first analyze space complexity of our algorithm. Comparing algorithm 2 and 1, the only difference is that algorithm 2 add an unit core extraction step. Therefore, difference of space complexity between them resides in unit core extraction algorithm. We know that the space overhead of unit core extraction mainly resides in set S and queue Q. Lets analyze them as below:

- We add a tag to each clause in clause database of SAT solver, to indicate that if this clause belongs to set S. Therefore, space overhead of S is linear to size of clause database.
- For queue Q, it may contain learned clauses. Because conflict analysis algorithm of SAT solver also need to perform similar implicate graph traversing, so space overhead of Q is not larger than that of SAT solver. We will present the peak size of Q in table 3 of experiment result, it is obvious that its size are much smaller than clause database.

Next, we will analyze the time complexity of our algorithm.

In algorithm 3, the most complex part is the if statement in step 14. For every clauses that has been in Q, this if statement will be run once. Because the size of Q is much smaller than clause database, so time overhead of algorithm 3 is much smaller than that of BCP in SAT solver.

In algorithm 2, one call to unit core extraction algorithm will eliminate many irrelevant variables, thus prevent them from calling SAT solver. This will significantly decrease the number of calling SAT solver and time overhead.

We will present the number of calls to unit core extraction algorithm and SAT solver in table 3 of experiment result.

4   Incremental SAT

From step 3 of algorithm 2, it is obvious that F' of two consecutive iterations are very similar. This suggests a good chance to share learned clause between them by employ incremental SAT approach.

In last paragraph of section 6, K Ravi[5] has mentioned that BFL's performance can be improved by Incremental SAT. But he hasn't presented how to achieve this. And all his experiments are based on non-incremental SAT. So we present here a novel approach to improve BFL's performance further by incremental SAT.

For two consecutive iterations, assume the two variables to be eliminated are $v1$ and $v2$. Then for the first iteration, $F' = F" \wedge \bigwedge_{v' \in Free \backslash v1} Assign(v')$. For the second iteration, $F' = F" \wedge \bigwedge_{v' \in Free \backslash v2} Assign(v')$. After we have finished solving the first F', to obtain the second one, we only need to delete $Assign(v1)$ and insert $Assign(v2)$ into clause database.

N. Een[12] concludes that: when delete a unit clause that contains only one literal, all learned clauses can be safely kept in clause database.

So when we delete $Assign(v1)$, we don't need to delete any learned clauses. Thus all learned clauses can be shared between consecutive iterations.

Therefore, we modify algorithm 2 into the following algorithm 4. All new steps are highlight with bold font.

Algorithm 4 BFL with unit core extraction and Incremental SAT

1. $F" = \bigwedge_{i=0}^{k-1} T(S_i, S_{i+1}) \wedge \neg P_k$
2. **Insert** $F' = F" \wedge (\bigwedge_{v' \in Free} Assign(v'))$ **into clause database**
3. for each $v \in Free$
4.   **delete** $Assign(v)$ **from clause database**
5.   if(SAT_Solve(F')==UNSATISFIABLE)
6. R=Unit_Core(v)
7. $Free = Free \cap R$
8.   **For each** $v' \in Free - R$
9.   **delete** $Assign(v')$ **from clause database**
10.   else
11.   **Insert** $Assign(v)$ **into clause database**
12. $Free$ is the minimization set

In step 8 and 9 of algorithm 4, according to N. Een's conclusion [12] stated above, we can simply delete all such $Assign(v')$, and no need to delete any learned clauses.

Thus, This mechanism improves performance in 2 aspects:

1. Learned clauses can be share between similar instances, to avoid searching overlapped state space repeatedly.
2. No need to waste time on deleting learned clauses.

5   Experiment Result

K Ravi[5] only presents the circuits that used to generate counterexample, but has not presented the assertion used. Therefore, we can't compare our result with his one directly. So we implement K Ravi's two-stages algorithm and ours in zchaff[10], such that we can compare them with same circuits and assertions.

We use NuSMV[9] to generate deep counterexample in the following way:

1. Perform a symbolic simulation to generate a state sequence $S_0, ..., S_k$.
2. Use "S_k can not be reach" as an assertion, and put it into BMC package of NuSMV[9] to obtain a counterexample shorter than k.

We perform counterexample minimization with K Ravi's two-stages algorithm[5] and our algorithm. The timeout limit is set to 10000 seconds.

5.1   Experiment Result of K Ravi's Two Stages Approach

Because K Ravi's approach includes two stages, so we first present its result in table 1. The 1st column are the circuits used to generate counterexample. The 2nd column presents the length of counterexample. The 3rd column presents number of free variables.

The 4th column is the number of variables eliminated by first stage of K Ravi's approach, the 5th column is the run time overhead of first stage.

The 6th column is the number of variables eliminated by BFL, the second stage of K Ravi's approach, The 7th column is run time overhead of BFL.

According to table 1, most irrelevant variables are eliminated by first stage, with little run time overhead. But to further eliminate more irrelevant variables, the highly expensive BFL must be called. The run time overhead of BFL is 2 to 3 orders of magnitude larger than that of first stage.

In the last 2 rows of table 1, K Ravi's approach run out of time limit. To obtain the data in the 6th column, we incorporate incremental SAT into BFL, but without unit core extraction.

5.2   Comparing Result of Our Approach and That of K Ravi

Experiment result of our approach and that of K Ravi are presented in table 2. The 1st column are the circuits used to generate counterexample. The 2nd column presents the length of counterexample. The 3rd column present number of free variables.

Table 1. Experiment Result of K Ravi's Two Stage Approach.

Circuits	CE length	Free Vars	first stage		second stage	
			Eliminated Vars	Run time	Eliminated Vars	Run time
s1512	21	667	601	0.07	5	5.097
s1423	24	483	325	0.07	75	92.443
s3271	15	507	398	0.911	34	38.946
s3384	13	743	596	0.08	19	29.01
s3330	6	373	279	0.03	16	2.613
s5378	10	530	344	0.08	72	12.698
s9234	7	362	169	0.09	57	16.984
s13207	22	1352	977	0.581	132	4080.34
s38584	14	1621	1008	2.592	61	>10000
s38417	14	2029	909	1.365	71	>10000

Table 2. Experiment Result.

Circuits	CE length	Free Vars	Result of K Ravi[5]		Result of our approach		
			Eliminated Vars	Run time	Eliminated Vars	Run time	Speedup
s1512	21	667	606	5.167	606	3.45	1.50
s1423	24	483	400	92.513	397	7.12	12.99
s3271	15	507	432	39.857	432	6.11	6.52
s3384	13	743	615	29.09	615	9.61	3.02
s3330	6	373	295	2.643	295	1.77	1.49
s5378	10	530	416	12.778	411	8.21	1.56
s9234	7	362	226	17.074	226	10.36	1.65
s13207	22	1352	1109	4080.921	1093	153.92	26.51
s38584	14	1621	1069	>10000	1069	682.19	>10
s38417	14	2029	980	>10000	981	947.84	>10

The 4th column is the number of irrelevant free variables eliminated by the two stages of K Ravi's algorithm[5]. run time of the two stages of K Ravi's algorithm is shown in 5th column.

The 6th column is the number of irrelevant free variables eliminated by our approach. run time of our algorithm is shown in 7th column. The speedup compared to K Ravi's algorithm is shown in last column.

5.3 Run Time Statistics of Our Approach

In table 3, we present some run time statistics of our algorithm:

The first column is the name of circuits. The variables and clauses number of CNF files are presented in 2nd and 3rd column. Their number of free variables are presented in 4th column, the variable eliminated by unit core extraction in step 7 of algorithm 4 are presented in 5th column. The numbers of UNSATISFIABLE

Table 3. Run Time Statistics.

Circuits	Vars	Clauses	Free Vars	Eliminated by Unit_Core	Number of UNSAT	Number of SAT	Peak size of Q
s1512	14858	39735	667	601	5	61	397
s1423	16565	44248	483	369	29	85	736
s3271	21769	59656	507	416	16	75	448
s3384	19452	50353	743	596	19	128	458
s3330	6935	17322	373	278	17	78	321
s5378	16180	42415	530	387	24	119	484
s9234	18291	49555	362	173	53	136	581
s13207	107079	284839	1352	1025	68	259	1999
s38584	237756	661828	1621	1005	64	552	5119
s38417	211653	576324	2029	910	71	1048	7703

instances are presented in the 6th column. The numbers of SAT instances are presented in 7th column. The peak size of Q is presented in last column.

Relationship between these columns is:

4th column=5th column+6th column+7th column

5.4   Conclusion About Experiment Result

From these tables, we can conclude that:

1. In most case, our approach run much faster than K Ravi's algorithm;
2. According to last column of table 2, it is obvious that the more complex the counterexample, the higher the speedup. For the three most complex counterexample:s13207, s38584 and s38417, our approach is 1 order of magnitude faster than K Ravi's algorithm.
3. Our approach achieves this speedup without any lost in its ability to eliminate irrelevant variables;
4. From 5th column of table 3, most variables are eliminated by unit core extraction, and don't need to run SAT solver for them any more;
5. Compare last column of table 3 to 3rd column, the size of Q are much smaller than that of clause database.

6   Related Works

Our work are somewhat similar to SAT solution minimization of SAT-based image computation[2–4].

Ken.McMillan's approach [3] needs to construct an alternating implication graph rooted at input variables. With this graph, he eliminates irrelevant variables from SAT solution.

Hyeong-Ju Kang[4] assigns lower decision priority to next state variables, such that when the transition relation is satisfied, as many as possible next state variables are undecided.

P Chauhan[2] employs an ATPG-like approach to analyze the dependence relation between input variables and transition relation. And try to eliminate as many as possible next state variables from final solution.

Minimization of counterexamples is useful in the context of abstraction-refinement[1, 15]. Refinement is often more effective when it is based on the simultaneous elimination of a set of counterexamples rather than on elimination of one counterexample at a time.

There are also other approaches to minimize counterexample.

Jin[6] presents a game-based technique that partitions an error trace into fated segments, controlled by the environment attempting to force the system into an error, and free segments, controlled by the system attempting to avoid the error.

P. Gastin[13] proposes a length minimization approach for explicate state model checker SPIN, which tries to generate shorter counterexample.

Alex Groce[14] proposes a value minimization approach for C language. His approach tries to minimize the absolute value of typed variables of C language.

7   Conclusion

To make the counterexample easier to be understood, irrelevant variables must be eliminated. At the same time, minimized counterexamples can significantly improve the performance of many important verification algorithm.

K Ravi's algorithm is the most effective counterexample minimization algorithm. However, its time overhead is too large.

Therefore, we propose a faster counterexample minimization algorithm in this paper. Our algorithm is 1 order of magnitude faster than K Ravi's algorithm without any lost in its ability to eliminate irrelevant variables;

In this paper we only due with path like counterexample of safety assertion, we would also like to address minimization of loop-like counterexample in future work.

References

1. E. Clarke, A. Gupta, J. Kukula, and O. Strichman. SAT based abstraction-refinement using ILP and machine learning. In E. Brinksma and K. G. Larsen, editors, Fourteenth Conference on Computer Aided Verification (CAV 2002), pages 265-279. Springer-Verlag, July 2002.LNCS 2404.
2. Pankaj Chauhan, Edmund M. Clarke, Daniel Kroening, Using SAT based Image Computation for Reachability Analysis. technology report CMU-CS-03-151, School of Computer Science ,Carnegie Mellon University, September 2003
3. K. L. McMillan. Applying SAT methods in unbounded symbolic model checking. In E. Brinksma and K. G. Larsen, editors, Fourteenth Conference on Computer Aided Verification (CAV'02), pages 250-264. Berlin, July 2002. LNCS 2404.
4. Hyeong-Ju Kang and In-Cheol Park,SAT-Based Unbounded Symbolic Model Checking,In Proceeding of DAC 2003,Anaheim, California, USA, June 2-6, 2003.

5. Kavita Ravi and Fabio Somenzi. Minimal Assignments for Bounded Model Checking. In Tenth International Conference on Tools and Algorithms For the Construction and Analysis of Systems (TACAS'04),pages 31-45 , 2004. LNCS 2988.

6. H.Jin, K.Ravi,and F.Somenzi. "Fate and free will in error traces". In 8th International Conference on Tools and Algorithms For the Construction and Analysis of Systems(TACAS 2002), pages 445-458, 2002.LNCS 2280.

7. A. Biere, A. Cimatti, E.M. Clarke, M. Fujita, Y. Zhu . "Symbolic Model Checking using SAT procedures instead of BDDs".In Proceedings of the 36th Conference on Design Automation(DAC1999).pages 317-320, 1999.

8. L.Zhang, C.Madigan, M.Moskewicz, and S.Malik. Efficient conflict driven learning in a Boolean satisfiability solver. ICCAD 2001.

9. A. Cimatti, E. M. Clarke, E. Giunchiglia, F. Giunchiglia, M. Pistore, M. Roveri, R. Sebastiani and A. Tacchella. "NuSMV 2: An OpenSource Tool for Symbolic Model Checking". In 14th International Conference on Computer Aided Verification(CAV 2002),pages 359-364 , Copenhagen, Denmark, July 27-31, 2002.LNCS 2404

10. M. Moskewicz, C. F. Madigan, Y. Zhao, L. Zhang, and S. Malik. Chaff: Engineering an efficient SAT solver. In Proceedings of the Design Automation Conference, pages 530-535,Las Vegas, NV, June 2001.

11. http://www.cbl.ncsu.edu/CBL_Docs/iscas89.html

12. N. Een and N. Sorensson. Temporal Induction by Incremental SAT Solving. In Proc. of the First International Workshop on Bounded Model Checking, 2003.

13. P. Gastin, P. Moro, and M. Zeitoun. Minimization of counterexamples in spin.In SPIN Workshop on Model Checking of Software, pages 92-108, 2004.

14. Alex Groce , Daniel Kroening. Making the Most of BMC Counterexamples. the second international workshop on Bounded Model Checking(BMC 2004), to appear

15. Marcelo Glusman, Gila Kamhi, Sela Mador-Haim, Ranan Fraer, and Moshe Y. Vardi,Multiple-Counterexample Guided Iterative Abstraction Refinement: An Industrial Evaluation. In 9th International Conference on Tools and Algorithms For the Construction and Analysis of Systems(TACAS 2003)

16. L. Zhang and S. Malik. Validating sat solvers using an independent resolution-based checker: Practical implementations and other applications. In Proceedings of Design Automation and Test in Europe (DATE2003),2003.

17. E. Goldberg and Y. Novikov. Verification of proofs of unsatisfiability for cnf formulas. In Proceedings of Design Automation and Test in Europe (DATE2003),2003.

I/O Efficient Directed Model Checking

Shahid Jabbar and Stefan Edelkamp

Department of Computer Science
Baroper Str. 301
University of Dortmund, Dortmund, Germany
{shahid.jabbar,stefan.edelkamp}@cs.uni-dortmund.de

Abstract. Directed model checking has proved itself to be a useful technique in reducing the state space of the problem graph. But still, its potential is limited by the available memory. This problem can be circumvented by the use of secondary storage devices to store the state space. This paper discusses directed best-first search to enhance error detection capabilities of model checkers like SPIN by using a streamed access to secondary storage. We explain, how to extend SPIN to allow external state access, and how to adapt heuristic search algorithms to ease error detection for this case. We call our derivate IO-HSF-SPIN. In the theoretical part of the paper, we extend the heuristic-based external searching algorithm to general weighted and directed graphs. We conduct experiments with some challenging protocols in Promela syntax like GIOP and dining philosophers and have succeeded in solving some hard instances externally.

1 Introduction

Model checking [3] has evolved into one of the most successful verification techniques. Examples range from mainstream applications such as protocol validation, software and embedded systems' verification to exotic areas such as business work-flow analysis, scheduler synthesis and verification.

There are two primary approaches to model checking. *Symbolic model checking* [2] uses a representation for the state set based on boolean formulae and decision diagrams. Property validation amounts to some form of symbolic fix-point computation. *Explicit-state model checking* uses an explicit representation of the system's global state graph. Property validation amounts to a partial or complete exploration of the state space. The success of model checking lies in its potential for *push-button* automation and in its error reporting capabilities. A model checker performs an automated complete exploration of the state space of a model, usually applying a depth-first search strategy. When a property violating state is encountered, the search stack contains an error trail that leads from an initial system state to the encountered state. This error trail greatly helps engineers in interpreting validation results.

The sheer size of the reachable state space of realistic models imposes tremendous challenges on the algorithm design for model checking technology. Complete exploration of the state space is often impossible, and approximations are needed. Also, the error trails reported by depth-first search model checkers are often exceedingly lengthy – in many cases they consist of multiple thousands of computation steps which greatly

R. Cousot (Ed.): VMCAI 2005, LNCS 3385, pp. 313–329, 2005.

hampers error interpretation. The use of *directed model checking* [6] renders erstwhile unanalyzable problems analyzable in many instances. The quality of the results obtained with heuristic search algorithms like A* [9] depends on the quality of the heuristic estimate. Various heuristic estimates have been devised that are specific for the validation of concurrent software, such as specific estimates for reaching deadlock states.

Nonetheless, the search spaces that are generated during the automated verification process are often too large to fit into main memory. One solution studied in this paper is external exploration. In this case, during the algorithm only a part of the graph is processed at a time; the remainder is stored on a disk. The block-wise access to secondary memory has led to a growing attention to the design of *I/O-efficient* algorithms in recent years. Algorithms that explicitly manage the memory hierarchy can lead to substantial speedups, since they are more informed to predict and adjust future memory access.

In this paper, we address explicit model checking on secondary memory. First we recall the most widely used computation model to design and analyze external memory algorithms. This model provides a basis to analyze external memory algorithms by counting the data transfers between different levels of memory hierarchy. Then, we recall *External A**, which extends delayed duplicate detection to heuristic search for the case of implicit (graph is generated on the fly), undirected, and unweighted graphs. In Section 4, we extend the External A* algorithm for the case of directed and weighted implicit graphs - a usual case with state space graphs that appear in model checking. Weighted graphs introduce new issues to the problem. One of the main issue is the presence of negative weights in the graph. These issues are also dealt with further in this section along with proofs of optimality for these extensions.

The second part of the paper mainly deals with practical aspects of external model checking. For the implementation of our algorithms, we chose the experimental model checker HSF-SPIN as the basis. HSF-SPIN (Section 5) extends SPIN by incorporating heuristics in the search procedure. It has shown a large performance gain in terms of expanded nodes in several protocols. We call our extension as IO-HSF-SPIN and is discussed in Sections 6. For the experiments, we choose three protocols in Promela syntax: Dining philosophers, Optical Telegraph, and CORBA-GIOP. In Section 7, we illustrate the efficiency of our approach on these protocols, by the sizes of problems that we have succeeded in solving. Finally, we address related and future work and draw conclusions. For the convenience of readers, an appendix is set at the end of the paper that discusses the proofs of some of the key theorems referenced in this paper.

2   I/O Efficient Algorithms

The commonly used model for comparing the performance of external algorithms [18] consists of a single processor, a small internal memory that can hold up to M data items, and an unlimited secondary memory. The size of the input problem (in terms of the number of records) is abbreviated by N. Moreover, the *block size B* governs the bandwidth of memory transfers. It is often convenient to refer to these parameters in terms of blocks, so we define $m = M/B$ and $n = N/B$. It is usually assumed that at the beginning of the algorithm, the input data is stored in contiguous block on external memory, and the same must hold for the output. Only the number of blocks' reads and writes are counted; computations in internal memory do not incur any cost. An extension of the model considers D disks that can be accessed simultaneously. When using disks in parallel, the technique of *disk striping* can be employed to essentially increase the block size by a factor of D. Successive blocks are distributed across different disks.

It is often convenient to express the complexity of external-memory algorithms using a number of frequently occurring primitive operations. The simplest operation is *scanning*, which means reading a stream of records stored consecutively on secondary memory. In this case, it is trivial to exploit disk- and block-parallelism. The number of I/Os is $\Theta(\frac{N}{DB}) = \Theta(\frac{n}{D})$. We abbreviate this quantity with $scan(N)$. Algorithms for external *sorting* fall into two categories: those based on the *merging* and those based on the *distribution* paradigm. It has been shown that external sorting can be done with $\Theta(\frac{N}{DB} \log_{M/B} \frac{N}{B}) = \Theta(\frac{n}{D} \log_m n)$ I/Os. We abbreviate this quantity with $sort(N)$.

3 External A*

In the following we study how to extend external exploration in A* search. The main advantage of A* with respect to other optimal exploration algorithms like breadth-first search or admissible depth-first search is that it traverses a smaller part of the search space to establish an optimal solution. In A*, the merit for state u is $f(u) = g(u) + h(u)$, with g being the cost of the path from the initial state to u and $h(u)$ being the estimate of the remaining cost from u to the goal. The new value $f(v)$ of a successor v of u is $f(v) = g(v) + h(v) = g(u) + w(u, v) + h(v) = f(u) + w(u, v) - h(u) + h(v)$. We first assume an undirected unweighted state space problem graph, and a *consistent* heuristic, where for all u and v we have, $w(u, v) \geq h(u) - h(v)$. These restrictions are often met in AI search practice. In this case we have $h(u) \leq h(v) + 1$ for every state u and every successor v of u. Since the problem graph is undirected this implies $|h(u) - h(v)| \leq 1$ so that $h(v) - h(u) \in \{-1, 0, 1\}$. This implies that the evaluation function f is monotonic non-decreasing. No successor will have a smaller f-value than the current one. Therefore, the A* algorithm, which traverses the state set in f-order, does not need to perform any *re-opening* strategy.

External A* [5] maintains the search horizon on disk. The priority queue data structure is represented as a list of buckets ordered first by their $h + g$ value and then by the g value. In the course of the algorithm, each bucket $Open(i, j)$ will contain all states u with path length $g(u) = i$ and heuristic estimate $h(u) = j$. As same states have same heuristic estimates it is easy to restrict duplicate detection to buckets of the same h-value. By an assumed undirected state space problem graph structure we can restrict aspirants for duplicate detection furthermore. If all duplicates of a state with g-value i are removed with respect to the levels i, $i - 1$ and $i - 2$, then there will remain no duplicate state for the entire search process. We consider each bucket for the $Open$ list as a different file that has an individual internal buffer. A bucket is *active* if some of its states are currently expanded or generated. If a buffer becomes full then it is flushed to disk. Fig. 1 depicts the pseudo-code of the *External A** algorithm. The algorithm maintain the two values g_{min} and f_{min} to address the correct buckets. The buckets of f_{min} are traversed for increasing g_{min} unless the g_{min} exceeds f_{min}. Due to the increase of the g_{min}-value in the f_{min} bucket, an active bucket is closed when all its successors

Procedure *External A**
> $Open(0, h(\mathcal{I})) \leftarrow \{\mathcal{I}\}$
> $f_{\min} \leftarrow h(\mathcal{I})$
> **while** $(f_{\min} \neq \infty)$
>> $g_{\min} \leftarrow \min\{i \mid Open(i, j) \neq \emptyset, i + j = f_{\min}\}$
>> $h_{\max} \leftarrow f_{\min} - g_{\min}$
>> **while** $(g_{\min} \leq f_{\min})$
>>> **if** $(h_{\max} = 0$ **and** $Open(g_{\min}, h_{\max})$ *contains terminal state* $u)$
>>>> **return** *path*(u)
>>> $A(f_{\min}), A(f_{\min} + 1), A(f_{\min} + 2) \leftarrow succ(Open(g_{\min}, h_{\max}))$
>>> $A'(f_{\min}), A'(f_{\min} + 1), A'(f_{\min} + 2) \leftarrow$
>>>> *remove duplicates from* $(A(f_{\min}), A(f_{\min} + 1), A(f_{\min} + 2))$
>>> $Open(g_{\min} + 1, h_{\max} + 1) \leftarrow A'(f_{\min} + 2) \cup Open(g_{\min} + 1, h_{\max} + 1)$
>>> $Open(g_{\min} + 1, h_{\max}) \leftarrow A'(f_{\min} + 1) \cup Open(g_{\min} + 1, h_{\max})$
>>> $Open(g_{\min} + 1, h_{\max} - 1) \leftarrow (A'(f_{\min}) \cup Open(g_{\min} + 1, h_{\max} - 1)) \setminus$
>>>> $(Open(g_{\min} - 1, h_{\max} - 1) \cup Open(g_{\min}, h_{\max} - 1))$
>>> $g_{\min} \leftarrow g_{\min} + 1$
>> $f_{\min} \leftarrow \min\{i + j > f_{\min} \mid Open(i, j) \neq \emptyset\} \cup \{\infty\}$

Fig. 1. *External A** for consistent heuristics.

have been generated. Given $f_{\min}$ and $g_{\min}$ the corresponding h-value is determined by $h_{\max} = f_{\min} - g_{\min}$. According to their different h-values, successors are arranged into three different horizon lists $A(f_{\min})$, $A(f_{\min} + 1)$, and $A(f_{\min} + 2)$. Duplicate elimination is delayed.

Since *External A** simulates A* and changes only the order of elements to be expanded that have the same f-value, completeness and optimality are inherited from the properties of A*. The I/O complexity for External A* in an implicit unweighted and undirected graph with a consistent estimates is bounded by $O(sort(|E|) + scan(|V|))$, where $|V|$ and $|E|$ are the number of nodes and edges in the explored subgraph of the state space problem graph. If we additionally have $|E| = O(|V|)$, the complexity reduces to $O(sort(|V|))$ I/Os.

We establish the solution path by backward chaining from starting with the target state. There are two main options. Either we store predecessor information with each state on disk or, more elegantly, we for a state in depth g intersect the set of possible predecessors with the buckets of depth $g-1$. Any state that is in the intersection is reachable on an optimal solution path, so that we can recur. The time complexity is bounded by the scanning time of all buckets in consideration and surely in $O(scan(|V|))$. It has been shown [5] that the lower bound for the I/O complexity for delayed duplicate bucket elimination in an implicit unweighted and undirected graph A* search with consistent estimates is at least $\Omega(sort(|V|))$.

4   General Graphs

So far, we have looked at uniformly weighted graphs only. However, in practical model checking, the transition systems that are encountered are often directed. Also, validation of softwares and communication protocols often contains atomic regions. Atomic region corresponds to a block of statements that should be executed without the intervention of any other process. Atomic regions are represented in the general state graph as arcs with weights equal to the number of instructions in the atomic region. This motivates the generalization of graph search algorithms for non-uniformly weighted directed graphs. Later in this section, we discuss the effect of introducing heuristics in these algorithms.

We define, $w : E \rightarrow I\!R$ as the weight function for edges; the *weight* or *cost* of a path $p = (s = v_0, \ldots, v_k = v)$ can then be defined as $w(p) = \sum_{i=1}^{k} w(v_{i-1}, v_i)$. Path p is called *optimal path* if its weight is minimal among all paths between s and v; in this case, its cost is called the *shortest path distance* $\delta(s, v)$. The *optimal solution path cost* is abbreviated as $\delta(s, T) = \min\{t \in T \mid \delta(s, t)\}$, with T being the set of target states.

4.1 Directed Graphs

As seen above, undirected and unweighted graphs require to look at one previous and one successor layer only. For directed graphs, the efficiency of external algorithms is dependent on the duplicate elimination scope or *locality of the search*. The locality of a directed search graph is defined as $\max\{\delta(s, u) - \delta(s, v), 0\}$ for all nodes u, v, with v being a successor of u. In other words, locality determines the *thickness* of the layer of nodes needed to prevent duplicates in the search. It has been analyzed in the context of the *breadth-first heuristic search*.

Theorem 1. *[24] The number of previous layers of the graph that need to be retained to prevent duplicate search effort is equal to the locality of the state space graph.*

As a consequence, in undirected unweighted graphs, the locality is one and we need to store the immediate previous layer only, to check for duplicates.

Lemma 1. *For undirected, but weighted graphs the locality is smaller than or equal to the maximum edge weight $C = \max_{e \in E} w(e)$ in the state space graph.*

Proof. By the triangle inequality for shortest paths, we have $\delta(x, y) + \delta(y, z) \geq \delta(x, z)$ for all nodes x, y, z in the state space graph. For all $v \in succ(u)$ we have

$$\delta(s, u) - \delta(s, v) = \delta(u, s) - \delta(v, s) \leq \delta(u, v) \leq w(u, v).$$

Lemma 2. *Let D be the cost of the largest cycle in the state space graph. Then the locality of the state space graph is smaller than D.*

Proof. Let $\delta(v, u)$ be the smallest cost to get back from v to u in the global state space graph with $v \in succ(u)$. We have that $\delta(s, u) - \delta(s, v) \leq \delta(v, u)$ using the triangular property of shortest paths, so that $\max_{u, v \in succ(u)}\{\delta(s, u) - \delta(s, v)\} \leq \max_{u, v \in succ(u)} \delta(v, u) < D$.

In model checking, the global transition system is often composed of smaller components, called devices, processes or threads. For example, in the verification of software [1], the state space consists of the cross product of local state spaces, together with some additional information, e.g., on communication queues or global variables. As the product of the local state spaces is asynchronous, only one transition in one process is executed at a time.

Using asynchronism, we have that $\max_{u,v \in succ(u)} \delta(v, u)$, in the global state space graph is bounded from below by $\max_{u',v' \in succ(u')} \delta(v', u')$ in any local state space graph. Each cycle in the global state space is actually consists of local cycles in the local state spaces.

Lemma 3. *Let* $p_1, \ldots, p_k$ *be the processes in the system. If we denote* D_i *as the cost of the largest cycle in the graph representation of process* p_i, $i \in \{1, \ldots, k\}$. *Then we have that the locality is bounded by* $D_1 + \ldots + D_k$.

Proof. Let c be the largest cycle in the global state space graph with $w(c) = D$. As it decomposes into cycles $c_1 \ldots, c_k$ in the local state space graphs of the processes $p_1, \ldots, p_k$, we have that $D \leq w(c_1) + \ldots + w(c_k) \leq D_1 + \ldots + D_k$.

Even if the number of stored layers $b \geq 2$ is less than the locality of the graph, the number of times a node can be re-opened in breadth-first search is only linear in the depth of the search. This contrasts the exponential number of re-openings for linear-space depth-first search strategies.

Theorem 2. *[24] The worst-case number of times a node* u *can be re-opened is bounded by* $\lfloor (\delta(s, T) - \delta(s, u))/b \rfloor$.

If the locality is lesser than b, a breadth-first search algorithm does not need to consider re-openings of nodes at all.

4.2 Positive Weights

To compute the shortest path in weighted graphs, Dijkstra [4] proposed a greedy search strategy based on the *principle of optimality* $\delta(s, v) = \min_{v \in succ(u)} \{\delta(s, u) + w(u, v)\}$. That is, the minimum distance from s to v is equal to the minimum of the sum of the distance from s to a predecessor u of v, plus the edge weight between u and v. This equation implies that any sub-path of an optimal path is itself optimal.

The exploration algorithm maintains an estimate of the minimum distance, more precisely, an upper bound $f(u)$ on $\delta(s, u)$ for each node u; initially set to ∞, $f(u)$ is successively decreased until it is equal to $\delta(u, v)$. From this point on, it remains constant throughout the rest of the algorithm. As the exploration of the problem graph is *implicit*, we additionally maintain a list *Closed* to store expanded nodes. The node relaxation procedure for a single-state algorithm, as opposed to the algorithms that work on sets of states, is shown in Fig. 2.

The correctness argument of the algorithm is based on the fact that for a node u with minimum f-value in *Open*, f is *correct*, i.e., $f(u) = \delta(s, u)$. Hence, when a node $t \in T$ is selected for removal from the *Open*, we have $f(t) = \delta(s, T)$. Moreover, if the weight function of a problem graph is strictly positive and if the weight of every infinite path is infinite, then Dijkstra's algorithm terminates with an optimal solution.

Procedure Relax
   if $(Search(Open, v))$
      if $(f(u) + w(u, v) < f(v))$
         $DecreaseKey(Open, v, f(u) + w(u, v))$
   else
      if not $(Search(Closed, v))$
         $Insert(Open, v, f(u) + w(u, v))$

Fig. 2. Node relaxation in implicit Dijkstra's algorithm.

4.3 Re-weighting

A heuristic h can be incorporated into Dijkstra's algorithm by a *re-weighting* transformation of the implicit search graph. The re-weighting function $\hat{w}(u, v)$ is defined as $\hat{w}(u, v) = w(u, v) - h(u) + h(v)$. If the heuristic is not consistent, re-weighting introduces negative weights into the problem graph. It is not difficult to obtain the following result.

Theorem 3. *Let $G = (V, E, w)$ be a weighted graph, and $h : V \to I\!R$ be a heuristic function. Let $\delta(s, t)$ be the length of the shortest path from s to t in the original graph and $\hat{\delta}(s, t)$ be the corresponding value in the re-weighted graph.*

1. *We have $w(p) = \delta(s, t)$, if and only if $\hat{w}(p) = \hat{\delta}(s, t)$, i.e., if p is the shortest path in the original graph, then p is also the shortest path in the re-weighted graph.*
2. *G has no negative weighted cycles with respect to w if and only if it has none with respect to $\hat{w}$.*

Proof. For proving the first assertion, let $p = (s = v_0, \dots, v_k = t)$ be any path from the start node s to a goal node t. We have $\hat{w}(p) = \sum_{i=1}^{k} (w(v_{i-1}, v_i) - h(v_{i-1}) + h(v_i)) = w(p) - h(v_0)$. Assume that there is a path p' with $\hat{w}(p') < \hat{w}(p)$ and $w(p') \geq w(p)$. Then $w(p') - h(v_0) < w(p) - h(v_0)$; resulting in $w(p') < w(p)$, a contradiction. The other direction is dealt with analogously.

For the second assertion, let $c = (v_0, \dots, v_l = v_0)$ be any cycle in G. Then we have $\hat{w}(c) = w(c) + h(v_l) - h(v_0) = w(c)$.   □

The equation $h(u) \leq h(v) + w(u, v)$ is equivalent to $\hat{w}(u, v) = h(v) - h(u) + w(u, v) \geq 0$. Hence, a consistent heuristic yields a first A* variant of the algorithm of Dijkstra. It sets $f(s)$ to $h(s)$ for the initial node s and updates $f(v)$ with $f(u) + \hat{w}(u, v)$ instead of $f(u) + w(u, v)$ each time a node is selected. Since the shortest path p_t remains invariant through re-weighting, if $t \in T$ is selected from *Open*, we have

$$f(t) = \hat{\delta}(s, t) + h(s) = \hat{w}(p_t) + h(s) = w(p_t) = \delta(s, t).$$

4.4 Graphs with Edges of Negative Weight

Unfortunately, Dijkstra's algorithm fails on graphs with negative edge weights. As a simple example consider the graph consisting of three nodes with $w(s, u) = 4$,

Procedure Relax
  if $(Search(Open, v))$
     if $(f(u) + w(u, v) < f(v))$
        $DecreaseKey(Open, v, f(u) + w(u, v))$
  else if $(Search(Closed, v))$
     if $(f(u) + w(u, v) \leq f(v))$
        $Delete(Closed, v)$
        $Insert(Open, v, f(u) + w(u, v))$
  else
     $Insert(Open, v, f(u) + w(u, v))$

Fig. 3. An node relaxation with re-opening that copes with negative edge weight.

$w(s, v) = 5$, and $w(v, u) = -2$, for which the algorithm of Dijkstra computes $\delta(s, u) = 4$ instead of the correct value $\delta(s, u) = 3$. The problem can be dealt with by *re-opening* already expanded node. The corresponding node relaxation procedure is shown in Fig. 3.

The following result was shown in the context of *route planning* [8], and is fundamental to prove the correctness of A* derivate.

Theorem 4. *[8] Let* $G = (V, E, w)$ *be a weighted graph and* f *be the cost of the shortest path so far for a particular node from the start node* s *in the modified algorithm of Dijkstra. At each selection of a node* u *from* Open, *we have the following invariant: Let* $p = (s = v_0, \ldots, v_n = t)$ *be a least-cost path from the start node* s *to a goal node* $t \in T$. *Application of* Relax *preserves the following invariant:*

(I) *Unless* v_n *is in* Closed *with* $f(v_n) = \delta(s, v_n)$, *there is a node* v_i *in* Open *such that* $f(v_i) = \delta(s, v_i)$, *and no* $j > i$ *exists such that* v_j *is in* Closed *with* $f(v_j) = \delta(s, v_j)$.

In short, at least we can be certain that there is one *good* node with perfect node evaluation in the *Open* list, that can be extended to an optimal solution path.

To optimize secondary storage accesses, expansions can be performed more efficiently if a particular order is selected. Invariant (I) is not dependent on the order that is present in the *Open* list.

In Fig. 4 we give a pseudo-code implementation for the node-ordering scheme. In contrast to Dijkstra's algorithm, reaching the first goal node will no longer guarantee optimality of the established solution path. Hence, the algorithm has to continue until the *Open* list runs empty. By storing and updating the current best solution path length as a global upper bound value α, it improves the solution quality over time.

Admissible heuristics are lower bounds, i.e. $h(u) \leq \delta(u, T)$ in the original graph. This corresponds to $0 \leq \hat{\delta}(u, T)$ in the re-weighted graph.

Theorem 5. *[8] If* $\delta(u, T) \geq 0$, *then the general node-ordering algorithm is optimal.*

But in model checking practice, we observe that non-admissible heuristics could appear. For example, the seemingly admissible heuristic *Active Processes* that for a given state identifies the number of active processes turned out to be non-admissible for

Procedure Node-Ordering
  $Closed \leftarrow \{\}$; $Open \leftarrow \{s\}$;
  $\alpha \leftarrow \infty$; $best \leftarrow \emptyset$
  while $(Open \neq \emptyset)$
      $u \leftarrow Select(Open)$
      $Open \leftarrow Open \setminus \{u\}$; $Closed \leftarrow Closed \cup \{u\}$
      if $(f(u) > \alpha)$ **continue**
      if $(terminal(u)$ **and** $f(u) < \alpha)$
          $\alpha \leftarrow f(u)$; $best \leftarrow path(u)$
      else
              for all v **in** $succ(u)$
                  $Relax(u, v)$
  return $best$

Fig. 4. Relaxing the node expansion order.

some domains. Let's take the example of dining philosphers with deadlock detection. Assume that there are 2 philosophers A and B and both are thinking. This gives the number of active processes as 2. Now, A picks up her/his right fork. Since the left fork is still on the table, both A and B are still non-blocked. For the second move, let's assume that B picks up her/his right fork. This move blocks both A and B; resulting in the sudden decrease of number of active processes from 2 to 0. A heuristic is said to be admissible if it never overestimates the actual path cost. Here, with just one move we reached the deadlock as apposed to the heuristic estimate 2, implying that the heuristic was non-admissible.

As we saw that there are non-admissible heuristics, used in model checking, the re-weighted graph we will have $\delta(u, T) < 0$, implying that we cannot apply the above theorem. To further guarantee cost optimality of the solution, we have to extend the pruning criterion. It is not difficult to show that if we drop the criterion "*if* $(f(u) > \alpha)$ **continue**" then the algorithm is optimal for all re-weighted graph structures. We can prove slightly more.

Theorem 6. *If we set $f(u) + \delta(u, T) > \alpha$ as the pruning condition in the node ordering algorithm, then the algorithm is optimal.*

Proof. Upon termination, each node inserted into *Open* must have been selected at least once. Suppose that invariant (I) is preserved in each loop, i.e., there is always a node v in the *Open* list on an optimal path with $f(v) = \delta(s, v)$. Thus the algorithm cannot terminate without eventually selecting the goal node on this path, and since by definition, it is not more expensive than any found solution path and *best* maintains the currently shortest path, an optimal solution will be returned. It remains to show that the invariant (I) holds in each iteration. If the extracted node u is not equal to v there is nothing to show. Otherwise $f(u) = \delta(s, u)$. The bound α denotes the currently best solution length. If $f(u) + \delta(u, T) \leq \alpha$ no pruning takes place. On the other hand $f(u) + \delta(u, T) > \alpha$ leads to a contradiction since $\delta(s, T) = \delta(s, u) + \delta(u, T) = f(u) + \delta(u, T) > \alpha \geq \delta(s, T)$. $\square$

Unfortunately, we do not know the value of $\delta(s, T)$, so the only thing that we can do is to take a lower bound to it. Since h that has been used earlier on is not admissible, we need a different bound or condition. For the original graph, it is easy to see that all nodes that have a larger path cost value than the obtained solution path cannot lead to a better solution, since the weights in the original graph are non-negative. Consequently, if $g(u)$ denotes the path length from s to u, $g(u) > \alpha$ is one pruning condition that we can apply in the original graph.

5   Explicit-State Model Checking in SPIN and HSF-SPIN

SPIN [10] is probably the most prominent explicit state model checking tool. Models are specified in its input language Promela. The language is well-suited to specify communication protocols, but has also been used for a wide range of other verification tasks. The model checker transforms the input into an internal automata representation, which, in turn, is enumerated by its exploration engine. Several efficiency aspects ranging from partial-order reduction to bit-state hashing enhance the exploration process. The parser produces sources that encode states and state transitions in native C code. These are linked together with the validation module to allow exploration of the model. The graphical user interface XSPIN allows to code the model, run the validator, show the internal automata representation, and simulate traces with message sequence charts.

Our own experimental model checker HSF-SPIN [6] is a compatible extension to SPIN. Additionally it incorporates directed search in explicit state model checking. The tool has been designed to allow different search algorithms by providing a general state expanding subroutine. In its current implementation it provides depth-first and breadth-first search as well as heuristic search algorithms like best-first search, A* and IDA*, and local search algorithms like hill-climbing and genetic algorithms. Partial order and symmetry reduction have been successfully combined with this portfolio [16, 15]. HSF-SPIN can handle a significant fraction of Promela and deals with the same input and output formats as SPIN. Heuristic search in HSF-SPIN combines positively with automated abstractions in form of abstraction databases.

The internal representation of a state consists of two parts. The first part contains information necessary for the search algorithms. This includes the estimated value for the state to the goal, the cost of the current optimal path to the state, a link to the predecessor state and information about the transition that lead to the state. The second part contains the representation of the state of the system and is usually called state vector. This part is represented similarly as in SPIN. Few modifications were, however, necessary due to technical details. Basically, the state vector contains the value of the variables and the local state of each process.

The expansion function is a fundamental component of the verifier. Actually, it was the component of HSF-SPIN that required most of the implementation efforts. It takes the representation of a state as input and returns a list containing each successor state. The use of this function in each search algorithm implies that the implementation of the depth-first search is not the most efficient.

All heuristic functions return a positive integer value for a given state. Some of them profit from information gathered before the verification starts. For example, the FSM distance estimate requires to run the all-pairs shortest path algorithm on the state transition graph of each process type. On the other hand, the deadlock inferring approach allows the user to determine explicitly which states have to be considered as potentially blocking by labeling statements in the model.

6   From HSF-Spin to IO-HSF-SPIN

Although theoretically simple, the practical extension of an existing explicit model checker like SPIN to external search is not trivial, and poses a lot of subtle implementation problems. In an external model it is required that the algorithm should be capable of writing any intermediate result to the disk, reading it again at any point of time in the future, and reusing it like it remained in the main memory. This requirement turned out to be a non-trivial one in order to adapt SPIN for external model checking. As described above, SPIN's state consists of two parts: state's information and the state vector. The state vector can be viewed as a sequence of active processes and message queues, describing the actual state of the system being checked.

SPIN is highly optimized for efficiency and hence uses a lot of global variables. These global variables are used to store the meta information about the state vector. This meta information consists of the address information of processes and queues in the state vector. Since the information about actual addresses would be void once a state has been flushed to the disk and retrieved back to a new memory address, we suggested to save the information that can *reset* the global variables to work on the new location of the state vector. We identified that with the order and type of each element in the state vector in hand, we can reset all the global variables. This motivates us to extend the state's description.

The new state's description S can be viewed as a 4-tuple, $(M, \sigma, \kappa, \tau)$, where M is the information about the state, e.g., its g and h values, size of the state vector, etc., σ is the state vector, and κ can be defined as $\kappa : \sigma \rightarrow \{Process, Queue\}$, i.e., given an element $\sigma_i \in \sigma$, κ identifies whether σ_i is a *Process* or a *Queue*. SPIN differentiates between different types of processes (resp. queues) by assigning an ID to each of them. If $\mathcal{P} = \{P_1, P_2, \ldots, P_n\}$ is the set of all processes and $\mathcal{Q} = \{Q_1, Q_2, \ldots, Q_m\}$ is the set of all queues, $\tau : \sigma_i \in \sigma \rightarrow \mathcal{P}$, if $\kappa(\sigma_i) = Process$ or $\tau : \sigma_i \in \sigma \rightarrow \mathcal{Q}$, otherwise.

We employed a two level memory architecture for storing the states. Initially all states are kept in the internal memory. An upper limit is defined on the maximum consumption of the internal memory available. If the total memory occupied by the stored states exceeds the maximum limit, the external memory management routines are invoked that flushes the excess states to the disk. The advantage of having a two-level memory management routine is to avoid the I/Os when the internal memory is sufficiently large for a particular problem.

A $bucket(i, j)$ is represented internally by a fixed size buffer. When the buffer gets full, it is sorted and flushed to the disk by appending it at the end of the corresponding file. Duplicates removal is then done in two stages. First, an external merge and compaction of the sorted flushed buffers that removes all the duplicates in the file is performed. Second, the files of the top layers with the same h values but smaller g values are subtracted from the resulting file. The number of top layers that are checked depends on the locality of the graph, as explained earlier.

Consequently, the reading of states for expansion is done by copying a part of the external bucket file to the corresponding internal buffer. Once the whole buffer is scanned and the successors are generated for all the states within the buffer, the next part of the file is read in the same buffer. The process continues until the file is completely read.

7 Experiments

We choose three classical and challenging protocol models namely, dining philosophers, optical telegraph and CORBA-GIOP for our experiments. The property to search for is the *deadlock* property. We employed the number of active processes as the heuristics to guide the exploration. For each experiment we report, the solution depth d, number of stored nodes s, number of expansions e, number of transitions t, and the space requirement of the stored nodes $Space$. The experiments are performed on a 4 processors Sun Ultra Sparc running Solaris operating system and using GCC 2.95 as the compiler. Additionally, symmetry reduction is employed in all experiments.

Table 1 presents the results for the deadlock detection for different instances of dining philosophers problem. The bottleneck in the dining philosopher's problem is not only the combinatorial explosion in the number of states but also the size of the states. As can be observed in the last column depicting the space requirement, the problem instance with 150 philosophers requires a storage space of 10.2 gigabytes, which is much higher than even the address limits of present micro computers.

The second domain is the optical telegraph model. We conducted experiments with different number of stations. The results are presented in Table 2.

Table 1. Deadlock Detection in Dining Philosophers.

N	d	s	e	t	Space (in gigabytes)
100	402	980,003	19,503	999,504	2.29
150	603	3,330,003	44,253	3,374,254	10.4

Table 2. Deadlock Detection in Optical Telegraph.

N	d	s	e	t	Space (in gigabytes)
5	33	10,874	4,945	24,583	0.0038
7	45	333,848	115,631	820,319	137
8	50	420,498	103,667	917,011	186
9	57	9,293,203	2,534,517	23,499,519	4.29

CORBA - GIOP [12] turned out to be one of the hardest models to verify because of its enormous state space. The reason is the high branching factor in the state space graph that results in the generation of a large number of states. The model takes two main parameters namely: the number of users N and the number of servers M with a range restriction of 1 to 4 on N and 1 to 2 on M. We have been able to solve all the

Table 3. Deadlock Detection in CORBA - GIOP.

N	M	d	s	e	t	Space (in gigabytes)
2	1	58	48,009	39,260	126,478	0.033
3	1	70	825,789	670,679	2,416,823	0.572
4	1	75	7,343,358	5,727,909	22,809,278	5.17
2	2	64	158,561	125,514	466,339	0.121
3	2	76	2,705,766	2,134,724	8,705,588	2.1
4	2	81	26,340,417	20,861,609	88,030,774	20.7

instances of the GIOP model especially the configuration with 4 users and 2 servers which requires a storage space of 20.7 gigabytes.

One of the main hurdles while running the experiments was the system limit on the number of file pointers that can be opened at a particular time. A large number of file pointers are the requirements while merging the sorted flushed buffers. For the files that needed file pointers more than the system limit, the experiments are re-run with larger internal buffer size that results in smaller number of large sorted buffers.

Summing up, the largest problem size reported to be solved by the first external model checker Murϕ [23] consisted of 1,021,464 states of 136 bytes each. This gives the overall space requirement of 0.129 gigabytes. With the presented approach, the largest problem size that we have been able to solve requires 20.7 gigabytes.

8   Conclusions

With this article we contribute the first theoretical and analytical study of I/O efficient directed model checking. In the theoretical part of the paper, we extended External A* to directed and weighted graphs. Through the process of re-weighting, we refer to some general results of node-ordering in the exploration of graphs with negative weights. We give different pruning conditions for node ordering algorithms for admissible and non-admissible heuristics. Moreover, we showed some necessary conditions on the locality of the graph to ease duplicate detection during the exploration. The concepts are then extended to the situation in model checking, where the global state space is composed of local transition graphs.

In the practical part of the paper, we have seen a non-trivial implementation to extend a state-of-the-art model checker SPIN to allow directed and external search. The first results on challenging benchmark protocols show that the external algorithms reduce the memory consumption, are sufficiently fast in practice, and have some further advantages by using a different node expansion order. It should be noted here that some of the hardest problems like GIOP and dining philosophers with scaled parameters that were not tractable earlier due to the internal memory requirements, have been solved for the first time. The present implementation is capable of coping with negative edges in the presence of inconsistent heuristic.

9   Related and Future Work

We are, however, not the first ones that look at the performance of model checkers on external devices. One of the first approaches toward this direction was proposed [23] in the context of the Murϕ validation tool. With a special algorithm disk instead of main memory is used for storing almost all of the state table at the cost of a small runtime penalty, which is typically around 15% when the memory savings factor is between one and two orders of magnitude. The algorithm linearizes the accesses to the state table and amortizes the cost of accessing the whole table over all the states in a breadth-first search level.

External breadth-first search for explicit graph structures that reside on disk has been introduced by [19]. It was improved to a sub-linear number of I/Os in [17]. Single-source shortest-pair algorithms that deal with explicit graphs stored on disk are surveyed in [18]. Delayed duplicate detection [14] adapts external BFS to implicit graphs. This extension to the External A* algorithm as proposed in [5] exploits the work of [24]. Zhou and Hansen [25] also worked on a different solution to apply external search for AI domains. They term their approach as *structured duplicate detection*, in which they use state space abstraction to establish which part of the search space can be externalized, and which part cannot.

Korf [13] also successfully extended delayed duplicate detection to best-first search and considered omission of the visited list as proposed in *frontier search*. In his proposal, it turned out that any 2 of the 3 options are compatible yielding the following set of algorithms: *breadth-first frontier search with delayed duplicate detection, best-first frontier search*, and *best-first search with external non-reduced closed list*. In the last case, the algorithm simulate a buffered traversal in a bucket-based priority queue. With External A* it turns out that one can combine all three approaches. In Korf's work, external sorting based on hash function partition is proposed. In summary, all external AI search approaches have independent contributions and can cooperate.

There is a tight connection between external and symbolic exploration algorithms. Both approaches consider sets of states instead of individual ones. It is apparent that the presented approach for an explicit state model checking will transfer to symbolic model checking. For example, in explicit graph theory, the external computation for the all-pair shortest path problem is studied in [22], while symbolic single-source and all-pair shortest path algorithms are considered in [20, 21]. As an interesting side effect, the symbolic algorithm of Bellman-Ford often outperformed Dijkstra's algorithm on symbolically represented graphs. For heuristic search, the splitting of the *Open*-list into buckets as seen in this text, corresponds to the fg-search method in the SetA* [11] version of the BDDA* algorithm [7]. However, refined considerations on the duplicate scope as presented here have not been studied. The implementation of an external directed search symbolic model checker is one of our future research goals.

Acknowledgments

The authors are supported by DFG in the projects ED 74/2 and ED 74/3. Thousands thanks to Alberto Lluch-Lafuente at University of Pisa for many detailed discussions on his implementation of HSF-SPIN and its possible extension. We are also grateful to Stefan Schrödl, with whom we developed the *External A** algorithm, and who is jointly responsible for some of the basic observations for the development of the node-ordering algorithm.

References

1. B. Bérard, A. F. M. Bidoit, F. Laroussine, A. Petit, L. Petrucci, P. Schoenebelen, and P. McKenzie. *Systems and Software Verification.* Springer, 2001.
2. J. R. Burch, E. M.Clarke, K. L. McMillian, and J. Hwang. Symbolic model checking: 1020 states and beyond. *Information and Computation,* 98(2):142–170, 1992.
3. E. Clarke, O. Grumberg, and D. Peled. *Model Checking.* MIT Press, 2000.
4. E.W. Dijkstra. A note on two problems in connection with graphs. *Numerische Mathematik,* 1:269–271, 1959.
5. S. Edelkamp, S. Jabbar, and S. Schroedl. External A*. In *German Conference on Artificial Intelligence (KI),* pages 226–240, 2004.
6. S. Edelkamp, S. Leue, and A. Lluch-Lafuente. Directed explicit-state model checking in the validation of communication protocols. *International Journal on Software Tools for Technology (STTT),* 2004.
7. S. Edelkamp and F. Reffel. OBDDs in heuristic search. In *German Conference on Artificial Intelligence (KI),* pages 81–92, 1998.
8. S. Edelkamp and S. Schrödl. Localizing A*. In *National Conference on Artificial Intelligence (AAAI),* pages 885–890, 2000.
9. P. E. Hart, N. J. Nilsson, and B. Raphael. A formal basis for heuristic determination of minimum path cost. *IEEE Transactions on on Systems Science and Cybernetics,* 4:100–107, 1968.
10. G. J. Holzmann. *Design and Validation of Computer Protocols.* Prentice Hall, 1990.
11. R. M. Jensen, R. E. Bryant, and M. M. Veloso. SetA*: An efficient BDD-based heuristic search algorithm. In *National Conference on Artificial Intelligence (AAAI),* 2002.
12. M. Kamel and S. Leue. Formalization and validation of the General Inter-ORB Protocol (GIOP) using PROMELA and SPIN. *International Journal on Software Tools for Technology Transfer,* 2(4):394–409, 2000.
13. R. Korf. Best-first frontier search with delayed duplicate detection. In *National Conference on Artificial Intelligence (AAAI),* pages 650–657, 2004.
14. R. E. Korf. Breadth-first frontier search with delayed duplicate detection. In *Workshop on Model Checking and Artificial Intelligence (MoChArt),* pages 87–92, 2003.
15. A. Lluch-Lafuente. Symmetry reduction and heuristic search for error detection in model checking. In *Model Checking and Artificial Intelligence (MoChArt-03),* 2003.
16. A. Lluch-Lafuente, S. Leue, and S. Edelkamp. Partial order reduction in directed model checking. In *Workshop on Model Checking Software (SPIN),* pages 112–127, 2002.
17. K. Mehlhorn and U. Meyer. External-memory breadth-first search with sublinear I/O. In *European Symposium on Algorithms (ESA),* pages 723–735, 2002.
18. U. Meyer, P. Sanders, and J. Sibeyn. *Memory Hierarchies.* Springer, 2003.
19. K. Munagala and A. Ranade. I/O-complexity of graph algorithms. In *Symposium on Discrete Algorithms (SODA),* pages 87–88, 2001.
20. D. Sawatzki. Experimental studies of symbolic shortest-path algorithms. In *Workshop on Algorithm Engineering (WAE),* pages 482–497, 2004.
21. D. Sawatzki. A symbolic approach to the all-pairs shortest-paths problem. In *Workshop on Algorithm Engineering (WAE),* pages 482–497, 2004.

22. J. F. Sibeyn. External matrix multiplication and all-pairs shortest path. *Information Process-ing Letters*, 91(2):99–106, 2004.
23. U. Stern and D. Dill. Using magnetic disk instead of main memory in the murphi verifier. In *International Conference on Computer Aided Verification (CAV)*, pages 172–183, 1998.
24. R. Zhou and E. Hansen. Breadth-first heuristic search. In *International Conference on Auto-mated Planning and Scheduling (ICAPS)*, pages 92–100, 2004.
25. R. Zhou and E. Hansen. Structured duplicate detection in external-memory graph search. In *National Conference on Artificial Intelligence (AAAI)*, pages 683–689, 2004.

Appendix: Proof of the Theorems

Theorem 1. The number of previous layers of the graph that need to be retained to prevent duplicate search effort is equal to the locality of the search graph.

Proof. To prove equality, we have to show that if the number of stored layers of a breadth-first search graph is smaller than the locality l, this can lead to re-openings, and if the number is greater than or equal to the locality, there are no re-openings.

For the first case, consider u and v with $\delta(s, u) - \delta(s, v) > l$. We will show that there is a duplicate node. When u is expanded, its successor v is either in the boundary of the previous k layers, in which case no re-openings occurs, or it is not, in which case, we have a re-opening of v. However, in the first case v has a sub-optimal depth and has been previously re-opened.

If the number of stored layers of a breadth-first search graph is greater than or equal to the locality of a graph this prevents re-openings as follows. Certainly, there is no re-opening in the first l layers. By induction, when a new layer is generated, no previously deleted node can be re-generated.

Theorem 2. The worst-case number of times a node u can be re-opened is bounded by $\lfloor (\delta(s, T) - \delta(s, u))/b \rfloor$.

Proof. We have no duplicate in every b layers. Therefore, the earliest level for a node u to be re-opened is $\delta(s, u) + b$ and the earliest next level it will be re-opened is $\delta(s, u) + 2b$ and so on. Since the total number of layers is bounded by $\delta(s, T)$ the number of re-openings for a node cannot exceed $\lfloor (\delta(s, T) - \delta(s, u))/b \rfloor$.

Theorem 4. Let $G = (V, E, w)$ be a weighted graph and f be the cost of the shortest path so far for a particular node from the start node s in the modified algorithm of Dijkstra. At each selection of a node u from *Open*, we have the following invariant: Let $p = (s = v_0, \ldots, v_n = t)$ be a least-cost path from the start node s to a goal node $t \in T$. Application of *Relax* preserves the following invariant:

(I) Unless v_n is in *Closed* with $f(v_n) = \delta(s, v_n)$, there is a node v_i in *Open* such that $f(v_i) = \delta(s, v_i)$, and no $j > i$ exists such that v_j is in *Closed* with $f(v_j) = \delta(s, v_j)$.

Proof. Without loss of generality, let i be maximal among the nodes satisfying (I). We distinguish the following cases:

1. Node u is not on p or $f(u) > \delta(s, u)$. Then node $v_i \neq u$ remains in *Open*. Since no v in *Open* $\cap\; p \;\cap \Gamma(u)$ with $f(v) = \delta(s, v) \leq f(u) + w(u, v)$ is changed and no other node is added to *Closed*, (I) is preserved.

2. Node u is on p and $f(u) = \delta(s, u)$. If $u = v_n$, there is nothing to show.
   First assume $u = v_i$. Then *Relax* will be called for $v = v_{i+1} \in \Gamma(u)$; for all other nodes in $\Gamma(u) \setminus \{v_{i+1}\}$, the argument of case 1 holds. According to (I), if v is in *Closed*, then $f(v) > \delta(s, v)$, and it will be reinserted into *Open* with $f(v) = \delta(s, u) + w(u, v) = \delta(s, v)$. If v is neither in *Open* or *Closed*, it is inserted into *Open* with this merit. Otherwise, the *DecreaseKey* operation will set it to $\delta(s, v)$. In either case, v guarantees the invariant (I).
   Now suppose $u \neq v_i$. By the maximality assumption of i we have $u = v_k$ with $k < i$. If $v = v_i$, no *DecreaseKey* operation can change it because v_i already has optimal merit $f(v) = \delta(s, u) + w(u, v) = \delta(s, v)$. Otherwise, v_i remains in *Open* with unchanged f-value and no other node besides u is inserted into *Closed*; thus, v_i still preserves (I).   □

Theorem 5. If $\delta(u, T) \geq 0$, then the node-ordering algorithm is optimal.

Proof. Upon termination, each node inserted into *Open* must have been selected at least once. Suppose that invariant (I) is preserved in each loop, i.e., that there is always a node v in the *Open* list on an optimal path with $f(v) = \delta(s, v)$. Thus the algorithm cannot terminate without eventually selecting the goal node on this path, and since by definition it is not more expensive than any found solution path and *best* maintains the currently shortest path, an optimal solution will be returned. It remains to show that the invariant (I) holds in each iteration. If the extracted node u is not equal to v there is nothing to show. Otherwise $f(u) = \delta(s, u)$. The bound α denotes the currently best solution length. If $f(u) \leq \alpha$ no pruning takes place. On the other hand $f(u) > \alpha$ leads to a contradiction since $\alpha \geq \delta(s, u) + \delta(u, T) \geq \delta(s, u) = f(u)$ (the latter inequality is justified by $\delta(u, T) \geq 0$).   □

Verification of an Error Correcting Code
by Abstract Interpretation

Charles Hymans

STIX, École Polytechnique, 91128 Palaiseau, France
charles.hymans@polytechnique.fr

Abstract. We apply the theory of abstract interpretation to validate
a Reed Solomon error correcting code. We design and implement an
abstract simulator for VHDL descriptions. This tool computes an over-
approximation of all the states that would be reached during any run of
a conventional simulator. It collects linear constraints that hold between
signals in the design. It is used to check the RTL implementations of
the Reed Solomon encoder and decoder against correct high-level specifications. We explain how to express the correctness property so as to
defeat the state explosion incurred by the deep pipeline in the decoder.
Benchmarks show the abstract simulator is very frugal in both memory
and time. Comparisons with VIS confirm that specialized tools outperform general purpose algorithms. Abstract simulation also competes ad-
vantageously with simulation. In less time than what was allocated for
simulation by the designers of the components, it achieves full coverage.

1 Introduction

In order to design today's complex system-on-a-chips (SoCs), the ability to reuse
existing intellectual properties (IPs) has become a necessity. Ideally, IP reuse
shortens time-to-market and bounds design costs. However, in practice, the assembly of components from multiple sources on a single chips turns out not to
be simple. First, the behavior of each IP must be clearly documented. Such a
documentation can take various more or less satisfactory forms. Informal specifications, test vectors together with expected results, testbenches or assertions are
all possible. The specification may be formally expressed in a standard property
language such as PSL/Sugar [3] but traditional hardware description languages
are for the most part expressive enough already. Also, obviously, the internal
behavior of an IP must match its documentation. If it doesn't, then finding the
origin of a flaw during whole chip simulation becomes a nightmare. Unfortunately, it is in general impossible to ensure a property of a design using only
a simulator. Simulation explores an extremely small fragment of all the possible executions. It is inherently not exhaustive. Only formal methods have this
unique capability of proving a component's correctness with respect to a given
property. Hence, the IP reuse methodology stresses the need for automatic and
efficient formal verification tools critically.

R. Cousot (Ed.): VMCAI 2005, LNCS 3385, pp. 330–345, 2005.
© Springer-Verlag Berlin Heidelberg 2005

We believe great efficiency can be obtained by designing tools that are specialized to their application domain. In that, we follow a similar path to the one explored in [6]. In previous work [17, 18], we applied the methodology of abstract interpretation [12] to design an abstract simulator for VHDL [1]. The abstract simulator computes a superset of all the states that may be reached during any conventional simulation of a given VHDL description. It employs a numerical domain [20, 19, 23] to symbolically encode the possible values of signals. Precision can be traded for efficiency by simply changing the numerical domain. We want to tailor this tool to the application domain of linear error correcting codes (ECCs). Hence the domain of linear relationships [19] is most appropriate. We slightly adapt the domain so that it can track undefined ('U') standard logic signals. For integer variables, we use the domain of constants. We apply the abstract simulator to a Reed Solomon encoder and decoder that was provided to us by industrial partners. The correctness of each component is expressed by a non-deterministic testbench written as a behavioral VHDL piece of code. The testbench is carefully written so as to circumvent the state explosion induced by the pipeline of the component under verification. The tool successfully performs the verification of both components. The performances of our experimental prototype turn out to be astonishingly good. In particular, in comparison to a standard BDD based model checker like VIS [15], the memory consumption is very low. The tool was also helpful to find the origin of flaws in incorrect descriptions.

2   Reed Solomon

Data transmitted over a communication channel or stored on a memory device may undergo corruption. Error correcting codes elude possible information loss by adding redundancy. In our information based society, ECCs have become ubiquitous: CDs, modems, digital television and wireless communication all incorporate them. We wish to validate a synthesizable register transfer level (RTL) VHDL description of a Reed Solomon ECC [25] encoder and decoder.

The informal documentation of the components explains how 16 bits messages are encoded by adding 8 bits of redundancy. The bits are packed in groups of 4 consecutive bits called symbols. The decoder is able to recover from a corruption that affects a unique symbol, i.e. at most 4 bits in the same block. The set of all recoverable corruptions of a vector of bits x is:

$$\text{correctable}(x) = \{y \mid \exists s \in [0 \ldots 5] : \forall i \notin [4 * s \ldots 4 * s + 3] : y_i = x_i\} .$$

Then, the characteristic property of the RS code can be stated by:

$$\forall x \in \mathbb{B}^{16} : \forall y \in \mathbb{B}^{24} : y \in \text{correctable}(\texttt{ref\_enc}(x)) \implies \texttt{ref\_dec}(y) = x . \quad (1)$$

We write concise VHDL behavioral implementations of the encoding $\texttt{ref\_enc}$ and decoding functions $\texttt{ref\_dec}$. These descriptions constitute the golden reference model for the functionality of the components. We check by extensive

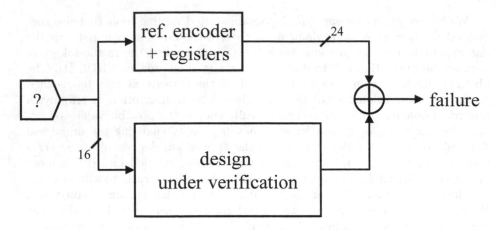

Fig. 1. Design and verification harness.

simulation that they observe property 1. This task spans over the negligible time of 6 seconds.

It may seem that it is as simple to validate the actual components as it is to check the specification. This is far from true. Let us consider the encoder. Its role is not to encode one 16 bits message and then terminate. Rather, at every clock cycle it takes a different 16 bits message and encodes it. The design is pipelined, so that encoding is performed in 2 clock cycles. Our goal is not to show that the encoder encodes correctly one, or two, or a bounded number of messages. Rather, we want to ensure it will function correctly forever. At each clock cycle and whatever the input, the component must compute exactly the same sequence of values as the `ref_enc` function would. We write in VHDL the testbench depicted in figure 1. A simple cycle-accurate, bit-accurate specification of the expected behaviour of the encoder is built by adding two rows of registers to the function `ref_enc`. At each clock cycle, random values are fed to the two components and their outputs are compared. At this point, showing the correctness of the encoder boils down to proving that no simulation run ever sets the signal `failure` to true. We have designed and implemented a tool to do this automatically.

3   Abstract Simulation

3.1   Semantics

In order to reason about VHDL descriptions, their semantics must be properly defined. We assume the descriptions are translated into the kernel language whose abstract syntax is found in Fig. 2. A description consists of a finite number of processes that are run concurrently. Each process executes its commands sequentially until it either terminates or is suspended by a `wait` statement. The local memory (unshared variables) of each process is modified by a variable assignment command. The global memory (signals) is updated only during a

descr	→ process { | process }	(Parallel composition)
process	→ command ; { command ; }	(Sequence)
command	→ lval := exp	(Variable assignment)
	→ lval <= exp	(Signal assignment)
	→ wait on sig_list until exp for timeout	(Suspension)
	→ while exp do process	(Iteration)
	→ if exp -> process { | exp -> process }	(Alternative)
	→ display(x, ..., x)	(Display)
lval	→ x | x[exp]...[exp]	(Memory accesses)
exp	→ n ∈ ℤ | '0' | '1' | 'U'	(Constants)
	→ lval | op exp | exp op exp	
	→ rnd() | lrnd() | lvec_rnd(n)	(Random generators)
	→ rising_edge(x)	(Edge detector)
	→ int_to_lvec(x) | lvec_to_int(x)	(Conversion functions)
op	→ not | or | and | xor | - | + | < | =	

where x is a variable or a signal identifier, sig_list a possibly empty set of signal names and timeout a positive integer or the keyword **ever** (to denote the absence of timeout clause). The notation {...} reads "zero or more instances of the enclosed".

Fig. 2. Syntax of the kernel language.

global synchronization phase. Hence, the effect of the signal assignment is just to schedule a memory update for the next synchronization point. Synchronization occurs whenever all processes are suspended. First, the global memory is updated. Then, the simulator wakes up any process for which at least one of the signals it is waiting for just changed. If no process can be awaken that way, then the simulation time is advanced by the smallest timeout. The **while** loop and the alternative construct both control the flow of execution. The alternative construct, introduced by Dijkstra in [13], runs one of the guarded processes whose guard evaluates to true. At last, **display** outputs the value of its arguments. The descriptions manipulate std_logics, booleans, integers and statically allocated multi-dimensional arrays. Of the std_logic literals only '0', '1' and 'U' are actually used. The **rising_edge** evaluates to true whenever a signal goes from '0' to '1'. The functions int_to_lvec and lvec_to_int convert an array of std_logic to an integer and back. Even though these three functions are not basic VHDL but defined in external IEEE packages [2], we consider them as primitive operators. We also incorporate random generators **rnd**, **lrnd** and **lvec_rnd** to be able to inject non-determinism in a design.

We give an operational semantics in the style of Plotkin [24] to this kernel language. We refer the reader to [17,18] for more in-depth descriptions. A state of the simulator $(c_0, \ldots, c_i, \ldots, c_n, \rho) \in \Sigma$ is a tuple of program points followed by an environment. For each process, a program point c_i indicates the command to execute next. The environment ρ stores the value of all variables and signals. The relation → describes one computation step of the simulator:

$$(c_0, \ldots, c_i, \ldots, c_n, \rho) \rightarrow (c_0', \ldots, c_i', \ldots, c_n', \rho') .$$

We are interested in all the states reachable from some initial configuration s_0:

$$\mathcal{O} = \{s \mid s_0 \rightarrow^* s\} \, .$$

This set can be equivalently expressed as the least fixpoint of the continuous function $\mathbb{F}$ on the complete lattice of set of states $(\wp(\Sigma), \emptyset, \cup, \Sigma, \cap)$ where:

$$\mathbb{F}(X) = \{s_0\} \cup \{s' \mid \exists s \in X : s \rightarrow s'\} \, .$$

Unfortunately, because of the excessive size of the state space, the computation of this fixpoint often turns out to be too expensive. However an approximation of the reachable states is often sufficient to show the absence of errors in a design.

3.2   Abstract Interpretation

We follow the methodology of abstract interpretation [12] to design a tool that computes a superset of the reachable states. We proceed in two steps. First, we choose a representation for sets of states. To do so, we suppose we have an abstract numerical domain $(\mathcal{N}, \gamma_{\mathcal{N}})$ which is left as a parameter of our construction. An element of this domain describes a set of environments as defined by the monotonic concretization function $\gamma_{\mathcal{N}}$. In the following, we call abstract environments the elements of $\mathcal{N}$. Then, we abstract a set of states by a function Y that maps each tuple of program points to an abstract environment. This mapping represents all the states $(c_1, \ldots, c_n, \rho)$ for which the environment ρ satisfies the constraints associated with the program points $(c_1, \ldots, c_n)$. The abstraction is formalized by the following monotonic concretization function γ:

$$\gamma(Y) = \{(c_1, \ldots, c_n, \rho) \mid \rho \in \gamma_{\mathcal{N}}(Y(c_1, \ldots, c_n))\} \, .$$

Second, we systematically derive from $\mathbb{F}$ a monotonic abstract counterpart $\mathbb{F}^\sharp$ which operates on the abstract domain. We express, in [17], the abstract transfer function $\mathbb{F}^\sharp$ in terms of a few primitives that operate on the numerical domain $\mathcal{N}$: $\bot$ represents the empty set, $\sqsubseteq$ compares two abstract environments, $\sqcup$ joins abstract environments, `assign` undertakes assignments, `select` asserts boolean conditions and `singleton` yields the abstract representation for a single concrete environment. In [17], we also explicit the soundness condition that each of these operations must obey in order for $\mathbb{F}^\sharp$ to be sound. Soundness ensures that the result of applying $\mathbb{F}^\sharp$ contains all the states obtained when applying $\mathbb{F}$:

$$\mathbb{F} \circ \gamma \subseteq \gamma \circ \mathbb{F}^\sharp \, .$$

This local soundness condition guarantees that the least fixpoint of $\mathbb{F}^\sharp$ is a sound over-approximation of the reachable states:

$$\text{lfp } \mathbb{F} \subseteq \gamma(\text{lfp } \mathbb{F}^\sharp) \, .$$

Our tool computes the least fixpoint of $\mathbb{F}^\sharp$. It consists of approximately 3000 lines of code in OCaml [22]. The compiler from VHDL to the intermediate representation of Fig. 2 accounts for another 2000 lines. The abstract simulator stores abstract environments in a hashtable. The fixpoint algorithm is the standard worklist algorithm found in [16]. The program points to be visited are placed on a priority queue. When the queue is empty, we have reached the fixpoint. We chose this data-structure so that the body of loops and alternative constructs are visited before the next instruction.

We can plug any kind of numerical domain [20, 19, 23, 7] as a backend to our analysis. The selection of an adequate numerical domain is of paramount importance: too coarse an abstraction might be insufficient to achieve the verification goals whereas precision is often gained in detriment to efficiency. Next section explains the tradeoff we chose to handle linear ECCs.

3.3 Boolean Affine Relationships

For the back-end of the analyzer, there is a tremendous variety of numerical domains that we can choose from. To cite but a few see [20, 19, 23, 27, 14]. We implemented a numerical domain which we believe is well adapted to the verification of linear error correcting codes (ECCs). We take the product of the domain of affine relationships for `std_logic` variables and the domain of constants [20] for integer variables.

Let V be a set of n boolean valued variables. We bestow the addition xor ($\oplus$) and multiplication and ($\wedge$) on the set $\mathbb{B}^V$ of binary vectors indexed by the variables in V. Now, $(\mathbb{B}^V, \oplus, \wedge)$ is a vector space over $\mathbb{B}$ of dimension n. A boolean affine equality is an equation of the form:

$$c_1 \wedge x_1 \oplus \ldots \oplus c_n \wedge x_n = c,$$

where $x_1, \ldots, x_n$ are variables in V and $c_1, \ldots, c_n, c$, boolean values. It represents the set of vectors in $\mathbb{B}^V$ that make the equality hold. The domain $(\mathcal{K}_V, \gamma_\mathcal{K})$ of Karr [19] tracks the affine equalities that are satisfied by variables in V. An element of Karr's domain is a system of affine equalities. The system is kept in row-echelon normal form thanks to the Gauss pivot algorithm. Karr describes all the primitives we need to manipulate the domain: $\perp_\mathcal{K}$, $\sqcup_\mathcal{K}$, $\mathsf{assign}_\mathcal{K}$, $\mathsf{select}_\mathcal{K}$ and $\mathsf{singleton}_\mathcal{K}$. Each of these operations obey their respective soundness condition. Two additional primitives allow to add and remove variables from the domain: extend and project. If V and W are sets of variables such that $V \subseteq W$ then:

$$\{\rho \mid \rho|_V \in \gamma_\mathcal{K}(R)\} \subseteq \gamma_\mathcal{K}(\mathsf{extend}_W(R))$$
$$\{\rho|_V \mid \rho \in \gamma_\mathcal{K}(R)\} \subseteq \gamma_\mathcal{K}(\mathsf{project}_V(R)).$$

Unfortunately, we can not use the domain of boolean equality as it is: VHDL implementations embed $\mathbb{B}$ into the type std_logic. In fact, variables of type std_logic do not only take the values '0' or '1' but also 'U'. To adapt the domain, we track the set b of std_logic variables which are definitely different from 'U'. Karr's domain is used to collect the linear relationships that solely concern the variables in b:

$$\mathcal{N} = \{(b, k) \mid b \subseteq V \wedge k \in \mathcal{K}_b\} \cup \{\bot\}$$
$$\gamma(b, k) = \{\rho \mid \rho|_b \in \gamma_{\mathcal{K}}(k)\}$$
$$\gamma(\bot) = \emptyset .$$

We produce sound definitions for the various operators. Abstract inclusion and union are:

$$(b_1, k_1) \sqsubseteq (b_2, k_2) = b_2 \subseteq b_1 \wedge \mathsf{project}_{b_2}(k_1) \sqsubseteq_{\mathcal{K}} k_2$$
$$(b_1, k_1) \sqcup (b_2, k_2) = (b, \mathsf{project}_b(k_1) \sqcup_{\mathcal{K}} \mathsf{project}_b(k_2)) \qquad \text{where } b = b_1 \cap b_2 .$$

Predicate $\mathsf{in01}_b(e)$ holds of expressions that necesseraly evaluate to '0' or '1', assuming the $\mathtt{std\_logic}$ variables in b are different from 'U'. It is defined by structural induction on the syntax of expressions:

$$\begin{cases} \mathsf{in01}_b(c) = \mathtt{true} & \text{if } c \in \{\text{'0'}, \text{'1'}\} \\ \mathsf{in01}_b(\mathtt{lrnd}()) = \mathtt{true} \\ \mathsf{in01}_b(x) = (x \in b) \\ \mathsf{in01}_b(\mathtt{not}\ e) = \mathsf{in01}_b(e) \\ \mathsf{in01}_b(e_1\ op\ e_2) = \mathsf{in01}_b(e_1) \wedge \mathsf{in01}_b(e_2) & \text{if } op \in \{\mathtt{and}, \mathtt{xor}\} \\ \mathsf{in01}_b(e) = \mathtt{false} & \text{for all other expressions} . \end{cases}$$

The assignment of an expression e to variable x is carried on in the Karr domain only when we are sure that e evaluates to '0' or '1':

$$\mathsf{assign}_{x \leftarrow e}(b, k) = \begin{cases} (b_1, \mathsf{assign}_{\mathcal{K} x \leftarrow e}(\mathsf{extend}_{b_1}(k))) & \text{if } \mathsf{in01}_b(e) \\ (b_2, \mathsf{project}_{b_2}(k)) & \text{otherwise} \end{cases}$$

$$\text{where } b_1 = b \cup \{x\} \text{ and } b_2 = b \setminus \{x\} .$$

In a similar way to assignments, the selection operation refines the Karr's component of our domain only when possible:

$$\begin{cases} \mathsf{select}_{e_1 = e_2}(b, k) = (b, \mathsf{select}_{\mathcal{K} e_1 = e_2}(k)) & \text{if } \mathsf{in01}_b(e_1) \wedge \mathsf{in01}_b(e_2) \\ \mathsf{select}_e(b, k) = (b, k) & \text{otherwise} . \end{cases}$$

At last, the singleton primitive is:

$$\mathsf{singleton}(\rho) = (b, \mathsf{singleton}_{\mathcal{K}}(\rho|_b)) \qquad \text{with } b = \{x \mid \rho(x) \in \{\text{'0'}, \text{'1'}\}\} .$$

In the implementation, we adopt a sparse matrix representation for the system of linear equalities. The set of variables b is encoded by a bitfield. The memory usage of the abstract domain is of the order of n^2 while the complexity of the most expensive operation is in n^3.

Optimization. We do not necessarily need to always collect all the linear equalities of a design. In particular, sometimes we only care about the functional relationship that hold between each variable y and some variables in a set X. If this is the case, we may safely trim the system of constraints to speed up the computation and free some memory. To do so, we first normalize the system in row-echelon form. We use an ordering of the column where the variables in X come last. Then, we discard any constraint that involves more than one variable not in X.

Example 1. We illustrate on the following system of equalities:

$$y_2 \oplus y_3 \oplus y_4 = 1$$
$$y_1 \oplus y_3 \oplus x_1 = 0$$
$$y_3 \oplus x_2 = 1 \,.$$

Suppose $X = \{x_1, x_2\}$. We put the system in normalized row-echelon form with the order $(y_1, y_2, y_3, x_1, x_2)$:

$$
\begin{aligned}
y_1 && &\oplus x_1 \oplus x_2 &= 1 \\
&y_2 &\oplus y_4 &\oplus x_2 &= 0 \\
&&y_3 &\oplus x_2 &= 1 \,.
\end{aligned}
$$

Any constraint with more than one variable not belonging to X is removed:

$$y_1 = x_1 \oplus x_2 \oplus 1$$
$$y_3 = x_2 \oplus 1 \,.$$

We implemented a tool, called `vhdla+`, which performs this optimization after each join operation.

The domain of boolean linear equalities is particularly fit to show the correctness of linear ECCs. This is because the encoding function of linear ECCs is linear, that is its input/output relation can be exactly captured by an affine equality. In the next sections, we present experimental results that support this claim.

4   Encoder

We run our tool on the RS encoder with the testbench of Fig. 1. First, we compile the description to the intermediate representation:

```
$ vhdlc encoder.vhd > encoder.khl
```

Then, we launch the abstract simulator:

```
$ vhdla encoder.vhd encoder.khl
```

The abstract simulator outputs its results in `html` format. It annotates all display directives with the constraints it has inferred. Figure 3 shows a screenshot of the

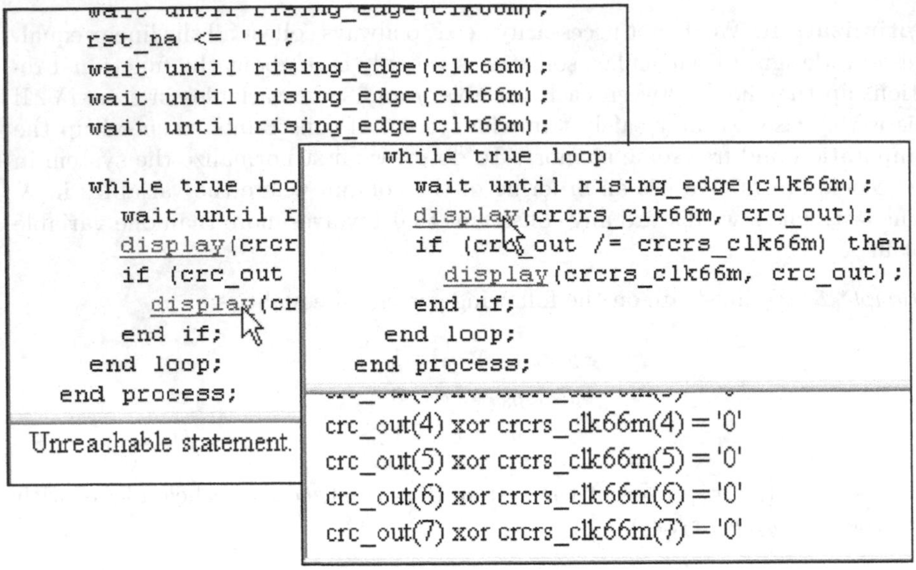

```
wait until rising_edge(clk66m);
rst_na <= '1';
wait until rising_edge(clk66m);
wait until rising_edge(clk66m);
wait until rising_edge(clk66m);

                      while true loop
    while true loo        wait until rising_edge(clk66m);
      wait until r        display(crcrs_clk66m, crc_out);
      display(crcr        if (crc_out /= crcrs_clk66m) then
      if (crc_out            display(crcrs_clk66m, crc_out);
         display(cr        end if;
      end if;          end loop;
    end loop;        end process;
  end process;
```

Unreachable statement.	crc_out(4) xor crcrs_clk66m(4) = '0'
	crc_out(5) xor crcrs_clk66m(5) = '0'
	crc_out(6) xor crcrs_clk66m(6) = '0'
	crc_out(7) xor crcrs_clk66m(7) = '0'

Fig. 3. Results presented by the tool.

results. It shows the piece of code in the testbench which is in charge of comparing the output of the RS encoder (crcrs_clk66m) with the output of the reference implementation (crc_out). The tool was able to find out that for each index i:

$$\text{crcrs\_clk66m}(i) \text{ xor } \text{crc\_out}(i) = \text{'0'}\,.$$

In other words, the outputs are equal element wise. This allows to conclude the error state inside the if statement is unreachable, which validates the encoder.

5   Decoder

The description of the decoder is harder to verify. Indeed, the function computed by the decoder is not linear. The reference implementation ref_dec for the decoder works as follows:

```
syndrome := control(din);
dout := correct(din, syndrome);
```

The linear map control computes the syndrome of the message. The function correct then modifies the message according to the value of the syndrome. For a fixed syndrome, correct is linear in din. The syndrome is made up of two symbols. Each symbol is 4 bits (here std_logics) wide. This means that the domain of the reference decoding function ref_dec can be split in 256 pieces. The restriction of ref_dec on any of these pieces is linear.

Moreover, the decoder is pipelined with a depth of five cycles. With the initial row of registers put on the inputs, this means that at most six different

```
process begin
  -- reset phase
  din <= (others => '0');
  wait until rising_edge(clk); wait until rising_edge(clk);
  wait until rising_edge(clk); wait until rising_edge(clk);
  rst_na <= '1';

  -- operating phase
  while rnd() loop
    din <= lvec_rnd(24); wait until rising_edge(clk);
  end loop;

  -- testing phase
  x := lvec_rnd(24); y := ref_dec(x); din <= x;
  wait until rising_edge(clk); din <= lvec_rnd(24);
  wait until rising_edge(clk); din <= lvec_rnd(24);
  wait until rising_edge(clk); din <= lvec_rnd(24);
  wait until rising_edge(clk); din <= lvec_rnd(24);
  wait until rising_edge(clk); din <= lvec_rnd(24);
  wait until rising_edge(clk); din <= lvec_rnd(24);

  if (dout /= y) then report "Failure"; end if;
end process;
```

Fig. 4. Driver for the RS decoder.

datas may be at the same time in different stages of the design. If we naively distinguish the 256 cases for each of these stages then we are bound to suffer from the state explosion problem since:

$$256^6 = 2^{48} \approx 280000 \text{ billions}.$$

More complex abstractions would probably shield us from the effects of state explosion. But we prefer to circumvent the problem so as to reuse the same tool that already worked for the encoder. We reformulate the correctness property. Let us consider a run of a conventional simulator on the decoder. We restrict our observation to the input din and output dout of the component at rising edges of the clock. We want to ensure that, at any clock cycle t, if some data is fed to the component, then the expected result shows up 6 clock cycles later:

$$\forall t : \forall x : din_t = x \implies dout_{t+6} = ref\_dec(x). \qquad (2)$$

To enforce this property, we drive the component with the process in Fig. 4. First, the component is reset. Then, it is fed with arbitrary values for some time. Intuitively, this first part in the driver expresses the $\forall t$ of equation (2). An input message x is picked randomly and fed to the component. After 6 clock cycles have elapsed, the output from the component dout and the expected value y are compared. The statement report "Failure." must be shown unreachable. Since the specification function ref_dec is not linear, the verification can't be performed in one run of the current abstract simulator. Instead, we can equivalently check 256 simpler properties. We specialize the previous driver for each possible value of the syndrome. For instance, for a syndrome equal to "10110111", the following code simply replaces the last part of the driver:

```
-- testing phase for a syndrome equal to "10110111"
x := lvec_rnd(24); syndrome := control(x);
if (syndrome = "10110111") then
  y := correct(x, syndrome); din <= x;
  wait until rising_edge(clk); din <= lvec_rnd(24);
  wait until rising_edge(clk); din <= lvec_rnd(24);
  wait until rising_edge(clk); din <= lvec_rnd(24);
  wait until rising_edge(clk); din <= lvec_rnd(24);
  wait until rising_edge(clk); din <= lvec_rnd(24);
  wait until rising_edge(clk); din <= lvec_rnd(24);

  if (dout /= y) then report "Failure"; end if;
end if;
```

Combinational Processes. To our surprise and dismay the tool fails. After inspection of the results, we find out it needs to establish intermediate invariants that involve non-linear constraints. Consider the following example:

```
process begin
  a <= lrnd(); b <= lrnd(); wait for 1 ns;
  display(a, b, y);
  a <= '1'; b <= lrnd(); wait for 1 ns;
  display(a, b, y);
end process;
process(x) begin y <= a and b; end process;
```

The abstract simulator is unable to infer the linear equality

$$b = y$$

that holds at the second `display` statement. This problem arises because of the combinational process. Let us follow the computation of the tool. At the first `display` statement, the value of signal a, b and y are linked by the relationship:

$$a \text{ and } b = y.$$

However, simply because this constraint is not a boolean linear equality, it is not inferred. Then, when the tool reaches the second wait statement, it must explore the two possible outcomes of the combinational process. Either it wakes up and y is assigned the value of '1' and b. Or, it stays idle in which case y is not modified. Unfortunately, the tool already lost all information about y. The restraint $y = b$ can not be deduced.

The exact same sequence of events prevents the analysis of the decoder from being conclusive. To resolve this problem, we inline the code of each combinational process wherever the signals it is sensitive on may be modified. As for now, this simple program transformation is done by hand. However, it can easily be made automatic and integrated as a final phase of the preprocessor vhdlc.

At last, the abstract simulator succeeds. It computes during 849 seconds on an AMD Athlon MP 2200+ and consumes 141 megabytes at its peak. Of course, to completely validate the decoder, the abstract simulator must be run 256 times, i.e. one time for each possible syndrome.

6 Discussion

Debugging Information. The tool may also be useful in the purpose of debugging. To trace the origin of flaws in a faulty design, we can display the constraints computed by the abstract simulator at different program points in the design. For instance, it is possible to discover the conditions on the input signals that lead the design into an abnormal state. Also, with a driver as described in Fig. 4, it is easy to follow the data flow through the pipeline. We can thus locate the first stage where signals in the design do not match their expected values.

Stronger Abstraction. The specificity of the property checked by the driver in Fig. 4 allows to take advantage of vhdla+, the optimized version of our tool. Indeed, not all affine relationships that hold in the design are important. It is sufficient to just collect the relationships that link the signals with the input vector x. Any other constraint may be freely disposed of. The computation time and memory consumption are down respectively to 593 seconds and 88 Mb. So we estimate the whole verification effort takes less than two days (10 minutes $*$ $256 \approx 42$ hours).

Benchmarks. We compared with the BDD-based model checker VIS [15]. To our knowledge there is no freely available model checking tool that inputs VHDL code. So we chose VIS which reads synthesizable synchronous Verilog descriptions. The VHDL descriptions were translated by hand. The asynchronous reset had to be removed completely. We also transformed the driver of Fig. 4 into a form suitable for synthesis. Table 1 displays various statistics of our benchmarks. The sizes of the descriptions are expressed in number of lines of VHDL, of the intermediate representation and of Verilog. The number of latches of the circuit synthesized by VIS is also shown. Then, time and memory consumption are shown. Line vhdla+ corresponds to the implementation of the stronger abstraction. We ran VIS with the check_invariant command. We tried both static and dynamic variables ordering for the BDDs. For the dynamic ordering, we used the window method. Dynamic ordering improves the memory consumption, but at the cost of increased computation time. Both methods failed: static ordering burns the 2GB of available memory very quickly, whereas dynamic ordering does

Table 1. Statistics on an AMD Athlon MP 2200+ with 2GB of memory.

	Program					
	encoder	decoder	dec. 1	dec. 1–2	dec. 1–3	dec. 1–4
Size in various metrics						
VHDL lines	251	395	215	265	305	358
IR lines	338	963	370	484	602	828
Verilog lines	235	519	206	310	358	415
VIS latches	337	647	286	486	529	617
Verification time (s)						
vhdla	58	849	37	152	259	513
vhdla+	45	593	37	166	261	420
vis static	1666	>960	>840	>845	>1826	>895
vis dynamic	4379	>172800 (48h)	2774	4540	78037 (21h)	>172800 (48h)
Peak memory consumption (Mb)						
vhdla	50	141	23	44	66	98
vhdla+	37	88	20	37	49	73
vis static	693	>2000	>2000	>2000	>2000	>2000
vis dynamic	173	>374	233	243	277	>333

Benchmarks dec. 1 to dec. 1–4 are troncated versions of the decoder: dec. 1 contains only the first stage of the pipeline, dec. 1–2, the first two stages and so on.

not finish within a timeout of 48 hours. The last benchmarks are performed on restricted versions of the decoder where only the first few stages of the pipeline are considered. These benchmarks confirm that specialized tools can outperform general algorithms like BDD based model checking.

At the time the component was designed, the hardware engineers allocated two days to simulation. The whole verification effort to fully validate the encoder and decoder takes less than two days with our prototype implementation. Obviously, simulation lacks the full coverage that we attain. So, our approach is competitive with conventional simulation: in a similar amount of time, it produces a much higher valued result.

7   Related Work

There exists numerous formal verification tools for hardware. We compared our approach with traditional BDD [7] based model checking [9]. Using the model checker VIS [15], we observed an undeniable blowup in the size of the BDDs or the time devoted to simplify them on the fly.

In bounded model checking [5], a violation of the property reachable in less than a bounded number of steps is searched for. The task is reduced to a propositional satisfiability problem and solved with regular sat-solvers. The tool described in [11] checks the consistency of a Verilog design with its specification written in ANSI-C. Essentially, in contrast to symbolic model checking, SAT based methods trade memory consumption for computation time. It proves very efficient to quickly find errors in designs. However, when the property holds, bounded model checking too tends to suffer from the state explosion problem.

Symbolic simulation algorithms [8] extend the power of traditional simulators by manipulating symbolic expressions instead of plain values. In particular, ternary symbolic simulation operates on BDDs whose nodes are variables denoting the input to the circuit and whose leaves are 0, 1 or X (for unknown). Symbolic trajectory evaluation [26] improves on ternary symbolic simulation by providing a logic to express the property to check. Symbolic trajectory evaluation was shown to be an abstract interpretation in [10]. The efficiency of symbolic simulation stems from the limited number of variables needed for the BDDs. Indeed, this number depends only on the property to check and not on the design. For instance, to establish the correctness of the RS decoder, only 24 variables would be needed. In comparison to the domain of linear constraints, which is polynomial, there is still the possibility of an exponential blowup. The implementation of a symbolic simulation for RT-level Verilog is described in [21]. The authors claim to support the full IEEE 1364-1995 semantics. However, they do not state, even less prove, the soundness of their algorithm with respect to a formalization of the Verilog semantics.

As for the specification part, we could use more complex formalisms like PSL/sugar [4]. Such logic is helpful to specify complex control properties or liveness properties. But as we have seen, for the simple case study of RS, VHDL augmented with non-determinism is already expressive enough. Our choice was also motivated by the fact that engineers prefer traditional hardware description languages with which they are already familiar.

8   Conclusion

We successfully verified VHDL descriptions of Reed Solomon error correcting code encoder and decoder. The descriptions, supplied to us by an industrial partner, were in no way modified for the purpose of verification. The verification tool we used was designed following the methodology of abstract interpretation. It computes an over-approximation of the reachable states of a VHDL description. It is systematically derived by abstraction from an event-driven simulation semantics of VHDL. The abstract numerical domain, used to represent the possible values of the signals in the description, may be freely chosen. This allows for various tradeoffs between the precision of the approximation and the cost of the computation. This facility is crucial to reach the verification goals within a reasonable time and memory budget. For the specific class of linear ECCs, we selected the domain of boolean linear equalities. It must be slightly adapted in order to handle multivalued logic (the VHDL std_logic data-type). The experimental results are excellent.

This study shows it is possible to validate descriptions produced by hardware engineers in an efficient manner. Abstract interpretation proved the adequate approach for this work. First, abstraction allows to fill the gap between the hardware description language and the verification tool. The soundness of the tool was proved with respect to a formalization of the VHDL simulation algorithm. Second, abstraction was necessary to achieve good performances. This is a step forward toward the integration of formal tools into existing design practices.

In the future, we plan to study the applicability of our tool in the VHDL design flow. Our tool is not limited to synthesizable descriptions only. So in theory, it can be used to first check high-level behavioral specifications. Then, the consistency of the lower level description can be verified against the specification. This approach helps to identify errors early in the design flow.

References

1. ANSI/IEEE Std 1076-1987. *IEEE Standard VHDL Language Reference Manual*, 1988.
2. IEEE Std 1164-1993. *IEEE Standard Multivalue Logic System for VHDL Model Interoperability (Std_logic_1164)*, 1993.
3. Accellera. *Property Specification Language Reference Manual, Version 1.01*, 2003. http://www.accellera.org/pslv101.pdf.
4. I. Beer, S. Ben-David, C. Eisner, D. Fisman, A. Gringauze, and Y. Rodeh. The temporal logic sugar. In *13th International Conference on Computer Aided Verification (CAV'01)*, volume 2102 of *Lecture Notes in Computer Science*, pages 363–367. Springer, 2001.
5. A. Biere, A. Cimatti, E. M. Clarke, M. Fujita, and Y. Zhu. Symbolic model checking using SAT procedure instead of BDDs. In *Proceedings of the 36th Design Automation Conference (DAC'99)*, pages 317–320. ACM Press, 1999.
6. B. Blanchet, P. Cousot, R. Cousot, J. Feret, L. Mauborgne, A. Miné, D. Monniaux, and X. Rival. A static analyzer for large safety-critical software. In *Conference on Programming Language Design and Implementation (PLDI'03)*, pages 196–207. ACM Press, 2003.
7. R. E. Bryant. Graph-based algorithms for boolean function manipulation. *IEEE Transactions on Computers*, 35(8):677–691, 1986.
8. R.E. Bryant. Symbolic simulation - techniques and applications. In *Proceedings of the 27th ACM/IEEE Design Automation Conference (DAC'90)*, pages 517–521. IEEE Computer Society Press, 1990.
9. J.R. Burch, E.M. Clarke, D.E. Long, K.L. McMillan, and D.L. Dill. Symbolic model checking for sequential circuit verification. *IEEE Transactions on Computer-Aided Design of Integrated Circuits and Systems*, 13(4):401–424, 1994.
10. C.-T. Chou. The mathematical foundation of symbolic trajectory evaluation. In *11th International Conference on Computer Aided Verification (CAV'99)*, volume 1633 of *Lecture Notes in Computer Science*, pages 196–207. Springer, 1999.
11. E.M. Clarke, D. Kroening, and K. Yorav. Behavioral consistency of C and verilog programs using bounded model checking. In *Proceedings of the 40th Design Automation Conference (DAC'03)*, pages 368–371. ACM, 2003.
12. P. Cousot and R. Cousot. Abstract interpretation: a unified lattice model for static analysis of programs by construction or approximation of fixpoints. In *4th ACM Symposium on Principles of Programming Languages (POPL'77)*, pages 238–252. ACM Press, 1977.
13. E. W. Dijkstra. Guarded commands, nondeterminacy and formal derivation of programs. *Communications of the ACM*, 18(8):453–457, 1975.

14. P. Granger. Static analysis of linear congruence equalities among variables of a program. In *Proceedings of the International Joint Conference on Theory and Practice of Software Development (TAPSOFT'91)*, volume 1, pages 169–192, 1991.
15. The VIS Group. Vis: A system for verification and synthesis. In *8th International Conference on Computer Aided Verification (CAV'96)*, volume 1102 of *Lecture Notes in Computer Science*, pages 428–432. Springer, 1996.
16. S. Horwitz, A.J. Demers, and T. Teitelbaum. An efficient general iterative algorithm for dataflow analysis. *Acta Informatica*, 24(6):679–694, 1987.
17. C. Hymans. Checking safety properties of behavioral VHDL descriptions by abstract interpretation. In *9th International Static Analysis Symposium (SAS'02)*, volume 2477 of *Lecture Notes in Computer Science*, pages 444–460. Springer, 2002.
18. C. Hymans. Design and implementation of an abstract interpreter for VHDL. In *12th Advanced Research Working Conference on Correct Hardware Design and Verification Methods (CHARME'03)*, volume 2860 of *Lecture Notes in Computer Science*, pages 263–269. Springer, 2003.
19. M. Karr. Affine relationships among variables of a program. *Acta Informatica*, 6:133–151, 1976.
20. G. A. Kildall. A unified approach to global program optimization. In *1st ACM Symposium on Principles of Programming Languages (POPL'73)*, pages 194–206, 1973.
21. A. Kölbl, J.H. Kukula, and R.F. Damiano. Symbolic RTL simulation. In *Proceedings of the 38th Design Automation Conference (DAC'01)*, pages 47–52. ACM, 2001.
22. X. Leroy, D. Doligez, J. Garrigue, D. Rémy, and J. Vouillon. *The Objective Caml System, Documentation and User's Manual*. INRIA-Institut National de Recherche en Informatique et en Automatique, 2002.
23. A. Miné. A few graph-based relational numerical abstract domains. In *9th International Static Analysis Symposium (SAS'02)*, volume 2477 of *Lecture Notes in Computer Science*, pages 117–132. Springer, 2002.
24. G. Plotkin. A structural approach to operational semantics. Technical Report DAIMI FN-19, Aarhus University, 1981.
25. I. S. Reed and G. Solomon. Polynomial codes over certain finite fields. *Journal of the Society for Industrial and Applied Mathematics*, 8:300–304, 1960.
26. C.-J.H. Seger and R.E. Bryant. Formal verification by symbolic evaluation of partially-ordered trajectories. *Formal Methods in System Design*, 6(2):147–189, 1995.
27. A. Simon, A. King, and J.M. Howe. Two variables per linear inequality as an abstract domain. In *Logic Based Program Synthesis and Tranformation (LOPSTR'02)*, pages 71–89, 2002.

Information Flow Analysis for Java Bytecode

Samir Genaim* and Fausto Spoto

Dipartimento di Informatica, Università di Verona
Strada Le Grazie, 15, 37134 Verona, Italy
genaim@sci.univr.it, fausto.spoto@univr.it

Abstract. We present a flow and context sensitive compositional information flow analysis for full (mono-threaded) Java bytecode. We base our analysis on the transformation of the Java bytecode into a control-flow graph of *basic blocks* of code which makes explicit the complex features of the Java bytecode. We represent information flows through Boolean functions and hence implement an accurate and efficient information flow analysis through binary decision diagrams. To the best of our knowledge, it is the first one for full Java bytecode.

1 Introduction

Information flow analysis infers dependencies between program variables and lets us check if a program is free from undesired information flows, a basic component of security [20]. Namely, a *security policy* can be defined as a complete lattice of *security classes* and information is allowed to flow from variables of a given security class to variables of higher security classes only [11, 20]. Static analysis has been used to check if a program meets its security policy, both through data/control-flow analyses [6, 9, 15, 21, 18] and type-inference [22, 25, 5, 4, 14, 12]. In the former case, it infers a superset of all possible information flows, from which the security policy is checked. In the latter case, program variables are classified into security classes, and well-typedness guarantees that programs do not leak secrets. Our work belongs to the data/control-flow approach.

There is a flow of information from a variables x to a variable y, denoted by $x \leadsto y$, if changes in the input values of x are observable from the output values of y. Such flows are classified in *direct* and *indirect* [11]. Direct flows are *explicit* when they arise from assignments: in x=y+z, information flows from y and z to x; or they are *implicit* when they arise from conditionals: in if (x>0) then y=w else y=z, information flows explicitly from w and z to y and implicitly from x to y. Indirect flows are defined as follows: if $x \leadsto y$ is followed by $y \leadsto z$, then $x \leadsto z$. In this paper we do not address information flows arising from *covert channels* such as termination, timing *etc.* Moreover, we study information flow in the context of low-level languages, namely, Java bytecode, since we want to analyse real-world applications as they are downloaded from the Internet or embedded in low-level devices such as banking cards, for which security is a real issue.

---

* Supported by Marie Curie Fellowship number HPMF-CT-2002-01848

A first contribution of this paper is the novel use of a graph-based representation of Java bytecode to identify all and only the implicit flows in the program with the nodes of the graph with at least two successors. This lets us fit inside the same setting all implicit flows which can arise in a Java bytecode, from conditionals to exceptions to dynamic method dispatch. Moreover, it lets us recover the structure of low-level code, without relying on decompilation.

A second contribution is the implementation of our analysis for full Java bytecode through Boolean functions, as pioneered in [12], efficiently implemented through binary decision diagrams [8].

2   Some Examples of Analysis

In Section 3 we describe our information flow analysis for Java bytecode. Here, we show some examples of analysis. We consider several Java byte codes as well as their original Java source codes (since it is easier to understand than the corresponding bytecode). However, our analyser actually works on the compiled bytecode. We only report the variables which flow into the return value of the methods or their exceptions, since the final values of the local variables are not observable when a method returns.

Example 1. Consider the following Java method:

```
public int loop1(int x) {      0: iconst 0      5: iinc 2, 1
   int res;                    1: istore 2     6: goto 2
   for (res = 0; res < x; res++);   2: iload 2  7: iload 2
   return res;                 3: iload 1      8: ireturn
}                              4: if_icmpge 7
```

The analyser reports the information flow set $\{l_1 \leadsto s_0\}$ *i.e.*, the initial value of local variable 1 (which holds x) may affect the final value of the only element s_0 in the operand stack at the end of loop1 (*i.e.*, the return value of loop1). This is an implicit flow. No flow is computed for the exceptions *i.e.*, loop1 does not raise an exception in a way which depends from its input arguments.   □

Example 2. Consider the following Java method:

```
public int loop2(int x) {      0: iconst 0      6: goto 2
   int res;                    1: istore 2     7: bipush 10
   for (res = 0; res < x; res++);   2: iload 2  8: istore 2
   res = 10;                   3: iload 1      9: iload 2
   return res;                 4: if_icmpge 7  10: ireturn
}                              5: iinc 2, 1
```

which is obtained by adding "res=10" to the program in Example 1. This time the analyser computes the empty set of information flows. This is correct since the return value of the method does not depend from its arguments.   □

Example 3. Consider the following Java method:

```
public int divide1(int a, int b) {          0: iload 1
    return a/b;                             1: iload 2
}                                           2: idiv
                                            3: ireturn
```

The analyser reports the information flow set $\{l_1 \leadsto s_0, l_2 \leadsto s_0, l_2 \leadsto e\}$ *i.e.*, both
a and b (local variables 1 and 2) may flow to the return value (s_0). The flow
$l_2 \leadsto e$ says that divide1 may raise an exception in a way which depends from
the initial value of b (if b = 0, then a division by zero occurs).   □

Example 4. Consider the following Java method:

```
public int divide2(int a, int b) {       0: iload 1      10: iload 3
    int res;                             1: iload 2      11: ireturn
    try {                                2: idiv
        a = a/b;                         3: istore 1
        res = 0;                         4: iconst 0
    } catch (ArithmeticException ae) {   5: istore 3
        res = 1;                         6: goto 10
    }                                    7: astore 4
    return res;                          8: iconst 1
}                                        9: istore 3
```

The analyser computes the set $\{l_2 \leadsto s_0\}$ *i.e.*, b (local variable 2) may flow to the
return value. This is an implicit flow, since if b is initially 0 then a division by
zero occurs and divide2 returns 1. Otherwise, it returns 0. The initial value of
a is irrelevant, so the flow $l_1 \leadsto s_0$ is not reported, while it was in Example 3.
Since the exception is handled inside divide2, there is no flow from b to e.   □

Example 5. Consider the following Java method:

```
public int divide3(int a, int b) {       0: iload 1       12: iconst 2
    int res;                             1: iload 2       13: istore 3
    try {                                2: idiv          14: goto 27
        a = a/b;                         3: istore 1      15: astore 5
        res = 0;                         4: iconst 0      16: iconst 2
    } catch (ArithmeticException ae) {   5: istore 3      17: istore 3
        res = 1;                         6: iconst 2      18: aload 5
    } finally {                          7: istore 3      19: athrow
        res = 2;                         8: goto 20       20: iload 3
    }                                    9: astore 4      21: ireturn
    return res;                         10: iconst 1
}                                       11: istore 3
```

The analyser computes the empty set of information flows, since divide3 *always*
returns 2. Hence our analyser is able to deal with a complex interaction between
exceptions and the jsr and ret bytecodes used to implement finally [17].   □

3   Information Flow Analysis for Java Bytecode

Java bytecode [17] is a strongly-typed, object-oriented low-level language. It lacks an explicit scope structure and uses an operand stack to hold intermediate computational results. A Java bytecode program consists of a set of classes, each defining a set of methods and fields. A method contains a sequence of Java bytecode statements, still called *bytecodes*. Stack and local variables used to execute a method are denoted by $\mathcal{S}_m$ and $\mathcal{L}_m$ and both start from index 0. When it is clear from the context, we write $\mathcal{S}$ and $\mathcal{L}$ instead of $\mathcal{S}_m$ and $\mathcal{L}_m$.

The verification algorithm [17] imposes some rules on valid Java bytecode. One of them is essential here, and requires that the stack height at each given program point is statically known *i.e.*, for each bytecode b we know the indexes q and p of the top stack element before and after b's execution, respectively (if the stack is empty, we assume that they are equal to -1). Hence, one cannot create information flows by manipulating the stack height.

The rest of this section describes our analysis. Section 3.1 shows how we recover the structure of a Java bytecode program through a control-flow graph. Section 3.2 characterises implicit flows in a graph-theoretical way. Section 3.3 describes the analysis of single bytecodes and Section 3.4 extends it to sequences of bytecodes. Sections 3.5, 3.6 and 3.7 add support for methods, exceptions and fields, respectively. Section 3.8 discusses the correctness of the analysis.

3.1   Recovering the Structure of Java Bytecode Programs

As a low-level programming language, Java bytecode lacks structure. Consider for example the Java program in Figure 1 (on the left) and its translation into Java bytecode (in the middle). The structure of the Java program is expressed syntactically. Namely, the body of the loop is y=y-1;x=y;z=z+1 and y=0 is executed at its end. Recovering the structure of the Java bytecode is much harder. We need to examine the control transfer bytecodes in order to understand, for instance, that lines 6-15 are the body of a loop.

We solve this problem through the technique already applied in [1] to other programming languages. Namely, we split the code into *basic blocks* and allow transfers of control only at the end of a block. We build a control-flow graph by connecting these blocks with directed edges which reflect the transfers of control in the program. For instance, the bytecode in the middle of Figure 1 is translated into the control-flow graph on its right, which contains control-flow information similar to that of the original Java program: *Block 0* is the guard of the loop; *Block 1* corresponds to y=0; and *Block 2* is the body of the loop. At the end of *Block 0*, control is transferred to *Block 2* if x > 0, and to *Block 1* otherwise. The new bytecodes goon_ifle and goon_ifgt are there to select the right execution path, so that we do not need a new kind of node for conditions.

3.2   Implicit Flows in the Control-Flow Graph

Implicit information flows are originated from conditionals, such as ifle in Figure 1, but also from dynamic method dispatch and exceptions. We translate a

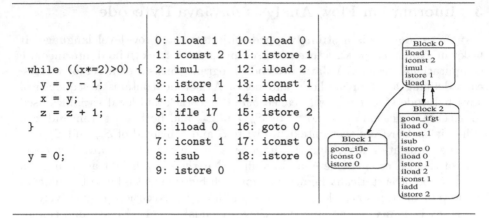

```
                   0: iload 1    10: iload 0
                   1: iconst 2   11: istore 1
while ((x*=2)>0) { 2: imul       12: iload 2
    y = y - 1;     3: istore 1   13: iconst 1
    x = y;         4: iload 1    14: iadd
    z = z + 1;     5: ifle 17    15: istore 2
}                  6: iload 0    16: goto 0
                   7: iconst 1   17: iconst 0
y = 0;             8: isub       18: istore 0
                   9: istore 0
```

Fig. 1. A Java method (on the left); its translation to Java bytecode (in the middle); and its control-flow graph (on the right).

virtual method call into a block with as many immediate successors as there are possible targets for the call (Section 3.5); and we put a bytecode which might raise an exception at the end of a basic block with two immediate successors, one for the case when the exception is raised, and another for the normal continuation (Section 3.6). The following result follows.

Proposition 1 (Implicit Flows). *There is a one-to-one correspondence between sources of implicit flows and nodes of the control-flow graph with at least two immediate successors.* □

Example 6. In the control-flow graph in Figure 1, the only implicit flow arises from *Block 0*, which transfers control either to *Block 1* or to *Block 2*. The choice depends on the value of the top element of the stack, where x is stored. □

Proposition 1 identifies the sources of implicit flows with some nodes of the graph. But we also need their *scope i.e.*, the set of bytecodes affected by the implicit flow arising at those nodes.

Definition 1 (Scope). *The scope $\varsigma(n)$ of a node n of a control-flow graph are the nodes which are executed conditionally, depending on the path taken at n.* □

Example 7. In the graph in Figure 1, the execution of *Block 0* and *Block 2* depends on the path taken at *Block 0*, while *Block 1* is always executed (assuming that the program terminates). Hence $\varsigma(Block\ 0) = \{Block\ 0, Block\ 2\}$.

Example 8. Consider the following graph. Its scopes are reported to its right.

$$\varsigma(1) = \{2, 3, 4, 6, 7, 8\} \qquad \varsigma(5) = \{\}$$
$$\varsigma(2) = \{7\} \qquad \varsigma(6) = \{\}$$
$$\varsigma(3) = \{\} \qquad \varsigma(7) = \{\}$$
$$\varsigma(4) = \{4, 6\} \qquad \varsigma(8) = \{\}.$$

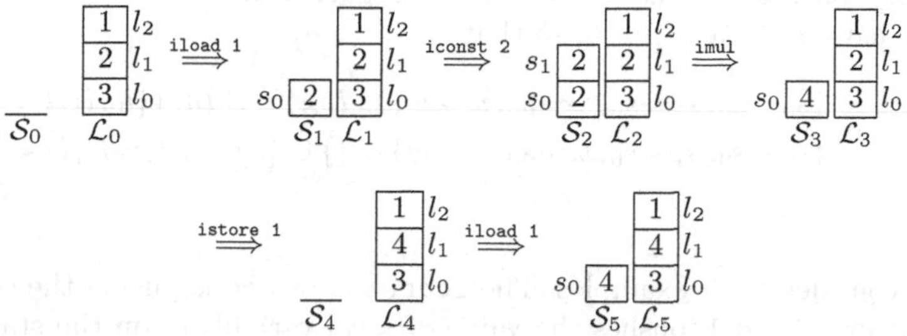

Fig. 2. Stack and local variables during an execution of some bytecodes.

Nodes 3, 5, 6, 7 and 8 do not generate implicit flows and have empty scopes. Node 5 is not in the scope of 1 since its execution is independent from the path taken at 1, namely 5 is always executed after 1.   □

Due to space concerns, an algorithm for computing the scopes is available in the extended version of this paper [13].

3.3   Step I: Single Bytecodes

We show here how we compute the information flows for some simple Java bytecodes, which represent most of the bytecodes described in [17].

Figure 2 shows an execution involving imul, which pops two values from the stack and pushes their product instead. The output value of s_0 depends on the input values of s_0 and s_1 i.e., a change in such values may affect the output value of s_0. The other variables keep their values unchanged. Hence imul features the set of information flows $\{s_0 \leadsto s_0, s_1 \leadsto s_0, l_0 \leadsto l_0, l_1 \leadsto l_1, l_2 \leadsto l_2\}$. We must however consider the implicit flows that arise if imul is in the scope of a node n of the control-flow graph. We express this with the flow $w \leadsto s_0$ (since s_0 is updated) where w stands for a generic implicit flow and will be bound when we analyse n (Definition 6). This way the analysis is *modular i.e.*, we analyse each component independently from its context. This is formalised below.

Definition 2 (Identity Flow Mappings). *The identity flow mappings for the stack elements and local variables are* $Id_S(j) = \{s_i \leadsto s_i \mid 0 \leq i < j\}$ *and* $Id_{\mathcal{L}}(X) = \{l_i \leadsto l_i \mid l_i \in X\}$.   □

Definition 3 (Denotation for imul). *The information flows for* imul *(with* q *input stack elements and* p *output stack elements) are*

$$[\![\text{imul}]\!]^\alpha = \{s_q \leadsto s_p, s_{q-1} \leadsto s_p, w \leadsto s_p, w \leadsto w\} \cup Id_S(p) \cup Id_{\mathcal{L}}(\mathcal{L})$$

where w *is a variable which stands for the (yet unknown) implicit flows.*   □

The flow $w \leadsto w$ is used in Definition 5 to let implicit flows propagate along a sequential composition of bytecodes.

Example 9. Consider the `imul` bytecode in Figure 2 and its input and output states. We have $q = 1$ and $p = 0$, so that

$$[\![\texttt{imul}]\!]^\alpha = \{s_0 \rightsquigarrow s_0, s_1 \rightsquigarrow s_0, w \rightsquigarrow s_0, w \rightsquigarrow w\} \cup Id_{\mathcal{S}}(0) \cup Id_{\mathcal{L}}(\{l_0, l_1, l_2\})$$
$$= \{s_0 \rightsquigarrow s_0, s_1 \rightsquigarrow s_0, w \rightsquigarrow s_0, w \rightsquigarrow w\} \cup \{\} \cup \{l_0 \rightsquigarrow l_0, l_1 \rightsquigarrow l_1, l_2 \rightsquigarrow l_2\}.$$

$\square$

Let us consider other examples. The `iconst c` bytecode pushes the constant c on the stack, `iload k` pushes the value of local variable l_k on the stack, and `istore k` pops the top of the stack and stores it into local variable l_k.

Definition 4 (Denotations for `iconst c`, `iload k` and `istore k`). *The information flows for* `iconst c`, `iload k` *and* `istore k` *are*

$$[\![\texttt{iconst c}]\!]^\alpha = \{w \rightsquigarrow s_p, w \rightsquigarrow w\} \cup Id_{\mathcal{S}}(p) \cup Id_{\mathcal{L}}(\mathcal{L})$$
$$[\![\texttt{iload k}]\!]^\alpha = \{l_k \rightsquigarrow s_p, w \rightsquigarrow s_p, w \rightsquigarrow w\} \cup Id_{\mathcal{S}}(p) \cup Id_{\mathcal{L}}(\mathcal{L})$$
$$[\![\texttt{istore k}]\!]^\alpha = \{s_q \rightsquigarrow l_k, w \rightsquigarrow l_k, w \rightsquigarrow w\} \cup Id_{\mathcal{S}}(p+1) \cup Id_{\mathcal{L}}(\mathcal{L} \setminus \{l_k\})$$

where w is a variable which stands for the (yet unknown) implicit flows. $\square$

Example 10. The denotations of the `iconst`, `iload` and `istore` bytecodes in Figure 2 are (the two occurrences of `iload 1` have the same p and q):

$$[\![\texttt{iload 1}]\!]^\alpha = \{l_1 \rightsquigarrow s_0, w \rightsquigarrow s_0, w \rightsquigarrow w\} \cup Id_{\mathcal{S}}(0) \cup Id_{\mathcal{L}}(\{l_0, l_1, l_2\})$$
$$= \{l_1 \rightsquigarrow s_0, w \rightsquigarrow s_0, w \rightsquigarrow w\} \cup \{\} \cup \{l_0 \rightsquigarrow l_0, l_1 \rightsquigarrow l_1, l_2 \rightsquigarrow l_2\}$$
$$[\![\texttt{iconst 2}]\!]^\alpha = \{w \rightsquigarrow s_1, w \rightsquigarrow w\} \cup Id_{\mathcal{S}}(1) \cup Id_{\mathcal{L}}(\{l_0, l_1, l_2\})$$
$$= \{w \rightsquigarrow s_1, w \rightsquigarrow w\} \cup \{s_0 \rightsquigarrow s_0\} \cup \{l_0 \rightsquigarrow l_0, l_1 \rightsquigarrow l_1, l_2 \rightsquigarrow l_2\}$$
$$[\![\texttt{istore 1}]\!]^\alpha = \{s_0 \rightsquigarrow l_1, w \rightsquigarrow l_1, w \rightsquigarrow w\} \cup Id_{\mathcal{S}}(0) \cup Id_{\mathcal{L}}(\{l_0, l_2\})$$
$$= \{s_0 \rightsquigarrow l_1, w \rightsquigarrow l_1, w \rightsquigarrow w\} \cup \{\} \cup \{l_0 \rightsquigarrow l_0, l_2 \rightsquigarrow l_2\}.$$

$\square$

3.4   Step II: Composition of Denotations

We describe here how we compose denotations of Java bytecodes that occur sequentially in the same basic block. As in [9,12], we say that there is an information flow from x to y in the composition $C_1; C_2$ if there is a flow from x to z in C_1 and a flow from z to y in C_2.

Definition 5 (Composition of Denotations). *Let C_1 and C_2 be two Java bytecodes. The information flow generated by executing C_2 immediately after C_1 is* $[\![C_1]\!]^\alpha \otimes [\![C_2]\!]^\alpha = \{x \rightsquigarrow y \mid \exists z.x \rightsquigarrow z \in [\![C_1]\!]^\alpha \wedge z \rightsquigarrow y \in [\![C_2]\!]^\alpha\}.$ $\square$

Example 11. The composition $[\![B_0]\!]^\alpha = [\![\texttt{iload 1}]\!]^\alpha \otimes [\![\texttt{iconst 2}]\!]^\alpha \otimes [\![\texttt{imul}]\!]^\alpha \otimes [\![\texttt{istore 1}]\!]^\alpha \otimes [\![\texttt{iload 1}]\!]^\alpha$ of the bytecodes in Figure 2 (see also Examples 9 and 10) is $\{w \rightsquigarrow l_1, w \rightsquigarrow s_0, w \rightsquigarrow w, l_1 \rightsquigarrow s_0, l_0 \rightsquigarrow l_0, l_1 \rightsquigarrow l_1, l_2 \rightsquigarrow l_2\}.$ $\square$

Definition 5 lets us compose denotations of bytecodes inside a given basic block. Composing the denotations of two basic blocks is similar in principle, but we must propagate the implicit flows from each basic block to those in its scope.

Example 12 (Handling Implicit Flows). Consider the control-flow graph in Example 8. During the analysis, node 1 imposes its implicit flow on its immediate successors 2, 3 and 4, which accept it since they are all in the scope of 1. Then node 2 imposes its implicit flow, and the implicit flow that it got from 1, on nodes 7 and 8. Node 7 accepts both incoming implicit flows since it is in the scope of both 1 and 2, while node 8 accepts the incoming implicit flow of 1, since it is in its scope, but ignores the implicit flow of 2, since it is not in its scope. □

The example above leads us to redefine the denotation of a basic block in order to *impose*, *accept* and *ignore* implicit flows. Namely, we replace each $w \leadsto x \in [\![B_i]\!]^\alpha$ with $w_j \leadsto x$ when the flow w_j generated at B_j must be accepted.

Definition 6 (Accepting and Ignoring Incoming Implicit Flows). *Let B_i be a basic block. Its denotation $[\![B_i]\!]^\alpha$ is transformed in order to accept or ignore incoming implicit flows on the basis of the scope structure:*

$$\mathcal{W}(B_i) = \{x \leadsto y \in [\![B_i]\!]^\alpha \mid x \neq w\} \cup \{w_j \leadsto y \mid w \leadsto y \in [\![B_i]\!]^\alpha \wedge i \in \varsigma(j)\}$$

where w_j stands for implicit flow generated by B_j. □

Example 13. In the graph in Figure 1, *Block 0* is in its own scope. Hence its denotation $[\![B_0]\!]^\alpha = \{w \leadsto l_1, w \leadsto s_1, w \leadsto w, l_1 \leadsto s_0, l_0 \leadsto l_0, l_1 \leadsto l_1, l_2 \leadsto l_2\}$ (Example 11) is refined into $\mathcal{W}(B_0) = \{l_1 \leadsto s_0, l_0 \leadsto l_0, l_1 \leadsto l_1, l_2 \leadsto l_2\} \cup \{w_0 \leadsto l_1, w_0 \leadsto s_1, w_0 \leadsto w\}$. If the same bytecodes were contained in node 7 of the graph of Example 8, then $\mathcal{W}(B_7) = \{l_1 \leadsto s_0, l_0 \leadsto l_0, l_1 \leadsto l_1, l_2 \leadsto l_2\} \cup \{w_1 \leadsto l_1, w_1 \leadsto s_1, w_1 \leadsto w, w_2 \leadsto l_1, w_2 \leadsto s_1, w_2 \leadsto w\}$ since node 7 is in the scope of nodes 1 and 2. □

We further refine $[\![B_i]\!]^\alpha$ now, in order to impose to B_i's successors its implicit flow, if any (Proposition 1), and those propagated from B_i's predecessors. A condition is always tested at the end of a basic block with at least two successors. For instance, in the graph in Figure 1, the condition `ifle` is tested at the end of *Block 0*. For simplicity, we assume that such conditions work always as follows: they check if they hold on the top k values on the stack, remove the top l values from the stack and decide which path to take. Hence, their information flows state that there are flows from the top k stack elements to w_i, which is the implicit flow generated by B_i; and that the rest of the stack and the local variables flow into themselves.

Definition 7 (Denotation of a Condition). *Let B_i be a basic block, q the index of the top element of the stack at its end (before the condition is checked), k the number of stack elements tested by the condition, and l the number of elements removed from the stack after checking the condition. The information flows generated by the condition are*

$$M_i = \{s_j \leadsto w_i \mid q - k < j \leq q\} \cup Id_{\mathcal{S}}(q - l + 1) \cup Id_{\mathcal{L}}(\mathcal{L}).$$

Note that when B_i does not end with a condition then $k = l = 0$ and M_i behaves like an identity mapping. $\quad\square$

Example 14. For the condition `ifgt` checked at the end of *Block 0* in Figure 1 we have $q = k = l = 1$. Hence $M_0 = \{s_0 \leadsto w_0, l_0 \leadsto l_0, l_1 \leadsto l_1, l_2 \leadsto l_2\}$. $\quad\square$

We modify the denotation of a block B_i, in order to handle both the incoming and the outgoing implicit flows. Namely, we compose $\mathcal{W}(B_i)$ with M_i, and add the flows $w_j \leadsto w_j$ so that the implicit flows coming from B_i's predecessors are propagated to its successors.

Definition 8 (Refined Denotation of Basic Blocks). *The refined denotation of a basic block B_i which can handle incoming and outgoing implicit flows is $\mathcal{R}(B_i) = (\mathcal{W}(B_i) \otimes M_i) \cup \{w_i \leadsto w_i \mid w_i \leadsto w \in \mathcal{W}(B_i)\}$.* $\quad\square$

Example 15. For the graph in Figure 1, we have computed $\mathcal{W}(B_0)$ in Example 13 and M_0 in Example 14. Then $\mathcal{R}(B_0) = (\mathcal{W}(B_0) \otimes M_0) \cup \{w_0 \leadsto w_0\} = \{l_0 \leadsto l_0, l_1 \leadsto l_1, l_2 \leadsto l_2, l_1 \leadsto w_0, w_0 \leadsto l_1, w_0 \leadsto w_0\}$. Note that $w_0 \leadsto l_1$ *i.e.*, the implicit flow of B_0 flows into l_1 since B_0 is in its own scope and updates l_1; $w_0 \leadsto w_0$ *i.e.*, B_0's incoming implicit flow is passed to its successors; and $l_1 \leadsto w_0$ *i.e.*, the same flow w_0 is also generated by B_0. $\quad\square$

By using the refined denotation for each block in the control-flow graph, we generate an equation system whose least solution approximates the information flows of the corresponding Java bytecode program.

Definition 9 (Information Flow Equation System). *Let P be a Java bytecode program. Its information flow equation system is the set of equations $E_i = \cup\{E_j \otimes \mathcal{R}(B_i) \mid B_j$ is an immediate predecessor of $B_i\}$ for each basic block B_i in the control-flow graph of P.* $\quad\square$

We assume that the computation starts always from an initial *basic block B_s* which simply copies the input values to the corresponding output values. This is a technical issue required when the real initial node occurs in a loop.

Example 16. Consider the Java program, its translation into Java bytecode and its control-flow graph in Figure 1. Local variables l_0, l_1 and l_2 correspond to the original variables y, x and z, respectively. For simplicity, we use the original names instead of l_0, l_1 and l_2. Moreover, we assume that the stack is empty before *Block 0*, and hence between all blocks. *Block 0* is the only conditional block, with scope $\varsigma(0) = \{0, 2\}$. We have:

$$\mathcal{R}(B_s) = \{x \leadsto x, y \leadsto y, z \leadsto z\} \quad \mathcal{R}(B_0) = \{x \leadsto w_0, w_0 \leadsto x, w_0 \leadsto w_0, x \leadsto x, y \leadsto y, z \leadsto z\}$$

$$\mathcal{R}(B_1) = \{x \leadsto x, z \leadsto z\} \qquad \mathcal{R}(B_2) = \left\{ \begin{array}{l} w_0 \leadsto y, w_0 \leadsto x, w_0 \leadsto z, w_0 \leadsto w_0, \\ y \leadsto x, y \leadsto y, z \leadsto z \end{array} \right\}.$$

By using the above refined denotations we generate the equations $E_s = \mathcal{R}(B_s)$, $E_1 = E_0 \otimes \mathcal{R}(B_1)$, $E_0 = (E_s \otimes \mathcal{R}(B_0)) \cup (E_2 \otimes \mathcal{R}(B_0))$ and $E_2 = E_0 \otimes \mathcal{R}(B_2)$ whose solution for E_1 (the exit point): is $\{x \leadsto x, y \leadsto x, x \leadsto z, z \leadsto z, y \leadsto z\}$. The flow $y \leadsto z$ is the composition of $y \leadsto x$ and $x \leadsto z$ due to the repeated execution of the loop. Nothing flows to y since it is assigned to a constant at the end. $\quad\square$

3.5   Step III: Methods

Java bytecode has a complex family of method call bytecodes. When a method m is invoked on an object x, namely $x.m(e_1, \ldots, e_k)$, the following steps are performed:

1. The value of the variable x is pushed into the stack;
2. The values of $e_1, \ldots, e_k$ are computed and pushed into the stack;
3. The actual method to be called is determined on the basis of the class of x;
4. A new frame with local variables $\mathcal{L}_m$ and empty stack S_m is created;
5. The top $k+1$ elements of the stack are copied into $l_0^m, l_1^m, \ldots, l_k^m \in \mathcal{L}_m$ and removed from the stack; and
6. Control is transferred to the method code, which uses $\mathcal{L}_m$ and $\mathcal{S}_m$.

When the method executes an `ireturn` bytecode, the top element of S_m is pushed into the stack of the caller, to which control returns.

The execution of a method might induce information flows from its arguments to its return value r. Moreover, if at least two candidate methods exist in step 3, then an implicit information flow exists from x to r, since by observing r one might learn which method was called and hence gather information about x. When we build the control-flow graph of a program, we use class hierarchy analysis [10] to approximate statically the dynamic classes of x and hence determine a superset of the methods that might be called at run-time. For each such fully qualified method $\kappa.\mathbf{m}$, we create a basic block which statically calls $\kappa.\mathbf{m}$ (`call` $\kappa.\mathbf{m}$) and we link it as a successor to the invocation point. If at least two successors exist, the mechanism of Section 3.4 handles the implicit flow.

We perform a denotational static analysis. Namely, we use a table from method names $\kappa.\mathbf{m}$ to their current approximation $[\![\kappa.\mathbf{m}]\!]^\alpha$, initialised to $\{\}$ and updated iteratively until a fixpoint. The set $[\![\kappa.\mathbf{m}]\!]^\alpha$ lives in the context of $\kappa.\mathbf{m}$, whose arguments are the lowest local variables, whose return value (if any) is the top of a stack of one element and whose input stack is empty [17]. First we explain how we compute the denotations of the `call` and `ireturn` bytecodes, and then how we modify the equation system of Definition 9 to compute the denotation of each method.

Definition 10 (Denotation for `call`). *Let $[\![\kappa.\mathbf{m}]\!]^\alpha$ be the current denotation of the method $\kappa.\mathbf{m}$ and assume that it uses l_i' to denote its arguments (including `this`) and that it uses s_0' for its return value. Then $[\![\text{call } \kappa.\mathbf{m}]\!]^\alpha$ is*

$$(\{s_{q-k+i} \rightsquigarrow l_i'\}_{i=0}^{i=k} \otimes [\![\kappa.\mathbf{m}]\!]^\alpha \otimes \{s_0' \rightsquigarrow s_p\}) \cup \{w \rightsquigarrow s_p, w \rightsquigarrow w\} \cup Id_{\mathcal{S}}(p) \cup Id_{\mathcal{L}}(\mathcal{L}).$$

□

Definition 11 (Denotation for `ireturn`). *The information flows generated by `ireturn` are $[\![\text{ireturn}]\!]^\alpha = \{s_q \rightsquigarrow s_0, w \rightsquigarrow s_0, w \rightsquigarrow w\}$.* □

We add now to the equation system an equation for each method so that the denotations of the methods are computed during the fixpoint computation.

```
int loop_rec(int l, int v, int p) {
    if (v > 0) {
        return loop_rec(l - 1,l - 1,p + 1);
    } else {
        return p;
    }
}

int loop_rec(int,int,int);
    0:  iload 2          8:  isub
    1:  ifle    14       9:  iload 3
    2:  aload 0         10:  iconst 1
    3:  iload 1         11:  iadd
    4:  iconst 1        12:  invoke loop_rec
    5:  isub            13:  ireturn
    6:  iload 1         14:  iload 3
    7:  iconst 1        15:  ireturn
```

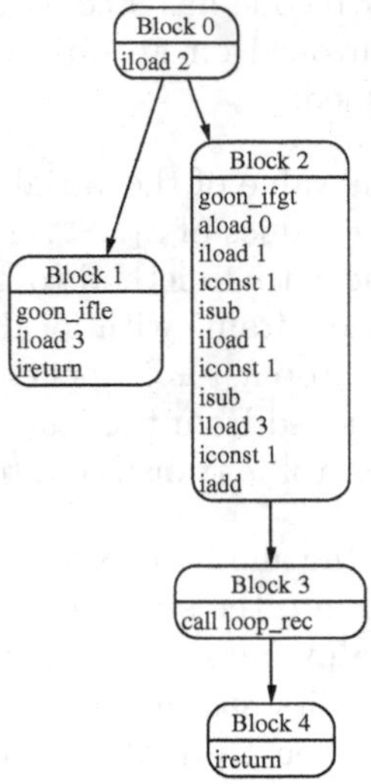

Block 0
iload 2

Block 2
goon_ifgt
aload 0
iload 1
iconst 1
isub
iload 1
iconst 1
isub
iload 3
iconst 1
iadd

Block 1
goon_ifle
iload 3
ireturn

Block 3
call loop_rec

Block 4
ireturn

Fig. 3. A recursive method.

Definition 12 (Equations for the Methods). *For each method $\kappa.\mathtt{m}$, we add the following equation to the equation system of Definition 9:*

$$[\![\kappa.\mathtt{m}]\!]^\alpha = \cup\{E_i \mid E_i \text{ finishes with an } \mathtt{ireturn} \text{ statement}\}[v/v']$$

where $[v/v']$ renames each variable v into v', to distinguish the variables of the method from those of the call site. □

Example 17. Consider the recursive method $\mathtt{loop\_rec}$ and its translation into Java bytecode and into a control-flow graph in Figure 3. Block 3 of such graph contains the recursive call to $\mathtt{loop\_rec}$, solved statically (hence it does not induce any implicit flow). The refined denotations for each basic block are:

$$\mathcal{R}(B_0) = \{l_0 \leadsto l_0, l_1 \leadsto l_1, l_2 \leadsto l_2, l_3 \leadsto l_3, l_2 \leadsto w_0, l_2 \leadsto s_0\}$$
$$\mathcal{R}(B_1) = \{l_3 \leadsto s_0, w_0 \leadsto s_0, w_0 \leadsto w_0\}$$
$$\mathcal{R}(B_2) = \{l_0 \leadsto s_0, l_1 \leadsto s_1, l_2 \leadsto s_2, l_3 \leadsto s_3, w_0 \leadsto s_0, w_0 \leadsto s_1, w_0 \leadsto s_2, w_0 \leadsto s_3, w_0 \leadsto w_0\}$$
$$\mathcal{R}(B_3) = (\{s_0 \leadsto l_0', s_1 \leadsto l_1', s_2 \leadsto l_2', s_3 \leadsto l_3'\} \otimes [\![\mathtt{loop\_rec}]\!]^\alpha \otimes \{s_0' \leadsto s_0\}) \cup$$
$$\qquad\qquad \{w_0 \leadsto s_0, w_0 \leadsto w_0\} \cup \{l_0 \leadsto l_0, l_1 \leadsto l_1, l_2 \leadsto l_2, l_3 \leadsto l_3\}$$
$$\mathcal{R}(B_4) = \{s_0 \leadsto s_0, w_0 \leadsto s_0, w_0 \leadsto w_0\}$$

and the corresponding equation system is

$$E_0 = \mathcal{R}(B_0) \qquad E_1 = E_0 \otimes \mathcal{R}(B_1) \qquad\qquad E_2 = E_0 \otimes \mathcal{R}(B_2)$$
$$E_3 = E_2 \otimes \mathcal{R}(B_3) \qquad E_4 = E_3 \otimes \mathcal{R}(B_4) \qquad [\![\mathtt{loop\_rec}]\!]^\alpha = (E_1 \cup E_4)[v/v'].$$

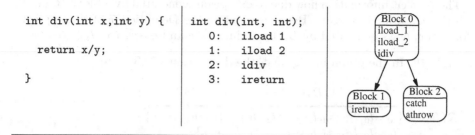

Fig. 4. A Java method which may raise an exception.

The solution for $[\![\texttt{loop\_rec}]\!]^\alpha$ is $\{l_1'\!\rightsquigarrow\! s_0', l_2'\!\rightsquigarrow\! s_0', l_3'\!\rightsquigarrow\! s_0'\}$. It is clear that l_3' and l_2' (*i.e.*, p and v) flow to the return value r. It is not obvious instead that l_1' (*i.e.*, 1) flows to r. But this is true since the second argument of the recursive call is 1-1, and hence v during the computation depends on the initial value of 1. $\square$

3.6   Step IV: Exceptions

Some bytecodes throw exceptions [17], which are potential sources of implicit information flows. For example an arithmetic exception raised by the division x/y leaks the information "*y is zero*". To handle exceptions, we use a variable e which represents the exception. Our representation of Java bytecode through basic blocks is such that each bytecode which might raise an exception is at the end of a basic block with at least two successors, for normal or exceptional continuation. The latter might further route the computation to the appropriate exception handler, if any.

Example 18. Consider in Figure 4 a Java program and its translation into its bytecode and control-flow graph. The execution of idiv leads to *Block 1* if s_1 (*i.e.*, y) is not 0, and to *Block 2* otherwise. $\square$

The denotation of a typical bytecode that can raise exceptions is as follows.

Definition 13 (Denotation of idiv). *The information flows for* idiv *are*

$$[\![\texttt{idiv}]\!]^\alpha = \{s_q\!\rightsquigarrow\! s_p, s_{q-1}\!\rightsquigarrow\! s_p, w\!\rightsquigarrow\! s_p, w\!\rightsquigarrow\! w, s_q\!\rightsquigarrow\! e\} \cup Id_{\mathcal{S}}(p) \cup Id_{\mathcal{L}}(\mathcal{L}).$$

$\square$

Both s_q and s_{q-1} flow into s_p (the result of the division) but only s_q flows to e. In the exception handlers, we use the bytecodes catch, which pushes an exception into an empty stack, and athrow, which throws the top of the stack.

Definition 14 (Denotations of catch and athrow). *The denotations of the bytecodes* catch *and* athrow *are:*

$$[\![\texttt{catch}]\!]^\alpha = \{e\!\rightsquigarrow\! s_0, w\!\rightsquigarrow\! s_0, w\!\rightsquigarrow\! w\} \cup Id_{\mathcal{L}}(\mathcal{L})$$
$$[\![\texttt{athrow}]\!]^\alpha = \{w\!\rightsquigarrow\! e, s_q\!\rightsquigarrow\! e, w\!\rightsquigarrow\! w\} \cup Id_{\mathcal{L}}(\mathcal{L}).$$

$\square$

The implicit information flow due to exceptions generated by a block B_i must be imposed on its successors. Hence we update the Definition 7 of the implicit information flows generated by B_i, by adding $e \leadsto e$ and $e \leadsto w_i$ to M_i.

Example 19. In the graph in Figure 4, the denotations $\mathcal{R}(B_i)$ are

$$\mathcal{R}(B_0) = \overbrace{\{l_0 \leadsto l_0, l_1 \leadsto s_0, l_2 \leadsto s_0, l_2 \leadsto e\}}^{\mathcal{W}(B_0)} \otimes \overbrace{\{e \leadsto w_0, e \leadsto e\}}^{M_0}$$
$$= \{l_0 \leadsto l_0, l_1 \leadsto s_0, l_2 \leadsto s_0, l_2 \leadsto e, l_2 \leadsto w_0\}$$
$$\mathcal{R}(B_1) = \{s_0 \leadsto s_0, w_0 \leadsto s_0, w_0 \leadsto w_0\} \qquad \mathcal{R}(B_2) = \{e \leadsto e, w_0 \leadsto e, w_0 \leadsto w_0\}$$

and the corresponding equation system is $E_0 = \mathcal{R}(B_0)$, $E_1 = E_0 \otimes \mathcal{R}(B_1)$, $E_2 = E_0 \otimes \mathcal{R}(B_2)$. The denotation of the method div is $(E_1 \cup (E_2 \otimes \{e \leadsto e\}))[v/v'] = \{l_1' \leadsto s_0', l_2' \leadsto s_0', l_2' \leadsto e'\}$ *i.e.*, we consider all its final blocks. However, exceptional blocks contribute through e only, so we write $E_2 \otimes \{e \leadsto e\}$ to project E_2 on e. $\square$

An exception can be propagated back across the method invocations stack. Hence, in Definition 10, we change $\{s_0' \leadsto s_p\}$ into $\{s_0' \leadsto s_p, e' \leadsto e\}$.

3.7   Step V: Fields

We treat fields as static (*i.e.*, global) class variables. Hence we do not distinguish between the same field of two objects of a given class. The two bytecodes that manipulate fields are `getfield f`, which pops an object from the stack and pushes the value of its field `f` instead, and `putfield f`, which pops a value v and an object o from the stack and sets the field `f` of o to the value v.

Definition 15 (Denotations of `getfield` and `putfield`). *The information flow denotations of* `getfield` *and* `putfield` *are:*

$$[\![\texttt{getfield f}]\!]^\alpha = \{f \leadsto s_p\} \cup Id_\mathcal{S}(p) \cup Id_\mathcal{L}(\mathcal{L})$$
$$[\![\texttt{putfield f}]\!]^\alpha = \{s_q \leadsto f\} \cup Id_\mathcal{S}(p+1) \cup Id_\mathcal{L}(\mathcal{L}).$$

$\square$

Since we treat fields as static variables, we accumulate their information flows when composing denotations. Hence the denotation of `x.f=a; y.f=b; z=x.f` will include $\{a \leadsto z, b \leadsto z\}$ *i.e.*, the accumulation of $a \leadsto f$ and $b \leadsto f$.

Definition 16 (Refinement of $\otimes$). *The refinement of the composition operator $\otimes$ of Definition 5 is:*

$$[\![C_1]\!]^\alpha \otimes [\![C_2]\!]^\alpha = \{x \leadsto y \mid \exists z . x \leadsto z \in [\![C_1]\!]^\alpha \wedge z \leadsto y \in [\![C_2]\!]^\alpha\} \cup \{x \leadsto f \in [\![C_1]\!]^\alpha\}.$$

$\square$

Example 20 (Fields). Consider the following Java bytecode:

```
0: aload 0       3: aload 1       6: aload 0
1: iload 2       4: iload 3       7: getfield f
2: putfield f    5: putfield f    8: istore 4
```

The denotations for bytecodes 0-2, 3-5 and 6-8 are, respectively:

$$[\![C_{0-2}]\!]^{\alpha} = \{l_2 \rightsquigarrow f, l_0 \rightsquigarrow l_0, l_1 \rightsquigarrow l_1, l_2 \rightsquigarrow l_2, l_3 \rightsquigarrow l_3, l_4 \rightsquigarrow l_4\}$$
$$[\![C_{3-5}]\!]^{\alpha} = \{l_3 \rightsquigarrow f, l_0 \rightsquigarrow l_0, l_1 \rightsquigarrow l_1, l_2 \rightsquigarrow l_2, l_3 \rightsquigarrow l_3, l_4 \rightsquigarrow l_4\}$$
$$[\![C_{6-8}]\!]^{\alpha} = \{f \rightsquigarrow l_4, l_0 \rightsquigarrow l_0, l_1 \rightsquigarrow l_1, l_2 \rightsquigarrow l_2, l_3 \rightsquigarrow l_3\}.$$

Hence $[\![C_{0-2}]\!]^{\alpha} \otimes [\![C_{3-5}]\!]^{\alpha} \otimes [\![C_{6-8}]\!]^{\alpha} = \{l_2 \rightsquigarrow l_4, l_3 \rightsquigarrow l_4, l_0 \rightsquigarrow l_0, l_1 \rightsquigarrow l_1, l_2 \rightsquigarrow l_2, l_3 \rightsquigarrow l_3\}$ $\cup \{l_2 \rightsquigarrow f, l_3 \rightsquigarrow f\}$. The old definition of $\otimes$ would miss $\{l_2 \rightsquigarrow l_4, l_2 \rightsquigarrow f, l_3 \rightsquigarrow f\}$.   □

We also use a variable inside each method κ.m, which stands for the implicit flows affecting the call site of κ.m and is used when κ.m updates a field and its call site is in the scope of an implicit flow.

3.8   Correctness

A finite *execution trace* τ for a Java bytecode is a finite sequence of *states* (similar to those in [24]) of the form $\langle \ell, \varsigma, \mu \rangle$ where ℓ is an array of local variables, ς a stack and μ a heap. The initial and last states of τ are τ_i and τ_f, respectively. We access local variables, stack elements and fields in a state through a *path*.

Definition 17 (Path). *A path is $p = v.f_1.\ldots.f_n$ where v is a local variable l_k or a stack element s_h and $f_1, \ldots, f_n$ are field names. If $n = 0$ the path is just a local variable or a stack element. Paths are ordered as $p \preceq p'$ if and only if p is a prefix of p'. If p refers to a value of primitive type, such as an integer, p is a primitive path. If it refers to a location, p is a location path. The value of p in a state is*

$$\langle \ell, \varsigma, \mu \rangle (l_k) = \ell(k), \quad \langle \ell, \varsigma, \mu \rangle (s_h) = \varsigma(h), \quad \langle \ell, \varsigma, \mu \rangle (p.f) = \mu(\overbrace{\langle \ell, \varsigma, \mu \rangle (p)}^{l})(f)$$

The last case says that the value of $p.f$ is the value of the field f of the object $\mu(l)$ pointed by p. If l is null*, we define* $\langle \ell, \varsigma, \mu \rangle (p.f) = \bot$.   □

Information flows to primitive paths and to location paths are different.

Definition 18 (Information Flow to Primitive Paths). *Let C be a Java bytecode, p a path and q a primitive path. The input value of p flows to the output value of q, denoted by $p \overset{\pi}{\rightsquigarrow} q$, if there exist two execution traces τ and σ for C s.t.* $[(\tau_i(p) \neq \sigma_i(p)) \wedge (\forall p' \text{ s.t. } p \npreceq p'. \ \tau_i(p') = \sigma_i(p'))] \rightarrow (\tau_f(q) \neq \sigma_f(q))$.   □

The allocation policy of the Java Virtual Machine is not specified [17]. Hence information cannot leak through the exact value of a location, but only by comparing locations with each other or with null.

Definition 19 (Information Flow to Location Paths). *Let C be a Java bytecode, p a path and q_1, q_2 two location paths or a location path and null. Extend Definition 17 so that $\sigma(\text{null}) = \text{null}$. The input value of p flows to the comparison of the output values of q_1 and q_2, denoted by $p \overset{\lambda}{\rightsquigarrow} \{q_1, q_2\}$, if there exist two execution traces τ and σ for C s.t. $[(\tau_i(p) \neq \sigma_i(p)) \wedge (\forall p' \text{ s.t. } p \not\preceq p'. \ \tau_i(p') = \sigma_i(p'))] \rightarrow [(\tau_f(q_1) \neq \tau_f(q_2)) \wedge (\sigma_f(q_1) = \sigma_f(q_2))].$* □

Proposition 2 (Correctness). *Let C be a Java bytecode. If $p \overset{\pi}{\rightsquigarrow} q$ then $\hat{p} \rightsquigarrow \hat{q} \in [\![C]\!]^\alpha$ and if $p \overset{\lambda}{\rightsquigarrow} \{q_1, q_2\}$ then $\hat{p} \rightsquigarrow \hat{q}_1 \in [\![C]\!]^\alpha$ and $q_1 \neq \text{null}$, or $\hat{p} \rightsquigarrow \hat{q}_2 \in [\![C]\!]^\alpha$ and $q_2 \neq \text{null}$, where $\hat{l}_k = l_k$, $\hat{s}_h = s_h$ and $\hat{p.f} = f$.* □

4 Experiments

We have implemented our analysis inside the generic static analyser Julia for full Java bytecode [23], by using Boolean functions to represent sets of information flows, as described in [12]. Boolean functions have been implemented as *binary decision diagrams* (BDDs) [8] by using the *BuDDy* library [16]. Figure 5 shows the application of our analysis to some programs (already compiled in Java bytecode): Dhrystone is a testbench for numerical computations; ImageViewer is an image visualisation applet; Morph is an image morphing program; Julia is our

program	C	M	B	Time
Dhrystone	7	21	604	5
ImageViewer	2	20	1,238	38
Morph	1	14	1,367	28
Julia	21	169	7,815	389
JLex	25	131	12,520	557
Jess	186	808	25,862	2,844

Fig. 5. Some examples of analysis. For each benchmark we report the number C, M and B of classes, methods and bytecodes, respectively, and the time of the analysis, in seconds.

Julia analyser itself (without the classes representing the Java bytecodes); JLex is a lexical analysers generator; and Jess is a rule language interpreter. For each program we report its size and the run-time of the analysis. Our experiments have been performed on a centrino® 1.4 Ghz machine with 512 megabytes of RAM, running Linux® 2.4, Sun® Java Development Kit version 1.3.1 and Julia version 0.36. Figure 5 shows that we are already able to analyse non-trivial applications.

5 Related Work

In the literature, there are several techniques for checking secure information flow and non-interference in software, ranging from standard data/control-flow analysis techniques [6,9,15,21,18,12,2] to type inference [22,25]. An overview is contained in [20]. Data/Control-flow approaches usually infer dependencies between the input and the output values of a program variables from which the information flow is observable. Type-based approaches associate inductively, at compile-time, a type to each program statement and then prove that well-typed programs do not leak secrets [22, 25].

Non-interference for Java has been studied in [3, 19]. Zwandevic and Myers [26] study it for a λ-calculus with jumps. Bonelli, Compagnoni and Mendel [7] and Kobayashi and Shirane [14] studied it for a simple low-level language. Barthe, Rezk and Basu [4] studied information flow for a small subset of the Java bytecode. Recently, Barthe and Rezk [5] defined an information flow type system for a non-trivial portion of the Java bytecode. No implementation was reported.

6   Conclusions

We think ours is the first implementation of an information flow analysis for a complex low-level language such as Java bytecode. Our examples in Section 2 and our experimental evaluation in Section 4 show that it is precise and efficient enough for practical use.

Acknowledgments

We thank Tamara Rezk for the useful discussions regard information flow for the Java bytecode.

References

1. A. V. Aho, R. Sethi, and J. D. Ullman. *Compilers, Principles Techniques and Tools.* Addison Wesley Publishing Company, 1986.
2. T. Amtoft and A. Banerjee. Information Flow Analysis in Logical Form. In R. Giacobazzi, editor, *Proceedings of the Eleventh International Static Analysis Symposium (SAS)*, Lecture Notes in Computer Science, pages 100–115. Springer-Verlag, August 2004.
3. A. Banerjee and D. A. Naumann. Stack-based Access Control and Secure Information Flow. *Journal of Functional Programming, Special issue on Language-based Security*, to appear.
4. G. Barthe, A. Basu, and T. Rezk. Security Types Preserving Compilation. In *VMCAI'04*, volume 2937 of *Lecture Notes in Computer Science*. Springer-Verlag, 2004.
5. G. Barthe and T. Rezk. Secure Information Flow for a Sequential Java Virtual Machine. Unpublished.
6. C. Bodei, P. Degano, F. Nielson, and H. Nielson. Static Analysis for Secrecy and non-Interference in Networks of Processes. In *Proc. of PaCT'01*, volume 2127 of *Lecture Notes in Computer Science*, pages 27–41. Springer-Verlag, 2001.
7. E. Bonelli, A. Compagnoni, and R. Medel. SIFTAL: A Typed Assembly Language for Secure Information Flow Analysis. Manuscript, 2004.
8. R. E. Bryant. Graph-Based Algorithms for Boolean Function Manipulation. *IEEE Transactions on Computers*, 35(8):677–691, 1986.
9. D. Clark, C. Hankin, and S. Hunt. Information Flow for ALGOL-like Languages. *Computer Languages*, 28(1):3–28, April 2002.

10. J. Dean, D. Grove, and C. Chambers. Optimization of Object-Oriented Programs using Static Class Hierarchy Analysis. In W. G. Olthoff, editor, *Proc. of ECOOP'95*, volume 952 of *LNCS*, pages 77–101, Århus, Denmark, August 1995. Springer-Verlag.

11. D. E. Denning. A Lattice Model of Secure Information Flow. *Communications of the ACM*, 19(5):236–242, 1976.

12. S. Genaim, R. Giacobazzi, and I. Mastroeni. Modeling Secure Information Flow with Boolean Functions. In P. Ryan, editor, *WITS'04*, April 2004.

13. S. Genaim and F. Spoto. Information flow analysis for java bytecode. Extended Version.

14. N. Kobayashi and K. Shirane. Type-based Information Flow Analysis for Low-Level Languages. In *3rd Asian Workshop on Programming Languages and Systems*, 2002.

15. P. Laud. Semantics and Program Analysis of Computationally Secure Information Flow. In *Programming Languages and Systems, 10th European Symposium On Programming, ESOP*, volume 2028 of *Lecture Notes in Computer Science*, pages 77–91. Springer-Verlag, 2001.

16. J. Lind-Nielsen. BuDDy - A Binary Decision Diagram Package. Available at `www.itu.dk/research/buddy/`.

17. T. Lindholm and F. Yellin. *The Java^{TM} Virtual Machine Specification*. Java^{TM} Series. Addison-Wesley, 1999.

18. M. Mizuno. A Least Fixed Point Approach to Inter-Procedural Information Flow Control. In *Proc. 12th NIST-NCSC National Computer Security Conference*, pages 558–570, 1989.

19. J. Practical Mostly-Static Information Flow Control. Andrew c. myers. In *26th ACM Symposium on Principles of Programming Languages*, pages 228–241, San Antonio, Texas, 1999.

20. A. Sabelfeld and A. Myers. Language-based Information-Flow Security. *IEEE Journal on Selected Areas in Communications*, 21(1):5–19, 2003.

21. A. Sabelfeld and D. Sands. A PER Model of Secure Information Flow in Sequential Programs. *Higher-Order and Symbolic Computation*, 14(1):59–91, 2001.

22. C. Skalka and S. Smith. Static Enforcement of Security with Types. In *ICFP'00*, pages 254–267. ACM press, 2000.

23. F. Spoto. The Julia Generic Static Analyser. `www.sci.univr.it/~spoto/julia`, 2004.

24. F. Spoto and T. Jensen. Class Analyses as Abstract Interpretations of Trace Semantics. *ACM Transactions on Programming Languages and Systems (TOPLAS)*, 25(5):578–630, September 2003.

25. D. Volpano, G. Smith, and C. Irvine. A Sound Type System for Secure Flow Analysis. *Journal of Computer Security*, 4(2,3):167–187, 1996.

26. S. Zdancewic and A. C. Myers. Secure Information Flow and CPS. In D. Sands, editor, *ESOP*, volume 2028 of *Lecture Notes in Computer Science*, pages 46–61. Springer, 2001.

Cryptographic Protocol Analysis on Real C Code[*]

Jean Goubault-Larrecq[1] and Fabrice Parrennes[1,2]

[1] LSV/CNRS UMR 8643 & INRIA Futurs projet SECSI & ENS Cachan
61 avenue du président-Wilson, F-94235 Cachan Cedex
Phone: +33-1 47 40 75 68
`goubault@lsv.ens-cachan.fr`
[2] RATP, EST/ISF/QS LAC VC42
40 bis Roger Salengro, F-94724 Fontenay-sous-Bois
Phone: +33-1 58 77 04 65
`fabrice.parrennes@ratp.fr`

Abstract. Implementations of cryptographic protocols, such as OpenSSL for example, contain bugs affecting security, which cannot be detected by just analyzing abstract protocols (e.g., SSL or TLS). We describe how cryptographic protocol verification techniques based on solving clause sets can be applied to detect vulnerabilities of C programs in the Dolev-Yao model, statically. This involves integrating fairly simple pointer analysis techniques with an analysis of which messages an external intruder may collect and forge. This also involves relating concrete run-time data with abstract, logical terms representing messages. To this end, we make use of so-called *trust assertions*. The output of the analysis is a set of clauses in the decidable class $\mathcal{H}_1$, which can then be solved independently. This can be used to establish secrecy properties, and to detect some other bugs.

1 Introduction

Cryptographic protocol verification has come of age: there are now many ways of verifying cryptographic protocols in the literature (see [12] for a sampler). They all start from a fairly abstract specification of the protocol. However, in real life, what you use when you type `ssh` or when you connect to a securized site on your Web browser is not a 5-line abstract protocol but a complete program. While this program is intended to implement some protocol, there is no guarantee it actually implements it in any way. The purpose of this paper is to make a few first steps in the direction of analyzing cryptographic protocols directly from source code.

To make things concrete, here is a specification of the public-key Needham-Schroeder protocol in standard notation (right). The goal is for A and B to exchange their secret texts N_A and N_B while authenticating themselves mutually [19]. It is well-known that there is an attack against this protocol (see [17]). This attack also makes N_B available to the intruder, although N_B was meant to remain secret.

1. A → B: $\{N_A, A\}_{\text{pub(B)}}$
2. B → A: $\{N_A, N_B\}_{\text{pub(A)}}$
3. A → B: $\{N_B\}_{\text{pub(B)}}$

Fig. 1. The NS protocol.

---

[*] Partially supported by the ACI jeunes chercheurs "Sécurité informatique, protocoles cryptographiques et détection d'intrusions" and the ACI cryptologie "Psi-Robuste". Work done while the second author was at LSV.

R. Cousot (Ed.): VMCAI 2005, LNCS 3385, pp. 363–379, 2005.
© Springer-Verlag Berlin Heidelberg 2005

Figure 1 reads as follows: any agent implementing A's role will first create a fresh *nonce* N_A, typically by drawing a number at random, then build the pair (N_A, A) where A is taken to be A's identity (some string identifying A uniquely by convention), then encrypt the result using B's public key pub(B). The encrypted text $\{N_A, A\}_{\text{pub}(B)}$ is then sent out. If traffic is not diverted, this should reach B, who will decrypt this using his private key prv(B), and send back $\{N_A, N_B\}_{\text{pub}(A)}$ to A. A waits for such a message at step 2., decrypts it using her private key prv(A), checks that the first component is indeed N_A, then sends back $\{N_B\}_{\text{pub}(B)}$ at step 3. for confirmation.

Compare this specification (Figure 1) with excerpts from an actual C implementation of A's role in it (Figure 2). First, the C code is longer than the specification (although Figure 2 only implements message 1 of Figure 1). Difficulties in analyzing such a piece of C code mainly come from other, less visible, problems:

```
1   int create_nonce (nonce_t *nce)
2   {
3       RAND_bytes(nce->nonce,SIZENONCE);
4       /* % *nce rec nonce(CTX) | context(CTX). % */
5       return(0);
6   }
7
8   int encrypt_mesg(msg1_t *msg, BIGNUM *key_pub,
9                    BIGNUM *key_mod, BIGNUM *cipher)
10  {
11      BIGNUM *plain;
12      int msg_len;
13      BN_CTX *ctx;
14      ctx = BN_CTX_new();
15      msg_len = sizeof (msg1_t);
16      plain = BN_bin2bn((const unsigned char *)msg, msg_len, NULL);
17      BN_CTX_init(ctx);
18      BN_mod_exp(cipher, plain, key_pub, key_mod, ctx);
19
20      /* % *cipher rec crypt(M,K) | *msg rec M, *key_pub rec K. % */
21
22      return (0);
23  }
24
25  int create_mesg1(msg1_t *mesg, nonce_t *n1, int *id, int *dest)
26  {
27      /* First copy nonce. */
28      memcpy (&mesg->nonce_msg1, n1, sizeof(nonce_t));
29
30      /* copy id... */
31      msg->id_1[0] = id[0]; msg->id_1[1] = id[1];
32      msg->id_1[2] = id[2]; msg->id_1[3] = id[3];
33      /* ... and dest. */
34      msg->dest_1[0] = dest[0]; msg->dest_1[1] = dest[1];
35      msg->dest_1[2] = dest[2]; msg->dest_1[3] = dest[3];
36
37      /* % *msg -> nonce_msg1 rec U and
38         *msg -> is_1        rec V and
39         *msg -> dest_1      rev W  | *n1 rec U, *id rec V,
40                                      *dest rec W. % */
41      return(0);
42  }
43
44  int write(int fd, const void *buf, int count)
45  {
46      write (fd, buf, count);
47      /* % knows rec B | *buf rec B. % */
48      return(0);
49  }

50  int main(int argc, char *argv[])
51  {
52      int conn_fd;   // The communication socket.
53      msg1_t mesg1;  // Message
54      nonce_t nonce;
55      BIGNUM * cipher1; // Cipher Message
56      BIGNUM * pubkey;  // Keys
57      BIGNUM * prvkey;  // Keys
58      BIGNUM * modkey;  // Keys
59      unsigned int ip_id[4];   // A's name
60      unsigned int ip_dest[4]; // B's name as seen from A.
61
62      /* Init ip_id and ip_dest. */
63      ip_id[0]  = 192; ip_id[1]  = 100;
64      ip_id[2]  = 200; ip_id[3]  = 100;
65      ip_dest[0] = 192; ip_dest[1] = 100;
66      ip_dest[2] = 200; ip_dest[3] = 101;
67      /* % ip_id   rec CTX(Agent(A)). % */
68      /* % ip_dest rec CTX(Agent(B)). % */
69      // Open connection to B
70      conn_fd = connect_socket(ip_dest, 522);
71
72      init_keys(&pubkey, &prvkey, &modkey, PUBALICESERV,
73      MODALICESERV, PRIVALICESERV);
74      /* % *pubkey rec pub(Y) | ip_dest rec Y. % */
75      /* % *prvkey rec priv(X) | ip_id rec X. % */
76
77      /*** 1. A -> B : {Na, A}_pub(B) ***/
78      create_nonce (&nonce);
79      create_mesg1(&mesg1, &nonce, ip_id, ip_dest);
80      cipher1 = BN_new();
81      encrypt_mesg(&mesg1, pubkey, modkey, cipher1);
82      write(conn_fd, cipher1, 128);
83
84      /** ...Remaining code omitted... **/
85  }
```

Fig. 2. A piece of code of a sample C implementation of the NS protocol.

– First, C is a real programming language, with memory allocation, aliasing, pointer arithmetic; all this is absent from protocol specifications, and must be taken into account. E.g., in Figure 2, line 80, the pointer cipher1 is set to the address allocated by BN_new(); at line 81, the encryption function encrypt_mesg expects to encrypt its first argument with the key in second and third arguments, putting the result at the address pointed to by its fourth argument cipher1.

- C programs are meant to be linked to external libraries, whose code is usually unavailable (e.g., `memcpy`, `strcpy`, `strncmp`, `read`, `write` in Figure 2) and cannot be analyzed. More subtly, low-level encryption functions should *not* be analyzed, simply because we do not know any way to recognize that some given bit-mangling code implements, say, RSA or DES. We shall take the approach that such functions should be *trusted* to do what they are meant to do.
- Even without looking at the intricacies of statically analyzing C code, we usually only have the source code of *one* role at our disposal. For example, the code of Figure 2 implements A's role in the protocol of Figure 1, not B's, not anyone else's either. So we shall analyze C code modulo an abstract description of the world around it. This so-called *external trust model* will state what malicious intruders can do, and what honest agents are trusted to do (e.g, if B is assumed to be honest, he should only be able to execute the corresponding steps in Figure 1).

  Alternatively, we could also analyze the source code of two or more roles. But we would still need an external trust model, representing malicious intruders, and honest agents of other protocols which may share secrets with the analyzed programs.

What we do in this paper. We analyze reachability properties of C code implementing roles of cryptographic protocols. Amongst all reachability properties, we shall concentrate on (non-)*secrecy*, i.e., the ability for a malicious intruder to get hold of some designated, sensitive piece of data. All problems considered here are undecidable: we therefore concentrate on upper approximations of behaviors of programs, i.e., on representations that contain at least all behaviors that the given program may exhibit – in a given external trust model, and a given execution model (see below). In particular, we aim at giving *security guarantees*. When none can be given by our techniques, just as in other static analyses, it may still be that the analyzed program is in fact safe.

What we do not do. First, we do *not* infer cryptographic protocols from C code, i.e., we do not infer Figure 1 from Figure 2. This might have seemed the most reasonable route: when Figure 1 has been reconstructed, use your favorite cryptographic protocol verifier. We do not believe this is practical. First, recall that we usually only have the source code of *some* of the roles. Even is we had code for all roles, real implementations use many constructs that have no equivalent in input languages for cryptographic protocol verification tools. To take one realistic example, implementations of SSL [10] such as `ssh` use conditionals, bindings from conventional names such as `SSL_RSA_WITH_RC4_128_MD5` to algorithms (i.e., records containing function pointers, initialized to specific encryption, decryption, and secure hash functions), which are far from what current cryptographic protocol verification tools offer.

Second, we do *not* guarantee against any arbitrary attack on C code. Rather, our techniques are able to guarantee that there is no attack on a given piece of C code *in* a given trust model, stating who we trust, and *in* a given execution model, i.e., assuming a given, somewhat idealized semantics of C. In this semantics, writing beyond the bounds of an array never occurs. If we did not rely on such idealized semantics, essentially every static analysis would report possible security violations, most of them fake. It follows that buffer overflow attacks will not be considered in this paper. While buffer overflows are probably the most efficient technique of attack against real implementations (even not of cryptographic protocols; for hackers, see [11]), they can be and have already been analyzed [25, 24]. On programs immune to buffer overflows, we believe our idealized semantics to be a fair account of the semantics of C. Programs should be checked against buffer overflows before our techniques are applied; we consider buffer overflows as an important but independent concern.

Outline. After reviewing related work in Section 2, we introduce the subset of C we consider in Section 3, augmented with *trust assertions* – the cornerstone of our way of describing relations between in-memory values and Dolev-Yao-style messages. Its concrete semantics is described in Section 4, including trust assertions and the external trust model. We describe the associated abstract semantics in Section 5, which approximates C programs plus trust models as sets of Horn clauses, and describe our implementation in Section 6. We conclude in Section 7.

2   Related Work

Analyzing cryptographic protocols directly from source code seems to be fairly new. As far as we know, the only previous attempts in this direction are due to El Kadhi and Boury [16, 6], who propose a framework and algorithms to analyze leakage of confidential data in Java applets. They consider a model of cryptographic security based on the well-known Dolev-Yao model [8], just as we do. While we use Horn clauses as a uniform mechanism to abstract program semantics, intruder capabilities, and security properties alike, El Kadhi and Boury use a dedicated constraint format, and use a special constraint resolution calculus [16].

Analyzing cryptographic *programs* is not just a matter of analyzing cryptographic *protocols*. El Kadhi and Boury analyze Java applets (from bytecode, not source), and concentrate on a well-behaved subset of Java, where method calls are assumed to be inlined. Aliasing in Java is simpler to handle in Java than in C: the only aliases that may occur in Java arise from objects that can be accessed through different access paths (e.g., different variables); in C, more complex aliases may occur, such as through pointers to variables (see &mesg1 for example in Figure 2). The StuPa tool [6] uses different static analysis frameworks to model the Dolev-Yao intruder and to analyze information flow through the analyzed applet; we use a uniform approach based on Horn clauses.

Finally, the security properties examined in [6] are models of leakage of sensitive data: sensitive data are those data stored in specially marked class fields, and are tracked through the program and the possible actions of the intruder; data can be leaked to the Dolev-Yao intruder, or more generally to untrusted classes in the programming environment. The aim of [6] is to detect whether some sensitive piece of data can be leaked to some untrusted class. Because we use Horn clauses, any property which can be expressed as a conjunction of atoms can be checked in our approach (as in [7]), in particular secrecy or leakage to some untrusted part of the environment.

Cryptographic protocol analysis. If we are just interested in cryptographic *protocols*, not programs, there are now many methods available: see [12] for an overview. One of the most successful models today is the *Dolev-Yao model* [8], where all communication channels are assumed to be rerouted to a unique *intruder*, who can encrypt and decrypt any message at will – provided it knows the inverse key in the case of decryption. Every message sent is just given to the intruder, and every message received is obtained from the intruder. This is the basis of many papers. One of the most relevant to our work is Blanchet's model [3], where a single predicate knows (called `attacker` in op.cit.) is used to model what messages may be known to the intruder at any time. The abilities of the intruder are modeled by the following Horn clauses (in our notation):

$$\text{knows}(\text{nil}) \qquad\qquad \text{Intruder can} \qquad\qquad (1)$$

$$\text{knows}(\text{cons}(X, Y)) \Leftarrow \text{knows}(X), \text{knows}(Y) \qquad \text{build lists.} \qquad (2)$$

$$\text{knows}(X) \Leftarrow \text{knows}(\text{cons}(X, Y)) \qquad \text{Intruder can read} \qquad (3)$$

$$\text{knows}(Y) \Leftarrow \text{knows}(\text{cons}(X, Y)) \qquad \text{all elements of a list.} \qquad (4)$$

$$\text{knows}(\text{crypt}(X, Y)) \Leftarrow \text{knows}(X), \text{knows}(Y) \qquad \text{Intruder can encrypt.} \qquad (5)$$

$$\text{knows}(X) \Leftarrow \text{knows}(\text{crypt}(X, \text{pub}(Y))), \text{knows}(\text{prv}(Y)) \quad \text{Intruder can decrypt} \qquad (6)$$

$$\text{knows}(X) \Leftarrow \text{knows}(\text{crypt}(X, \text{prv}(Y))), \text{knows}(\text{pub}(Y)) \quad \text{provided he knows} \qquad (7)$$

$$\text{knows}(X) \Leftarrow \text{knows}(\text{crypt}(X, \text{sk}(Y, Z))), \text{knows}(\text{sk}(Y, Z)) \quad \text{the inverse key.} \qquad (8)$$

$$\text{knows}(\text{pub}(X)) \qquad\qquad \text{Intruder knows public keys.} (9)$$

We shall use a Prolog-like notation throughout: identifiers starting with capital letters, such as X or Y, are universally quantified variables; nil is a constant, cons and crypt are function symbols. Clause (5), for example, states that whenever the intruder knows (can deduce) X and Y, then he can deduce the result $\text{crypt}(X, Y)$ of the encryption of X with key Y. Clauses (6) through (8) state that he can deduce the plaintext X from the ciphertext $\text{crypt}(X, k)$ whenever he knows the inverse of key k; $\text{prv}(A)$ is meant to denote A's private key, $\text{pub}(A)$ is A's public key, and $\text{sk}(A, B)$ is some symmetric key to be used between agents A and B.

Most roles in cryptographic protocols are sequences of rules $M \Rightarrow M'$ (not to be confused either with implication $\Leftarrow$ or the arrows $\rightarrow$ shown in Figure 1), meaning that the role will wait for some (optional) message matching M, then (optionally) send M'. For example, role A in Figure 1 implements the rules $\Rightarrow \{N_A, A\}_{\text{pub(B)}}$ (step 1.) and $\{N_A, N_B\}_{\text{pub(A)}} \Rightarrow \{N_B\}_{\text{pub(B)}}$. This is easily compiled into Horn clauses. A rule $M \Rightarrow M'$ is simply compiled as the clause $\text{knows}(M') \Leftarrow \text{knows}(M)$, modulo some details. For example, and using Blanchet's trick of coding nonces as function symbols applied to parameters in context (e.g., N_A will be coded as $\text{na}(B)$, in any session where A talks to some agent B), the role of A in Figure 1 may be coded as:

$$\text{knows}(\text{crypt}(\text{cons}(\text{na}(B), \text{cons}(\text{a}, \text{nil})), \text{pub}(B))) \qquad (10)$$

$$\text{knows}(\text{crypt}(Nb, \text{pub}(B))) \Leftarrow \text{knows}(\text{crypt}(\text{cons}(\text{na}(B), \text{cons}(Nb, \text{nil})), (11)$$
$$\text{pub}(\text{a})))$$

Finally, secrecy properties are encoded through negative clauses. For instance, given a specific agent b, that N_A remains secret when A is talking to b will be coded as $\perp \Leftarrow \text{knows}(\text{na}(\text{b}))$. More complicated queries are possible, e.g., $\perp \Leftarrow \text{knows}(\text{na}(B))$, $\text{honest}(B)$ asks whether N_A remains secret whatever agent A is really talking to, provided this agent is honest, for some definition of honesty (see [7] for example). We won't explore all the variants, and shall be content to know that we can use at least one. Note that the encodings above are upper approximations of the actual behavior of the protocol; this is needed in any case, as cryptographic protocol verification is undecidable [9, 1].

Program analysis. There is an even wider literature on static program analysis. Our main problem will be to infer what variables contain what kind of data. As these variables are mostly pointers to structures allocated on the heap, we have to do some kind of shape analysis. The prototypical such analysis is due to Sagiv *et al.* [22]. This analysis gives very precise information on the shape of objects stored in variables. It is also rather costly. A crucial observation in [22] is that store shapes are better understood as formulae. We shall adapt this idea to a much simplified memory model.

At the other end of the spectrum, Andersen's *points-to* analysis [2] gives a very rough approximation of what variables may point to what others, but can be computed extremely efficiently [14]. (See [15] for a survey of pointer analyses.) We shall design an analysis that is somewhere in between shape analysis and points-to analysis as far as precision is concerned: knowing whether variable x may point to y is not enough, e.g. we need to know that once lines 77–82 of Figure 2 have been executed, `cipher1` points to some allocated record containing A's identity as `ip_id` and that the field `mesg1.msg.msg1.nonce` contains A's nonce N_A. (This is already non-trivial; we also need to know that this record actually denotes the term $\text{crypt}(\text{cons}(\text{na}(B), \text{cons}(\text{a}, \text{nil})), \text{pub}(B))$ when seen from the cryptographic protocol viewpoint.) While this looks like what shape analysis does, our analysis will be flow-insensitive, just like standard points-to analyses.

One of our basic observations is that such pointer analyses can be described as generating Horn clauses describing points-to relations. Once this is done (Section 5), it will be easier to link in the cryptographic protocol aspects (e.g., to state that `cipher_1` *denotes* $\text{crypt}(\text{cons}(\text{na}(B), \text{cons}(\text{a}, \text{nil})), \text{pub}(B)$, as stated above).

3   C Programs, and Trust Assertions

We assume that C programs are represented as a set of control flow graphs G_f, one for each function f. We assume that the source code of each function f is known – at least all those that we don't want to abstract away, such as communication and cryptographic primitives. We also consider a restricted subset of C, where casts are absent, and expressions are assumed to be well-typed. We do definitely consider pointers, and in particular pointer arithmetic, one of the major hassles of C semantics.

Formally, we define a *C program* as a map from function names f to triples (in_f, loc_f, G_f), where in_f is the list of f's formal parameters, loc_f is the list of f's local variables, and G_f is f's control flow graph. We assume that the node sets of each control flow graph G_f are pairwise disjoint.

A *control flow graph (CFG)* is a directed graph G with a distinguished *entry node* $I(G)$ and a distinguished *exit node* $O(G)$. Edges are labeled with *instructions*. The set of instructions in Figure 3 will be enough for our purposes, where x, y, z, ..., range over names of local variables, c ranges over integer and floating-point constants, f over function names, a over struct field names, and op ranges over primitive operations (arithmetic operations, bitwise logical operations, comparisons): The instructions $x = \&y[z]$ and $x = \&y \rightarrow a$ implement pointer arithmetic. The first adds the integer z to the pointer y, yielding x. The second adds the offset of field a to the pointer y. More complex instructions can be broken down to sequences of instructions as above. For ex-

$$
\begin{array}{lll}
i \in Instr ::= & x = y & \text{variable copy} \\
\mid & x = c & \text{storing constant } c \text{ into } x \\
\mid & x = f & \text{storing the address of function } f \text{ into } x \\
\mid & x = \&y & \text{storing the address of variable } y \text{ into } x \\
\mid & x = *y & \text{reading from a pointer} \\
\mid & *x = y & \text{storing into a pointer} \\
\mid & x = \&y[z] & \text{taking the address of entry } z \text{ of array } y \\
\mid & x = \&y \to a & \text{taking the address of field } a \text{ in struct } y \\
\mid & x = g(x_1, \ldots, x_n) & \text{calling function } g \\
\mid & x = (*y)(x_1, \ldots, x_n) & \text{indirect call} \\
\mid & x = op(x_1, \ldots, x_n) & \text{primitive call} \\
\mid & ?x == 0 & \text{zero test} \\
\mid & ?x\,! = 0 & \text{non zero test} \\
\mid & \mathbf{trust}\ A \Leftarrow A_1, \ldots, A_n & \text{trust assertion} \\
A \in Atom ::= & x\ \mathbf{rec}\ t & x \text{ is trusted to denote } t \\
\mid & P(t) & \text{term } t \text{ is trusted to obey property } P
\end{array}
$$

Fig. 3. Syntax of core C.

ample, msg->id_1[0] = id[0] can be translated to the sequence of instructions $z = 0$, $x_1 = \&\mathrm{id}[z]$, $x_2 = *x_1$, $x_3 = \&\mathrm{msg} \to \mathrm{id\_1}$, $x_4 = \&x_3[z]$, $*x_4 = x_2$. This of course presumes a given scheduling of elementary instructions; to verify output from a given C compiler, the same scheduling should be used. The test instructions $?x == 0$ and $?x\,! = 0$ do nothing, but can only be executed provided x is zero, resp. non-zero; they are used to represent if and while branches.

The only non-standard instruction above is the trust assertion. This is one of the main ingredients we use to link concrete C data with abstract Dolev-Yao style messages that they are meant to denote. A trust assertion trust x rec $t \Leftarrow x_1$ rec $t_1, \ldots,$ x_n rec t_n relates the value of C variables (x, x_1, ..., x_n) to terms (messages; t, t_1, ..., t_n) that they are meant to denote. Intuitively, this states that the value of x denotes the term t, as soon as x_1 denotes t_1, and ... and x_n denotes t_n. While atomic formulae x rec t state that the value of x denotes t, other atomic formulae $P(t)$ (e.g., knows(t), see Section 2) will be defined by the external trust model (see Section 4.2).

We have chosen to let the programmer state trust relations in the C source code using special comments; they are enclosed between /* % and % */ in Figure 2. For example, the comment at line 20 translates to the trust statement trust cipher rec $\mathrm{crypt}(M, K) \Leftarrow$ msg rec M, key_pub rec K, and states that, if msg points to a memory zone where message M is stored, and if key_pub points to some zone containing K, then cipher will be filled with the ciphertext $\mathrm{crypt}(M, K)$; in other words, encrypt_mesg computes the encryption of *msg using key *key_pub and stores it into *cipher.

We *do* require trust assertions. Otherwise, there is no way to recognize statically that the call to BN_mod_exp on line 18 actually computes modular exponentiation on arbitrary sized integers ("bignums", of type BIGNUM), and much less that this encrypts its second argument plain using the key given as third and fourth arguments key_pub, key_mod, storing the result into the first argument cipher. In fact, there is no way to even define a sensible map from bignums to terms that would give their purported meaning in the Dolev-Yao model.

We need such trust assertions for two distinct purposes. The first is to describe the *effect of functions in the API* in terms of the Dolev-Yao model; in particular, to abstract away the effect of low-level cryptographic functions that are used in the analyzed program (e.g., the OpenSSL crypto lib), or of the standard C library (see the comment on line 47, which abstracts away the behavior of the `write` function, stating that any message sent to `write` through the buffer `buf` will be known to the Dolev-Yao intruder). The second purpose of trust assertions is to state *initial security assumptions*: see the comment on line 67, which states that the array `ip_id` is trusted to contain A's identity, initially. (The notation `CTX(Agent(A))` refers to A's identity as given in a global context `CTX`; we shall not describe this in detail here.)

4   Concrete Semantics

We first describe the memory layout. Let *Addr* be a denumerable set of so-called *addresses*. A *store* $\mu \in Store$ is any map from adresses to zones. Intuitively, addresses are those memory addresses returned by memory allocation functions, e.g., `malloc`. (As a technical aside, we assume that declaring a local C variable x in a C function has the effect of allocating some memory, too, for holding x's value, at an address that is usually written &x in C. We do this because, contrarily to, say, Java, you can take the address of variables in C, and modify them through pointer operations.) *Zones* describe the layout of data stored at given addresses, and are described by the following grammar:

$$
\begin{array}{ll}
z ::= \texttt{code } f & \text{code for function } f \\
\quad | \quad \texttt{int } n & \text{integer } n \\
\quad | \quad \texttt{float } x & \text{floating-point value } x \\
\quad | \quad \texttt{ptr } \ell & \text{pointer, pointing to location } \ell \\
\quad | \quad \texttt{struct } \{lab_1 = z_1, \ldots, lab_n = z_n\} & \text{structure, with labels } lab_i, 1 \le i \le n \\
\quad | \quad \texttt{array}(z_1, \ldots, z_n) & \text{array of } n \text{ sub-zones}
\end{array}
$$

Let *Zone* be the set of all zones. *Locations* ℓ, as used in pointers, are strings $a.sel_1.\ldots.sel_k$, where $a \in Addr$, and $sel_j, 1 \le j \le k$, are *selectors*, namely either *labels* $lab \in Lab$ or integers $n \in \mathbb{Z}$. For example, in Figure 4, if a is the address of x, $a.\texttt{data.t.2}$ is the location of the cell shown in red.

Let *Loc* be the set of all locations. Let $Store = Addr \rightarrow Zone$ be the set of all stores. Any store μ extends in a unique way to a map $\hat{\mu}$ from *locations* to zones: if $a \in Addr$, then $\hat{\mu}(a) = \mu(a)$; $\hat{\mu}(\ell.lab_i) = z_i$ provided $\hat{\mu}(\ell)$ is defined and of the form `struct` $\{lab_1 = z_1, \ldots, lab_n = z_n\}, 1 \le i \le n$; and $\hat{\mu}(\ell.j) = z_j$ provided $\hat{\mu}(\ell)$ is defined and of the form `array`$(z_1, \ldots, z_n), 1 \le j \le n$. E.g., x.data has a location, namely $a.\texttt{data}$, mapped by $\hat{\mu}$ to the zone shown in Figure 4, top right.

Given a C program mapping each function f to (in_f, out_f, G_f) (Section 3), we define its semantics as a transition system. *Transitions* (inside G_f) are defined by judgments $q, \rho, \mu \xrightarrow{i} q', \rho', \mu'$, one for each edge $q \xrightarrow{i} q'$ in G_f, where ρ and ρ' are *environments* mapping variables to their addresses. This is shown in Figure 5. The notation $\rho[x \mapsto z]$ denotes the map sending x to z, and every other $y \in \text{dom } \rho$ to $\rho(y)$. Similarly for $\mu[a \mapsto z]$, where $a \in Addr$ and $z \in Zone$. To model writing into arbitrary locations ℓ, not just addresses, we extend this notation by letting

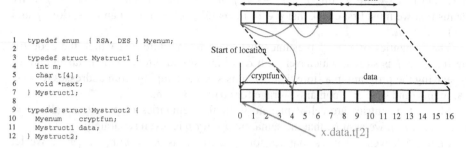

```
1   typedef enum { RSA, DES } Myenum;
2
3   typedef struct Mystruct1 {
4     int m;
5     char t[4];
6     void *next;
7   } Mystruct1;
8
9   typedef struct Mystruct2 {
10    Myenum    cryptfun;
11    Mystruct1 data;
12  } Mystruct2;
```

Fig. 4. Sample memory zone.

$q, \rho, \mu \xrightarrow{x=y} q', \rho, \mu[\rho(x) \mapsto \mu(\rho(y))]$

$q, \rho, \mu \xrightarrow{x=c} q', \rho, \mu[\rho(x) \mapsto c]$

$q, \rho, \mu \xrightarrow{x=f} q', \rho, \mu[\rho(x) \mapsto a]$ if $\mu(a) = \text{code } f$ for some $a \in \text{dom } \mu$

$q, \rho, \mu \xrightarrow{x=\&y} q', \rho, \mu[\rho(x) \mapsto \text{ptr}(\rho(y))]$

$q, \rho, \mu \xrightarrow{x=*y} q', \rho, \mu[\rho(x) \mapsto \hat{\mu}(\ell)]$ if $\mu(\rho(y)) = \text{ptr } \ell$ for some $\ell \in Loc$

$q, \rho, \mu \xrightarrow{*x=y} q', \rho, \mu[\ell \mapsto \mu(\rho(y))]$ if $\mu(\rho(x)) = \text{ptr } \ell$ for some $\ell \in Loc$

$q, \rho, \mu \xrightarrow{x=\&y[z]} q', \rho, \mu[\rho(x) \mapsto \text{ptr } (\ell.(j+1))]$ if $\rho(y) = \text{ptr } \ell$,
$\mu(\ell) = \text{array } (z_1, \ldots, z_n)$, and $\mu(\rho(z)) = \text{int } j, 0 \leq j \leq n$

$q, \rho, \mu \xrightarrow{x=\&y \to a} q', \rho, \mu[\rho(x) \mapsto \text{ptr } (\ell.a)]$ if $\rho(y) = \text{ptr } \ell$,
and $\mu(\ell) = \text{struct } \{\ldots, a = z, \ldots\}$

$q, \rho, \mu \xrightarrow{x=g(x_1,\ldots,x_n)} q', \rho', \mu'$iff: see main text

$q, \rho, \mu \xrightarrow{x=(*y)(x_1,\ldots,x_n)} q', \rho', \mu'$iff: see main text

$q, \rho, \mu \xrightarrow{x=op(x_1,\ldots,x_n)} q', \rho, \mu[\rho(x) \mapsto \hat{op}(\mu(\rho(x_1)), \ldots, \mu(\rho(x_n)))]$

$q, \rho, \mu \xrightarrow{?x==0} q', \rho, \mu$ if $\mu(\rho(x)) = \text{int } 0$

$q, \rho, \mu \xrightarrow{?x \models 0} q', \rho, \mu$ if $\mu(\rho(x)) \neq \text{int } 0$

$q, \rho, \mu \xrightarrow{\text{trust } A \Leftarrow A_1,\ldots,A_n} q', \rho, \mu$

Fig. 5. Concrete semantics.

$\mu[\ell.lab_i \mapsto z] = \mu[\ell \mapsto \text{struct } \{lab_1 = z_1, \ldots, lab_i = z, \ldots, lab_n = z_n\}]$ whenever $\hat{\mu}(\ell) = \text{struct } \{lab_1 = z_1, \ldots, lab_n = z_n\}$, and $\mu[\ell.i \mapsto z] = \mu[\ell \mapsto \text{array}(z_1, \ldots, z, \ldots, z_n)]$ with z at position i, whenever $\hat{\mu}(\ell) = \text{array}(z_1, \ldots, z_n)$ and $1 \leq i \leq n$. (This is then partially defined.) This extension is used in the semantics of $*x = y$.

The rules deserve some explanation. E.g., the semantics of $x = y$ consists in fetching the address $\rho(y)$ at which the contents of variable y is stored in memory (the address usually referred to as $\&y$ in C code), and copying it into the address $\rho(x)$ at which x is stored. In effect, $x = y$ in C really means $*(\&x) = *(\&y)$. To lighten up the semantics, we agree that mentioning any expression entails that it is defined. In other words, the mere fact that we are writing $\mu[\rho(x) \mapsto \mu(\rho(y))]$ in the semantics of $*x = y$ really means that we must first check that $y \in$ dom ρ and $\rho(y) \in$ dom μ and $x \in$ dom ρ and $\rho(x) \in$ dom μ.

The semantics of $x = f$ presumes that there is an address at which the code for the function f is stored; whichever such a is then stored into x. This is taken care of by starting the program in a store that contains such a mapping from addresses to code fragments (and similarly contains storage for string constants).

Most other entries are self-explanatory. In the semantics of primitive calls $x = op(x_1, \ldots, x_n)$, we assume that the semantic $\widehat{op}$ of op is given separately.

Figure 5 leaves out the semantics for function calls $x = g(x_1, \ldots, x_n)$. We let $q, \rho, \mu \xrightarrow{\ x = g(x_1, \ldots, x_n)\ } q', \rho', \mu'$ if and only if $I(G_g), \rho_I, \mu_I \longrightarrow^* O(G_g), \rho_O, \mu_O$, where μ_I is obtained by allocating one new structure for formal parameters, one for local variables, and one for the return value (i.e., $\mu_I = \mu[a_{in} \mapsto \mathtt{struct}\ \{\&\mathrm{x}_1 = z_1, \ldots, \&\mathrm{x}_n = z_n\}, a_{loc} \mapsto \mathtt{struct}\ \{\&\mathrm{y}_1 = z'_1, \ldots, \&\mathrm{y}_m = z'_m\}, a_{ret} \mapsto \mathtt{struct}\ \{\&\mathtt{return} = z\}]$, where a_{in}, a_{loc}, and a_{ret} are distinct fresh addresses, $\mathrm{x}_1, \ldots, \mathrm{x}_n$ are the formal parameters, $\mathrm{y}_1, \ldots, \mathrm{y}_m$ are the local variables, and $z_1, \ldots, z_n, z'_1, \ldots, z'_m, z$ are appropriate zones, considering the types of variables), where ρ_I maps each x_i to $a_{in}.\&\mathrm{x}_i$, each y_j to $a_{loc}.\&\mathrm{y}_j$, and the fresh variable $\mathtt{return}$ (used to actually return a value from g) to $a_{ret}.\&\mathtt{return}$, where μ' is μ_O restricted to dom $\mu_O \setminus \{a_{in}, a_{loc}, a_{ret}\}$, and where $\rho' = \rho[x \mapsto \hat{\mu}_O(a_{ret}.\&\mathtt{return})]$. Note that we encode $\mathtt{return}\ v$ as an assignment $\mathtt{return} = v$. We deal with indirect calls $x = (*y)(x_1, \ldots, x_n)$ similarly: the only change is that we check that $\mu(\rho(y)) = \mathtt{code}\ g$ for some function g.

At the level of zones and pointers which we consider in this section, trust assertions just do nothing. We shall extend this semantics in the next section to properly handle trust assertions.

4.1 Semantics of Trust Assertions

The purpose of trust assertions is to define the denotation of concrete C data as Dolev-Yao style messages. A given piece of C data z may have one such denotation, or zero (e.g., if z just denotes, say, some index into a table, with no significance, security-wise), or several (e.g., if only for cardinality reasons, there are infinitely many terms but only finitely many 128-bit integers; concretely, even cryptographic hash functions have collisions.) Therefore we model the semantics of trust assertions as generating a *trust relation* $\mathcal{R}$ – a binary relation between C values and ground first-order terms – together with a *trust base* $\mathcal{B}$ – a set of ground first-order atoms. Let $Term_0$ be the set of all ground terms, $Atom_0$ be the set of ground atoms, and Val the set of C values, so a trust relation $\mathcal{R}$ is a subset of $Val \times Term_0$, and a trust base $\mathcal{B}$ is a subset of $Atom_0$.

A difficulty here is in defining what a C value is. Typically, an integer n should be a C value, and two integers should be equal as values if and only if they are equal as integers. In general, it is natural to think that zones should somehow represent C values. This implies that a zone of the form $\mathtt{ptr}(\ell)$, i.e., a pointer, should also represent a C value. This is needed: in Figure 2, we really want to understand the *pointer* $\mathtt{cipher1}$ (l.55) as denoting a message. But only the contents of the zone pointed to by $\mathtt{cipher1}$ should be relevant, not the location ℓ.

The irrelevance of ℓ is best handled through the notion of *bisimilarity*, which we define by imitation from [18]. A *bisimulation* is a binary relation $\sim$ on $Loc \times Store$, together with a binary relation (again written $\sim$) on $Zone \times Store$, such that:

- if $(\ell, \mu) \sim (\ell', \mu')$ then either $\ell \notin \mathrm{dom}\ \hat{\mu}$ and $\ell' \notin \mathrm{dom}\ \hat{\mu}'$, or $\ell \in \mathrm{dom}\ \hat{\mu}$, $\ell' \in \mathrm{dom}\ \hat{\mu}'$ and $(\hat{\mu}(\ell), \mu) \sim (\hat{\mu}'(\ell'), \mu')$;
- if $(z, \mu) \sim (z', \mu')$ then either $z = z'$ is of the form code f or int n or float x; or z is of the form $\mathrm{ptr}(\ell)$, z' is of the form $\mathrm{ptr}(\ell')$, and $(\ell, \mu) \sim (\ell', \mu')$; or $z = \mathrm{struct}\ \{lab_1 = z_1, \ldots, lab_n = z_n\}$, $z' = \mathrm{struct}\ \{lab_1 = z'_1, \ldots, lab_n = z'_n\}$, and $(z_i, \mu) \sim (z'_i, \mu')$ for every i, $1 \leq i \leq n$; or $z = \mathrm{array}(z_1, \ldots, z_n)$, $z' = \mathrm{array}(z'_1, \ldots, z'_n)$, and $(z_i, \mu) \sim (z'_i, \mu')$ for every i, $1 \leq i \leq n$.

Let $\cong$ (*bisimilarity*) be the largest bisimulation, with respect to inclusion of binary relations. A pair (ℓ, μ) of a location and a store μ describes a rooted graph in memory, whose root is ℓ, and whose edges are given by following pointers. Then, each rooted graph can be unfolded to yield an infinite tree. It is standard that bisimilarity relates (ℓ, μ) to (ℓ', μ') if and only if the unfolded infinite trees corresponding to each graph are isomorphic. It is natural to equate C values with such unfolded infinite trees (up to isomorphism), hence to pairs (ℓ, μ) up to bisimilarity: we therefore let Val be the quotient $(Loc \times Store)/\cong$. We let $[\ell, \mu]$ be the equivalence class of (ℓ, μ) under $\cong$.

We need to modify our semantics of C so that it takes into account trust assertions. For each instruction i in function f, except trust assertions, define the new transition relation $q, \rho, \mu, \mathcal{R}, \mathcal{B} \xrightarrow{i} q', \rho', \mu', \mathcal{R}', \mathcal{B}'$ (which now deals additionally with $\mathcal{R}, \mathcal{R}' \subseteq Val \times Term_0$ and $\mathcal{B}, \mathcal{B}' \subseteq Atom_0$) by: $q, \rho, \mu \xrightarrow{i} q', \rho', \mu'$ as defined in Figure 5, and $\mathcal{R}' = \mathcal{R}$ and $\mathcal{B}' = \mathcal{B}$. That is, ordinary C instructions do not modify the trust relation or the trust base, and otherwise behave in the standard way.

When i is the trust assertion trust $A \Leftarrow A_1, \ldots, A_n$, do the following. First, fix a set of definite clauses $\mathcal{M}$. (For now, just imagine $\mathcal{M}$ is empty. $\mathcal{M}$ is the external trust model, which we shall explain in Section 4.2.) The trust assertion simply adds to $\mathcal{R}$ and $\mathcal{B}$ all the new consequences deducible from the current $\mathcal{R}$ and $\mathcal{B}$, using the clauses $A \Leftarrow A_1, \ldots, A_n$ and the clauses in $\mathcal{M}$.

Formally, given any atom A', say that $\rho, \mu, \mathcal{R}, \mathcal{B} \models A'$ if and only if A' is of the form x rec t and $([\rho(x), \mu], t) \in \mathcal{R}$, or A' is of the form $P(t)$ and $P(t) \in \mathcal{B}$. For each definite clause C of the form $A \Leftarrow A_1, \ldots, A_n$, let $T_C^{\rho, \mu}(\mathcal{R}, \mathcal{B})$ be the smallest pair $(\mathcal{R}', \mathcal{B}')$ in the componentwise subset ordering such that, for every substitution σ such that $A\sigma, A_1\sigma, \ldots, A_n\sigma$ are ground and such that $\rho, \mu, \mathcal{R}, \mathcal{B} \models A_i\sigma$ for each i, $1 \leq i \leq n$, then $\rho, \mu, \mathcal{R}', \mathcal{B}' \models A\sigma$. For every set $\mathcal{M}$ of definite clauses, let $T_{\mathcal{M}}^{\rho, \mu}(\mathcal{R}, \mathcal{B})$ be the sup over all $C \in \mathcal{M}$ of $T_C^{\rho, \mu}(\mathcal{R}, \mathcal{B})$. (This is the familiar T_P operator of Prolog semantics.) Let lfp $T_{\mathcal{M}}^{\rho, \mu}(\mathcal{R}, \mathcal{B})$ be the least fixpoint of $T_{\mathcal{M}}^{\rho, \mu}$ above $(\mathcal{R}, \mathcal{B})$.

Then, when i is the trust assertion trust $A \Leftarrow A_1, \ldots, A_n$, we define $q, \rho, \mu, \mathcal{R}, \mathcal{B}$ $\xrightarrow{i} q', \rho', \mu', \mathcal{R}', \mathcal{B}'$ if and only if $q \xrightarrow{i} q'$ is an edge of G_f, $\rho = \rho'$, $\mu = \mu'$ (so trust statements behave as no-operations in the standard C semantics), and

$$(\mathcal{R}', \mathcal{B}') = \mathrm{lfp}\ T_{\mathcal{M}}^{\rho, \mu}(T_{A \Leftarrow A_1, \ldots, A_n}^{\rho, \mu}(\mathcal{R}, \mathcal{B})) \tag{12}$$

To simplify things a bit, imagine that $\mathcal{M}$ is empty. So $(\mathcal{R}', \mathcal{B}') = T^{\rho,\mu}_{A \Leftarrow A_1,\ldots,A_n}(\mathcal{R}, \mathcal{B})$. In particular, if i is trust x rec $t \Leftarrow x_1$ rec $t_1, \ldots, x_n$ rec t_n, then $\mathcal{B}' = \mathcal{B}$ and

$$\mathcal{R}' = \mathcal{R} \cup \{([\rho(x), \mu], t\sigma) | ([\rho(x_1), \mu], t_1\sigma) \in \mathcal{R} \text{ and } \ldots \text{ and } ([\rho(x_n), \mu], t_n\sigma)\}$$

where σ ranges over all substitutions such that $t\sigma$, $t_1\sigma$, $\ldots$, $t_n\sigma$ are ground terms. In other words, remembering that the C value of a variable y is $[\rho(y), \mu]$, this states that we trust that the C value of x should denote any message that is a ground instance $t\sigma$ of t, as soon as the C value of x_1 denotes $t_1\sigma$ and $\ldots$ and the C value of x_n denotes $t_n\sigma$.

Trust assertions are given as special C comments. E.g., the trust assertion on line 20 of Figure 2 states that encrypt_mesg really encrypts: we *trust* that, at the end of encrypt_mesg, cipher points to the encryption crypt(M,K) of the plaintext pointed to by msg with key pointed to by key_pub. Line 47 states that we trust write to make anything the contents of the buffer buf available to the Dolev-Yao intruder.

4.2   The External Trust Model

As we have already said in the introduction, programs such as SSL or the one of Figure 2 cannot be analyzed in isolation. We have to describe how the outside world, i.e., the other programs with which the analyzed programs communicates, behaves. This is in particular needed because the canonical trust statement for write is to declare that knows(t) holds whenever its input argument is trusted to denote message t; and the canonical trust statement for read is to declare that the contents of the buffer given as input will denote any message t such that knows(t). (This is the standard assumption in the Dolev-Yao model, that all communication is to and from an all powerful intruder.)

Concretely, in particular, we have to describe the semantics of the knows predicate, meant to represent all messages that a Dolev-Yao intruder may build. We do this by providing clauses such as (1)–(9), but also such as (10)–(11) to describe an abstract view of the roles of *honest* principals participating in the same or other protocols, and which are believed to share secrets with the analyzed program. Such clauses can be built from spi-calculus terms for example, following either Blanchet's [3] or Nielson et al.'s [20] approaches. (We tend to prefer the latter for pragmatic reasons: the output clauses are always in the decidable class $\mathcal{H}_1$; more detail later.)

In any case, we parameterize our analysis by an *external trust model*, which is just a set $\mathcal{M}$ of definite Horn clauses given in advance. The concrete semantics of programs is defined relatively to $\mathcal{M}$, see (12). The effect of applying lfp $T^{\rho,\mu}_{\mathcal{M}}$ is to close all facts in $\mathcal{R}$ and $\mathcal{B}$ under any finite number of applications of intruder and honest principal rules from the outside world.

5   Abstract Semantics

Let *AbsStore* and *AbsEnv* be the set of abstract *stores* and abstract *environments*. It does not matter much really how we represent these. Any static analysis of C code that is able of handling pointer aliases would probably do the job. We choose one that matches the simplicity of points-to analysis as much as we can. We associate an *abstract zone* with each variable (local or global), and with each memory allocation site, in the form of a fresh constant, taken from a finite set. An *atomic formula* $p(t, t')$, where t is a term, states that t is a location that may point to zone t'. The abstract semantics is then given as Horn clauses stating what new possible values may be found at what abstract zones.

Following the spirit of points-to analyses, we only include *gen* equations, and no *kill*; this considerably simplifies the abstract semantics. We define the abstract semantics $[\![i]\!]^{\#}\rho^{\#}$ of instruction i in the abstract environment $\rho^{\#}$, mapping variable names to abstract zones, a.k.a., constants, as sets of Horn clauses. The semantics of a function, resp. a whole program, is just the union of the semantics of all instructions in the given control flow graphs.

$$
\begin{aligned}
[\![x = y]\!]^{\#}\rho^{\#} &= \{p(c_x, X) \Leftarrow p(c_y, X)\} \text{ where } c_x = \rho^{\#}(x), c_y = \rho^{\#}(y) \\
[\![x = c]\!]^{\#}\rho^{\#} &= \{p(c_x, c)\} \\
[\![x = f]\!]^{\#}\rho^{\#} &= \{p(c_x, \text{code}(f))\} \\
[\![x = \&y]\!]^{\#}\rho^{\#} &= \{p(c_x, \text{ptr}(c_y))\} \\
[\![x = *y]\!]^{\#}\rho^{\#} &= \{p(c_x, X) \Leftarrow p(c_y, \text{ptr } Y), p(Y, X)\} \\
[\![*x = y]\!]^{\#}\rho^{\#} &= \{p(X, Y) \Leftarrow p(c_x, \text{ptr } X), p(c_y, Y)\} \\
[\![x = \&y[z]]\!]^{\#}\rho^{\#} &= \{p(c_x, \text{ptr}(X_{j+1})) \Leftarrow p(c_y, \text{ptr}(Y)), \\
&\qquad\qquad\qquad p(Y, \text{array}(X_1, \ldots, X_n, X_{n+1})) \\
&\quad \mid j \in [\![z]\!]^{\#}_{int}\} \text{ if } y \text{ is an expanded array} \\
&\quad \{p(c_x, \text{ptr}(X)) \Leftarrow p(c_y, \text{ptr}(X))\} \text{ if } y \text{ is a shrunk array} \\
[\![x = \&y \to a]\!]^{\#}\rho^{\#} &= \{p(c_x, \text{ptr}(Z)) \Leftarrow p(c_y, \text{ptr}(Y)), \\
&\qquad\qquad\qquad p(Y, \text{struct } \{\ldots, a = Z, \ldots\}) \\
[\![\text{trust } A \Leftarrow A_1, \ldots, A_n]\!]^{\#}\rho^{\#} &= \{(A \Leftarrow A_1, \ldots, A_n)\rho^{\sharp}\}
\end{aligned}
$$

Fig. 6. Some abstract semantic equations.

In Figure 6, we use the convention that $c_x = \rho^{\sharp}(x)$, $c_y = \rho^{\sharp}(y)$. This is recalled in the first rule, and omitted in later rules. In the second and third clauses, we assume that constants c and functions f can also serve as term constants when used in clauses. For the sake of precision, integer constants thus recorded are not used in computing array indices (instructions $x = \&y[z]$); rather an auxiliary analysis is run, based on a given integral abstract domain, yielding a set of possible integer values $[\![z]\!]^{\#}_{int}$ for the variable z: we follow here [4, 5] in that we distinguish *expanded array cells* (arrays whose length n is completely known, and are handled much like collections of separate global variables) and *shrunk array cells* (arrays thought of as one single abstract cell). In $x = \&y[z]$ and $x = \&y \to a$, we assume the types of all variables to be completely known; this determines the right form of term $\text{array}(X_1, \ldots, X_n, X_{n+1})$ or $\text{struct } \{\ldots, a = Z, \ldots\}$ in the bodies of clauses (in the first case, it yields the length n of the expanded array; the fictitious element X_{n+1} is added so as to cope with the fact that $\&y[n]$ is legal C code although $y[n]$ is not a valid element; while $\text{struct } \{\ldots, a = Z, \ldots\}$ is syntactic sugar for some term where field labels have been ordered in some way, and Z denotes the entry corresponding to the a label).

The abstract semantics for function calls is implemented as in [14]. We leave its formal expression as a (tedious) exercise. Intuitively, calling the known function g by $x = g(x_1, \ldots, x_n)$ works as though the actual parameters were copied, using run-of-the-mill assignments, into global locations $g.\text{in}.\mathbf{x}_1, \ldots, g.\text{in}.\mathbf{x}_n$. A local variable struct $g.\text{loc}$ is also used to hold local variables, another $g.\text{ret}$ to hold the return value, and the assignment $x = g.\text{ret}.\&\text{return}$ is simulated. (This matches the names of structs used in the concrete semantics of function calls, see Section 4.) Additional standard optimizations are added, e.g., keeping track of effective call sites when returning from functions to avoid spurious, fake control flow.

One advantage of this points-to-like abstract semantics is that the semantic of trust assertions is as simple as it can be: just add the trust assertion as a clause, replacing all C variables x by their location $\rho^{\#}(x)$. Reading $\rho^{\#}$ as a substitution, this means applying the substitution $\rho^{\#}$ to the entire clause $A \Leftarrow A_1, \ldots, A_n$.

This abstract semantics is of course rather coarse. One may improve somehow the precision of the analysis by renaming local variables after each assignment, in effect using variants of the SSA form.

5.1   Checking Abstract Properties

Once the abstract semantics of the program has been computed, as a set of Horn clauses, add the external trust model $\mathcal{M}$, which specifies all intruder capabilities, as well as behaviors that we trust other honest participants may have on the network. This yields a set S of Horn clauses.

Confidentiality. Assume we want to check that the value of variable x is always secret. This can be checked by verifying that S plus the goal clause $\bot \Leftarrow \text{knows}(Y)$, $\mathsf{p}(c_{\mathbf{x}}, X), X \text{ rec } Y$ is satisfiable. (That security boils down to satisfiability of clause sets, and more precisely to the existence of a model, was first noticed explicitly by Selinger [23].) Indeed, our abstract semantics is an upper approximation of all correct behaviors of our C program in the current trust model. If there is an attack, then there will be a closed term t (denoting the bit-level value of variable x, in the sense of Section 4.1) such that $\mathsf{p}(c_{\mathbf{x}}, t)$ holds, and a closed term u (denoting the message that we think is one possible reading of the value t) such that $t \text{ rec } u$, and which the intruder can discover, namely $\text{knows}(u)$.

Conformance. We may also check that specific variables may contain values of a specific form, say values trusted to denote messages matching a given open term t. We can test this by checking whether S plus the goal $\bot \Leftarrow \mathsf{p}(c_{\mathbf{x}}, X), X \text{ rec } t$ is unsatisfiable, where X is not free in t. This can be used to detect bugs, e.g., when one variable name was mistyped.

Checking satisfiability of sets of Horn clauses is in general undecidable. However we notice that all the clauses provided in the abstract semantics are in the decidable class $\mathcal{H}_1$, and in fact in the polynomial-time decidable subclass $\mathcal{H}_2$ [20]. We prefer clauses in the external trust model $\mathcal{M}$, accordingly, to fall in $\mathcal{H}_1$, too. Otherwise, we can approximate them as follows. We assume without loss of generality that only monadic predicate symbols occur; e.g., $\mathsf{p}(u, v)$ is encoded as $\mathsf{p}(c(u, v))$. Given a Horn clause $P(t) \Leftarrow body$, first linearize t by making copies of each variable, copying the corresponding parts of the body as needed. E.g., transform $P(f(X, X)) \Leftarrow Q(X), R(Y)$ into $P(f(X_1, X_2)) \Leftarrow Q(X_1), Q(X_2), R(Y)$. Then, if t is of the form $f(t_1, \ldots, t_n)$ where some t_i at least is not a variable, replace $P(t) \Leftarrow body$ by the clauses $P(f(X_1, \ldots, X_n)) \Leftarrow Q_1(X_1), \ldots, Q_n(X_n)$ and $Q_i(t_i) \Leftarrow body, 1 \leq i \leq n$, for fresh predicates $Q_1, \ldots, Q_n$, and repeat the process on the latter clauses. This yields clauses in $\mathcal{H}_1$, and is guaranteed to have a least Herbrand model that is an upper approximation of that of the original clause set. (In effect, this defines a set-constraint based typing discipline.) Since most clauses arise from the abstract semantics of the program, we do not lose much precision by doing this second abstraction step. Moreover, past experience in the verification of cryptographic protocols demonstrates that this does not throw away any essential information [13]. We have yet to evaluate whether this abstraction to $\mathcal{H}_1$ remains practical in the context of program verification.

6   Implementation

We have implemented this in the CSur project [21].

In a first phase, a specific *compiler* csur_cc reads, manages and generates a control-flow graph for each function of the program. All control flow graphs are stored in a unique table. Starting from the main function, the second phase uses a hybrid analyzer (computing abstract memory zones and collecting all Horn clauses for all program points) and performs function calls using the above table. Our tool follows the Compile-Link-Analysis technique of Heintze and Tardieu [14].

For each function, a control flow graph is generated and the compiler collects types for each variable of programs. For all types, the physical representation is also computed (using low level representations, for example field offsets of structures are computed as seen as Figure 4). Finally a linker merges all control flow graphs and types into a unique table. In the same way a library manager csur_ar (used just like ar) was implemented to help collect control flow graphs as single archives. These tools are defined as gcc front-ends to collect compilation options of source file.

The csur_cc compiler also collects trust assertions as it analyzes C code, and spits out a collection of Horn clauses which are then fed to an $\mathcal{H}_1$ solver – currently SPASS [27, 26] or the first author's prototype h1 prover. The fact that most clauses are in $\mathcal{H}_2$, a polynomial class, is a treat: despite several optimizations meant to decrease the number of generated clauses, a running 229 line implementation (excluding included files) of A's role in the Needham-Schroeder protocol results in a set of 459 clauses.

7   Conclusion

This paper is one of the first attempts at analyzing actual implementations of cryptographic protocols. Our aim is not to detect subtle buffer overflows, which are better handled by other techniques, but to detect the same kind of bugs that cryptographic protocols are fraught with, only on actual implementations. We must say that combining the intricacies of analyzing C code with cryptographic protocol verification is still a challenge. This can be seen from the fact that our abstract semantics for C is still fairly imprecise. First experiments however show that this is enough on the small examples we tested. Despite the shortcomings that our approach clearly still has, and which will be the subject of future work, we would like to stress the importance of *trust assertions* as a logical way of linking the in-memory model of values to the abstract Dolev-Yao model of messages; and the fact that compiling to Horn clauses is an effective, yet simple way of checking complex trust and security properties.

References

1. R. M. Amadio and W. Charatonik. On name generation and set-based analysis in the Dolev-Yao model. In *13th International Conference on Concurrency Theory CONCUR'02*, volume 2421 of *Lecture Notes in Computer Science*, pages 499–514. Springer-Verlag, 2002.
2. L. O. Andersen. *Program Analysis and Specialization for the C Programming Language.* PhD thesis, DIKU, University of Copenhagen, 1994. (DIKU report 94/19).
3. B. Blanchet. An Efficient Cryptographic Protocol Verifier Based on Prolog Rules. In *14th IEEE Computer Security Foundations Workshop (CSFW-14)*, pages 82–96, Cape Breton, Nova Scotia, Canada, June 2001. IEEE Computer Society.
4. B. Blanchet, P. Cousot, R. Cousot, J. Feret, L. Mauborgne, A. Miné, D. Monniaux, and X. Rival. Design and Implementation of a Special-Purpose Static Program Analyzer for Safety-Critical Real-Time Embedded Software, invited chapter. In T. Mogensen, D. A. Schmidt, and I. H. Sudborough, editors, *The Essence of Computation: Complexity, Analysis, Transformation. Essays Dedicated to Neil D. Jones*, volume 2566 of *Lecture Notes on Computer Science*, pages 85–108. Springer Verlag, Dec. 2002.
5. B. Blanchet, P. Cousot, R. Cousot, J. Feret, L. Mauborgne, A. Miné, D. Monniaux, and X. Rival. A Static Analyzer for Large Safety-Critical Software. In *ACM SIGPLAN 2003 Conference on Programming Language Design and Implementation (PLDI'03)*, pages 196–207, San Diego, California, June 2003. ACM.
6. P. Boury and N. Elkhadi. Static Analysis of Java Cryptographic Applets. In *ECOOP'2001 Workshop on Formal Techniques for Java Programs*. Fern Universität Hagen, 2001.
7. H. Comon-Lundh and V. Cortier. Security properties: Two agents are sufficient. In *Proc. 12th European Symposium on Programming (ESOP'2003)*, pages 99–113, Warsaw, Poland, Apr. 2003. Springer-Verlag LNCS 2618.
8. D. Dolev and A. C. Yao. On security of public key protocols. *IEEE trans. on Information Theory*, IT-30:198–208, 1983.
9. N. Durgin, P. Lincoln, J. Mitchell, and A. Scedrov. Undecidability of bounded security protocols. In N. Heintze and E. Clarke, editors, *Proceedings of the Workshop on Formal Methods and Security Protocols – FMSP, Trento, Italy*, July 1999.
10. A. Freier, P. Karlton, and P. Kocher. The SSL protocol. Version 3.0., 1996. http://home.netscape.com/eng/ssl3/.
11. O. Gay. Exploitation avancée de buffer overflows. Technical report, LASEC, Ecole Polytechnique Fédérale de Lausanne, June 2002. http://diwww.epfl.ch/~ogay/advbof/advbof.pdf.
12. J. Goubault-Larrecq, editor. *Special Issue on Models and Methods for Cryptographic Protocol Verification*, volume 4. Instytut Łącsności (Institute of Telecommunications), Warsaw, Poland, Dec. 2002.
13. J. Goubault-Larrecq. Une fois qu'on n'a pas trouvé de preuve, comment le faire comprendre à un assistant de preuve ? In *Actes 15èmes journées francophones sur les langages applicatifs (JFLA'04)*, Sainte-Marie-de-Ré France, Janvier 2004. INRIA.
14. N. Heintze and O. Tardieu. Ultra-fast aliasing analysis using cla: a million lines of c code in a second. In *Proc. of the ACM SIGPLAN'01 conference on Programming language design and implementation*, pages 254–263. ACM Press, 2001.
15. M. Hind. Pointer analysis: haven't we solved this problem yet? In *Proceedings of the 2001 ACM SIGPLAN-SIGSOFT workshop on Program analysis for software tools and engineering*, pages 54–61. ACM Press, 2001.
16. N. E. Kadhi. Automatic verification of confidentiality properties of cryptographic programs. *Networking and Information Systems*, 3(6), 2001.

17. G. Lowe. An attack on the needham-schroeder public-key authentication protocol. *Information Processing Letters*, 56(3):131–133, 1995.
18. R. Milner. *Communication and concurrency*. Prentice Hall International (UK) Ltd., 1995.
19. R. Needham and M. Schroeder. Using encryption for authentification in large networks of computers. *Communications of the ACM*, 21(12), December 1978.
20. F. Nielson, H. R. Nielson, and H. Seidl. Normalizable horn clauses, strongly recognizable relations, and spi. In *Proceedings of the 9th International Symposium on Static Analysis*, volume 2477, pages 20–35. Springer-Verlag, 2002.
21. F. Parrennes. The CSur project. http://www.lsv.ens-cachan.fr/csur/, 2004.
22. S. Sagiv, T. W. Reps, and R. Wilhelm. Parametric shape analysis via 3-valued logic. *ACM Trans. Prog. Lang. Sys.*, 24(3):217–298, may 2002.
23. P. Selinger. Models for an adversary-centric protocol logic. *Electronic Notes in Theoretical Computer Science*, 55(1):73–87, July 2001. Proceedings of the 1st Workshop on Logical Aspects of Cryptographic Protocol Verification (LACPV'01), J. Goubault-Larrecq, ed.
24. A. Simon and A. King. Analyzing string buffers in C. In *Intl. Conf. on Algebraic Methods and Software Methodology (AMAST'2002)*, pages 365–379, 2002.
25. D. Wagner, J. S. Foster, E. A. Brewer, and A. Aiken. A first step towards automated detection of buffer overrun vulnerabilities. In *Network and Distributed System Security Symposium*, pages 3–17, San Diego, CA, February 2000.
26. C. Weidenbach. Towards an automatic analysis of security protocols. In H. Ganzinger, editor, *16th International Conference on Automated Deduction CADE-16*, volume 1632, pages 378–382. Springer, 1999.
27. C. Weidenbach, U. Brahm, T. Hillenbrand, E. Keen, C. Theobald, and D. Topic. SPASS version 2.0. In *Proc. 18th Conference on Automated Deduction (CADE 2002)*, pages 275–279. Springer-Verlag LNCS 2392, 2002.

Simple Is Better:
Efficient Bounded Model Checking for Past LTL

Timo Latvala[1,*], Armin Biere[2], Keijo Heljanko[1,**], and Tommi Junttila[1,***]

[1] Laboratory for Theoretical Computer Science
Helsinki University of Technology
P.O. Box 5400, FI-02015 HUT, Finland
{Timo.Latvala,Keijo.Heljanko,Tommi.Junttila}@hut.fi
[2] Institute for Formal Models and Verification
Johannes Kepler University
Altenbergerstrasse 69, A-4040 Linz, Austria
biere@jku.at

Abstract. We consider the problem of bounded model checking for linear temporal logic with past operators (PLTL). PLTL is more attractive as a specification language than linear temporal logic without past operators (LTL) since many specifications are easier to express in PLTL. Although PLTL is not more expressive than LTL, it is exponentially more succinct. Our contribution is a new more efficient encoding of the bounded model checking problem for PLTL based on our previously presented encoding for LTL. The new encoding is *linear* in the bound. We have implemented the encoding in the NuSMV 2.1 model checking tool and compare it against the encoding in NuSMV by Benedetti and Cimatti. The experimental results show that our encoding performs significantly better than this previously used encoding.

Keywords: Bounded Model Checking, Past LTL, NuSMV

1   Introduction

Bounded model checking [1] is an efficient method of implementing *symbolic model checking*, a way of automatically verifying system designs w.r.t. properties given in a temporal logic. Symbolic model checking allows verification of designs with large state spaces by representing the state space implicitly. In bounded model checking (BMC) the system is represented as a propositional logic formula, and only the bounded paths of the system are considered. Given a system model, a temporal logic specification and a bound k, a formula in propositional logic is generated which is satisfiable if and only if the system has a counterexample of length k to the specification. A satisfiability (SAT) solver is used to check if the generated formula is satisfiable. By letting the bound

* Work supported by the Helsinki Graduate School in Computer Science, the Academy of Finland (project 53695), and the Nokia Foundation.
** Work supported by the Academy of Finland (project 53695, grant for research work abroad, research fellow post).
*** Work partially done while visiting ITC-IRST, Trento, Italy. This work has been sponsored by the CALCULEMUS! IHP-RTN EC project, contract code HPRN-CT-2000-00102.

R. Cousot (Ed.): VMCAI 2005, LNCS 3385, pp. 380–395, 2005.

grow incrementally we can prove that the system has no counterexample for the given property. Although basic BMC is an incomplete method in practice (it is difficult to a priori determine a reasonably small bound k which guarantees completeness) it has been very successful in industrial context [2–4]. The success of BMC is mostly based on that propositional logic is a compact representation for Boolean functions and that BMC allows leveraging the vast improvements in SAT solver technology made in recent years.

Linear temporal logic (LTL) is one of the most popular specification languages used in model checking tools and many model checking tools support some variant of it. However, in most of its incarnations only the so called future fragment of the language (which we will denote by LTL) is considered. This fragment includes only temporal operator which refer to future states. Recently, several papers [5–7] have also considered supporting LTL with past operators (PLTL). The main argument for adding support for past operators is motivated by practice: PLTL allows more succinct and natural specifications than LTL. For instance, the specification "if the discharge valve is open, then the pressure alarm must have gone off in the past" can easily be expressed in PLTL while expressing it in LTL is not as straightforward. We believe that an intuitive specification language reduces the probability of a model checking effort failing because of an erroneous specification. The usefulness of PLTL has already been argued earlier in [8].

PLTL also has theoretical advantages compared to LTL. Although PLTL and LTL are equally expressive [9, 10], PLTL is exponentially more succinct than LTL [11]. This succinctness comes for free in the sense that model checking for LTL and PLTL are both PSPACE-complete in the length of the formula [12]. In practice, however, PLTL model checking algorithms are more difficult and complex to implement.

The first to present a reasonable solution for doing BMC with PLTL were Benedetti and Cimatti [7]. They showed how the standard BMC encoding [1] can be extended to handle PLTL. Our main contribution is a new encoding for BMC with PLTL based on our LTL encoding [13]. Unlike the encoding in [7], the size of our new encoding is linear in the bound k. The new encoding is quadratic in the size of the formula. When the number of nested past operators is fixed, the encoding becomes linear in the size of the formula. The new encoding has been implemented in the NuSMV 2 model checker [14] and we have experimentally evaluated our encoding. The results clearly show that the new encoding has better running times and that it generates smaller SAT instances than the current encoding in NuSMV. Since the new encoding is also very simple, it allows a straightforward implementation.

2   Bounded Model Checking

The main idea of bounded model checking [1] is to search for *bounded witnesses* for a temporal property. A bounded witness is an infinite path on which the property holds, and which can be represented by a finite path of length k. A finite path can represent infinite behaviour, in the following sense. Either it represents all its infinite extensions or it forms a *loop*. More formally, an infinite path $\pi = s_0 s_1 s_2 \ldots$ of states contains a (k,l)-loop, or just an k-loop, if $\pi = (s_0 s_1 \ldots s_{l-1})(s_l \ldots s_k)^\omega$. The two cases we consider are depicted in Fig. 1.

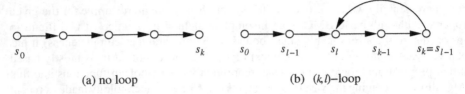

(a) no loop   (b) (k,l)–loop

Fig. 1. The two possible cases for a bounded path.

In BMC all possible k-length bounded witnesses of the *negation* of the specification are encoded as a SAT problem. The bound k is increased until either a witness is found (the instance is satisfiable) or a sufficiently high value of k to guarantee completeness is reached.

Note that as in [7, 13, 15] the shape of the loop and accordingly the meaning of the bound k is slightly different from [1]. In this paper, a finite path of length k for representing an infinite path with a loop contains the *looping state* twice, at position $l-1$ and at position k.

2.1 LTL

LTL is a commonly used specification logic. The syntax is defined over a set of atomic propositions AP. Boolean operators we use are negation, disjunction and conjunction. Regarding temporal connectives, we concentrate on the next time ($\mathbf{X}$), the until ($\mathbf{U}$) , and the release ($\mathbf{R}$) operators. The semantics of an LTL formula is defined along infinite paths $\pi = s_0 s_1 \ldots$ of states s_i. The states are part of a model M with transition relation T and initial state constraint I. Further, let π^i denote the suffix of π starting from the i:th state. The semantics can then be defined recursively as follows:

$$\pi^i \models \psi \quad \Leftrightarrow \psi \text{ holds in } s_i \text{ for } \psi \in AP.$$
$$\pi^i \models \neg\psi \quad \Leftrightarrow \pi^i \not\models \psi.$$
$$\pi^i \models \psi_1 \vee \psi_2 \Leftrightarrow \pi^i \models \psi_1 \text{ or } \pi^i \models \psi_2.$$
$$\pi^i \models \psi_1 \wedge \psi_2 \Leftrightarrow \pi^i \models \psi_1 \text{ and } \pi^i \models \psi_2.$$
$$\pi^i \models \mathbf{X}\psi \quad \Leftrightarrow \pi^{i+1} \models \psi.$$
$$\pi^i \models \psi_1 \mathbf{U}\psi_2 \Leftrightarrow \exists n \geq i \text{ such that } \pi^n \models \psi_2 \text{ and } \pi^j \models \psi_1 \text{ for all } i \leq j < n.$$
$$\pi^i \models \psi_1 \mathbf{R}\psi_2 \Leftrightarrow \forall n \geq i, \pi^n \models \psi_2 \text{ or } \pi^j \models \psi_1 \text{ for some } i \leq j < n.$$

Commonly used abbreviations are the standard Boolean shorthands $\top \equiv p \vee \neg p$ for some $p \in AP$, $\bot \equiv \neg\top$, $p \Rightarrow q \equiv \neg p \vee q$, $p \Leftrightarrow q \equiv (p \Rightarrow q) \wedge (q \Rightarrow p)$, and the derived temporal operators $\mathbf{F}\psi \equiv \top \mathbf{U}\psi$ ('finally'), $\mathbf{G}\psi \equiv \neg\mathbf{F}\neg\psi$ ('globally').

It is always possible to rewrite any formula to *positive normal form*, where all negations only appear in front of atomic proposition. This can be accomplished by using the dualities $\neg(\psi_1 \mathbf{U}\psi_2) \equiv \neg\psi_1 \mathbf{R} \neg\psi_2$, $\neg(\psi_1 \mathbf{R}\psi_2) \equiv \neg\psi_1 \mathbf{U} \neg\psi_2$ and $\neg\mathbf{X}\psi \equiv \mathbf{X}\neg\psi$. In the following we assume all formulas are in positive normal form.

2.2 Bounded Model Checking for LTL

We briefly review our simple and compact encoding for bounded model checking LTL given in [13]. This encoding has been shown to outperform previous encodings and in addition is much simpler to implement. Moreover, it forms the basis for our new encoding of PLTL in this paper. It consists of three types of constraints. *Model constraints* encode legal initialised finite paths of the model M of length k:

$$|[M]|_k := I(s_0) \wedge \bigwedge_{i=1}^{k} T(s_{i-1}, s_i),$$

where $I(s)$ is the initial state predicate and $T(s, s')$ is a total transition relation. The *loop constraints* are used to detect loops. We introduce k fresh *loop selector variables* $l_1, \ldots, l_k$ that have the following constraint: if l_i is true then $s_{i-1} = s_k$. In this case the LTL encoding treats the bounded path as a (k, i)-loop. If no loop selector variable is true the LTL encoding treats the path as a simple path without a loop. At most one loop selector variable is allowed to be true. Thus, the loop selector variables show where the bounded path loops. This is accomplished with the following constraints:

$$|[LoopConstraints]|_k \Leftrightarrow Loop_k \wedge AtMostOne_k,$$

$$Loop_k \Leftrightarrow \bigwedge_{i=1}^{k} (l_i \Rightarrow (s_{i-1} = s_k)),$$

$$AtMostOne_k \Leftrightarrow \bigwedge_{i=1}^{k} (SmallerExists_i \Rightarrow \neg l_i),$$

$$SmallerExists_1 \Leftrightarrow \bot, \text{ and}$$

$$SmallerExists_{i+1} \Leftrightarrow SmallerExists_i \vee l_i, \text{ where } 0 < i \leq k.$$

The constraints select a (k, l)-loop (also called *lasso-shaped* path) from the model, when a loop is needed to find a counterexample. Finally, *LTL constraints* restrict the bounded path defined by the model constraints and loop constraints to witnesses of the LTL formula. The encoding utilises the fact that for lasso-shaped Kripke structures the semantics of CTL and LTL coincide [16, 17]. Essentially, the encoding can be seen as a CTL model checker for lasso-shaped Kripke structures based on using the least and greatest fixpoint characterisations of **U** and **R**. The computation of the fixpoints for **U** and **R** is done in two parts. An auxiliary translation $\langle\langle \cdot \rangle\rangle$ computes an approximation of the fixpoints that is refined to exact values by $|[\cdot]|$. The presentation of the constraints differs slightly from [13] to allow easier generalisation to the PLTL case.

φ	$0 \leq i < k$	$i = k$
$\|[p]\|_i$	p_i	p_i
$\|[\neg p]\|_i$	$\neg p_i$	$\neg p_i$
$\|[\psi_1 \wedge \psi_2]\|_i$	$\|[\psi_1]\|_i \wedge \|[\psi_2]\|_i$	$\|[\psi_1]\|_i \wedge \|[\psi_2]\|_i$
$\|[\psi_1 \vee \psi_2]\|_i$	$\|[\psi_1]\|_i \vee \|[\psi_2]\|_i$	$\|[\psi_1]\|_i \vee \|[\psi_2]\|_i$
$\|[\mathbf{X}\psi_1]\|_i$	$\|[\psi_1]\|_{i+1}$	$\bigvee_{j=1}^{k} (l_j \wedge \|[\psi_1]\|_j)$
$\|[\psi_1 \mathbf{U} \psi_2]\|_i$	$\|[\psi_2]\|_i \vee (\|[\psi_1]\|_i \wedge \|[\psi_1 \mathbf{U} \psi_2]\|_{i+1})$	$\|[\psi_2]\|_i \vee \left(\|[\psi_1]\|_i \wedge \left(\bigvee_{j=1}^{k} \left(l_j \wedge \langle\langle \psi_1 \mathbf{U} \psi_2 \rangle\rangle_j \right) \right) \right)$
$\|[\psi_1 \mathbf{R} \psi_2]\|_i$	$\|[\psi_2]\|_i \wedge (\|[\psi_1]\|_i \vee \|[\psi_1 \mathbf{R} \psi_2]\|_{i+1})$	$\|[\psi_2]\|_i \wedge \left(\|[\psi_1]\|_i \vee \left(\bigvee_{j=1}^{k} \left(l_j \wedge \langle\langle \psi_1 \mathbf{R} \psi_2 \rangle\rangle_j \right) \right) \right)$
$\langle\langle \psi_1 \mathbf{U} \psi_2 \rangle\rangle_i$	$\|[\psi_2]\|_i \vee (\|[\psi_1]\|_i \wedge \langle\langle \psi_1 \mathbf{U} \psi_2 \rangle\rangle_{i+1})$	$\|[\psi_2]\|_i$
$\langle\langle \psi_1 \mathbf{R} \psi_2 \rangle\rangle_i$	$\|[\psi_2]\|_i \wedge (\|[\psi_1]\|_i \vee \langle\langle \psi_1 \mathbf{R} \psi_2 \rangle\rangle_{i+1})$	$\|[\psi_2]\|_i$

The conjunction of these three sets of constraints forms the full encoding of the bounded model checking problem into SAT:

$$|[M, \varphi, k]| = |[M]|_k \wedge |[LoopConstraints]|_k \wedge |[\varphi]|_0.$$

The LTL formula φ has a witness in M that can represented by a finite path of length k iff the encoding is satisfiable. For more details on the encoding and how it can be used for model checking please refer to [13].

3 Bounded Model Checking with Past Operators

Benedetti and Cimatti [7] were the first to consider bounded model checking for PLTL. Their approach is based on the original encoding of Biere et al. [1]. The approach is such that it generates constraints separately for each possible bounded path with a loop (for all values of $0 \leq l \leq k$). This makes sharing structure in the formula difficult. Our encoding is based on a different solution where the concerns of evaluating the formula and forming the bounded path have been separated. As we shall see, this allows for a simple and compact encoding for PLTL.

3.1 PLTL

Extending LTL with past operators results in a logic which is more succinct than LTL and arguably more intuitive for some specifications. The simplest past operators are the two previous state operators $\mathbf{Y}\psi$ and $\mathbf{Z}\psi$. Both are true if ψ was true in the previous time step. The semantics of the operators differ at the origin of time: $\mathbf{Y}\psi$ is always false while $\mathbf{Z}\psi$ is always true. Similar to the derived future operators $\mathbf{F}\psi$ and $\mathbf{G}\psi$ are $\mathbf{O}\psi$ ('once') and $\mathbf{H}\psi$ ('historically') that hold if ψ holds once in the past or ψ holds always in the past, respectively. The binary operator $\psi_1 \mathbf{S} \psi_2$ ('since') holds if ψ_2 was true once in the past and ψ_1 has been true ever since. Note that ψ_2 must have been true at some point in the past in order for $\psi_1 \mathbf{S} \psi_2$ to hold. The other past binary operator $\psi_1 \mathbf{T} \psi_2$ ('trigger') holds when ψ_2 holds up until the present starting from the time step where ψ_1 was true. If ψ_1 never was true ψ_2 must have been true always in the past.

We define the semantics of PLTL by extending the formal semantics of LTL. Only semantics for the new operators are given.

$$\pi^i \models \mathbf{Y}\psi \quad \Leftrightarrow i > 0 \text{ and } \pi^{i-1} \models \psi.$$
$$\pi^i \models \mathbf{Z}\psi \quad \Leftrightarrow i = 0 \text{ or } \pi^{i-1} \models \psi.$$
$$\pi^i \models \mathbf{O}\psi \quad \Leftrightarrow \pi^j \models \psi \text{ for some } 0 \leq j \leq i.$$
$$\pi^i \models \mathbf{H}\psi \quad \Leftrightarrow \pi^j \models \psi \text{ for all } 0 \leq j \leq i.$$
$$\pi^i \models \psi_1 \mathbf{S}\psi_2 \Leftrightarrow \pi^j \models \psi_2 \text{ for some } 0 \leq j \leq i \text{ and } \pi^n \models \psi_1 \text{ for all } j < n \leq i.$$
$$\pi^i \models \psi_1 \mathbf{T}\psi_2 \Leftrightarrow \text{ for all } 0 \leq j \leq i : \pi^j \models \psi_2 \text{ or } \pi^n \models \psi_1 \text{ for some } j < n \leq i.$$

Useful dualities which hold for past operators are $\neg(\psi_1 \mathbf{S}\psi_2) \equiv \neg\psi_1 \mathbf{T} \neg\psi_2$, $\neg\mathbf{H}\psi \equiv \mathbf{O}\neg\psi$, $\neg(\psi_1 \mathbf{T}\psi_2) \equiv \neg\psi_1 \mathbf{S} \neg\psi_2$, $\neg\mathbf{O}\psi \equiv \mathbf{H}\neg\psi$, $\neg\mathbf{Z}\psi \equiv \mathbf{Y}\neg\psi$, and $\neg\mathbf{Y}\psi \equiv \mathbf{Z}\neg\psi$. Examples of simple PLTL formulas are $\mathbf{G}(p \Rightarrow \mathbf{O}q)$ ('all p occurrences are preceded by an occurrence of q') and $\mathbf{F}\mathbf{G}(p\mathbf{S}\neg q)$ ('eventually p will stay true after q becomes false'). Recall that we assume that all formulas are in positive normal form.

The maximum number of nested past operators in PLTL formula is called the *past operator depth*.

Definition 1. *The past operator depth for a PLTL formula* ψ *is denoted by* $\delta(\psi)$ *and is inductively defined as:*

$$
\begin{aligned}
\delta(\psi) &= 0 & &\text{for } \psi \in AP, \\
\delta(\circ\psi) &= \delta(\psi) & &\text{for } \circ \in \{\neg, \mathbf{X}, \mathbf{F}, \mathbf{G}\}, \\
\delta(\psi_1 \circ \psi_2) &= max(\delta(\psi_1), \delta(\psi_2)) & &\text{for } \circ \in \{\vee, \wedge, \mathbf{U}, \mathbf{R}\}, \\
\delta(\circ\psi) &= 1 + \delta(\psi) & &\text{for } \circ \in \{\mathbf{Y}, \mathbf{Z}, \mathbf{O}, \mathbf{H}\}, \text{ and} \\
\delta(\psi_1 \circ \psi_2) &= 1 + max(\delta(\psi_1), \delta(\psi_2)) & &\text{for } \circ \in \{\mathbf{S}, \mathbf{T}\}.
\end{aligned}
$$

PLTL has features which impact the way model checking can be done. We illustrate these features through examples. As a running example we use an example from [7] adapted to better suit our setting. In this example the system to be model checked is a counter which uses a variable x to store the counter value. The counter is initialised to 0 and the system adds one to the counter variable x at each time step until the highest value 5 is reached. After this the counter is reset to the value 2 in the next time step and the system starts looping as illustrated in Fig. 2. Thus the system is deterministic and the counter values can be seen as an infinite sequence $(012)(3452)^\omega$ corresponding to a $(6,3)$-loop of the system.

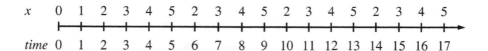

Fig. 2. Execution of the counter system.

Consider the $(6,3)$-loop of the counter system. The formula

$$((x = 3) \wedge \mathbf{Y}\mathbf{Y}\mathbf{Y}(x = 0))$$

holds only at time point 3 but not at any later time point. This demonstrates the (quite obvious) fact that unlike pure future LTL formulas, the PLTL past formulas can distinguish states which belong to different unrollings of the loop. We introduce the notion of a time point belonging to a d-unrolling of the loop to distinguish between different copies of each state in the unrolling of the loop part.

Definition 2. *For a* (k, l)-*loop* π *we say that the* period $p(\pi)$ *of* π *is* $(k - l) + 1$, *i.e., the number of states the loop consists of. We define that a time point* $i \geq 0$ *in* π *belongs to the* d-unrolling of the loop iff $d \geq 0$ *is the smallest integer such that* $i < l + ((d + 1) \cdot p(\pi))$.

At the time point 3, which belongs to the 0-unrolling of the loop, the formula $\mathbf{Y}\mathbf{Y}\mathbf{Y}(x = 0)$ holds. However, at the time point 7 belonging to the 1-unrolling of the loop the formula $\mathbf{Y}\mathbf{Y}\mathbf{Y}(x = 0)$ does not hold even though they both correspond to the first state in the unrolling of the loop.

Benedetti and Cimatti [7] observed that encoding the BMC problem for PLTL when the bounded path has no loop was fairly straightforward. It is simple to generalise the no loop case of Biere et al. [1] to include past operators, as they have simple semantics. In the no loop case our encoding reduces to essentially the same as [7]. This case is an optimisation that can sometimes result in shorter counterexamples but is not needed for correctness. When loops are allowed the matter is more complicated and therefore we will focus on this part in the rest of the paper. The fact which enables us to do bounded model checking of PLTL formulas (containing past operators in the loop case) is the following property first observed by [11] and later independently by [7]: for (k, l)-loops the ability to distinguish between time points in different d-unrollings in the past is limited by the past operator depth $\delta(\varphi)$ of a formula φ.

Proposition 1. *Let φ be a PLTL formula and π be a (k, l)-loop. For all $i \geq l$ it holds that if the time point i belongs to a d-unrolling of the loop with $d \geq \delta(\varphi)$ then: $\pi^i \models \varphi$ iff $\pi^j \models \varphi$, where $j = i - ((d - \delta(\varphi)) \cdot p(\pi))$.*

Proof. The proposition directly follows from Theorem 1 and Lemma 2 of [7].

The proposition above can be interpreted saying that after unrolling the loop $\delta(\varphi)$ times the formula cannot distinguish different unrollings of the loop from each other. Therefore if we want to evaluate a formula at an index i belonging to a d-unrolling with $d > \delta(\varphi)$, it is equivalent to evaluate the formula at the corresponding state of the $\delta(\varphi)$-unrolling.

Consider again the running example where we next want to evaluate whether the formula

$$\mathbf{F}\left((x = 3) \wedge \mathbf{O}\left((x = 4) \wedge \mathbf{O}\left(x = 5\right)\right)\right) \tag{1}$$

holds in the counter system. The formula expresses that it is possible to reach a point at which the counter has had the values $3, 4, 5$ in decreasing order in the past. By using the semantics of PLTL it is easy to check that this indeed is the case. The earliest time where the subformula $((x = 3) \wedge \mathbf{O}((x = 4) \wedge \mathbf{O}(x = 5)))$ holds is time 11 and thus the top-level formula holds at time 0. In fact the mentioned subformula holds for all time points of the form $11 + i \cdot 4$, where $i \geq 0$ and $4 = p(\pi)$ is the period of the loop 3452. The time point 11 corresponds to a time step which is in the 2-unrolling of the loop 3452. This stabilisation at the second unrolling is guaranteed by the past operator depth of two of the formula in question. The subformula $((x = 4) \wedge \mathbf{O}(x = 5))$ has past operator depth $\delta(\varphi) = 1$ and it holds for the first time at time step 8 which is in the 1-unrolling of the loop. Again the stabilisation of the formula value is guaranteed by the past operator depth of one of the formula in question. It will also hold for all time steps of the form $8 + i \cdot 4$, where $i \geq 0$. Thus, if we need to evaluate any subformula at a time step which belongs to a deeper unrolling than its past operator depth, e.g. if we want to evaluate $((x = 4) \wedge \mathbf{O}((x = 5)))$ at time step 16 in 3-unrolling, we can just take a look at the truth value of that formula at the time step corresponding to the unrolling of the formula to its past operator depth, in this case at time step $8 = 16 - (3 - 1) \cdot 4$.

3.2   Translation

At this point we are ready to present the propositional encoding of the BMC problem for PLTL. From the previous discussion it is fairly obvious that an efficient encoding requires that we encode the unrolling of the loop in a sensible manner and encode the semantics of the operators succinctly.

The basic idea of the encoding is to virtually unroll the path by making copies of the original k step path. A copy of the original path corresponds to a certain d-unrolling. If all loop selector variables l_i are false the encoding collapses to the original path without a loop. The number of copies of the path for a PLTL formula φ is dictated by the past operator depth $\delta(\varphi)$. Since different subformulas have different past depths, the encoding is such that subformulas with different past depths see different Kripke structures. Fig. 3 shows the running example unwound to depth $d = 2$, for evaluating formula (1).

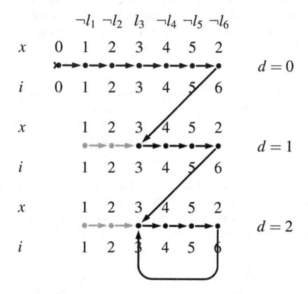

Fig. 3. Black arcs show the Kripke structure induced by virtual unrolling of the loop for $k = 6$ up to depth 2 (i.e., $\delta(\varphi) = 2$) when l_3 holds.

The PLTL encoding $|[\varphi]|_i^d$ has two parameters: d is the current d-unrolling and i is the index in the current d-unrolling. The case where $d = 0$ corresponds to the original k-step path. Subformulas at virtual unrolling depth beyond their past operator depth can by Prop. 1 be projected to the depth corresponding to the past operator depth. From this we get our first rule:

$$|[\varphi]|_i^d = |[\varphi]|_i^{\delta(\varphi)}, \text{ when } d > \delta(\varphi).$$

The rest of the encoding is split into cases based on the values of i and d. Encoding atomic propositions and their negation is simple. We simply project the atomic propositions onto the original path. The Boolean operators $\vee$ and $\wedge$ are also easy to encode since they are part of standard propositional logic.

φ	$0 \leq d \leq \delta(\psi), 0 \leq i \leq k$
$\|[p]\|_i^d$	p_i
$\|[\neg p]\|_i^d$	$\neg p_i$
$\|[\psi_1 \wedge \psi_2]\|_i^d$	$\|[\psi_1]\|_i^d \wedge \|[\psi_2]\|_i^d$
$\|[\psi_1 \vee \psi_2]\|_i^d$	$\|[\psi_1]\|_i^d \vee \|[\psi_2]\|_i^d$

The translation of the future operators is a fairly straightforward generalisation of our pure future encoding of Sect. 2.2 published in [13]. The path is copied as many times as required by the past depth. When $d < \delta(\psi)$ the translation is essentially identical to the pure future encoding with the exception of the case $i = k$. As only the loop part of the copy of the path is relevant (see Fig. 3), the successor for $i = k$ must be encoded to select the correct state in the next d-unrolling. This is accomplished by using the loop selector variables l_i.

φ	$0 \leq d < \delta(\varphi), 0 \leq i < k$	$0 \leq d < \delta(\varphi), i = k$
$\|[\mathbf{X}\psi_1]\|_i^d$	$\|[\psi_1]\|_{i+1}^d$	$\bigvee_{j=1}^k \left(l_j \wedge \|[\psi_1]\|_j^{d+1}\right)$
$\|[\psi_1 \mathbf{U} \psi_2]\|_i^d$	$\|[\psi_2]\|_i^d \vee \left(\|[\psi_1]\|_i^d \wedge \|[\psi_1 \mathbf{U} \psi_2]\|_{i+1}^d\right)$	$\|[\psi_2]\|_i^d \vee \left(\|[\psi_1]\|_i^d \wedge \left(\bigvee_{j=1}^k \left(l_j \wedge \|[\psi_1 \mathbf{U} \psi_2]\|_j^{d+1}\right)\right)\right)$
$\|[\psi_1 \mathbf{R} \psi_2]\|_i^d$	$\|[\psi_2]\|_i^d \wedge \left(\|[\psi_1]\|_i^d \vee \|[\psi_1 \mathbf{R} \psi_2]\|_{i+1}^d\right)$	$\|[\psi_2]\|_i^d \wedge \left(\|[\psi_1]\|_i^d \vee \left(\bigvee_{j=1}^k \left(l_j \wedge \|[\psi_1 \mathbf{R} \psi_2]\|_j^{d+1}\right)\right)\right)$

When $d = \delta(\varphi)$ we have reached the d-unrolling where the Kripke structure loops back. At this depth we can guarantee that the satisfaction of the subformulas has stabilised (see Prop. 1). Therefore we call the auxiliary translation $\langle\langle\varphi\rangle\rangle_i^d$, which is needed to correctly evaluate until- and release-formulas along the loop (see [13]), at this depth.

φ	$d = \delta(\varphi), 0 \leq i < k$	$d = \delta(\varphi), i = k$
$\|[\mathbf{X}\psi_1]\|_i^d$	$\|[\psi_1]\|_{i+1}^d$	$\bigvee_{j=1}^k \left(l_j \wedge \|[\psi_1]\|_j^d\right)$
$\|[\psi_1 \mathbf{U} \psi_2]\|_i^d$	$\|[\psi_2]\|_i^d \vee \left(\|[\psi_1]\|_i^d \wedge \|[\psi_1 \mathbf{U} \psi_2]\|_{i+1}^d\right)$	$\|[\psi_2]\|_i^d \vee \left(\|[\psi_1]\|_i^d \wedge \left(\bigvee_{j=1}^k \left(l_j \wedge \langle\langle\psi_1 \mathbf{U} \psi_2\rangle\rangle_j^d\right)\right)\right)$
$\|[\psi_1 \mathbf{R} \psi_2]\|_i^d$	$\|[\psi_2]\|_i^d \wedge \left(\|[\psi_1]\|_i^d \vee \|[\psi_1 \mathbf{R} \psi_2]\|_{i+1}^d\right)$	$\|[\psi_2]\|_i^d \wedge \left(\|[\psi_1]\|_i^d \vee \left(\bigvee_{j=1}^k \left(l_j \wedge \langle\langle\psi_1 \mathbf{R} \psi_2\rangle\rangle_j^d\right)\right)\right)$
$\langle\langle\psi_1 \mathbf{U} \psi_2\rangle\rangle_i^d$	$\|[\psi_2]\|_i^d \vee \left(\|[\psi_1]\|_i^d \wedge \langle\langle\psi_1 \mathbf{U} \psi_2\rangle\rangle_{i+1}^d\right)$	$\|[\psi_2]\|_i^d$
$\langle\langle\psi_1 \mathbf{R} \psi_2\rangle\rangle_i^d$	$\|[\psi_2]\|_i^d \wedge \left(\|[\psi_1]\|_i^d \vee \langle\langle\psi_1 \mathbf{R} \psi_2\rangle\rangle_{i+1}^d\right)$	$\|[\psi_2]\|_i^d$

The starting point for the encoding for the past operators is using their one-step fixpoint characterisation. This enables the encoding of the past operators to fit in with the future encoding. Since past operators look backwards, we must encode the move from one copy of the path to the previous copy efficiently. To save space we do not give the encodings for the derived operators $\mathbf{H}\psi \equiv \bot\,\mathbf{T}\psi$ and $\mathbf{O}\psi \equiv \top\,\mathbf{S}\psi$ since they are easily derived from the encodings of the binary operators $\psi_1\,\mathbf{T}\psi_2$ and $\psi_1\,\mathbf{S}\psi_2$.

The simplest case of the encoding for past operators occurs at $d = 0$. At this depth, the past is unique in the sense that the path cannot jump to a lower depth. We do need to take into account the loop edge, so the encoding follows from the recursive characterisation $\psi_1\,\mathbf{S}\psi_2$ and $\psi_1\,\mathbf{T}\psi_2$. Encoding $\mathbf{Y}\psi$ and $\mathbf{Z}\psi$ is trivial.

φ	$d=0, i=0$	$d=0, 1 \leq i \leq k$
$\|[\psi_1 \mathbf{S} \psi_2]\|_i^d$	$\|[\psi_2]\|_i^d$	$\|[\psi_2]\|_i^d \vee \left(\|[\psi_1]\|_i^d \wedge \|[\psi_1 \mathbf{S} \psi_2]\|_{i-1}^d \right)$
$\|[\psi_1 \mathbf{T} \psi_2]\|_i^d$	$\|[\psi_2]\|_i^d$	$\|[\psi_2]\|_i^d \wedge \left(\|[\psi_1]\|_i^d \vee \|[\psi_1 \mathbf{T} \psi_2]\|_{i-1}^d \right)$
$\|[\mathbf{Y} \psi_1]\|_i^d$	$\perp$	$\|[\psi_1]\|_{i-1}^d$
$\|[\mathbf{Z} \psi_1]\|_i^d$	$\top$	$\|[\psi_1]\|_{i-1}^d$

When $d > 0$ the key ingredient of the encoding is to decide whether the past operator should consider the path to continue in the current unrolling of the path or in the last state of the previous unrolling. The decision is taken based on the loop selector variables, which indicate whether we are in the loop state. In terms of our running example, we need to traverse the straight black arrows of Fig. 3 in the reverse direction. We implement the choice with an if-then-else construct $(l_i \wedge \psi_1) \vee (\neg l_i \wedge \psi_2)$. The expression encodes the choice if l_i is true then the truth value of the expression is decided by ψ_1, otherwise ψ_2 decides the truth value of the expression.

φ	$1 \leq d \leq \delta(\varphi), 2 \leq i \leq k$
$\|[\psi_1 \mathbf{S} \psi_2]\|_i^d$	$\|[\psi_2]\|_i^d \vee \left(\|[\psi_1]\|_i^d \wedge \left(\left(l_i \wedge \|[\varphi]\|_k^{d-1} \right) \vee \left(\neg l_i \wedge \|[\varphi]\|_{i-1}^d \right) \right) \right)$
$\|[\psi_1 \mathbf{T} \psi_2]\|_i^d$	$\|[\psi_2]\|_i^d \wedge \left(\|[\psi_1]\|_i^d \vee \left(\left(l_i \wedge \|[\varphi]\|_k^{d-1} \right) \vee \left(\neg l_i \wedge \|[\varphi]\|_{i-1}^d \right) \right) \right)$
$\|[\mathbf{Y} \psi_1]\|_i^d, \|[\mathbf{Z} \psi_1]\|_i^d$	$\left(l_i \wedge \|[\psi_1]\|_k^{d-1} \right) \vee \left(\neg l_i \wedge \|[\psi_1]\|_{i-1}^d \right)$

The only case left, which actually can be seen as an optimisation w.r.t. the above case, occurs at $i = 1$. The encoding has the general property that if l_j is true all constraints generated by the encoding for $i < j$ will not affect the encoding for $d > 0$. At $i = 1$ we can thus ignore the choice of continuing backwards on the path and always proceed to the previous d-unrolling.

φ	$1 \leq d \leq \delta(\varphi), i = 1$
$\|[\psi_1 \mathbf{S} \psi_2]\|_i^d$	$\|[\psi_2]\|_i^d \vee \left(\|[\psi_1]\|_i^d \wedge \|[\psi_1 \mathbf{S} \psi_2]\|_k^{d-1} \right)$
$\|[\psi_1 \mathbf{T} \psi_2]\|_i^d$	$\|[\psi_2]\|_i^d \wedge \left(\|[\psi_1]\|_i^d \vee \|[\psi_1 \mathbf{T} \psi_2]\|_k^{d-1} \right)$
$\|[\mathbf{Y} \psi_1]\|_i^d, \|[\mathbf{Z} \psi_1]\|_i^d$	$\|[\psi_1]\|_k^{d-1}$

Combining the tables above we get the full encoding $\|[\varphi]\|_i^d$. Given a Kripke structure M, a PLTL formula φ, and a bound k, the complete encoding as a propositional formula is given by:

$$\|[M, \varphi, k]\| = \|[M]\|_k \wedge \|[LoopConstraints]\|_k \wedge \|[\varphi]\|_0^0.$$

The correctness of our encoding is established by the following theorem.

Theorem 1. *Given a PLTL formula φ, a bound k and a path $\pi = s_0 s_1 s_2 \ldots$ which is a (k,l)-loop, $\pi \models \varphi$ iff $\|[M, \varphi, k]\|$ is satisfiable.*

Proof. (sketch) The proof proceeds as an induction on the structure of the formula. All future cases follow a similar pattern. As an example, consider the case $\varphi = \psi_1 \mathbf{U} \psi_2$.

By appealing to the induction hypothesis we can assume that $|[\psi_1]|_i^d$ and $|[\psi_2]|_i^d$ are correct. The future encoding replicates the path $\delta(\varphi)$ times, which ensures that at $d = \delta(\varphi)$ all subformulas have stabilised (see Prop. 1). Let $k' = k + p(\pi) \cdot \delta(\varphi)$ denote the index of π which corresponds to the final index of the unrolled model. We first prove that the encoding is correct at $\pi^{k'}$ corresponding to $|[\varphi]|_k^{\delta(\varphi)}$. We will make use of the equivalence: $\pi^i \models \psi_1 \mathbf{U} \psi_2$ iff $\pi^i \models \psi_2$ or $\left(\pi^i \models \psi_1 \text{ and } \pi^{i+1} \models \psi_1 \mathbf{U} \psi_2\right)$.

First assume that $|[\varphi]|_k^{\delta(\varphi)}$ holds. The encoding has the following property: for a (k,l)-loop π, whenever $|[M, \varphi, k]|$ has a satisfying truth assignment where no loop selector variable l_i is true another satisfying truth assignment exists where l_l is true. Thus we only need to consider the case where l_l is true. From $|[\varphi]|_k^{\delta(\varphi)}$ it follows that either $|[\psi_2]|_k^{\delta(\varphi)}$ holds, or that $|[\psi_1]|_k^{\delta(\varphi)}$ and $\langle\langle\varphi\rangle\rangle_l^{\delta(\varphi)}$ hold. In the former case we can appeal to the induction hypothesis and we are done. In latter case we can argue by the definition of $\langle\langle\psi_1 \mathbf{U} \psi_2\rangle\rangle$ that $|[\psi_2]|_j^{\delta(\varphi)}$ must hold for some $l \leq j \leq k$. Let j be the smallest such index. Since $\langle\langle\psi_1 \mathbf{U} \psi_2\rangle\rangle_l^{\delta(\varphi)}$ holds and the definition of $\langle\langle\psi_1 \mathbf{U} \psi_2\rangle\rangle$ forces $|[\psi_1]|_i^{\delta(\varphi)}$ to hold until j, we can conclude that $|[\psi_1]|_i^{\delta(\varphi)}$ holds for all $l \leq i < j$. By the induction hypothesis and the semantics of $\mathbf{U}$ we can then conclude $\pi^{k'+1} \models \varphi$. Combining this with $\pi^{k'} \models \psi_1$, we get $\pi^{k'} \models \varphi$.

Now assume that $\pi^{k'} \models \varphi$. By the equivalence above and the semantics of until we can split the proof into two cases. In the case $\pi^{k'} \models \psi_2$ we can by the induction hypothesis conclude that $|[\psi_2]|_k^{\delta(\varphi)}$ and thus $|[\varphi]|_k^{\delta(\varphi)}$. In the other case we have that $\pi^{k'} \models \psi_1$ and that ψ_2 is satisfied at some later index. Let j' be the smallest such index and denote $j = l + j' - (k' + 1)$. Then we know that $|[\psi_2]|_j^{\delta(\varphi)}$ must hold (Prop. 1 and induction hypothesis) and therefore also $\langle\langle\varphi\rangle\rangle_j^{\delta(\varphi)}$ holds. By the semantics of $\mathbf{U}$ we have that $\pi^i \models \psi_1$ for all $k' \leq i < j'$. This fact together with $|[\psi_2]|_j^{\delta(\varphi)}$ implies that $\langle\langle\varphi\rangle\rangle_i^{\delta(\varphi)}$ holds for all $l \leq i \leq j$. Consequently, $|[\varphi]|_k^{\delta(\varphi)}$ holds since we know that $|[\psi_1]|_k^{\delta(\varphi)}$ holds.

Once the correctness of the case $d = \delta(\varphi), i = k$ has been established, the correctness of the remaining cases are easily established. Since the encoding $|[\psi_1 \mathbf{U} \psi_2]|_i^d$ directly follows the recursive semantic definition of $\mathbf{U}$ to compute all the other cases of i and d, and these cases ultimately depend on the proven case we can conclude the encoding is correct for these as well.

Proving correctness for the past operators follows a similar pattern. Consider $\varphi = \psi_1 \mathbf{S} \psi_2$. By the induction hypothesis we can assume that $|[\psi_1]|_i^d$ and $|[\psi_2]|_i^d$ are dealt with correctly. For the past operators the case $i = 0, d = 0$ initialises the encoding while the other cases are computed using the recursive semantic definition of $\mathbf{S}$. The correctness of the initialisation can be argued using the semantics of $\mathbf{S}$ and the induction hypothesis. Again by Prop. 1 we do not need to go deeper than $i = k, d = \delta(\varphi)$. With these ingredients we can establish the correctness of the translation for $|[\psi_1 \mathbf{S} \psi_2]|_i^d$. Performing a case analysis for the rest of the past operators completes the proof. $\square$

The following result can be proved as a straightforward generalisation of the no loop case of [1] to PLTL.

Theorem 2. *If $\|[M,\varphi,k]\|$ has a satisfying truth assignment where all loop selector variables l_i are false then no matter how the corresponding finite path is extended to an infinite path π, it holds that $\pi \models \varphi$.*

The new encoding is very compact. Let $|I|$ and $|T|$ denote the size of the initial state predicate and the size of the transition relation seen as Boolean circuits.

Theorem 3. *Given a model M, a PLTL formula φ, a bound k, the size of $\|[M,\varphi,k]\|$ seen as a Boolean circuit is of the order $O(|I| + k \cdot |T| + k \cdot |\varphi| \cdot \delta(\varphi))$.*

Proof. The unrolling of the transition relation and the loop constraints contribute the term $O(|I| + k \cdot |T|)$. For each subformula of φ we add a constant number of constraints at each time point and k constraints at time points $i = k$. Although k constraints that refer to other linear sized constraints ($\|[\cdot]\|$ and $\langle\langle \cdot \rangle\rangle$) are added at $i = k$, the circuit remains linear because $\|[\cdot]\|$ and $\langle\langle \cdot \rangle\rangle$ can easily be shared among the constraints. As the loop is virtually unrolled there are $O(k \cdot \delta(\varphi))$ time points for a subformula in the worst case. Combining these two we get $O(|I| + k \cdot |T| + k \cdot |\varphi| \cdot \delta(\varphi))$. $\square$

The translation is linear in all components but since $\delta(\varphi)$ can be $O(|\varphi|)$, it can be seen as worst case quadratic in the formula length. Usually, however, linearity w.r.t. the bound k is the most critical as finding deeper bugs is considered more important than handling very large formulas. When dealing with formulas of fixed $\delta(\varphi)$, e.g. pure LTL formulas, the encoding is linear in $|\varphi|$.

4 Experiments

We have implemented the new encoding in version 2.1.2 of the NuSMV 2 model checker [14]. This facilitates easy comparison against NuSMV, currently the only published PLTL bounded model checker, which is based on the encoding given in [7]. For our implementation of the new PLTL encoding we have adapted the optimisations for the future LTL encoding presented in [13].

We have performed two different sets of experiments. In order to asses how the encodings scale in general, we model checked randomly generated formulas on small randomly generated models. This lets us evaluate how the encodings scale when the size of the formulas is increased or the length of the bound is increased. We also tested the encodings on a few real-life examples to corroborate our findings from the random experiments. In both experiments we measured the size of the generated conjunctive normal form (CNF) expressions. Specifically, we measured the number of variables, clauses and literals (the sum of the lengths of the CNF-clauses) in the generated CNF, and the time to solve the CNF instance. All experiments were run on a computer with an AMD Athlon XP 2000+ processor and 1 GiB of RAM using the SAT solver zChaff [18], version 2003.12.04. Our implementation and files related to the experiments are available at http://www.tcs.hut.fi/~timo/vmcai2005/.

4.1 Random Formulae

The experiments with random formulae were performed in the following way. Random formulae were generated with the tool described in [17]. We generated 40 formulas for

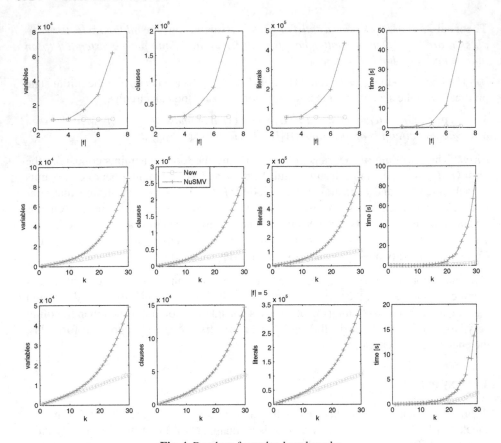

Fig. 4. Random formulae benchmarks.

each formula size between three and seven. For each formula we generated a BMC problem for all bounds up to $k = 30$. The BMC problem is constructed using a random Kripke model with 35 states that was generated with techniques described in [17]. The Kripke models have a fairness requirement that requires that at least one of two randomly selected states should appear infinitely often in a counterexample path. This eliminates many short counterexamples and makes the measurement more meaningful for larger values of k.

Figure 4 has twelve plots depicting the results of the benchmarks. In the first row, all results are averaged over the bound and show how the procedures scale with increasing formula size. In the second row, all results are averages over the formula size and show how the procedures scale in the bound k. For the third row the size of the formula is fixed at 5 and the plots show the average over the 40 formulas. The plots in the first column show the number of variables in the generated CNF. Plots in the second column show the number of clauses and plots in the third column the number of literals in the CNF. The last column has plots which show the time to solve the CNF instances.

From the plots it is clear that the new encoding scales much better than the encoding implemented in NuSMV. This is the case both when considering scaling w.r.t. the size of the formula and the length of the bound.

4.2 Real-Life Examples

The second set of experiment were performed on a few real-life examples. We used five models of which four are included in the NuSMV 2 distribution. The models were an alternating bit protocol (*abp*), a bounded resource protocol (*brp*), a distributed mutual exclusion algorithm (*dme*), a pci bus (*pci*) and a 5-bit shift-register (*srg5*). For *abp* and *pci* we checked a property with a counterexample while the properties for *brp*, *dme* and *srg5* were true properties. The template formulae are collected in Table 1.

Table 1. Properties used in real-life benchmarks.

Model	Property
abp	$\mathbf{G}\,(p \Rightarrow \mathbf{Y}\mathbf{H}\,q)$
brp	$\mathbf{F}\mathbf{G}\,(p \Rightarrow \mathbf{O}\,(q \Rightarrow \mathbf{O}\,r))$
dme	$\mathbf{G}\,(p \Rightarrow p\mathbf{T}\,(\neg p\mathbf{T}\,q))$
pci	$\mathbf{G}\,p \Rightarrow \mathbf{G}\,(q \wedge \mathbf{Y}\,(\neg q \wedge \mathbf{O}\,(r \wedge \mathbf{O}\,(s \wedge \mathbf{O}t))) \Rightarrow \mathbf{O}\,(u \wedge \mathbf{O}\,(v \wedge \mathbf{G}w)))$
srg5	$\mathbf{F}\mathbf{G}\,p \wedge \mathbf{G}\mathbf{F}\,q \wedge \mathbf{G}\mathbf{F}\,r \Rightarrow \mathbf{F}\,(s\mathbf{S}\,(t\mathbf{S}\,(u\mathbf{S}\,(v\mathbf{S}w))))$

We measured the number of variables, clauses, and literals in the generated CNF, and the time used to solve an instance at a specific bound k. We also report the cumulative time ($\Sigma time$) used to solve all instances up to the given k. The results of the runs can be found in Table 2.

The new encoding was always the fastest. In all cases the new encoding produced the smallest instances w.r.t. all size measures. For *srg5*, NuSMV was not able to proceed further than $k = 18$ because the computer ran out of memory. The reason for this can be found in the apparently at least *cubic* growth w.r.t. the bound k of the encoding for nested binary past operators.

Table 2. Real-life benchmarks.

Model	k	NuSMV					New				
		vars	clauses	literals	time	Σtime	vars	clauses	literals	time	Σtime
abp	16	25,175	74,208	174,644	104	342	22,827	67,116	158,096	52.5	269
brp	10	14,115	41,228	98,304	0.9	2.5	8,961	25,736	62,156	0.7	2.2
	15	30,225	89,218	211,334	4.6	15.9	13,346	38,536	93,076	1.5	7.5
	20	56,935	169,008	398,564	19.2	75.6	17,731	51,336	123,996	3.2	19.7
dme	10	49,776	139,740	338,752	10.3	15.1	28,855	76,947	192,235	6.3	17.5
	15	139,071	404,485	962,837	98.9	171	42,685	115,282	288,030	15.5	70.2
	20	346,166	1,022,630	2,411,522	1,017	1,812	56,515	153,617	383,825	41.2	214
pci	10	81,285	242,133	567,029	96.7	188	60,456	179,616	421,156	69.8	151
	15	159,885	477,358	1,116,914	2,441	5,408	90,611	269,491	631,891	888	2,422
	18	227,357	679,429	1,589,029	2,557	19,119	108,704	323,416	758,332	867	11,992
srg5	10	137,710	412,952	963,900	53.6	90.7	1,655	4,757	11,445	0.0	0.1
	18	1,264,988	3,794,698	8,854,918	14,914	33,708	2,999	8,677	20,869	0.2	0.9
	30	N/A	N/A	N/A	N/A	N/A	5,015	14,557	35,005	0.7	6.6

5   Discussion and Conclusions

We have presented an encoding of the BMC problem for PLTL. The encoding is linear in the bound k unlike the encoding by Benedetti and Cimatti [7]. In the general case the encoding is quadratic in the size of the formula but if we fix the past operator depth, the encoding is also linear in the size of the formula. Experiments confirm that the encoding is more compact and efficient than the original encoding. In the experiments our encoding scales better both in the bound k and in the size of the formula.

After having independently discovered our new encoding we very recently became aware of a manuscript [19] discussing an alternative approach to bounded model checking of PLTL. Our approach differs in many ways from that of [19], the main differences being that their approach does not perform any virtual unrolling at all and that their starting point is the so called SNF encoding for BMC [15]. It is easy to modify our encoding not to virtually unroll (k, l)-loops by defining the past operator depth function $\delta(\varphi)$ to return the constant 0 for all formulas irregardless of their past operator depth. However, in this case the encoding would *not* remain sound for formulas with looping counterexamples. For example, verifying the formula $\neg \mathbf{G} \mathbf{F} \mathbf{Y} \mathbf{Y} \mathbf{Y} (x = 0)$ on our running example would result in a counterexample at $k = 6$ even though the formula holds. We do not see how soundness for full PLTL could be achieved without performing virtual unrolling.

If we restrict ourselves to searching for non-looping counterexamples (not all PLTL formulas have non-looping counterexamples) or to specifications in some subset of full PLTL, the virtual unrolling could be discarded while maintaining soundness. However, although virtual unrolling has a small overhead it also has benefits. For example, model checking formula (1) on our running example requires the transition relation to be unrolled 6 times with our encoding but the encoding of [19] requires the transition relation to be unrolled 11 times before the first witness is found. Due to the efficiency of our encoding the overhead of virtual unrolling is small and the potential gain in using smaller bounds can be significant. We argue that our approach can be more efficient than [19], at least in the cases where the encoding is dominated by the system transition relation size ($|T| \gg |\varphi|$) and the counterexample can be detected earlier by virtual unrolling. In our opinion the new encoding is also easier to understand and implement than that of [19].

There are still possibilities for improving the performance of our encoding and extending it to other uses. The bounded satisfiability problem asks if there is *any* model represented as a bounded path of length k for a given PLTL formula ψ. The new encoding can easily be extended to solve this problem by removing all constraints set by the transition relation on the state variables. If the encoding is viewed as a Boolean circuit, the loop selector variables l_i and the atomic propositions (and their negations) are viewed as input gates, then the encoding generates a monotonic Boolean circuit. This could be exploited in specific SAT solver optimisations. Another possible topic for future research is considering incremental encodings for BMC in the spirit of [20].

References

1. Biere, A., Cimatti, A., Clarke, E., Zhu, Y.: Symbolic model checking without BDDs. In: Tools and Algorithms for the Constructions and Analysis of Systems (TACAS'99). Volume 1579 of LNCS., Springer (1999) 193–207

2. Biere, A., Clarke, E.M., Raimi, R., Zhu, Y.: Verifying safety properties of a Power PC microprocessor using symbolic model checking without BDDs. In: Computer Aided Verification (CAV 1999). Volume 1633 of LNCS., Springer (1999) 60–71
3. Copty, F., Fix, L., Fraer, R., Giunchiglia, E., Kamhi, G., Tacchella, A., Vardi, M.Y.: Benefits of bounded model checking at an industrial setting. In: Computer Aided Verification (CAV 2001). Volume 2102 of LNCS., Springer (2001) 436–453
4. Strichman, O.: Accelerating bounded model checking of safety properties. Formal Methods in System Design **24** (2004) 5–24
5. Havelund, K., Rosu, G.: Synthesizing monitors for safety properties. In: Tools and Algorithms for the Construction and Analysis of Systems (TACAS 2002). Volume 2280 of LNCS., Springer (2002) 342–356
6. Gastin, P., Oddoux, D.: LTL with past and two-way very-weak alternating automata. In: Mathematical Foundations of Computer Science 2003 (MFCS 2003). Volume 2747 of LNCS., Springer (2003) 439–448
7. Benedetti, M., Cimatti, A.: Bounded model checking for past LTL. In: Tools and Algorithms for Construction and Analysis of Systems (TACAS 2003). Volume 2619 of LNCS., Springer (2003) 18–33
8. Lichtenstein, O., Pnueli, A., Zuck, L.D.: The glory of the past. In: Logic of Programs. Volume 193 of LNCS., Springer (1985) 196–218
9. Kamp, J.: Tense Logic and the Theory of Linear Order. PhD thesis, University of California, Los Angeles, California (1968)
10. Gabbay, D.M., Pnueli, A., Shelah, S., Stavi, J.: On the temporal basis of fairness. In: Conference Record of the Seventh Annual ACM Symposium on Principles of Programming Languages, Las Vegas, Nevada, ACM (1980) 163–173
11. Laroussinie, F., Markey, N., Schnoebelen, P.: Temporal logic with forgettable past. In: 17th IEEE Symp. Logic in Computer Science (LICS 2002), IEEE Computer Society Press (2002) 383–392
12. Sistla, A.P., Clarke, E.M.: The complexity of propositional linear temporal logics. Journal of the ACM **32** (1985) 733–749
13. Latvala, T., Biere, A., Heljanko, K., Junttila, T.: Simple bounded LTL model checking. In: Formal Methods in Computer-Aided Design (FMCAD 2004). Volume 3312 of LNCS., Springer (2004) 186–200
14. Cimatti, A., Clarke, E., Giunchiglia, E., Giunchiglia, F., Pistore, M., Roveri, M., Sebastiani, R., Tacchella, A.: NuSMV 2: An opensource tool for symbolic model checking. In: Computer Aided Verification (CAV 2002). Volume 2404 of LNCS., Springer (2002) 359–364
15. Frisch, A., Sheridan, D., Walsh, T.: A fixpoint encoding for bounded model checking. In: Formal Methods in Computer-Aided Design (FMCAD'2002). Volume 2517 of LNCS., Springer (2002) 238–255
16. Kupferman, O., Vardi, M.: Model checking of safety properties. Formal Methods in System Design **19** (2001) 291–314
17. Tauriainen, H., Heljanko, K.: Testing LTL formula translation into Büchi automata. STTT - International Journal on Software Tools for Technology Transfer **4** (2002) 57–70
18. Moskewicz, M., Madigan, C., Zhao, Y., Zhang, L., Malik, S.: Chaff: Engineering an efficient SAT solver. In: Proceedings of the 38th Design Automation Conference, IEEE (2001)
19. Cimatti, A., Roveri, M., Sheridan, D.: Bounded verification of past LTL. In: Formal Methods in Computer-Aided Design (FMCAD 2004). Volume 3312 of LNCS., Springer (2004) 245–259
20. Eén, N., Sörensson, N.: Temporal induction by incremental SAT solving. In: First International Workshop on Bounded Model Checking. Volume 89 of ENTCS., Elsevier (2003)

Optimizing Bounded Model Checking
for Linear Hybrid Systems[*]

Erika Ábrahám[1], Bernd Becker[1], Felix Klaedtke[2], and Martin Steffen[3]

[1] Albert-Ludwigs-Universität Freiburg, Germany
[2] ETH Zurich, Switzerland
[3] Christian-Albrechts-Universität zu Kiel, Germany

Abstract. Bounded model checking (BMC) is an automatic verification method that is based on finitely unfolding the system's transition relation. BMC has been successfully applied, in particular, for discovering bugs in digital system design. Its success is based on the effectiveness of satisfiability solvers that are used to check for a finite unfolding whether a violating state is reachable. In this paper we improve the BMC approach for linear hybrid systems. Our improvements are tailored to lazy satisfiability solving and follow two complementary directions. First, we optimize the formula representation of the finite unfoldings of the transition relations of linear hybrid systems, and second, we accelerate the satisfiability checks by accumulating and generalizing data that is generated during earlier satisfiability checks. Experimental results show that the presented techniques accelerate the satisfiability checks significantly.

1 Introduction

Model checking is widely used for the verification of concurrent state systems, like finite state systems [20, 12] and timed automata [3]. One main reason for the acceptance of model checking is its push-button appeal. A major obstacle to its universal applicability, however, is the inherent size of many real-world systems. This obstacle is often called the state space explosion problem. *Bounded model checking* (BMC) [10] has attracted attention as an alternative to model checking. The bounded model checking problem starts from a more modest question: Does there exist a counterexample of length $k \in \mathbb{N}$ refuting a stipulated property P? In particular, when P is a safety property, a counterexample is simply a finite run leading to the violation. Whether P can be violated in k steps is reduced to checking satisfiability of the formula

$$I(s_0) \wedge T(s_0, s_1) \wedge \ldots \wedge T(s_{k-1}, s_k) \wedge \neg P(s_k), \tag{1}$$

where s_i are state variables, I is a unary predicate describing the initial states, and T is a binary predicate describing the transition relation. The bound k is successively increased until either a counterexample is found or some limit is reached (e.g., an upper bound on k or resource limitations).

---

[*] This work was partly supported by the German Research Council (DFG) as part of the Transregional Collaborative Research Center "Automatic Verification and Analysis of Complex Systems" (SFB/TR 14 AVACS).

R. Cousot (Ed.): VMCAI 2005, LNCS 3385, pp. 396–412, 2005.

BMC shares with model checking its push-button appeal. However, without further extensions, BMC does not terminate for properties that are fulfilled by the system. While this seems to be a step backwards, BMC has practical relevance. For finite state systems, the formula (1) corresponds to a propositional satisfiability problem that enables the use of state-of-the-art SAT-solvers. Empirical evidence, e.g., in [11] and [13], shows that BMC is often superior to model checking, in particular when the focus is on refuting a property. Extensions for using the BMC approach also for verification are summarized in [9].

The BMC approach for finite state systems cleanly extends to many classes of infinite state systems [16]. For infinite state systems, formula (1) is a Boolean combination of domain-specific constraints depending on the class of the systems. Instead of a SAT-solver we have to use a solver specific to that domain. For instance, BMC has been extended and applied to timed automata in, e.g. [19, 22, 7, 25]. The BMC approach can be further extended to the more general class of *linear hybrid automata* [2, 18]. For linear hybrid automata, the domain-specific constraints are linear (in)equations, where variables range over the reals. Prominent state-of-the-art solvers that can be used in the BMC approach for linear hybrid systems are MathSAT [5], CVC Lite [8], and ICS [15]. All these solvers have in common that the satisfiability checks are done *lazily*. Roughly speaking, this means that these solvers are based on a SAT-solver that calls on demand solvers for conjunctions of the domain-specific constraints.

In this paper we improve the BMC approach for linear hybrid systems by accelerating the satisfiability checks. Our improvements are motivated by a thorough investigation of checking satisfiability of formulas of the form (1), which describe in our context finite runs of a fixed length k of a linear hybrid system. First, we optimize the formula representation of finite runs. The optimized representation is tailored to lazy satisfiability solving. Besides others, one point is to force alternation of the different types of transitions of hybrid systems, namely discrete and time transitions. Second, we accumulate the conflicts returned by the domain-specific solver during the lazy satisfiability check of (1). We use these conflicts as follows. If (1) is unsatisfiable, i.e., there is no counterexample of size k, we generalize the returned conflicts and use these generalized conflicts such that the domain-specific solver is not called again for similar conflicts in forthcoming satisfiability checks. This means, we learn generalized domain-specific conflicts in each satisfiability check. This learning technique also applies to the BMC approach for other classes of infinite state systems.

Both kinds of optimization reduce the demand-driven calls to the domain-specific solver for conjunctions of linear (in)equations. Furthermore, they are complementary in the sense that the optimized encoding leads to fewer conflicts that are generalized and learned. We extensively evaluated our techniques for a number of linear hybrid systems. The outcome of our experiments is that the combination of both techniques increases the bound k on the size of the runs by several orders of magnitudes for which state-of-the-art solvers are able to perform the satisfiability checks in a reasonable amount of time and space.

We proceed as follows. In §2 we review the definition of linear hybrid automata and the BMC approach for linear hybrid automata using lazy satisfiability solvers. In §3 we optimize the encoding of finite runs and in §4 we introduce our learning technique. We

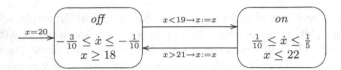

Fig. 1. Thermostat.

present experimental results in §5. In §6 we discuss related work and finally, in §7 we draw conclusions.

2 Bounded Model Checking for Linear Hybrid Systems

Before presenting our work, we first introduce linear hybrid systems and describe a straightforward encoding of finite runs as Boolean combinations of (in)equations. Furthermore, we describe relevant details of state-of-the-art solvers for checking satisfiability of Boolean combinations of linear (in)equations and pinpoint obstacles for using these solvers in the BMC approach for linear hybrid automata.

2.1 Hybrid Systems Background

Hybrid automata [2, 18] have been introduced in control engineering and in computer science as a formal model for systems with both discrete and continuous components.

Hybrid automata are often given graphically, like the one shown in Figure 1. This automaton models a thermostat, which senses the temperature x of a room and turns a heater on and off. In location *off* the heater is off and the temperature falls according to the flow condition $-\frac{3}{10} \leq \dot{x} \leq -\frac{1}{10}$. The location's invariant $x \geq 18$ assures that the heater turns on at latest when the temperature reaches 18 degrees. Analogously for the location *on*, where the heater is on. Control may move from location *off* to *on* if the temperature is below 19 degrees, and from *on* to *off* if the temperature is above 21 degrees. The temperature x does not change by jumping from *off* to *on* or from *on* to *off*. Initially, the heater is *off* and the temperature is 20 degrees.

In the remainder of the paper we only consider the class of linear hybrid automata, which can be described using first-order logic formulas over $(\mathbb{R}, +, <, 0, 1)$. Formally, a *linear hybrid automaton* $\mathcal{H}$ is a tuple

$$\left(L, V, (jump_{\ell,\ell'})_{\ell,\ell' \in L}, (flow_\ell)_{\ell \in L}, (inv_\ell)_{\ell \in L}, (init_\ell)_{\ell \in L} \right),$$

where L and V are finite nonempty sets, and $(jump_{\ell,\ell'})_{\ell,\ell' \in L}$, $(flow_\ell)_{\ell \in L}$, $(inv_\ell)_{\ell \in L}$, $(init_\ell)_{\ell \in L}$ are families of first-order logic formulas over the structure $(\mathbb{R}, +, <, 0, 1)$:

- $L = \{\ell_1, \ldots, \ell_m\}$ is the set of *locations*.
- $V = \{v_1, \ldots, v_n\}$ is the set of *continuous variables*.
- $(jump_{\ell,\ell'})_{\ell,\ell' \in L}$ is an $(L \times L)$-indexed family of formulas with free variables in V and their primed versions. A formula $jump_{\ell,\ell'}(v_1, \ldots, v_n, v'_1, \ldots, v'_n)$ represents the possible *jumps* from location ℓ to location ℓ', where $v_1, \ldots, v_n$ are the values of the continuous variables before the jump and $v'_1, \ldots, v'_n$ are the values of the continuous variables after the jump.

- $(flow_\ell)_{\ell \in L}$ is an L-indexed family of formulas with free variables in V, their primed versions, and t. A formula $flow_\ell(v_1, \ldots, v_n, t, v'_1, \ldots, v'_n)$ represents the *flow* of duration $t \geq 0$ in location ℓ, where the values of the continuous variables change from $v_1, \ldots, v_n$ to $v'_1, \ldots, v'_n$.
- $(inv_\ell)_{\ell \in L}$ is an L-indexed family of formulas with free variables in V. A formula $inv_\ell(v_1, \ldots, v_n)$ represents the *invariant* in location ℓ. We require that all invariants are convex sets.
- $(init_\ell)_{\ell \in L}$ is an L-indexed family of formulas with free variables in V representing the *initial states* of the system.

For instance, the flow in location *on* of the thermostat in Figure 1 can be described by the formula $flow_{on}(x, t, x') = 10x' - 10x \geq t \wedge 5x' - 5x \leq t$. The other components of the thermostat can be described analogously. Since $(\mathbb{R}, +, <, 0, 1)$ admits quantifier elimination, we assume without loss of generality that the formulas occurring in the description of a linear hybrid automaton are quantifier-free.

Hybrid systems often consist of several hybrid automata that run in parallel and interact with each other. The parallel composition of hybrid automata requires an additional event set for synchronization purposes. The parallel composition is standard but technical and we omit it here. For simplicity and due to space limitations, in the theoretical part of the paper we restrict ourselves to a single linear hybrid automaton.

Encoding Linear Hybrid Automata. In the remainder of this subsection, let $\mathcal{H} = (L, V, (jump_{\ell,\ell'})_{\ell,\ell' \in L}, (flow_\ell)_{\ell \in L}, (inv_\ell)_{\ell \in L}, (init_\ell)_{\ell \in L})$ be a linear hybrid automaton with $L = \{l_1, \ldots, l_m\}$ and $V = \{v_1, \ldots, v_n\}$, for some $m, n \in \mathbb{N}$. For readability, we write tuples in boldface, i.e., $\boldsymbol{v}$ abbreviates $(v_1, \ldots, v_n)$, and we introduce state variables $s = (at, \boldsymbol{v})$, where at ranges over the locations in L and $\boldsymbol{v} = (v_1, \ldots, v_n)$.

A jump of the automaton $\mathcal{H}$ is described by the formula

$$J(s, s') = \bigvee_{\ell, \ell' \in L} \left(at = \ell \wedge at' = \ell' \wedge jump_{\ell,\ell'}(\boldsymbol{v}, \boldsymbol{v}') \wedge inv_{\ell'}(\boldsymbol{v}') \right)$$

and a flow of $\mathcal{H}$ is described by the formula

$$F(s, t, s') = \bigvee_{\ell \in L} \left(at = \ell \wedge at' = \ell \wedge t \geq 0 \wedge flow_\ell(\boldsymbol{v}, t, \boldsymbol{v}') \wedge inv_\ell(\boldsymbol{v}') \right),$$

where $s = (at, \boldsymbol{v})$ and $s' = (at', \boldsymbol{v}')$ are state variables, and t is a real-valued variable representing the duration of the flow. Note that we check the invariant of a location after t time units have passed in $F(s, t, s')$ and when we enter the location of s' in a jump $J(s, s')$. Since we assume that invariants are convex sets, we do not have to check at every time point between 0 and t of a flow whether the invariant in the location is satisfied. For $k \in \mathbb{N}$, we recursively define the formula π_k by

$$\pi_0(s_0) = \bigvee_{\ell \in L} \left(at_0 = \ell \wedge inv_\ell(\boldsymbol{v}_0) \right)$$

and for $k > 0$,

$$\pi_k(s_0, \ldots, s_k, t_1, \ldots, t_k) = $$
$$\pi_{k-1}(s_0, \ldots, s_{k-1}, t_1, \ldots, t_{k-1}) \wedge \left(J(s_{k-1}, s_k) \vee F(s_{k-1}, t_k, s_k) \right),$$

where $s_0, \ldots, s_k$ are state variables and $t_1, \ldots, t_k$ are real-valued variables. Intuitively, π_k describes the runs of length k of a linear hybrid automaton by glueing together k jumps and flows. Moreover, we have to assure that the first state satisfies the location's invariant.

BMC for Linear Hybrid Automata. With the formulas π_k at hand, it is straightforward to obtain a semi-decision procedure for checking whether a linear hybrid automaton violates a state property given by the formula $safe(s)$. For $k \in \mathbb{N}$, we define

$$\varphi_k(s_0, \ldots, s_k, t_1, \ldots, t_k) =$$
$$\left(\bigvee_{\ell \in L}(at_0 = \ell \wedge init_\ell(v_0)) \right) \wedge \pi_k(s_0, \ldots, s_k, t_1, \ldots, t_k) \wedge \neg safe(s_k).$$

Starting with $k = 0$ and iteratively increasing $k \in \mathbb{N}$, we check whether φ_k is satisfiable. The algorithm terminates if φ_k is satisfiable, i.e., an unsafe state is reachable from an initial state in k steps.

The effectiveness of the algorithm depends on the effectiveness of checking whether the φ_ks are satisfiable. Experimental results show that the satisfiability checks of φ_k often become impractical even for small ks and rather small linear hybrid systems, like the railroad crossing example [4], which consists of three linear hybrid automata running in parallel (two of them have 3 locations and one automaton has 4 locations). For instance, the satisfiability check for φ_{10} takes 18 seconds with the state-of-the-art solver ICS [16] and the satisfiability check for φ_{15} takes almost 4 minutes. In order to pinpoint the reasons for the bad running times of the satisfiability checks, we first have to give some ICS details.

2.2 Satisfiability Checking Details and Performance Issues

We first recall details of *lazy theorem proving* [16]. Lazy theorem proving is built on top of a SAT-solver for propositional logic that lazily interacts with a solver for a specific domain. In our context, the domain specific solver checks satisfiability of conjunctions of linear (in)equations over the reals.

Assume that φ is a Boolean combination of the atomic formulas $\alpha_1, \ldots, \alpha_n$. We define the mapping $abs(\alpha_i) = b_i$, where b_i is a fresh Boolean variable. The mapping abs is homomorphically extended to Boolean combinations of (in)equations. We call $abs(\varphi)$ the *Boolean abstraction* of the formula φ. The pseudo-code of the lazy theorem proving algorithm from [16, 14] is shown in Figure 2. We start with the Boolean abstraction $\beta = abs(\varphi)$. In each loop, the SAT-solver suggests a candidate assignment $\nu : \{b_1, \ldots, b_n\} \rightarrow \{true, false\}$ satisfying β. If the conjunction $\psi = \bigwedge_{\nu(b_i)=true} \alpha_i \wedge \bigwedge_{\nu(b_i)=false} \neg \alpha_i$ is satisfiable, then φ is satisfiable. Otherwise, we extend β to $\beta \wedge \neg abs(explain(\psi))$, where $explain(\psi)$ is an unsatisfiable subformula of ψ, i.e., a conjunction of some atomic formulas or their negations occurring in ψ that is responsible for the unsatisfiability of ψ. We call the formula $explain(\psi)$ an *explanation*. A simple implementation of *explain* is the identity function, i.e., it returns ψ. Using this simple implementation, there is one loop iteration for each satisfying assignment of $abs(\varphi)$. General techniques for reducing the number of iterations, and in particular more sophisticated implementations of the *explain* function are described in [16, 14].

procedure $sat(\varphi)$
   $\beta \leftarrow abs(\varphi)$
   loop
      $\nu \leftarrow SAT\text{-}Solver(\beta)$
      if $\nu = unsatisfiable$ **then return** $unsatisfiable$
      $\psi \leftarrow \bigwedge_{\nu(b_i)=true} \alpha_i \wedge \bigwedge_{\nu(b_i)=false} \neg\alpha_i$
      if $Solver(\psi) \neq unsatisfiable$ **then return** $satisfiable$
      $\beta \leftarrow \beta \wedge \neg abs(explain(\psi))$
   end loop

Fig. 2. The lazy theorem proving algorithm for checking satisfiability of a Boolean combination of linear (in)equations.

Less lazy variants of the lazy theorem proving algorithm, like in CVC Lite [8] and ICS [16] consist of a tighter integration of a SAT-solver and the satisfiability checks of a solver for conjunctions of linear (in)equations. In ICS, a truth assignment to a Boolean variable by the SAT-solver adds the corresponding (in)equation to the conjunction of (in)equations for which the corresponding Boolean variables are already assigned to some truth value. A *frequency parameter*, for which the user can provide a threshold, determines after how many truth assignments the SAT-solver checks whether the conjunction of (in)equations is still satisfiable, i.e., the SAT-solver calls the solver for conjunctions of (in)equations. An inconsistency triggers backtracking in the search for Boolean variable assignments and is propagated to the SAT-solver by adding a clause to the formula explaining the inconsistency using the *explain* function.

Performance Issues. The lazy theorem proving algorithm in Figure 2 scales poorly for checking satisfiability of the formulas φ_k. The reason is the large number of loop iterations: for most examples, the number of iterations grows exponentially in k. The following examples illustrate this obstacle more clearly.

Example 1. Consider the following linear hybrid automaton:

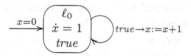

Assume that we want to check whether we can reach in k steps a state with $x < 0$. Clearly, a run with x having the initial value 0 and that increases x in each step cannot reach a state with x having a negative value. However, when we only look at a finite unfolding of the transition relation, we must be aware of all changes made on the value of x in order to check that the value of x is not negative after k steps. Independently of the implementation of the *explain* function, for checking unsatisfiability of φ_k with the lazy theorem proving algorithm, the number of loop iterations is at least 2^k.

The reason for the above exponential behavior can be explained as follows. For each of the 2^k possible sequences of k flows and jumps there is a corresponding satisfying assignment of $abs(\varphi_k)$ assigning $true$ to the Boolean variable for $x_k < 0$ and to the Boolean variables whose (in)equations describe the initial state and the transitions in the sequence. Without loss of generality, the truth values of the other Boolean variables $abs(\varphi_k)$ need not to be considered. For a satisfying assignment of $abs(\varphi_k)$ the *explain* function has to return a conjunction containing at least the (in)equations in which x_i occurs and for which the Boolean variable is assigned to *true*. Since two such conjunctions of (in)equations are distinct for assignments corresponding to different sequences of k flows and jumps, we have to check at least 2^k conjunctions of (in)equations.

The less lazy variant of the lazy theorem proving algorithm is faced with a similar problem: the number of satisfiability checks for conjunctions of (in)equations corresponding to partial truth assignments of the Boolean variables in the Boolean abstraction is often exponential in the bound k. For the railroad crossing example, we have 95 explanations in the satisfiability check for φ_5, 1047 explanations for φ_{10}, and 6462 explanations for φ_{15}.

Experimental evaluations [16] have shown that the less lazy variant – as, e.g., implemented in ICS – is superior to the lazy theorem proving algorithm in Figure 2. However, in our experiments we observed that if the Boolean abstraction of a formula has few satisfying assignments then the lazy theorem proving algorithm usually performs better than the less lazy variant, since the solver for conjunctions of (in)equations is called less often. In §4, we will exploit this observation by switching from the less lazy variant to the lazy theorem proving algorithm whenever it is likely that the Boolean abstraction has few satisfying assignments.

Before we present and evaluate the optimizations for the BMC approach for linear hybrid systems we want to comment on the BMC approach for a larger class of hybrid systems. For the BMC approach, it is, in principal, possible to allow first-order logic formulas over $(\mathbb{R}, +, \cdot, <, 0, 1)$ instead of $(\mathbb{R}, +, <, 0, 1)$ in the definition of a hybrid automaton in §2.1. By allowing formulas over $(\mathbb{R}, +, \cdot, <, 0, 1)$ we can describe a much larger class of hybrid systems. Note that the first-order theory over $(\mathbb{R}, +, \cdot, <, 0, 1)$ is decidable since it admits quantifier elimination [24]. The lazy theorem proving algorithm can be easily modified to handle quantifier-free formulas over $(\mathbb{R}, +, \cdot, <, 0, 1)$. However, for a non-linear flow, we have to check a location's invariant in a run for all time points of that flow. This introduces in the formula description of a flow step an additional universally quantified variable, which has to be eliminated before we apply the lazy theorem proving algorithm. The reason why we restrict ourselves to $(\mathbb{R}, +, <, 0, 1)$ is that eliminating such a quantified variable can be expensive. Furthermore, the authors are not aware of a satisfiability checker for quantifier-free formulas over $(\mathbb{R}, +, \cdot, <, 0, 1)$ that performs well in practice for large conjunctions of quantifier-free formulas. However, the following optimizations will also be useful for this larger class of hybrid systems, since they reduce the number of interactions of the SAT-checker and the domain specific solver for the conjunctions.

3   Optimizing the Encoding

For improving the BMC approach for linear hybrid automata, we optimize the formula encoding of finite runs. Our optimized encoding is tailored to the lazy theorem proving algorithms. In order to give an impression of the impact of the different optimizations,

Table 1. Experimental results for the railroad crossing example.

Formula encoding with optimizations		$k = 5$		$k = 10$		$k = 15$	
		time (secs.)	# expl.	time (secs.)	# expl.	time (secs.)	# expl.
φ_k		0.5	95	18.0	1047	234.5	6462
φ_k	$+ \S 3.1$	0.2	21	3.7	349	46.8	1922
φ_k	$+ \S 3.1 + \S 3.2$	0.2	24	2.8	242	35.5	1741
ψ_{2k+1}	$+ \S 3.1 + \S 3.2$	0.2	4	1.8	53	3.6	109
$\psi_1, \ldots, \psi_{2k+1}$	$+ \S 3.1 + \S 3.2$	0.7	14	5.1	144	14.0	396
$\psi_{1,2k+1}^{tau}$	$+ \S 3.1 + \S 3.2$	0.4	14	0.9	21	6.8	169

we list in Table 1 the improvements for the railroad crossing example. We obtain similar improvements for other examples of hybrid automata (further experiments are in §5).

Let $\mathcal{H} = \big(L, V, (jump_{\ell,\ell'})_{\ell,\ell' \in L}, (flow_\ell)_{\ell \in L}, (inv_\ell)_{\ell \in L}, (init_\ell)_{\ell \in L} \big)$ be a linear hybrid automaton with $V = \{v_1, \ldots, v_n\}$.

3.1 Using Boolean Variables

The lazy theorem proving algorithm in Figure 2 and its variants can be easily extended such that they also handle Boolean combinations of (in)equations *and* Boolean variables. Since the location set L is finite, we can use $\lceil \lg |L| \rceil$ Boolean variables for each $0 \le i \le k$ to encode the formulas $at_i = \ell$ with $\ell \in L$ in φ_k. However, the algorithm in Figure 2 replaces (in)equations by fresh Boolean variables; for each $0 \le i \le k$, this requires $|L|$ Boolean variables for the atomic formulas $at_i = \ell$ with $\ell \in L$.

Encoding finite sets by Boolean variables is not new. However, we want to point out the benefit of using Boolean variables for the lazy theorem proving algorithm. The Boolean encoding of locations has two advantages over the encoding by equations of the form $at_i = \ell$: The first advantage is that we need exponentially less Boolean variables. The more important advantage is the following. A satisfying assignment of $abs(\varphi_k)$ may assign the corresponding Boolean variables for the equations $at_i = \ell$ and $at_i = \ell'$ with $\ell \ne \ell'$ both to *true*. Such a conflict is not discovered until we call the solver for conjunctions of (in)equations. With Boolean location encoding such conflicts arc already discovered by the SAT-solver. This results in less interaction of the SAT-solver and the solver for conjunctions of (in)equations. In particular, note that when using the Boolean encoding of the locations, the assignments returned by the SAT-solver always describe a path in the location graph of the hybrid automaton.

Analogously to the Boolean encoding of locations we can use Boolean variables for all system variables with a finite domain. In order to keep formulas readable, we still write formulas like $at_i = \ell$ as abbreviation for their Boolean encodings.

3.2 Excluding Bad and Initial State Loops

Another optimization is to require that we do not visit an initial state twice and only the last state violates the specification. This means, we add to φ_k the two conjuncts

$$\bigwedge_{0 < i \le k} \bigwedge_{\ell \in L} \neg \big(at_i = \ell \wedge init_\ell(v_i) \big) \qquad \text{and} \qquad \bigwedge_{0 \le i < k} safe(s_i) .$$

This optimization has already been proposed in [21] for finite state systems.

It is worth mentioning that the speed-up due to this optimization heavily depends on the underlying linear hybrid automaton and the specification: For specifications containing Boolean variables (or Boolean encodings of locations), the number of assignments for the Boolean abstraction can be reduced this way. On the other hand, if adding the above conjuncts introduces (in)equations that do not occur in φ_k, then it is less likely that this optimization improves the running times of the satisfiability checks. However, it does not significantly slow them down in our examples.

3.3   Alternating Flows and Jumps

Since two successive flows of durations t and t' can always be represented by a single flow of duration $t + t'$, we can require that each flow is followed by a jump. This restriction excludes irrelevant computations, and thus leads to a reduced number of solutions for the Boolean abstractions of the formulas φ_k. Excluding successive flows has already been proposed in [7].

Below we define a formula that describes computations with alternating flows and jumps, thereby excluding successive time steps without any overhead. Note that we also exclude runs with successive jumps. However, successive jumps can be expressed using flows of duration 0. Each computation can be rewritten to this form with alternating flows and jumps. The advantage of alternating flows and jumps over excluding successive flows is discussed in Remark 1. For $k \in \mathbb{N}$, we define ψ_k similar to φ_k where π_k is replaced by π'_k:

$$\psi_k(s_0, \ldots, s_k, t_1, \ldots, t_k) =$$
$$\left(\bigvee_{\ell \in L}(at_0 = \ell \wedge init_\ell(\boldsymbol{v_0})) \right) \wedge \pi'_k(s_0, \ldots, s_k, t_1, \ldots, t_k) \wedge \neg safe(s_k),$$

where $\pi'_0(s_0) = \pi_0(s_0)$, and for $k > 0$,

$$\pi'_k(s_0, \ldots, s_k, t_1, \ldots, t_k) =$$
$$\pi'_{k-1}(s_0, \ldots, s_{k-1}, t_1, \ldots, t_{k-1}) \wedge \begin{cases} J(s_{k-1}, s_k) & \text{if } k \text{ is even,} \\ F(s_{k-1}, t_k, s_k) & \text{otherwise.} \end{cases}$$

Using the above definition for searching iteratively for counterexamples, it suffices to start with $k = 1$ and to increase k in each iteration by 2: We start with a run consisting of a single flow. In each iteration we extend the runs under consideration with a jump that is followed by a flow. Since flows may have the duration 0, there is a counterexample containing k jumps iff ψ_{2k+1} is satisfiable.

Recall that φ_k is satisfiable iff there is a counterexample of length k. Now, if there is a counterexample of length less than or equal to k then there is also a counterexample containing at most k jumps. However, not all runs with at most k jumps can be represented by a run of length less than or equal to k. Consequently, the unsatisfiability of $\psi_1, \psi_3, \ldots, \psi_{2k+1}$ implies the unsatisfiability of $\varphi_0, \varphi_1, \ldots, \varphi_k$. The converse is not true.

The formula ψ_{2k} has twice as many variables as φ_k but the number of distinct (in)equations is approximately the same. Note that for the satisfiability check the number of distinct (in)equations is relevant and not the number of variables. That means, using ψ_{2k+1} instead of φ_k has the advantage that with no overhead the first k iterations check all runs of length less than or equal to $2k+1$ with at most k jumps in addition to the runs of length less than or equal to k, as it is also done by φ_k.

Moreover, the satisfiability check for ψ_{2k+1} is in most cases faster than the satisfiability check for φ_k (see Table 1 and the experiments in §5). The reason is that the number of calls of the solver for conjunctions of (in)equations in the lazy theorem proving algorithms often reduces significantly.

Remark 1. When excluding successive flows we still have the choice of doing a jump or a flow after we have done a jump. This choice is eliminated when we alternate between flows and jumps. In practice, eliminating this choice pays off. For instance, for the hybrid automaton in Example 1, for every $k \geq 0$ there is exactly one satisfying assignment for the Boolean abstraction of ψ_{2k+1} when flows and jumps alternate. Therefore, we have to check only one conjunction of (in)equations. In contrast, by excluding successive flows we would have to cope with exponentially many assignments.

Note that applying the optimization in §3.2 together with the encoding using alternating flows and jumps, we have to allow that the first two states can be initial states, since there are runs that can be described only with a first flow having the duration 0. Similarly, we must allow the last two states to violate the specification.

3.4 Introducing τ-Transitions

The BMC approach analyzes in each iteration runs of a certain length. That means, in order to show all runs of a length less than or equal to k to be safe, we must check the satisfiability of $k+1$ formulas. In this section we develop a method to search for counterexamples reachable by runs of length less than or equal to k in a single satisfiability check. To do so, we introduce jumps that do nothing, so-called τ-transitions. Recall that flows may have the duration 0. We require that after a τ-transition only further τ-transitions or flows of duration 0 are possible. Formally, for $k, k' \in \mathbb{N}$ we define $\psi_{k',k}^{tau}$ similar to ψ_k, where π_k' is replaced by $\pi_{k',k}''$:

$$\psi_{k',k}^{tau}(s_0,\ldots,s_k,t_1,\ldots,t_k) = \left(\bigvee_{\ell \in L}(at_0 = \ell \wedge init_\ell(\boldsymbol{v}_0))\right) \wedge \pi_{k',k}''(s_0,\ldots,s_k,t_1,\ldots,t_k) \wedge \neg safe(s_k),$$

where $\pi_{k',k}''$ describes computations of length k allowing τ-transitions to occur after the first k' steps only. We define $\pi_{k',k}'' = \pi_k'$ for $k' \geq k$, and for $k' < k$ we define

$$\pi_{k',k}''(s_0,\ldots,s_k,t_1,\ldots,t_k) = \pi_{k',k-1}''(s_0,\ldots,s_{k-1},t_1,\ldots,t_{k-1}) \wedge$$
$$\begin{cases} \left((\neg tau_{k-2} \wedge J(s_{k-1},s_k)) \vee tau_k\right) & \text{if } k \text{ is even,} \\ F(s_{k-1},t_k,s_k) \wedge (tau_{k-1} \rightarrow t_k = 0) & \text{otherwise} \end{cases}$$

where tau_k is a shortcut for *false* if $k \leq 0$ and $s_{k-1} = s_k$, otherwise.

Assume that we already know that there are no counterexamples of length less than or equal to k', and we want to check for some $k > k'$ whether we can reach a bad state in at most k steps. Instead of checking satisfiability of the formulas $\psi_{2k'+3},\ldots,\psi_{2k+1}$ or $\psi_{1,2k+1}^{tau}$ it suffices to check satisfiability of $\psi_{2k'+3,2k+1}^{tau}$.

The formula $\psi_{k',k}^{tau}$ allows us more flexibility in the BMC approach with hardly any overhead by increasing the length of the runs. The main advantage of using $\psi_{k',k}^{tau}$ is that we only have to call the solver once, and guide the solver not to do unnecessary work, i.e., we force the solver not to look for counterexamples that end in a bad state in less than k' steps.

For the railroad crossing example, the last two rows of Table 1 compare the sums of running times for ψ_{2k+1}, where k ranges from 0–5, 0–10, and 0–15 with the running times of $\psi_{1,2k+1}^{tau}$ for $k \in \{5, 10, 15\}$.

4   Learning Explanations

The bottleneck of the lazy theorem proving algorithm and its less lazy variants for the satisfiability check of a Boolean combination φ of (in)equations is the large number of calls to the solver for conjunctions of (in)equations. In the BMC approach, the number of calls usually grows exponentially with respect to the bound k. In this section we present a simple but effective method for reducing the calls of the solver for conjunctions of (in)equations.

The idea is that we make use of the knowledge of the unsatisfiability of the explanations that were generated during the previous satisfiability checks of the BMC algorithm. Assume that there is no counterexample of length less than k, i.e., the formulas $\psi_1, \ldots, \psi_{2k-1}$ are unsatisfiable. Moreover, assume that $\gamma_1, \ldots, \gamma_n$ are the explanations that are generated during the satisfiability checks for $\psi_1, \ldots, \psi_{2k-1}$. Since the γ_is are unsatisfiable conjunctions of (in)equations, we can check satisfiability of $\psi_{2k+1} \wedge \left(\bigwedge_{1 \leq i \leq n} \neg\gamma_i \right)$ instead of ψ_{2k+1} in the next iteration of the BMC algorithm. Intuitively, this means that we "learn" for the next iteration the unsatisfiability of the explanations $\gamma_1, \ldots, \gamma_n$.

In practice it turned out that just adding explanations from the previous satisfiability checks does not result in much speed-up. However, we can do better. In order to describe our method of exploiting the knowledge of the unsatisfiability of the explanations, we need the following definitions.

Definitions. Let $\gamma = \bigwedge_{1 \leq i \leq m} \alpha_i$ and $\gamma' = \bigwedge_{1 \leq i \leq m'} \alpha_i'$ be explanations. The explanation γ *(syntactically) subsumes* γ' if for every $1 \leq i \leq m$ there is a $1 \leq j \leq m'$ such that α_i and α_j' are syntactically equal. The explanation γ is *minimal* if for every $1 \leq j \leq m$, the conjunction $\bigwedge_{1 \leq i \leq m \text{ and } i \neq j} \alpha_i$ is satisfiable. For an integer s, $shift(\gamma, s)$ denotes the formula γ where each variable index i occurring in γ is replaced by $i + s$. The motivation of shifting indices in explanations is that the lazy theorem proving algorithm often checks similar conjunctions of (in)equations that only differ by the indices of the variables. Note that shifting the indices does not change the satisfiability of a formula. Let $min(\gamma)$ be the smallest index occurring in γ and let $max(\gamma)$ be the largest index occurring in γ. Figure 3 illustrates the possible range of values for shifting the indices in the explanation γ up to some bound k. The set of all variations of γ due to index shifting such that all indices are between 0 and k is defined as

$$SHIFT(\gamma, k) = \left\{ shift(\gamma, s) \mid -min(\gamma) \leq s \leq k - max(\gamma) \text{ and } s \text{ is even} \right\}.$$

Fig. 3. Shifting an explanation γ.

Observe that we always shift indices by an even integer. An (in)equation in an explanation γ describing a flow rarely describes also a jump. Since flows and jumps alternate in the formula ψ_{2k-1}, it is unlikely that for an odd s, the additional conjunct $shift(\gamma, s)$ prunes the search space in the satisfiability check of $\psi_{2k+1} \wedge \neg shift(\gamma, s)$.

Learning Method. The learned explanations should not contain irrelevant (in)equations. Therefore we first minimize every explanation that is generated during a satisfiability check. We do minimization greedily: We eliminate the first (in)equation α in an explanation γ if γ without α is still unsatisfiable; otherwise we do not remove α. We proceed successively with the other (in)equations in γ in the same way. After minimizing an explanation γ we delete all other explanations that are subsumed by γ. Finally, using shifting, we generalize all the remaining explanations for the next BMC iteration. In the kth BMC iteration we check satisfiability of the formula

$$\psi_{2k+1}^{learning} = \psi_{2k+1} \wedge \left(\bigwedge_{\gamma \in E} \bigwedge_{\gamma' \in SHIFT(\gamma, 2k+1)} \neg\gamma' \right),$$

where E is the set of all minimized explanations that occurred in the first $k-1$ iterations and that are not subsumed by other explanations.

We point out that with the additional conjunct $\left(\bigwedge_{\gamma \in E} \bigwedge_{\gamma' \in SHIFT(\gamma, 2k+1)} \neg\gamma' \right)$ we not only learn explanations that have been generated during earlier satisfiability checks, but due to index shifting we also apply them to the whole length of computations. Our case studies have shown that the same conflicts occur in different iterations with shifted indices, i.e., at another part of the computation sequence.

Due to our learning method, the Boolean abstractions of the formulas $\psi_{2k+1}^{learning}$ often have very few satisfying assignments. For such formulas, it is often more efficient to use the lazy theorem proving algorithm than the less lazy variant of it, since the solver for conjunctions of (in)equations has to be called less often. We pursue the policy that if in the last two iterations there are less than a threshold number (we use 50) of explanations then we assign a large value to the frequency parameter (see §2.2) of ICS, i.e., ICS switches to a "very" lazy variant of the lazy theorem proving algorithm. The running times heavily depend on this threshold.

5   Experimental Results

We carried out tests for evaluating the BMC approach for linear hybrid systems with the different encodings and techniques described in §3 and §4. Our test suite[1] consists

---

[1] A detailed description of our test suite and all the experimental results is in [1].

Table 2. Maximal number of BMC iterations k.

Example	Last iteration below 200 secs. of CPU time		
	naive	optimized	optimized+learning
Thermostat	70	> 1500	> 1500
Water-level monitor	39	> 1500	> 1500
Railroad crossing	14	52	872
Extended railroad crossing	10	12	80
Fischer's protocol (2 processes)	10	15	1254
Fischer's protocol (3 processes)	9	14	31
Bakery protocol (2 processes)	10	45	742
Nuclear reactor	20	82	> 1500
Audio-control protocol	20	62	357

of standard examples, e.g., examples that come with the HyTech tool and the Bakery protocol[2]. All experiments were performed on a SUN Blade 1000 with 8 Gbytes of main memory and two 900 Mhz UltraSparc III+ processors; each one with an 8 Mbyte cache. We used ICS (version 2.0b) [16] for checking satisfiability of the formulas in the BMC approach. The reason for us to use ICS was that in most cases ICS behaves at least as good as other state-of-the-art solvers [15]. We expect similar running times with other state-of-the-art solvers, like e.g., CVC Lite [8], since they use similar techniques as described in §2.2 for checking satisfiability of Boolean combinations of (in)equations.

We report on experimental results for the following three different encodings of finite runs: (A) the *naive* encoding as described in §2.1; (B) the *optimized* encoding as described in §3.1–§3.3; (C) the optimized encoding as in (B) with additional *learning* of explanations as described in §4. Table 2 lists for each example the maximal number of BMC iterations for which every satisfiability check could be performed within a time limit of 200 seconds.

Additionally, we recorded the running times for each iteration and the numbers of explanations that are generated during the satisfiability checks. In the following, we describe the outcome of our experiments separately.

Running Times. Figure 4 shows the running times for the encodings (A), (B), and (C) for some of our examples with k ranging from 0 to 200.

Checking satisfiability of the formulas φ_k becomes impractical even for small ks. For example, the satisfiability check for the railroad crossing example with $k = 15$ needs more than 230 seconds of CPU time. Although the optimization of the representation with alternating flows and jumps leads to a reduction of the running times, checking satisfiability of ψ_{2k+1} is also limited to rather small ks. For the railroad crossing example each satisfiability check for $k < 53$ needs less than 200 seconds; for $k = 53$ the satisfiability check exceeds our time limit of 200 seconds. The technique of learning explanations reduces the running times significantly. More importantly, the running times of satisfiability checks often scale much better for our examples. For instance, for

---

[2] The Bakery protocol is not a hybrid system but a discrete infinite state system. Our techniques can also be used for the BMC approach of such systems.

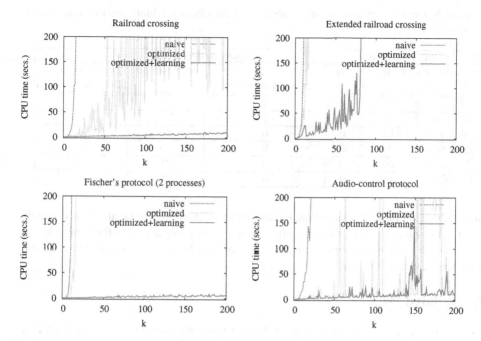

Fig. 4. Running times for the satisfiability checks for the naive encoding, the optimized encoding, and the optimized encoding with learning explanations.

the railroad crossing example each satisfiability check for $k \leq 200$ is under 11 seconds. The running times for computing the set of explanations that are added to the formula are not included. For the railroad crossing example, the sum of CPU times that ICS needs for the explanation minimization amounts to 15 seconds in the first 12 iterations; there are no explanations generated in later iterations. The reason for not including the times for minimizing explanations and the subsumption checks is twofold: First, we are interested in the speed-up of the satisfiability check that is due to the learning of explanations. Second, the implementation of the minimization and subsumption check is currently rather naive. For instance, we call ICS for each minimization step.

Number of Explanations. Additionally to the running times, we also recorded the numbers of explanations that are generated during the satisfiability checks. The running times strongly correlate with the numbers of explanations. A detailed statistics on the number of explanations for the railroad crossing example is listed in Table 3. We obtained similar numbers for the other examples.

The second and third column in Table 3 list the numbers of explanations generated during the satisfiability checks of φ_k and of ψ_{2k+1} with the optimizations of §3.1–§3.2, respectively, for some different ks. The optimizations significantly reduce the number of generated explanations. Further reduction can be reached by learning explanations, as illustrated in the fourth column. Only a few explanations (column 5) are left over after minimization and removing subsumed explanations. The sizes of the explanations, i.e., the numbers of (in)equations in the explanations (column 6) are reduced by min-

Table 3. Number of explanations that are generated during the satisfiability checks for the railroad crossing example.

k	naive #expl.	optimized #expl.	optimized+learning #expl.	#expl. after subsumption check	mean expl. size	mean expl. size after minimization
0	1	1	1	1	3	2
3	31	3	1	1	25	18
6	179	12	0	0	0	0
9	651	40	27	6	19	8
12	2500	20	9	2	21	13
15	6462	109	0	0	0	0

imization. Column 7 shows the mean sizes of the minimized explanations that remain after subsumption. These sizes are often moderate in comparison to the bound k. For the railroad crossing example with optimization and learning explanations, ICS only generates explanations for $k \in \{0, \ldots, 12\}$.

6   Related Work

BMC has been extended to verify properties for finite state systems [21] by introducing termination conditions that are again checked by a SAT-solver. A generalization and extension of these methods to infinite state systems is presented in [17]. We have also applied our presented optimizations for checking termination conditions. We obtained similar improvements as for the satisfiability checks of the counterexample search[3].

A complementary method of learning conflicts discovered in previous satisfiability checks is described in [23]. The conflicts that are learned by the two methods originate from different kinds of inconsistencies. The method in [23] learns conflicts that are discovered by the SAT-solver and our method learns conflicts that are discovered by the domain-specific solver.

Our work is in the line of the works by Audemard et. al. [7, 6] and by Sorea et. al. [22, 16] on the BMC approach for timed systems using lazy satisfiability solvers for Boolean combinations of (in)equations. The papers [7] and [22] extend the BMC approach to timed automata for properties written as LTL formulas. For simplicity, we only considered state properties. The paper [7] proposes several optimizations for encoding finite runs of timed systems. For instance, Audemard et. al. avoid successive flows and encode some form of symmetry reduction. The symmetry reduction only applies to certain timed systems, e.g., for systems consisting of identical components. As explained in Remark 1 in §3.3, alternating between flows and jumps is superior to excluding successive flows. Alternating between flows and jumps also appears in [22] with a different motivation. Sorea argues that alternation guarantees nonzenoness and often leads to smaller completeness thresholds for timed automata. In contrast, our motivation is that alternating between flows and jumps accelerates lazy satisfiability solving. We show that alternation significantly speeds up the satisfiability checks. The papers [6, 16] extend and generalize the work in [7, 22].

---

[3] Due to space limitations we omit a description on checking termination conditions. Details and the experimental results are in [1].

In [19] bounded-length verification problems for timed automata are translated into formulas in difference logic. Another approach of BMC for timed automata is presented in [25]. In contrast to the work by Audemard et. al., Sorea et. al., and ours, the core of their work is a reduction from the BMC problem for timed automata to a SAT problem exploiting the region graph construction for timed automata.

7 Conclusion

In this paper we presented complementary optimizations for improving the BMC approach for linear hybrid automata and explained why these optimizations speed-up lazy satisfiability solving. Experimental results substantiate the benefit of the optimizations. The speed-up stems from reducing the interactions of the SAT-solver used as well as the domain-specific solver. Our first optimization tunes the encodings of finite runs of linear hybrid automata and the second optimization speeds up the satisfiability checks by learning generalized conflicts. The learning technique can also be used in the BMC approach for other classes of infinite state systems.

Other verification tools for linear hybrid systems, like the model checker HyTech, are faster on some of our test examples. One reason is that, on small examples, the reachable set computation terminates already after a few iterations. However, many larger systems cannot be handled by model checkers due to state explosion. The BMC approach for hybrid system verification is still in its infancy, but this paper shows, that there is a large potential for further improvements to be successful also for larger examples.

Our future work includes developing a tighter integration of generalized conflict learning and satisfiability solving. One task here is to develop methods that determine the usefulness of conflicts in later satisfiability checks and data structures that efficiently store generalized conflicts with fast look-ups. We also want to develop a more dynamic adjustment of the "laziness" in the satisfiability checks. Moreover, minimizing explanations is a crucial subtask in lazy satisfiability solving. At the moment, minimization is done greedily. Other methods for explanation minimization have to be developed.

Acknowledgements

We thank Christian Herde and Martin Fränzle for the fruitful discussions, and Leonardo de Moura and Harald Rueß for answering our numerous ICS-related questions.

References

1. E. Ábrahám, B. Becker, F. Klaedtke, and M. Steffen. Optimizing bounded model checking for linear hybrid systems. Technical Report TR214, Albert-Ludwigs-Universität Freiburg, Fakultät für Angewandte Wissenschaften, Institut für Informatik, 2004. Online available at http://www.informatik.uni-freiburg.de/tr/.
2. R. Alur, C. Courcoubetis, T. Henzinger, P.-H. Ho, X. Nicollin, A. Olivero, J. Sifakis, and S. Yovine. The algorithmic analysis of hybrid systems. *Theor. Comput. Sci.*, 138:3–34, 1995.
3. R. Alur and D. Dill. A theory of timed automata. *Theor. Comput. Sci.*, 126:183–235, 1994.

4. R. Alur, T. Henzinger, and P.-H. Ho. Automatic symbolic verification of embedded systems. *IEEE Transactions on Software Engineering*, 22:181–201, 1996.

5. G. Audemard, P. Bertoli, A. Cimatti, A. Korniłowicz, and R. Sebastiani. A SAT based approach for solving formulas over boolean and linear mathematical propositions. In *Proc. of CADE'02*, volume 2392 of *LNAI*, pages 195–210, 2002.

6. G. Audemard, M. Bozzano, A. Cimatti, and R. Sebastiani. Verifying industrial hybrid systems with MathSAT. In *Proc. of BMC'04*, 2004.

7. G. Audemard, A. Cimatti, A. Korniłowicz, and R. Sebastiani. Bounded model checking for timed systems. In *Proc. of FORTE'02*, volume 2529 of *LNCS*, pages 243–259, 2002.

8. C. Barrett and S. Berezin. CVC Lite: A new implementation of the cooperating validity checker. In *Proc. of CAV'04*, volume 3114 of *LNCS*, pages 515–518, 2004.

9. A. Biere, A. Cimatti, E. Clarke, O. Strichman, and Y. Zhu. Bounded model checking. *Advances in Computers*, 58, 2003.

10. A. Biere, A. Cimatti, E. Clarke, and Y. Zhu. Symbolic model checking without BDDs. In *Proc. of TACAS'99*, volume 1579 of *LNCS*, pages 193–207, 1999.

11. A. Biere, E. Clarke, R. Raimi, and Y. Zhu. Verifying safety properties of a PowerPC^{TM} microprocessor using symbolic model checking without BDDs. In *Proc. of CAV'99*, volume 1633 of *LNCS*, pages 60–71, 1999.

12. E. Clarke and E. Emerson. Design and synthesis of synchronisation skeletons using branching time temporal logic specifications. In *Proc. of the Workshop on Logic of Programs 1981*, volume 131 of *LNCS*, pages 244–263, 1982.

13. F. Copty, L. Fix, R. Fraer, E. Guinchiglia, G. Kamhi, and M. Vardi. Benefits of bounded model checking in an industrial setting. In *Proc. of CAV'01*, volume 2102 of *LNCS*, pages 436–453, 2001.

14. L. de Moura and H. Rueß. Lemmas on demand for satisfiability solvers. In *Proc. of SAT'02*, pages 244–251, 2002.

15. L. de Moura and H. Rueß. An experimental evaluation of ground decision procedures. In *Proc. of CAV'04*, volume 3114 of *LNCS*, pages 162–174, 2004.

16. L. de Moura, H. Rueß, and M. Sorea. Lazy theorem proving for bounded model checking over infinite domains. In *Proc. of CADE'02*, volume 2392 of *LNAI*, pages 438–455, 2002.

17. L. de Moura, H. Rueß, and M. Sorea. Bounded model checking and induction: From refutation to verification. In *Proc. of CAV'03*, volume 2725 of *LNCS*, pages 14–26, 2003.

18. T. Henzinger. The theory of hybrid automata. In *Proc. of LICS'96*, pages 278–292, 1996.

19. P. Niebert, M. Mahfoudh, E. Asarin, M. Bozga, N. Jain, and O. Maler. Verification of timed automata via satisfiability checking. In *Proc. of FTRTFT'02*, volume 2469 of *LNCS*, pages 225–244, 2002.

20. J. Queille and J. Sifakis. Specification and verification of concurrent systems in CESAR. In *Proc. of the 5th International Symposium on Programming 1981*, volume 137 of *LNCS*, pages 337–351, 1982.

21. M. Sheeran, S. Singh, and G. Stalmårck. Checking safety properties using induction and a SAT-solver. In *Proc. of FMCAD'00*, volume 1954 of *LNCS*, pages 108–125, 2000.

22. M. Sorea. Bounded model checking for timed automata. *Electronic Notes in Theoretical Computer Science*, 68, 2002.

23. O. Strichman. Accelerating bounded model checking of safety properties. *Formal Methods in System Design*, 24(1):5–24, 2004.

24. A. Tarski. *A Decision Method for Elementary Algebra and Geometry*. University of California Press, Berkeley, 2nd edition, 1951.

25. B. Woźna, A. Zbrzezny, and W. Penczek. Checking reachability properties for timed automata via SAT. *Fundamenta Informaticae*, 55(2):223–241, 2003.

Efficient Verification of Halting Properties
for MPI Programs with Wildcard Receives

Stephen F. Siegel[*]

Laboratory for Advanced Software Engineering Research
Department of Computer Science, University of Massachusetts
Amherst MA 01003, USA
siegel@cs.umass.edu
http://laser.cs.umass.edu

Abstract. We are concerned with the verification of certain properties, such as freedom from deadlock, for parallel programs that are written using the Message Passing Interface (MPI). It is known that for MPI programs containing no "wildcard receives" (and restricted to a certain subset of MPI) freedom from deadlock can be established by considering only synchronous executions. We generalize this by presenting a model checking algorithm that deals with wildcard receives by moving back and forth between a synchronous and a buffering mode as the search of the state space progresses. This approach is similar to that taken by partial order reduction (POR) methods, but can dramatically reduce the number of states explored even when the standard POR techniques do not apply.

1 Introduction

It is well-known that finite-state verification techniques, such as model checking, suffer from the *state explosion problem*: the fact that the number of states of a concurrent system may – and often does – grow exponentially with the size of the system. Many different approaches have been studied to counteract this difficulty. These include partial order reduction (POR) methods, data abstraction, program slicing, and state compression techniques, to name only a few.

For the most part, these approaches have been formulated in very general frameworks. Their generality is both a strength and a weakness: the methods can be broadly applied, but may miss opportunities for reduction in specific situations. This observation has led to interest in more *domain-specific* approaches. The idea is to leverage knowledge of the restrictions imposed by a particular programming domain, or of common idioms used in the domain, in order to gain greater reductions than the generic algorithms allow. An example of this approach for concurrent Java programs is given in [2], where analysis that identifies common locking patterns, among other things, is exploited to dramatically improve the generic POR algorithms.

[*] Research supported by the U.S. Army Research Laboratory and the U.S. Army Research Office under agreement number DAAD190110564.

R. Cousot (Ed.): VMCAI 2005, LNCS 3385, pp. 413–429, 2005.

This paper is concerned with the domain of parallel programs that employ the Message Passing Interface (MPI). The MPI Standard [9,10] specifies the syntax and semantics for a large library of message passing functions with bindings in C, C++, and Fortran. For many reasons – portability, performance, the broad scope of the library, and the wide availability of quality implementations – MPI has become the de facto standard for high-performance parallel computing. In addition, we focus on a particular class of properties of MPI programs, which we call *halting properties*: claims on the state of a program whenever execution halts, whether due to deadlock, or to normal termination. Freedom from deadlock is an example of a halting property; another would be an assertion on the values of variables when a program terminates.

Some explanation of the most essential MPI functions is required for what follows. The basic MPI function for sending a message to another process is MPI_SEND. To use it, one must specify the destination process and a message tag, in addition to other information. The corresponding function for receiving a message is MPI_RECV. In contrast to MPI_SEND, an MPI_RECV statement may specify its source process, or it may use the *wildcard* value MPI_ANY_SOURCE, indicating that this statement will accept a message from any source. Similarly, it may specify the tag of the message it wishes to receive, or it may use the wildcard value MPI_ANY_TAG. A receive operation that uses either or both wildcards is called a *wildcard receive*. The use of wildcards and tags allows for great flexibility in how messages are selected for reception.

Previous work has established that if a program (restricted to a certain subset of MPI) contains no wildcard receives, then a suitable model $\mathcal{M}$ of that program can be constructed with the following property: $\mathcal{M}$ is deadlock-free if, and only if, no synchronous execution of $\mathcal{M}$ can deadlock [12, Theorem 7.4]. This is exactly the kind of result we are after, as the need to represent all possible states of message channels is often a significant source of state explosion. Unfortunately, wildcard receives are common in actual MPI programs, and the theorem may fail if the hypothesis on wildcard receives is removed [12, Sec. 7.3].

The approach of this paper generalizes the earlier result in three ways. First, it shows that the hypothesis forbidding wildcard receives may be relaxed to allow the use of MPI_ANY_TAG, with no ill effects. Second, the range of properties is expanded to include all halting properties. But most importantly, it provides a model checking algorithm that deals with MPI_ANY_SOURCE by moving back and forth between a synchronous and a buffering mode as the search of the state space progresses. This approach is similar to that taken by POR methods, but can dramatically reduce the number of states explored even when the standard POR techniques do not apply.

The discussion proceeds as follows. Section 2 establishes the precise definition of a model of an MPI program, and of the execution semantics of such a model. The definition of a halting property and the statement of the main theorem are given in Sec. 3. Section 4 deals with consequences of the main theorem. These include a bounded model checking algorithm for halting properties; the consequences for programs that do not use MPI_ANY_SOURCE are also explored. Section 5 discusses the relationship with the standard POR techniques. Results of an empirical investigation are presented in Sec. 6, and conclusions are drawn in Sec. 7. Proofs of the theorems, a description of the program and model for each example, complete MPI/C source code for the examples, and all experimental results can be downloaded from `http://laser.cs.umass.edu/~siegel/projects`.

2 Models of MPI Programs

For the purposes of this paper, an MPI program consists of a fixed number of concurrent processes, each executing its own code, with no shared variables, that communicate only through the MPI functions. The precise notion of a *model* of such a program is defined below. While there are many issues that arise in creating models from code, these are beyond the scope of this paper, and the reader is referred to [12] for a discussion of this subject and some examples. It is argued there that this notion of model suffices to represent MPI_SEND, MPI_RECV, MPI_SENDRECV (which concurrently executes one send and one receive operation), as well as the 16 collective functions, such as MPI_BCAST, MPI_ALLREDUCE, etc. The definition of receiving states here is slightly more general, in order to accommodate a new way to deal with tags, explained below.

2.1 Definition of a Model of an MPI Program

An *MPI context* is a 7-tuple

$$\mathcal{C} = (\mathsf{Proc}, \mathsf{Chan}, \mathsf{sender}, \mathsf{receiver}, \mathsf{msg}, \mathsf{loc}, \mathsf{com}).$$

The first two components are finite sets, representing the set of *processes*, and the set of communication *channels*, respectively. The next two components are functions from Chan to Proc; they define the sending and receiving process for each channel. The function msg assigns, to each $c \in$ Chan, a nonempty set $\mathsf{msg}(c)$; this is the set of messages that can be sent over channel c. The final two components are functions of Proc. For $p \in$ Proc, $\mathsf{loc}(p)$ is a finite set representing the set of *local events* for p, while $\mathsf{com}(p)$ is defined to be the set of *communication events* for p, namely, the set of send and receive symbols

$$\{c!x, d?y \mid c, d \in \mathsf{Chan}, x \in \mathsf{msg}(c), y \in \mathsf{msg}(d), \mathsf{sender}(c) = p = \mathsf{receiver}(d)\}.$$

Finally, for all $p, q \in$ Proc, we assume $\mathsf{loc}(p) \cap \mathsf{com}(q) = \emptyset$, and $p \neq q \Rightarrow \mathsf{loc}(p) \cap \mathsf{loc}(q) = \emptyset$.

Let $p \in$ Proc. An *MPI state machine for p under $\mathcal{C}$* is a 6-tuple

$$M_p = (\mathsf{States}_p, \mathsf{Trans}_p, \mathsf{src}, \mathsf{des}, \mathsf{label}, \mathsf{start}_p)$$

where States_p and Trans_p are sets, src and des are functions from Trans_p to States_p, label is a function from Trans_p to $\mathsf{loc}(p) \cup \mathsf{com}(p)$, and $\mathsf{start}_p \in \mathsf{States}_p$.

We do not use the subscript p for the functions src, des, and label, because the process p will always be clear from the context. Finally, we require that every state u must fall into one of 5 categories, which are determined by the transitions departing from u. First, we define the following:

$$R(u) = \{(d, y) \mid d \in \mathsf{Chan}, y \in \mathsf{msg}(d), \exists t \in \mathsf{Trans}_p : \mathsf{src}(t) = u \wedge \mathsf{label}(t) = d?y\}$$
$$Q(u) = \{d \in \mathsf{Chan} \mid \exists y \in \mathsf{msg}(d) : (d, y) \in R(u)\}$$
$$R_d(u) = \{y \in \mathsf{msg}(d) \mid (d, y) \in R(u)\} \qquad (d \in Q(u)).$$

Now the 5 possibilities for u are as follows:

1. u is a *final state*: there are no transitions departing from u,
2. u is a *local-event state*: there is at least one transition departing from u, and the transitions departing from u are labeled by local events for p,
3. u is a *sending state*: there is precisely one transition departing from u and it is labeled by a send event for p,
4. u is a *receiving state*: there is at least one transition departing from u, and the transitions departing from u are labeled by distinct receive events for p, or
5. u is a *send-receive state* (see Fig. 1): $R(u) \neq \emptyset$, and there is a $c \in \mathsf{Chan}$ with $\mathsf{sender}(c) = p$, an $x \in \mathsf{msg}(c)$, a state u', and states $v(d, y)$ and $v'(d, y)$ for all $(d, y) \in R(u)$, such that the following all hold:
   (a) the set of transitions departing from u consists of one transition to u' whose label is $c!x$, and, for each $(d, y) \in R(u)$, one transition labeled $d?y$ to $v(d, y)$,
   (b) for each $(d, y) \in R(u)$, there is precisely one transition departing from $v(d, y)$, it is labeled $c!x$, and it terminates in $v'(d, y)$, and
   (c) for each $(d, y) \in R(u)$, there is a transition from u' to $v'(d, y)$, it is labeled $d?y$, and these make up all the transitions departing from u'.

The point of the send-receive state is to model the MPI_SENDRECV function, which executes one send and one receive operation concurrently. This is modeled by allowing the send and receive to happen in either order.

Finally, a *model $\mathcal{M}$ of an MPI program* is a pair $(\mathcal{C}, M)$, where $\mathcal{C}$ is a context and M is a function that assigns, to each $p \in \mathsf{Proc}$, an MPI state machine M_p for p under $\mathcal{C}$, such that $\mathsf{States}_p \cap \mathsf{States}_q = \emptyset = \mathsf{Trans}_p \cap \mathsf{Trans}_q$ for $p \neq q$.

Given an MPI program, one may construct a model using one channel $c_{p,q}$, with $\mathsf{sender}(c_{p,q}) = p$ and $\mathsf{receiver}(c_{p,q}) = q$, for each $(p, q) \in \mathsf{Proc} \times \mathsf{Proc}$. To translate a receive statement r it suffices to specify the sets $Q(u)$ and $R_d(u)$ for

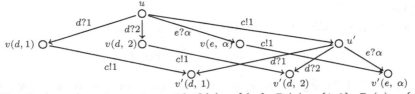

Fig. 1. A send-receive state u with $Q(u) = \{d, e\}$, $R_d(u) = \{1, 2\}$, $R_e(u) = \{\alpha\}$.

the receiving state u corresponding to r. If r occurs in process q and specifies its source p, then we let $Q(u) = \{c_{p,q}\}$. If r instead uses MPI_ANY_SOURCE then we let $Q(u) = \{c_{p,q} \mid p \in \mathsf{Proc}\}$. We may assume that the tags have been encoded in the messages, so that to each message x is associated an integer $\mathsf{tag}(x)$. Now if r specifies a tag t, we let

$$R_d(u) = \{x \in \mathsf{msg}(d) \mid \mathsf{tag}(x) = t\} \qquad (d \in Q(u)).$$

If instead r uses MPI_ANY_TAG, we take $R_d(u) = \mathsf{msg}(d)$. We will see below that the execution semantics in effect allow a receive operation to choose non-deterministically among the receiving channels $Q(u)$, but, for a given $d \in Q(u)$, it must pick out the oldest message in d with a matching tag. This corresponds exactly to the requirements of the MPI Standard [9, Sec. 3.5].

2.2   Execution Semantics of a Model of an MPI Program

Let $\mathbf{N} = \{0, 1, \ldots\}$ and $\mathbf{N}^\infty = \mathbf{N} \cup \{\infty\}$. A sequence $S = (x_1, x_2, \ldots)$ of elements of a set X may be either infinite or finite. We write $|S|$ for the length of S. If A is a subset of a set B, and S is a sequence of elements of B, then *the projection of S onto A* is the sequence that results by deleting from S all elements that are not in A. If S is any sequence and $n \in \mathbf{N}$, then S^n denotes the sequence obtained by truncating S after the nth element.

Let $\mathcal{M}$ be a model of an MPI program. A *global state* σ of $\mathcal{M}$ is a pair of functions (u, α), where u assigns, to each $p \in \mathsf{Proc}$, a state $u_p \in \mathsf{States}_p$, and α assigns to each $c \in \mathsf{Chan}$ a finite sequence α_c of elements of $\mathsf{msg}(c)$. The sequence represents the *pending* messages for c: messages that have been sent but not yet received. We define $\mathsf{Pending}_c(\sigma) = \alpha_c$ and $\mathsf{state}_p(\sigma) = u_p$. The *initial state* of $\mathcal{M}$ is the global state for which $u_p = \mathsf{start}_p$ for all p, and α_c is empty for all c.

Suppose $\sigma = (u, \alpha)$ and $\sigma' = (u', \alpha')$ are global states of $\mathcal{M}$, $p \in \mathsf{Proc}$, $t \in \mathsf{Trans}_p$, and that $\mathsf{src}(t) = u_p$, $\mathsf{des}(t) = u'_p$, $u_q = u'_q$ for $q \neq p$, and one of the following holds:

1. $\mathsf{label}(t) \in \mathsf{loc}(p)$ and $\alpha = \alpha'$,
2. there exist $c \in \mathsf{Chan}$ and $x \in \mathsf{msg}(c)$ such that $\mathsf{label}(t) = c!x$, α'_c is obtained by appending x to the end of α_c, and $\alpha'_d = \alpha_d$ for $d \neq c$, or
3. there exist $d \in \mathsf{Chan}$ and $y \in \mathsf{msg}(d)$ such that $\mathsf{label}(t) = d?y$, y is the first element of the projection of α_d onto $R_d(u_p)$, α'_d is obtained by deleting the first occurrence of y from α_d, and $\alpha'_c = \alpha_c$ for $c \neq d$.

Then we call the triple $\tau = (\sigma, \sigma', t)$ a *simple global transition of $\mathcal{M}$*, and we define $\mathsf{label}(\tau) = \mathsf{label}(t)$.

Suppose now that σ, σ', and σ'' are global states, t_1, t_2 are transitions, $c \in \mathsf{Chan}$, $x \in \mathsf{msg}(c)$, $p = \mathsf{receiver}(c)$, and that the following all hold:

1. $\mathsf{label}(t_1) = c!x$ and $\mathsf{label}(t_2) = c?x$,
2. $\mathsf{Pending}_c(\sigma)$ contains no element of $R_c(\mathsf{state}_p(\sigma))$, and
3. (σ, σ', t_1) and (σ', σ'', t_2) are simple global transitions.

In this case we will refer to the 4-tuple $\tilde{\tau} = (\sigma, \sigma'', t_1, t_2)$ as a *synchronous global transition*, as it corresponds to a synchronous MPI communication: a message that is transferred directly from the sender to the receiver in one atomic step. We do *not* want to think of $\tilde{\tau}$ as "passing through" the intermediate state σ', but rather as leading directly from σ to σ''. In particular, since $\mathsf{Pending}_c(\sigma) = \mathsf{Pending}_c(\sigma'')$, $\tilde{\tau}$ leaves all of the channels unchanged. We define $\mathsf{label}(\tilde{\tau})$ to be the symbol $c!?x$.

The *state graph* of $\mathcal{M}$ is the ordered pair $\mathcal{G} = (\mathcal{S}, \mathcal{T})$, where $\mathcal{S}$ is the set of all global states, and $\mathcal{T}$ is the set of all (simple and synchronous) global transitions. Let $\mathsf{src}, \mathsf{des}\colon \mathcal{T} \to \mathcal{S}$ be the projections onto the first and second coordinates, respectively. These give $\mathcal{G}$ the structure of a directed graph.

An *event* α is any element of $\{\mathsf{label}(\tau) \mid \tau \in \mathcal{T}\}$. We say that α is *enabled* at the global state σ if there exists $\tau \in \mathcal{T}$ with $\mathsf{src}(\tau) = \sigma$ and $\mathsf{label}(\tau) = \alpha$.

Given a path $T = (\tau_1, \tau_2, \dots)$ in $\mathcal{G}$, we define the *atomic length of T* to be $\|T\| = \sum_i \epsilon(\tau_i)$, where $\epsilon(\tau) = 1$ if τ is simple and $\epsilon(\tau) = 2$ if τ is synchronous. This is sometimes a more natural measure of length than $|T|$. A *trace* of $\mathcal{M}$ is any path in $\mathcal{G}$ originating in the initial state. Finally, If T originates in the global state σ and $c \in \mathsf{Chan}$, we define

$$\mathsf{maxlen}_c(T) = \max_i\{|\mathsf{Pending}_c(\sigma)|, |\mathsf{Pending}_c(\mathsf{des}(\tau_i))|\}.$$

3   The Main Theorem

The main theorem concerns *halting properties* so we first explain what these are. In general, a concurrent program is considered to be in a halted state if every process has become permanently blocked. A receive statement in an MPI program blocks, as one would expect, as long as there is no pending message that matches the parameters of that statement. However, the circumstances under which a sending statement blocks are more subtle. Typically, one would assume that each channel c has some fixed size $\nu(c) \in \mathbf{N}$, and declare that a send on c blocks whenever the length of c equals $\nu(c)$. The MPI Standard, however, imposes no such bounds, but instead declares that a send *may* block at any time, unless the receiving process is at a state from which it can receive the message synchronously [9, Sec. 3.4]. We thus make the following definition for a model $\mathcal{M}$:

Definition 1. A global state σ of $\mathcal{M}$ is *potentially halted* if no receive, local, or synchronous event is enabled at σ.

We use the word "potentially" because a program in such a state may or may not halt, depending on the particular choices made by the MPI implementation.

For any predicate f on the global states of $\mathcal{M}$, and any subgraph $\mathcal{H}$ of $\mathcal{G}$ that contains the initial state σ_0, let $\Pi(\mathcal{H}, f)$ denote the statement *for all states σ reachable in $\mathcal{H}$ from σ_0, $f(\sigma)$*. Let phalt be the predicate defined by $\mathsf{phalt}(\sigma) \Leftrightarrow \sigma$ is potentially halted.

Definition 2. A *halting predicate* is a state predicate f of the form phalt $\Rightarrow q$, where q is any state predicate. A *halting property* is a statement of the form $\Pi(\mathcal{H}, f)$, where f is a halting predicate.

An example of a halting property is given by taking $q =$ false, the predicate that holds at no state. For this q, $\Pi = \Pi(\mathcal{G}, f)$ states that $\mathcal{M}$ never halts. One could also take $q =$ term, the predicate that is true when all processes are at final states. Then Π states that whenever $\mathcal{M}$ halts, all processes have terminated, i.e., $\mathcal{M}$ is deadlock-free. More generally, one could take q to be the predicate term$_\Sigma$ that holds when all processes in a certain subset Σ are at final states. One could also let q be the conjunction of term$_\Sigma$ with another predicate – for example, a predicate that holds when variables in the processes in Σ, whose values are encoded in the local states, have particular values. In this case Π would say that whenever the program halts, all processes in Σ have terminated and the variables have the specified values.

To motivate what follows, consider a model [12, Fig. 5] of three processes with state machines as follows:

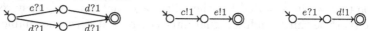

Suppose we try to verify freedom from deadlock for this model by considering only synchronous executions. Then we only explore the sequence $(c!?1, e!?1, d!?1)$, which terminates normally, and miss the deadlocking sequence $(c!1, e!?1, d!?1)$. We can try to explain why we missed the deadlock in the following way. At the initial state, process $p =$ receiver(c) is at a wildcard receive u with $Q(u) = \{c, d\}$. At this state, c is ready to receive a message (synchronously) but d is not. By pursuing only synchronous communication, we never get to see the state in which p is at u and a receive on d is enabled.

The solution is to consider all enabled events (not just synchronous ones) whenever a process p is at a wildcard receive u, unless u has become "urgent." By this we mean that for each $c \in Q(u)$, either a (synchronous or buffered) receive on c is enabled or we know that a receive on c can never become enabled. Note that once a receive on c becomes enabled, it will remain enabled until p executes a transition, since p is the only process which may remove a message from c. Since no receive event can be enabled at a potentially halted state σ, the only way we can arrive at σ is if p eventually executes. Now if u is urgent, no new events in p can become enabled, and so one of the currently enabled events in p must occur if the system is to arrive at σ. Since those events are *independent* of events in other processes, we might as well explore the paths that result from scheduling each of those enabled events immediately. (If two events are independent then neither can disable the other and the effect of applying one and then the other does not depend on the order in which they are applied.) Local event states are similar, but they are always urgent since the local events are always enabled. The following definitions attempt to make all of this precise:

Definition 3. Let σ be a global state of $\mathcal{M}$, $p \in$ Proc, and $u =$ state$_p(\sigma)$. We say p is *at an urgent state in* σ if either u is a local event state, or all of the following hold:

1. u is a receiving or send-receive state,
2. for all $d \in Q(u)$, at least one of the following holds:
    (a) there is an event of the form $d?y$ or $d!?y$ enabled at σ, or
    (b) $\mathsf{state}_{\mathsf{sender}(d)}(\sigma)$ is a final state,
    and
3. there is at least one $d \in Q(u)$ for which 2(a) holds.

We define $\mathsf{Urgent}(\sigma)$ to be the set of all $p \in \mathsf{Proc}$ such that p is at an urgent state in σ. Finally, we say that σ is *urgent* if $\mathsf{Urgent}(\sigma) \neq \emptyset$.

Definition 4. A global transition τ is *urgent for process p* if τ has the form (σ, σ', t) or (σ, σ', t', t), where $p \in \mathsf{Urgent}(\sigma)$, $t \in \mathsf{Trans}_p$, and $\mathsf{label}(t)$ is either a local event or a receive.

Condition 2(b) of Definition 3 can be relaxed somewhat: all that is really required is that $\mathsf{sender}(d)$ be in a state from which it can never reach a send on d. However, the version that we have stated has the advantage that it is very easy to check. Also, note that the third condition guarantees there is at least one enabled event at an urgent state.

We now fix a total order on Proc. The reason for this will become clear: we do not have to consider all urgent transitions departing from an urgent state, but only those for a single process, and so we will just choose the least one.

Definition 5. Let $\tilde{\mathcal{T}}$ denote the set of all global transitions τ for which either $\mathsf{src}(\tau)$ is not urgent, or τ is urgent for the minimal element of $\mathsf{Urgent}(\mathsf{src}(\tau))$. Let $\tilde{\mathcal{G}} = (\mathcal{S}, \tilde{\mathcal{T}})$.

Now we can state the main theorem:

Theorem 1. *Given any path S in $\mathcal{G}$ from a global state σ_0 to a potentially halted global state σ, there exists a path T from σ_0 to σ in $\tilde{\mathcal{G}}$ such that $\|T\| = \|S\|$, $|T| \leq |S|$, and $\mathsf{maxlen}_c(T) \leq \mathsf{maxlen}_c(S)$ for all $c \in \mathsf{Chan}$. In particular $\Pi(\mathcal{G}, f) \Leftrightarrow \Pi(\tilde{\mathcal{G}}, f)$ for any halting predicate f.*

In light of the discussion above, it should come as no surprise that the proof of Theorem 1 relies on many of the restrictions imposed by our domain and property. For example, the fact that each channel has an exclusive receiving process was used to show that once a receive event becomes enabled, it must remain enabled until that process executes. The knowledge that the property could be violated only if no receive were enabled was also used. The fact that a sending state has exactly one outgoing transition also comes into play: if the sending state had outgoing transitions on two different channels then a synchronous event that was enabled on one channel could become disabled if the sending process were to send on the other channel. These arguments withstand the introduction of send-receive states only because the specific structure of those states guarantees that the send event is independent of the receive events. Remove any of these domain-specific restrictions, and Theorem 1 may fail.

4   Consequences of the Main Theorem

4.1   The Urgent Algorithm

In general, the number of reachable states in $\mathcal{G}$ or $\tilde{\mathcal{G}}$ may be very large (or even infinite). So it is common practice to place upper bounds on the channel sizes, or the search depth, in order to reach a conclusive result on at least a bounded region of the state space. For these reasons we define the following concepts. Let $\nu : \mathsf{Chan} \to \mathbf{N}^\infty$ and $m \in \mathbf{N}^\infty$. Let $\mathcal{T}_{\nu,m}$ be the set of all global transitions that occur in traces T that satisfy (i) $\|T\| \leq m$, and (ii) for all global states σ through which T passes, and all $c \in \mathsf{Chan}$, $|\mathsf{Pending}_c(\sigma)| \leq \nu(c)$. We let $\mathcal{G}_{\nu,m} = (\mathcal{S}, \mathcal{T}_{\nu,m})$.

Let $\mathcal{T}_{\nu,m}^\flat$ be the set of all $\tau \in \mathcal{T}_{\nu,m}$ such that $\tau \in \tilde{\mathcal{T}}$ and

$$\text{if } \mathsf{label}(\tau) = c!?x \text{ for some } c, x \text{ then } \sigma \text{ is urgent or } |\mathsf{Pending}_c(\sigma)| = \nu(c), \quad (1)$$

where $\sigma = \mathsf{src}(\tau)$. Condition (1) is not strictly necessary, but it may provide some additional reduction. The idea is that when σ is not urgent, it would be redundant to consider synchronous transitions since we are already pursuing all buffered sends and receives. An exception is made if a channel is full since then a buffered send would not be enabled. Let $\mathcal{G}_{\nu,m}^\flat = (\mathcal{S}, \mathcal{T}_{\nu,m}^\flat)$. We have the following consequence of Theorem 1:

Corollary 1. *Given any path in $\mathcal{G}_{\nu,m}$ from a global state σ_0 to a potentially halted global state σ, there exists a path in $\mathcal{G}_{\nu,m}^\flat$ from σ_0 to σ. In particular, $\Pi(\mathcal{G}_{\nu,m}, f) \Leftrightarrow \Pi(\mathcal{G}_{\nu,m}^\flat, f)$ for any halting predicate f.*

If States_p, Trans_p, and $\nu(c)$ are finite for all $p \in \mathsf{Proc}$ and $c \in \mathsf{Chan}$, then $\mathcal{T}_{\nu,m}$ and $\mathcal{T}_{\nu,m}^\flat$ are finite as well. It follows from Corollary 1 that we can verify a halting property in this case by performing a depth-first search of $\mathcal{G}_{\nu,m}^\flat$. Specifically, algorithm Urgent of Fig. 2 will find all reachable states in $\mathcal{G}_{\nu,m}$ for which f does not hold. We assume $\mathsf{Proc} = \{p_1, \ldots, p_N\}$ and $p_1 < \cdots < p_N$. The search is initiated by setting the global variable R to the empty set and calling $search(\sigma_0, 0)$, where σ_0 is the initial state. Function $urgent\_transitions(\sigma, p)$ returns the set of all $\tau \in \mathcal{T}$ such that $\mathsf{src}(\tau) = \sigma$ and τ is urgent for p. Function $standard\_transitions(\sigma, \nu)$ returns the set of all $\tau \in \mathcal{T}$ that satisfy (i) $\mathsf{src}(\tau) = \sigma$, (ii) $|\mathsf{Pending}_c(\mathsf{des}(\tau))| \leq \nu(c)$ for all c, and (iii) $\mathsf{label}(\tau) = c!?x \Rightarrow |\mathsf{Pending}_c(\sigma)| = \nu(c)$. There is no need to specify ν for $urgent\_transitions$ since an urgent transition can never increase the length of a channel.

Example. In a model of a *client-server* system with n clients ($n \geq 1$), $\mathsf{Proc} = \{0, 1, \ldots, n\}$ with the natural order, $\mathsf{Chan} = \{c_1, d_1, \ldots, c_n, d_n\}$, $\mathsf{msg}(c) = \{1\}$ for all $c \in \mathsf{Chan}$, and $\mathsf{sender}(c_i) = i = \mathsf{receiver}(d_i)$, $\mathsf{receiver}(c_i) = 0 = \mathsf{sender}(d_i)$ for $1 \leq i \leq n$. For $n = 2$, the state machines for processes 0 (the server), 1, and 2, are respectively:

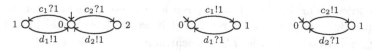

```
1    function selected_transitions(σ)    /* returns {τ ∈ T^♭_{ν,m} | src(τ) = σ} */
2        for i = 1 to N do
3            if p_i ∈ Urgent(σ) then return urgent_transitions(σ, p_i) end if
4        end for;
5        return standard_transitions(σ,ν)
6    end function;

7    procedure search(σ, l)
8        if l > m then return end if;
9        R := R ∪ {σ};
10       if not f(σ) then report_violation() end if;
11       for all τ ∈ selected_transitions(σ) do
12           if des(τ) ∉ R then search(des(τ), l + ϵ(τ)) end if
13       end for all
14   end procedure
```

Fig. 2. The Urgent Algorithm: depth-first search of $\mathcal{G}^{\flat}_{\nu,m}$.

Let us see how the Urgent algorithm applies to this system for any ν and $m = \infty$. We start with the initial state: this state is urgent for process 0, so we explore the states resulting from the global transitions labeled $c_i!?1$ for all i. For any such i, the resulting state has process 0 in local state i, process i in local state 1, and all other processes and channels unchanged. This state is urgent for i, and so we explore the single transition $d_i!?1$. This returns us to the initial state, which is already in R. Hence the algorithm explores a total of $n + 1$ global states, and $2n$ transitions. Notice also that, in this case, the search does not explore any buffered communication, even though process 0 contains a wildcard receive.

4.2 Source-Specific Models and Synchronous Traces

We say that $\mathcal{M}$ is *source-specific* if for every receiving and send-receive state u in $\mathcal{M}$, $|Q(u)| = 1$; this corresponds to an MPI program which never uses MPI_ANY_SOURCE (though it may use MPI_ANY_TAG). We say that a path in $\mathcal{G}$ is *synchronous* if it consists solely of local and synchronous transitions.

Let $\mathcal{M}$ be any model and σ a global state of $\mathcal{M}$. If σ is urgent, then clearly σ cannot be potentially halted. Now if $\mathcal{M}$ is source-specific, the converse is also true. For if there is some $c \in$ Chan and $x \in$ msg(c) for which $c?x$ or $c!?x$ is enabled at σ, then $p =$ receiver$(c) \in$ Urgent(σ), since $Q(\text{state}_p(\sigma)) = \{c\}$.

Now suppose $\mathcal{M}$ is source-specific and T is a trace terminating in a potentially halted state σ. By Theorem 1, there exists a trace $\tilde{T} = (\tau_1, \ldots, \tau_n)$ in $\tilde{\mathcal{G}}$ terminating in σ, with $n \leq |T|$ and $||\tilde{T}|| = ||T||$. Let $\sigma_k = \text{des}(\tau_k)$ for $1 \leq k \leq n$ and let σ_0 be the initial state. Let i be the least integer for which σ_i is potentially halted. For $0 \leq j < i$, σ_j is not potentially halted, which as we have seen means that σ_j is urgent. This implies that τ_{j+1} is a local event, synchronous, or receive transition. But τ_{j+1} cannot be a receive: if it were, there would have to be a preceding send. In other words, $\tilde{T}^i$ is synchronous. We have proved:

Corollary 2. *Let $\mathcal{M}$ be a source-specific model of an MPI program and T a trace terminating in a potentially halted state σ. Then there exist $i \in \mathbf{N}$ and a trace $\tilde{T}$ in $\tilde{\mathcal{G}}$ that terminates in σ such that $|\tilde{T}| \leq |T|$, $||\tilde{T}|| = ||T||$, and $\tilde{T}^i$ is synchronous and terminates in a potentially halted state.*

This leads to the following, which generalizes [12, Theorem 7.4]. Note that 0 is used to denote the function on Chan which is identically 0. Note also that all of the examples of halting predicates given in Sec. 3 satisfy the condition on q.

Corollary 3. *Suppose $\mathcal{M}$ is a source-specific model of an MPI program, and q is a state predicate satisfying $q(\sigma) \Rightarrow q(\sigma')$ for any simple global transition (σ, σ', t). Let f denote the predicate $\mathsf{phalt} \Rightarrow q$, $\nu: \mathsf{Chan} \to \mathbf{N}^\infty$, and $m \in \mathbf{N}^\infty$. Then $\Pi(\mathcal{G}_{\nu,m}, f) \Leftrightarrow \Pi(\mathcal{G}_{0,m}^b, f)$.*

5 Related Work

The literature on partial order reduction techniques is too large to summarize here, but [1,4,11] and the references cited cover much of the ground. *Persistent set* techniques [4,5] form a family of POR methods that deal specifically with freedom from deadlock. Those techniques associate, to each global state σ encountered in the search, a subset T_σ of the set of all transitions enabled at σ, in such a way that the following condition holds: on any path in the full state graph departing from σ, no transition dependent on a transition on T_σ can occur without a transition in T_σ occurring first. (The word *transition* in this context corresponds to a set of our global transitions.) The reduced search explores only the transitions in T_σ, and so benefits whenever T_σ is a proper subset. If it is also the case that T_σ is empty only when there are no enabled transitions at σ, then we may conclude that the reduced search will explore all reachable deadlocked states [4, Thm. 4.3].

It should be emphasized, however, that here "deadlocked state" is used in the usual sense, to mean a state with no outgoing transitions. In our MPI context we call such states *absolutely halted*. An absolutely halted state is certainly potentially halted, but the converse is not always the case, and, in fact, the persistent set POR algorithms may miss potentially halted states. Consider, for example, the standard state graph (i.e., without the added synchronous transitions) arising from a model of an MPI program. For simplicity, let us assume the model has no send-receive states. Now for any global state σ, we could declare σ to be urgent if some process p were at either (i) a receiving state in which every receiving channel had at least one pending matching message, (ii) a local-event state, or (iii) a sending state. We could then let T_σ consist of the enabled events for the least urgent process (or all enabled events if no process is urgent), and this would satisfy the conditions of the previous paragraph. Consider a model with $\mathsf{Proc} = \{0,1\}$, in the natural order, a local event λ in process 1, and with state machines as follows:

The model contains a potentially halted state σ_1, obtained from the initial state σ_0 by executing λ. However, process 0 would be urgent at σ_0, so we would have $T_{\sigma_0} = \{c!1\}$. Hence the reduced search would not explore σ_1, and in fact would complete without encountering any potentially halted states.

We could attempt to correct this problem by simply not allowing the sending states to be urgent, and it can in fact be shown that this would lead to an algorithm that explored all potentially halted states. However, the algorithm would miss many of the opportunities for reduction. Consider, for example, a client server system with n clients. The system would not be in an urgent state until every client had sent at least one request. In particular, the reduced search would explore all possible states of the n request channels for which at least one channel is empty.

Our approach solves this problem by adding the synchronous transitions to the state graph and defining the T_σ to take advantage of those transitions under the appropriate circumstances. This solution cannot, strictly speaking, be characterized as a persistent set approach, since our T_σ do not necessarily satisfy the persistent set condition. Consider, for example, a client-server system with one client. At the initial state σ, our T_σ consists of the single transition labeled $c!?1$. But the path $c!1, c?1$ is also possible from σ, and both $c!1$ and $c?1$ are dependent on $c!?1$.

Other POR techniques preserve more complex temporal properties. The *ample set* framework [1, Chap. 10] is an example of these. Here, the T_σ must satisfy several conditions in addition to those described above for persistent sets. If all the conditions are met, then the reduced state graph is guaranteed to be stutter-equivalent to the full state graph, and hence can be used to verify any LTL$_{-X}$ property [1, Cor. 2 and Thm. 12].

Returning to the MPI context, any halting property can be expressed as an LTL$_{-X}$ property of the form $\Box(\mathsf{phalt} \Rightarrow q)$, and therefore, in theory, is amenable to the ample set approach. Now, however, another problem arises. In the ample set framework, a transition is *invisible* if it can never change the truth value of a predicate (such as phalt) used in the LTL formula. The *invisibility condition* requires that whenever T_σ is a proper subset of the set of all transitions enabled at σ, every transition in T_σ is invisible. Since any local event, receive, or synchronous transition might change phalt from false to true, these transitions are not necessarily invisible, and therefore an ample set algorithm would not include them in a T_σ (unless the T_σ consisted of all enabled transitions). This eliminates most, if not all, of the opportunities for reduction.

As it turns out, the ample set invisibility condition is unnecessarily strict, and all that is really required is that a transition never change phalt from true to false, which is certainly the case for local event, receive, and synchronous transitions, since they are not even enabled at potentially halted states. (Notice that send transitions can change phalt from true to false, which explains why it really would be a mistake to treat them as invisible.) Another condition, concerning cycles in the reduced graph, can also be safely ignored in our context. After these modifications, however, the ample set approach essentially reduces to the persistent set approach, discussed above.

Another deadlock-preserving reduction method is the *sleep set* technique [3, 4]. Sleep sets can be used in conjunction with the persistent set approach to further reduce the numbers of states and transitions explored. The idea is to associate to each state a dynamically changing set of transitions that can be safely ignored even if they appear in the persistent set for that state. It is possible that this method could be adapted to work with our urgent algorithm, an idea we hope to explore in future work.

6   Experimental Results

Eight scalable C/MPI programs were used for our empirical investigation. They range from standard toy concurrency examples to more complex programs from a well-known book on MPI [6]. For each, we constructed by hand an abstract model appropriate for verifying freedom from deadlock. These models were encoded as certain Java classes that can be read by the MPI-Optimized Verifier (MOVER), a Java tool developed for this project. Given the model and an object describing a halting property, MOVER can either (A₁) execute a generic depth-first search of the state space to verify the property or report any violations, (A₂) execute the Urgent algorithm to do the same, or (A₃) produce a Promela model that can be used by the model checker SPIN [7] to do the same.

The processes and channels in the Promela model correspond exactly to those in the MPI model. There are no variables in the Promela, other than the channels. The local states of a process are encoded by labeled positions in the code. States with multiple departing transitions are encoded using the Promela selection construct (`if...fi`). A never claim is inserted corresponding to the LTL formula `<>!(univenabled || terminated)`, where `univenabled` is defined to hold whenever a synchronous, local, or receive event is enabled (the definition refers to the lengths of the channels and the positions of the local processes), and `terminated` is defined to hold when all terminating processes are at final states. SPIN uses a POR algorithm that is similar to the ample set technique [8]. It might seem appropriate to use SPIN's `xr` and `xs` declarations, which declare a process to have exclusive read or write access to a channel and provide information to help the POR algorithm. However, this is not allowed, as the never claim makes reference to all the channels, and in fact an attempt to use those declarations causes SPIN to flag the error. This is SPIN's way of recognizing that the communication events may not be invisible with respect to the property.

(A different way to use SPIN to verify freedom from deadlock for MPI programs is described in [13]. In that approach, every send is immediately followed by a non-deterministic choice between blocking until the channel becomes empty and proceeding without blocking. Freedom from deadlock can then be checked in the usual way with SPIN, i.e., without a never claim. While we have not carried out an extensive comparison, it appears that the state-explosion is much worse for that approach than for the approach presented here, due to all the new states introduced by the non-deterministic choices.)

We applied all three approaches to each of the examples, increasing system size n until $n = 200$ or we ran out of memory. In each case we recorded the numbers of states and transitions explored, and the time and memory used. We used the Java2 SDK 1.4.2 with options -Xmx1900M and SPIN 4.2.0, with options -DCOLLAPSE -DMEMLIM=2800 -DSAFETY; the maximum search depth also had to be increased in some cases. The experiments were run on a Linux box with a 2.2 GHz Xeon processor and 4 GB of memory. In the one case where a deadlock was found, the searches were stopped after finding the first counterexample.

Figures 3 and 4 show the number of states explored. We first observe that the numbers for A_1 and A_3 are exactly equal in all cases where both searches completed. Since A_1 explores all reachable states, this means that SPIN's POR algorithm (on, by default) made no difference in the number of states explored. This is not surprising, since there are no invisible events for the algorithm to exploit. For the one case where a violation exists, SPIN did find the violation much sooner than either MOVER algorithm (Fig. 3(d)). This appears to be just a fluke related to process ordering: we ran the same problem but reversed the order in which the processes were declared (for both tools), and the results were almost exactly reversed.

For the Client-Server, Producer-Consumer, and the two exchange examples, the performance of A_2 was the most impressive, reducing the complexity class from one that is apparently exponential to one that is linear. For Monte Carlo and Master-Slave, both functions appear to be exponential, but the exponent for the A_2 function is lower (significantly so for Master-Slave), allowing it to scale further. In one case (Fig. 3(c)), the use of A_2 makes almost no difference, but there the number of reachable states was quadratic to begin with so there was not much room for improvement. The Master Producer-Consumer proved the most difficult: there seemed to be a small constant reduction but no approach could scale beyond $n = 4$.

For Producer-Consumer, we give on one graph (Fig. 4, left) the results for various values of ν. This graph demonstrates the impact of channel size on state explosion for systems that can buffer many messages. For $\nu = 0$, however, the number of reachable states for the system of size n is just $n + 1$, and A_2 searches that number of states for any value of ν, since the system contains no wildcard receives. We also give the time for the Master-Slave example; typical of these examples, the pattern is similar to that for the number of states.

In summary, the Urgent algorithm often dramatically reduced the number of states explored. It can never increase that number, as long as the search is carried to completion, nor did it appear to have a significant impact on the time required to complete the search. In contrast, the POR algorithm implemented in SPIN had no effect on the number of states explored.

7   Conclusions and Future Work

We have presented a POR-like optimization to the standard model checking algorithm for verifying halting properties of MPI programs. The algorithm seeks to control state explosion by limiting the number of transitions explored that

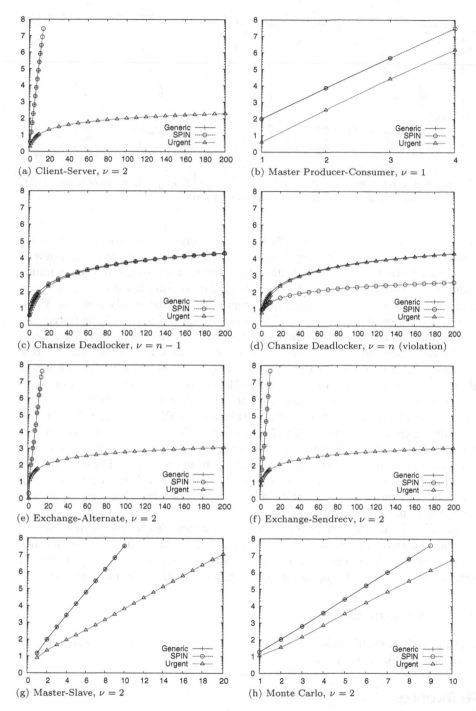

Fig. 3. Graphs of $y = \log_{10}(f(n))$, where $f(n)$ is the number of states explored for the system of size n, with channel size bound ν.

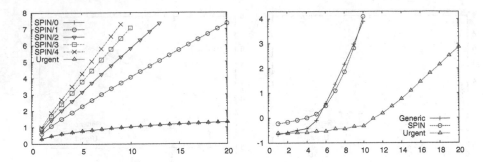

Fig. 4. Producer-Consumer states for $\nu \in \{0, 1, \ldots, 4\}$ ($\log_{10}$ of number of states, left), and Master-Slave time ($\log_{10}$ of number of seconds, right).

involve buffering messages. The technique also interacts well with the imposition of bounds on both the search depth and the sizes of the communication channels.

Earlier work showed that it suffices to consider only synchronous communication when verifying freedom from deadlock for certain MPI programs with no wildcard receives. We have shown how that result follows easily from the theorem that justifies our optimization. Moreover, we have shown that the restriction that forbids wildcard receives may be relaxed to allow the use of MPI_ANY_TAG.

We have demonstrated the effectiveness of our algorithm on several scalable examples, including some with wildcard receives. However, a better validation of effectiveness would utilize more "realistic" examples. There is no guarantee that scaling our simple examples presents the same kind of challenge to the Urgent algorithm that an actual production-level MPI code would. Due to the difficulty of creating models by hand, this task would benefit from an automated MPI model extractor. We intend to develop such a tool, and use it to verify not only freedom from deadlock, but also other halting properties. For example, we would like to model the arithmetic computations performed by an MPI program symbolically, and check that at termination the program has arrived at the correct arithmetic result.

Finally, the study of domain-specific approaches may also shed light on the general framework. It would be interesting to see if the ample set framework, for example, could be extended to incorporate the idea of switching between a synchronous and a buffering mode, generalizing our MPI-specific approach.

Acknowledgments

The author is grateful to George Avrunin and to Reviewer 3 for helpful comments on earlier drafts of this paper.

References

1. Clarke, Jr., E.M., Grumberg, O., Peled, D.A.: Model Checking. MIT Press, Cambridge (1999)

2. Dwyer, M.B., Hatcliff, J., Robby, Ranganath, V.P.: Exploiting object escape and locking information in partial-order reductions for concurrent object-oriented programs. Formal Methods in System Design **25** (2004) 199–240
3. Godefroid, P.: Using partial orders to improve automatic verification methods. In Clarke, E.M., Kurshan, R.P., eds.: Computer-Aided Verification, 2nd International Conference, CAV '90, New Brunswick, NJ, USA, June 1990, Proceedings. Volume 531 of Lecture Notes in Computer Science, Springer-Verlag (1990) 176–185
4. Godefroid, P.: Partial-Order Methods for the Verification of Concurrent Systems: An Approach to the State-Explosion Problem. Springer, Berlin (1996)
5. Godefroid, P., Pirottin, D.: Refining dependencies improves partial-order verification methods. In Courcoubetis, C., ed.: Computer-Aided Verification, 5th International Conference, CAV '93, Elounda, Greece, June/July 1993, Proceedings. Volume 697 of Lecture Notes in Computer Science, Springer-Verlag (1993) 438–449
6. Gropp, W., Lusk, E., Skjellum, A.: Using MPI: Portable Parallel Programming with the Message-Passing Interface. MIT Press, Cambridge, MA (1999)
7. Holzmann, G.J.: The SPIN Model Checker. Addison-Wesley, Boston (2004)
8. Holzmann, G.J., Peled, D.: An improvement in formal verification. In Hogrefe, D., Leue, S., eds.: Formal Description Techniques VII, Proceedings of the 7th IFIP WG6.1 International Conference on Formal Description Techniques, Berne, Switzerland, 1994. Volume 6 of IFIP Conference Proceedings, Chapman & Hall (1995) 197–211
9. Message Passing Interface Forum: MPI: A Message-Passing Interface standard, version 1.1. http://www.mpi-forum.org/docs/ (1995)
10. Message Passing Interface Forum: MPI-2: Extensions to the Message-Passing Interface. http://www.mpi-forum.org/docs/ (1997)
11. Peled, D.: Ten years of partial order reduction. In Hu, A.J., Vardi, M.Y., eds.: Computer Aided Verification, 10th International Conference, CAV '98, Vancouver, BC, Canada, June 28 – July 2, 1998, Proceedings. Volume 1427 of Lecture Notes in Computer Science, Springer (1998) 17–28
12. Siegel, S.F., Avrunin, G.S.: Modeling MPI programs for verification. Technical Report UM-CS-2004-75, Department of Computer Science, University of Massachusetts (2004)
13. Siegel, S.F., Avrunin, G.S.: Verification of MPI-based software for scientific computation. In Graf, S., Mounier, L., eds.: Model Checking Software: 11th International SPIN Workshop, Barcelona, Spain, April 1–3, 2004, Proceedings. Volume 2989 of Lecture Notes in Computer Science, Springer-Verlag (2004) 286–303

Generalized Typestate Checking
for Data Structure Consistency

Patrick Lam, Viktor Kuncak, and Martin Rinard

Computer Science and Artificial Intelligence Laboratory
Massachusetts Institute of Technology

Abstract. We present an analysis to verify abstract set specifications for programs that use object field values to determine the membership of objects in abstract sets. In our approach, each module may encapsulate several data structures and use membership in abstract sets to characterize how objects participate in its data structures. Each module's specification uses set algebra formulas to characterize the effects of its operations on the abstract sets. The program may define abstract set membership in a variety of ways; arbitrary analyses (potentially with multiple analyses applied to different modules in the same program) may verify the corresponding set specifications. The analysis we present in this paper verifies set specifications by constructing and verifying set algebra formulas whose validity implies the validity of the set specifications.

We have implemented our analysis and annotated several programs (75-2500 lines of code) with set specifications. We found that our original analysis algorithm did not scale; this paper describes several optimizations that improve the scalability of our analysis. It also presents experimental data comparing the original and optimized versions of our analysis.

1   Introduction

Typestate systems [7, 10, 12, 13, 21, 30] allow the type of an object to change during its lifetime in the computation. Unlike standard type systems, typestate systems can enforce safety properties that depend on changing object states.

This paper develops a new, generalized formulation of typestate systems. Instead of associating a single typestate with each object, our system models each typestate as an abstract set of objects. If an object is in a given typestate, it is a member of the set that corresponds to that typestate. This formulation immediately leads to several generalizations of the standard typestate approach. In our formulation, an object can be a member of multiple sets simultaneously, which promotes modularity and typestate polymorphism. It is also possible to specify subset and disjointness properties over the typestate sets, which enables our approach to support hierarchical typestate classifications. Finally, a typestate in our formulation can be formally related to a potentially complex property of an object, with the relationship between the typestate and the property verified using powerful independently developed analyses such as shape analyses or theorem provers.

We have implemented the idea of generalized typestate in the Hob program specification and verification framework [23, 24]. This framework supports the division of the

R. Cousot (Ed.): VMCAI 2005, LNCS 3385, pp. 430–447, 2005.

program into instantiable, separately analyzable modules. Modules encapsulate private state and export abstract sets of objects that support abstract reasoning about the encapsulated state. Abstraction functions (in the form of arbitrary unary predicates over the encapsulated state) define the objects that participate in each abstract set. Modules also export procedures that may access the encapsulated state (and therefore change the contents of the exported abstract sets). Each module uses set algebra expressions (involving operators such as set union or difference) to specify the preconditions and postconditions of exported procedures. As a result, the analysis of client modules that coordinate the actions of other modules can reason solely in terms of the exported abstract sets and avoid the complexity of reasoning about any encapsulated state.

When the encapsulated state implements a data structure (such as list, hash table, or tree), the resulting abstract sets characterize how objects participate in that data structure. The developer can then use the abstract sets to specify consistency properties that involve multiple data structures from different modules. Such a property might state, for example, that two data structures involve disjoint objects or that the objects in one data structure are a subset of the objects in another. In this way, our approach can capture global sharing patterns and characterize both local and global data structure consistency.

The verification of a program consists of the application of (potentially different) analysis plugins to verify 1) the set interfaces of all of the modules in the program and 2) the validity of the global data structure consistency properties. The set specifications separate the analysis of a complex program into independent verification tasks, with each task verified by an appropriate analysis plugin [23]. Our approach therefore makes it possible, for the first time, to apply multiple specialized, extremely precise, and unscalable analyses such as shape analysis [27,28] or even manually aided theorem proving [31] to effectively verify sophisticated typestate and data structure consistency properties in sizable programs [23,31].

Specification Language. Our specification language is the full first-order theory of the boolean algebra of sets. In addition to basic typestate properties expressible using quantifier-free boolean algebra expressions, our language can state constant bounds on the cardinalities of sets of objects, such as "a local variable is not null" or "the content of the queue is nonempty", or even "the data structure contains at least one and at most ten objects". Because a cardinality constraint counts all objects that satisfy a given property, our specification language goes beyond standard typestate approaches that use per-object finite state machines. Our specification language also supports quantification over sets. Universal set quantifiers are useful for stating parametric properties; existential set quantifiers are useful for information hiding. Note that quantification over sets is not directly expressible even in such sophisticated languages as first-order logic with transitive closure[1]. Despite this expressive power, our set specification language is decidable and extends naturally to Boolean Algebra with Presburger Arithmetic [22].

The Flag Analysis Plugin. The present paper describes the flag analysis plugin, which uses the values of integer and boolean object fields (flags) to define the meaning of ab-

---

[1] The first-order logic with transitive closure is the basis of the analysis [28]; our modular pluggable analysis framework [23] can incorporate an analyzer like TVLA [28] as one of the analysis plugins.

stract sets. It verifies set specifications by first constructing set algebra formulas whose validity implies the validity of the set specifications, then verifying these formulas using an off-the-shelf decision procedure. The flag analysis plugin is important for two reasons. First, flag field values often reflect the high-level conceptual state of the entity that an object represents, and flag changes correspond to changes in the conceptual state of the entity. By using flags in preconditions of object operations, the developer can specify key object state properties required for the correct processing of objects and the correct operation of the program. Unlike standard typestate approaches, our flag analysis plugin can enforce not only temporal operation sequencing constraints, but also the generalizations that our expressive set specification language enables.

Second, the flag analysis plugin can propagate constraints between abstract sets defined with arbitrarily sophisticated abstraction functions in external modules. The plugin can therefore analyze modules that, as they coordinate the operation of other modules, indirectly manipulate external data structures defined in those other modules. The flag analysis can therefore perform the intermodule reasoning required to verify global data structure invariants such as the inclusion of one data structure in another and data structure disjointness. Because the flag plugin uses the boolean algebra of sets to internally represent its dataflow facts, it can propagate and verify these constraints in a precise way.

To evaluate our flag analysis, we have annotated several benchmark programs with set specifications. We have verified our benchmarks (in part) using the flag analysis algorithm described in Section 3, with MONA [19] as the decision procedure for the boolean algebra of sets. We found that our original analysis algorithm did not scale. This paper describes several optimizations that our analysis uses to improve the running time of the algorithm and presents experimental data comparing the original and optimized versions of our analysis.

2   Specification Language

Our system analyzes programs in a type-safe imperative language similar to Java or ML. A program in our language consists of one of more modules; each module has an implementation section, a specification section, and an (analysis-specific) abstraction section. We next give an overview of the specification section.

Figure 1 presents the syntax for the specification section of modules in our language. This section contains a list of set definitions and procedure specifications and lists the names of types used in these set definitions and procedure specifications. Set declarations identify the module's abstract sets, while boolean variable declarations identify the module's abstract boolean variables. Each procedure specification contains a `requires`, `modifies`, and `ensures` clause. The `requires` clause identifies the precondition that the procedure requires to execute correctly; the `ensures` clauses identifies the postcondition that the procedure ensures when called in program states that satisfy the `requires` condition. The `modifies` clause identifies sets whose elements may change as a result of executing the procedure. For the purposes of this paper, `modifies` clauses can be viewed as a special syntax for a frame-condition conjunct in the `ensures` clause. The variables in the `ensures` clause can refer to both the

$$M ::= \text{spec module } m \ \{(\text{type } t)^* (\text{set } S)^* (\text{predvar } b)^* P^*\}$$
$$P ::= \text{proc } pn(p_1 : t_1, \ldots, p_n : t_n)[\text{returns } r : t]$$
$$[\text{requires } B] \ [\text{modifies } S^*] \ \text{ensures } B$$
$$B ::= SE_1 = SE_2 \mid SE_1 \subseteq SE_2 \mid \text{card}(SE){=}k$$
$$\mid \ B \wedge B \mid B \vee B \mid \neg B \mid \exists S.B \mid \forall S.B$$
$$SE ::= \emptyset \mid p \mid [m.] \, S \mid [m.] \, S'$$
$$\mid \ SE_1 \cup SE_2 \mid SE_1 \cap SE_2 \mid SE_1 \setminus SE_2$$

Fig. 1. Syntax of the Module Specification Language.

initial and final states of the procedure. Both requires and ensures clauses use arbitrary first-order boolean algebra formulas B extended with cardinality constraints. A free variable of any formula appearing in a module specification denotes an abstract set or boolean variable declared in that specification; it is an error if no such set or boolean variable has been declared. The expressive power of such formulas is the first-order theory of boolean algebras, which is decidable [20, 26]. The decidability of the specification language ensures that analysis plugins can precisely propagate the specified relations between the abstract sets.

3   The Flag Analysis

Our flag analysis verifies that modules implement set specifications in which integer or boolean flags indicate abstract set membership. The developer specifies (using the flag abstraction language) the correspondence between concrete flag values and abstract sets from the specification, as well as the correspondence between the concrete and the abstract boolean variables. Figure 2 presents the syntax for our flag abstraction modules. This abstraction language defines abstract sets in two ways: (1) directly, by stating a base set; or (2) indirectly, as a set-algebraic combination of sets. *Base sets* have the form $B = \{x : T \mid x.f{=}c\}$ and include precisely the objects of type T whose field f has value c, where c is an integer or boolean constant; the analysis converts mutations of the field f into set-algebraic modifications of the set B. *Derived sets* are defined as set algebra combinations of other sets; the flag analysis handles derived sets by conjoining the definitions of derived sets (in terms of base sets) to each verification condition and tracking the contents of the base sets. Derived sets may use named base sets in their definitions, but they may also use *anonymous* sets given by set comprehensions; the flag analysis assigns internal names to anonymous sets and tracks their values to compute the values of derived sets.

In our experience, applying several formula transformations drastically reduced the size of the formulas emitted by the flag analysis, as well as the time that the MONA

$$M ::= \text{abst module } m \ \{D^* \ P^*\}$$
$$D ::= \text{id}{=}D_r;$$
$$D_r ::= D_r \cup D_r \mid D_r \cap D_r \mid \text{id} \mid \{x : T \mid x.f{=}c\}$$
$$P ::= \text{predvar } p;$$

Fig. 2. Syntax of the Flag Abstraction Language.

decision procedure spent verifying these formulas. Section 4 describes these formula optimizations. These transformations greatly improved the performance of our analysis and allowed our analysis to verify larger programs.

3.1 Operation of the Analysis Algorithm

The flag analysis verifies a module M by verifying each procedure of M. To verify a procedure, the analysis performs abstract interpretation [5] with analysis domain elements represented by formulas. Our analysis associates quantified boolean formulas B to each program point. A formula F has two collections of set variables: unprimed set variables S denoting initial values of sets at the entry point of the procedure, and primed set variables S' denoting the values of these sets at the current program point. F may also contain unprimed and primed boolean variables b and b' representing the pre- and post-values of local and global boolean variables. The definitions in the abstraction sections of the module provide the interpretations of these variables. The use of primed and unprimed variables allows our analysis to represent, for each program point p, a binary relation on states that overapproximates the reachability relation between procedure entry and p [6, 17, 29].

In addition to the abstract sets from the specification, the analysis also generates a set for each (object-typed) local variable. This set contains the object to which the local variable refers and has a cardinality constraint that restricts the set to have cardinality at most one (the empty set represents a null reference). The formulas that the analysis manipulates therefore support the disambiguation of local variable and object field accesses at the granularity of the sets in the analysis; other analyses often rely on a separate pointer analysis to provide this information.

The initial dataflow fact at the start of a procedure is the precondition for that procedure, transformed into a relation by conjoining $S' = S$ for all relevant sets. At merge points, the analysis uses disjunction to combine boolean formulas. Our current analysis iterates `while` loops at most some constant number of times, then coarsens the formula to `true` to ensure termination, thus applying a simple form of widening [5]. The analysis also allows the developer to provide loop invariants directly[2]. After running the dataflow analysis, our analysis checks that the procedure conforms to its specification by checking that the derived postcondition (which includes the `ensures` clause and any required representation or global invariants) holds at all exit points of the procedure. In particular, the flag analysis checks that for each exit point e, the computed formula B_e implies the procedure's postcondition.

Incorporation. The transfer functions in the dataflow analysis update boolean formulas to reflect the effect of each statement. Recall that the dataflow facts for the flag analysis are boolean formulas B denoting a relation between the state at procedure entry and the state at the current program point. Let B_s be the boolean formula describing the

---

[2] Our typestate analysis could also be adapted to use predicate abstraction [1,2,16] to synthesize loop invariants, by performing data flow analysis over the space of propositional combinations of relationships between the sets of interest, and making use of the fact that the boolean algebra of sets is decidable. Another alternative is the use of a normal form for boolean algebra formulas.

effect of statement s. The incorporation operation $B \circ B_s$ is the result of symbolically composing the relations defined by the formulas B and B_s. Conceptually, incorporation updates B with the effect of B_s. We compute $B \circ B_s$ by applying equivalence-preserving simplifications to the formula

$$\exists \hat{S}_1, \ldots, \hat{S}_n.\ B[S_i' \mapsto \hat{S}_i] \wedge B_s[S_i \mapsto \hat{S}_i]$$

3.2 Transfer Functions

Our flag analysis handles each statement in the implementation language by providing appropriate transfer functions for these statements. The generic transfer function is a relation of the following form:

$$[\![\text{st}]\!](B) = B \circ \mathcal{F}(\text{st}),$$

where $\mathcal{F}(\text{st})$ is the formula symbolically representing the transition relation for the statement st expressed in terms of abstract sets. The transition relations for the statements in our implementation language are as follows.

Assignment Statements. We first define a generic frame condition generator, used in our transfer functions,

$$\text{frame}_x = \bigwedge_{S \neq x,\, S \text{ not derived}} S' = S \wedge \bigwedge_{p \neq x} (p' \Leftrightarrow p),$$

where S ranges over sets and p over boolean predicates. Note that derived sets are not preserved by frame conditions; instead, the analysis preserves the anonymous sets contained in the derived set definitions and conjoins these definitions to formulas before applying the decision procedure.

Our flag analysis also tracks values of boolean variables:

$$\mathcal{F}(\text{b} = \text{true}) = \text{b}' \wedge \text{frame}_b$$
$$\mathcal{F}(\text{b} = \text{false}) = (\neg \text{b}') \wedge \text{frame}_b$$
$$\mathcal{F}(\text{b} = \text{y}) = (\text{b}' \Leftrightarrow \text{y}) \wedge \text{frame}_b$$
$$\mathcal{F}(\text{b} = \langle \text{if cond}\rangle) = (\text{b}' \Leftrightarrow f^+(\langle \text{if cond}\rangle)) \wedge \text{frame}_b$$
$$\mathcal{F}(\text{b} =\,!e) = \mathcal{F}(\text{b} = e) \circ ((\text{b}' \Leftrightarrow \neg \text{b}) \wedge \text{frame}_b)$$

where $f^+(e)$ is the result of evaluating e, defined below in our analysis of conditionals. We also track local variable object references:

$$\mathcal{F}(\text{x} = \text{y}) = (\text{x}' = \text{y}) \wedge \text{frame}_x \qquad \mathcal{F}(\text{x} = \text{null}) = (\text{x}' = \emptyset) \wedge \text{frame}_x$$
$$\mathcal{F}(\text{x} = \text{new } t) = \neg(\text{x}' = \emptyset) \wedge \bigwedge_S (\text{x}' \cap S = \emptyset) \wedge \text{frame}_x$$

We next present the transfer function for changing set membership. If $R = \{x : T \mid x.\text{f} = c\}$ is a set definition in the abstraction section, we have:

$$\mathcal{F}(\text{x.f} = \text{c}) = R' = R \cup \text{x} \wedge \bigwedge_{S \in \text{alts}(R)} S' = S \setminus \text{x} \wedge \text{frame}_{\{R\} \cup \text{alts}(R)}$$

where $\text{alts}(R) = \{S \mid \text{abstraction module contains } S = \{x : T \mid x.\text{f} = c_1\}, c_1 \neq c.\}$

The rules for reads and writes of boolean fields are similar but, because our analysis tracks the flow of boolean values, more detailed:

$$\mathcal{F}(\texttt{x.f} = \texttt{b}) = \left(\begin{matrix} b \wedge B^{+\prime} = B^+ \cup \texttt{x} \\ \wedge \bigwedge_{S \in \text{alts(B+)}} S' = S \setminus \texttt{x} \end{matrix} \right) \wedge \left(\begin{matrix} \neg b \wedge B^{-\prime} = B^- \cup \texttt{x} \\ \wedge \bigwedge_{S \in \text{alts(B-)}} S' = S \setminus \texttt{x} \end{matrix} \right)$$
$$\wedge \text{frame}_{\{B\} \cup \text{alts}(B)}$$
$$\mathcal{F}(\texttt{b} = \texttt{y.f}) = (b' \Leftrightarrow y \in B^+) \wedge \text{frame}_b.$$

where $B^+ = \{x : T \mid x.\texttt{f} = \text{true}\}$ and $B^- = \{x : T \mid x.\texttt{f} = \text{false}\}$.
Finally, we have some default rules to conservatively account for expressions not otherwise handled,

$$\mathcal{F}(x.f = *) = \text{frame}_x \qquad \mathcal{F}(x = *) = \text{frame}_x.$$

Procedure Calls.   For a procedure call x=proc(y), our transfer function checks that the callee's requires condition holds, then incorporates proc's ensures condition as follows:

$$\mathcal{F}(\texttt{x} = \texttt{proc(y)}) = \text{ensures}_1(\texttt{proc}) \wedge \bigwedge S' = S$$

where both ensures$_1$ and requires$_1$ substitute caller actuals for formals of proc (including the return value), and where S ranges over all local variables.

Conditionals.   The analysis produces a different formula for each branch of an if statement if (e). We define functions $f^+(e), f^-(e)$ to summarize the additional information available on each branch of the conditional; the transfer functions for the true and false branches of the conditional are thus, respectively,

$$[\![\texttt{if (e)}]\!]^+(B) = f^+(e) \wedge B \qquad [\![\texttt{if (e)}]\!]^-(B) = f^-(e) \wedge B.$$

For constants and logical operations, we define the obvious f^+, f^-:

$$
\begin{aligned}
f^+(\text{true}) &= \text{true} & f^-(\text{true}) &= \text{false} \\
f^+(\text{false}) &= \text{false} & f^-(\text{false}) &= \text{true} \\
f^+(!e) &= f^-(e) & f^-(!e) &= f^+(e) \\
f^+(x\texttt{!=}e) &= f^-(x\texttt{==}e) & f^-(x\texttt{!=}e) &= f^+(x\texttt{==}e) \\
f^+(e_1 \texttt{ \&\& } e_2) &= f^+(e_1) \wedge f^+(e_2) & f^-(e_1 \texttt{ \&\& } e_2) &= f^-(e_1) \vee f^-(e_2)
\end{aligned}
$$

We define f^+, f^- for boolean fields as follows:

$$
\begin{aligned}
f^+(x.f) &= x \subseteq B & f^-(x.f) &= x \not\subseteq B \\
f^+(x.f\texttt{==false}) &= x \not\subseteq B & f^-(x.f\texttt{==false}) &= x \subseteq B
\end{aligned}
$$

where $B = \{x : T \mid x.\texttt{f} = \text{true}\}$; analogously, let $R = \{x : T \mid x.\texttt{f} = \texttt{c}\}$. Then,

$$f^+(x.f\texttt{==c}) = x \subseteq R \qquad f^-(x.f\texttt{==c}) = x \not\subseteq R.$$

We also predicate the analysis on whether a reference is null or not:

$$f^+(x\texttt{==null}) = x = \emptyset \qquad f^-(x\texttt{==null}) = x \neq \emptyset.$$

Finally, we have a catch-all condition,

$$f^+(*) = \text{true} \qquad f^-(*) = \text{true}$$

which conservatively captures the effect of unknown conditions.

Loops. Our analysis analyzes `while` statements by synthesizing loop invariants or by verifying developer-provided loop invariants. To synthesize a loop invariant, it iterates the analysis of the loop body until it reaches a fixed point, or until N iterations have occurred (in which case it synthesizes true). The conditional at the top of the loop is analyzed the same way `if` statements are analyzed. We can also verify explicit loop invariants; these simplify the analysis of `while` loops and allow the analysis to avoid the fixed point computation involved in deriving a loop invariant. Developer-supplied explicit loop invariants are automatically conjoined with the frame conditions generated by the containing procedure's modifies clause to ease the burden on the developer.

Assertions and Assume Statements. We analyze statement s of the form `assert A` by showing that the formula for the program point s implies A. Assertions allow developers to check that a given set-based property holds at an intermediate point of a procedure. Using `assume` statements, we allow the developer to specify properties that are known to be true, but which have not been shown to hold by this analysis. Our analysis prints out a warning message when it processes assume statements, and conjoins the assumption to the current dataflow fact. Assume statements have proven to be valuable in understanding analysis outcomes during the debugging of procedure specifications and implementations. Assume statements may also be used to communicate properties of the implementation that go beyond the abstract representation used by the analysis.

Return Statements. Our analysis processes the statement `return x` as an assignment `rv = x`, where `rv` is the name given to the return value in the procedure declaration. For all return statements (whether or not a value is returned), our analysis checks that the current formula implies the procedure's postcondition and stops propagating that formula through the procedure.

3.3   Verifying Implication of Dataflow Facts

A compositional program analysis needs to verify implication of constraints as part of its operation. Our flag analysis verifies implication when it encounters an assertion, procedure call, or procedure postcondition. In these situations, the analysis generates a formula of the form $B \Rightarrow A$ where B is the current dataflow fact and A is the claim to be verified[3]. The implication to be verified, $B \Rightarrow A$, is a formula in the boolean algebra of sets. We use the MONA decision procedure to check its validity [18].

4   Boolean Algebra Formula Transformations

In our experience, applying several formula transformations drastically reduced the size of the formulas emitted by the flag analysis, as well as the time needed to determine their validity using an external decision procedure; in fact, some benchmarks could

---

[3] Note that B may be unsatisfiable; this often indicates a problem with the program's specification. The flag analysis can, optionally, check whether B is unsatisfiable and emit a warning if it is. This check enabled us to improve the quality of our specifications by identifying specifications that were simply incorrect.

only be verified with the formula transformations enabled. This subsection describes the transformations we found to be useful.

Smart Constructors. The constructors for creating boolean algebra formulas apply peephole transformations as they create the formulas. Constant folding is the simplest peephole transformation: for instance, attempting to create $B \land \mathsf{true}$ gives the formula B. Our constructors fold constants in implications, conjunctions, disjunctions, and negations. Similarly, attempting to quantify over unused variables causes the quantifier to be dropped: $\exists x.F$ is created as just F when x is not free in F. Most interestingly, we factor common conjuncts out of disjunctions: $(A \land B) \lor (A \land C)$ is represented as $A \land (B \lor C)$. Conjunct factoring greatly reduces the size of formulas tracked after control-flow merges, since most conjuncts are shared on both control-flow branches. The effects of this transformations appear similar to the effects of SSA form conversion in weakest precondition computation [14, 25].

Basic Quantifier Elimination. We symbolically compute the composition of statement relations during the incorporation step by existentially quantifying over all state variables. However, most relations corresponding to statements modify only a small part of the state and contain the frame condition that indicates that the rest of the state is preserved. The result of incorporation can therefore often be written in the form $\exists x.x = x_1 \land F(x)$, which is equivalent to $F(x_1)$. In this way we reduce both the number of conjuncts and the number of quantifiers. Moreover, this transformation can reduce some conjuncts to the form $t = t$ for some Boolean algebra term t, which is a true conjunct that is eliminated by further simplifications.

It is instructive to compare our technique to weakest precondition computation [14] and forward symbolic execution [4]. These techniques are optimized for the common case of assignment statements and perform relation composition and quantifier elimination in one step. Our technique achieves the same result, but is methodologically simpler and applies more generally. In particular, our technique can take advantage of equalities in transfer functions that are not a result of analyzing assignment statements, but are given by explicit formulas in ensures clauses of procedure specifications. Such transfer functions may specify more general equalities such as $A = A' \cup x \land B' = B \cup x$ which do not reduce to simple backward or forward substitution.

Quantifier Nesting. We have experimentally observed that the MONA decision procedure works substantially faster when each quantifier is applied to the smallest scope possible. We have therefore implemented a quantifier nesting step that reduces the scope of each quantifier to the smallest possible subformula that contains all free variables in the scope of the quantifier. For example, our transformation replaces the formula $\forall x. \forall y. (f(x) \Rightarrow g(y))$ with $(\exists x. f(x)) \Rightarrow (\forall y. g(y))$.

To take maximal advantage of our transformations, we simplify formulas after applying incorporation and before invoking the decision procedure. Our global simplification step rebuilds formulas bottom-up and applies simplifications to each subformula.

5   Other Plugins

In addition to the flag plugin, we also implemented a shape analysis plugin that uses the PALE analysis tool to verify detailed properties of linked data structures such as lists and trees. This plugin represents an extreme case in the precision of properties that fully automated analyses can verify. Nevertheless, we were interested in verifying even more detailed and precise data structure consistency properties. Namely, we sought to verify properties of array-based data structures such as hash tables, which are outside the scope of the PALE tool. We therefore implemented a theorem proving plugin which generates verification conditions suitable for partially manual verification using the Isabelle proof checker [31]. One of the goals of this effort is build up a library of instantiable verified data structure implementation modules. Ideally, such a library would eliminate internal data structure consistency as a concern during development, leaving developers free to operate exclusively at the level of abstract sets to concentrate on broader application-specific consistency properties that cut across multiple data structures.

6   Experience

We have implemented our modular pluggable analysis system, populated it with several analyses (including the flag, shape analysis, and theorem prover plugins), and used the system to develop several benchmark programs and applications. Table 1 presents a subset of the benchmarks we ran through our system; full descriptions of our benchmarks (as well as the full source code for our modular pluggable analysis system) are available at our project homepage at http://cag.csail.mit.edu/~plam/hob. Minesweeper and water are complete applications; the others are either computational patterns (compiler, scheduler, ctas) or data structures (prodcons). Compiler models a constant-folding compiler pass, scheduler models an operating system scheduler, and ctas models the core of an air-traffic control system. The board, controller, and view modules are the core minesweeper modules; atom, ensemble, and h2o are the core water modules. The **bold** entries indicate system totals for minesweeper and water; note that minesweeper includes several other modules, some of which are analyzed by the shape analysis and theorem proving plugins, not the flag plugin.

We next present the impact of the formula transformation optimizations, then discuss the properties that we were able to specify and verify in the minesweeper and water benchmarks.

6.1   Formula Transformation Optimizations

We analyzed our benchmarks on a 2.80GHz Pentium 4, running Linux, with 2 gigabytes of RAM. Table 2 summarizes the results of our formula transformation optimizations. Each line summarizes a specific benchmark with a specific optimization configuration. A √ in the "Smart Constructors" column indicates that the smart constructors optimization is turned on; a × indicates that it is turned off. Similarly, a √ in the "Optimizations" column indicates that all other optimizations are turned on; a × indicates that they are turned off. The "Number of nodes" column reports the sizes (in terms of AST node

Table 1. Benchmark characteristics.

	Number of modules	Lines of spec	Lines of impl
prodcons		41	50
compiler		75	143
scheduler		34	22
ctas		49	53
board		78	168
controller		43	133
view		43	372
minesweeper	7	236	750
atom		31	64
ensemble		164	883
h2o		158	420
water	10	582	1976

Table 2. Formula sizes before and after transformation.

	Optimizations	Smart Constructors	Number of nodes	Optimization ratio	MONA time	Flag time
prodcons	✓	✓, ×	12306	2.46	0.17	0.03
	×	✓, ×	30338	1.00	0.27	0.04
compiler	✓	✓	15854	32.06	0.45	5.10
	✓	×	28003	18.15	0.60	6.19
	×	✓, ×	508375	1.00	N/A	60.27
scheduler	✓	✓, ×	442	2.44	0.05	0.04
	×	✓, ×	1082	1.00	0.12	0.14
ctas	✓	✓, ×	2874	3.18	0.21	0.12
	×	✓, ×	9141	1.00	12.79	0.33
board	✓	✓	28658	41.43	1.92	18.89
	✓	×	106550	11.14	11.45	29.27
	×	✓	926321	1.28	N/A	134.94
	×	×	1187379	1.00	N/A	151.46
controller	✓	✓	6759	4.23	0.41	0.18
	✓	×	7101	4.02	0.41	0.18
	×	✓, ×	28594	1.00	3.08	0.54
view	✓	✓	15878	59.08	1.07	12.38
	✓	×	53925	17.39	1.45	18.88
	×	✓, ×	93800	1.00	N/A	263.15
atom	✓	✓	9677	3.14	0.53	0.13
	✓	×	10244	2.97	0.54	0.13
	×	✓, ×	30447	1.00	40.95	0.43
ensemble	✓	✓	120279	20.60	50.90	34.15
	✓	×	148748	16.66	105.59	47.06
	×	✓, ×	2478004	1.00	N/A	464.52
h2o	✓	✓	205933	4.32	73.80	477.01
	✓	×	206167	4.31	81.85	475.86
	×	✓, ×	889637	1.00	N/A	1917.99

counts) of the resulting boolean algebra formulas. Our results indicate that the formula transformations reduce the formula size by 2 to 60 times (often with greater reductions for larger formulas); the Optimization Ratio column presents the reduction obtained in formula size. The "MONA time" column presents the time spent in the MONA decision procedure (up to 73 seconds after optimization); the "Flag time" column presents the time spent in the flag analysis, excluding the decision procedure (up to 477 seconds after optimization). Without optimization, MONA could not successfully check the formulas for the compiler, board, view, ensemble and h2o modules because of an out of memory error.

6.2 Minesweeper

We next illustrate how our approach enables the verification of properties that span multiple modules. Our minesweeper implementation has several modules: a game board module (which represents the game state), a controller module (which responds to user input), a view module (which produces the game's output), an exposed cell module (which stores the exposed cells in an array), and an unexposed cell module (which stores the unexposed cells in an instantiated linked list). There are 750 non-blank lines of implementation code in the 6 implementation modules and 236 non-blank lines in the specification and abstraction modules.

Minesweeper uses the standard model-view-controller (MVC) design pattern [15]. The board module (which stores an array of Cell objects) implements the model part of the MVC pattern. Each Cell object may be mined, exposed or marked. The board module represents this state information using the isMined, isExposed and isMarked fields of Cell objects. At an abstract level, the sets MarkedCells, MinedCells, ExposedCells, UnexposedCells, and U (for Universe) represent sets of cells with various properties; the U set contains all cells known to the board. The board also uses a global boolean variable gameOver, which it sets to true when the game ends.

Our system verifies that our implementation has the following properties (among others):

- The sets of exposed and unexposed cells are disjoint; unless the game is over, the sets of mined and exposed cells are also disjoint.
- The set of unexposed cells maintained in the board module is identical to the set of unexposed cells maintained in the UnexposedList list.
- The set of exposed cells maintained in the board module is identical to the set of exposed cells maintained in the ExposedSet array.
- At the end of the game, all cells are revealed; *i.e.* the set of unexposed cells is empty.

Although our system focuses on using sets to model program state, not every module needs to define its own abstract sets. Indeed, certain modules may not define any abstract sets of their own, but instead coordinate the activity of other modules to accomplish tasks. The view and controller modules are examples of such modules. The view module has no state at all; it queries the board for the current game state and calls the system graphics libraries to display the state.

Because these modules coordinate the actions of other modules – and do not encapsulate any data structures of their own – the analysis of these modules must operate solely at the level of abstract sets. Our analysis is capable of ensuring the validity of these modules, since it can track abstract set membership, solve formulas in the boolean algebra of sets, and incorporate the effects of invoked procedures as it analyzes each module. Note that for these modules, our analysis need not reason about any correspondence between concrete data structure representations and abstract sets.

The set abstraction supports typestate-style reasoning at the level of individual objects (for example, all objects in the ExposedCells set can be viewed as having a conceptual typestate Exposed). Our system also supports the notion of global typestate. The board module, for example, has a global gameOver variable which indicates whether or not the game is over. The system uses this variable and the definitions of relevant sets to maintain the global invariant gameOver | disjoint(MinedCells, ExposedCells).

This global invariant connects a global typestate property – is the game over? – with a object-based typestate state property evaluated on objects in the program – there are no mined cells that are also exposed. Our analysis plugins verify these global invariants by conjoining them to the preconditions and postconditions of methods. Note that global invariants must be true in the initial state of the program. If some initializer must execute to establish an invariant, then the invariant can be guarded by a global typestate variable.

Another invariant concerns the correspondence between the ExposedCells, UnexposedCells, ExposedSet.Content, and UnexposedList.Content sets:

```
(ExposedCells = ExposedSet.Content) & (UnexposedCells = UnexposedList.Content)
```

Our analysis verifies this property by conjoining it to the ensures and requires clauses of appropriate procedures. The board module is responsible for maintaining this invariant. Yet the analysis of the board module does not, in isolation, have the ability to completely verify the invariant: it cannot reason about the concrete state of ExposedSet.Content or UnexposedList.Content (which are defined in other modules). However, the ensures clauses of its callees, in combination with its own reasoning that tracks membership in the ExposedCells set, enables our analysis to verify the invariant (assuming that ExposedSet and UnexposedList work correctly).

Our system found a number of errors during the development and maintenance of our minesweeper implementation. We next present one of these errors. At the end of the game, minesweeper exposes the entire game board; we use removeFirst to remove all elements from the unexposed list, one at a time. After we have exposed the entire board, we can guarantee that the list of unexposed cells is empty:

```
proc drawFieldEnd()
    requires ExposedList.setInit & Board.gameOver &
            (UnexposedList.Content <= Board.U)
    modifies UnexposedList.Content, Board.ExposedCells,
            Board.UnexposedCells, ExposedList.Content,
            UnexposedList.Content
    ensures card(UnexposedList.Content') = 0;
```

because the implementation of the `drawFieldEnd` procedure loops until `isEmpty` returns `true`, which also guarantees that the `UnexposedList.Content` set is empty. The natural way to write the iteration in this procedure would be:

```
while (UnexposedList.isEmpty()) {
    Cell c = UnexposedList.removeFirst();
    drawCellEnd(c);
}
```

and indeed, this was the initial implementation of that code. However, when we attempted to analyze this code, we got the following error message:

```
Analyzing proc drawFieldEnd...
Error found analyzing procedure drawFieldEnd:
    requires clause in a call to procedure View.drawCellEnd.
```

Upon further examination, we found that we were breaking the invariant ensuring that `Board.ExposedCells` equals `UnexposedList.Content`. The correct way to preserve the invariant is by calling `Board.setExposed`, which simultaneously sets the `isExposed` flag and removes the cell from the `UnexposedList`:

```
Cell c = UnexposedList.getFirst();
Board.setExposed(c, true);
drawCellEnd(c);
```

6.3   Water

Water is a port of the Perfect Club benchmark MDG [3]. It uses a predictor/corrector method to evaluate forces and potentials in a system of water molecules in the liquid state. The central loop of the computation performs a time step simulation. Each step predicts the state of the simulation, uses the predicted state to compute the forces acting on each molecule, uses the computed forces to correct the prediction and obtain a new simulation state, then uses the new simulation state to compute the potential and kinetic energy of the system.

Water consists of several modules, including the `simparm`, `atom`, `H2O`, `ensemble`, and `main` modules. These modules contain 2000 lines of implementation and 500 lines of specification. Each module defines sets and boolean variables; we use these sets and variables to express safety properties about the computation.

The `simparm` module, for instance, is responsible for recording simulation parameters, which are stored in a text file and loaded at the start of the computation. This module defines two boolean variables, `Init` and `ParmsLoaded`. If `Init` is true, then the module has been initialized, *i.e.* the appropriate arrays have been allocated on the heap. If `ParmsLoaded` is true, then the simulation parameters have been loaded from disk and written into these arrays. Our analysis verifies that the program does not load simulation parameters until the arrays have been allocated and does not read simulation parameters until they have been loaded from the disk and written into the arrays.

The fundamental unit of the simulation is the atom, which is encapsulated within the `atom` module. Atoms cycle between the *predicted* and *corrected* states, with the `predic` and `correc` procedures performing the computations necessary to effect these state changes. A correct computation will only predict a corrected atom or correct a predicted atom. To enforce this property, we define two sets Predic and Correc and populate them with the predicted and corrected atoms, respectively. The correc procedure operates on a single atom; its precondition requires this atom to be a member of the Predic set. Its postcondition ensures that, after successful completion, the atom is no longer in the Predic set, but is instead in the Correc set. The predic procedure has a corresponding symmetric specification.

Atoms belong to molecules, which are handled by the H2O module. A molecule tracks the position and velocity of its three atoms. Like atoms, each module can be in a variety of conceptual states. These states indicate not only whether the program has predicted or corrected the position of the molecule's atoms but also whether the program has applied the intra-molecule force corrections, whether it has scaled the forces acting on the molecule, etc. We verify the invariant that when the molecule is in the predicted or corrected state, the atoms in the molecule are also in the same state. The interface of the H2O module ensures that the program performs the operations on each molecule in the correct order – for example, the bndry procedure may operate only on molecules in the Kineti set (which have had their kinetic energy calculated by the kineti procedure).

The ensemble module manages the collection of molecule objects. This module stages the entire simulation by iterating over all molecules and computing their positions and velocities over time. The ensemble module uses boolean predicates to track the state of the computation. When the boolean predicate INTERF is true, for example, then the program has completed the interforce computation for all molecules in the simulation. Our analysis verifies that the boolean predicates, representing program state, satisfy the following ordering relationship:

$$Init \leadsto INITIA \leadsto PREDIC \leadsto INTRAF \leadsto VIR \leadsto INTERF \leadsto \cdots$$

Our specification relies on an implication from boolean predicates to properties ranging over the collection of molecule objects, which can be ensured by a separate array analysis plugin [23].

These properties help ensure that the computation's phases execute in the correct order; they are especially valuable in the maintenance phase of a program's life, when the original designer, if available, may have long since forgotten the program's phase ordering constraints. Our analysis' set cardinality constraints also prevent empty sets (and null pointers) from being passed to procedures that expect non-empty sets or non-null pointers.

7   Related Work

Typestate systems track the conceptual states that each object goes through during its lifetime in the computation [7, 9–12, 30]. They generalize standard type systems in that the typestate of an object may change during the computation. Aliasing (or more generally, any kind of sharing) is the key problem for typestate systems – if the program uses one reference to change the typestate of an object, the typestate system must ensure that either the declared typestate of the other references is updated to reflect the new typestate or that the new typestate is compatible with the old declared typestate at the other references.

Most typestate systems avoid this problem altogether by eliminating the possibility of aliasing [30]. Generalizations support monotonic typestate changes (which ensure that the new typestate remains compatible with all existing aliases) [12] and enable the program to temporarily prevent the program from using a set of potential aliases, change the typestate of an object with aliases only in that set, then restore the typestate and reenable the use of the aliases [10]. It is also possible to support object-oriented constructs such as inheritance [8]. Finally, in the role system, the declared typestate of each object characterizes all of the references to the object, which enables the typestate system to check that the new typestate is compatible with all remaining aliases after a nonmonotonic typestate change [21].

In our approach, the typestate of each object is determined by its membership in abstract sets as determined by the values of its encapsulated fields and its participation in encapsulated data structures. Our system supports generalizations of the standard typestate approach such as orthogonal typestate composition and hierarchical typestate classification. The connection with data structure participation enables the verification of both local and global data structure consistency properties.

8 Conclusion

Typestate systems have traditionally been designed to enforce safety conditions that involve objects whose state may change during the course of the computation. In particular, the standard goal of typestate systems is to ensure that operations are invoked only on objects that are in appropriate states. Most existing typestate systems support a flat set of object states and limit typestate changes in the presence of sharing caused by aliasing. We have presented a reformulation of typestate systems in which the typestate of each object is determined by its membership in abstract typestate sets. This reformulation supports important generalizations of the typestate concept such as typestates that capture membership in data structures, composite typestates in which objects are members of multiple typestate sets, hierarchical typestates, and cardinality constraints on the number of objects that are in a given typestate. In the context of our Hob modular pluggable analysis framework, our system also enables the specification and effective verification of detailed local and global data structure consistency properties, including arbitrary internal consistency properties of linked and array-based data structures. Our system therefore effectively supports tasks such as understanding the global sharing patterns in large programs, verifying the absence of undesirable interactions, and ensuring the preservation of critical properties necessary for the correct operation of the program.

Acknowledgements

This research was supported by the DARPA Cooperative Agreement FA 8750-04-2-0254, DARPA Contract 33615-00-C-1692, the Singapore-MIT Alliance, and the NSF Grants CCR-0341620, CCR-0325283, and CCR-0086154.

References

1. T. Ball, R. Majumdar, T. Millstein, and S. K. Rajamani. Automatic predicate abstraction of C programs. In *Proc. ACM PLDI*, 2001.
2. T. Ball, A. Podelski, and S. K. Rajamani. Relative completeness of abstraction refinement for software model checking. In *TACAS'02*, volume 2280 of *LNCS*, page 158, 2002.
3. W. Blume and R. Eigenmann. Performance analysis of parallelizing compilers on the Perfect Benchmarks programs. *IEEE Transactions on Parallel and Distributed Systems*, 3(6):643–656, Nov. 1992.
4. L. Clarke and D. Richardson. Symbolic evaluation methods for program analysis. In *Program Flow Analysis: Theory and Applications*, chapter 9. Prentice-Hall, Inc., 1981.
5. P. Cousot and R. Cousot. Systematic design of program analysis frameworks. In *Proc. 6th POPL*, pages 269–282, San Antonio, Texas, 1979. ACM Press, New York, NY.
6. P. Cousot and N. Halbwachs. Automatic discovery of linear restraints among variables of a program. In *Conference Record of the 5th POPL*, pages 84–97, Tucson, Arizona, 1978. ACM Press, New York, NY.
7. R. DeLine and M. Fähndrich. Enforcing high-level protocols in low-level software. In *Proc. ACM PLDI*, 2001.
8. R. DeLine and M. Fähndrich. Typestates for objects. In *Proc. 18th ECOOP*, June 2004.
9. S. Drossopoulou, F. Damiani, M. Dezani-Ciancaglini, and P. Giannini. Fickle: Dynamic object re-classification. In *Proc. 15th ECOOP*, LNCS 2072, pages 130–149. Springer, 2001.
10. M. Fahndrich and R. DeLine. Adoption and focus: Practical linear types for imperative programming. In *Proc. ACM PLDI*, 2002.
11. M. Fähndrich and K. R. M. Leino. Declaring and checking non-null types in an object-oriented language. In *Proceedings of the 18th ACM SIGPLAN conference on Object-oriented programing, systems, languages, and applications*, pages 302–312. ACM Press, 2003.
12. M. Fähndrich and K. R. M. Leino. Heap monotonic typestates. In *International Workshop on Aliasing, Confinement and Ownership in object-oriented programming (IWACO)*, 2003.
13. J. Field, D. Goyal, G. Ramalingam, and E. Yahav. Typestate verification: Abstraction techniques and complexity results. In *Static Analysis, 10th International Symposium, SAS 2003, San Diego, CA, USA, June 11-13, 2003, Proceedings*, volume 2694 of *Lecture Notes in Computer Science*. Springer, 2003.
14. C. Flanagan and J. B. Saxe. Avoiding exponential explosion: Generating compact verification conditions. In *Proc. 28th ACM POPL*, 2001.
15. E. Gamma, R. Helm, R. Johnson, and J. Vlisside. *Design Patterns. Elements of Reusable Object-Oriented Software*. Addison-Wesley, Reading, Mass., 1994.
16. T. A. Henzinger, R. Jhala, R. Majumdar, and K. L. McMillan. Abstractions from proofs. In *31st POPL*, 2004.
17. B. Jeannet, A. Loginov, T. Reps, and M. Sagiv. A relational approach to interprocedural shape analysis. In *11th SAS*, 2004.
18. N. Klarlund and A. Møller. *MONA Version 1.4 User Manual*. BRICS Notes Series NS-01-1, Department of Computer Science, University of Aarhus, January 2001.
19. N. Klarlund, A. Møller, and M. I. Schwartzbach. MONA implementation secrets. In *Proc. 5th International Conference on Implementation and Application of Automata*. LNCS, 2000.
20. D. Kozen. Complexity of boolean algebras. *Theoretical Computer Science*, 10:221–247, 1980.
21. V. Kuncak, P. Lam, and M. Rinard. Role analysis. In *Proc. 29th POPL*, 2002.
22. V. Kuncak and M. Rinard. The first-order theory of sets with cardinality constraints is decidable. Technical Report 958, MIT CSAIL, July 2004.

23. P. Lam, V. Kuncak, and M. Rinard. On our experience with modular pluggable analyses. Technical Report 965, MIT CSAIL, September 2004.
24. P. Lam, V. Kuncak, K. Zee, and M. Rinard. The Hob project web page. http://cag.csail.mit.edu/~plam/hob/, 2004.
25. K. R. M. Leino. Efficient weakest preconditions. KRML114a, 2003.
26. L. Loewenheim. Über mögligkeiten im relativkalkül. *Math. Annalen*, 76:228–251, 1915.
27. A. Møller and M. I. Schwartzbach. The Pointer Assertion Logic Engine. In *Proc. ACM PLDI*, 2001.
28. M. Sagiv, T. Reps, and R. Wilhelm. Parametric shape analysis via 3-valued logic. *ACM TOPLAS*, 24(3):217–298, 2002.
29. M. Sharir and A. Pnueli. Two approaches to interprocedural data flow analysis problems. In *Program Flow Analysis: Theory and Applications*. Prentice-Hall, Inc., 1981.
30. R. E. Strom and S. Yemini. Typestate: A programming language concept for enhancing software reliability. *IEEE TSE*, January 1986.
31. K. Zee, P. Lam, V. Kuncak, and M. Rinard. Combining theorem proving with static analysis for data structure consistency. In *International Workshop on Software Verification and Validation (SVV 2004)*, Seattle, November 2004.

On the Complexity of Error Explanation

Nirman Kumar[1], Viraj Kumar[2,*], and Mahesh Viswanathan[2,**]

[1] Oracle Corporation, Redwood Shores, CA, USA,
nirman.kumar@oracle.com
[2] University of Illinois at Urbana-Champaign, Urbana, IL, USA,
{kumar,vmahesh}@cs.uiuc.edu

Abstract. When a system fails to satisfy its specification, the model checker produces an error trace (or counter-example) that demonstrates an undesirable behavior, which is then used in debugging the system. *Error explanation* is the task of discovering errors in the system or the reasons why the system exhibits the error trace. While there has been considerable recent interest in automating this task and developing tools based on different heuristics, there has been very little effort in characterizing the computational complexity of the problem of error explanation. In this paper, we study the complexity of two popular heuristics used in error explanation. The first approach tries to compute the smallest number of system changes that need to be made in order to ensure that the given counter-example is no longer exhibited, with the intuition being that these changes are the errors that need fixing. The second approach relies on the observation that differences between correct and faulty runs of a system shed considerable light on the sources of errors. In this approach, one tries to compute the correct trace of the system that is closest to the counter-example. We consider three commonly used abstractions to model programs and systems, namely, finite state Mealy machines, extended finite state machines and pushdown automata. We show that the first approach of trying to find the fewest program changes is NP-complete no matter which of the three formal models is used to represent the system. Moreover we show that no polynomial factor approximation algorithm for computing the smallest set of changes is possible, unless P = NP. For the second approach, we present a polynomial time algorithm that finds the closest correct trace, when the program is represented by a Mealy machine or a pushdown automata. When the program is represented by an extended finite state machine, the problem is once again NP-complete, and no polynomial factor approximation algorithm is likely.

1   Introduction

Model checking [1] is a popular technique for automated verification of software and hardware systems. One of the principal reasons for its wide spread use is the ability of the model checker to produce a witness to the violation of a property in the form of an error trace (counter-example). While counter-examples are useful

---

* Supported by DARPA/AFOSR MURI award F49620-02-1-0325.
** Supported by NSF CCF 04-29639.

R. Cousot (Ed.): VMCAI 2005, LNCS 3385, pp. 448–464, 2005.
© Springer-Verlag Berlin Heidelberg 2005

in debugging a system, the error traces can be very lengthy and they indicate only the *symptom* of the error. Locating the *cause* of the error (or the bug) is often an onerous task even with a detailed counter-example. Recently, considerable research effort [2–8] has been directed towards automating the process of *error explanation* (or *localizing errors* or *isolating error causes*) to assist in the debugging process by identifying possible causes for the faulty behavior. Error explanation tools are now featured in model checkers such as SLAM [9, 6] and Java PathFinder (JPF) [10, 7].

Error explanation is an intrinsically informal process that admits many heuristic approaches which cannot be justified formally. Most current approaches to this problem rely on two broad philosophical themes for justification. First, in order to explain something (like an error), one has to identify its "causes" [11]. And second is Occam's principle, which states that a "simpler" explanation is to be always preferred between two competing theories. The different approaches to error explanation primarily differ in what they choose to be the "causal theory" for errors. Two popular heuristics have been widely and successfully used in debugging. The first one relies on the observation that program changes which result in a system that no longer exhibits the offending error trace identify possible causes for the error [12–14, 3, 2]; in accordance with Occam's principle, one tries to find the minimum number of changes. The second, more popular approach [5–8] relies on the intuition that differences between correct and faulty runs of the system shed considerable light on the sources of errors. This approach tries to find correct runs exhibited by the system that *closely match* the error trace. They then infer the causes of the error from the correct executions and the given error-trace.

While algorithms for these heuristics have been developed based on sophisticated use of SAT solvers and model checkers [12, 13, 3, 2, 5–8], there has been very little effort to study the computational complexity of these methods. In this paper we study the computational complexity of applying the above mentioned heuristics to three commonly used abstractions to model systems[1]. The first and least expressive model we look at is that of Mealy Machines [15], which are finite state machines (FSMs) that produce outputs when transiting from one state to another; the reason we consider Mealy machines and not finite automata is because they are a generalization. The second model we consider are Extended FSMs, which are finite state machines equipped with a finite number of boolean variables which are manipulated in each transition. The third model we examine is that of Pushdown Automata (PDA) which have been widely used as a model of software programs in model checking[2]. Once again we consider a generalization of PDAs that produce outputs.

---

[1] We make no effort to judge the practical usefulness of these error explanation approaches. The interested reader is referred to the papers cited here for examples where these heuristics have been effective in debugging.

[2] In software model checking the more commonplace model is actually a boolean program with a stack, which is a combination of extended finite state machines and PDAs. While we do not explicitly consider this model, our results have consequences for doing error explanation for such boolean programs, which we point out.

The two approaches to error explanation yield three distinct notions of the 'smallest distance' between the given program and a correct program, which we now describe. The precise definitions of these distances depends on the representation used, and will be presented in Section 2.2. We investigate the complexity of computing these distances when the program is abstractly represented by one of the three computation models.

Minimum Edit Set. Let M be an abstract representation of the program. For an input string w_i and an output string w_o of the same length as w_i, an *edit set* is a set of transitions of M that can be changed so that the resulting program M' produces output w_o on input w_i. A *minimum edit set* $X_M(w_i, w_o)$ is an edit set of smallest size.

Closest-Output Distance. Let M be an abstract representation of the restriction of the program to correct runs. For an output string w_o, the *closest-output distance* $d_M(w_o)$ is the smallest Hamming distance between w_o and a string w that can be produced by M.

Closest-Input Distance. Let M be an abstract representation of the restriction of the program to correct runs. For an input string w_i, the *closest-input distance* $d_M(w_i)$ is the smallest Hamming distance between w_i and a string w that is in the language of the machine represented by M.

Remark 1. Note that the latter two distances are defined when the *restriction* of the program to correct runs is represented by one of the computation models we consider. The representations we consider are commonly used to model programs, and for most correctness properties of interest (e.g. those expressed in linear temporal logic) the subset of executions of the system satisfying such properties can be expressed using the same kind of abstraction.

Summary of Results. Our results can be summarized as follows. The problem of determining the size of a minimum edit set for given input/output strings and a program represented as a Mealy machine is NP-complete. In addition, there is no polynomial time algorithm for computing an edit set whose size is within a polynomial factor of the size of a minimum edit set unless P = NP. A couple of points are in order about these results. First, the intractability of this error explanation method for extended finite state machines and PDAs (and boolean programs) follows as a corollary because they are generalizations of the simple Mealy machine model. Second, since we prove these results for a deterministic model, we can also conclude the intractibility of this problem for nondeterministic models, which are typically encountered in practice.

We provide a more positive answer for the second error explanation approach. When the set of correct executions of a system can be represented by traces of pushdown automata, we present a polynomial time algorithm based on dynamic programming to determine the closest-output distance for a given output string. Since finite state machines are a special case of pushdown automata, this upper bound applies to them as well. However, when the set of correct traces is represented by an extended finite state machine, the results are radically different.

Not only is the problem of computing the closest-input distance NP-complete in this case, but we show that it is unlikely that polynomial factor approximation algorithms to compute the closest-input distance in polynomial time exist. Note that the typical model for programs used in model checking is boolean programs, which can be seen as PDAs with boolean variables. Since this model is a generalization of extended finite state machines, our lower bounds imply that the second error explanation method will be intractible for boolean programs as well.

Note also that for the purposes of error explanation, we are not just interested in computing the above distance measures, but rather in computing the closest correct execution. However, the results on computing the above distances have direct consequences to error explanation. The intractibility of computing the closest input distance for extended finite state machines implies that finding the closest correct trace is also intractible. Further, the dynamic programming based algorithm that we present for computing the closest-output distance for PDAs (and FSMs) can be easily modified in a standard manner, to yield not just the distance but also the closest correct trace to the given error trace.

The rest of the paper is organized as follows. In Section 2 we provide the formal definitions of system models and the problems whose complexity we investigate. Section 3 provides the hardness results on computing the minimum edit set. Section 4 provides a polynomial time algorithm to compute the closest output distance and a hardness result for the problem of computing the closest input distance. Finally, we present our conclusions in Section 5.

2   Preliminaries

2.1   Abstract Representations

In this section, we recall the definitions of the various formal models of systems that we consider in this paper, namely, Mealy machines, Extended finite state machines, and Pushdown Automata.

Mealy Machines. A (Σ, Ω)-FSM is a deterministic finite state Mealy machine $M = (V_M, i_M, \delta_M)$ with finite input alphabet Σ, finite output alphabet Ω, finite set of states V_M, initial state $i_M \in V_M$ and transition function $\delta_M : V_M \times \Sigma \to V_M \times \Omega$. For $w \in \Sigma^*$, $M(w)$ denotes the string in Ω^* generated by M on input w. We denote $\delta_M(u, \sigma) = (v, \omega)$ by the shorthand $u \xrightarrow{\sigma/\omega}_M v$.

Extended FSMs. Suppose X is a finite set of Boolean variables and $\mathcal{A}$ is the set of all possible assignments to variables in X, i.e. $\mathcal{A} = \{0, 1\}^X$. Suppose $\mathcal{B}$ is the set of all finite boolean expressions involving the variables in X and the constants $\top$ (true) and $\bot$ (false). A (Σ, X)-FSM is a tuple $M = (V_M, s_M, F_M, a_M, g_M, \delta_M)$ where:

1. V_M is a finite set of states, $F_M \subseteq V_M$ is the set of final (accepting) states ;
2. s_M is the initial state, $a_M \in \mathcal{A}$ is the initial assignment of variables ;
3. $g_M : V_M \times \Sigma \to \mathcal{B}$ is the guard function ;
4. $\delta_M : V_M \times \Sigma \to V_M \times \mathcal{A} \times \mathcal{A}$ is the transition function.

Executions of a (Σ, X)-FSM are defined as follows. The initial state is s_M and the initial assignment to the variables is a_M. If the current state is s, the current assignment is a, the input symbol is σ and $\delta_M(s, \sigma) = (s', a_T, a_F)$, then

- if $g_M(s, \sigma) = \bot$, no transition is possible ;
- if $g_M(s, \sigma) \neq \bot$, the next state is s' and the next assignment is a', where $a' = a_T$ if $g_M(s, \sigma)$ is satisfied by a, and $a' = a_F$ otherwise.

We use the shorthand notation $(s, \sigma) \xrightarrow[a_F]{a_T} s'$ to represent such a transition. We use the notation $(s, \sigma) \to s'$ when the new assignment is identical to the current assignment a. If $a \in \mathcal{A}$, we use the notation $a[x_i := b]$ to denote the assignment in $\mathcal{A}$ that is identical to a except that x_i is set to b. We use the notation $L_M \subseteq \Sigma^*$ to denote the set of strings accepted by M.

Remark 2. Note that any (Σ, Ω)-FSM $M = (V_M, i_M, \delta_M)$ can be modeled as a $(\Sigma \times \Omega, \emptyset)$-FSM M' where the guard function for any pair $(v, (\sigma, \omega))$ is $\top$ whenever M produces the output ω on input σ from state v, and $\bot$ otherwise.

Pushdown Automata. We formally define Pushdown Automata that produce outputs on each transition. We restrict ourselves slightly to nondeterministic pushdown automata which, on every transition, push or pop at most one symbol from the stack, and consume exactly one input symbol. This model is nevertheless powerful enough to capture visibly pushdown automata [16] or control flow graphs [17], which are typically used to model software systems in the model checking community. A (nondeterministic) (Σ, Ω)-PDA with finite input alphabet Σ and finite output alphabet Ω is a tuple $M = (V, V_i, \Gamma, \delta)$ where

1. V is a finite set of states, $V_i \subseteq V$ is the set of initial states ;
2. $\Gamma = \Gamma' \cup \{\bot\}$ is a finite stack alphabet, $\bot$ is the bottom-of-stack symbol ;
3. $\delta = \delta_c \cup \delta_r \cup \delta_i$ is the transition relation, where $\delta_c \subseteq (V \times \Sigma \times V \times \Gamma' \times \Omega)$, $\delta_r \subseteq (V \times \Sigma \times \Gamma' \times V \times \Omega)$ and $\delta_i \subseteq (V \times \Sigma \times V \times \Omega)$.

A transition $(u, \sigma, v, \gamma, \omega) \in \delta_c$ is a push-transition where on reading σ, γ is pushed onto the stack, ω is outputted and the state changes from u to v. Similarly, $(u, \sigma, \gamma, v, \omega) \in \delta_r$ is a pop-transition where on reading σ, if $\gamma \neq \bot$ is the top of the stack, the symbol γ is popped from the top of the stack, ω is outputted and the state changes from u to v. If the top of the stack is $\bot$, no pop-transition is possible. On internal transitions $(u, \sigma, v, \omega) \in \delta_i$, the stack does not change and ω is outputted while the state changes from u to v. Note that (Σ, Ω)-PDAs need not be deterministic.

The set of possible stacks S is $\Gamma'^* \bot$. We say that a *run* r exists from $(u_1, s_1) \in V \times S$ on input $w = \sigma_1 \sigma_2 \ldots \sigma_k \in \Sigma^*$ if $\exists (u_1, s_1), (u_2, s_2), \ldots, (u_k, s_k)$ such that, for every $j = 1, \ldots, k$, $(u_j, s_j) \in V \times S$ and one of the following transitions t_j exists in δ:

1. $t_j = (u_j, \sigma_j, u_{j+1}, \gamma, \omega_j) \in \delta_c$ such that $\gamma \in \Gamma'$ and $s_{j+1} = \gamma s_j$
2. $t_j = (u_j, \sigma_j, \gamma, u_{j+1}, \omega_j) \in \delta_r$ such that $\gamma \in \Gamma'$ and $s_j = \gamma s_{j+1}$
3. $t_j = (u_j, \sigma_j, u_{j+1}, \omega_j) \in \delta_i$ and $s_{j+1} = s_j$.

In this case, we say that the sequence of transitions $\bar{t} = t_1 t_2 \ldots t_k$ is *consistent* with the run r.

We say that $w \in \Sigma^*$ is a *valid input from state* $v \in V$ if there is a run r from $(v, \perp)$ on input w. We say that $w \in \Sigma^*$ is a *balanced input from state* $v \in V$ if there is a run r from $(v, \perp)$ on input w such that for some sequence $\bar{t}$ of transitions consistent with r, the number of push-transitions in $\bar{t}$ is equal to the number of pop-transitions in $\bar{t}$. If the output string produced by the sequence $\bar{t}$ is w' and the destination of the final transition in $\bar{t}$ is v', we use the notation $v \xrightarrow{w/w'}_M v'$ to denote the fact that M produces output w' on the balanced input w from v, and the state changes from v to v'.

We say that M can reach the state v and can produce the output $\omega_1 \omega_2 \ldots \omega_k$ on input w if w is a valid input from some state $u \in V_i$ and for some sequence of transitions $t_1 t_2 \ldots t_k$ consistent with a run from $(u, \perp)$ on input w, the output of t_j is ω_j for every $1 \leq j \leq k$ and the destination of t_k is v. Let $M(w)$ denote the set of all strings that M can produce on input w.

2.2 Problem Definitions

As mentioned in the introduction, we are interested in the examining the complexity of two heuristics for error explanation. The first heuristic tries to find the smallest number of program transformations that result in the error trace not being exhibited any longer. This problem is related to computing what we call a *minimum edit set* of a program, which we define formally below.

Minimum Edit Set. We define a minimum edit set when the program M is represented as a (Σ, Ω)-FSM. Given equal length strings $w_i \in \Sigma^*$, $w_o \in \Omega^*$, an *edit set* is a set $X \subseteq V_M \times \Sigma$ such that there is a (Σ, Ω)-FSM M' for which $V_{M'} = V_M$, $i_{M'} = i_M$, δ_M and $\delta_{M'}$ differ only on the set X and $M'(w_i) = w_o$. A *minimum edit set* $X_M(w_i, w_o)$ is a smallest edit set X.

Remark 3. Although we have defined minimum edit set only for Mealy machines, we could easily define it for the other models we consider as well. We shall show that this problem is intractible for Mealy machines. Since the other models are more general than Mealy machines, the intractibility result applies to these other models as well.

The second heuristic tries to find the closest correct computation to the given error trace. This is related to computing the *closest-output distance* that we define below.

Closest-Output Distance. We define the closest-output distance when the correct executions of the program are represented as a (Σ, Ω)-PDA M. Given a string $w_o \in \Omega^*$, the *closest-output distance* $d_M(w_o)$ is the smallest non-negative integer d for which there is a string $w \in M(w_i)$ for some $w_i \in \Sigma^*$ such that the Hamming-distance between w and w_o is d.

Remark 4. We will present a polynomial time algorithm for the problem of computing the closest-output distance, when the correct executions are modeled as a PDA (and a Mealy machine). Therefore, we formally define this problem for a model that has outputs as well, which is more general than a model without outputs. Again we formally define this problem only for PDAs, which is a most general model for which this upper bound applies. Also, for error explanation we would actually be interested in computing the closest correct computation and not just the distance, and we outline how this can be done in Section 4.

Finally, we show that applying the second heuristic when the correct traces are modeled as an extended finite state machine is difficult. We do this by showing that computing another distance measure is difficult; since we are proving a lower bound, this measure is defined for models without outputs.

Closest-Input Distance. We define the closest-input distance when the correct executions of the program are represented as a (Σ, X)-FSM M. Given a string $w_i \in \Sigma^*$, the *closest-input distance* $d_M(w_i)$ is the smallest non-negative integer d for which there is a string $w \in L_M$ such that the Hamming-distance between w and w_i is d.

3 Computing the Minimum Edit Set

3.1 NP-Completeness

Let M be a (Σ, Ω)-FSM. We consider the decision version of computing the size of $X_M(w_i, w_o)$, i.e. given a non-negative integer k, decide whether or not $|X_M(w_i, w_o)| \leq k$. Clearly, this problem is in NP: we guess an edit set X of size k and guess the changes to δ_M to be made on the set X. We then verify if $M'(w_i) = w_o$ for the resulting (Σ, Ω)-FSM M'.

We now show that the decision version of the problem is NP-hard, even when the size of the input and output alphabets (Σ and Ω) are bounded by a constant. We will reduce the HAMILTONIAN-CYCLE problem to our problem. Given a directed graph G, we construct a (Σ, Ω)-FSM M and input/output strings w_i and w_o such that any edit set must contain a certain set of transitions of M. The key idea is to show that this set of transitions is "small" if and only if G has a Hamiltonian cycle.

Reduction. The undirected HAMILTONIAN-CYCLE problem for graphs with at most one edge between any pair of vertices and with degree bounded by a constant is NP-complete (see the reduction from 3-CNF in [18]). Since undirected graphs are a special case of directed graphs, HAMILTONIAN-CYCLE is NP-complete for digraphs with outdegree bounded above by a constant d and with at most one edge between any ordered pair of vertices. Let $G = (V, E)$ be any such digraph, where $V = \{v_1, v_2, \ldots, v_n\}$ and for every $i = 1, 2, \ldots, n$, there is a non-negative integer $m_i \leq d$ and a permutation π_i of $(1, 2, \ldots, n)$ such that $(v_i, v_{\pi_i(k)}) \in E$ iff $k \leq m_i$.

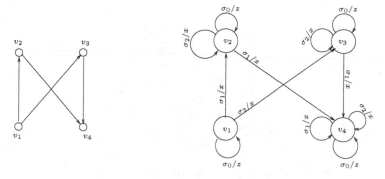

Fig. 1. A graph G and the associated FSM M.

Let $\Sigma = \{\sigma_0, \sigma_1, \sigma_2, \dots, \sigma_d\}$ and let $\Omega = \{x, y, z\}$. We construct an n-state (Σ, Ω)-FSM $M = (V_M, i_M, \delta_M)$, where $V_M = V$, $i_M = v_1$ and for every $i = 1, \dots, n$: (1) $v_i \xrightarrow{\sigma_0/z}_M v_i$, (2) $v_i \xrightarrow{\sigma_k/x}_M v_{\pi_i(k)}$ whenever $1 \leq k \leq m_i$, and (3) $v_i \xrightarrow{\sigma_k/x}_M v_i$ whenever $m_i < k \leq d$. Figure 1 depicts an example graph and the Mealy machine M with $d = 2$. We use the notation σ^k to denote σ repeated k times. Let $t_1 = yx^{n-1}$, and for $i = 2, \dots, n$ let $t_i = x^{n-i+1}yx^{i-2}$. Further, let

$$s_{1\dots d} = (\sigma_0\sigma_1\sigma_0^n)(\sigma_0\sigma_2\sigma_0^n)\dots(\sigma_0\sigma_d\sigma_0^n)$$
$$w_i = \sigma_0^{2n}s_{1\dots d}(\sigma_0 s_{1\dots d})^{n-1}$$
$$w_o = t_1 t_1 (yxt_1)^d \left(y(xxt_2)^d x(xxt_3)^d \dots x(xxt_n)^d\right)$$

Lemma 1. $|X_M(w_i, w_o)| \leq dn$ *iff* G *has a Hamiltonian cycle.*

Proof. Suppose G has a Hamiltonian cycle C. We obtain a (Σ, Ω)-FSM M' satisfying $M'(w_i) = w_o$ by modifying dn transitions of M as follows:

Since C is a Hamiltonian cycle in G, for every v_i there is exactly one v_j such that $(v_j, v_i) \in C$. For every such v_i, replace the transition $v_i \xrightarrow{\sigma_0/z}_M v_i$ with the transition $v_i \xrightarrow{\sigma_0/y}_{M'} v_j$ (if $v_i = v_1$), and with the transition $v_i \xrightarrow{\sigma_0/x}_{M'} v_j$ (if $v_i \neq v_1$). This accounts for n changes.

Further, by definition of M, for each such $(v_j, v_i) \in C$ there is exactly one transition of the form $v_j \xrightarrow{\sigma_k/x}_M v_i$ in M, and hence $d - 1$ transitions of the form $v_j \xrightarrow{\sigma_k/x}_M v_l$ where $v_l \neq v_i$. Replace each such transition with the transition $v_j \xrightarrow{\sigma_k/x}_{M'} v_i$. This accounts for $(d-1)n$ changes. Hence, M' differs from M in dn transitions. It is easy to verify that $M'(w_i) = w_o$.

Conversely, suppose G is not Hamiltonian. Consider a (Σ, Ω)-FSM $M' = (V_M, i_M, \delta_{M'})$ such that $M'(w_i) = w_o$. We claim that M' satisfies the following properties for every $1 \leq i, j, \leq n$:

1. The edges corresponding to the σ_0-labeled transitions of M' form a Hamiltonian cycle, i.e. the sequence of states reached in M' from v_i on input $\sigma_0, \sigma_0^2, \dots, \sigma_0^n$ is a permutation of the set of states V_M and the state reached in M' from v_i on input σ_0^n is v_i.

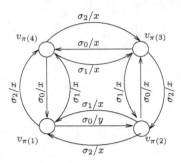

Fig. 2. A solution FSM for the example graph G.

2. $v_i \xrightarrow{\sigma_0/t} {}_{M'} v_i'$ for some $v_i' \in V$, where $t = y$ if $i = 1$ and $t = x$ otherwise.

3. If $v_i \xrightarrow{\sigma_0/t} {}_{M'} v_j$ for some $t \in \{x, y\}$, then $v_j \xrightarrow{\sigma_k/x} {}_{M'} v_i$ for every $k = 1, \ldots, d$.

To see this, consider the prefix σ_0^{2n} of w_i and the corresponding prefix $t_1 t_1 = yx^{n-1}yx^{n-1}$ of w_o. For every $i = 1, \ldots, n$ let $v_{\pi(i)}$ be the state reached in M' from v_1 on input σ_0^{i-1} (note that $\pi(1) = 1$). On reaching state $v_{\pi(i)}$, we note that the output produced by M' on the subsequent input σ_0^n is t_i. Since, for distinct i, j we have $t_i \neq t_j$, $(\pi(1), \ldots, \pi(n))$ must be a permutation of $(1, \ldots, n)$. Also, the state v reached in M' on input σ_0 from $v_{\pi(n)}$ produces output t_1 on subsequent input σ_0^n. Since M' has n states, v must in fact be v_1. In other words, we have the following cycle in M' obtained by following the edges labeled by σ_0:
$v_1 \xrightarrow{\sigma_0/y} {}_{M'} v_{\pi(2)} \xrightarrow{\sigma_0/x} {}_{M'} v_{\pi(3)} \xrightarrow{\sigma_0/x} {}_{M'} \cdots \xrightarrow{\sigma_0/x} {}_{M'} v_{\pi(n)} \xrightarrow{\sigma_0/x} {}_{M'} v_1$. Hence M' satisfies the first two properties.

As observed above, from each state $v_{\pi(i)}$, M' produces the unique output t_i on input σ_0^n and returns to state $v_{\pi(i)}$. Hence the output produced by M' on input σ_0^n can be used to identify the current state in M'. The string $s_{1\ldots d}$ defined above consists of d substrings of the form $\sigma_0 \sigma_k \sigma_0^n$, where $k = 1, \ldots, d$. Since $M'(w_i) = w_o$, it follows that for every $i = 1, \ldots, n$ and every $k = 1, \ldots, d$, M' goes from state $v_{\pi(i)}$ to $v_{\pi(i)}$ on input $\sigma_0 \sigma_k$ with output of the form tx (where $t \in \{x, y\}$). Hence, M' also satisfies the third property. For the example presented in Figure 1, a solution Mealy machine M' must be as depicted in Figure 2.

Since M' satisfies the first and third properties, for every $i = 1, \ldots, n$ and every $k = 1, \ldots, d$: $v_{\pi(i+1)} \xrightarrow{\sigma_k/x} {}_{M'} v_{\pi(i)}$ (where $\pi(n + 1) = \pi(1)$). Now $G = (V, E)$ is not Hamiltonian, so there is at least one $j \in \{1, \ldots, n\}$ such that $(v_{\pi(j+1)}, v_{\pi(j)}) \notin E$. Thus, there is no transition of the form $v_{\pi(j+1)} \xrightarrow{\sigma_k/x} {}_M v_{\pi(j)}$ in M. Also, for every $i \neq j$, there is at most one transition of the form $v_{\pi(i+1)} \xrightarrow{\sigma_k/x} {}_M v_{\pi(i)}$ in M. Hence, M' differs from M in at least $d + (d-1)(n-1)$ transitions.

Furthermore, since M' satisfies the second property, it clearly differs from M on the n σ_0-labeled transitions. Thus, M' differs from M in at least $dn + 1$ transitions. Hence, $|X_M(w_i, w_o)| > dn$. □

This completes the proof of NP-completeness for the decision version of computing $|X_M(w_i, w_o)|$ when M is a (Σ, Ω)-FSM.

Remark 5. Note that (Σ, Ω)-FSMs are restricted versions of $(\Sigma \times \Omega, X)$-FSMs (as observed in Remark 2) and (Σ, Ω)-PDAs. It is easy to show that the decision version of computing $|X_M(w_i, w_o)|$ is also in NP when M is a $(\Sigma \times \Omega, X)$-FSM or a (Σ, Ω)-PDA. Hence, the decision version of computing $|X_M(w_i, w_o)|$ is also NP-complete for these models.

3.2 Inapproximability Result

Given a (Σ, Ω)-FSM $M = (V_M, i_M, \delta_M)$ and equal length strings $w_i \in \Sigma^*$ and $w_o \in \Omega^*$, we prove that if the minimum edit set has size d, then for every positive constant k there is no polynomial time algorithm to construct a (Σ, Ω)-FSM $M' = (V_M, i_M, \delta_{M'})$ such that $M'(w_i) = w_o$ and δ_M and $\delta_{M'}$ differ on a set of size at most d^k, unless P = NP.

Our proof is in three steps. We first prove a variant of a result by Pitt and Warmuth [19]: Given a positive integer k and a set of input/output pairs of strings P for which the smallest FSM *consistent* with P (i.e. an FSM which produces output w' on input w for every pair $(w, w') \in P$) has n states, there is no efficient algorithm to construct an FSM consistent with P having at most n^k states (unless P = NP). Next, given such a set of pairs P, we carefully construct an FSM M and a single input/output pair (w_i, w_o) such that the minimum edit set $X_M(w_i, w_o)$ has size $\Theta(n)$. Finally, we show that *any* edit set X can be efficiently modified to yield an FSM with $|X|$ states that is consistent with P. We put these three results together to complete our proof.

Definition 1. *Given a finite set Σ and two finite sets POS, NEG $\subseteq \Sigma^*$, a deterministic finite automata (DFA) is said to be consistent with (POS, NEG) if it accepts all strings in POS and rejects all strings in NEG.*

Under the assumption that P $\neq$ NP, Pitt and Warmuth [19] prove the following inapproximability result for the minimum consistent DFA problem.

Theorem 1 (Pitt-Warmuth). *Given a finite set Σ such that $|\Sigma| \geq 2$, and two finite sets of strings POS, NEG $\subseteq \Sigma^*$, for any positive integer k there is no polynomial time algorithm to find a DFA with at most n^k states, where n is the number of states in the smallest DFA that is consistent with (POS, NEG).*

Using the result above we prove the following:

Lemma 2. *Given a finite set of input/output pairs P in $\Sigma^* \times \Omega^*$, let n be the minimum number such that there is a (Σ, Ω)-FSM M with n states that is consistent with P (i.e. for every pair $(w_i, w_o) \in P$, $M(w_i) = w_o$). Then, assuming*

$P \neq NP$, *for any positive constant* k, *there is no polynomial-time algorithm to find a consistent* (Σ, Ω)-*FSM* M' *with at most* n^k *states. This result holds even if* $|\Sigma|$ *and* $|\Omega|$ *are bounded by suitable constants.*

Proof. We reduce the minimum consistent DFA problem to the above problem. Consider an instance of the minimum consistent DFA problem with input alphabet Σ and sets POS, NEG $\subseteq \Sigma^*$. Let $\Sigma' = \Sigma \cup \{c\}$ where $c \notin \Sigma$ and $\Omega = \{0, 1, 2\}$. Consider the set of input output pairs $P = P^+ \cup P^-$, where

$P^+ = \{(w_i, w_o) \mid w_i = xc, x \in \text{POS and } w_o = 2^{|w_i|}1\}$
$P^- = \{(w_i, w_o) \mid w_i = xc, x \in \text{NEG}, w_o = 2^{|w_i|}0\}$

If there is a (Σ', Ω)-FSM M with n states consistent with the set of pairs in P then we can construct a DFA M' with n states where we neglect the output symbols and label states accept or reject by the output produced on the input c from that state. Clearly this DFA is consistent with (POS,NEG). Conversely, if there is a DFA consistent with (POS,NEG) then we can produce a (Σ', Ω)-FSM M that is consistent with P as follows: the output on all inputs in Σ is 2, and the transition from every state on input c leads to the same state, with output 1 if the state is an accepting state of the DFA and with output 0 otherwise. Clearly the FSM produced is consistent with P.   □

For the rest of this section, we fix an input alphabet Σ (with $|\Sigma| = c$, a constant), a finite output alphabet Ω, and a finite set $P = \{(w_{i1}, w_{o1}), \ldots, (w_{ik}, w_{ok})\}$ of input/output pairs of strings over $\Sigma^* \times \Omega^*$, with $|w_{is}| = |w_{os}|$ for $1 \leq s \leq k$. A necessary and sufficient condition for the existence of a (Σ, Ω)-FSM consistent with the pairs in P is the following: For any $w \in \Sigma^*$, if w is a prefix of both w_{ip} and w_{iq} then the prefixes of length $|w|$ of w_{op} and w_{oq} must be identical. If this condition is satisfied, it is easy to construct a (Σ, Ω)-FSM consistent with P which has at most $m = (\sum_{s=1}^{k} |w_{is}|) + 1$ states. As a corollary, if the smallest (Σ, Ω)-FSM consistent with P has n states, then $n \leq m$.

Let $\sigma_0, \sigma_1 \notin \Sigma$ and let $x, y, z \notin \Omega$. Let $\Sigma' = \Sigma \cup \{\sigma_0, \sigma_1\}$ and $\Omega' = \Omega \cup \{x, y, z\}$. We construct a (Σ', Ω')-FSM $M = (V_M, v_1, \delta_M)$ with m states such that for every $v \in V_M$, $v \xrightarrow{\sigma_1/x} v_1$ and for every $\sigma \in \Sigma$, $v \xrightarrow{\sigma/z}_M v$; and further, for some fixed permutation π of $(1, 2, \ldots, m)$ such that $\pi(1) = 1$,

$$v_{\pi(1)} \xrightarrow{\sigma_0/y}_M v_{\pi(2)} \xrightarrow{\sigma_0/x}_M v_{\pi(3)} \xrightarrow{\sigma_0/x} \cdots \xrightarrow{\sigma_0/x}_M v_{\pi(n)} \xrightarrow{\sigma_0/x}_M v_{\pi(1)}$$

i.e. the transitions on input σ_0 form a Hamiltonian cycle, with output x for every transition other than the transition from the initial state $v_1 = v_{\pi(1)}$, for which the output is y. Let $t_1 = yx^{m-1}$ and for every $i = 2, \ldots, m$ let $t_i = x^{m-i+1}yx^{i-2}$. Consider

$$w_i = \sigma_0^{2m}[(\sigma_0\sigma_1\sigma_0^m)(\sigma_0^2\sigma_1\sigma_0^m)\ldots(\sigma_0^{m-1}\sigma_1\sigma_0^m)][(w_{i1}\sigma_1)(w_{i2}\sigma_1)\ldots(w_{ik}\sigma_1)]$$
$$w_o = t_1t_1[(yxt_1)(yxxt_1)\ldots(yx^{m-2}xt_1)][(w_{o1}x)(w_{o2}x)\ldots(w_{ok}x)]$$

We claim that $|X_M(w_i, w_o)|$ is $\Theta(n)$, where n is the number of states in the smallest (Σ, Ω)-FSM consistent with P. The proof of this claim follows from the following two lemmas:

Lemma 3. $|X_M(w_i, w_0)| \leq cn$.

Proof. Notice that σ_0^{2m} is a prefix of w_i and the corresponding prefix of w_o is $t_1 t_1 = y x^{m-1} y x^{m-1}$. By an argument similar to the one used in the reduction of Subsection 3.1, we can prove that any (Σ', Ω')-FSM $M' = (V_M, v_1, \delta_{M'})$ such that $M'(w_i) = w_o$ must have the structure of a Hamiltonian cycle on the input σ_0, where the output on σ_0 is y from the initial state v_1, and x from every other state; furthermore, all transitions of M' on input σ_1 from any state must go to the initial state v_1 with output x. Notice that these properties are true of M. Hence, M only needs to be modified so that it produces output w_{os} on input w_{is} for each $1 \leq s \leq k$.

As remarked earlier, $m \geq n$. Since there is an n-state (Σ, Ω)-FSM consistent with P, it is possible to select an n-state subset V of V_M and modify only the Σ-transitions from states in V to obtain a (Σ', Ω')-FSM M' such that $M'(w_{is}) = w_{os}$ for every $1 \leq s \leq k$. It now immediately follows that $M'(w_i) = w_0$. Hence, $|X_M(w_i, w_o)| \leq |\Sigma| n = cn$. $\qquad\square$

Lemma 4. $|X_M(w_i, w_o)| \geq n$.

Proof. As remarked earlier, $m \geq n$. Let $|X_M(w_i, w_o)| = d$ and suppose we have made d changes to M, yielding M' such that $M'(w_i) = w_o$ and hence, for every $1 \leq s \leq k$, $M'(w_{is}) = w_{os}$. Thus, there are at most d states v for which at least one transition of the form $v \xrightarrow{\sigma/z}_M v$ ($\sigma \in \Sigma$) has been changed. Hence, there are at least $m - d$ states in M' such that $v \xrightarrow{\sigma/z}_{M'} v$ for every $\sigma \in \Sigma$. We claim that we can discard all such states v and modify the resulting (Σ', Ω')-FSM to obtain a (Σ, Ω)-FSM consistent with P.

Consider any state v such that $v \xrightarrow{\sigma/z}_{M'} v$ for every $\sigma \in \Sigma$. Thus on an input w_{is}, $1 \leq s \leq k$, if we can ever reach v, it must be the last state, since the output from v on any input symbol in Σ is z and w_{os} does not contain z. Clearly v cannot be the start state of M'. So v can be discarded from M' and it is still possible to construct a (Σ', Ω')-FSM M'' such that $M''(w_{is}) = w_{os}$ for every $1 \leq s \leq k$ (all edges into v can be sent to some other state).

This process can be repeated for all such states v, resulting in a (Σ', Ω')-FSM $\hat{M}$ with at most d states such that $\hat{M}(w_{is}) = w_{os}$ for every $1 \leq s \leq k$. Now, by discarding all σ_0 and σ_1 transitions from $\hat{M}$, we obtain a (Σ, Ω)-FSM consistent with P which has $d = |X_M(w_i, w_o)|$ states. Hence, $|X_M(w_i, w_o)| \geq n$. $\qquad\square$

Recalling that $c = |\Sigma|$ is a constant, we conclude that $|X_M(w_i, w_o)|$ is $\Theta(n)$.

Suppose there is a positive integer k and a polynomial time algorithm to compute a (Σ', Ω')-FSM M' that differs from M in at most $|X_M(w_i, w_o)|^k$ transitions for which $M'(w_i) = w_o$. Using an argument similar to the one in Lemma 4, we can modify M' in polynomial time by discarding at least $m - |X_M(w_i, w_o)|^k$ states and the σ_0 and σ_1 transitions to obtain a $\Theta(n^k)$-state (Σ, Ω)-FSM consistent with P. By Lemma 2, this would imply that P = NP. Thus we have the following

Theorem 2. *Given a (Σ, Ω)-FSM M and equal length strings $w_i \in \Sigma^*$ and $w_o \in \Omega^*$, for any positive integer k there is no polynomial time algorithm to compute an edit set of size $|X_M(w_i, w_o)|^k$ unless P = NP.*

Remark 6. By observing that (Σ, Ω)-FSMs are restricted versions of $(\Sigma \times \Omega, X)$-FSMs and (Σ, Ω)-PDAs, we obtain similar inapproximability results when the program is represented using either of these abstractions.

4   Computing the Closest-Output Distance

4.1   Upper Bound for FSMs and PDAs

We will prove a polynomial upper bound on the time to compute the closest-output distance when the correct executions of a program are represented as a (Σ, Ω)-PDA. The closest-output distance can be expressed using two simple recurrences, and our algorithm uses a straightforward dynamic programming approach to solve these recurrences.

Let $w_o \in \Omega^*$ and let $M = (V, V_i, \Gamma, \delta)$ be a (Σ, Ω)-PDA. We consider the problem of computing $d_M(w_o)$. Let the length of w_o, denoted by $|w_o|$, be L. For every $1 \leq i \leq j \leq L$ let $w_o(i, j)$ denote the substring of w_o from the i-th to the j-th position and let $w_o(i)$ denote the i-th letter of w_o (i.e. $w_o(i) = w_o(i, i)$).

For every $v \in V$ and every $1 \leq i \leq L$, let $P(v, i)$ denote the Hamming distance of the closest string to $w_o(i, L)$ that can be produced by M on a some valid input w starting from state v. Also, for every $u, v \in V$ and every $1 \leq i \leq j \leq L$, let $B(u, v, i, j)$ denote the Hamming distance of the closest string to $w_o(i, j)$ that can be produced by M on some balanced input w such that the state changes from u to v. By definition, $d_M(w_o) = \min_{v_i \in V_i} P(v_i, 1)$.

Let $[\omega_1 \neq \omega_2]$ be 1 if $\omega_1 \neq \omega_2$ and 0 otherwise. For notational convenience, let $P(v, i) = 0$ if $i > L$ and let $B(u, v, i+1, i) = 0$ if $u = v$, and $B(u, v, i+1, i) = \infty$ otherwise. We observe that if w is a balanced string from state u, then w must be of one of the following two forms:

1. $w = \sigma_i w_1$ where $(u, \sigma_i, v_1, \omega) \in \delta_i$ for some $v_1 \in V$ and $\omega \in \Omega$, and w_1 is a balanced string from v_1; or

2. $w = \sigma_c w_1 \sigma_r w_2$ where $(u, \sigma_c, v_1, \gamma, \omega) \in \delta_c$, $v_1 \xrightarrow{w_1/t}_M v_2$ and $(v_2, \sigma_r, \gamma, v_3, \omega')$
    $\in \delta_r$ for some $v_1, v_2, v_3 \in V$, $\gamma \in \Gamma$, $\omega, \omega' \in \Omega$ and $t \in \Omega^*$, and w_1 is a balanced string from v_1 and w_2 is a balanced string from v_3.

Note that w can be of the latter form only if $|w| \geq 2$. Thus, for every $1 \leq i \leq j \leq L$, $B(u, v, i, j) = b_1$ if $j - i < 2$ and $B(u, v, i, j) = \min(b_1, b_2)$ otherwise, where

$b_1 = \min[\omega \neq w_o(i)] + B(v_1, v, i+1, j)$

minimum over all σ, u_1, ω such that $(u, \sigma, v_1, \omega) \in \delta_i$

$b_2 = \min[\omega_c \neq w_o(i)] + B(v_1, v_2, i+1, k) + [\omega_r \neq w_o(k+1)] + B(v_3, v, k+2, j)$

minimum over all $\sigma_c, v_1, v_2, \sigma_r, v_3, \gamma, k$ such that $i < k < j$ and $(u, \sigma_c, v_1, \gamma, \omega_c) \in \delta_c, (v_2, \sigma_r, \gamma, \omega_r) \in \delta_r$ for some $\sigma_c, \sigma_r \in \Sigma, \gamma \in \Gamma', v_1, v_2, v_3 \in V$

We also observe that any valid input w from state u must be of the following three forms:

1. $w = \sigma_c w_1$ where $(u, \sigma_c, v_1, \gamma, \omega) \in \delta_c$ for some $\sigma_c \in \Sigma$, $v_1 \in V$, $\gamma \in \Gamma'$, $\omega \in \Omega$, and w_1 is a valid input from v_1; or

2. $w = w_1 w_2$ where w_1 is a balanced string from u, $u \xrightarrow{w_1/t} v_1$ for some $t \in \Omega^*$ and $v_1 \in V$, and w_2 is a valid input from v_1; or
3. w is a balanced string from u.

Thus, for every $1 \leq i \leq L$, $P(v, i) = \min(p_1, p_2, p_3)$ where

$\qquad p_1 = \min_{\sigma_c \in \Sigma, v_1 \in V, \gamma \in \Gamma', \omega_c \in \Omega} \{ [\omega_c \neq w_o(i)] + P(v_1, i+1) \mid (u, \sigma_c, v_1, \gamma, \omega_c) \in \delta_c \}$

$\qquad p_2 = \min_{i \leq k < L; v_1 \in V} B(v, v_1, i, k) + P(v_1, k+1)$

$\qquad p_3 = \min_{v_1 \in V} B(v, v_1, i, L)$

The required value $\min_{v_i \in V_i} P(v_i, 1)$ can easily be computed using dynamic programming in $O(|\Sigma|^2 \cdot |\Gamma| \cdot |V|^5 L^3)$ time, which is polynomial in the size of the input. By observing that a (Σ, Ω)-FSM is a special case of a (Σ, Ω)-PDA, we obtain the following

Theorem 3. *There is a polynomial time algorithm for computing the closest-output distance when the correct executions of the program are represented as a (Σ, Ω)-PDA or a (Σ, Ω)-FSM.*

Remark 7. Note that the polynomial-time dynamic programming algorithm to compute $d_M(w_o)$ can easily be modified to compute a string $w \in \Sigma^*$ such that the Hamming distance between w_o and some string $w' \in M(w)$ is $d_M(w_o)$.

Remark 8. Most programs are infinite-state systems and need to be abstracted to form PDAs (or extended finite state machines); consequently these abstractions describe more than just the correct executions of the program. Hence, the input string computed by the above dynamic programming algorithm may not be *legal*, i.e. it may not correspond to a correct execution of the program. While we do not know of a general technique to compute the closest-output distance when inputs are constrained to be legal, the following technique can be used in practice: Using the procedure by Lawler [20], the above dynamic programming algorithm can be used to compute input strings corresponding to the closest-output distance, the second-closest-output distance, ..., the kth-closest-output distance, in time polynomial in k and the size of the input. These input strings can be examined in order, and the first legal input string can then be chosen.

4.2 Hardness Results for Extended FSM Representation

Given a (Σ, X)-FSM M and a string $w_i \in \Sigma^*$, we show that the decision version of computing $d_M(w_i)$ is NP-complete and further, there is no polynomial-time algorithm to compute $d_M(w_i)$ to within any given polynomial factor (unless P = NP). Briefly, given a SAT formula ϕ over a set X of n variables, we construct a (Σ, X)-FSM M and a string $w_i \in \Sigma^*$ such that every string $w \in L_M$ identifies an assignment a_w of the variables in X, and if w is "close" to w_i, then a_w satisfies ϕ. The results follow from the NP-completeness of SAT.

Let $\Sigma = \{0, 1\}$, let X be a set of n boolean variables, and let ϕ be any SAT formula over variables in X. For every positive integer k, let $N(k) = n^k + 1$ and construct the following (Σ, X)-FSM $M_k = (V, v_0, F, a_0, g, \delta)$:

1. $V = \{v_0, v_1, \ldots, v_n\} \cup \{u_1, \ldots, u_{N(k)}\} \cup \{s_1, \ldots, s_{N(k)}\}$, $F = \{s_{N(k)}, u_{N(k)}\}$;
2. $g(v_i, j) = \top$ for $i = 0, \ldots, n$ and $j = 0, 1$;
3. $g(u_i, j) = \neg\phi$ and $g(s_i, j) = \phi$ for $i = 1, \ldots, N(k)$ and $j = 0, 1$;
4. $(v_{i-1}, 0) \xrightarrow[x_i := 0]{x_i := 0} v_i$ and $(v_{i-1}, 1) \xrightarrow[x_i := 1]{x_i := 1} v_i$ for $i = 1, \ldots, n$;
5. $(v_n, 0) \to s_1$ and $(v_n, 1) \to u_1$;
6. $(s_i, 0) \to s_{i+1}$, $(s_i, 1) \to s_i$, $(u_i, 0) \to u_i$, $(u_i, 1) \to u_{i+1}$ for $1 \le i \le N(k) - 1$;
7. $(s_{N(k)}, j) \to s_{N(k)}$ and $(u_{N(k)}, j) \to u_{N(k)}$ for $j = 0, 1$;
8. the initial state is v_0, and the initial assignment a_0 sets all variables to 0.

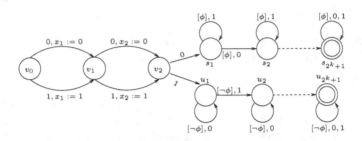

Fig. 3. The FSM for $n = 2$.

Figure 3 shows the FSM for $n = 2$ variables. The transition arrows are labeled by the input symbol 0 or 1. The change in assignment (if any) is given after the input symbol while the enabling condition is given before the input symbol if it is not always true.

Note that the size of M_k is polynomial in the size of the inputs. Let $w_i = 0^{n+N(k)}$. By the construction of M_k, every $w' \in L_{M_k}$ of length $n + N(k)$ is either of the form $w0^{N(k)}$ or $w1^{N(k)}$ where $w \in \Sigma^n$. Note that w uniquely determines an assignment a_w of the variables of X. It is immediately clear from the construction of M_k that the Hamming distance between w_i and w' is at most n if a_w satisfies ϕ, and is at least $N(k)$ otherwise.

The decision problem $d_{M_k}(w_i) \le n$ is clearly in NP: we guess a string w' of length equal to w_i and verify in polynomial time if $w' \in L_{M_k}$ and the Hamming distance between w' and w_i is at most n. If so, then as argued above, the prefix w of length n of w' uniquely determines a satisfying assignment to the SAT formula ϕ. Since ϕ was an arbitrary SAT formula, we conclude that this decision problem is NP-complete.

We now show that, unless P = NP, there is no polynomial time algorithm for computing $d_{M_k}(w_i)$ to within a polynomial approximation factor. Suppose, for the sake of contradiction, that such an algorithm A exists. Let $A(M_k, w_i)$ denote the output of A for the input M_k and w_i defined above. Since $d_{M_k}(w_i) \le n$ iff ϕ is satisfiable, it follows that $A(M_k, w_i) < N(k)$ iff ϕ is satisfiable. Thus, no such polynomial-time algorithm A exists unless SAT $\in$ P. Hence, we have the following

Theorem 4. *Let M be a (Σ, X)-FSM and let $w_i \in \Sigma^*$ such that $d_M(w_i) = d$. For any positive integer k, there is no polynomial time algorithm to decide whether or not $d_M(w_i) \leq d^k$, unless $P = NP$.*

Remark 9. The typical model for programs used in model checking is boolean programs, which can be seen as PDAs with boolean variables. Since this model is a generalization of extended finite state machines, our hardness result applies to boolean programs as well.

Remark 10. As mentioned in Remark 8, programs may be abstracted as extended finite state machines, and thereby describe more than just the correct executions of the program. The above hardness result for extended FSMs clearly extends to this more general case as well.

5   Conclusions

We have proved upper and lower bounds for two popular heuristics used in automated error explanation for various models encountered in formal verification. Based on our observations, we can draw two important conclusions. First, our lower bounds provide justification for algorithms based on SAT solvers that have been proposed in the literature. These algorithms are likely to be the most efficient that one can hope to design. Second, since the problem of determining the minimum edit set is intractible even for Mealy machines, it is unlikely that error explanation tools based on this heuristic will scale up to large software programs. On the other hand, the closest correct trace to a counter-example can be computed efficiently for PDAs (and hence for finite state models as well). The intractibility of this problem for extended finite state machines is a consequence of the well-known state space explosion problem, and does not seem intrinsic to the heuristic itself.

References

1. Clarke, E., Grumberg, O., Peled, D.: Model Checking. MIT Press (2000)
2. Zeller, A.: Isolating cause-effect chains for computer programs. In: Proceedings of the ACM Symposium on the Foundations of Software Engineering. (2002) 1–10
3. Zeller, A., Hildebrandt, R.: Simplifying and isolating failure-inducing input. IEEE Transactions on Software Engineering **28** (2002) 183–200
4. Jin, H., Ravi, K., Somenzi, F.: Fate and free will in error traces. In: Proceedings of Conference on Tools and Algorithms for Construction and Analysis of Systems. Volume 2031 of Lecture Notes in Computer Science., Springer (2002) 445–459
5. Renieris, M., Reiss, S.: Fault localization with nearest neighbor queries. In: Proceedings of the Conference on Automated Software Engineering. (2003)
6. Ball, T., Naik, M., Rajamani, S.: From symptom to cause: Localizing errors in counterexample traces. In: Proceedings of the ACM Symposium on the Principles of Programming Languages. (2003) 97–105
7. Groce, A., Visser, W.: What went wrong: Explaining counterexamples. In: Proceedings of the SPIN Workshop on Model Checking of Software. (2003) 121–135

8. Groce, A.: Error explanation with distance metrics. In: Proceedings of Conference on Tools and Algorithms for Construction and Analysis of Systems. (2004) 108–122

9. Ball, T., Rajamani, S.K.: The SLAM project: Debugging system software via static analysis. In: Proceedings of the ACM Symposium on the Principles of Programming Languages. (2002) 1–3

10. Brat, G., Havelund, K., Park, S., Visser, W.: Java PathFinder – A second generation of a Java model checker. In: Proceedings of the Workshop on Advances in Verification. (2000)

11. Lewis, D.: Causation. Journal of Philosophy **70** (1973) 556–567

12. Zeller, A.: Yesterday, my program worked. Today, is does not. Why? In: Proceedings of the ACM Symposium on the Foundations of Software Engineering. (1999) 253–267

13. Tip, F., Dinesh, T.B.: A slicing-based approach for locating type errors. ACM Transactions on Software Engineering and Methodology **10** (2001) 5–55

14. Bhargavan, K., Gunter, C.A., Kim, M., Lee, I., Obradovic, D., Sokolsky, O., Viswanathan, M.: Verisim: Formal analysis of network simulations. IEEE: Transactions on Software Engineering **28** (2002) 129–145

15. Hopcroft, J.E., Ullman, J.D.: Introduction to Automata Theory, Languages and Computation. Addison Wesley (1979)

16. Alur, R., Madhusudan, P.: Visibly pushdown languages. In: Proceedings of the ACM Symposium on the Theory of Computation. (2004)

17. Reps, T., Horwitz, S., Sagiv, M.: Precise interprocedural dataflow analysis via graph reachability. In: Proceedings of the ACM Symposium on the Principles of Programming Languages. (1995) 49–61

18. Cormen, T.H., Leiserson, C.E., Rivest, R.L., Stein, C.: Introduction to Algorithms. McGraw-Hill Higher Education (2001)

19. Pitt, L., Warmuth, M.K.: The minimum consistent DFA problem cannot be approximated within any polynomial. Journal of the ACM **40** (1993) 95–142

20. Lawler, E.L.: A procedure for computing the K best solutions to discrete optimization problems and its application to the shortest path problem. Management Science **18** (1972) 401–405

Efficiently Verifiable Conditions
for Deadlock-Freedom
of Large Concurrent Programs

(Extended Abstract)

Paul C. Attie[1,2] and Hana Chockler[2,3]

[1] College of Computer and Information Science, Northeastern University,
360 Huntington Avenue, Boston, MA 02115, USA
attie@ccs.neu.edu
[2] MIT CSAIL,
32 Vassar Street, Cambridge, MA 02139, USA
{attie,hanac}@theory.csail.mit.edu
[3] Department of Computer Science, WPI,
100 Institute Road, Worcester, MA 01609, USA

Abstract. We present two polynomial-time algorithms for automatic verification of deadlock-freedom of large finite-state concurrent programs. We consider shared-memory concurrent programs in which a process can nondeterministically choose amongst several (enabled) actions at any step. As shown in [23], deadlock-freedom analysis is NP-hard even for concurrent programs of restricted form (no nondeterministic choice). Therefore, research in this area concentrates either on the search for efficiently checkable sufficient conditions for deadlock-freedom, or on improving the complexity of the check in some special cases. In this paper, we present two efficiently checkable sufficient conditions for deadlock freedom.

Our algorithms apply to programs which are expressed in a particular syntactic form, in which variables are shared between pairs of processes. The first algorithm improves the complexity of the deadlock check of Attie and Emerson [4] to polynomial in all parameters, as opposed to the exponential complexity of [4]. The second algorithm involves a conceptually new construction of a "global wait-for graph" for all processes. Its running time is also polynomial in all its parameters, and it is more discriminating than the first algorithm. We illustrate our algorithms by applying them to several examples of concurrent programs that implement resource allocation and priority queues. To the best of our knowledge, this is the first work that describes polynomially checkable conditions for assuring deadlock freedom of large concurrent programs.

1 Introduction

One of the important correctness properties of concurrent programs is the absence of *deadlocks*, e.g. as defined in [28]: "a set of processes is deadlocked if each process in the set is waiting for an event that only another process in the

R. Cousot (Ed.): VMCAI 2005, LNCS 3385, pp. 465–481, 2005.
© Springer-Verlag Berlin Heidelberg 2005

set can cause." Most approaches to deadlock assume that the "event" that each process waits for is the release of a resource held by another process. We refer to this setting as the *resource allocation* setting. Four conditions are necessary for a deadlock to arise [10, 20]: (1) resources can be held by at most one process; (2) processes can hold some resources while waiting to acquire several (more than 1, in general) others; (3) resources cannot be taken away from a process (no preemption); and (4) a cyclical pattern of waiting amongst the involved processes. The exact pattern of waiting required to cause a deadlock depends on the specific resource model, and can be depicted in terms of a *wait-for-graph* (WFG): a graph whose edges depict the "wait-for" relationships between processes. The following models have been formulated [22]: (1) AND model: a process blocks iff one or more of the resources it has requested are unavailable; (2) OR model: a process blocks iff all of the resources it has requested are unavailable; (3) AND-OR model: a process can use any combination of AND and OR operators in specifying a resource request; and (4) k-out-of-n: a process requests any k resources out of a pool of n resources. For the AND-model, deadlock arises if the WFG contains a cycle. For the OR-model, deadlock arises if the WFG contains a knot, i.e., a set of processes each of which can reach exactly all the others by traversing wait-for edges. To our knowledge, no graph-theoretic construct characterizing deadlock in the AND-OR or the k-out-of-n models is known [22].

In this paper, we address a version of the deadlock problem that is more general than the resource-based model. We consider the deadlock problem in the case that the event which each process waits for is the truthification of a predicate over shared state. Thus, we deal with a shared variables model of concurrency. However, our approach is applicable in principle to other models such as message passing or shared events. We exploit the representation of concurrent programs in a form where the synchronization between processes can be factored out, so that the synchronization code for each pair of interacting processes is expressed separately from that for other pairs, even for two pairs that have a process in common. This "pairwise" representation was introduced in [4], where it was used to synthesize programs efficiently from CTL specifications.

Traditionally, three approaches to dealing with deadlock have been investigated: (1) deadlock detection and recovery: since a deadlock is stable, by definition, it can be detected and then broken, e.g., by the preemption, rollback, or termination of an involved process. (2) deadlock avoidance: avert the occurrence of a deadlock by taking appropriate action. Deadlock avoidance algorithms have been devised for the resource-based formulation of deadlock [28], (3) deadlock prevention: prevent a deadlock from arising by design. In particular, attempt to negate one of the four conditions mentioned above for the occurrence of deadlock. As Tanenbaum [28] observes, attempting to negate any of the first three conditions is usually impractical, and so we are left with condition (4): a cyclical pattern of waiting.

Related Work. As shown in [23], deciding the deadlock-freedom of a finite-state concurrent program is NP-hard even for constrained programs in which each process consists of a finite prefix followed by an infinite loop.

Most model checking algorithms can be applied to verifying deadlock freedom. The main impediment is state-explosion. Some approaches to ameliorating state-explosion are to use a partial order instead of an interleaving model [16–18, 26], using symbolic model checking [21, 7, 8, 25] or by using symmetry reductions [2, 9, 13, 14]. These approaches, however, have worst case running time exponential in the number of processes in a system, and often rely on the processes being similar. (Roughly, two processes are similar if the code for one can be obtained from the code for the other by replacing process indices). Our first algorithm has better accuracy (i.e., returns a positive answer for deadlock-free programs) when processes are similar, but our second algorithm does not depend on similarity in any way.

In [1, 19] sufficient conditions for verifying deadlock-freedom are given, but it is not shown that these can be evaluated in polynomial time. Also, no example applications are given.

Attie and Emerson [4] formulate a condition that is sufficient but not necessary for deadlock-freedom. Checking this condition requires the construction of the automata-theoretic product of $n + 2$ processes, where n is the maximum branching degree of a state-node in a state-transition graph that represents the behavior of processes (essentially, n reflects the degree of "local" nondeterminism of a single process in a state). The $n+2$ processes are arranged in a "star" configuration with a central process P_k and $n + 1$ "satellite" processes. The condition is that after every transition of P_k, either P_k does not block another process, or P_k has another enabled transition. Hence P_k cannot be part of a cyclical waiting pattern in either case. Since this product has size exponential in n, checking the condition is infeasible for concurrent programs that have a high degree of local nondeterminism. While the condition in [4] is formulated for systems of similar (isomorphic) processes, the restriction to similar processes does not play any role in the proof of correctness given in [4], and thus can be removed.

Our Contribution. In this paper we follow the approach of [4] to deadlock prevention. We present two sufficient conditions for assuring deadlock freedom and describe efficient (polynomial time) algorithms for checking these conditions.

The first condition is a modification of the condition presented in [4], but can be checked by constructing the product of only three processes (triple-systems). Roughly, the idea is to check the condition "after a transition, P_k either does not block another process, or is itself enabled" in systems of only three processes. We show that this implies the original condition of [4], and so implies deadlock-freedom by the results of that paper. Since only triple-systems are model-checked, the condition can be checked in time polynomial in all the input parameters: the number of processes, the size of a single process, and the branching degree of state-nodes of a process. Moreover, the space complexity of the check is polynomial in the size of a single process, and the checks for all triples can be performed sequentially, thus memory can be reused. Therefore, this condition can be efficiently checked even on very large concurrent programs.

The second condition is more complex and also more discriminating. This condition is based on constructing the "global wait-for graph," a bipartite graph whose nodes are the local states of all processes, and also the possible transitions that each process can execute. The edges of this graph represent "pairwise wait-for" conditions: if in the system consisting of P_i and P_j executing their synchronization code in isolation (pair-system), there is a transition a_i of P_i that is blocked in some state where the local state of P_j is s_j, then there is an edge from a_i to s_j. Since only pair-systems need to be checked, the global wait-for-graph can be constructed in polynomial time. Existence of a deadlock implies the existence of a subgraph of the global wait-for-graph in which every process is blocked by some other processes in the subgraph. We call such a subgraph a *supercycle* and define it formally in the sequel. One could check the global wait-for-graph for the occurrence of supercycles, but the results of [23] imply that this cannot be done in polynomial time. Instead we check the global wait-for-graph for the occurrence of subgraphs of a supercycle. If these subgraphs are not present, then the supercycle cannot be present either, and so our check succeeds in verifying deadlock-freedom. If these subgraphs are present, then the supercycle may or may not be present, and so our check is inconclusive.

To the best of our knowledge, this is the first work that describes sufficient and polynomially checkable conditions for deadlock-freedom of large concurrent programs. We have implemented our pairwise representation using the XSB logic programming system [27]. This implementation provides a platform for implementing the algorithms in this paper. Due to the lack of space, all proofs and many technical details are omitted from this version. The full version can be found at authors' home pages.

2   Technical Preliminaries

2.1   Model of Concurrent Computation

We consider finite-state concurrent programs of the form $P = P_1 \| \cdots \| P_K$ that consist of a finite number n of fixed sequential processes $P_1, \ldots, P_K$ running in parallel. Each P_i is a *synchronization skeleton* [15], that is, a directed multigraph where each node is a (local) state of P_i (also called an *i-state* and is labeled by a unique name (s_i), and where each arc is labeled with a guarded command [12] $B_i \rightarrow A_i$ consisting of a guard B_i and corresponding action A_i. With each P_i we associate a set $\mathcal{AP}_i$ of *atomic propositions*, and a mapping V_i from local states of P_i to subsets of $\mathcal{AP}_i$: $V_i(s_i)$ is the set of atomic propositions that are true in s_i. As P_i executes transitions and changes its local state, the atomic propositions in $\mathcal{AP}_i$ are updated. Different local states of P_i have different truth assignments: $V_i(s_i) \neq V_i(t_i)$ for $s_i \neq t_i$. Atomic propositions are not shared: $\mathcal{AP}_i \cap \mathcal{AP}_j = \emptyset$ when $i \neq j$. Other processes can read (via guards) but not update the atomic propositions in $\mathcal{AP}_i$. There is also a set of shared variables $x_1, \ldots, x_m$, which can be read and written by every process. These are updated by the action A_i. A *global state* is a tuple of the form $(s_1, \ldots, s_K, v_1, \ldots, v_m)$ where s_i is the current local state of P_i and $v_1, \ldots, v_m$ is a list giving the current values of $x_1, \ldots, x_m$, respectively. A guard B_i is a predicate on global states, and so can reference any atomic proposition and any shared variable. An action A_i is a parallel assignment statement that updates the shared variables. We write just A_i for $true \to A_i$ and just B_i for $B_i \to skip$, where $skip$ is the empty assignment.

We model parallelism as usual by the nondeterministic interleaving of the "atomic" transitions of the individual processes P_i. Let $s = (s_1, \ldots, s_i, \ldots, s_K, v_1, \ldots, v_m)$ be the current global state, and let P_i contain an arc from node s_i to s_i' labeled with $B_i \to A_i$. We write such an arc as the tuple $(s_i, B_i \to A_i, s_i')$, and call it a P_i-move from s_i to s_i'. We use just $move$ when P_i is specified by the context. If B_i holds in s, then a permissible next state is $s' = (s_1, \ldots, s_i', \ldots, s_K, v_1', \ldots, v_m')$ where $v_1', \ldots, v_m'$ are the new values for the shared variables resulting from action A_i. Thus, at each step of the computation, a process with an enabled arc is nondeterministically selected to be executed next. The *transition relation* R is the set of all such (s, s'). The arc from node s_i to s_i' is *enabled* in state s. An arc that is not enabled is *blocked*.

Let S^0 be a given set of initial states in which computations of P can start. A *computation path* is a sequence of states whose first state is in S^0 and where each successive pair of states is related by R. A state is *reachable* iff it lies on some computation path. Let S be the set of all reachable global states of P, and redefine R to restrict it to $S \times S$, i.e, to reachable states. Then, $M = (S^0, S, R)$ is the *global state transition diagram* (GSTD) of P. We write $states(M)$ for S.

2.2 Pairwise Normal Form

We will restrict our attention to concurrent programs that are written in a certain syntactic form, as follows. Let $\oplus, \otimes$ be binary infix operators. A *general guarded command* [4] is either a guarded command as given in Section 2.1 above, or has the form $G_1 \oplus G_2$ or $G_1 \otimes G_2$, where G_1, G_2 are general guarded commands. Roughly, the operational semantics of $G_1 \oplus G_2$ is that either G_1 or G_2, but not both, can be executed, and the operational semantics of $G_1 \otimes G_2$ is that both G_1 or G_2 must be executed, that is, the guards of both G_1 and G_2 must hold at the same time, and the bodies of G_1 and G_2 must be executed simultaneously, as a single parallel assignment statement. For the semantics of $G_1 \otimes G_2$ to be well-defined, there must be no conflicting assignments to shared variables in G_1 and G_2. This will always be the case for the programs we consider. We refer the reader to [4] for a comprehensive presentation of general guarded commands.

A concurrent program $P = P_1 \| \cdots \| P_K$ is in *pairwise normal form* iff the following four conditions all hold: (1) every move a_i of every process P_i has the form $a_i = (s_i, \otimes_{j \in I(i)} \oplus_{\ell \in \{1, \ldots, n_j\}} B_{i,\ell}^j \to A_{i,\ell}^j, t_i)$, where $B_{i,\ell}^j \to A_{i,\ell}^j$ is a guarded command, I is an irreflexive symmetric relation over $\{1 \ldots K\}$ that defines a "interconnection" (or "neighbors") relation amongst processes[1], and $I(i) = \{j \mid (i,j) \in I\}$, (2) variables are shared in a pairwise manner, i.e., for each $(i,j) \in I$, there is some set $\mathcal{SH}_{ij}$ of shared variables that are the only variables that can be read and written by both P_i and P_j, (3) $B_{i,\ell}^j$ can reference only variables in $\mathcal{SH}_{ij}$ and atomic propositions in $\mathcal{AP}_j$, and (4) $A_{i,\ell}^j$ can update only variables in $\mathcal{SH}_{ij}$.

---

[1] In other words, I is the topology of the connection network.

For each neighbor P_j of P_i, $\oplus_{\ell \in [1:n]} B_{i,\ell}^j \to A_{i,\ell}^j$ specifies n alternatives $B_{i,\ell}^j \to A_{i,\ell}^j$, $1 \leq \ell \leq n$ for the interaction between P_i and P_j as P_i transitions from s_i to t_i. P_i must execute such an interaction with each of its neighbors in order to transition from s_i to t_i ($\otimes_{j \in I(i)}$ specifies this). We emphasize that I is not necessarily the set of all pairs, i.e., there can be processes that do not directly interact by reading each others atomic propositions or reading/writing pairwise shared variables. We do not assume, unless otherwise stated, that processes are isomorphic, or *similar* (we define process similarity later in this section).

We will usually use a superscript I to indicate the relation I, e.g., process P_i^I, and P_i^I-move a_i^I. For $a_i^I = (s_i, \otimes_{j \in I(i)} \oplus_{\ell \in \{1,...,n_j\}} B_{i,\ell}^j \to A_{i,\ell}^j, t_i)$, we define $a_i^I.start = s_i$, $a_i^I.guard_j = \bigvee_{\ell \in \{1,...,n_j\}} B_{i,\ell}^j$, and $a_i^I.guard = \bigwedge_{j \in I(i)} a_i.guard_j$. We write $a_i^I \in P_i^I$ when a_i^I is a move of P_i^I. If $P^I = P_1^I \| \ldots \| P_K^I$ is a concurrent program with interconnection relation I, then we call P^I an *I-system*. Global states of P^I are called *I-states*.

In pairwise normal form, the synchronization code for P_i^I with one of its neighbors P_j^I (i.e., $\oplus_{\ell \in \{1,...,n_j\}} B_{i,\ell}^j \to A_{i,\ell}^j$) is expressed separately from the synchronization code for P_i^I with another neighbor P_k^I (i.e., $\oplus_{\ell \in \{1,...,n_k\}} B_{i,\ell}^k \to A_{i,\ell}^k$). We can exploit this property to define "subsystems" of an I-system P as follows. Let $J \subseteq I$ and $range(J) = \{i \mid \exists j : (i,j) \in J\}$. If a_i^I is a move of P_i^I then define $a_i^J = (s_i, \otimes_{j \in J(i)} \oplus_{\ell \in \{1...n\}} B_{i,\ell}^j \to A_{i,\ell}^j, t_i)$. We also use $a_i^I {\upharpoonright} J$ for a_i^J, to emphasize the projection onto the subrelation J. Then the *J-system* P^J is $P_{j_1}^J \| \ldots \| P_{j_n}^J$ where $\{j_1, \ldots, j_n\} = range(J)$ and P_j^J consists of the moves $\{a_j^J \mid a_j^I$ is a move of $P_j^I\}$. Intuitively, a J-system consists of the processes in $range(J)$, where each process contains only the synchronization code needed for its J-neighbors, rather than its I-neighbors. If $J = \{\{i,j\}\}$ for some i, j then P_J is a *pair-system*, and if $J = \{\{i,j\}, \{j,k\}\}$ for some i, j, k then P_J is a *triple-system*. For $J \subseteq I$, $M_J = (S_J^0, S_J, R_J)$ is the GSTD of P^J as defined in Section 2.1, and a global state of P^J is a *J-state*. If $J = \{\{i,j\}\}$, then we write $M_{ij} = (S_{ij}^0, S_{ij}, R_{ij})$ instead of $M_J = (S_J^0, S_J, R_J)$.

Also, if s_J is a J-state, and $J' \subseteq J$, then $s{\upharpoonright}J'$ is the J'-state that agrees with s on the local state of all $P_j \in range(J')$ and the value of all variables $x_{ij} \in \mathcal{SH}_{ij}$ such that $i, j \in range(J')$, i.e, the projection of s onto the processes in J'. If $J' = \{\{i,j\}\}$ then we write $s{\upharpoonright}J$ as $s{\upharpoonright}ij$. Also, $s{\upharpoonright}i$ is the local state of P_i in s. Two processes P_i and P_j are *similar* if they are isomorphic to each other up to a change of indices [4, p. 78]. A concurrent program $P = P_1 \| \cdots \| P_K$ *consists of similar processes* if for each $1 \leq i, j \leq K$, we have that P_i and P_j are similar.

[4, 3, 5] give, in pairwise normal form, solutions to many well-known problems, such as dining philosophers, drinking philosophers, mutual exclusion, k-out-of-n mutual exclusion, two-phase commit, and replicated data servers. Attie [6] shows that any finite-state concurrent program can be rewritten (up to strong bisimulation) in pairwise normal form. Thus, the algorithms we present here are applicable to any concurrent program, up to strong bisimulation.

2.3 The Wait-for-Graph

The wait-for-graph for an I-state s gives all of the blocking relationships in s.

Definition 1 (*Wait-for-Graph $W_I(s)$*). *Let s be an arbitrary I-state. The wait-for-graph $W_I(s)$ of s is a directed bipartite AND-OR graph, where*

1. *The AND nodes of $W_I(s)$ (also called* local-state nodes*) are the i-states $\{s{\restriction}i \mid i \in \{1 \ldots K\}\}^2$;*
2. *The OR-nodes of $W_I(s)$ (also called* move nodes*) are the moves $\{a_i^I \mid i \in \{1 \ldots K\}\}$ and a_i^I is a move of P_i^I and $a_i^I.start = s{\restriction}i$*
3. *There is an edge from $s{\restriction}i$ to every node of the form a_i^I in $W_I(s)$;*
4. *There is an edge from a_i^I to $s{\restriction}j$ in $W_I(s)$ if and only if $\{i,j\} \in I$ and $a_i^I \in W_I(s)$ and $s{\restriction}ij(a_i^I.guard_j) = false$.*

The AND-nodes are the local states s_i ($= s{\restriction}i$) of all processes when the global state is s, and the OR-nodes are the moves a_i^I such that local control in P_i^I is currently at the start state of a_i^I, i.e., all the moves that are candidates for execution. There is an edge from s_i to each move of the form a_i^I. Nodes s_i are AND nodes since P_i^I is blocked iff *all* of its possible moves are blocked. There is an edge from a_i^I to s_j ($= s{\restriction}j$) iff a_i^I is blocked by P_j^I: a_i^I can be executed in s only if $s{\restriction}ij(a_i^I.guard_j) = true$ for all $j \in I(i)$; if there is some j in $I(i)$ such that $s{\restriction}ij(a_i^I.guard_j) = false$, then a_i^I cannot be executed in state s. The nodes labeled with moves are OR nodes, since a_i^I is blocked iff *some* neighbor P_j^I of P_i^I blocks a_i^I. We cannot, however, say that P_i^I itself is blocked by P_j^I, since there could be another move b_i^I in P_i^I such that $s{\restriction}ij(b_i^I.guard_j) = true$, i.e., b_i^I is not blocked by P_j^I (in state s), so P_i^I can progress in state s by executing b_i^I.

In the sequel, we use $s_i \longrightarrow a_i^I \in W_I(s)$ to denote the existence of an edge from s_i to a_i^I in $W_I(s)$, and $a_i^I \longrightarrow s_j \in W_I(s)$ to denote the existence of an edge from a_i^I to s_j in $W_I(s)$. We also abbreviate $((s_i \longrightarrow a_i^I \in W(s)) \wedge (a_i^I \longrightarrow s_j \in W(s)))$ with $s_i \longrightarrow a_i^I \longrightarrow s_j \in W(s)$, and similarly for longer "wait-chains." For $J \subseteq I$ and J-state s_J we define $W_J(s_J)$ by replacing I by J and $\{1 \ldots K\}$ by $range(J)$ in the above definition.

2.4 Establishing Deadlock-Freedom: Supercycles

Deadlock is characterized by the presence in the wait-for-graph of a graph-theoretic construct called a *supercycle* [4]:

Definition 2 (Supercycle). *Let s be an I-state and $s_i = s{\restriction}i$ for all $i \in \{1 \ldots K\}$. SC is a supercycle in $W_I(s)$ if and only if all of the following hold:*

1. *SC is nonempty,*
2. *if $s_i \in SC$ then $\forall a_i^I : a_i^I \in W_I(s)$ implies $s_i \longrightarrow a_i^I \in SC$, and*
3. *if $a_i^I \in SC$ then $\exists s_j : a_i^I \longrightarrow s_j \in W_I(s)$ and $a_i^I \longrightarrow s_j \in SC$.*

---

[2] In [4] state nodes are denoted by processes P_i and not by local states, since they consider wait-for-graphs for each state of the system separately; in this paper, we study wait-for-graphs that encompass all blocking conditions for all local nodes of all processes together; hence we need to distinguish between different local state-nodes of the same process.

Note that SC is a subgraph of $W_I(s)$. If an i-state s_i is in a supercycle SC, then every move of P_i^I that starts in s_i is also in SC and is blocked by some other I-process P_j^I which has a j-state s_j in SC (note that a process has at most one local state in SC, and we say that the process itself is in SC). It follows that no I-process in SC can execute any of its moves, and that this situation persists forever.

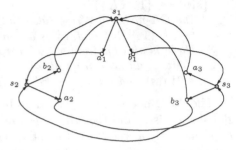

In the figure on the right we give an example of a wait-for-graph for a three process system. And-nodes (local states of processes) are shown as •, and or-nodes (moves) are shown as ○. Each process P_i, $i \in \{1, 2, 3\}$ has two moves a_i and b_i in the local state s_i. Since every move has at least one outgoing edge, i.e., is blocked by at least one process, the figure is also an example of a supercycle. In fact, several edges can be removed and still leave a supercycle (for example, $a_3 \longrightarrow P_1$, $b_3 \longrightarrow P_2$, $a_2 \longrightarrow P_1$ can all be removed). Thus, the figure contains several subgraphs that are also supercycles.

From [4], we have that the absence of supercycles in the wait-for-graph of a state implies that there is at least one enabled move in that state:

Proposition 1 ([4]). *If $W_I(s)$ is supercycle-free, then some move a_i^I has no outgoing edges in $W_I(s)$, and so can be executed in state s.*

We say that s is *supercycle-free* iff $W_I(s)$ does not contain a supercycle. We assume that all initial states of the I-system are supercycle free. That is, we do not allow initial states that contain deadlocks.

3   Improving the Attie-Emerson Deadlock-Freedom Condition

In this section we improve the Attie and Emerson [4] deadlock-freedom check (the wait-for-graph assumption of [4]). Consider the following condition.

For every reachable I-state t in M_I such that
$s \xrightarrow{k} t \in R_I$ for some reachable I-state s,
$(\neg \exists a_j^I : (a_j^I \longrightarrow t_k \in W_I(t)))$ or
$(\exists a_k^I \in W_I(t) : (\forall \ell \in \{1 \ldots K\} : (a_k^I \longrightarrow t_\ell \notin W_I(t)))).$ (a)

This condition implies that, after P_k^I executes a transition, either P_k^I blocks no move of another process, or P_k^I itself has an enabled move. Thus P_k^I cannot be in a supercycle. Hence, this transition of P_k^I could not have *created* a supercycle; any supercycle present after the transition must also have been present before the transition. Since initial states are supercycle-free, we conclude, by induction on computation path length, that every reachable I-state is supercycle-free.

Let $t_k.moves = \{a_k^I \mid a_k^I \in P_k^I \wedge a_k^I.start = t_k\}$. It is proved in [4] that it is enough to check condition (a) for all local states t_k of P_k^I and for all J-systems for $J \in \mathcal{J}$, where $\mathcal{J}$ is the set of all interconnection relations of the form $\{\{j, k\}, \{k, \ell_1\}, \{k, \ell_2\}, \ldots, \{k, \ell_n\}\}$, and $n = |t_k.moves|$, $1 \leq j, k, \ell_1 \ldots, \ell_n \leq K$, $k \notin \{j, \ell_1 \ldots, \ell_n\}$. This condition implies an algorithm that checks all possible subsystems J of the form $\{\{j, k\}, \{k, \ell_1\}, \ldots, \{k, \ell_n\}\}$. The algorithm must construct M_J, and so is exponential in n. It is thus impractical for large n.

Let $J_i = \{\{j, k\}, \{k, \ell_i\}\} \subseteq J$, for $1 \leq i \leq n$ [3]. Then, for each move a_k^J and state $t_J \in states(M_J)$, $\forall \ell \in \{\ell_1, \ldots, \ell_n\} : a_k^J \to t_J\lceil\ell \notin W_J(t_J)$ holds iff

$$\forall i : 1 \leq i \leq n : a_k^{J_i} \to t_J\lceil\ell_i \notin W_{J_i}(t_J\lceil J_i). \tag{1}$$

The last equation follows from wait-for-graph projection [4, Proposition 6.5.4.1].

Equation 1 is checked with respect to all systems of three processes, for all reachable states of these triple-systems. To avoid constructing the J-system, we check the following condition (b), which requires constructing only J_i-systems. Define $triple-reachable(k) = \{t_k : (\forall J = \{\{j, k\}, \{k, \ell\}\} \subseteq I : (\exists t_J \in states(M_J) : t_J\lceil k = t_k))\}$. That is, $triple - reachable(k)$ is the set of local states t_k of P_k such that in every triple system J_i involving P_k there is a reachable state t_{J_i} that projects onto t_k. Then, the appropriate condition is:

$\forall t_k \in triple - reachable(k)$
$\quad \exists a_k \in t_k.moves$
$\qquad \forall J_i = \{\{j, k\}, \{k, \ell_i\}\} \subseteq I$
$\qquad\quad \forall t_{J_i}$ such that $t_{J_i} \in states(M_{J_i})$ and $t_{J_i}\lceil k = t_k$
$\qquad\quad$ and $s_{J_i} \xrightarrow{k} t_{J_i}$ for some $s_{J_i} \in states(M_{J_i})$:
$\qquad\qquad (\neg\exists a_j^{J_i} : a_j^{J_i} \longrightarrow t_k \in W_{J_i}(t_{J_i}))$ or
$\qquad\qquad (a_k^{J_i} \longrightarrow t_{J_i}\lceil\ell_i \notin W_{J_i}(t_{J_i})))$ for $a_k^{J_i} = a_k\lceil J_i$. $\qquad$ (b)

Condition (b) holds if either P_k blocks no move of another process or there exists a move of P_k that is not blocked in any of the triple systems J_i. In either case, in every system $J = \{\{j, k\}, \{k, l_1\}, \ldots, \{k, l_n\}\}$, either P_k has an enabled move, or P_k does not block any move of P_j. Hence, in the I-system, P_k cannot be involved in a deadlock. Note that if the state t_J that projects onto t_{J_i} for all J_i is reachable in the J-system, then condition (b) implies the deadlock-freedom condition of [4] for the J-system. The converse always holds.

Theorem 1. *If condition (b) holds, then the I-system P^I is deadlock-free.*

Intuitively, checking condition (b) involves constructing all triples of processes with P_k being the middle process. Since the size of a triple system is polynomial in the size of a single process, and the number of triples is polynomial in the number of processes in the system, the check is polynomial in all parameters.

We check condition (b) as follows. For every process P_k, we compute the set $S_k = triple - reachable(k)$, and the set $\mathcal{J}_k$ of all triple-systems J_i which have P_k as the "middle" process:

$$\mathcal{J}_k = \{J_i : J_i = \{\{j, k\}, \{k, \ell_i\}\} \wedge J_i \subseteq I \wedge k \neq j, \ell_i\}.$$

---

[3] Since $J \subseteq I$ and I is irreflexive, we have $k \neq i, \ell_i$.

For every $t_k \in S_k$, we compute the set $t_k.moves$ of outgoing moves of P_k from t_k. Then, for each $a_k \in t_k.moves$ and each $J_i \in \mathcal{J}_k$, we find every state $t_{J_i} \in states(M_{J_i})$ such that $t_{J_i} \lceil k = t_k \wedge (\exists s_{J_i} \in states(M_{J_i}) : s_{J_i} \xrightarrow{k} t_{J_i})$. This can be done by a graph search of M_{J_i}. We then evaluate

$$(\forall a_j^{J_i} : a_j^{J_i} \longrightarrow t_k \notin W_{J_i}(t_{J_i})) \vee (a_k^{J_i} \to t_{J_i} \lceil \ell_i \notin W_{J_i}(t_{J_i})) \tag{2}$$

where $a_k^{J_i} = a_k \lceil J_i$ and $a_j^{J_i}$ ranges over all moves of $P_j^{J_i}$ such that $a_j^{J_i}.start = t_{J_i} \lceil j$, i.e., the moves of process j in the J_i-system which start in the local state that process j has in state t_{J_i}.

If for all $k \in \{1 \ldots K\}$ and all t_k, there exists $a_k \in t_k.moves$ for which Equation 2 holds for all $J_i \in \mathcal{J}$, then we conclude that the system is deadlock-free. We formalize the procedure given above as the procedure CHECK-TRIPLES(P^I).

CHECK-TRIPLES(P^I)
0. **for all** $k \in \{1 \ldots K\}$
1. $S_k := triple - reachable(P_k)$
2. $\mathcal{J}_k := \{J_i \mid J_i = \{\{j, k\}, \{k, \ell_i\}\} \wedge J_i \subseteq I\}$
3.   **for all** $t_k \in S_k$
            for all $a_k \in t_k.moves$
                for all J_i in $\mathcal{J}_k$
                generate M_{J_i}
                    for all t_{J_i} such that $t_{J_i} \lceil k = t_k \wedge (\exists s_{J_i} \in states(M_{J_i}) : s_{J_i} \xrightarrow{k} t_{J_i})$
                    evaluate Equation 2
                    if Equation 2 was found true for all J_i and all t_{J_i} **then** mark t_k
4. **if** $\forall k \in \{1 \ldots K\}$: all $t_k \in S_k$ are marked, **then return** ("No supercycle possible")
    else return ("Inconclusive")

Upon termination of CHECK-TRIPLES(P^I), condition (b) holds iff "No supercycle possible" is returned. Termination is assured since all loops are finite.

Let b be the branching factor of a process, i.e., the maximum value of $|t_k.moves|$ over all $k \in \{1 \ldots K\}$ and all $t_k \in triple - reachable(P_k)$.

Theorem 2. *The time complexity of procedure* CHECK-TRIPLES(P^I) *is* $O(K^3 N^4 b)$, *and the space complexity is* $O(N^3)$.

We apply our check to the general resource allocation problem [24, Chapter 11]. For a system of n processes, an explicit resource specification $\mathcal{R}$ consists of a universal finite set R of (unsharable) resources and sets $R_i \subseteq R$ for all $i \in 1, \ldots, n$, where R_i is the set of resources that process P_i requires to execute.

Example 1 (Deadlock detection in the general resource allocation problem). In this example, we describe an solution to the the resource allocation problem in which there is a potential deadlock and show how this deadlock can be detected by studying triples of processes. We assume that each process needs at least one resource in order to execute. We first consider a naive algorithm in which each process chooses the order of requests for resources non-deterministically. That is, if a process P_i needs resources $\{1, \ldots, k\}$, it non-deterministically acquires resource $1 \leq r_1 \leq k$, then a resource $r_2 \in \{1, \ldots, k\} \setminus r_1$, etc. After the last resource has been acquired, P_i executes. Clearly, if a resource r is already allocated to another process, P_i cannot acquire it. If at some state in the resources allocation all remaining resources are allocated to other processes, P_i cannot proceed. It can be shown that condition (b) fails, and indeed there is a deadlocked state in the system (in which each process is trying to acquire a resource already acquired by another process). In the full version we present the formal and detailed description of this example.

Now consider the hierarchical resource allocation presented in Lynch [24, Chapter 11]. In this case, there is a global hierarchy between processes, and the resource is acquired to the process with the highest priority that requests it. The system is deadlock-free. However, condition (b) fails, giving a false deadlock indication. The reason for its failure is existence of waiting chains of length three in the system, despite the fact that cyclical waiting pattern never ocurs. In Section 4 we present a more complex (and more discriminating) test that shows deadlock freedom of hierarchical resource allocation.

In the following example we demonstrate false deadlock indication. It describes a system in which there are two types of processes, and only processes from one type can block other processes. The deadlock-freedom condition from [4] (the "wait-for-graph assumption") is satisfied, since it considers systems of $m + 2$ processes, m being the branching degree of a single process. Since condition (b) checks blocking for each outgoing move separately, it does not detect unreachability of the blocking state.

Example 2. We give here only the brief informal description of the example. For the formal description including the skeletons of participating processes the reader is refered to the full version of the paper. The system in the example consists of 4 processes P_1, P_2, P_3, and P_4 accessing two critical sections, where the processes P_3 and P_4 can block all other processes, and the processes P_1 and P_2 can only block each other. Consider a triple in which P_3 is the middle process. In its trying state it has two outgoing moves for accessing two critical sections. Both moves can be blocked by process P_4 separately, depending on the state of the process P_4. That is, the process P_4 blocks the move of the process P_3 that attempts to access the same critical section as P_4. The condition (b) fails. At the same time, the condition in [4] passes, since it checks blocking conditions for both moves of P_3 at the same time. Then, it is easy to see that there are no two processes that can block both moves of P_3 simultaneously. In Section 4 we show that the absence of reachable supercycles can be detected by examining the global wait-for graph for this system.

Example 2 illustrates that while condition (b) implies the deadlock-freedom condition of [4], the opposite is not true. That is, there exist cases in which condition (b) fails, while the more discriminating condition of [4] is satisfied, and hence the system is deadlock-free. This happens when the blocking state is reachable for each triple separately, but not for the J-system with $m + 2$ processes.

4 A More Complex and Discriminating Deadlock-Freedom Check

We define a *global wait-for graph* $\mathcal{W}$ which contains the union of all $W_I(s)$, for all reachable I-states s. Let $reachable(P_i) = \{s_i \mid \exists j \in I(i), s_{ij} \in S_{ij} : s_{ij} \lceil i = s_i\}$, that is, $reachable(P_i)$ is the set of local states of P_i that are reachable in some pair-system involving P_i.

Definition 3. $(\mathcal{W})$ *The graph $\mathcal{W}$ is as follows. The nodes of $\mathcal{W}$ are*
  1. *the states s_i such that $i \in \{1 \ldots K\}$ and $s_i \in reachable(P_i)$;*
  2. *the moves a_i^I such that $i \in \{1 \ldots K\}$, a_i^I is a move of P_i^I, and $a_i^I.start = s_i$ for some node s_i;*
and the edges are:
  1. *an edge from s_i to every a_i^I such that $a_i^I.start = s_i$;*
  2. *for $(i,j) \in I$ and every move a_i^I of P_i^I, there is an edge from a_i^I to s_j iff $\exists s_{ij} \in S_{ij} : s_{ij} \lceil j = s_j \wedge s_{ij}(a_i^I.guard_j) = false$.*

We can view $\mathcal{W}$ as either a directed graph or as an AND-OR graph. When viewed as an AND-OR graph, the AND-nodes are the local states s_i of all processes (which we call local-state nodes) and the OR-nodes are the moves a_i (which we call move nodes). We use MSCC to abbreviate "maximal strongly connected component" in the sequel.

Proposition 2. *For every reachable I-state s, $W_I(s)$ is a subgraph of $\mathcal{W}$.*

Proposition 3. *Let s be a reachable I-state, and assume that $W_I(s)$ contains a supercycle SC. Then, there exists a nontrivial subgraph SC' of SC which is itself a supercycle, and which is contained within a maximal strongly connected component of $\mathcal{W}$.*

Note that a supercycle is strongly connected, but is not necessarily a maximal strongly connected component.

Proposition 4. *If $\mathcal{W}$ is acyclic, then for all reachable I-states s, $W_I(s)$ is supercycle-free.*

We now present a test for supercycle-freedom. In the following we will view $\mathcal{W}$ as a regular directed graph, rather than an AND-OR graph. The test is given by the procedure CHECK-SUPERCYCLE($\mathcal{W}$) below, which works as follows. We first find the maximal strongly connected components (MSCC's) of $\mathcal{W}$. If no nontrivial MSCC's exist, then $\mathcal{W}$ is acyclic and so the I-system is supercycle-free by Proposition 4. Otherwise, we execute the following check for each local-state node t_k in $\mathcal{W}$. If the check marks t_k as "safe", this means that no transition by P_k that ends in state t_k can create a supercycle where one did not exist previously. If all local-state nodes in $\mathcal{W}$ are marked as "safe", then we conclude that no transition by any process in the I-system can create a supercycle. Given that all initial I-states are supercycle-free, this then implies that every reachable I-state is supercycle free, and so the I-system is deadlock-free. The check for t_k is as follows. If t_k does not occur in a nontrivial MSCC of $\mathcal{W}$, then, by Proposition 3, t_k cannot occur in any supercycle, so mark t_k as safe and terminate. Otherwise, invoke CHECK-STATE(t_k, C), where C is the nontrivial MSCC of $\mathcal{W}$ in which t_k occurs. Our test is sound but not complete. If some t_k is not marked "safe", then we have no information about the possibility of the occurrence of supercycles.

CHECK-SUPERCYCLE($\mathcal{W}$)
1. Find the maximal strongly connected components of $\mathcal{W}$
2. **for** each MSCC C of $\mathcal{W}$ that consists of a single node
        if the node is a local-state node **then** mark it "safe"
3. **for** each MSCC C of $\mathcal{W}$ that contains more than one node
        for each local-state node s_i of C, invoke CHECK-STATE(s_i, C)
4. **if** all local-state nodes in $\mathcal{W}$ are marked "safe", **then**
        return ("No supercycle possible")
    else return ("Inconclusive")

CHECK-STATE(t_k, C)
1. Construct a subgraph SC of C as follows.
        Let SC initially be C
        Remove from SC every s_k such that $s_k \in reachable(P_k) - \{t_k\}$
        repeat until no more nodes can be removed from SC
            if a_j is a node in SC with no outgoing edges in SC **then**
                let s_j be the unique node such that $s_j \longrightarrow a_j \in SC$
                remove s_j and a_j and their incident edges from SC
2. Compute the maximal strongly connected components of SC
3. **if** t_k is not in some MSCC of SC **then** mark t_k as "safe" and terminate.
    else Let MC be the MSCC of SC containing t_k
4. **for** all $(s_j, a_j^I, t_k, a_k^I, s_\ell)$ such that $s_j \longrightarrow a_j^I \longrightarrow t_k \longrightarrow a_k^I \longrightarrow s_\ell \in MC$
        Let $J = \{\{j, k\}, \{k, \ell\}\}$
        if there exists a state s_J of M_J such that:
            s_J is reachable along a path in M_J that ends in a transition by P_k, and
            $s_j \longrightarrow a_j^J \longrightarrow t_k \longrightarrow a_k^J \longrightarrow s_\ell \in W_J(s_J)$
        then mark all the nodes and edges in $s_j \longrightarrow a_j^I \longrightarrow t_k \longrightarrow a_k^I \longrightarrow s_\ell$
5. Remove from MC all nodes and edges within two hops from t_k (in either direction) that are unmarked. Call the resulting graph MC'
6. Calculate the maximal strongly connected components of MC'
7. **if** t_k does not lie in an MSCC of MC' **then** mark t_k as safe

The procedure CHECK-STATE(t_k, C) tests whether the wait-for chain from some local state s_j to some j-move a_j to state t_k to some ℓ-move a_ℓ to some state s_ℓ can arise from a reachable transition of process P_k in the triple system consisting of processes P_j, P_k, P_ℓ. If so, then all these states and moves are marked and are retained, since they might form part of a supercycle involving t_k. After all such "length 5" chains have been examined, all nodes within 2 hops of t_k are removed, since these nodes cannot possibly be part of a supercycle involving t_k. If this removal process causes t_k to no longer be contained in an MSCC, then

t_k cannot possibly be an essential part of a supercycle, since every supercycle is "essentially" contained inside a single MSCC, since removing all parts of the supercycle outside the MSCC still leaves a supercycle (see Proposition 3).

In summary, we check for the existence of subgraphs of a potential supercycle that are wait-chains of length 5. If enough of these are absent, then no supercycle can be present. Our check could be made more accurate by using longer length chains, but at the cost of greater time complexity.

Theorem 3. *If all local-state nodes in $\mathcal{W}$ are marked as "safe," then the I-system P^I is supercycle-free.*

Proposition 5. *Let N be the size of the largest I-process (number of local states plus number of I-moves). Then the size of $\mathcal{W}$ (number of nodes and edges) is $O(K^2 N^2)$.*

Theorem 4. *The time complexity of* CHECK-SUPERCYCLE($\mathcal{W}$) *is $O(K^4 N^4)$.*

It may be possible to improve the runtime complexity of the algorithm using more sophisticated graph search strategies. For example, for each three-process system, we could collect all the wait-chains together and search for them all at once within the global state-transition graph (GSTD) of the three-process system. Wait-chains that are found could then be marked appropriately for subsequent processing.

It is not too hard to verify that the global wait-for graph for the hierarchical resource allocation strategy that we discussed in Section 3 is acyclic. Indeed, a supercycle in a wait-for graph represents a cyclical waiting pattern between processes. However, a hierarchy establishes a total order between processes, and the transitions in the graph represent blocking conditions, which can occur only when moves of a process with a lower priority are blocked by a process with higher priority. Thus, waiting conditions form chains, and not cycles in the wait-for graph. In a more general situation, the requirement of total hierarchical order can be relaxed for a subset of resources. Clearly, in this case deadlock can occur, depending on the sets of resources that each process attempts to acquire and the order of requests. Our algorithm can efficiently detect deadlocks in these cases.

The following proposition relates the deadlock-freedom check of Section 3 and the check introduced in this section.

Proposition 6. *If procedure* CHECK-TRIPLES(P^I) *returns "No supercycle possible," then so does procedure* CHECK-SUPERCYCLE($\mathcal{W}$).

5   Examples

In this section, we study several examples of deadlock-free and deadlock-prone instances of the resource allocation problem [24, Chapter 11] and summarize the results obtained by using our algorithms. Due to the lack of space, many details are omitted here. They can be found in the full version.

Example 3 (Deadlock-free instance with two resources). We study a special case of resource allocation problem [24] that we presented in Section 3. In this system, there are two resources (we refer to them as priority queues) and the additional parameter is the set of priorities of processes for the queues. Consider an I-system where the processes are partitioned into 3 classes, and are accessing two priority queues R and Q. The first class of processes has the highest priority for R, and the second class of processes has the highest priority for Q. For processes in the same class and processes in different classes that have the same priority, the access to a queue is FIFO. There can be only one process at a time at the head of each queue. Intuitively, a deadlock can occur if there are several processes with the same priority in a trying state. However, the guards on transitions to trying states guarantee that a process enters a trying state iff either there is no other process is in the trying state, or the other process in the trying state has a lower priority. We note that the unreachability of supercycles in the wait-for graph is evident already by considering triple-systems, and thus condition (b) is also satisfied.

Example 4 (Deadlock-prone instance with two resources). In this example we describe a system with a reachable deadlocked state and demonstrate the evidence for the deadlock in the global wait-for graph. The system consists of two dissimilar processes P_1 and P_2 accessing two priority queues R and Q.

A deadlocked state $[B_1 A_2]$ can be reached in which process P_1 is in local state B_1, waiting for process P_2 to release Q, and process P_2 is in local state A_2, waiting for process P_1 to release R. This cyclic waiting can be discovered by examining the global wait-for graph for supercycles.

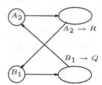

The drawing above presents a fragment of the graph that contains the supercycle for the deadlocked state $[B_1 A_2]$. The node labeled $B_1 \rightarrow Q$ is the move of P_1 that acquires Q, and the move labeled $A_2 \rightarrow R$ is the move of P_2 that acquires R. Condition (b) fails for the triple system $J_1 = \{\{P_1, P_2\}, \{P_2, P_1\}\}$, and thus the cyclic waiting is discovered by applying CHECK-TRIPLES(P^I).

Example 5 (Overlapping sets of resources). For a process P_i, let R_i be the set of resources P_i needs to acquire in order to execute. For each process P_k in the system, there exist two different processes P_i and P_j such that $R_i \cap R_k \neq \emptyset$ and $R_j \cap R_k \neq \emptyset$. Also, the order of acquiring the resources is non-deterministic for each process. In this case, condition (b) fails, thus indicating a possible deadlock. It is easy to see that the system is indeed deadlock-prone.

Example 6 (Processes with rollback). Now we construct an example for which the condition (b) described in Section 3 fails, although there is no deadlock. In this example, we have two types of processes. One type is the processes that acquire and lock resources one-by-one without the ability to rollback, as in the previous examples. The second type is the processes that rollback in case they encounter that one of the required resources is not available. In this case, condition (b) fails, although there is no deadlock.

6 Summary and Conclusions

The inset table summa-
rizes the deadlock detec-
tion results for the in-
stances of resource allo-
cation problem (both in
the previous section and
in Section 3). We note
that although we did not
demonstrate this explic-
itly, it is easy to verify

examples	existence of deadlock	algorithm from Section 3	algorithm from Section 4
Example 1	deadlock	deadlock	deadlock
Example 2	no deadlock	deadlock	no deadlock
Example 3	no deadlock	no deadlock	no deadlock
Example 4	deadlock	deadlock	deadlock
Example 5	deadlock	deadlock	deadlock
Example 6	no deadlock	deadlock	no deadlock

that the deadlock detection algorithm of [4] recognizes deadlock correctly in
all the examples studied in this paper. Our fist algorithm is very simple and
has a polynomial complexity in all its parameters. The negative answer from
this algorithm, that is, if the system satisfies the condition (b), eliminates the
need to invoke more complex and time-consuming algorithms. In cases where
the system fails the condition (b), it might be necessary to invoke the more discriminating algorithm from Section 4. While this algorithm is more complicated,
its complexity is still polynomial in all the parameters of the system.

By closely examining the instances of the resource allocation problem we
studied, we can see that the algorithm from Section 3 gives false positive deadlock
indications in systems with dissimilar processes, where there are some processes
with "more blocking power" than the others and the number of potentially
blocking processes is smaller than the branching degree of a single process. The
algorithm from Section 4 is more subtle, and is suitable for systems of any
number of dissimilar processes.

In conclusion, the success of our approach in verifying the deadlock-freedom
of many variants and instances of the resource allocation problem is evidence of
its wide applicability.

References

1. A. Aldini and M. Bernardo. A general approach to deadlock freedom verification
   for software architectures. In *FM 2003*, pp. 658–677, LNCS 2805.
2. Tamarah Arons, Amir Pnueli, Sitvanit Ruah, Jessie Xu, and Lenore D. Zuck.
   Parameterized verification with automatically computed inductive assertions. In
   CAV, pp. 221–234, 2001.
3. P. C. Attie. Synthesis of large concurrent programs via pairwise composition. In
   CONCUR, LNCS 1664, 1999.
4. P. C. Attie and E. A. Emerson. Synthesis of concurrent systems with many similar
   processes. *ACM Trans. Program. Lang. Syst.*, 20(1):51–115, 1998.
5. P.C. Attie. Synthesis of large dynamic concurrent programs from dynamic specifications. Technical report, NEU, Boston, MA, 2003.
6. P.C. Attie. Finite-state concurrent programs can be expressed pairwise. Technical
   report, NEU, Boston, MA, 2004.

7. Armin Biere, Alessandro Cimatti, Edmund M. Clarke, and Yunshan Zhu. Symbolic model checking without bdds. In *TACAS*, pp. 193–207, 1999.
8. E. M. Clarke, O.Grumberg, and D. Peled. *Model Checking*. MIT Press, Cambridge, MA, 2000.
9. E.M. Clarke, R. Enders, T. Filkorn, and S. Jha. Exploiting symmetry in temporal logic model checking. *FMSD*, 9(2), 1996.
10. E.G. Coffman, M.J. Elphick, and A. Shoshani. System deadlocks. *ACM Comput. Surv.*, 3:67–78, 1971.
11. T.H. Cormen, C.E. Leiserson, R.L. Rivest, and C. Stein. *Introduction to Algorithms; Second Edition*. MIT Press and McGraw-Hill, 2001.
12. E. W. Dijkstra. *A Discipline of Programming*. Prentice-Hall Inc., 1976.
13. E. A. Emerson and V. Kahlon. Reducing model checking of the many to the few. In *CAD*, pp. 236–254, 2000.
14. E. Allen Emerson and A. Prasad Sistla. Symmetry and model checking. *FMSD*, 9(1/2):105–131, 1996.
15. E. A. Emerson and E. M. Clarke. Using branching time temporal logic to synthesize synchronization skeletons. *Sci. Comput. Program.*, 2:241 – 266, 1982.
16. P. Godefroid. *Partial Order Methods for the Verification of Concurrent Systems*. PhD thesis, University of Liege, 1994.
17. P. Godefroid, D. Peled, and M. Staskauskas. Using partial-order methods in the formal validation of industrial concurrent programs. *Trans. on Soft. Eng.*, 22(7):496–507, 1996.
18. P. Godefroid and P. Wolper. A partial approach to model checking. *Information and Computation*, 110(2):305–326, 1991.
19. Gregor Goessler and Joseph Sifakis. Component-based construction of deadlock-free systems. In *FSTTCS*, pp. 420–433, LNCS 2914, 2003.
20. R. C. Holt. Some deadlock properties of computer systems. *ACM Comput. Surv.*, 4(3):179–196, 1972.
21. J.R. Burch, E.M. Clarke, K.L. McMillan, D.L. Dill, and L.J. Hwang. Symbolic Model Checking: 10^{20} States and Beyond. In *LICS*, pp. 1–33, 1990.
22. E. Knapp. Deadlock detection in distributed databases. *ACM Comput. Surv.*, 19(4):303–328, 1987.
23. P. Ladkin and B. Simons. Compile-time analysis of communicating processes. In *Proc. Int. Conf. on Supercomputing*, pp. 248–259, 1992.
24. N. A. Lynch. *Distributed Algorithms*. Morgan-Kaufmann, 1996.
25. Kenneth L. McMillan. *Symbolic Model Checking*. Kluwer Academic Publishers, 1993.
26. D. Peled. Partial order reduction: Model-checking using representatives. In *MFCS*, 1996.
27. B. Rex. Inference of k-process behavior from two-process programs. Master's thesis, School of Computer Science, Florida International University, Miami, FL, April 1999.
28. A. S. Tanenbaum. *Modern Operating Systems, second edition*. Prentice-Hall, 2001.

Author Index

Lecture Notes in Computer Science

For information about Vols. 1–3256

please contact your bookseller or Springer